IN SEARCH OF GRAND MASTER HIRAM

Understanding Masonic Symbolism

BY

JOHN R. HEISNER

Copyright © 2012 by John R. Heisner
All rights reserved.

ISBN-10: 1627350012
ISBN-13: 9781627350013

In Memory of
Bob & Elinor Heisner

TABLE OF CONTENTS

Preface	....	xiii
Chapter 1	Myth and Mystery	1
Chapter 2	Cause and Effect	11
Chapter 3	The Setting Maul	21
Chapter 4	A Foul Conspiracy	31
Chapter 5	Burying the Body	39
Chapter 6	The Evergreen	47
Chapter 7	Guilt and the Conscience	57
Chapter 8	The Master's Word	67
Chapter 9	Kneeling at the Gravesite	75
Chapter 10	Behind the Veil	87
Chapter 11	The Five Points of Fellowship	97
Chapter 12	King Solomon's Temple	107
Chapter 13	Making Gold From Brass	117
Chapter 14	Signaling for Help	131

Chapter 15	A Just Sentence	141
Chapter 16	Grand Master Hiram and the Messiah	151
Chapter 17	The Seafaring/Wayfaring Man	167
Chapter 18	No Man is an Island	175
Chapter 19	Human Strife	183
Chapter 20	Leadership	197
Chapter 21	Fulfillment	209
Chapter 22	Gradual Progression	217
Chapter 23	Masonic Origins	225
Chapter 24	Advancing Ancient Freemasonry	245

Part 2
Masonic Philosophy

	Introduction	249
Chapter 25	A Man Plucked Off His Shoe	251
Chapter 26	A Man, Freeborn	255
Chapter 27	A Passage of Scripture	259
Chapter 28	Admonishing a Brother	263
Chapter 29	Circumspection	267
Chapter 30	Clefts of the Rocks	271
Chapter 31	Clouded Canopy	275
Chapter 32	Death	279
Chapter 33	Despotism	283
Chapter 34	Divested of All Minerals and Metals	289
Chapter 35	Equilibrium	293

Chapter 36	Fear Not	297
Chapter 37	Angle of the Square	301
Chapter 38	Fraternity	305
Chapter 39	Friendship	311
Chapter 40	Grip of the Lion's Paw	315
Chapter 41	Intolerance	319
Chapter 42	Jacob's Ladder	325
Chapter 43	Lustration	329
Chapter 44	Melchizedek	333
Chapter 45	Mount Moriah	337
Chapter 46	Operative and Speculative Masonry	341
Chapter 47	Perseverance	345
Chapter 48	Pot of Incense	349
Chapter 49	Rubbish of the Temple	353
Chapter 50	Shibboleth	357
Chapter 51	Stone of Foundation	361
Chapter 52	Strength	367
Chapter 53	Sun, Moon and Master	371
Chapter 54	Temperance	377
Chapter 55	The Acacia	381
Chapter 56	The All-Seeing Eye	385
Chapter 57	The Anchor and Ark	389
Chapter 58	The Beehive	393
Chapter 59	The Common Gavel	397
Chapter 60	The East	401

Chapter 61	The Fall	405
Chapter 62	The Green Man	409
Chapter 63	The Heavenly Jerusalem	413
Chapter 64	The Hidden Mysteries	417
Chapter 65	The Human Soul	423
Chapter 66	The Level	427
Chapter 67	The Perambulation	431
Chapter 68	The Plumb	435
Chapter 69	The Purity of the Lily	439
Chapter 70	The Role Model	443
Chapter 71	The Temple	447
Chapter 72	The Tower of Babel	455
Chapter 73	The Vale	459
Chapter 74	The Volume of the Sacred Law	463
Chapter 75	The Weeping Virgin	467
Chapter 76	Tools of Iron	471
Chapter 77	Truth is a Divine Attribute	477
Chapter 78	"What Do You Most Desire?"	481

Part 3
Lessons in the Masonic Lodge

Introduction		487
Chapter 79	What is a Mason?	489
Chapter 80	Traveling in Foreign Countries	493
Chapter 81	Beauty: The Design of God	497

Chapter 82	The Ruffians	409
Chapter 83	The Mystic Tie	501
Chapter 84	An Emblem of Innocence	503
Chapter 85	Justice in a Great Measure	505
Chapter 86	Wisdom: The First Great Pillar	509
Chapter 87	Chastity	511
Chapter 88	Harmony, The Music of Masonry	513
Chapter 89	Triune Symbolism	515
Chapter 90	Knowledge – A Masonic Duty	517
Chapter 91	A Point	519
Chapter 92	Whence Came You?	521
Chapter 93	The Principle of Brotherhood	523
Chapter 94	In Unity	525
Chapter 95	The Fatherhood of God	527
Chapter 96	Humility of Mind	531
Chapter 97	The Faithful Servant	533
Chapter 98	Adversity	535
Chapter 99	History vs. Myth	537
Chapter 100	Two Things Worth Living For	541
Chapter 101	The Mysteries of Creation	543
Chapter 102	The Awakening	547
Chapter 103	The Sabbath	549
Chapter 104	Fear and Injustice	551
Chapter 105	The First Great Light	555
Chapter 106	Secrecy and Silence	557

Chapter 107	So Mote It Be	561
Chapter 108	Laborare Est Orare	563
Chapter 109	The Square and Compass	565
Chapter 110	The 47th Problem of Euclid	569
Chapter 111	The Letter "G"	573
Chapter 112	Boaz and Jachin	575
Chapter 113	From Darkness to Light	579
Chapter 114	Corn, Wine and Oil	581
Chapter 115	The Lost Word	583
Chapter 116	The Indented Tessel	587
Chapter 117	Freedom, Fervency and Zeal	591
Chapter 118	Tubal-Cain	595
Chapter 119	Freedom and Responsibility	599
Chapter 120	The Fellowcraft	601
Chapter 121	Within The Length of My Cable-Tow	603
Chapter 122	A Test of Faith	605
Chapter 123	Why Are Masons Called "Freemasons?"	609
Chapter 124	The Holy Saints John	613
Chapter 125	The Master's Hat	617
Chapter 126	The Entered Apprentice's Apron	619
Chapter 127	The Winding Staircase	621
Chapter 128	Two Perpendicular Parallel Lines	623
Chapter 129	The Cable-Tow	625
Chapter 130	The Cornerstone	627
Chapter 131	Network, Lily-work and Pomegranates	629

Chapter 132	The Asheroth, or Rods	633
Chapter 133	Seven: The Sacred Number	637
Chapter 134	The North – A Place of Darkness	639
Chapter 135	The Trowel	641
Chapter 136	The Widow's Son	643
Afterword		647

PREFACE

As modern-day researchers seek to identify the historical origins of Freemasonry, the character known in Masonic legend as Hiram Abif will likely present a most interesting challenge. Central to the mysteries of Freemasonry, his origin has proven elusive. Reputed to have been the chief architect at the building of King Solomon's Temple, his name is unrecorded anywhere other than in the ritual and writings of Freemasonry. Notwithstanding the fact that the Temple has never been discovered and there is little, if any proof that it was ever actually built, the Old Testament of the Holy Bible tells the story of its building, but conveniently omits any reference to a person named Hiram Abif.

In that there is no historical record confirming the existence of such a person, it is fair to ask why Freemasonry adopted him as the central figure of its symbolic mysteries. For years Masons and non-Masons alike have sought to discover Hiram Abif within the pages of the Old Testament perhaps sensing that if they are unsuccessful in so doing the central message of the Craft would be seriously undermined. Likely for this reason alone, Masons and other historical researchers will continue their search. Whether or not such an effort will eventually prove successful is impossible to know. However, the more important question to be posed – the question that is more closely associated with why Hiram Abif was embraced by Freemasonry in the first place – is whether or not the legend surrounding this seemingly fictional character conveys a lesson, or lessons that benefit mankind?

The Biblical character most popularly known as *Moses* is credited with delivered monotheism to the masses as well as having led the Jews out of their Egyptian captivity. However, the recognition and worship of the one true God existed long before the period of time history attributes to *Moses*. But until *Moses* arrived upon the world stage the manner, method and reason for worshipping one God was reserved to a select few. The state sponsored mysteries of Egypt, Greece, India and Persia each designed their respective philosophies, theologies and rituals around a belief in one Supreme Architect of the Universe and withheld those mysteries from the uninitiated, oftentimes referring to them as "profane."

The Biblical *Moses* is presented to us as the person who led the Hebrews from Egyptian captivity for the principal purpose of establishing an ever-expanding community of believers in one God. Presumably, *Moses*' followers left behind an Egyptian mass that worshipped the Sun, cattle and other creatures and objects. While such is not the case the presumption has been allowed to stand unchallenged for centuries because it serves as a stark contrast to the truth and importance of mankind's belief in one God. Indeed, as every Mason knows no man can become a Freemason without first openly professing his belief in the one true God.

Among other matters Freemasonry teaches that life is endless. It has no beginning or ending, but continues indefinitely according to God's grace and plan for His whole creation. The Masonic teaching about the resurrection of life is fundamentally derived from this truth. Death of man's material body does not end life. Rather, death merely transitions life from the material world to another dimension. Neither *Moses* nor his followers universally accepted this interpretation of resurrection, but it is found in the later writings of the Essenes and presumably was thus embraced by that sect. Consequently, we may emphatically conclude that while *Moses* gave monotheism to the masses, he did not include the resurrection of the dead in his teachings. Yet, each of the ancient state sponsored mysteries in Egypt, Greece, India and Persia included the mystery of resurrection in their respective teachings to their respective initiated followers. Clearly, the teachings of *Moses,* as they are known to us, either derive from something that entirely differs, or represents a perpetuation of the ancient Egyptian practice of reserving such knowledge for the *initiated*.

Nowhere in any of the allegories presented by the ancient mysteries was there ever a character identified as *Hiram Abif* – Huramabi is a close as the Bible comes. That is not to state that none of those mysteries included a similar character, for each did identify a person for the purpose of illustrating the meaning behind the mystery of the resurrection of the dead. Somewhere in the hazy mists of ancient history lies the answer to how, when and where that person actually came to be known as *Hiram Abif*. However it is not the central purpose of this literary work to peer into those mists. Rather, this work examines the entirety of the lessons Freemasonry teaches by the use of *Hiram Abif* as its exemplar. A chapter is devoted to studying some of the origins of Freemasonry but it, too, avoids an in depth inquiry into *Hiram's* true origin.

The sacred institutions and colleges that developed in close association with the ancient state mysteries, including those practiced in Egypt were the custodians of a universal wisdom. Their initiates were given the keys to a sublime science dedicated to the regeneration of mankind, as well as to the reformation of human society. Today, Freemasonry continues that essential work by making good men better and sending them into the world to build stronger families; to conduct themselves as peacemakers; to assist the poor and relieve the needy; and to form or reform governments in the image of brotherly love and affection.

In all of the world's history there have been no fewer than five great governmental revolutions that resulted in giving power and freedom to the masses. Coincidentally, each of those revolutions was led by a Freemason. George Washington is regarded as the father of the United States of America; Simon Bolivar delivered independence throughout South America; Georges Danton was a chief force in the overthrow of the French monarchy in favor of the establishment of the First French Republic; Italian patriot Giuseppe Garibaldi brought about the unification of his beloved Italy to the utter dismay of the Vatican; and Benito Juarez led the overthrow of the French occupation of Mexico and became that nation's most beloved leader. Each one of those men studied their lessons at the knee of *Hiram Abif* and used all they learned from him to regenerate and reform the societies in which they lived.

From time immemorial Freemasonry has labored to eliminate tyranny, oppression, slavery and man's inhumanity toward his fellow man. The Craft, as Freemasonry is affectionately called by all Masons, has consistently supported the concept of a free public education to serve as the cornerstone of a free society. Everywhere darkness seeks to absorb the face of the earth Freemasons assemble to replace that darkness with their light of brotherhood. Each member of the Craft has at one time or another unqualifiedly obligated himself to labor tirelessly within the country where he lives to ensure freedom for all people – not merely for a select few.

Accordingly thousands of men congregate together each day in the halls of Freemasonry to determine how best to work in the spirit of Washington, Bolivar, Danton, Garibaldi and Juarez to ensure that no man, woman, or child will suffer from the ravages of hunger, poverty, disease, intolerance, or tyranny. They do so in the spirit of *Hiram Abif* and bring to the world the lessons originally derived from that universal wisdom that has been safely guarded by sacred institutions, colleges and Freemasonry. The form and beauties of that universal wisdom unfold before you in the pages that follow revealing the secrets of the evolution of human consciousness.

Chapter 1

MYTH AND MYSTERY

In telling the story about *Hiram Abif,* Freemasonry placed him in the middle of the Old Testament tale about King Solomon building a temple. Without regard to whether or not that story is fiction, it begins with Solomon's ascension to the throne of Israel following the death of his father, King David. Although favored by God early in his youth, David was denied the privilege of building a stately edifice where God might comfortably dwell among His people, because he had waged vicious warfare upon his neighbors, allegedly stole the wife of a subject whose death he caused and otherwise behaved badly on numerous occasions. He was not, however, left without hope, for God reserved the dignified privilege of building His temple to the capable hands of Solomon, who is reported to have reigned during an unusual period of worldwide peace.

God's dwelling place among the Hebrews had heretofore been in a portable object called the Ark of the Covenant, an object that may have actually been the *Tabernacle* said to have been brought out of Egypt by Moses during the second exodus. It was carried from place to place by able-bodied Hebrews who believed that the Ark protected them from the ravages of wandering tribes and helped them secure the land. Once the struggle ended, King David decided that he and his people would settle down and establish a permanent home. It was necessary to establish a permanent home for the *One True God*, who had not only blessed David with ruling power, but had delivered him victory after victory during an intense period of bloody war.

During his wars, David developed a faithful friend in Hiram, the King of Tyre, who upon hearing that his son Solomon had ascended the throne of Israel sent congratulatory messages and offerings of assistance. Both Solomon and Hiram were reputed to have been men of wit and wisdom. Indeed, Solomon is historically renowned for the wisdom which he is said to have received after praying to God. Following a prayer of supplication during which Solomon asked for nothing more than the true wisdom necessary to understand right from wrong, God blessed him with true wisdom. As if to demonstrate to each other the extent of their wit and wisdom, Solomon and Hiram devised puzzling questions to test each other and upon discovering that they shared much in common soon became fast friends.

Eventually Solomon made an arrangement with Hiram for the building of a *Temple* to God whereby King Hiram would provide stonemasons, carpenters and master builders to assist in the construction in return for vast quantities of wheat, corn, wine and oil as their wages. Hiram also supplied cedars from the forests of Lebanon which were floated down the sea to Joppa and then laboriously conveyed by land to Jerusalem by Solomon's hardy workmen. Because of his devotion to Solomon, Hiram also sent him his own master builder - the Grand Master of Dionysiac Architects called *Hiram Abif*, a widow's son of the tribe of Naphtali.

Legend suggests that he was a Tyrian by birth. Also of Israelitish descent *Hiram Abif* was known throughout the land as the most skillful architect who had ever lived. His abilities were not confined to building edifices, but extended to all kinds of material creation, whether in silver, brass, iron or gold. Solomon appointed him at once to serve as Deputy Grand Master, a title which authorized him to employ Solomon's kingly powers during his absence. *Hiram Abif* was also appointed as overseer of all artisans and was directed to design each and every detail relative to the *Temple*.

Solomon commenced building the *Temple* during the fourth year of his reign on or about what our modern calendar would indicate as approximately April 21st. The work was completed seven years later and the glorious *Temple* stood as a monument to God on the brow of Mount Moriah. It consisted of 1,453 columns and 2,906 pilasters all hewn from the finest Parian marble and is said to have exemplified the best influences of ancient Egyptian symbolism. A broad porch decorated its eastern sector and in its midst stood the Holy of Holies, sometimes referred to as the *Oracle*. It was there that only anointed priests were permitted entry to worship once each year. Admission was forbidden to everyone else, who entered only upon the certain knowledge that by so doing they would die immediately.

The stones for the *Temple* were taken from stone quarries beneath Mount Moriah. The ornamental brass and gold were cast in the clay grounds between Succoth and Zeredetha. During the construction it is said that there was not heard the sound of ax, hammer, or any tool of iron. But, when the entire building was completed its several parts fitted together with such exact nicety that it had more the appearance of God's handiwork than that of human hands.

Under Solomon's supervision *Hiram Abif* separated the workmen into three groups, which he identified as Entered Apprentices, Fellowcrafts and Master Masons. Each working group was provided with certain passwords and signs by which their respective talents would be easily recognized by the overseers. Although the groups were classified according to merit, legend records that some members became dissatisfied that they were not included in the highest order – that known as *Master Mason*. Approximately fifteen of those unhappy craftsmen lusted for higher position and eventually entered into a conspiracy with each other to get what they desired at any cost.

The conspirators carefully noticed that each day at high noon *Hiram Abif* entered the unfinished *Sanctum Sanctorum* or Holy of Holies to kneel and pray to God. Seizing upon his habit, a plot was hatched to force the Master Builder to reveal the Master Mason's password and signs. Three of the ruffians named Jubela, Jubelo and Jubelum secreted themselves at the main gates to the *Temple* and lay in wait. The next day *Hiram Abif* predictably attempted to enter the *Sanctum Sanctorum* at high noon first. At the south, west and east gates he was serially assaulted by Jubela, Jubelo and Jubelum each of whom threatened him with death if he did not disclose the password and signs. On his third refusal at the east gate, he was finally murdered by Jubelum, who struck a fatal blow to the head with a setting maul. Under cover of darkness the three ruffians secretly buried the corpse near Mount Moriah and planted an evergreen at the head of the grave as a marker. While attempting their escape out of the kingdom they were captured, confessed their guilt to King Solomon and were by his order immediately executed. One of the parties sent by Solomon to search for *Hiram Abif* spotted the acacia and discovered the grave. After Entered Apprentices and Fellowcrafts failed to extract the body, *Hiram* was finally raised from the grave by King Solomon's use of the strong grip of the *Lion's Paw*.

To the initiated Mason the name *Hiram Abif* signifies the Universal Spirit, one in essence with God, three in aspect. He is neither intended to represent, nor replace the person known to the world as Jesus Christ. Rather, the murdered Master Builder represents the tragic *dying god;* a symbolism used throughout numerous cultures, religions and mysteries. His legend has been told for centuries by Hindus, Egyptians, Greeks, Romans and Persians. While the names and story lines differ, the central figure reaches the same end conveying a similar spiritual message to each person in each cultureIn its present Masonic form, the legend is comparatively modern even though based upon practices extending far back into antiquity. Most Masonic writers tend to agree that the story about the murder of *Hiram Abif* is based upon the Egyptian legend of Osiris, whose death and subsequent resurrection symbolized the spiritual death of man and his regeneration by initiation into the Mysteries. As such, *Hiram* may be regarded as the prototype of humanity about whom Plato wrote in his literary work entitled *Idea*.

Other explanations about the legend's origin continue to command attention for various historical and religious reasons. Some see *Hiram Abif* as the symbol of Jacques De Molay, the last Grand Master of the original Knights Templar, who was burned alive on March 19, 1314 at the command of the King of France, Philip the Fair with the approval of the Roman Catholic Pope Clement. Before dying, De Molay is reputed to have cried to God for justice by calling both the King and the Pope to judgment in heaven within forty days. History records that both Philip and Clement died suddenly – precisely forty days after De Molay's horrid death. According to this interpretation of the legend, the three ruffians represent King Philip, Pope Clement and the executioners who set De Molay ablaze.

To many Christian Freemasons, the murder and resurrection of *Hiram* is a reminder that Jesus Christ was tortured, crucified and rose again in full life. For them, the ruffians represent none other than the betrayer Judas, the corrupt Sanhedrin tribunal and the Roman executioners. Thus considered, *Hiram Abif* represents man's higher nature while the murderers symbolize fear, superstition and ignorance.

Some scholars contend that the Hiramic Legend was invented by Elias Ashmole, a mystical philosopher, reputed member of the Rosicrucian College and one of the original members of the Royal Society. Among those scholars, Ashmole is said to have created *Hiram* as homage to the murdered King Charles I, who was beheaded in 1647 leaving the Royalist political party without a leader. In this version of the legend, the appellation *Sons of the Widow* is fitted to England herself, which to the Royalists literally became a widow upon Charles' death.

The Hiramic Legend also has an astrological aspect – one that is enacted annually as the sun passes through the various signs of the zodiac. The sun's journey through the twelve signs reportedly led to the story about the twelve labors of Hercules, as well as the incarnations of Vishna (Hinduism) and Buddha. Here, *Hiram Abif* represents the sun and the three ruffians symbolize the winter signs of the zodiac – Capricorn, Aquarius and Pisces. In this context the search for *Hiram's* body by the nine Fellowcraft reminds us of the ascension and resurrection of *Hiram* (the sun) at the summer solstice.

That zodiacal theme is repeated by several other writers, some of whom describe Libra, Scorpio and Sagittarius as the three murderers of the sun as represented by *Hiram Abif.* In the Egyptian Osiric legend, Osiris was murdered by Typhon to whom is affixed the *thirty-three degrees* of the constellation of Scorpio. Christian mystics argue that the traitor Judas represents Scorpio and that the thirty pieces of silver paid to him for his treachery signify the number of degrees within that constellation. The sun, represented by *Hiram,* is first struck by Libra which represents the state, then by Scorpio representing the Church and finally by Sagittarius which embodies the mob. Capricorn is said to represent Father Time – a wayfaring man – who also serves to straighten the ringlets of the young girl's hair – another object of Masonic symbolism.

Astronomically, this symbolism corresponds with the geometry embraced by Freemasonry, for there exists a precise ninety-degree interval between Virgo – the Weeping Virgin – and Capricorn – Father Time, which is the interval occupied by *Hiram's* three murderers. The urn held by the *Weeping Virgin* represents the human heart where the memory of the valiant *Hiram* is symbolically safely deposited. The sprig of evergreen so prominently displayed during Masonic Funeral services is contributed to this celestial allegory by Saturn, known to those familiar with this part of the legend as the old man of the north. Some have speculated that it is this legend that that gives rise to both the Christmas tree (the sprig of evergreen) and Santa Claus, who brings the gift of a new year each winter. The murdered sun (*Hiram*) is eventually discovered by Aries, described in this allegory as a *Fellow-Craftsman*. The discovery is made at the vernal equinox when the process of *raising* or regeneration begins. That process is completed by the *Lion of the Tribe of Judah*, who occupies the revered cosmic position as "keystone" of the Royal Arch of heaven. The *lost word* is carried to the sun's grave when finally properly spoken restores life to its fullest power and glory.

Sir Francis Bacon figures prominently in yet another interpretation of the Hiramic Legend. Some historians speculate that it was Bacon, not William Shakespeare, who actually wrote the numerous plays every serious English literature student is compelled to study. Dr. Orville Owen claims to have discovered that a significant part of the ritual of the first thirty-two degrees of Scottish Rite Freemasonry was concealed within the Shakespearean works. Bacon is reputed to have been both a Mason and a member of the Royal Society. He was undoubtedly of royal vintage and therefore would have found it necessary to conceal his identity when writing about Masonic matters. To have revealed his relationship to the Craft would have certainly imposed great difficulty upon the Crown of England, which was then embroiled in a series of political and religious dramas that pitted Catholicism against Protestantism, as well as one political force against the other. The Crown necessarily had to maintain the appearance, if not the reality of impartiality.

Bacon's description of the Temple of Solomon may have been intended to identify an ideal state of being as opposed to a specific place. In this context *Hiram Abif* symbolizes an ideal – the universal man, who upon seeing the *light* casts aside the ways of materialism and pursues the true path of spirituality. Thus, the *Temple of Freemasonry*, represented by the Temple of Solomon, is emblematic of an ideal condition within which societies of men may live and grow.

There is some evidence obtained from a very old manuscript indicating that Masonry was originally formed by alchemists and Hermetic philosophers, who banded together to guard the secrets of gold-making. As far-fetched as gold-making may appear to some, present-day scientists have reportedly replicated an ancient process in modern laboratories and actually made gold from lead. To underscore the very real possibility that gold-making was not only a probability during the Middle Ages, but a reality, several European governments sought to ban the practice in an effort to safeguard their respective economies. Too much gold filtering into commerce could have had disastrous effects upon the world's economy.

The fact that the Hiramic Legend reputedly contains an alchemical formula may lend credence to this theory. That formula is as follows: the building of Solomon's Temple represents the consummation of the *Grand Design*, which cannot be completed without the assistance of the universal man, *Hiram Abif*. The lessons in Masonry teach the initiated man how to prepare his soul thereby transmuting him from an ignorant human mass to a spiritual person.

Those alchemical lessons are also claimed by some to disclose the Masonic "lost key" – the science of human regeneration – which was allegedly passed from one adept to another initiate in the ancient Hindu mysteries. In this context, *Hiram Abif* symbolizes the Hindu "Spirit Fire" which moves within the human body through the sixth ventricle of the human spinal column traveling through *thirty-three degrees*, or segments of the spinal column. Eventually, that "Spirit Fire" passes into the brain and locates in the pituitary gland, or pineal gland, where it engages with the Supreme Grand Master of the Universe creating the *Sacred Center* of all human growth. Some writers assert that this deeply esoteric message was included in the lessons imparted by the ancient Egyptian and Grecian mysteries.

The pineal gland is extremely small and is situated within the human brain. To the ancients it was considered to be the *sacred eye,* which may constitute the origin of the Masonic symbol known as the *All-Seeing Eye*. Although scientists are keenly aware of this tiny gland, very little is known about its true functions. Among several educated guesses is that it is the root of human life and when properly manipulated may extend human longevity. Some writers have postulated that the ancients identified in the Holy Bible as men who lived for amazing lengths of time did so because they knew the secrets about the proper manipulation of the pineal gland.

In the Masonic mysteries the thrice-enriched spirit of man is symbolized by the three original Grand Masters. Accordingly, *Hiram Abif* is closely identified with the incarnating part of that trinity - the *Master Builder* who erects shrines of flesh and blood to God. He cometh forth like a flower and is cut down. He lies waiting to be transmuted into divine potency, his earthly body originally sown dishonorable, but ultimately raised to glory within a spiritual body.

The Hiramic Legend is also seen by others as incorporating the divine secrets of architecture. After *Hiram* was murdered with builders' tools, Solomon eventually instructed that the Grand Master be buried beneath the edifice the Craft finally erected. That burial represents the reduction of the dimensionless Spirit of Cosmic Beauty to the confines of structural conformity. By meditating upon the *Temple* the Master Mason can resurrect the divine principles locked in the stone of which it is comprised. In this context, an architectural structure such as the *Temple* represents an encasement embodying the Creative Ideal of God.

In quite another sense, the Hiramic Legend is said to embrace a variety of different philosophies. The pagan mysteries were the foundation of ancient civilization and its power is personified by *Hiram Abif.* Eventually those mysteries fell victim to the state, church and mob. As when *Hiram* is finally raised from his grave and the secret word is whispered, so, too, according to the history of philosophy shall its true nature be revealed when the ancient mysteries are restored or resurrected. Until that day mankind is destined to remain in a state of constant moral confusion.

As long as the mob governs, ignorance will reign. As long as the church rules, superstition will hold sway. As long as the state governs, fear will be in the way. Harmony among all mankind cannot reign until ignorance is transmuted in the manner of spiritual alchemy into wisdom, superstition into faith, and fear into love. Freemasonry seeks to unite God and man by elevating man's consciousness to such a height that he may more clearly understand the plan or *Grand Design* of the Great Architect of the Universe. Within the Craft secular and spiritual science resides side-by-side revealing to those with eyes to see and ears to hear the numberless worlds of the vast creation. Creed and dogma are set aside in favor of the pursuit of the assimilation of ideas and the reverent acknowledgement that diversity is a very natural state of human existence. The human body is not made of two left hands, two left legs, or one right eye. Different parts work together in the same human system to make man a complete functioning creature.

However told the Hiramic Legend imparts to all who pursue its lessons the importance of attaining knowledge. To the murderers, knowing a secret password was so important that they turned to treachery to obtain the key to greater rewards. To the craftsmen who raised the Grand Master from his grave, even knowledge of a substitute for the *ineffable name of Deity* was highly prized. To the Masons who later contemplated the symbolic importance of the *urn* and the *acacia,* knowledge of *Hiram Abif's* virtues was essential to learning the manner in which all Masons should conduct their lives.

Thus, the *Grand Design* of Freemasonry is the achievement of a state of being through spiritual and physical education that releases living truths from man's lifeless covering; to transmute that which is bad into that which is good; and to peacefully embrace the differences among men rather than attempt to forcefully remove them.

Chapter 2

CAUSE AND EFFECT

Every intentional murder has a motive. Even seemingly senseless serial murders are motivated albeit by a diseased curiosity or pleasure at seeing someone die. While motive is a characteristic common to every murder, it is not always easily discovered. That is certainly true with regard to the motive behind the murder of the Grand Master *Hiram Abif.*

Before completing our investigation into the motive, it is essential to first learn about the identity and background of the murderers and to understand the nature of the scene of the crime. Solomon's Temple is the scene and it is there that we initially encounter our suspects. We are told that the construction of the *Temple* commenced on the second day of the month known as Zif, the second month of the sacred year which biblical scholars have correlated to the modern month of April. The specific reference to such a sacred year identifies this legend as having derived from a Jewish tradition. The calendar for sacred months did not begin until the Hebrews made their second escape from Egyptian captivity. Sacred years ran from approximately March to May, while a Hebrew or Jewish secular year consisted of all of the remaining months. Those were considered as the growing months and were dedicated to nurturing new plants that would one day yield the food that would feed the people.

The site selected for the construction of the *Temple* was near Mount Moriah, which simply means "the land of the Amorites" – occupiers of the territory before Hebrew settlers arrived. Once constructed, the *Temple* consisted of 1,453 columns and 2,906 pilasters which were hewn from beautiful Parian marble. The constructions required the disciplined effort of stonemasons organized in working groups by Solomon and *Hiram Abif.*

Solomon is said to have wisely considered how best to avoid envy, discord and confusion when establishing those groups. Consequently the craftsmen were separated into three Grand Masters, consisting of Solomon, King Hiram of Tyre and *Hiram Abif;* three thousand three-hundred masters or overseers of the work; eighty thousand Fellowcraft or hewers on the mountain and workers in the rock quarries; and seventy thousand Entered Apprentices who carried the rock, stone and marble to the constructions sites. Each working group was attired in a manner that permitted easy identification of each workman's rank. To insure that none could simply disguise himself by his attire, each working group was also provided with its own password and signs that were unknown to those among lower ranking working groups.

The three murderers were members of the Fellowcraft – hewers on the mountains and in the rock quarries. As the *Temple* neared its completion, they realized they had not advanced in rank and feared they never would once their job was done. It would have been easy to simply change their manner of dress and imitate the attire of the masters. However the only way to obtain the password and signs would have been to hear and see someone give them. Since none in the higher rank would willingly part with the password or signs, the three Fellowcraft realized they would have to take them by force and began to think of a plan. But why was it so important for those Fellowcraft to abandon their morality and resort to the use of false pretenses? There are at least two likely motives.

The first relates to a desire to attain the status necessary to insure higher wages for future architectural work. Master Masons were paid more by their employers, because their greater skill was materially more important than the lesser skills possessed by either the Fellowcraft, or Entered Apprentices. In order to carefully protect the earning power of the more skilled craftsmen, employers demanded that a Master Mason prove his entitlement by recognizable signs of membership. Those signs included what is now referred to as the *password of a Master Mason.*

The second likely motive is spiritual - as powerful an attraction to men as is a lust for money. According to Masonic legend, King Hiram of Tyre and *Hiram Abif* were Phoenicians who worshipped God differently than did King Solomon. Like the ancient Egyptians, the Phoenicians practiced initiatory rites that were once practiced by Moses and his followers. Owing to the gradual corruption of the Hebrews those practices were eventually discarded by certain segments of the priesthood. By the time of Solomon's reign, those practices were essentially lost.

Among those lost rites and mysteries, the King was believed to become a Son of God upon his initiation into the mysteries. As Solomon surveyed his vast kingdom and contemplated the importance of his reign, he must have realized that his neighbor and good friend Hiram of Tyre enjoyed much greater stature. One reason Solomon sought his help was to learn the secrets about how kings became gods. Passages from the book of Kings I in the Old Testament reveal that Solomon later married the daughter of the reigning Egyptian pharaoh in hopes of further securing his desired position as a Son of God. Solomon knew that such men understood the correct pronunciation of the *Ineffable Name of Deity* – the *Lost Word* in the symbolic blue lodge of Freemasonry – and thereby acquired enormous powers.

Many of the ancients believed that the man who could accurately pronounce God's true name would possess all of God's powers. Some held this belief literally going so far as to claim that such powers granted the knowledgeable man dominion over all other men, kingdoms, provinces and empires. Others claimed that the power was spiritual, not material, allowing the man who possessed it to understand all wisdom, faith and knowledge. Masonic legend reveals that Hiram of Tyre knew the correct pronunciation of the *Word* – King Solomon did not. However, it is evident that he wanted his dear friend to tell him the secrets. Before imparting the *Word*, Hiram conferred the ancient mysteries upon Solomon in a ceremony participated in by fellow initiate, *Hiram Abif.*

During the ceremony, the *Word* was whispered to Solomon. So powerful and profound a ceremony also required the strictest secrecy, otherwise the *Word* could fall into the wrong hands. To insure that secrecy, the three Grand Masters vowed not to give the *Word* unless all three were present and agreed to do so. They never intended that the *Word* would not be given to others – they merely intended that it would only be given to those whom they mutually agreed were morally worthy.

It is quite likely that the three murderers knew enough about the significance of the *Word* to fully appreciate its value. Undeniably the material benefits that could have been derived from being paid higher wages alone was sufficient reason to steal and murder. Coupled with the belief that the password opened the door to God's hidden powers, the temptation to possess the *Word* at all cost, even morally reprehensible murder, is much easier to understand. But the three murderers were Masons – men who had once been found honorable enough to have been initiated as Entered Apprentices and then passed to the degree of Fellowcraft. Is it likely that such base motives were truly at the core of their criminal enterprise?

History abounds with sad incidents of failed virtue by men of honorable standing. Philip the Fair, King of France, and Clement I, Pope of the Roman Catholic Church, teamed together to hunt down and murder Jacques De Molay and his Knights Templar. So heinous a crime as torturing and burning men to death seems somehow improbable for a Chief of State, or the Vicar of God, but history records its alarming occurrence. Later in the 11th century, another of God's Vicars, Pope Innocent III, authorized the slaughter of people in the southern region of France known as the Languedoc on the grounds that they were heretical Manichaeans.

In the more recent history of the United States of America, doctors, lawyers, bankers and businessmen – men of honor during the daytime – cloaked themselves in white robes and roamed the darkened streets of the South searching for men of color whom they could torture and hang. Ministers of God recently turned away from the Creator's gaze and sexually abuse children who were placed their trust. Indeed, it is not only possible for men of honor to commit horrid deeds – history proves they have done so repeatedly. The cloak of honor – even the badge of a Mason - is no guarantee that he who wears it will not one day, for vile and selfish reasons engage in high crimes and misdemeanors. Not even the square and compasses possess the magic necessary to prevent man from using his God-given free will to accomplish dark purposes.

Returning to the murderers, it is fair to ask whether or not there was something about who they were that might reveal their motive? Masonic legend informs us that from the peculiarity of their names they were supposed to be brothers and men of Tyre – Phoenicians! As such, they were part of the contingent Hiram of Tyre brought with him when Solomon asked for builders to assist in the construction of a great temple to God. They were also members of a culture that believed that their monarch, having been initiated in the mysteries was the very Son of God – just as were the Egyptian pharaohs. Did the assassins aspire to also be sons of God? Did they seek admission to a higher rank in order that they might possess God's powers for their own selfish interests? Of course that is possible, as much as it is possible that they also desired to receive higher wages when traveling in foreign countries to practice their skills at building. The motive for murder could easily have consisted of a combination of reasons. For purposes of our investigation it is necessary to understand as many of the possible motives as are reasonably likely to have occurred.

At the time when the *Temple* is believed to have been under construction, the Phoenicians had two claims of important achievement: they were sailors who understood the art of navigation; and they invented the first known alphabet. When it came to navigation, the Phoenicians were much more than shoreline sailors. They navigated the open seas by use of the stars that were observable on many moonlit nights. This art required an understanding of both longitude and latitude – at a time in history when only longitude was generally known. Most history books claim that the discovery of latitude (horizontal lines running east to west that are distinguished from lines of longitude which describe a place on earth east or west of a north-south line) occurred in approximately 1516. Depending upon which source one uses to fix the date for the construction of King Solomon's Temple, the year 1516 is approximately 2,000 years after the Phoenicians went to Solomon's. Owing to the manner of their naval navigations during King Hiram's reign, the Phoenicians of that era must have understood the fundamentals of latitude. Quite likely those fundamentals very skillfully employed.

The significance of this is that the Phoenicians possessed the knowledge of latitude long before it became generally known. That suggests that the Phoenicians had contact with other societies and cultures that possessed the same knowledge. Here, we arrive at a possible link with the ancient people whom certain present-day historians believe were responsible for spreading ancient knowledge around the world. That elite group includes such people as the Norwegian Vikings and Grooved Ware People whom some contend are responsible for erecting crude observatories in England, Scotland and South America to study the stars.

Men have frequently wondered how it is that the Egyptian pyramids show such striking similarities to the Mayan pyramids, or why the uniqueness of Stonehenge is repeated elsewhere around the globe. How is it possible that the sailors in the Knights Templar navy knew as much about navigation as did the Vikings, Phoenicians and Grooved Ware People? What is the connection and why is it important to Freemasonry – or, at least, why is it important to understanding a possible motive for slaying *Hiram Abif?*

When man first began sailing the seas he quickly learned that the one who could first solve the problem of accurate navigation would become rich beyond measure. To solve that problem, it was necessary to apply mathematics – the very same mathematics used to construct large edifices such as King Solomon's Temple. Pythagoras, himself revered by Freemasons and believed to have been initiated into several of the ancient mysteries, postulated that mathematics was at the core of musical harmonics and also explained the motions of the planets. Indeed, an instrument of mathematics dating back at least 70,000 years held the key to understanding latitude – an essential ingredient to accurate navigational skills.

The instrument is represented on the Junior Warden's pedestal – archaeologists call it a lozenge. It has been linked by Marija Gimbutas, the Lithuanian archaeologist and anthropologist who lectured for years at Harvard University, to goddess worship. Thus, it is possible that much of the Masonic ritual associated with King Solomon's Temple is linked to the Venus worship of Phoenicians – men such as King Hiram of Tyre and *Hiram Abif.* Interestingly, the Vikings also participated in goddess worship and are the ancestors of the man some insist founded Freemasonry – the famous Scot, William St. Clair.

The Israelites who followed King Solomon were descendants of the followers of Moses. Most of them had never engaged in goddess worship of any kind. But the three murderers, Jubela, Jubelo and Jubelum were not Israelites – they were Phoenician and citizens of the goddess worship culture. While some may allege that people like the Phoenicians were heretical pagans who have recently been unjustifiably glorified at the expense of the so-called true religions, all of Christianity prominently includes a feminine figure in its traditions and teachings – Mary, the mother of Jesus. Jesus himself is said to have descended from King David, whose great-grandfather and great-grandmother were Boaz and Ruth. Ruth's male children have been historically referred to as "sons of the widow." Obviously there is more to a feminine connection than first meets the eye – even Christian eyes.

This is indeed a mysterious connection that is made all the more mysterious when considered in conjunction with passages of scripture. While the name *Hiram Abif* never appears, the names Hiram and Hurumabi appear in several instances. Some passages seem to confuse Hiram of Tyre with another man also named Hiram, but the distinction is never explained. Yet, in chapter 7 of the book of Kings I, the following revelation cannot be overlooked:

King Solomon had Hiram brought from Tyre. He was a bronze worker, the son of a widow from the tribe of Naphtali; his father had been from Tyre. He was endowed with skill, understanding, and knowledge of how to produce any work in bronze. He came to King Solomon and did all his metal work. *1 Kings 7, 13-15.*

The passage appears to describe the man every Master Mason knows as *Hiram Abif.* It also appears to link *Hiram Abif* to Ruth and all of her other "sons of the widow," including Jesus himself. Whether or not that lineage could ever be proven to the satisfaction of anyone, it clearly implies that if that Hiram was *Hiram Abif,* he was much more than an exceptional worker in bronze – he was a man of God. Such a man would be likely have been included in the group of three Grand Masters – the three who knew the true pronunciation of the *Ineffable Name of Deity.*

Jubela, Jubelo and Jubelum presumably knew the quality and character of their own leaders and likely knew that *Hiram Abif* was also the descendant of Hebrew ancestors – ancestors of a royal lineage that extended back to the grand patriarch Abraham. It is that ancestry that truly distinguishes *Hiram Abif* from either King Hiram, or King Solomon. At the very least a thorough exploration of the motive for his murder must not overlook this important detail. Neither must we overlook the fact that the three murderers risked everything, including their own lives, to force *Hiram Abif* to tell them a word, albeit presumably the most important word a man could ever hope to know.

The oldest worker in bronze mentioned in the Old Testament is Tubalcain, a man who also figures prominently in Masonic ritual and legend. It is said that Tubalcain was the eighth man from Adam, the first artificer in metals and a brother of Jubal, the inventor of music. While this brief description from the book of Genesis is undoubtedly allegorical, it may also be important to our investigation into understanding what truth is actually concealed within that allegory. What is it about metal workers – bronze in particular – that is so important? Perhaps there is something contained in the science of alchemy that might assist us in discovering the answer.

Modern-day societies generally regard alchemy as a false science. More often than not men today will laugh at those who claim an ability to transform base metals into gold. As a science, the art has been reduced to unverified activities within secret laboratories where men of odd backgrounds continue to claim the ability to employ secret chemical formulas in making gold. Today, if alchemy has any relevance to mainstream society it is on the philosophical level. Those who claim to be able to manufacture gold are regarded as frauds and charlatans. The same is not so for those who profess the continuing relevance of alchemy's contribution to thoughts of transforming mankind's character from bad deeds to good works. But if alchemy holds any clue about the motive for the murder of *Hiram Abif,* we cannot merely discard gold-making, for that science was not held in disrepute during that era.

In ancient Mesopotamia, years before Egyptian dynasties began emerging on the world stage the royalty reputedly consumed quantities of substances that were associated with longevity and kingship. Some of those substances consisted of the potent female essence, forming the basis for later traditions centered upon the power and influence of the feminine. Those chemicals were believed to have triggered the output of high levels of melatonin, which is manufactured in the human body by the pineal gland. Some claim that high pineal activity is closely related to enhanced intuition, as well as to the reduction of stress.

In the continuing present-day remnants of the Mayan culture various shamans teach their followers which jungle plants are most suitable for healing diseases and adding years to human life. Today in the United States many people are turning to herbs to supplement nutrition and heal the body. Although traditional medical societies generally contend that there is no scientific data sufficient to prove the existence of such healing and strengthening properties, several herbologists and an increasing number of medical doctors endorse melatonin as a natural substance that will protect the immune system, decrease the chances of contracting cancer, heighten energy levels and promote healthier cardiovascular functioning.

Gold was among the several regenerative substances ingested by the ancients. The recent series of wonderful fantasy novels about Harry Potter and his mystical adventures energized greater interest in such arcane alloys as are represented by something referred to as "the Philosopher's Stone." Some have claimed that the Stone was actually a powder used by alchemists to transmute base metals into gold. According to legend, the Master Craftsmen were not merely workers in stone as Freemasons today believe: they were adepts who made gold from base metals. Over the years many metallurgists have confirmed that ingested liquid gold can actually activate the endocrinal glandular system and heighten human awareness to an extraordinary level.

Some of the most venerated spiritualists in older civilizations, including certain Native American tribes, are known to have consumed a variety of different mind-altering substances for the purpose of attaining a heightened state of spiritual consciousness. For those men, it was that state of mind, body and spirit that best prepared them to enter into a condition of deep contemplation and eventually to arrive at a place where man quietly meets and listens to God. Some adepts have been known to achieve that same state of being without the aid of substances, because as the Phoenicians in the day of *Hiram Abif* believed, they knew the true pronunciation of the *Ineffable Name of Deity*.

We have gone full-circle in our investigation into the possible motives for murder and end where we began. The available evidence strongly suggests that for some reason extremely important to them Jubela, Jubelo and Jubelum were desperate to possess the life-giving powers of

God – a lust shared by such historical characters as Adolph Hitler, Joseph Stalin and Nero. The insight that emerges from our investigation is haunting, for it reveals a fierce material and spiritual tension that has existed from time immemorial between good and evil, light and darkness. Evil and darkness seem always to threaten the good and the light by imposing a tyrannical restraint upon man's ability to perform good deeds. In addition to possibly having discovered a provable motive for murder, we may have also stumbled across a very good reason why Freemasonry abhors tyranny of any kind and strenuously argues for its defeat.

Chapter 3

THE SETTING MAUL

Masonic tradition tells us that *Hiram Abif* was slain with a setting maul. After thrice refusing the demands of Jubelum to reveal the *Master's Word,* his skull was crushed by a blow from a wooden hammer. Ironically the same instrument was commonly used by the craftsmen during the building of the *Temple* to properly set stone into mortar. Any seasoned murder detective will likely tell you that more often than not murders are committed by the use of tools and instruments that were never intended to be used for killing people. Implements such as knives, ropes and ice picks are frequently used to kill, but are actually meant to be helpful tools. The same is so for the setting maul which was readily available to any of the assassins, who each day held one in his hands as he tapped stones hewn from the quarries into place.

The murder of *Hiram Abif* was not the first time that a tool was put to bad use. It will not likely be the last. But this particular tool symbolized something very ominous.

The maul has been used as a symbol of powerful destruction for centuries. It has appeared as a force of evil and doom in many stories of ancient mythology. The God of Thunder, Thor, is usually depicted tightly gripping a huge hammer in his strong fingers. In Icelandic, the word *mjolnir* meant hammer, or pulveriser – the most fearsome weapon in Norse mythology. Although other weapons of death were often available, the *mjolnir* was selected when the killer wanted to demonstrate his supremacy in the act of killing. No other weapon would send the same message as convincing as killing a man with one blow. Such power was meant to terrorize the living, as well as to make sure the victim remained dead.

As we learned previously, the three assassins have been compared to the three greatest enemies of individual welfare and social progress to have ever existed: kingcraft, priestcraft and the mob-mind. At various times throughout human history these three enemies have inflicted more terror upon mankind than all other enemies. The first strikes a blow at the throat, representing free speech; the second assails freedom of conscience by stabbing at the heart; and the third kills the freedom of thought by crushing the brain. While it is possible for man to live without either free speech, or freedom of conscience, he cannot exist without being free to think for himself. If reduced to thinking only as he is told, he may never hear the voice of God in response to his prayers. Indeed, like the biblical Cain, he could be compelled to wander the earth a lost and lonely man searching in vain for his God. The blow that kills free thought – the one that struck dead the Grand Master - is without doubt the most deadly of all blows.

Freemasonry has consistently supported the principle of free thought. During historical periods of repression in which people were forbidden to freely state what was on their minds, Masonic lodges quietly taught men how to become free. In fact most of the freedoms not then openly practiced in society were generally common place in Masonic lodges. Men of unequal social status met *on the square* to share their respective opinions without fear of reprisal. In those days, lodges became islands of personal dignity and could be found in some of the harshest environments, such as Communist Eastern Europe, Nazi Germany and the turbulent times of the French Revolution.

During a time when the Church told people how to think, Masonic lodges inculcated the importance of remaining true to the judgments of one's own intellect. For this, as well as other reasons, Freemasonry has been regarded as a threat to institutions that preach one way of thinking – of one path to take along the spiritual journey. Terror and fear have often been the tools used to insure that Church members did not wander into a Masonic lodge. In the hands of the Pope, excommunication becomes a *mjolnir* delivering the most vicious of all blows - one that severs man's relationship with God. This terror has not entirely disappeared, for even in today's society certain religious institutions continue to threaten its members who have dared to become Masons. Some continue to seek the annihilation of the fraternity by falsely attributing to it secret intentions to rule the world and compel people to worship at the altar of the devil.

Like the three assassins, repressive governments and religions have always feared that Freemasonry has something they do not – some secret thing that will deliver greater power and broader freedoms to the people. If they cannot possess that secret, they will attempt all that is in their power to destroy those who do. Answering the angry demands of Jubela, Jubelo and Jubelum to tell them the secrets of a Master Mason, *Hiram Abif* said he would, but only after each earned the right and privilege to know. The *Word* was never intended to be withheld; it was intended to be passed along to those who proved themselves worthy so that the doing of good works for all mankind would be perpetuated.

From all that we now know the selection of a setting maul as a murder weapon appears to have been made to serve at least two possible purposes: to make certain that *Hiram Abif* died if he failed to disclose the *Word;* and to strike fear into the hearts of the two remaining Grand Masters who also possessed the *Word*. Assuming hypothetically that terrorizing King Solomon and King Hiram of Tyre was a part of the assassins' plan, we would also expect to discover evidence of a plan to attack both of them. While Masonic legend does not give us the answer, the initial involvement of fifteen Fellowcraft circumstantially supports that possibility.

Originally, those fifteen Fellowcraft entered into a conspiracy to obtain the *Word* by force, if necessary. Twelve of them abandoned the criminal enterprise and confessed the plan to King Solomon. On the surface it does not appear that it would have required fifteen men to murder one man. After all, Jubelum killed the Grand Master with one crushing blow to the skull. But if the real targets were all three Grand Masters, then both the number of original conspirators, as well as the weapon selected offers us probable cause to believe that all three were originally in peril. Fifteen Fellowcraft might have been able to complete the dastardly task, but not three men forced to cobble together a new plan of attack after being abandoned by the majority of their co-conspirators. The three likely knew they would never escape detection and punishment for their horrid deed and planned to leave behind a reminder that the powers of darkness dwelled in the midst of the two kings. Even though facing certain death, the three assassins could be assured that they would strike fear into the hearts of the Grand Masters even if knowledge of the *Word* was denied them.

The majority of the *Temple* workmen had been provided by Hiram of Tyre, who made an agreement with King Solomon to pay them their wages. Like Jubela, Jubelo and Jubelum most of those workmen were Phoenician. The communication of the sacred *Word* to King Solomon, the leader of what they regarded as a mongrel Hebrew nation, must have been a very bitter pill to swallow. The God-kings that arose from the ancient Mysteries were reserved for what many Phoenicians believed was their nobler race. Their own King had just betrayed them by delivering the very power of God into the hands of infidels – pearls had literally been cast before swine.

The Jews were believed by most Phoenicians to worship something other than the One True God. It was well known that they no longer worshipped in the manner of Moses and Abraham. In fact since Moses' death the Jews became corrupt and brutally savage, as evidenced by the brutality of David their warrior King. Only an instrument like the *mjolnir* would send a message forceful enough to frighten such people.

When he gave Solomon the *Word* Hiram of Tyre was trying to unite the Phoenicians and Jewish cultures. Having passed through the ceremonies of the ancient Mysteries, he was not simply the monarch of his people; he was the Son of God, just as were the Egyptian pharaohs. He closely followed the progress of his neighbor and noticed that Solomon possessed a very unique wisdom – *the wisdom of peace*. Hiram knew that men of peace were often also men of compromise. Although Solomon descended from a line of monarchs different from Hiram's line, he seemed to possess the same knowledge as the monarchs from Hiram's royal bloodline.

During his own formal education, King Hiram was schooled in the lessons of Hermes Trismegistus, the mythical son of Deity who came to earth to teach mankind the importance of peaceably blending different doctrines and ideas. According to an allegory related by Plato, there was once a time when the gods existed but mortal races did not. When the time came for mortals to appear, the gods molded them inside the earth. Prometheus and Epimetheus were placed in charge of giving each human their respective powers and abilities. Epimetheus begged Prometheus to allow him to exclusively assign those attributes and after receiving Prometheus' consent proceeded to make a mess of it. He foolishly gave all of the important powers to the animals and ran out of options when it came to humans. Zeus rushed Hermes in to correct the situation and distribute justice and a sense of shame in equal measure among men. From justice and shame came the ability to compromise and achieve a peaceable existence among other men. While Plato's allegory is just a story, it was one of great importance to Hiram of Tyre, for it taught him the conditions that must prevail to enjoy peace.

Plato's story also taught him that men must be prepared to synthesize ideas and doctrines. Hiram knew that it was impossible to force people to think in a pre-determined manner. A man must first see the wisdom of that idea or doctrine before he will embrace it.

According to the Holy Bible, Solomon prayed to God asking Him for wisdom to understand right from wrong. By his prayer Solomon demonstrated to God that he was a man of the people – a monarch who intended to place the interests of the people above his own. It is this specific trait that not only contributed to the peace that reigned throughout Solomon's kingdom, but also gained him the respect and admiration of his neighboring monarch, Hiram of Tyre.

King Hiram was also taught to take the measure of a man by the length of his virtue, not his lineage. Because he was not Phoenician, Solomon may have been viewed by many of the *Temple* workmen as an infidel. But Hiram saw him as a man of honor, piety and virtue. In comparison to his war-like father, Solomon was literally a breath of fresh air.

Hiram of Tyre took his throne during David's reign and stood by anxiously watching as the Hebrew warlord gobbled up cities and empires which were subjugated to Israeli control. Thinking that his wealthy port of Tyre might be next, Hiram made friends with David and exercised enormous diplomatic skills to keep David happy and far away from Tyre.

After David died and the young Solomon seized the scepter of Israel, Hiram observed that Solomon's more peaceable demeanor presented a golden opportunity to consolidate power and provide the people of Tyre with a more lasting peace. In return for lasting peace, Hiram was willing to give Solomon the king-making ritual he desired, as well as the accompanying *Word*.

The three assassins labored for years on behalf of their King and country believing that if they persevered in following the path of virtue they each would one day also share in the knowledge of the *Word*. They obediently followed their King to work for the infidel, Solomon, and must have felt horribly betrayed when they learned that he was given the *Word* that none of them had yet received. In their minds they thought that that which should one day belong to them should never have been so cheapened. They seemed oblivious to the fact that such a compromise insured peace. Perhaps they did not care about anything other than themselves.

Our investigation into the importance of using a setting maul as the murder weapon leads us to also consider some pertinent and quite possibly relevant competing philosophies that always seem to be in conflict. Here, we examine the tension between *continuous transformation* and *immediate gratification*. Regardless of the variety of possible motives for murder, we know that Jubelum killed *Hiram Abif* because he was told he could not immediately have the *Word*. Killing the Grand Master was a response to his rage and frustration at not being able to possess that which he urgently sought. Jubelum desired to proceed by leaps and bounds, not slowly and gradually. His desires must be fulfilled *now* not later. He demanded nothing less than *immediate gratification*.

Real spiritual growth flows slowly and gently, while material growth often advances by leaps and bounds – *continuous transformation vs. immediate gratification*. The Psalmist wrote: *"The righteous flourish like the palm tree...they are ever full of sap and green." Psalms 92*. This link between consciousness and action has frequently been described as *the universal sap of life*. The tension between immediate gratification and continuous growth is everywhere in Nature, including the domain of human intellectuality. There are minds that have sided with growth and transformation and others that have embraced fire and revolution. The first seeks to make men aware that there are several paths that lead to the same destination. The second seeks to remove everything that threatens the path one has chosen to follow.

This principle of continuity was portrayed in a particularly beneficial light by the German philosopher Leibnitz. Employing continuity of thought, Leibnitz created the concept of the *"rainbow of continuity,"* that is the bridging of conflicting ideas in such a manner that assimilation had the best chance to succeed, rather than surgically removing conflicting ideas. Platonism, Aristotelianism, Scholasticism, Cartesianism, Spinozism and mysticism were only so many colors in the rainbow of perennial philosophy. For Leibnitz, his entire work was devoted to peace; similar to the work of Hermes Trismegestis whom many claim gave rise to Freemasonry.

Jubelum and his fellow assassins did not care one way or the other about the assimilation of ideas, or about the silly notion that many paths may actually lead to the same destination. Instead, they lusted to keep the *Word* for themselves and to send a threatening message to Hiram of Tyre and Solomon that death awaited them, too, if they persisted in their plan of mongrelizing the *Word*. History has witnessed this same deadly pursuit to maintain the purity of race, ethnicity and religion. Regrettably, mankind has suffered its horrid consequences on more occasions than the slaying of *Hiram Abif*.

Years after his death the world continues to bear witness to the same terror. In the United States, Martin Luther King was felled by an assassin's gunshot while working to bring Caucasian and African Americans together. Years before, Abraham Lincoln was murdered after signing the Emancipation Proclamation and concluding a war fought to unite an entire nation. In Europe, innocent and helpless Jews were rounded up and exterminated by the thousands in Hitler's gas chambers. During the earlier Spanish Inquisition hundreds of thousands of other Jews were forced to either convert to Catholicism or die. Many who did convert were slaughtered anyway for not being Catholic enough. In the Middle East, Persians killed Arabs while other Arabs killed other "Impure" Arabs. On the British Isles, Catholics and Protestants killed each other in the belief that the other side did not worship Jesus Christ in the correct manner. More often than not the most horrible means of murder was chosen to not only kill, but to also terrorize the living.

The same setting maul that killed *Hiram Abif* has been selected by Freemasonry as a symbol of man's mortality. It is ironic that a tool used by craftsmen to build the *Temple* also serves as a reminder that human life can end quite suddenly before one can prepare for its finality. Odd, indeed, that the tool that set the stone into the mortar which constructed the mighty edifice where the Ark of the Covenant was enshrined actually teaches us more about death than it does about life – a lesson reserved for a sturdy plant known as the *acacia*. However, upon reflection the lesson about death is very much also a lesson about never ending life.

Consider what the Holy Bible tells us in that regard: *Man that is born of a woman is of few days and full of trouble. He cometh forth like a flower and is cut down. He fleeth as a shadow and continueth not.* These passages from the book of Job suggest that we humans do not have much time within which to live our lives. The setting maul illustrates that stark reality. Just as certainly as we all have been born we are all destined to die. When we finally understand and accept this truth, we can expect to experience a much greater freedom and ease while we live. Hanging onto our material lives, while instinctive and justified, is not nearly as important as living our lives well by remaining true to our principles.

The Grand Master's resistance to the demands made by the three assassins, even though knowing that death would result, symbolizes what it means to remain true to one's principles. Indeed, it is that level of integrity and steadfast adherence to his principles that sets *Hiram Abif* apart from his murderers. Had *Hiram* valued his life more he would have given up the *Word* long before the fatal blow was struck. In a deeply esoteric context his final confrontation with Jubelum represents nothing less than the eternal confrontation between truth and falsehood.

Well known for his determination of character, Jubelum must have grown angrier by the second as he watched *Hiram Abif* stumble toward the east gate to the *Temple* knowing that the Grand Master had thus far refused to reveal the *Word* and cheated death. Neither a slashing to his throat nor a stabbing at his heart had successfully compelled him to abandon his principles. In Jubelum's angry mind he knew that this matter required yet greater force and a much more horrible terror – things for which the *mjolnir* or setting maul was especially well-suited.

Waiting until the last moment Jubelum lunged from the shadows, grabbed the Grand Master and shouted at him threateningly. If the *Word* was not given instantly, Jubelum growled, he would strike him dead on the spot. *Hiram Abif* calmly replied that the *Word* could not be given to just any man. First, the *Temple* had to be completed and then Jubelum had to prove that he was worthy. In a purple-faced rage, Jubelum's tightened his grip on the Grand Master's tunic. Fed up with *Hiram's* annoying refusals he grasped a nearby setting maul and fatally crushed *Hiram's* skull. The price paid for remaining true to his principles was death – a lesson worthy of emulation by all men.

When *Hiram Abif* died so, too, did the threat posed to him by the *mjolnir*. Terror and violence has no power over the dead. The Hiramic Legend teaches us that the assumption that human death is final is wrong. Men do not die never to live again. Although Jubelum held in his hands the power to end *Hiram Abif's* human existence, he held no power over his spirit and soul. While falsehood, chaos and unprincipled behavior may pose a threat, it is a hollow threat. They succeed only when men are fearful and are powerless when confronted by courage and integrity. This was a lesson the three assassins had not learned until that day, but one they would not soon forget.

Chapter 4

A FOUL CONSPIRACY

While confessing to King Solomon their complicity in the plot to kill *Hiram Abif*, the twelve Fellowcraft who abandoned the enterprise said that originally fifteen had entered into a conspiracy to either obtain the *Word*, or kill the Grand Master. Three of the conspirators were unaccounted for and Solomon ordered a thorough search for them and the Grand Master. The twelve confessors assisted in the search and were told by Solomon that if they failed, they would be executed.

After having no success at the sea port city of Joppa, the twelve Fellowcraft eventually discovered Jubela, Jubelo and Jubelum hiding in the rocks near Mount Moriah. They seized them, took them before King Solomon where they confessed to the murder and were then summarily executed. The twelve who had abandoned the plot were allowed to live.

Not even the treasures accumulated by Solomon's father, King David, were enough to repay Hiram of Tyre the cost of the labor he provided to build the *Temple*. In return for his agreement to pay the craftsmen their wages as they came due, Hiram he demanded that Solomon repay him those advances. After all, as Hiram pointed out, the *Temple* was for Solomon and the Israelites; not the Phoenicians.

We read in the Holy Bible that in order to repay Hiram, Solomon eventually subjected his people to forced labor to grow the crops necessary to pay the bill. With so much on the line from the very beginning of his relationship with King Hiram, it was absolutely imperative for Solomon to take all steps at his disposal to insure that the conspiracy was entirely eliminated.

English common law has long held that the crime of conspiracy is one of the more heinous and dangerous crimes men can commit. That is so because a conspiracy involves two or more perpetrators – not just one man. Because murder was the object of this conspiracy, it was even more dangerous. Several men had taken time to secretly observe the daily habits of the Grand Master *Hiram Abif* and then to lay a deadly trap for him at a time he would be least prepared to defend himself – during a time of prayer and reflection. Most of the conspirators abandoned the plot, but the fact that so many men of virtue would be involved was sufficient enough grounds for Solomon to be concerned that new attempts by new conspirators might follow.

Treason and betrayal have been an unseemly part of society's fabric for centuries. Oftentimes it was those closest to the betrayed who were the chief organizers of treacherous plots. The New Testament records that the disciple Judas betrayed Jesus for pieces of silver and delivered him to torture and death. Julius Caesar was given up by Brutus, his friend and ally. And, General Benedict Arnold gave away the secrets of his military commander to their common English enemy. Many other similar examples abound of conspiracies that history records were organized and promoted by fiends, associates and confidantes alike. Some workmen at the *Temple* may have even praised Jubela, Jubelo and Jubelum, and it was those men that Solomon sought to discover and eliminate.

Having put his famous wisdom to good use, with the assistance of *Hiram Abif* Solomon arranged the *Temple* workman so as to maximize production, maintain peace and promote harmony. Three thousand three-hundred Masters or overseers of the work were separated into one group. Eighty thousand Fellowcraft or hewers on the mountains and in the quarries were placed in another. And seventy thousand Entered Apprentices, or bearers of burden made up the third group. Other than this single instance, the envy, discord and confusion Solomon hoped to avoid were successfully avoided. As far as Solomon knew all of the conspirators were Fellowcraft – members of the working rank just below that of

Master. Unless some new evidence proved otherwise, Solomon believed that his investigation could focus exclusively upon that group.

Neither history nor Masonic legend reveals the identity of the chief organizer among the Fellowcraft. We are left to speculate that he or they were among the three assassins Solomon ordered executed. Regardless, it appears that this was an isolated incident, for no further attempts were made on the lives of either Solomon or King Hiram. Evidently order was restored, light prevailed over darkness and the workmen returned to lives of virtue and labor. The Wisdom of Solomon was yet again verified.

Assuming that this episode is allegorical and not based upon any historical fact we would not expect to learn anything more than what is evident to the eye without peering deeper into the meaning of this allegory's rich symbolism. It is important to know that an allegory about conspiracy and intrigue was not haphazardly selected. It was intentionally inserted into the Hiramic Legend to sharpen our focus upon the importance of always being prepared; ready to guard against the intrusion of private interests into the philosophical and charitable intentions of the Craft.

Envy is among the traditional *seven deadly sins,* and was the only deadly sin defused by the manner in which Solomon arranged and classified the craftsmen. As a human emotion, envy occurs whenever a person lacking in the superior qualities, achievements, or possessions of another uncontrollably desires to possess them. People who find themselves in the grasp of such envy frequently discover that it is neither easy nor possible to have all that they desire.

Envy usually occurs when a persons believes that his self-esteem is under attack. Scientists and anthropologists have written that envy is controlled by that portion of the brain known as the *medulla oblongata,* which is the sector that also controls aggressive behavior. In some circumstances envy can become uncontrollable leaving the person afflicted without any consideration of the potential consequences. Viewed in this context, it was certainly prudent for Solomon to take as many precautions as possible to contain envy.

Believing they have discovered a link between the original Knights Templar and modern-day Freemasonry, certain writers have suggested that the Hiramic Legend has been modified from its original ancient

Egyptian version. According to those writers, those modifications were made necessary because of the growing menace to the Templars and Freemasonry presented by the Church of Rome. The recent release by the Vatican of certain documents relating to the trial of the Templars in the early 14th century may help clarify the actual source of that menace, but the fact that it existed – at least insofar as the Templars were concerned – has already been universally accepted.

Our Templar writers have also suggested that *Hiram Abif* was created by the Craft as a character to represent that which was lost when the Catholic Church undertook the eradication of heretical pagans – including the destruction of an entire pagan library at Alexandria that comprised masterful literary works about man's relationship to God. To the extent there is truth in that contention, the symbolic message to the Craft remains the same: envy in the hands of the powerful constitutes an enormous threat that must be prudently thwarted.

When we recall that governments envious of the accomplishments of their neighbors have at times resorted to murder, plots and intrigues to get what they want, the parallel lesson about the menace to the Masonic *Word* is driven home more forcefully. But to existing and potential conspirators Freemasonry answers with a startling fact: it is unnecessary to plot and scheme against it; all that the fraternity has is yours for the asking. A man is not asked to join Freemasonry; it is up to him to ask for admission.

Hiram Abif never told his assassins that they would never receive the *Word*. Jubela, Jubelo and Jubelum had simply grown impatient and chose to demand, not ask. But as Masons they first had to learn and apply what they had learned before they could advance any farther. Possessing the *Word* places new obligations and duties upon a Mason – obligations and duties that cannot be entirely understood without having first learned the foundational lessons in the preceding degrees.

Solomon's containment of other potential disturbances was the result of great preparation. The wisdom of grouping Entered Apprentices together and Fellowcraft with other Fellowcraft paid huge dividends. Had the younger Masons been included in working groups with the Fellowcraft, the conspiracy may well have been more widespread. Younger men are more easily persuaded by older men – especially by older men who, in the eyes of younger men, have accomplished something of significance. Moreover, by grouping the craftsmen as he did Solomon limited the range of possible problems. Entered Apprentices were not as likely as their more experienced Fellowcraft brethren to lust after the *Word*.

Although he had no way of actually knowing that a plot to steal the *Word* would erupt, Solomon was nevertheless prepared when it did. The potential for jealousy and envy had been lessened. Men who one day would like to lead other men may learn a valuable lesson from Solomon's wise anticipation. Prudence cautions that all who lead should first make every effort to reduce the probability of conflict among those who must implement plans, orders and directions. Otherwise the work may be compromised or even defeated. Solomon not only knew this to be so, but having developed a keen sense of intuition, he was spiritually prepared to anticipate trouble.

While it is difficult to accurately define "intuition," it is relatively easy to state what it is not. Intuition is not the rough equivalent of making good guesses or better choices. In psychological terms "intuition" essentially suggests an ability to understand without effort or to bring to bear a quick and ready insight to a matter that is seemingly wholly disconnected from any past personal experience. It is in many respects an act by which the mind perceives the agreement or disagreement between two ideas. When using intuition one immediately knows the truth of the situation at hand. In contrast when using "instinct," an altogether distinct state of consciousness, one knows how to behave because of an inherent disposition to act in that manner, i.e., the instinct for survival.

The philosopher Immanuel Kant taught that the human mind casts all of its external intuitions in the form of space. The space to create, organize and prepare are among his examples. Perhaps an easier example to understand is that of the decision by General Dwight Eisenhower to have his troops invade Europe at the exact time he chose. His actions were either the product of a good guess, divine intervention, or something in between like *intuition*. Kant has further described intuition as constituting faith at first hand combined with intelligence at the second hand. From his biography, we learn that Eisenhower spent hours in prayer during the days before he gave the order to invade. We also learn that he had the very best intelligence information at his finger tips. His decision to invade Europe was undoubtedly made with the help of his *intuition*.

The philosophy called *scholasticism* came into full acceptance during the Middle Ages; long after the building of the *Temple*. At the root of scholasticism is both the desire for the fullness of intuition, or divinely purifying intelligence, and the compelling of its cooperation with faith. We read in the Holy Bible that Solomon prayed that God would endow him with wisdom, but we are not told that the wisdom he was given was what we know as intuition. However, we learn from the book of Ecclesiastes that Solomon rued his own sins which seemed to have ruptured the usefulness of his God-given wisdom and knowledge. His own lack of faithfulness eroded those powers and by the end of his life the once all-wise King was but a mere shell of his former self. His greatest error had been the failure to persist in combining intelligence with faithfulness. True wisdom cannot be attained without the interaction of divine and human will.

At the time of the conspiracy Solomon's powers were at their peak. He was the world's foremost *believing thinker*. His ability to foresee danger, as well as to discern the better road to travel, placed him in the category of mystic. Years later advanced philosophical scholasticism helped men to achieve that same state of awareness. However that philosophical discipline never acknowledged God as its originator. Instead it held that intuition is created by man during moments of deep spiritual contemplation.

Such well-known holy men as St. Thomas Aquinas and St. Albertus Magnus also are members of the fraternity of intuition, although their paths to that end differed from those who followed the path of scholasticism. They journeyed along the pathways of Christiandom, but like their secular scholasticism companions discovered the same truth – intuition is the marriage of intellect and faith.

No better contrast can be made than the contrast Solomon himself represents at different points in his life between a *believing thinker* and a faithless thinker. During the years when he planned and supervised the building of the *Temple*, Solomon busied himself with God's work. The *Temple* was being constructed on a grander scale than even the King's own palace, because that is where God would dwell. Solomon sought to learn the ritual that would teach him the *Word* so that he could use all of the divine wisdom for which he prayed and benefit others. In that pursuit his faith was clearly at work and he consequently easily foresaw potential problems among the workmen and wisely softened the impact by the manner in which he had them grouped. Accordingly there were no uprisings or conflicts except in the single instance that resulted in the death of *Hiram Abif.*

In his later years, as so clearly reflected in the book of Ecclesiastes, Solomon fell away from his faith and was filled with self-pride. To him, everything was vanity for God was no longer predominantly in his thoughts. Solomon had sunk so low in self-pity that he actually believed he would have been better off never having been born. As an older monarch he was no longer a *believing thinker* and when he left his throne peace and harmony gave way to intrigue and chaos. As he strolled through his palace in his final days, he might have looked to his right and then to his left and sadly shaken his head as he realized that he no longer walked with God.

As far as conspiracies go, the plot to take the *Word* unraveled very quickly. Although we are not given the precise moment when the twelve Fellowcraft abandoned the plan, we are told that it was before Jubelum murdered *Hiram.* During their confession to King Solomon, the twelve also expressed their fear that the three others with whom they had originally plotted intended to carry out murder. Unsure whether or not the crime had yet occurred, Solomon thought that there might still be time to save the Grand Master.

It is hard for most people to change their opinions or behaviors, even if doing so would clearly be beneficial. In America, elected politicians seldom, if ever, deviate from the so-called "party line." To do so could make it difficult, if indeed not entirely impossible to raise the money necessary to be elected or re-elected to office. When obtaining and maintaining power or positions of authority are more important than doing the best job possible, the best interests of the people oftentimes takes a back seat. Occasionally a man or woman arrives on the political scene and acts responsibly even though doing so frequently results in the loss of personal power. Sadly, such dedication is not often seen in any government anywhere in the world.

But government is not the only environment lacking in people of character who hold positions of authority. Self-interest is far too often a characteristic that best describes many past and present business, religious and community leaders. Even in the family home fathers, mothers and siblings find it difficult to place the interest of other family members ahead of their own. Once a particular path is chosen, for the most part it is blindly followed regardless of the harm. It is not so much that people are intent upon hurting others around them; it is more often the case that people simply are clueless and profoundly unaware that their behavior is in sore need of changing. Our own human nature can even inhibit change unless a cataclysmic crisis intervenes to slap us across the face and jolt us into confronting the difficult task of coming face-to-face with our own shortcomings.

When Jubela, Jubelo and Jubelum told twelve other Fellowcraft that they were all being abused by the three Grand Masters and deprived of that which should be theirs, they immediately yielded to the intoxicating lure of self-interest. They even went so far as to agree to kill, if they did not obtain that which they sought. In hindsight it is easy to hold such behavior reprehensible and to hold all of the conspirators in low regard. But if we consider the times we ourselves have given in to the temptation to pursue self-interest, even at the potential cost of hurting others, we might not so quickly condemn those wayward craftsmen. Indeed, twelve repented, aided in finding the assassins, discovered the corpse of *Hiram Abif*, assisted King Solomon in meting out justice to the murderers and returned to the task of completing the *Temple*. Those Fellowcraft actually changed. Sadly we cannot applaud them very loudly for they also abandoned their principles.

We read in the book of Ruth about the ancient Israelitish custom of plucking off one's shoe and learn that it relates to redeeming the soul and changing human behavior. Masons are taught this lesson in the first degree of their Masonic journey. As with many similar lessons in morality and virtue, this lesson is repeated most prominently in the symbolism of the twelve Fellowcraft who abandoned the conspiracy. Interestingly, modern-day laws provide that a conspirator who abandons the conspiracy to which he once belonged before the completion of the conspiracy's criminal object is not guilty of the crime of conspiracy. Society forgives such a person, just as Solomon forgave the twelve Fellowcraft, providing us with yet another link between Freemasonry and certain secular values with which we have become so familiar.

Chapter 5

BURYING THE BODY

"This is no time for reflection, what shall we do with the body?" asked Jubelo as he stood over the slain Grand Master *Hiram Abif* and looked over at Jubela and Jubelum. The answer was to temporarily bury it in a shallow grave in the rubbish of the *Temple*. It was necessary that the body be concealed as quickly as possible to avoid detection and still the rapid pounding of the assassins' hearts. Glancing over their shoulders to see that no one was watching they quickly covered the body with trash, rubble and other conveniently available debris. Speaking in hushed tones they agreed to meet later under cover of darkness and decide how to dispose of the body.

They met at the agreed upon hour and consulted in whispered voices. Jubelum had previously scouted the territory and found a place at the brow of a hill near Mount Moriah that he thought was perfect to permanently conceal the corpse. The assassins carried the body to the spot and buried it planting an evergreen acacia at the head of the grave so they could identify the spot if necessary. Frightened, they ran toward the seaport town of Joppa and sought passage on a ship bound for nearby Ethiopia. A grizzled seafaring man surveyed the assassins carefully and demanded that they produce King Solomon's pass. None of the assassins had the *Word* and offered instead to pay money for the trip. But the *Word* was necessary, not the money and passage was denied them. Stunned and crestfallen, the three Phoenician brothers turned back into the country, found a private cave and secreted themselves in the rocks.

Words and actions often produce results different than originally intended. We learn from the Holy Writings that man may make plans in his heart, but what the tongue utters is from the Lord. *Proverbs 16:1.* Jubela, Jubelo and Jubelum never obtained that which they conspired to take and never made their escape out of the kingdom after slaying the Grand Master. Life is a law of Nature and those who would extinguish it are criminals against the laws of Nature. The plotting and planning to conceal the body and hide their horrid crime failed because God and Nature had something very different in mind - justice. As each assassin sat alone with his own private thoughts in the crevices of the cave each soon realized that fate had a different plan than originally intended. If those Fellowcraft had observed the Masonic lessons taught them they might then have been at the *Temple* among the workmen happy in their labors. But now the sands of time were beginning to run out and the moment of justice was at hand.

Before arriving at their craggy hideout, Jubela, Jubelo and Jubelum had twice attempted to bury *Hiram Abif's* body. The first location was in the *rubbish of the Temple,* which has great singular symbolic importance. Masonic tradition relates that during the construction the *Temple* craftsmen frequently encountered obstacles that primarily arose out of material and worldly concerns. Those obstacles are also intended to represent the distractions that afflict all men during their years of spiritual growth.

Theologically, the *rubbish* represents sin, or that state of human existence that separates man from God. This state of existence is another law of Nature, for man is naturally tempted by some things that surround him. The occurrence of sin continues throughout the one's entire lifetime. According to certain theological doctrines man's only remedy is *spiritual redemption,* or the restoration to God's favor through God's grace or act of loving kindness. Modern-day Christians identify Jesus Christ as the source of that redemption while other religions, philosophies and disciplines suggest other sources. The common thread among those religions, philosophies and disciplines is that while man must rely upon God's grace for his own redemption, he also must act vigilantly and constantly seek to correct any improper behavior.

The slaying of *Hiram Abif* symbolizes two different states of being for us to consider in connection with the concept of God's grace. After he was struck on the head with the setting maul *Hiram Abif* was dead and no longer capable of correcting any past improper behavior. However the assassins were still living, albeit not very well after secreting themselves in the stony, cold cave. In order to correct their improper behavior it was essential that justice intervene, because the murder could not simply be undone. What was done was done and could never be reversed. The matter of the Grand Master's spiritual redemption was in God's hands. The redemption of the living assassins awaited man's justice. In truth there is no real difference between those two — God is in charge of both situations. The real difference is that the assassins continued to be able to exercise free will, while *Hiram Abif* could not. The assassins could sin again; the Grand Master would never sin again. Redemption is for the living, God's grace is for the dead.

This contrast between the dead Grand Master and the living assassins is also symbolic of the patterns of mind and soul that are layered deep within each man's subconscious. Because of seemingly unknowable influences people frequently complain that they do not really know themselves. They do not know why they do what they do, or how to prevent themselves from behaving badly in the future. Such was also true for Jubela, Jubelo and Jubelum following the slaying of *Hiram Abif.*

The image of the dead Grand Master illustrates that there is a spiritual order to the universe, as well as a natural order. We may come to know that spiritual order as *God's grace*. That grace is not limited to the dead, but is available to those of us among the living. To achieve harmony between those orders and thereby attain a much more complete understanding of ourselves, *God's grace* must be permitted to penetrate the natural order. The answer to the question how to do so is that we must first believe in the love of the Great Architect of the Universe. Our Rosicrucian brethren teach us that His spark is imbedded inside the spirit and soul of each human being and can be only accessed by us if we believe He is really there.

Jesus taught his disciples this same lesson. Buddha demonstrated it by his living example. Moses spoke directly to God and afterward visibly changed in physical appearance. In each example, the teacher did not suggest that we clear out the bad habits and simply leave our house empty. To do so simply allows other bad habits to take up residence. Rather, man must practice spiritual lessons to both rid himself of his bad habits and replace them with *God's grace*.

In the case of the three assassins, their voluntary submission to *God's grace* was not enough. The heinous crime demanded man's justice before *God's grace* would ever become effective. As the lustration or purification by water symbolizes regeneration, so too does justice serve to cleanse and purify. Every act performed by man has a consequence and every consequence imparts a valuable lesson. For some that lesson may not be entirely absorbed or placed into action. But since the spiritual order of the universe mirrors the natural order, we may be assured that the law of consequences also exists in that realm. Sometimes those consequences seem fearsome and difficult to accept, for the lesson to be learned is harsh and frequently unwanted. But by the *grace* of God we may be assured that even the three assassins were able to withstand the horror of the divine justice they faced following their own execution.

Spiritually, the *rubbish of the temple* also represents the importance of harmony. Quickly attempting to conceal the body of *Hiram Abif*, the assassins deluded themselves in the belief that they could actually get away with murder. Their minds raced with possibilities, sorted out what they believed should be done, and led them to conclude that the body must be moved to a better location. Somebody at the *Temple* would surely discover it there in the shallow grave. But perhaps in a more permanent grave near Mount Moriah it might never be found. Such thoughts were entirely inconsistent with the virtues taught at the *Temple*. But Jubela, Jubelo and Jubelum had sunk to the depths of selfish behavior and by their own actions had disgraced themselves. Like Solomon at the end of his days, they were no longer in harmony with God and were quickly spinning out of control.

After solemnly depositing the corpse in a properly dug grave near Mount Moriah, the assassins marked it with an *acacia* in order that they could find it again if necessary. That grave marker never was intended to properly honor the distinguished Grand Master. Rather, it represented another act toward concealing the crime. Regarded as holy ground by the Hebrews, Mount Moriah was certainly qualified as an appropriate site for the burial of so good and great a man as *Hiram Abif*. But as their fingers ripped into the soil to dig the grave, the assassins were not thinking holy thoughts. After marking the grave they rushed away thinking that perhaps one day they might need to return and move the body to a different location to make certain their horrid deed was never discovered.

Their rush to conceal the *Hiram's* body symbolizes the change that overwhelms people who suddenly find themselves in the strong embrace of enormous stress. Once considered by their peers as kind, patient and respectful brethren, Jubela, Jubelo and Jubelum had become men on the run – fugitives from justice who needed to act quickly to conceal their guilt, or face the gallows. In the twinkling of an eye a horribly bad decision transformed them from men of honor into men bent upon covering up the evil they had done.

The New Testament contains a pertinent parable that Jesus reputedly told about a seed sower. Some seed the sower cast fell on hard ground and was soon eaten by the birds. Other seed was scattered upon extremely shallow soil and was unable to take root. Some seed actually fell upon fertile ground and plant life thrived at those spots. The parable's lesson strikes at the heart of the real reason why the three assassins behaved as they did. The lessons in virtue and morality never took root.

When men such as Jubela, Jubelo and Jubelum either ignore or become inattentive to the task of transforming lessons about virtue into every-day custom and habit, they risk domination by dark and despairing thoughts. Sins that go unconfessed or bad habits that are excused instead of eliminated have an uncanny knack for entirely absorbing men. Soon those sins and bad habits become predominant and exert enough energy to compel good men to act badly. The person who falls subject to such forces is frequently powerless to stop them and often finds himself in peril of spiritual destruction.

The Hiramic Legend teaches us how to prevent such an unwelcome calamity by using the *alchemical key* of what is oftentimes referred to as God-harmony. It is impossible to experience God's peace by behaving badly and then simply praying to be relieved from any adverse consequence. It is equally impossible for a man to kneel in prayer in his chosen house of worship, later cheat his friend or neighbor and then hope to ever achieve God-harmony.

Politicians who profess their abhorrence at certain lifestyle preferences and then are caught living that very same lifestyle should not be surprised at the ridicule for their hypocrisy or their resulting uselessness to their constituents. Priests and other holy men who secretly molest innocent children expose themselves to horrible secular punishments and subject the churches they represent to public humiliation, dishonor and disrespect. The man who truly possesses God-harmony and consistently lives this Masonic ideal is a man without guile, hypocrisy, or deceit.

While it is true that some followers of religious movements may, for a time and through persistent prayer, invoke the presence of what some refer to as the Holy Spirit, that Spirit is not always retained. With regard to the three assassins it is interesting to observe that during their race to bury *Hiram's* body and escape out of the kingdom they never knelt in prayer. Being in the strong grip of dark forces they did not even bother. Instead they abandoned God and the Holy Spirit and dedicated themselves to their own self interests.

Another parable from the New Testament more clearly illustrates this same lesson. When questioned by a wealthy young man about how he could become a disciple, Jesus told him to sell everything he had, give the money to the poor and follow him. We are told that the young man walked away deeply saddened and unable to comply, for he had massive possessions that he was unwilling to relinquish. His personal interests proved more important to him than his desire to become Jesus' disciple. That young man helped prove the truth of the biblical saying that it is easier for a camel to fit through the eye of a needle than for a rich man to make his way into heaven.

The moving of the Grand Master's corpse by the assassins from the rubbish of the Temple to a grave near Mount Moriah, while certainly amounting to an effort to more permanently conceal the murder, offers up yet another glimpse at alchemical symbolism. From the perspective of their own self interests, when the assassins moved the body they transformed themselves from virtue to vice. This transformation is the exact opposite of making gold from brass. It amounts to nothing more than tossing the gold aside in favor of the brass, or returning to a state of spiritual impurity. Their backward slide represents a complete fall from virtue and morality.

It could also be said that Jubela, Jubelo and Jubelum demonstrated spiritual movement from vice to virtue, for Mount Moriah was holy ground. Moving *Hiram* from the rubbish to holy ground might be interpreted as an instinctive acknowledgement that *Hiram* was a man of virtue and morality even if the assassins themselves had fallen into the grips of vice. For Masons, the science of alchemy represents transformation – change that can either be for the better or for the worse. The outcome is entirely dependent upon the path chosen by each individual. In order to live in the light one must *move* out of the darkness.

Mount Moriah symbolically teaches us that the man who has chosen the path leading to the light will be deserving of recognition for holiness in the same manner as the Grand Master *Hiram Abif.* The site's holy significance is derived from the Old Testament stories about men placing God first in their lives. For example, Mount Moriah was the place where Abraham was about to offer up his son Isaac as a sacrifice to the living God and where David is said to have met and appeased the destroying angel. Some believe it was also the general location where the deposed Egyptian Phaoroh Ahkenaten, identified by Sigmund Freud as the biblical Moses, led his followers after escaping from Egypt. The stories attached to each of these events uniquely symbolize man's journey toward God and into the light.

Mount Moriah has been regarded by generations of Jews, Christians and Moslems as one of the holiest sites on earth. As we reflect upon such veneration for a piece of land by such diverse religions, we cannot help noting a possible reason for the symbolic importance of Mount Moriah to Freemasonry. Like the mountain itself, the Craft has consistently refused to endorse any one particular religion above any other.

Man is endowed with a God-given free spirit and is thereby permitted to pick and choose which of many paths to pursue. Each and every person is free to choose to do great good or greater evil; to decide to become a Roman Catholic, a Jew, a Moslem, or a practicing Buddhist; and to labor for the benefit of his fellow man instead of solely on his own behalf. This symbolic meaning of Mount Moriah clearly implies that no man has a God-given right to impose his own will upon any other man.

For all Masons, Mount Moriah also represents the center of activity where genuine acts of loving kindness are exchanged. When asked by a prospective new member of the Jewish religion to describe the law, the great Pharisee Hillel is said to have replied that *to do unto others is the entire law – the rest is mere commentary.* The illustrious Zoroaster similarly taught that man's most important obligation is to treat others as he would have them treat him. This knowledge was passed on to mankind long before Jesus is reputed to have walked the earth, but is no less valid than are similar lessons in charity taught by the Christ.

At the building of King Solomon's Temple the three assassins eventually determined that it was more important to obtain the *Word* than to acknowledge the sanctity of human life - specifically *Hiram Abif's* life. Each of them ignored the holy truth that there are no riches on the face of the earth more valuable than a human being. History teaches us that Jubela, Jubelo and Jubelum were not the only men to so despicably disregard human life. Prelates, monarchs and mobs have, at various times throughout history, decided that a life or two was not nearly as valuable as power, prestige, or self-importance. In the name of God men have perversely acted to kill others to acquire standing, leadership and influence. The absurdity of such thinking and behavior is readily apparent when we recognize that those things are meaningless unless there are other people around to bully, boss, or demean. If the people are dead, what use is power, prestige, or self-importance? The lesson imparted is clear: it is foolish for a Mason to countenance any act toward mankind that is anything other than loving and kind.

Chapter 6

THE EVERGREEN

After hurriedly burying *Hiram Abif's* corpse in the rubbish of the Temple, Jubela, Jubelo and Jubelum vanished and met again at midnight to decide what next to do. In whispered, hurried tones Jubelum announced that he had prepared a new grave at the foot of Mount Moriah. Moving as silently as possible beneath the moonlit sky, the assassins removed the corpse from its shallow grave, carefully carried it to the brow of the hill and swiftly buried it at the new site. As Jubela and Jubelo turned to run away, Jubelum shouted for them to return for one last bit of important business.

"What if we ourselves need to find the body?" Jubelum thought aloud, as he stretched out his hand to pull an evergreen plant from the ground. Turning to his Phoenician brethren he said, "Unless we mark the grave we will never remember this spot." Holding the evergreen in his outstretched hand he continued, "Let us plant this acacia at the head of the grave in case we need to find the body." Agreeing with his logic Jubela and Jubelo knelt beside their brother and dug at the earth with their hands. When it was deep enough Jubelum placed the acacia into the hole and covered it with the loose soil. As soon as they had finished, Jubela and Jubelo followed Jubelum toward the seaport town of Joppa in hopes of obtaining passage on a boat headed toward Ethiopia.

To Masons the acacia symbolizes human immortality which is the central lesson of the third, or Master Mason degree. The lesson is purely non-denominational in its application, but the plant is described in one Coptic legend as the first tree in Nature to worship the Christ. That legend underscores the belief that God is in Nature and Nature is of God, as much as are humans.

The acacia is also reputed to have been the plant that comprised the crown of thorns Roman soldiers crushed upon the head of Jesus during his Passion. Also known as the tamarisk, this tenacious plant is nearly impossible to kill. A species of the plant was also said to have been used by Noah to build his famous ark. In an ancient Egyptian legend the acacia grew around the corpse of Osiris after he was slain by Typhon and is symbolic of the everlasting immortality of Osiris and all mankind. Thus from Osiris to Jesus the use of the acacia symbolized the same thing – because God has so determined the spirit and soul of all men will live forever.

Within the Hiramic Legend, Masonry also intends the acacia to represent the spirituality that all Masons and all human beings should aspire to attain. Man's happiness and fulfillment of purpose depends entirely upon the strength of the bonds he develops with the Great Architect. By seeking to achieve equilibrium between good and evil, light and darkness, mankind struggles to emulate what God alone has actually attained – perfection. The balancing of the strong tendencies toward both bias and tolerance is or should be every Mason's goal. Although certain of never achieving such perfection during his life on earth, the Mason who makes an effort to do so adds to the progress and positive development of spirituality in the world without which God's permanent rule will surely be postponed. The work of each and every man, woman and child regardless of status, wealth or education is essential to achieving that goal.

If a mature acacia plant is closely inspected it is readily evident that it consists of spiraling branches. In Masonry the spiral represents spiritual and biological growth of all life – plant, animal and human alike. The acacia grows in a spiral movement as it matures. Similarly an idea or problem follows a spiraling pattern or movement as it proceeds from being and idea developed in the mind to a positive act for the betterment of mankind. Interestingly the branches of an ordinary tree, as well as the "tree-ring" circles that are a part of its trunk are arranged in a spiral and mark various points of growth toward maturity. Conceptually, ideas and problems "grow" in the human consciousness through a series of expansions and contractions that are analogous to "tree-ring" spirals.

On a more spiritual level the concept of spiraling movement is profoundly illustrated in those passages in the Holy Bible dealing with the coming of the Christ. The Gospel of Matthew summarizes that coming in the unusual guise of the Jesus' genealogy: *So all the generations from Abraham to David were fourteen generations, and from David to the deportation to Babylon fourteen generations, and from the deportation to Babylon to the Christ fourteen generations.*

This spiritual spiraling in the context of cosmogony may be interpreted as preparing for the coming of Christ. To the Jews the movement symbolizes the coming of the Messiah. Each spiral consists of three distinct segments: the threefold imprint of the patriarchs Abraham, Isaac and Jacob; an imprint from above which corresponds to the sacrament of baptism in the name of the Father, Son and Holy Spirit; all of which is made possible by the transfiguration of Jesus on Mount Sinai in the presence of Moses and Elijah.

Some of the early Christians used a species of the acacia known as mimosa to represent the Christ. We learn from an ancient fanciful Coptic legend that the mimosa was the first plant form in Nature to worship the Christ. Both symbolisms reveal that our ancient ancestors believed that all of Nature was filled with life and Divine light. Unfortunately present-day Masonic ritual inadequately explains the true meaning of the acacia. For all the candidate knows it was simply a handy plant that Jubelum plucked from the ground and used to mark the spot of *Hiram Abif's* grave. Consequently, each Mason is left to discover the meaning of the acacia that best suits his own disposition.

After covering the acacia with the loose soil, Jubelum ordered his fellow assassins to walk with him by a circuitous route toward Joppa and endeavor to gain passage by boat out of the kingdom. But King Solomon had already sealed the kingdom instructing all of his subjects not to allow anyone to leave unless he had a special password. Upon arriving at Joppa the assassins encountered a seafaring man and learned that he was soon to depart for Ethiopia aboard his boat moored at the docks. In reply to their inquiry, the seafaring man said that he would gladly offer them passage, if they had King Solomon's pass. Had he ignored his monarch's directive to demand the correct password, he himself would have suffered swift and fatal punishment. The assassins tried to convince the man to accept money, but when he refused dejectedly turned back into the country to find a place where they could hide.

Symbolically the circuitous route traveled by Jubela, Jubelo and Jubelum from Mount Moriah to Joppa signifies the twisted, tortured path one travels after transgressing against the Great Architect – a backward spiraling. From the Old Testament we read the story about Cain, who after viciously slaying his own brother Abel was compelled by God to wander the earth eventually settling at a place referred to as Nod. The book of Genesis tells us that Nod was situated east of the Garden of Eden, but that geography does very little to help identify the actual spot. Eden itself has never been geographically identified and may simply serve to symbolize the state of being whereby man dwells in complete harmony with God. However, in the Hebrew language Nod is the root verb of the phrase "to wander" and therefore is likely used in the Old Testament to describe the peripatetic wanderings of people who like Cain disobey the commandments of the Grand Architect. Thus, the circuitous route traveled by Jubela, Jubelo and Jubelum may be similarly regarded as a wandering through the Land of Nod – a journey of the condemned.

The land of Ethiopia holds a special symbolic meaning for Masons, for it is one of the oldest nations in the world and hugely significant to human evolution. The circuitous travel of the three assassins eventually led them to justice which brought them into equilibrium with God. Man must by nature sustain the consequences of his good and bad acts. Avoidance of those consequences is both unnatural and grossly unjust.

Human evolution is the process of mankind's spiritual travel back to the Supreme Grand Master of the Universe – not of avoidance of justice. From the Hindu *Rigveda* we learn that like Adam Kadmon, the central character in the Kabbalah, the Perusha of the Vedas represents the transcendent human principle – the man who evolves from complete self-centeredness to complete devotion to the service of God. Well aware of that spiritual concept Masons throughout the ages have exhorted other Masons to unite their individual efforts with those of other Masons for the common purpose of serving God by serving mankind. For those men, the Masonic journey is the correct path to travel if man wishes to walk in harmony with the Great Architect.

As an institution, Masonry has ebbed and flowed; at times true to its mission while at others being adrift, as if lost at sea. This back-and-forth lurching toward God, even by a fraternity such as Freemasonry, lends concrete evidence to the contention that man having once been created in the image of God has fallen away from his calling and is frequently inclined to selfishly pursue his own personal interests. The true history about the human race tells a story about man's circuitous travels or wanderings from generation to generation in the Land of Nod. When man has finally evolved to the point where he will consistently contribute to human improvement great strides will have been made to bring him out of darkness and into the light.

Our Hindu brethren believe that ascended souls exist within our midst to aid and assist each generation's effort to translate human souls from this imperfect to that all perfect celestial place where God forever presides. If this seems like a phrase often heard during Masonic ritual, it is because that part of the ritual was, indeed, contributed to the fraternity by our Hindu and Buddhist ancestors. Masons are also taught that the Hebrews were originally Arabians who traveled into Egypt by way of India, presumably accumulating along the way both Hindu and Buddhist teachings. In that manner the lessons of the wisest teachers have become an important part of the Masonic fabric that has been passed down to us from time immemorial.

The Bodhisattvas, or "wise beings" derived from Buddhist teachings and beliefs, represent unascended souls who have vowed to serve God and the flame of freedom until every man, woman and child become *ascended* and free. Those vows represent an exceptionally sacred spiritual calling and are believed to destine the person making them to a perpetual return to earth after death for the purpose of continuing the work that was left undone. The Bodhisattva belong to a high holy order consisting of some who have earned the right for their souls to ascend to God, but have chosen to serve Him by foregoing that opportunity in favor of working to help mankind redeem its rightful place in the Divine light, i.e., to restore man's proper place in the symbolic Garden of Eden.

It has never been considered desirable that all men choose the Bodhisattva path. But according to Buddhist teachings, most who have chosen that path have earned their right to ascension by virtue of freely choosing to bypass it in favor of continuing to serve on earth for the greater good of mankind and the higher *Mind of God*. Thus, according to this belief and practice, evolution consists of a process whereby God returns to earth following the death of each holy man in a new incarnation. In that newly incarnated state He lives in the midst of His creation for the loving purpose of prompting each person to exercise his or her free will to both serve and love God. Freemasonry has incorporated those teachings into its own lessons which are intended to transcend individual benefit and assist entire societies to adopt practices that bring them into greater harmony with the Great Architect.

For example it has been variously asserted that the lessons derived from the symbolism associated with *Hiram Abif* are as important to nations and their governments as they are to the individuals who populate them. In this context the *acacia* serves as a reminder of that Hermetic saying: *as it is above, so shall it be below*. Once it was planted by the assassins at the head of the Grand Master's grave, the evergreen symbolically connected the dead to the living. It was to be the plant itself that would show the assassins where the body laid should they return and have need of unburying it. This symbolism intimates that all of mankind's actions on earth are intimately bound to the cosmos and have as dramatic an impact there as they do here. In order that human evolution may complete its cycle according to the Creator's plan, governments must also become as divinely enlightened as the people who are governed.

It has been written that in approximately 1270 B.C. King Solomon gained control over Ethiopia with the aid of Sheba after claiming that he was descended from the kings of Aksum. The Aksumite dynasty, whose seat of power was situated in northeastern Africa, commenced existence in the first century B.C. Together with Rome, Persia and China it was regarded as one of the world's great powers. Aksum controlled vast lands including the southern portion of Egypt – that region known today as Yemen – as well as a part of Saudi Arabia located near the Red Sea.

It was this land that comprised ancient Ethiopia where the assassins hoped to travel with the aid of the seafaring man. The region was not only a melting pot for the assimilation of diverse social, religious and philosophical ideas, it was also geographically spread out in such a vast manner that the assassins could have easily avoided apprehension for years, if not indefinitely. Although the assassins were not likely considering anything other than making an escape, Aksum was also one of the very few locales where the surrounding environment permitted a positive evolution of men and their government toward greater harmony with God, demonstrating once again that darkness (a land where murderers might disappear) and light (a land wherein the progress of human consciousness was promoted) co-exist on the material plane.

World history has recorded the appearance of many nations and governments that became world powers. None were capable of sustaining themselves indefinitely ultimately failing for various different reasons. Ancient Egypt, once the garden spot of the world and the center of western civilization lapsed into spiritual decay which in turn made it an easy target for Roman invaders. Rome itself ruled the world in peace for many years before also succumbing to a similar moral decay. Like Egypt, it, too, became an easy prey for marauding hordes that left the country and its people in chaos, confusion and fear.

A great and wise Persian Empire once ruled over the entire Iranian plateau consisting of western Asia, central Asia and the Caucasus. During the rule of Cyrus the Great, Persia grew to such strength that it overthrew the Medes and conquered much of the Middle East. Internal religious conflict spoiled its high standing and eventually opened the door to conquerors known simply as the *Buwayhid* – a Deylamite or Arabic mountain tribal confederation.

While Egypt stands out in history as the center of ancient western civilization, the more ancient Mesopotamian region is regarded as the true cradle of all civilization. The people of that land were extraordinarily gifted and developed many technologies of the era, including metalworking, glassmaking, flood control and water storage. They comprised the first Bronze Age people excelling at both mathematics and astronomy.

It was from the Mesopotamia province of Ur that the patriarch Abraham is said to have journeyed to Egypt. Until the rise of the ancient Persian Empire, Mesopotamia was the most powerful nation in the world. One of the more significant contributing factors to its decline and ultimate irrelevance was the foolish decision by its governmental leaders to routinely go to war against weaker neighbors. The costs of supporting warfare, as well as the erosion of the national conscience, drained that once powerful nation of both its strength and legitimacy.

In more contemporary times similar missteps have consumed and obliterated nations that also held world power status at one time or another. France declined during the Napoleonic Age primarily because the ravages of unrelenting warfare sapped its energy. The Austro-Hungarian Empire sank into economic chaos and moral decay resulting from the all-consuming demands of constant warfare. England, Germany and Russia likewise declined in varying degrees for quite similar reasons seemingly not having learned the historic lessons taught us by the rise and fall of former world powers.

The French historian Jean-Baptiste Duroselle defined a world power as a nation capable of preserving its own independence against any other single power. Sadly, this definition is seemingly based upon the proposition that men will forever seek to control each other — by force and violence, if necessary.

To the extent the legend of *Hiram Abif* includes symbolism reminding us that God continues to create and that His creation continues to evolve from darkness to light, the symbolism tends to verify Manly P. Hall's assertion. Governments, like all human beings, must learn the lessons of virtue and morality if they are ever to bask in divine light. It is frequently stated that *"the devil is in the details,"* which here suggests that the implementation of well-conceived plans for enlightened government will eventually replace force as the method employed by nations to preserve their independence and standing in the world. The use of force and warfare has been the leading cause for the decline, decay and ultimate irrelevance of world powers. In some cases it has even resulted in the deliverance of entire populations, such as the ancient Israelites, into captivity and slavery.

In the opinion of most Masons leaders in government who placed service to the people above the desire to accumulate personal power and prestige are absolutely essential to a nation that intends to survive. When government employs merit as the just standard for selecting its leaders it takes a critical step toward achieving that goal. When "merit" is defined by such governments as the possession of characteristics such as competence, charitableness, tolerance and dedication to duty, governments take another step in the right direction. When the poor and helpless are cared for and humanity is provided with all comfort and assistance during times of illness, mankind makes a positive contribution toward evolving out of the darkness and into the light. When public education becomes the centerpiece for an uncompromising education that is unimpeded by religious doctrine, the people may have confidence that their government promotes tolerance and the teaching of real freedom.

Masonry teaches that the *acacia* is also intended to remind us of the immortal part of man; that part which bears the greatest affinity to that all-pervading force in Nature that will never die. Like all men possessed of an immortal soul and spirit, *Hiram Abif* did not "die" after he was struck by Jubelum. His body died, but his immortal part lives forever. Where it lives no one knows for sure any more than one can pin point God's dwelling place. The immortality of the human soul and spirit is not reserved for good men, such as *Hiram,* but includes men who have acted badly, such as Jubela, Jubelo and Jubelum. It is a mystery of God's creation that light exists alongside darkness; good flourishes as evil ebbs and flows; and all is or will eventually be made right according to His will. The one constant force is Nature herself, which was recognized by King Solomon as symbolizing immortality: *All rivers go to the sea, yet never does the sea become full, to the place where they go, the rivers keep on going. Ecclesiastes 1:7.*

Chapter 7

GUILT AND THE CONSCIENCE

"What shall we do now?" Jubelo asked when told by Jubelum that the seafaring man at Joppa denied them passage to Ethiopia.

"Let us turn back into the country," Jubelum replied. Each assassin grudgingly agreed.

Demoralized and dejected the three assassins hung their heads and trudged onward. Finally crawling into a cave in the mountains of Palestine, they settled themselves between the crevices and in the silence that surrounded them soon were overwhelmed by guilt. This was the first indication that their own consciences would ultimately launch an all-out assault upon their emotions. At the same time the three brothers were consumed by the gripping fear that they would soon be discovered and made to face severe justice. The nagging self-accusations rolled ceaselessly through their heads and became nearly unbearable. Eventually, the overwhelming attack on their emotions gave them away to their pursuers.

Having made *Hiram Abif* their victim the assassins became victims of the haunting and inescapable gnawing of self-loathing and self-deprecation. They desperately hoped that somehow the horrid deed they could not forget was simply a bad dream. Those conflicting emotions teach us that the human mind and conscience can be either man's best friend, or his worst nightmare.

As we know, the human mind is capable of storing enormous amounts of data and information. While this is most often a blessing, it can also become a curse when the memories swirling around in our heads prove hurtful or difficult to bear. The New Testament informs us that the wages of sin is death and that the root of all sin is the failure to love our brother as we love ourselves. There can be no greater demonstration of the complete disregard for such a brother than to maliciously plot and execute his murder. We need only read again the lifetime of wandering inflicting upon Cain after he murdered his own brother Abel to understand the wages of such a sin.

Many of our own individual life experiences teach us that infringement far less serious than murder can trigger a mourning conscience. For most of us, it does not require committing such a supreme crime to discover that we are hounded by a profound sense of guilt. Such is a commonly experienced consequence of transgressing an important rule, law, or virtue. When we fail to do that which we know to be right, we can expect to feel badly.

Men seemingly have the habit of permitting themselves to be unnecessarily victimized by legions of people encountered during their lifetime who delight in the dark art of manipulation. We are thereby reminded that Jubela, Jubelo and Jubelum serve to represent certain horrors confronting mankind – including the horror of tyranny. When we yield to the manipulations by others, we also submit to a form of tyranny that actually can and should be avoided. Interestingly psychologists have determined that many of those manipulators more frequently ply their dark arts upon members of their own families. Apparently one does not have to search far from home to discover examples of tyrannical practices.

Far too often, people are made to feel guilty because they do not visit relatives as frequently as others expect; fail to call relatives as often as some would like; do not suffer well nagging angry relatives; or, insist upon times of privacy away from everyone including family members. Without question our families are the cornerstone of our personal and social development and as Masons we are expected to attend to their welfare. However, even as God permits light to exist alongside of darkness, the Great Architect has also challenged all of us to know the difference between a loving family member and a hostile, manipulative relative. The first inspires love and virtue while the other unnecessarily inflicts us with a mourning conscience – an emotion that should be reserved for soul-searching when we have committed serious infractions.

Mental institutions throughout the country are filled with patients who have told their individual stories to others about wretched difficulties with family members. Many of those patients have fallen ill because they never appreciated the bright-line distinction between love and duty, on the one hand, and disrespect and uncaring for others, on the other hand. Like all men, Masons should diligently seek to understand the difference and maintain the sort of loving independence that is essential to fulfilling each man's personal destiny.

A man's job or profession can be equally threatening to one's delicate sense of guilt. It is an unfortunate fact that some employers believe that the people who work for them have thereby given up rights to individual respect and become little more than common chattel. Even when the work environment is equipped with compassionate and competent bosses, some individuals find themselves imagining the worst- "this cannot be real and I am about to lose my job!" Whether inflicted by an overbearing superior, or by one's own feelings of inadequacy, the painful guilt can be the same. In other words, a mourning conscience is a mourning conscience regardless of the cause. However, as is so when dealing with one's family, each person has the ability to do something positive about his or her situation.

If we experience a bad work environment, we can quit and move to another place of employment. If the problem really lies in our own mind, we can come to terms with that fact, too, and obtain the best professional help we can afford. When we stop to think about Jubela, Jubelo and Jubelum trembling in the caves of Palestine we might also come to understand that unless we do something to change what is happening to us, we, too, might end up trembling with few choices to make. The symbolism of the hourglass described during the *Hiram Abif* presentation emblematically teaches us that time is not indefinite – the sands will eventually run from the top to the bottom of the glass. If anything is to be accomplished by us, it must be accomplished before it is too late. We must act now and stop sitting by idly while events around us consume our entire lives.

As Jubela, Jubelo and Jubelum lay trembling in their hideout awaiting eventual discovery, their minds became their greatest source of terror. Their mourning consciences caused them to think about every possible regret and remorse that the human mind can muster. More often than not men who are suddenly revealed as serious offenders experience instant fear that soon yields to a wish that they had never been discovered. That feeling is primarily motivated by a sense of regret at having been caught – not regret for having been an offender. Of course that is not true remorse, but rather a convenient response to a selfish desire to have things our own way.

In that the Hiramic Legend describes three assassins as opposed to one criminal, we might well imagine that one or two of them felt a sense of betrayal. After all the idea to take the *Word* or slay the Grand Master was most likely the original idea of one of them – quite possibly Jubelum. It is not often that a criminal enterprise such as murder is the simultaneous idea of multiple individuals. More often than not it begins with one person who convinces another, who then convinces others to join the conspiracy. If that also applied to Jubela, Jubelo and Jubelum, we can well imagine that two of the brothers were having a hard time in the Palestinian cave holding good thoughts about their leader. The anger they must have felt must also have compounded the pain each experienced from his own mourning conscience.

While Masonic tradition does not reveal who among the brother assassins was the eldest, there is no doubt that the Hiramic Legend intends for us to believe that Jubelum was the leader. He made the decision to kill the Grand Master, to bury his body in the rubbish of the Temple, to move the body to Mount Moriah and plant an acacia at the head of the grave; to attempt passage to Ethiopia; and eventually to find sanctuary among the clefts of the rocks in the rugged Palestinian mountains. More likely than not, Jubela and Jubelo simply went along with the plan of their brother without seriously considering the potential consequences. There must have come a moment during their terrifying time in the cave that they came to not only regret blindly following Jubelum, but to decide that it was he who was at fault for having led them down the wrong path. Blaming others for our problems is a very natural emotion known to most of us.

When we pause to reflect upon the times we blamed others for our plight we may be surprised by the examples that we recall. Perhaps we remember feeling that our mother did not love us as much as she loved our siblings; our spouse behaved insensitively and caused us to lose control and lash out angrily; or, maybe a trusted friend gave us poor advice about the stock market and we lost our entire investment. The mourning conscience laments what others have done to us, as much as it regrets the wrong we are willing to admit. While those feelings are natural and shared by many of us, they are often inaccurate and tend to undermine our ability to accept responsibility for our own behavior. When that occurs our self-worth erodes and may even result in our becoming less loving of both ourselves and others.

The Great Architect has implanted within each one of us a common almost natural understanding that every human being is worthy and important. There is never a good reason to permit others to push or pull us in the wrong direction. In most circumstances we have a clear choice between being effective and achieving your personal goals, or being ineffective and permitting ourselves to be controlled by our own personal desires. In other words no one is in charge of you other than you. If you become angry at another's behavior, that is because you chose to become angry. Blaming the other person is a convenient way of ignoring that you made a poor a choice about how to behave. In most situations we can base our actions on our own intrinsic worth as human beings – but not when we refuse to accept responsibility for our own actions.

Even Jubela and Jubelo finally accepted responsibility for their own plight. We learn from Masonic tradition that when their pursuers closed in on them, both brothers loudly moaned that it was they, too, who had erred – not just Jubelum. Jubela groaned that he deserved to be punished according to the penal vow he made as an Entered Apprentice Mason. Jubelo followed by stating his desire to be similarly punished according to his penal vow as a Fellowcraft Mason. Criminals though they were, perhaps Jubela, Jubelo and Jubelum should actually be applauded for finally demonstrating one of the Masonic virtues taught them at the Temple – acceptance of responsibility.

Their plight serves as a reminder that all men, particularly all Masons, are literally linked so tightly together by an indissoluble spirit of fraternal kinship that compassion for one another is a duty imposed upon us by Nature. The mourning conscience described in this chapter should never be wasted on self-pitying. Rather it should be reserved for those occasions when we encounter the suffering of others. Equally important that type of compassion is not limited to those whom we believe to live virtuous lives, but should be freely poured out for all men regardless of whether or not we find them worthy.

In time all men will face the same *Dark Night of the Soul* about which St. John of the Cross wrote between 1542 and 1591. St. John speculated that upon passing from this material dimension each man's soul journeys into a state of abandonment and darkness and then on to a loving union with God. During that journey, man's soul moves away from routine theological rituals and truly embraces the Supreme Architect of the Universe, whom we may only come to know through pure love. While enveloped in the loneliest darkness at the beginning of that journey the soul is eventually illuminated by the light of wisdom and is purged of all imperfections in the same manner that the *common gavel* demonstrated during Masonic ritual is intended to break off the rough and superfluous parts of stones for the builder's later use. Among those imperfections are such human traits as callousness toward others, insensitivity to the pain of others and uncaring attitudes about the plight of others. It is these that weaken the soul and starve the spirit.

Not all men travel the same path during their lifetime journey on earth. Similarly in the Hiramic Legend not all craftsmen engaged in conspiracy and murder – only three stooped so low. Not all craftsmen were ordered to hunt down the assassins – only twelve were selected. Masonic legend informs us that there were thousands of others at the Temple who played no direct role in either the conspiracy, or the apprehension of the murderers. Which of them deserves our compassion for the suffering they endured upon learning that *Hiram Abif* was dead and forever lost to them? The response is easy for Masons, because no suffering may go ignored whether that suffering is by the lowest, the highest, or those in between. Compassion is not handed out on the basis of merit: it is felt and given freely to all who suffer.

We read in the book of Job how quickly one man's fortunes can change. That exquisite biblical drama portrays the suffering of one innocent man and how those around him reacted. An oriental chieftain, Job lived a pious, upright and richly blessed life. For seemingly no reason other than the fact that he was perhaps living too well for too long, his fortunes suddenly changed. Job suddenly lost his property and children before being afflicted with a loathsome disease. His friends were certain that God was punishing Job for something he had done but none could identify the dreadful sin. Finally, even his closest companions concluded that Job had been keeping some horrible secret about himself from them – a secret that God found terribly offensive. Consequently, everyone lashed out at him and left him to suffer alone.

A similar message is contained in the book of Lamentations wherein God's chosen prophet is compelled to walk in affliction and feel the mighty sting of the Creator's wrath. Set in the sixth century B.C., the poetic dramas revealed in those biblical passages depict the destruction of the Temple, an abrupt cessation of dearly loved rituals, the exile of leaders and the disgraceful loss of a nation's sovereignty. In those dramas, just like Job, Israel serves as a symbol of how suddenly good fortune can become a living nightmare.

These lessons clearly teach us that we must never judge the behavior of our neighbor before extending to him the compassion he deserves. The compassion that flows out of the depths of our mourning conscience is never dependent upon our first determining that the suffering person is worthy. Mankind is expected by the Great Architect to compassionate the miseries of all Creation – men, women, children and all other life forms.

When Nature suffers because of man's neglect we all suffer. When an animal suffers, men mourn. When nations, religions and cultures are suddenly upended displacing people, ideas and manners of worship, men and women everywhere should kneel in compassionate heartfelt prayer. For the suffering that occurs elsewhere in the world is as much our own as it is that of others.

The mourning conscience depicted in the Hiramic Legend may be seen as a stone necessary for erecting the Temple of Spiritual Love in our own souls without which we may never truly know God. It is directly related to the *Golden Rule* taught by every religion since the day mankind first began to worship the Great Architect. If we wish to find love in our world, in our homes, or in our places of employment we must first give love from our own hearts. If we desire peace, we must live peaceably. If we hope to be comforted when we suffer, we must compassionate the miseries of others.

Not even Jubela, Jubelo and Jubelum should be hated, though their crime was immense. They should be regarded with compassion. As they each mourned in their cave because of the murder they had committed, so should we also mourn that they were afflicted with a sudden reversal in their own fortunes. The compassion meant here is something very different than the justice of Solomon that the assassins eventually faced. However, both are essential to mankind's spiritually balanced existence.

Man cannot ever really be just in the punishment of another person until he has first learned how to feel and express compassion. Solomon understood that justice without mercy is no justice at all. It is sad to witness men past and present who have determined to replace justice, compassion and mercy with vengeance. When that occurs, love gives way to hate; peace yields to violence; and compassion discovers that it has no place in the world.

As darkness settled over Palestine, the three assassins shivered in silence against the chill wind whistling through the caves. Having no time to consider what they might need while escaping to Ethiopia the brothers had nothing with which to survive. They had no fire, no blankets and nothing other than the cold rocky clefts to lie upon. Very likely Jubela and Jubelo then shared in Jubelum's earlier lament: *had I observed the lessons taught me at the Temple, I might now be among the workmen honored and respected instead of being an outcast and disgraced.* As the night grew darker the brothers finally stopped talking and soon discovered a greater horror – their own thoughts.

Their thoughts soon turned to God. Sleep gave way to constant prayer. They first pleaded with the Great Architect to reset the clock to a time in the recent past when their lives were simpler and much less stressful. They next begged God to forgive them their grave sin, as well as all other sins they had committed during their lives. Hoping against hope, they prayed over and over for God to grant them life everlasting.

There was no mistaking the fact that the assassins would eventually be captured and very likely executed. The days of their lives had been reduced to hours and there were no longer any dreams to dream. Instead they found themselves earnestly hoping that they might set their souls right with God. They were condemned men for whom the hourglass had nearly run out.

It is universally the case that when human prayer moves from self-pity to self-examination it alternates between loud plaintive pleadings and a silent give-and-take conversation with the Creator. Penance becomes a pleasure; the personal condemnation of others vanishes in a flash; and a patient acceptance of fate soon absorbs the mind.

Unlike so many who had never led a virtuous life, Jubela, Jubelo and Jubelum had known what it was like to live exemplary lives. Though death was their certain fate, they were no better or worse than any other man who had fallen short of God's glory. In that moment they turned obediently to Him seeking forgiveness. Expressing their most sincere regret at having offended their loving Supreme Grand Master of the Universe, each also reasserted his allegiance to the One True God in whom they had always placed their trust. As soon as their prayers ceased each was swept with an enormous sense of the Creator's deepest love and affection. "It is true," each thought, "the Great Architect disinherits none of his children." We will never know for certain whether or not joy replaced despair in the caves of Palestine that night, but it is quite likely that although engulfed in darkness three troubled souls saw light.

No longer master of anyone, Jubela, Jubelo and Jubelum turned humbly toward God and tried to ready themselves to travel a new path – the path traveled by the dead. Oddly their contrite submission offered the perfect environment within which God's grace could begin its precious work. As was known even to the ancients the Great Architect enters the hearts of only the pure of soul and spirit. But before He could accomplish anything further with the assassins, it would be necessary that justice work its transforming magic.

God's influence upon the spirits and souls of the assassins that night made each moan so loudly that they were overheard by the Fellowcraft sent by Solomon. That same engulfing spiritual influence later allowed all three to openly admit their guilt and march obediently to the death that awaited them outside the gates of Jerusalem. Such obedience in the final hours of life teaches all of us a valuable lesson - man must bear responsibility for the imperfections in his soul with humility and meekness before God will extend him divine grace.

When the assassins' heartfelt laments echoed from the cave, the twelve Fellowcraft rushed upon, seized and bound Jubela, Jubelo and Jubelum who were then hurried off to appear before King Solomon. With heads bowed they listened as their great King sternly questioned them about their guilt. "What have you to say," he bellowed at them, "are you guilty or not guilty?"

Furtively glancing at each other they announced their guilt in unison. At that moment their souls and spirits submitted to the cleansing and sense of calm that only true confession can inspire. The bitter dark night in the cave that first delivered an overwhelming self-loathing gave way to a renewed spiritual strength that yearned for the love of their Great Creator. Out of the depths of the deepest darkness each assassin eventually saw the light and their consciences mourned no more.

Chapter 8

THE MASTER'S WORD...OR A KEY THERETO

After delivering Jubela, Jubelo and Jubelum to King Solomon the twelve Fellowcraft were ordered to return to Mount Moriah and search for the body of *Hiram Abif* and the *Word*. If they could not find the *Word,* Solomon told them to examine the body carefully to determine if there was any evidence of *a key thereto.* The Fellowcraft repaired to the spot and upon discovering evidence of a fresh grave found the decaying body. There was nothing there other than the jewel that identified the Grand Master's important office among the *Temple* workmen. This they took to King Solomon who immediately recognized it and while holding it high in the air strangely proclaimed that the Master's *word* was lost.

The symbolic importance of the *Word* is discussed elsewhere in the rituals of Freemasonry, particularly in the rituals of both Royal Arch Masonry and Scottish Rite Masonry. That the meaning is not found in any one ritual, or in any *rite* to the exclusion of any other *rite* clearly implies that all lessons and traditions relating to virtue, morality and the spirit must be carefully studied before the true meaning of the *Word* may be thoroughly understood. During those lessons we come face-to-face with what mystics have called the *Eternal Logos.*

The power of the *Word* when spoken is believed by many to constitute the key that unlocks the door to reality. The Greek word "logic" is closely related to the word "logos" and the philosophy associated with both is regarded as a controlling principle of the universe. "Logos" has been defined as "divine wisdom manifest in the creation, government and redemption of the world." It has also been identified with the second person of the Holy Trinity – the Christ. The Gospel of John records that concept in the following manner: *In the beginning was the Word, and the Word was with God, and the Word was God. John 1:1.*

That "Logos" or *Word* of God is nothing less than the power that resides behind all physical manifestations. In that sense it bears the imprint of the Divine Mind. Many theologians and philosophers contend that it also constitutes what is known as *the potential of being* which is found in the heart of every material atom. It is also firmly lodged in the heart of every man. From it flow the assortment of creative energies the Supreme Ruler of the Universe has given to each of His sons for use in the partnership of creation.

Some religions and philosophies hold that the "Logos" functions independently of man requiring no assistance from any source other than itself. Accordingly it operates within a framework of laws fashioned by the very mind of God: a spark of the *Eternal Logos* which is locked within every particle of every living being. That spark carries the stamp of man's destiny somewhat like a seed and also acts as a receptacle for messages from God. Those messages teach us that God's laws constantly remain inviolate and cannot ever be changed. However, insofar as those laws relate to God they are wholly inapplicable and entirely irrelevant. The Great Architect transcends even Himself and thereby repeatedly transforms from glory to glory within a boundless realm of infinity.

When he saw *Hiram Abif's* jewel in the hands of the Fellowcraft King Solomon immediately believed that the Grand Master's *Word* was lost. He had already heard the assassins confess to his murder and there could be no doubt in his mind that his dear friend and brother was dead. Thus, when he ordered the Fellowcraft to find the body and search for the *Word* it is not likely that he expected them to discover a live body. Rather, Solomon fully expected that if anything was discovered at all, it was very likely to be a corpse. Assuming that was his state of mind, why was Solomon not able to proclaim the *Word* lost when the assassins confessed to murder? To discover the answer to that question we must first examine other Masonic symbolism.

From several early Masonic writings, such as the Harleian, Sloane, Lansdowne and Edinburgh-Kilwinning manuscripts, we learn a legend about a craft of initiated builders that existed before the Great Flood. Its members had even been employed in the construction of the Tower of Babel. Before Noah was born there lived a man named Lamech who took two wives named Adah and Zillah. Adah bore him two sons, Jaball and Juball. Zillah gave him one son and one daughter. Lamech's four children founded all Crafts in the world. Jaball founded the Craft of geometry; Juball established the Craft of music; the third brother, who was named Tubal-cain, began iron working; and the daughter, Naamah, founded weaving. The siblings knew that God intended to take His vengeance upon man's sinfulness by sending either a deadly flood or a horrendous fire and took steps to protect the sciences they had each discovered. They wrote the pertinent information on two pillars of stones which could neither be drowned, nor burned so that succeeding generations of man might know the secrets they had unearthed.

Several parts of this legend are important to Masonry. First, the names Jaball, Juball and Tubal-cain have a rhythm in common with the Phoenican names of Jubela, Jubelo and Jubelum. Second, the book of Genesis records the possibility that two different men named Lamech spawned two separate lineages: one is an ancestor of Cain and the other is said to be a descendant of Seth, the third son of Adam and Eve. Third, it is possible that the lineage from Cain is more critical, because it constitutes the royal line to which the House of David owes its origin. Fourth, the Seth ancestry includes Noah who is said to have survived the Great Flood as God's chosen one. Fifth, Naamah, the daughter of Lamech and Zillah and the founder of weaving, is reputed to have been Noah's wife. Sixth, one of the Lamech's (all but the most conservative scholars have recently concluded that there is only one Lamech, but two traditions) is alleged to have been a *Master Mahan,* a title of derision to Mormons, who assert that like Cain, Lamech made a pact with the devil. And seventh, the act of recording all knowledge on two Pillars, while appearing to constitute the memorialization of everything that will ever be known to mankind, is merely the beginning point for man's quest for knowledge. When understood in its appropriate sense, the two Pillars actually symbolize the coherence of all knowledge – something quite different than representing the sum total of all that man can ever know.

Behind the materialistic and mechanistic world there exists another realm of interaction. That realm has been scientifically proven and represents a synthesis of such disciplines as cosmology, quantum physics and biology with the study of human consciousness. The principle empirical and observable effect of this synthesis is the coherence of phenomena across a broad range of distances. Just when mankind thought it had established boundaries for the universe by identifying the Milky Way, these phenomena - the *metaverse hypothesis* - reared up to offer a challenge.

Scientists have observed that the universe that we have known is coherent – that is all of its stars and galaxies are connected in some mysterious way. Whereas those scientists once believed we were alone, with the advent of powerful telescopes they have now discovered galaxy after galaxy that extend even into what were once termed "black holes." Those discoveries have led to the speculation that a more vast and infinite universe might actually exist. In other words, it is highly unlikely that our universe defines the boundaries of *the* universe, any more than the substitute for the ancient Master's *Word* defines God.

Current scientific thinking concludes that matter is expanding, not contracting or remaining constant. The laws of gravity appear to be at the center of this activity producing a perpetual matter-creating mill. The geometry of space-time seemingly creates a reservoir of "negative energy" from which is extracted positive energy. Most amazing is the scientifically proven fact that the mass of particles involved are all mysteriously adjusted to favor certain relationship ratios that recur again and again in galaxy after galaxy. In short, everything appears to be related – and yet man does not appear to know everything.

The Jewish historian Josephus informs us that Adam forewarned his descendants that sinful humanity would be destroyed by a deluge. To preserve what had already been discovered, the children of Lamech raised separate pillars of stone and brick which were calculated to withstand such an inundation. An ancestor of Noah named Enoch rediscovered the *two pillars* after the flood subsided and built upon the knowledge they contained. According to Masonic tradition he also discovered the ineffable Name of Deity, or *Word* of the symbolic lodge of Freemasonry.

Like his ancestors before him, Enoch envisioned the need to record this valuable information and is said to have made two golden deltas. He constructed an underground temple consisting of nine vaults and placed a triangular tablet of gold containing the ineffable Name in the deepest vault. Masonic legend records that it was later discovered and guarded as a valuable secret by King Solomon, King Hiram of Tyre and *Hiram Abif* during the erection of the Great Temple.

The importance of obtaining knowledge and passing it on to succeeding generations is emphasized in Masonic ritual. During the second degree candidates are advised to assiduously attend to learning seven liberal arts and sciences – grammar, rhetoric, logic, astronomy, music, arithmetic and geometry. In other words, man's quest to know God did not end with the discovery of the *two pillars*, for there is much more to learn. Likewise, man's efforts to comprehend the ineffable Name of Deity did not end with the discovery of the triangular plate of gold. Knowing how to spell the *Word* is far different from knowing its pronunciation.

Similarly, learning about the Milky Way and the boundaries of our universe does not constitute knowing all there is to know about the galaxy after galaxy that conjures up speculation about a metaverse, or coherent parallel universe that may contribute to the creation of the universe within which we live. As scientists who explore the field of quantum physics are coming to understand, numberless worlds are around us each framed by the same Divine artist and which roll through the vast expanse that we call "space." Infinite in nature, "space" signifies that which lies within the confines of our material world about which we may never learn all that is available to be discovered. Much like the symbolic *point within the circle*, our material world is limited. But beyond that world there is much more that mankind is only now beginning to understand cannot be fully comprehended without the aid and assistance of the *Word*.

Numerous religions have laid their respective wisdom upon the altars of Freemasonry. Untold numbers of arts and sciences have contributed to the Craft's symbolism and helped established it as the university of Divine inspiration. Beneath the angles, squares and other implements of architecture that have been selected to symbolize infinite concepts one may find at least a key to the mysteries of a Master Mason, if not actually discover the *Word*. What will be found when one uses that key is impossible to predict, for the extent of the discovery depends upon the person making it.

For example, according to several theological canons there are always a certain number of holy men and women who are admitted into intimate communion with God. It is while there at the center of contemplation and in the midst of profound silence that the Great Architect is said to speak. In those moments great truths are revealed to each listener - truths that are not otherwise made known to anyone.

As the Fellowcraft obediently left the Temple upon King Solomon's order to search for the secrets of a Master Mason, or a key thereto, we may wonder whether or not any of them knew what they were looking for. After all, they were only Fellowcraft and knew nothing about such secrets. None of them had been initiated as a Master Mason. What to look for? Where to search? Such questions most certainly rolled through their minds. What exactly did King Solomon expect of them? And why did he choose Fellowcraft instead of Master Masons? Did Solomon's fabled wisdom fail him in this instance, or did he have something more profound in mind?

Solomon's wisdom was very much intact. It is the legend itself that is questionable when interpreted literally. But as Masonic lessons are primarily imparted through symbolism, it is better that we analyze the symbolic meaning of this part of the legend. The best that Solomon could have expected from mere Fellowcraft was a surprised reaction if they discovered something odd or unusual in *Hiram Abif's* grave. Moreover, Masonic tradition informs us that there were only three Master Masons who actually knew the secrets of a Master Mason – Solomon, King Hiram of Tyre and *Hiram Abif.* If that was so, sending other Master Masons to search for those secrets would have been no better than sending Fellowcraft or even Entered Apprentices.

After removing the earth and inspecting the Grand Master's corpse, the only object of interest was the jewel of *Hiram Abif's* office – the plumb that now adorns the Junior Warden's jewel in present-day Masonic lodges. Of what or to what was this a key? On its face it did not appear to have any secret or esoteric significance. Solomon did not attribute secret significance to it either, as he held it in his hand and proclaimed that the *Word* was lost. But was it a key to something that only men as knowledgeable as Solomon could understand?

A possible answer to that question might be gleaned from a re-examination of the attributes that Freemasonry associates with the office of Junior Warden. The plumb admonishes us to walk uprightly in our several stations in life, to hold the scales of justice in equal poise, to observe the just medium between intemperance and pleasure, and to make our passions and prejudices coincide with the line of our duty. Elsewhere in Masonic ritual we are also taught that the Junior Warden represents the beauty and glory of the day, which is to say that which is just and gloriously upright. Yet in spite of such lofty attributes, it is fair to further ask to what secrets is any of this a key?

It is here that the symbolism of the *dying god* may contribute to our analysis. The jewel of the Junior Warden's office reminds us to thoroughly examine what it is that constitutes the symbolic *beauty and glory of the day*. To the ancients, as well as for present-day Masons, it relates to the position of the Sun at meridian height, for it shines everywhere and illuminates everything that God has created.

The myth and legend of Tammuz and Ishtar represents one of the earliest versions of the *dying god* allegory. Tammuz was alleged to have been the esoteric god of the Sun. He was frequently referred to as a *shepherd* and was both the husband and son of Ishtar, the Babylonian Mother-goddess. Tammuz' annual festival took place at the beginning of the summer solstice. He is reputed to have died in midsummer and was mourned at the time by extraordinarily elaborate ceremonies. While the manner of his death is historically disputed, it is clear that legend records both his resurrection and subsequent status among his worshippers as the *redeemer* of his people.

Another similar legend concerns Adonis, who was reputedly born at midnight on the 24th day of December. His unhappy death resulted in a mystery rite that was established by the Jews – not the Greeks, who nevertheless also acknowledge this character as a god-man. The book of Ezekiel records that women wept for Adonis at the north gate of the Lord's House in Jerusalem. Legend records that Adonis was slain in the winter time by a boar, which has become a symbol of the evil principle of cold. After three days, he rose from his tomb amidst the acclamation of priests and worshippers. They are said to have loudly shouted: *He is risen!*

In Phrygia another philosophical school centered upon the legend of Atys, who like Adonis was reputed to have been born at midnight on the 24th day of December. While there are two accounts of his death too lengthy to recount, suffice to say that a great debt of gratitude is owed to this legend for initiating the well-known symbolism of the Christmas tree. Atys is alleged to have died beneath such a tree imparting at the last his own spirit to its limbs. Like other *dying gods* before him, Atys remained in his tomb for three days and rose on Easter morning overcoming death by his own resurrection.

A most curious aspect of the various *dying god* legends is the *hanged man* symbolism not easily found in any Masonic ritual. That symbolism is primarily associated with the Norwegian *Odinic legend* wherein Odin is reputed to have hanged himself for nine nights during which time he also pierced his own side with a sacred spear. While suspended, Odin discovered through meditation the runes or alphabets by which the later histories of his people were recorded. Esoterically, the *hanged man* represents the human spirit suspended from heaven by a single thread. The world below is but an illusion and when that fact becomes known it constitutes the greatest achievement of self-realization.

The evidence derived from all of the various secret rituals is that the mystery of the *dying god*, like that portrayed in the Hiramic Legend, was universal among the enlightened sacred teachings. It has been perpetuated in Christianity through the *passion* or crucifixion of Jesus Christ – the ultimate *dying God*. The secret importance of this tragedy constitutes nothing less than the true secrets of a Master Mason – the lost Master's *Word*. That secret holds the key to universal and individual redemption and regeneration. Those who never learn the true nature of this allegory are not likely to ever know and understand the wisdom of King Solomon.

Chapter 9

KNEELING AT THE GRAVESITE

After proclaiming that the Master's *Word* was lost, King Solomon ordered Hiram of Tyre to assemble a working party to accompany him to *Hiram Abif's* grave. They were to exhume the body and take it to the Temple for a more decent internment. Upon arriving at the grave, Masonic tradition informs us that Solomon and King Hiram conducted a solemn, sacred ceremony that is frequently repeated to this day in lodges of Master Masons. While the specifics about that ceremony will not herein be disclosed, because they are reserved exclusively for Master Masons, we can state that the legend of *Hiram Abif* clearly implies that Fellowcraft were in attendance that day and witnessed something that would henceforth be withheld from succeeding Fellowcraft.

As far as it is known in the annals of Freemasonry, those twelve Fellowcraft are the only men other than Master Masons to have witnessed the sacred ceremony. Their presence was no mistake, for Solomon led the procession to the gravesite and presided over the secret rites. He must have intended for those Fellowcraft to learn the truth about human death, which folds the meaning of the *dying god* symbolism into the secrets of a Master Mason. Why he chose to do so on that occasion is not made entirely clear to us by either the legend, or the ritual. Suffice to say, we are meant to understand that Solomon intended to act as he acted, either because he believed the twelve Fellowcraft worthy to be made Master Masons, or because he felt that the lesson about life everlasting was important to them.

The remainder of what transpired at the gravesite that day is not fully reported in Masonic legend. However, it is at this point that the candidate for the Master Mason degree learns the dual lessons about life everlasting and the importance of conducting his life on earth in a particularly moral and virtuous manner. The concept of resurrection from the dead is vividly depicted leaving the Master Mason with the unmistakable impression that while one good Mason travels beyond the veil on an unknown path toward an unknown goal, another good Mason continues to live and pass on the benefits of virtue and morality. This endless cycle of dying and living further symbolizes the existence of parallel universes – one that is bounded by finite restrictions and the other which is free from the restraints of time.

When he is made to represent the resurrected man the candidate for the Master Mason degree is reminded of the symbolism's vertical and horizontal importance. The vertical realm deals with the Divine through which the sojourn of the spirit and soul is wrapped in mystery. The horizontal realm relates to mankind's journey on earth about which much has been learned throughout history. Both share a commonality in participating in the becoming of that which is to be, better described as continuous *creation,* and challenges us to comprehend the great spiritual distinction between intelligence, on the one hand, and creative intuition, on the other hand. Aside from the important truths imparted by the symbolic *five steps of fellowship,* which will be discussed later, the great spiritual distinction taught here is perhaps one of Freemasonry's most valued *secrets.*

Human intelligence is associated with successive points of rest, while creative intuition is intimately linked to mobility and progress. The body of knowledge that we discover in our lives relates to that which has happened and is reminiscent of the pronouncement attributed to Solomon in the book of Ecclesiastes that *there is nothing new under the sun.* For example, scientific discoveries do not amount to the invention of anything new and different, but pertain to finding that which is right in front of our face but has previously gone unnoticed. When we first learned that adding 2 plus 2 equaled 4 we did not learn anything new under the sun. We merely acquired knowledge that was already known, but had not until then been discovered by us.

Intelligence turns aside from mobility, for it has little to gain from pure theorizing. Theories and speculation are not knowledge or intelligence, for neither is based in fact. They are precisely what they purport themselves to be – educated guesses or deductions based upon other bodies of known facts. The intellect is meant for something entirely different – assessing immobile facts and appreciating them as though they were ultimate realities. Freemasons first encounter this truth when encouraged in the Fellowcraft degree to assiduously study the liberal arts and sciences. Yet, in so doing the candidate inevitably arrives at the point of theorizing and speculating that the body of immobile knowledge once had a source, or point of creation.

Examined somewhat differently, intelligence concentrates only on the harvest, which is the product or result of growing. The raising of *Hiram Abif's* corpse from its grave is a moment when the candidate encounters the additional truth that there is much more than the harvest to which to aspire. However, it is essential not to forget that this new truth cannot possibly be understood or appreciated unless one first learns the lessons of the harvest. While intelligence is oriented toward facts, this new truth is oriented toward the process of creation – the process of *becoming*. As opposed to restricting human perception to all that is already known under the sun, the process of *becoming* seeks to embrace germination and growth which represent the hidden sources of the harvest.

Exercising our own human intelligence translates us to the process of decomposing; a process quite similar to the dissection of animal and plant life as a part of a routine education in the science of biology. It seems that our intelligence is only entirely at ease when it works upon raw matter which could logically continue ad infinitum until we decided to stop thinking. No man has ever fully exhausted all that there is to know under the sun and is not likely ever to do so. Instead, one works for a period at decomposing until he is either exhausted or satisfied and then ceases. That point of cessation represents the refusal of our minds to continue, but it does not represent the end of knowledge. All of the doctrine and dogma that is derived from human intelligence falls into this category. Thus the promotion of such doctrines and dogmas as being complete is not only inaccurate; it poses a grave danger of causing another mind never to pick up where the previous one left off. For this reason and many more the legend of *Hiram Abif* cautions us against compelling others to accept only those doctrines and dogmas that we ourselves find most appealing.

The parallel lesson that may be gleaned from the raising of *Hiram Abif's* body relates to the intuition of faith – the process of *becoming*. The Gospel of John advances this process in its opening message about the creative *Word*. As noted previously, we read therein that: *In the beginning was the Word*. Here, it is the *beginning* that seizes our attention, not the result, or the harvest. It is within this realm that comprehension of the light of consciousness may be explored and developed for the purpose of nurturing our spirits and souls in preparation for the same Divine vertical journey *Hiram Abif* embarked upon after his death.

In actuality, the Gospel of John invites us to transcend our human intelligence and open our hearts and minds to life itself which is represented by the mystery of faith. Once *Hiram Abif* could no longer think, act and love as a human being he was swallowed up in that mystery which we can either permit to frighten or encourage us. We learn that the human soul is neither fully rejuvenated nor regenerated by human intelligence alone. To the contrary, if we look close enough we will see that there are two aspects to the raising of the Grand Master from the grave: the continuation of the living on earth according to his precept and example, and the progression of the human spirit and soul. The latter aspect places us squarely in the domain of creativity where we can expect to acquire something new - something that is not already known under the sun.

The *Word* King Solomon proclaimed lost represents none other than the creative spirit, or spark given to us by the Great Architect. Throughout the annals of Masonic lore *Hiram Abif* is represented as the chief architect or builder who oversees the creation of the *Temple*. He is also symbolized as the emblem of *beauty* which is intended to convey the notions of pleasure, meaning of life and human satisfaction – man in harmony with nature. Christians frequently associate the *Word* with Jesus; Jews embrace it as symbolic of the coming *messiah*; Buddhists teach us that such beauty is found much closer to home - within each and every human being; Hindus inform us that the creative spirit represented by the *Word* never dies, but is repeatedly reborn on earth; and Moslems understand the simple beauty of dwelling submissively in the light of Allah without need of anything more. Regardless of which theology we select, all religions recognize the same creative mystery of faith that is embraced in the Hiramic Legend.

When Abraham left the land of Ur and traveled to a strange country he acted on faith, for there was no guarantee that he would ever find that for which he was in search. During his era some of his friends and associates likely thought him foolish and may even have gone so far as to describe his faith as nothing more than a false reliance upon a flawed premise. In contrast, when Solomon announced in the book of Ecclesiastes that there was nothing new under the sun, he acted as a man of intelligence relying upon his own intellect rather than his faith. While both approaches have merit, they are quite different from each other.

On the one hand, Abraham acted as a sower; while on the other hand, Solomon behaved like a reaper – one who harvests what has already been sown. The Hiramic Legend teaches us the importance of assimilating sowing and reaping into an alchemical marriage. But before we blindly accept such a proposition on faith alone, it might be prudent to ask ourselves whether or not such a marriage is logically possible?

The men of solid historical reputation who have answered *yes* to that question include St. Thomas Aquinas, Henri Bergson and Pierre Teilhard de Chardin. Since each man represents a different discipline they tend to lend enormous credibility to the *yes* answer. St. Thomas Aquinas dedicated his existence to theology; Bergson was devoted to the study of philosophy; and de Chardin ceaselessly explored science. While St. Thomas Aquinas made gold from other metals in a theological sense, blending his brand of Roman Catholicism with an extraordinary toleration of all theologies, Bergson opened our eyes to the important link between instinct and creative intuition.

In his studies, Bergson concluded that instinct moulds the very form of life. While intelligence is quite mechanical, instinct tends more toward the organic dimension. They represent two divergent developments of one and the same principle that embraces both an inward and external assessment of matter and how it was first created. Interestingly, there is significant swing to-and-fro among the assortment of scientific theories about instinct. Some schools of thought simply regard it as *intelligence,* while others at the opposite end of the spectrum consider it *intelligible.* According to Bergson, the resolution of this wide spectrum lies relies upon the lessons taught us by Hermeticism.

On one level instinct may be regarded as the rough equivalent of sympathy. If this manner of sympathy could extend its object and reflect upon itself, it might give us the key to vital operations, just as intelligence opens the door to matter. Intelligence and instinct enjoy an opposing focus: the former leans toward inert matter, while the latter inclines toward life. While intelligence is closely associated with science and the scientific method of analysis, instinct or intuition constitutes the path of an inward journey each person may pursue to discover the truths about God residing within their own being.

While the metaphysical truths about intelligence and intuition may grab our attention, Freemasonry's message about the practical steps one makes take toward realizing the benefits of those truths is equally gripping. Those steps consist of going beyond or outside intelligence which to the rational thinking mind poses the challenge of how best to accomplish *going beyond.* The human mind instinctively recoils at such a thought, because it is exceedingly difficult to rationally imagine going outside of intelligence by any path other than intelligence. After all our own consciousness is nothing other than intelligence and so we are understandably left to ponder how one may use intelligence to *go beyond* intelligence.

One well-known Masonic message would actually allow us to do so if it was accurately understood. It is the message contained in the symbolism of the *strong grip of the lion's paw* used during the movement of *Hiram Abif's* body from Mount Moriah to a new grave near the Sanctum Sanctorum of the Temple. By using the grip of the lion's paw, Solomon and Hiram of Tyre *went beyond* the manner and method prescribed by existing human knowledge. After attempting known methods for removing a corpse and miserably failing, they knelt and prayed to the Supreme Architect of the Universe. By the power of his God-given wisdom, Solomon realized that when human strength and wisdom fail, Divine assistance was vouchsafed him through the medium of prayer. When he finished a new idea rolled through his head – the idea about using the *lion's paw*.

Acquiring anything new, including new habits requires that we first make an effort to try something new and different. For example, consider the physical act of swimming and how you might learn the skill if you had never before seen anyone swim. The inspiration to jump into the water and float around awhile might come to you during prayer, or focused reflection upon how best to meet the challenge of crossing the river that lay between you and the land on the other side. In order to breathe after jumping into the water you might make every attempt to keep your head above the water so you could breathe fresh air. In time, you might even begin to move your arms then your legs and suddenly discover that you were swimming. In this instance, as in all other similar instances of discovering something new, you used your intelligence to *go beyond* what you already knew. You acquired a new habit or skill by first putting your mind to good use and then allowing it to become informed by something entirely new.

In theory it seems absurd to try and know something without using human intelligence. But is it really such an absurd notion? In the example about learning how to swim our intelligence took us only so far. Assuming the risk of drowning and overcoming the fear of drowning were equal parts to the decision to finally jump into the water. Had we merely employed our powers of reasoning we might never have assumed the risk in the first place. But, casting aside reason we jumped in, held our heads high, flailed around a bit and suddenly to our surprise actually swam!

In this example human intellect detached itself from reality and we took a huge leap leaving behind our safe environment in exchange for the uncertainty of that which lay ahead. Is that not precisely the ultimate fate of the human soul and spirit? Regardless of our fears will not our bodies eventually decay and die? What lies ahead for us – do we know? If we do not, then we have not yet decided to jump into the water and learn to swim. Reasoning powers alone will never open the door for us to understand this mystery of eternal life anymore than they permitted Solomon to understand what he must do to raise the body of *Hiram Abif* from the grave.

While the Kabbalah refers to this exercise as *profound meditation*, or plunging the mind into the depths of darkness, something more than meditation is actually at work. In reality, Solomon's graveside prayer symbolizes *contemplation*, which in Latin means to separate something from its environment. In Christianity contemplation is connected to mysticism – a practice so misunderstood throughout the ages as to have once been labeled heretical, or the result of witchcraft.

Contemplation was an essential feature of Plato's philosophy and in practice is quite nearly the exact opposite of meditation. For Plato, contemplation led the human soul on an upward ascension in search of direct knowledge about God – literally the Tree of Knowledge referred to in the book of Genesis. In practice it differs from meditation in that while the meditative state involves specifically focusing the mind on a subject or object, contemplation requires that the mind be emptied of all thoughts. In that state the soul and spirit are open to receiving God's revelations.

As Solomon knelt and prayed at the grave he awaited just such a revelation or answer that had never before been given to mankind to meet the challenge at hand – a revelation that taught him the valuable use of the *strong grip of the lion's paw*. That revelation is merely one of many spiritual lessons and practices that may be gleaned from both Hermetic philosophy and the Kabbalah. In Christian practice Solomon's graveside contemplation is often referred to as revelatory prayer or the reception of messages from the Divine which God chooses to convey for His own purposes.

As was noted previously, the book of Job introduces us to an exquisite dramatic poem that deals with suffering and retribution. The relevance of that poem to the plight of *Hiram Abif* is easily apparent, for the circumstances surrounding the Grand Master's death are reminiscent of innocent suffering. As was stated before, Job was an oriental chieftain who was highly regarded by his peers for his pious and upright character. Richly endowed with family and fortune, Job experienced a sudden and wholly unexpected reversal. He lost his property and his children. His body became afflicted with a loathsome disease and he sank into a deep depression. Although he restrained himself from complaining against God, he mournfully questioned why such an innocent person as he should suffer so terribly.

Unsympathetically, Job's friends insisted that his plight must be God's punishment for some personal wrongdoing Job has kept concealed. They recommended that he repent and ask God for forgiveness, but Job was unrelenting in professing his innocence. Rejecting his friends' conclusion and recommendation he demanded that God tell him the reason for his suffering. Amazingly God answered, not by explaining the reasons for Job's plight, but by reaffirming His own omniscience and almighty power. Though this was not the response Job had hoped to hear he felt somehow soothed and soon recovered his humility and trust in God.

Upon closer analysis the course of action recommended by Job's friends actually invited him to engage in a meditative communication with God. They told Job he should talk with God specifically about repentance and forgiveness and nothing more. The path Job selected was the contemplative path, for he emptied himself, remained silent and allowed God to do the talking. Even though Job had no idea how God would respond the response he finally received accomplished the greatest understanding about his plight that Job could have ever hoped to learn.

Coincidentally, the prayer Solomon uttered at *Hiram Abif's* graveside, memorialized at chapter 14 of the book of Job, symbolizes the type of prayer that the Holy Bible teaches will likely elicit Divine revelation. The beginning phrase of that prayer lays bare man's meager status before God: *Man that is born of a woman is of few days and full of trouble.* Immediately following is an acknowledgement of man's fleeting presence on earth: *He cometh forth like a flower, and is cut down: he fleeth also as a shadow, and continueth not.* Man is not in charge of very much – it is God who determines everything; and Solomon's prayer continues: *Seeing his days are determined, the number of his months are with thee, thou hast appointed his bounds that he cannot pass.* Frequently human life is beset with failure, misery and suffering which are intended to refine the human spirit and strengthen the soul. But here Solomon gently invites God to temper that refinement and permit man to participate in the process by fulfilling his destiny: *Turn from him, that he may rest, till he shall accomplish...his day.* Next Solomon acknowledges that God has given hope to His creation: *For there is hope of a tree, if it be cut down, that it will sprout again, and that the tender branch thereof will not cease.*

Solomon's contemplative prayer teaches us that we are partners with God in fulfilling His plan - a plan about which we actually know very little: *But man dieth, and wasteth away: yea, man giveth up the ghost, and where is he? As the waters fail from the sea, and the flood decayeth and drieth up: So man lieth down, and riseth not till the heavens be no more.*

Later in the biblical drama Job rhetorically asked: *if a man die, shall he live again?* Job believed he knew the answer thinking quietly to himself: *all the days of my appointed time will I wait till my change come – thou shalt call and I will answer thee.* Although Solomon's graveside prayer did not include that same sentiment, these passages are nevertheless important for Masons to consider as they ponder the precise nature of the resurrection. While some who witness the Master Mason ritual are reminded of the spiritual resurrection, others see it as God giving man a second chance in life – a chance to follow the path of Freemasonry toward the fulfillment of his destiny on earth. Is it possible the symbolism relates to both?

While kneeling beside his dear friend's grave Solomon heard God's answer to his prayer and immediately sprung to his feet announcing the good news about the secret of the *strong grip of the lion's paw.* The same secret lies within the ancient Mithraic tradition which some writers contend has in part been grafted onto Freemasonry. It, too, relates to such symbolism as self-sacrifice and service to mankind unto death. Like the lessons in Freemasonry, it is the secret of *work;* the lesson of *loving labor.*

From first to last, Masonry is *work* which is honored in its rich symbolism of God as the Great Architect; Solomon's Temple under construction at the hands of craftsmen; tools and implements of architecture that have been selected to impart wise and serious truths; and by revering the first artificer in metals who holds a key necessary to entering a lodge of Master Masons. Everywhere one looks he sees Freemasons at labor both within their lodge rooms, as well as abroad in the world, living the truth of that sacred scripture: *Faith without works is dead.*

The candidate for the Master Mason degree is also taught the valuable secrets of the *five points of fellowship,* which relate to *work.* A Mason's entire Masonic career culminates not in a life of leisure, but in a lifetime of labor, because those *five points* commit him *never* to hesitate to go on foot and out of his way to assist a worthy brother Master Mason; to *always* remember the welfare of his fellow Master Masons when praying to God;

never to reveal the secrets given him by another brother Master Mason, unless they be criminal in nature; to *habitually* extend a helping hand to another whose fortunes, like the wretched fortunes of Job, have turned sour; and to *remain constant* and trustworthy in whispering good counsel into another Master Mason's ear.

It is these *five points of fellowship* that constitute the real secrets of Freemasonry – not a chalice, a person, a royal line, or a luminous treasure, though all may exist. It is the heart, soul and spirit found in every Mason who is at work assisting God to accomplish His great and loving purposes. It is these secrets that radically change the world so that our earthly abode will truly be fit to be embraced by God as His Kingdom.

Chapter 10

BEHIND THE VEIL

After King Solomon raised *Hiram Abif's* decaying corpse from its grave the body was carefully and reverently transported to the Temple grounds. There it was buried near the *Sanctum Sanctorum,* or *Holy of Holies,* where a marble monument is said to have been erected in memory of the Grand Master. The ornaments of that monument serve as additional symbols of importance to Freemasonry further highlighting the broad significance of *Hiram Abif* to the Craft and the world.

That monument is said to have consisted of a beautiful broken column; a weeping virgin holding an acacia in one hand and an urn in the other; an open book was situated in front of the weeping virgin; and an image representing Father Time stood at her back unfolding the ringlets of her hair. Each item symbolizes one or more ancient truths which are carefully explained to every Master Mason before he embarks on his mission in the world. The explanation of those items constitutes one of the final events in a Mason's initiation into Freemasonry. However, little, if anything further is explained about the spiritual significance of burying *Hiram Abif's* body near the *Sanctum Sanctorum.* That explanation requires us to consider something that happened following the second exodus of the Hebrews out of Egypt.

After Moses settled his followers near Mount Moriah, he erected a Tabernacle to God which he purposely situated due east and due west.

Masonic tradition implies that he did so to commemorate the mighty east wind which miraculously opened the Red Sea permitting the trapped masses of Hebrews to escape as the Egyptian Army bore down upon them to inflict a certain and merciless slaughter. Within that Tabernacle, Moses and the High Priest (his brother Aaron) fashioned a private area to house the Ark of the Covenant. There, God could rest in his earthly house where he would only be visited once a year by the High Priest who would humbly worship him on behalf of all Hebrews.

Of all the ancient religious sites still standing today, the Kaaba at Mecca most closely resembles the many pictorial depictions of Moses' Tabernacle. Although it stands today as Islam's holiest place in Mecca, it was actually erected before the Prophet Mohammed's birth. The edifice was originally dedicated to Hubal, a Nabatean god worshipped at one time in so-called pagan Arabia. The Nabatean's were traders from southern Jordan and Canaan – the same land that gave King Hiram of Tyre and *Hiram Abif* to Freemasonry. They were eventually conquered by the Roman Empire and subjected to harsh rule by Emperor Trajan. Eventually the people dispersed and their culture has seemingly been lost for all time. But the Kaaba lives on continuing as it always has to symbolically serve as a house for God or Allah as He is most reverently referred to by our Islamic brethren.

Crowds of worshippers congregated at the Kaaba once a year, just as the Islamic crowds do today. In ancient times the crowd was quite diverse and consisted of Christians, pagans and Jews, as well as other people who embraced different religious beliefs. During that era it was a virtual melting pot of religious thought that neither intentionally precluded nor omitted people of any religion. In the representation of tolerating diversity it stood above even the Tabernacle of Moses which was exclusively reserved for Hebrews and the precious Ark of the Covenant.

The crowds that gathered there once each year enjoyed a peace that was not always felt during the rest of the year. To perpetually keep the peace, Mecca was declared a sanctuary and it was carefully monitored to make sure that no acts of violence occurred within a 20-mile radius. As a result, the surrounding area surrounding thrived as a center of trade and commerce which was contributed to extensively by the Canaanites who had then become exclusive masters of navigation.

In that the Tabernacle of Moses has never been discovered, some religious writers have been inclined to speculate that the Kaaba is the Tabernacle. A few have even gone so far as to make the equally unsubstantiated claim that the Kaaba is the Temple of Solomon. Today, both contentions would be regarded as heretical by Jews, Christians and Moslems alike. Moreover, there is no indication that the Kaaba has ever contained a *Sanctum Sanctorum* or *Holy of Holies*.

According to Jewish tradition, within both the Tabernacle of Moses and the Temple of Solomon a thick curtain separated the *Sanctum Sanctorum* from the Holy Place, or inner room. Banners emblazoned with cherubim reputedly stood at the entrance emblematic in design and coloring of God. They were made of linen and yarn that was colored blue, purple and scarlet, and served to remind everyone that spirits serving God were then and there present. The curtain or veil constituted a symbolic barrier between God and man leaving all men to measure God's awesome power against their own meager capabilities.

While the veil was never intended to keep man separated from God, it served to remind those who entered not to carelessly approach God or to trifle with His laws. Even the High Priest who was permitted entry beyond the veil once a year was required to make certain that he meticulously prepared himself for standing in the Divine presence. Specific manners of washing were followed, as was the donning of special clothing reserved for the grand occasion. A unique type of incense was to be burned that would yield a special aroma. The smoke it emitted was intended to cover the High Priest's eyes from God's direct view.

The single day each year when the High Priest was permitted entry into God's presence was referred to by the Hebrews as the *Day of Atonement*. Within the silent confines of the *Sanctum Sanctorum* the High Priest offered up a sacred sacrifice on behalf of all of the people - literally a mass repentance for all of the past year's sins. At that moment the High Priest stood in the place of Moses who had ascended Mount Horeb and conversed with God face-to-face. We are told that in later years Moses also acted in the role of mediator with the Great Architect on behalf of his people. The Paulinian-Christians who followed much later in time contended that Jesus's sacrificial death changed those rules, for as sacred scripture informs us the veil in the Temple of Jerusalem was torn in half from top to bottom – symbolizing the yielding of one era of worship to another. By that act, our Paulinian-Christian brethren were convinced beyond persuasion to the contrary that the *Holy of Holies* had been exposed thereby making God accessible to everyone, not just the High Priest. However, the tearing of the Temple veil did not obliterate the *Sanctum Sanctorum;* it symbolized that the *Holy of Holies* had moved to its correct location in the hidden and secret presence of God where, as Christian theology informs us, Jesus ascended after his death. The book of Revelations provides us with additional insight into this *changing of the rules,* for John describes the New Heavenly Jerusalem as a perfect square – the same configuration found in the *Sanctum Sanctorum.*

Freemasonry neither accepts nor rejects any religion's theological explanation about the *Holy of Holies.* Neither does it offer us any specific interpretation about its purpose or symbolic importance. Such explanations are both inappropriate exercises in theology and entirely irrelevant to the reason why *Hiram Abif* was finally laid to rest *near* the sacred inner sanctuary.

Notably his body was not laid to rest *in* the *Sanctum Sanctorum* which makes it quite clear that Solomon knew that doing so would have been contrary to all propriety. For *Hiram Abif* was not the High Priest either during his life or in death. That status was reserved for the Zadok lineage that gave us such sacred High Priests as Aaron and his son Phineas. Rather, *Hiram* was the Chief Architect of the Temple construction and was primarily responsible for building the *Holy of Holies.* It was by his skill that man constructed God's earthly dwelling place symbolizing for all time the beautiful effort of human hands in the service of God. In short, *Hiram Abif* symbolizes the beauty of *work.*

Understanding the symbolism of the monument erected to the memory of the Grand Master also serves to explain, in quite different terms, the truth about everything Masonry claims *Hiram Abif* to symbolize. For example, we are informed that the monument consisted of a virgin weeping which represented the unfinished state of the Temple. The Grand Master's death interrupted the work and ended his contribution. However, it did not end the building of the Temple. Solomon eventually selected *Hiram's* successor– Adonhiram - who guided the craftsmen through the completion of the construction. From this allegory we also learn the importance of participating in God's work during our brief lifespan and to prepare others who will survive us to continue that same labor. For if mankind is ever to build the New Jerusalem, it must be built by the efforts of succeeding generations, not merely by the efforts made during our lifetimes.

The broken column shown on the monument memorial represents both the untimely death of *Hiram,* as well as the undeniable truth that no man has been promised that he will live any longer than this very moment in time. While modern-day medicine has improved man's general health, it has not arrived at the point that it can guarantee immortality. Moreover, even if medicine could one day do so, that advance cannot possibly stop men from waging war and killing each other; neither could it reverse the devastation to earth's environment, which threatens man's ability to live on this planet; likewise, it cannot alone improve the progress of the universe or resolve all causes of human death.

Man will always be born, live for a time and then die. The time one individual shall live is bound to always differ from the time allotted to other people. As some are born, some will die, just as surely as new leaves sprout after old leaves decay and fall from the trees. The lesson of the broken column is that the length of one man's lifespan is not nearly as important as the work man performs while living. Each man has within himself the power to make his work either beneficial to the advancement of humanity, or detrimental to all human existence.

In one hand, the weeping virgin held an acacia while in the other hand she grasped an urn. The acacia is a symbol of life without end while the urn represents mortality causing us to ponder the difference between the two. While human mortality is symbolized by *Hiram Abif's* ashes which were eventually placed in the urn, the acacia represents the spirit or soul of man that will never die. The mystery that remains unexplained is precisely how it is that a mortal essence can possibly be commingled with an immortal essence. How that occurred in the first instance is the subject of much study, prayer and contemplation. The various religious studies that weigh in with frequently differing opinions have contributed to that study, but to date we have not received an acceptable answer to the question. A similar struggle for acceptance among the many differing schools of thought persists over defining what actually lives forever. The Grand Master's monument offers no hint making it quite clear that unlocking this secret must be accomplished by using a much different key.

An additional object - an open book - rests in front of the weeping virgin which Masonic tradition informs us holds the record of *Hiram's* virtuous life. Although we are not told why such a record was made it appears evident that it consisted of his virtues and not his vices or human failings.

Nowhere in the annals of Freemasonry is the beloved Grand Master ever described as either a man without sin, or as the Deity incarnate. He is merely a man, albeit a man possessed of both an enormous talent and an extraordinarily pious nature. *Hiram* used both during his lifetime and achieved so high a recognition among his peers as to have been included with two kings, Solomon and Hiram of Tyre, as Freemasonry's first three Grand Masters. That only his virtues were recorded and not his sins evidence the fact that those virtues should be forever remembered by men in all ages.

Many hundreds of thousands of human beings have been born, lived their lives and died without ever having their virtues recorded – except possibly by God in His Book of Life. Some may never have given a hint of virtue in anything they ever did, while many more have simply been forgotten as time passed by. The recordation of *Hiram's* virtues was an honor not commonly accorded every man. Its purpose was to provide us with an example to follow; an example of beautiful labor; of the skillful application of God-given talents; and of dedication to creating, building and ornamenting a Temple unto God – whether it be a temporal or spiritual temple.

Perhaps the most profound symbolic segment of *Hiram Abif's* monument consists of Father Time standing behind the weeping virgin. In various drawings of this symbolism an elderly male figure is depicted using his frail fingers to patiently unfold the ringlets in the young virgin's hair. The message intended is that time, patience and perseverance will accomplish all things. But those who already appreciate this message because of their own personal experience are very likely disappointed that there is not something more to consider.

Few who ever lived have had everything they desired. If each one of us honestly took stock of our own lives we would likely admit that during our lifetimes we have failed almost as often as we have succeeded. At least, we have failed according to the commonly accepted definition of that word by not having met our intended goals. But failure is part of learning and contributes to the erection of a spiritual edifice that will eventually withstand any attack, onslaught, or inundation.

While the business of the world absorbs, corrupts and degrades one mind, it feeds and nurses the noblest independence, integrity and generosity in another. Pleasure is a poison to some and healthy refreshment to others. To one man, the world is a great harmony, but to another it is filled with madness and the horrible clanging of evil deeds.

Yet when all is said, life is actually the same for everyone. It is simply viewed and experienced differently. Some find a purpose behind personal failure, while others are quickly defeated and never try again. One way is self-invigorating, while the other is self-defeating. One way leads to understanding the truth behind the symbolism of Father Time patiently unfolding the ringlets of the virgin's hair; the other never will lead to understanding anything.

The fact that both this monument and *Hiram Abif's* final resting place stand in the shadow of the *Sanctum Sanctorum* is further evidence of God's pervasive influence upon all that we do each and every day of our lives. It also serves to remind us that the Great Architect's pervasiveness and loving embrace does not lose its grasp when at last our own ashes are deposited in the urn. Perhaps it is helpful here to remember the both the monument and the place where it was situated symbolically represent the *guardian of the threshold* which is drawn from Hermetic tradition – a threshold across which immortality forever extends before us.

That threshold separates the "surface world" from the "depth world." Man's conscience has been defined by numerous philosophers as the passageway from one world to another entry into which reveals a truth to each person about himself. In Hermetic philosophy the *guardian of the threshold* was said to have judged correctly he who could cross over to the "depth world" with the courage and humility necessary to bear that truth.

In the Hermetic tradition the "depth world" represented the school of esoteric life which conveys its lessons by *symbols*. Those lessons are intended to contribute to the alliance of human intelligence with unconscious wisdom, or intuition, which is regarded by many as that state of being most desirable to obtaining the fruits of contemplation – revelation from the Supreme Ruler of the Universe.

Direct communication between intelligence and wisdom is the development of conscience, which is extended from the domain of action to the domain of knowledge and is awakened there to the point of becoming the light of intelligence. The positive aspect of conscience, as opposed to the negative aspect with which we are all so familiar from our daily lives, is that which is said to become the illuminating and revelatory principle of intelligence that unites with unconscious wisdom. More simply stated a person is not at all likely to achieve this state of being if he permits himself to become fully absorbed with negativity. It is said among philosophers that he who manifests disapproval, anger, jealousy and worldly sin will never be permitted to cross the threshold.

Once a person is permitted by the *guardian of the threshold* to enter into the esoteric school, intelligence grows in two directions. First, it grows in the direction of the outer empirical world and later toward the inner empirical world. Conscience is the door that opens unto a world as vast and profound as the world we physically perceive with our human senses. It is this new world that is symbolized by the *Sanctum Sanctorum* which is also closely guarded by the equally symbolic monument erected to the memory of *Hiram Abif.* It is this new world that opens to each individual who positively wills that his own intelligence become the servant of his conscience. It is also this new world, or *Sanctum Sanctorum* that the High Priest entered once each year as he enjoyed an audience with God on behalf of the people. It is this same *Sanctum Sanctorum* that represented the sacred center of both the Tabernacle of Moses' and King Solomon's Temple.

Each of those stately edifices has long since yielded in sacred influence to the inner sanctuary or sacred part within each one of us about which both the Essenian Teacher of Righteousness and Jesus spoke when they instructed their followers upon the duty they owed to God to individually regard their bodies as Holy Temples. As we search within the depths of our souls we discover the "depth world," or *Sanctum Sanctorum,* which constitutes the new world protected by the *guardian of the threshold.*

That same *guardian of the threshold,* symbolized by the monument to Hiram Abif, stands as a reminder to us that there is a hierarchical entity, or Archangel who privately teaches each one of us within the depths of our souls of the "depth world." Considered in this context, the *guardian of the threshold* also represents for us an older brother or sister who while engaged in the service of the Great Architect also pass on to us a greater appreciation for God's infinite kindness and wisdom.

In the Hermetic tradition, the *guardian of the threshold* is the great judge charged with preserving the equilibrium between that which is above and that which is below. The Roman Catholic Church depicts that judge holding a sword in one hand and a balance in another. The sword signifies cleansing and healing which fortifies the human soul with courage and humility. The balance represents a precise accounting of what must be paid by each man before he may travel further. As esoteric writer Maitre Philip of Lyons observed, that which must be paid consists of one's personal debts, as well as the debts of his neighbor. This profound observation is quite similar with the earlier command by Moses that each of his followers must tithe regularly. It is also reminiscent of the offering made by Abraham after receiving the blessing from the King of Salem – the High Priest Melchizidek.

Another way to repay the debt is by giving money to the poor, or in support of a good and gallant cause. Freemasonry excels in promoting this virtue and encouraging philanthropy amongst all Masons to support hospitals, homes, educational endowments, eye care facilities and language centers. The very act of giving from one's abundance, or perhaps from one's meagerness brings into balance the blessings of God some men have received while others have seemingly gone wanting. That apparent imbalance is not so much the result of God determining that some should benefit while others suffer as it is the result of the Great Architect's plan to challenge man to act as God's partner in spreading His blessings everywhere they are needed. Such acts are *sacrament* - an outward manifestation of the person who has either already entered the "depth world," or seeks to do so at the earliest moment possible.

Consequently the judge or *guardian of the threshold* represented by Hiram Abif's monument is nothing less than the administrator of the justice of conscience. His balance beam signifies the negative aspect of human conscience while his sword represents the positive and healing revelation of God. Man's intuition reveals to him the "depth world" and informs him in no uncertain terms that the only manner in which he may transcend from the "surface world" to the "depth world" is by sacrificing intelligence in favor of conscience.

One must proceed with compassion and not by merely thinking about things. Mankind was made for mankind and each man was made to serve every other man. There are no relevant distinctions of color, religion, culture or origin. As God disinherits none of His children, he who desires to enter the "depth world" and to then encounter the Great Architect must also disregard color, religion, culture or origin.

Entering the *Sanctum Sanctorum* of the human soul is not a matter of either occult practices, or the uttering of magical phrases. No breathing exercises or mental technique will suffice to attain intuition. Those are reserved to the world of meditation, which is associated with the "surface world." The world of contemplation associated with the "depth world" requires using higher and greater means. Abraham and Moses understood this truth and personally encountered God who revealed His truths by imprinting them upon the hearts of each of them. Jesus, too, understood this truth and taught his disciples the importance of joining human acts of kindness with a deep faith in God in order that new habits of bringing God to all men might become second-nature to each of his disciples. Like Abraham, Moses and Jesus, Masonry teaches that it is better to serve than to be served; more rewarding to love than to be loved; and exceedingly more blessed to give than to receive. It is these practices that must become as natural as any other human habit before any man can enter the "depth world," otherwise the *guardian of the threshold* will close the door and leave you behind.

Chapter 11

THE FIVE POINTS OF FELLOWSHIP

As a significant part of his elevation to Master Mason, the candidate for the third degree of Masonry is instructed about the enormous importance of the *five points of fellowship*. The point at which that instruction occurs in Masonic ritual coincides with the conclusion of the degree. It is also emblematic of the candidate's transition from the external expression of Masonic lessons to the spiritual practice of putting those lessons to work to improve the human soul.

It is fair to ask why there are *five points of fellowship* as opposed to three, four, or any other number. As one would expect there are many reasons. For example our Rosicrucian brethren teach that the number 5 represents *health and safety*. The number 5 has also been called the *occult number* because it represents the spirit as well as the four elements – earth, air, fire and water. The number 5 also symbolizes the Pentagram which the early Christians commonly used to represent the five wounds of Jesus. Certain sects within both the Greek and Babylonian cultures believed that the Pentagram held magical powers like those attributed to Jesus.

Pythagoras is regarded as the first man to refer to the Pentagram as *Hygieia* (Greek for "health") and saw in it a great mathematical perfection. Because Pythagoras is also believed to have been initiated into several of the ancient mystery schools, it is likely that his perceptions of perfection have also been incorporated into today's Masonic ritual and symbolic teachings. Those who continued to adhere to his magnificent teachings after his death – often referred to as Neo-Pythagoreans - added to his interpretation of the Pentagram's significance and accepted that, among other things, it reflected the five classical elements of spirit, water, earth, fire and air.

The ancient Pythagorean Pentagram was drawn with two points directed upward representing the doctrine of *Pentemychos,* which refers to *five recesses,* or *five chambers.* Those recesses or chambers are also known as the *pentagonas,* which was the title of the literary work supposedly written by Pythagoras' teacher, Pherecydes of Syros. That work was said to have blended myth with philosophy as it chronicled the creation of Earth. Quite distinct from the theology and philosophy of that era, *Pentagonas* held that mankind did not suffer annihilation at death, but lived as it has always lived without any beginning or ending. Confirming the importance of this new consideration, both Cicero and St. Augustine wrote that Pherecydes was very likely the first man to teach that the human soul is immortal.

In later years Heinrich Agrippa perpetuated the popularity of the Pentagram as a symbol of magic. Nineteenth century occultists lent us its most unfavorable interpretation as a symbol of unrepentant evil. Depicted with a single point directed upwards, the symbol was regarded as symbolizing "good," for the single upward point emphasized spirit presiding over matter. However, when the single point was directed downward, the symbolism indicated that materiality, or evil, prevailed over the spirit. This same five-pointed star was considered to represent the seat of wisdom when all five points were directed upward, and despicable evil when all were directed downward.

Christianity employed the Pentagram to represent the five senses and similar to the Rosicrucians primarily regarded it as a symbol of health. During medieval times, it was also believed to provide protection against witches and demons. Like many other venerated symbols of good spirits, such as the swastika, the Pentagram suffered an ignominious fate when it was misappropriated by ceremonial magicians and eventually gained a nasty reputation as a symbol of evil. To counter such awkward distortions we find, for example, that Mormons throughout the Nation revere the

Pentagram in their Temple architecture, most especially at the Temple in Nauvoo, Illinois.

For a time, a Pentagram served as the official seal for the City of Jerusalem. The national flags of both Ethiopia and Morocco contain a Pentagram within their respective coat of arms. As far back in time as the era of Solomon, it served as the object now known as *the Seal of Solomon,* upon which it is believed the Masons working at the Temple placed their hands and pledged their vows of secrecy, obedience and allegiance. The Order of the Eastern Star has also used a five-pointed Pentagram as its symbol consisting of five isosceles triangles colored red, blue, yellow, white and green. Of course this older form of the Order's symbol is now depicted in such a manner that it may no longer accurately be called a Pentagram.

In the mathematics of geometry the Pentagram is considered to represent the simplest regular star polygon. It contains ten points consisting of the five points of the star and the five vertices of the inner pentagon. Like a regular pentagon and a regular pentagon with a Pentagram constructed inside it, the regular Pentagram has as its symmetry group the dihedral group of order 10. In fact the Pentagram may be constructed by simply connecting alternate vertices of a pentagon. While all of this may appear at first glance to be uninteresting detail it immediately becomes much more interesting when we also consider that this exact construction has been selected for the headquarters of the United States Department of Defense. The very same construction is also used during certain Scottish Rite rituals to explain to Masonic candidates various wise and serious truths about man, Nature and God.

In sum it may prove an impossible task to discover who first determined that there would be *five points of fellowship* demonstrated in the Master Mason degree. However, ample reasons actually do exist and each Mason may seek to discover for himself the one with which he is more comfortable, knowing that other possible reasons also exist from which others may choose just as wisely. But there is a convergence of many of those various reasons that enables us to conclude that inculcating habits designed to promote health, safety and spiritual control over material matters is essential to all Masons. For the *five points of fellowship* convey truths so simple as to be deemed incontrovertibly beneficial to mankind regardless of race, creed or religion.

We read in the Holy Bible that each person is responsible for the welfare of each other person as though that other person was a brother or another self. History records that the greatest nations have consistently made efforts to care for those unable to care for themselves. This course of compassionate conduct is not open to political debate, although the extent to which such care should be given will differ according to various beliefs and opinions. One need neither embrace nor shun the political concept of socialism to wholeheartedly embrace the concept of brotherly love and affection. Also one need not accept nor reject any particular religious doctrine or philosophy to sincerely believe that *doing unto others as one would that they should do unto him* is a sacred obligation. It is not for Masons alone to learn and make their habit the grand practice of never hesitating to go on foot and out of the way to serve another human being.

In the Hirmaic Legend *Hiram Abif* clearly represents such a man, for it is evident from our Masonic allegory that he originally had a choice to either serve as Chief Architect of the Temple, or stay at home in the land of Canaan. His specific talents were necessary and he did not hesitate one moment to make himself available and answer the call of his King of Tyre. Based upon his refusal to meet the demands of the ruthless assassins to reveal the Master's *Word*, it is safe to assume that *Hiram* would not have hesitated to become involved even had he known that he would one day pay for his decision with his own life. Such is the nature of the exalted example he has set for all Masons and all mankind – service unto death.

Throughout the Holy Bible we are introduced to men who teach their followers how to pray to God. From Abraham to Jesus the lesson of prayer was taught exhaustively for the purpose of primarily petitioning the Great Architect to favor others.

The Old Testament relates that Abraham bargained with God to save the cities of Sodom and Gomorrah so long as it was determined that one holy man resided there. God agreed and temporarily spared the cities annihilation. Years later, Abraham's son Isaac sought God's blessing upon his son Jacob, who, like his grandfather before him, petitioned the Supreme Ruler of the Universe to save Jacob's people (Israel) from distinction. And years after that Moses prayed that God would deliver the Hebrews from Egyptian bondage and that He would guide them throughout their later journey in the deserts of Sinai.

Each of the prophets poured out their hearts in prayer to the One God in whom they placed their unflinching trust and who could save their people from the consequences of their own folly and destruction. In both the Sermon on the Mount as well as the Lord's Prayer, Jesus taught men to pray for the health, welfare and safety of others before asking God for any personal favor. Indeed, the second of the *five points of fellowship* adheres to a similar path: when offering up devotion to the ever living God, remember first the welfare of another as though that person was you.

Similarly, during the last moments of his life *Hiram Abif* thought more about others than he did of himself – a sentiment of genuine love and affection that stands as a lesson to all Masons. He could have saved his own life by revealing the Master's *Word* when threatened by the three assassins. That he chose not to do so and thereby lost his life is testimony to each one of us that there are matters in this world that are imminently more important than protecting ourselves from physical harm.

That is not to say that all life is unimportant, or that some lives are more important than others. Rather it is to first acknowledge that life has no beginning and no ending. What seemingly comes to a conclusion in this material world actually continues elsewhere and it matters not where, for the whole process is part of God's mysterious plan that will be revealed to us when we are entitled to know. We also acknowledge that spiritual truth frequently requires that we make great sacrifices to insure that God's mysterious plan moves forward and does not sustain a setback because of our lack of virtue, diligence, care, love, or courage. If we fail as individuals, we place the burden to succeed upon the shoulders of others and consequently delay the coming of God's Kingdom.

The third of the *five points of fellowship* – keeping faith and trust among those whom we meet, especially our brother Masons – is another aspect of the burden we either bear during our lifetimes, or pass on for our ancestors to bear. The importance of this is best illustrated by both the Craft's insistence upon the obligation of silence as well as the example thereof by *Hiram Abif* who refused to reveal his secrets when assailed by Jubela, Jubelo and Jubelum.

Similar to the demands placed upon members of the Essene community, Masons are expected to keep confidential all matters confided to them by other Masons, especially when asked to do so. Of course there are exceptions to this rule particularly when maintaining such confidence would conceal murder, treason, or otherwise constitute the aiding and abetting of another in the commission of a heinous crime. But the general purpose of this obligation is to create an environment of trust among the brethren such that communication on all subjects may be freely exchanged without concern that the subject matter will become the fodder of gossip-mongers. *Hiram Abif* best exemplified this virtue by refusing to disclose the secrets of a Master Mason to his assassins.

Trust and fidelity also serve as cornerstones of the lessons taught us in the Holy Bible. In the book of Genesis we read about Adam and Eve and how their failure to follow God's laws resulted in their fall from grace. It is impossible to read about the consequences of that fall without also wondering what would have happened to both of them and to all of us had they behaved more obediently. The clear message is that the consequences of untrustworthiness and disobedience are both grave and endure from generation-to-generation.

In the books of Exodus and Deuteronomy we are introduced to God's laws which are His gifts to mankind. The importance of maintaining faith with God by following His statutes is held in common by all religions. Each sincerely believes and teaches that a faithful adherence to those laws will insure that the bond of trust between God and man is not broken. The succeeding biblical stories about war, devastation, murder and suffering represent the consequences we may expect when we break faith with the Great Architect. Not even the coming of the Messiah was intended to replace God's law, for without the stability of trust and fidelity life swiftly cascades into chaos and suffering.

The universality of these virtues reaches beyond our material existence in a manner that is actually discernible to both the human eye and the human soul. Masons are taught that numberless worlds created by the same God are connected by the same laws of nature. If we view our universe through the powerful telescopes available to us at the many observatories around the globe, we learn that we are not alone. Hundreds of thousands of stars, planets, meteors and other phenomena flicker before our eyes and we know that other worlds exist. Although no man can possibly fathom the extent of creation, present-day scientists have determined that galaxy upon galaxy is continually expanding at an enormous pace. That phenomenon which we can see with our own eyes informs our souls that there is much more to God's creative plan than we know.

From time to time, Masonic writers have linked the symbolism of the *cosmic egg* to the symbolism of the *holy trinity*. The purpose for doing so has been to illustrate that all worlds and universes revolve around God, who represents the hub of all creation. When considered jointly as forming one symbolism, the *cosmic egg* and *holy trinity* also illustrate the interconnection of those worlds and universes – those numberless worlds that Masonry teaches are connected by the same laws of nature.

By itself, the *cosmic egg* represents different planes of spirit-form and matter-form, as well as spirit-formlessness and matter-formlessness. In other words, this symbolism teaches us that numberless universes actually exist. The *holy trinity* represents the laws of nature that connect those numberless universes created by the forces of the Father (God), Son (individual man) and Holy Spirit (the divine spark within each man).

While our Christian brethren will recognize this symbolism as evidencing the true nature of Jesus, reaching that conclusion is entirely unnecessary to comprehend the truth about mankind's connectedness. The *holy trinity* might just as easily include the laws or commandments of God, for its importance to us regarding trust and fidelity is to teach us that we are responsible to one another; necessarily obedient to the laws of nature; and in reverent awe of every universe that God has created. Of the *five points of fellowship* none imposes upon us a more vast and profound obligation, or foretells more damaging consequences to all creation than the terrifying consequences of breaching that trust and fidelity.

In science the *five phases of God's consciousness* are made known to us by the atom and undivided neutrons whose electrons have not separated for the purposes of expansion in the world of form. This scientific example serves as a material basis for the more spiritual example that is clearly illustrated in the Gospel of John: "In the beginning was the *Word* and the *Word* was with God and the *Word* was God." *St. John 1:1*. In other words, the resting atom awaits the *Word*, or God's action, before it goes into action as a creative force. This symbolism also connects us to the fourth of the *five points of fellowship*, which obligates us to think before we extend a helping hand to a fallen brother Mason.

That assistance is not a duty to be lightly undertaken, or to be taken without careful consideration of that which is required to be done. Masonry consistently reminds us that this duty is owed to a *worthy* brother Mason as opposed to an *unworthy* Mason. The fraternity makes it possible for us to understand the difference thereby relieving us from the excruciatingly difficult task of passing judgment about who is and is not *worthy*. Simply stated, honorable Masons are deemed *worthy;* dishonorable Masons are considered *unworthy.*

More specifically an honorable Mason is a man of integrity, truthfulness and honesty. Everything he does exemplifies right living, right action, right speech and right thinking. Such a man refuses to cheat his brother, his family, or his country. He allows only the truth to pass his lips and governs his conduct by the laws of his country and the laws of his Craft. The honorable man never seeks to deceive anyone and is ready to both admit his own failings and to endure the just consequences of his own behavior. To such a Mason is owed the very special duty of assistance when he stumbles or falls, for such a man is exemplary of the very best that Masonry demands.

No similar duty is owed to dishonorable Masons who by their own actions have substituted deceit for truthfulness and infidelity for the keeping of important vows. Masonic jurisdictions throughout the nation have enacted fraternal laws that are frequently referred to as Masonic Codes. Those codes consist of written laws promulgated by state Grand Lodges and provide guidance to the management of lodges, as well as for the personal management of one's own conduct. The Mason who lives in contravention of the provisions of those Codes without remorse and seeks to further conceal that fact from others is *unworthy*. To such a Mason no duty of assistance is demanded of another brother Mason.

While it might appear to some that the making of such a distinction among Masons smacks of elitism, the truth is that it is actually an extension of another Cardinal rule embraced by Freemasonry: *justice.* Even an honorable Mason may one day find himself faced with the difficult decision to either submit to *justice,* or attempt to hide from its sting like the three assassins. It is an undeniable truth that all men have fallen short of God's expectations and have acted disobediently at one time or another. However, it is not equally true that all men have thereafter acted dishonorably by concealing their misdeeds in an effort to avoid or obstruct *justice.*

Eventually even Jubela, Jubelo and Jubelum admitted their guilt to King Solomon and accepted their death sentences. Where do such men fall on the scale of honor? Are they honorable or dishonorable? Slaying *Hiram Abif* certainly rendered each of them dishonorable, but did the eventual submission to *justice* somehow transform them into honorable men? Likewise, is it possible for a Mason to be expelled from the Craft because of his misdeeds and yet be redeemed at some subsequent time and again become an honorable man? While calculating where any man falls on the scale of honor is at best imprecise, the answer to each of these questions is an emphatic "yes."

Men and Masons who have acted so disobediently as to be properly labeled "dishonorable" may redeem and change themselves. Like the ancient alchemist who could transmute brass into gold, man also can transmute himself from dishonor to a state of honor. However such transmutations occur within different periods of time depending upon the severity of the dishonor. Some acts take longer to redeem while others may not be redeemable during a lifetime. The lesson of the three assassins is that submission to *justice* here on earth, while possibly never resulting in an eventual distinction of honor during one's lifetime, places the soul in a good position for honorable treatment by the one loving God.

Another point for our consideration about this special duty of assistance is how best to define the extent of such assistance. Quite clearly the answer depends upon the nature and seriousness of the *fall*. How extensive was the resulting damage of the dishonorable deed? What does the *worthy* brother Mason need? Where can one obtain all that is necessary to meet those needs? It is this measure of our determination that is required by the fourth of the *five points of fellowship*.

No Mason is required to give more than he is capable of rendering. No lay person is expected to kneel at the side of an injured person and set a broken bone. No person unskilled in financial matters is expected to offer sound financial advice. And no person unskilled as an attorney is expected to provide a skillful representation in a legal matter. However, we are expected to spend the time necessary to understand the extent of the *worthy* Mason's suffering and to then help him find the skills necessary to assist in meeting his challenge. One who merely assesses the problem, determines that the resolution is beyond his talents, throws up his arms in frustration and walks away has not performed his duty. A Mason stands by another *worthy* Mason until his problems are solved, no matter how much time or effort is required.

The fifth and final point of the *five points of fellowship* imposes another similar but somewhat distinct duty of assistance upon Master Masons. That duty consists of offering wise counsel to an erring brother Mason and endeavoring to bring about a reformation of conduct in a most gentle manner. On the surface, this sounds relatively easy to accomplish: simply tell the other man he is wrong and that he needs to pattern his life after you! But such a superficial understanding about the extent of this duty is fraught with peril, for something much different is actually required.

Both the Holy Bible and several traditional parables relate stories that are intended to remind us that no matter the trouble another person experiences, it is never sufficient to merely tell that person to stop doing that which got him into trouble. While that is certainly good advice, it is most often not nearly enough to actually bring about a reformation or change. For example, a famous fable tells about a man who encountered another who was unable to swim but had accidentally wandered into deep water. "You should never have gone into such deep water," said the helpful man shaking his head as he turned and walked away. While the fable never discloses whether or not the drowning man survived, it is abundantly clear that if he did it was not because of the efforts of that "helpful man."

Sadly we frequently hear about occasions in Masonry that eerily echo this fable of foolishness. Masons with gambling problems receive "good counsel" from well-meaning brethren to quit gambling. Members who have become alcoholics are counseled to simply quit drinking. Others who have acquired poor health habits are advised to stop eating, quit smoking, or to exercise more regularly. Far less frequently we hear about a Mason personally accompanying a brother to a meeting of gamblers anonymous, or alcoholics anonymous. Sometimes we actually learn that another brother has taken an overweight brother to a weight loss clinic, or introduced a brother to a quit-smoking program. What would you do in a similar situation? Would you walk away and merely hope for the best, or would you try to whisper some constructively wise counsel in your brother's ear? Remember that you have already given an answer at the altar of Freemasonry. Do you recall what it was?

Chapter 12
KING SOLOMON'S TEMPLE

King Solomon's Temple is said to have been constructed as an exact replica of the Tabernacle of Moses and occupies center stage in the Masonic dramatization of the Hiramic Legend. Following in the footsteps of his father, King David, Solomon determined to build a temple dedicated to the One True God and garnered the support of his Phoenican neighbor, King Hiram of Tyre. The slain Grand Master *Hiram Abif* was engaged for the express purpose of supervising the construction because of his unique architectural skills. Conspiracy, intrigue and murder creep into the story about virtue and morality and become equally important parts of the dramatization.

Mankind has never discovered archeological evidence that the Temple ever actually existed. But Masonic legend affirms that its construction was completed after *Hiram Abif* was murdered. Since the Temple is claimed to have been the successor to the Tabernacle of Moses, it is possible that men have not yet searched in the right region of the world. It is quite possible that the Temple is strictly allegorical and never did exist. In truth the significance of the Temple to Masonry does not demand that we ever reconcile these unknowns. Rather, the Craft seeks always to impart wise and serious truths from antiquity for mankind to consider. It is in the allegorical context that we discover the valuable lessons that could easily be ignored if Masons become too distracted by trying to determine when and where the Temple was built.

Our Masonic speculative explorations call us back to the times of the ancient Chaldeans, who have likely been unfairly criticized as feckless stargazers. Long ago these strange men gave names to the star formations that are commonly used by today's astronomers and astrologers. IThe Holy Scriptures reveal that the *mages* of this era were later directed by signs in the sky to a manger in Bethlehem. Those signs have been identified as the *Twelve Hierarchies* of the Sun through which it is said that God's power is reflected upon the earth. Those hierarchies are known to us today as the twelve constellations of the celestial zodiac. Our ancient ancestors attributed certain human qualities to each of those constellations for man's material consideration. However those attributions should not be confused by us with the divine attributes that God charged those hierarchies to guard.

On a very esoteric level those hierarchies are believed to transform the energy of light from the *three pillars* in such a manner that God becomes known in varying degrees to each man, woman and child. Our Masonic brethren will immediately recognize a relationship of those *three pillars* to the Pillars of the Lodge. Within their respective quadrants, those *three pillars* anchor the threefold flame that issues from the Fire of God in the same manner as do the Master, Senior and Junior Wardens of a Masonic lodge.

Each of the *twelve hierarchies* is responsible for projecting and supporting one ray of light manifesting the union of spirit and matter. Within the trinity that is the *three pillars* twelve rays coalesce with twelve flames yielding thousands of virtues of the particular attribute of God represented by each ray. Together the hierarchies are responsible for focusing twelve rays, 144 flames and 144,000 virtues of God upon the universe.

From this spiritual revelation has derived the meaning of the well-known phrase in Masonic ritual — *the beauty and glory of the day,* which pertains to the Temple of the Sun at twelve o'clock noon and to the astrological signs of Capricorn, Aries, Cancer and Libra. These signs project the very will of the Great Architect of the Universe and embue all creation with the same godly attributes that are reflected in the twelve rays. Thus, *High Noon* is unequivocally the beauty and glory of the day for it represents the entirety of God's attributes that can be reflected on earth.

The ancient *mages* held that the One True God cycled through the four cosmic forces (water, fire, earth and air) yielded by the Twelve Hierarchies, or zodiacal signs, resulting in the emanation of the twelve rays of God, which provided the scripture writers of the book of Genesis with the inspiration to write that well-known phrase, *"Let there be light!"* Spiritual alchemists contend that this emanation represents a phase in the creative evolution without which mankind would be unable to process the differences between good and evil. Freemasonry's Hiramic Legend symbolizes man's journey through the world of good and evil; a journey that is marked by occasions of progress and decline in matters of virtue and morality. Mankind does not always behave well; in fact although no scorecard has ever been kept, history suggests that man has behaved poorly nearly as often as he has worked good deeds. But that same history also records that frequently just one good deed performed during one lifetime or one generation has frequently served as a springboard for greater advances that benefit all humanity.

Here, we are reminded of the story from the book of Genesis about Abraham bargaining with God to save a city and its people whom God was about to destroy. Abraham asked if the innocent would be swept away with the guilty upon learning that God intended to annihilate Sodom. Suppose there were fifty innocent people in the city; would God wipe out the place rather than spare it for the sake of those fifty? Abraham then praised God for his just and righteous demeanor and reminded him that such character could never be satisfied with having innocent blood on its hands. God then replied that if he found fifty innocent people in Sodom, He would spare the whole place for their sake. *Genesis 18:23-26.*

But Abraham asked what if there are five less than fifty? He was obviously attempting to discover God's limit. Would He destroy the whole city because of those five? God replied that he would not, but Abraham tested Him further; what if only forty are found there? Again God relented and said he would spare the city if forty innocent men were found in Sodom. Abraham continued to ask about a lower number of innocents until he at last discovered God's limit. What if there are at least ten there? God replied that for the sake of those ten, He would not destroy it. *Genesis 18: 28-32.*

As God chose to spare ten and not some other number He revealed a most important truth to us. So long as there is enough good in the world to make a difference, evil will not succeed in dragging with it to the depths of destruction all that is moral and virtuous. It is the alchemical evolution of the good in man that advances the spirit of all men.

That same truth is also found in the legend of *Hiram Abif,* wherein one good man stood against evil and though he lost his life permitted virtue and morality to succeed. The death of the Grand Master did not result in the destruction of the Temple. Rather it caused a momentary halt to the construction which was commenced again shortly thereafter under the guidance of another capable man of honor named Adonhiram.

While some Masonic writers have speculated that Adonhiram was none other than the resurrected *Hiram Abif* upon whom King Solomon bestowed the title of honor "Adon," thereby confirming that the Grand Master never died, that speculation is not embraced as a part of what is known as "mainstream" Masonic tradition. Instead, the naming of a new Chief Architect to complete the construction of the Temple is intended to symbolically demonstrate the alchemical evolution of good works done by different men of equal talents living in different times. After *Hiram Abif* was finally laid to rest near the *Sanctum Sanctorum* his spirit is said to have filled the workers with zeal and to have inspired Adonhiram to render the Temple as beautiful a monument to God as *Hiram Abif* would himself have done.

The ancient *mages* of the Orient, from whom Freemasonry has inherited much of its rich numerological symbolism, imagined that the Twelve Hierarchies were subject to twelve clocks which governed the time it took for God's creative presence to pass through the Four Cosmic Forces of water, fire, earth and air. Since mankind is subject to time, this imagining served to reveal the intersection of timeless existence with an existence limited by time. The marble monument erected to the memory of *Hiram Abif* contains a figure symbolizing time standing at the back of a weeping virgin patiently unfolding the ringlets of her hair. That symbolism serves to remind us that the Great Architect works alongside generations of men to accomplish a single purpose. Unborn generations will soon pick up where deceased generations left off and continue the task of completing the plan of creation. The story about Abraham negotiating with God teaches us that as long as some good men are a productive part of those unborn generations, the Great Architect will permit them to live and work.

The cycles of the Four Cosmic Forces are copied by twelve sub-cycles again representing time as depicted in twelve-hour parts. We recognize that span of time as representing one-half of a twenty-four hour day suggesting to us that creation is a continuous process that incorporates both a conscious and unconscious component. The conscious component is fulfilled when man works and contributes to progress in full awareness of what he is doing. The unconscious component represents the creative work done without either man's awareness, or his active involvement. In other words, while there are forces at work with which we are intimately familiar, there are also forces working without our assistance to complete creation. That completed work is symbolically represented to Masons by the Temple of Solomon.

These cycles within cycles are said by the Oriental *mages* to be infinite. Centuries, decades, years, months, weeks, days, hours, minutes, seconds and microseconds are examples of time within time during which spiritual energies flow from *above to below* and from *below to above*. This general concept forms the basis for the Kabbalah's Tree of Life, which depicts and describes various channels through which human souls descend from heaven and later return to God. As long as some of those souls are innocent, as were the ten for whom God spared the city of Sodom, creation will continue without destructive interruption by the Great Architect.

The Temple which *Hiram Abif* commenced also reminds us about the attributes of the elemental atom technically described for us by the many scientists who have written on the subject. The cycle of the electron in its spinning orbit around the white fire core of the atom governs the relative cycles of time and space. Since the orbital and rotational speed of the electron may vary from atom to atom, scientists have extrapolated that fact to theorize that the cycles of time and space may also vary among planets, suns, stars and solar systems just as we know it does among human beings. Yet the atom remains the center around which the electron spins eventually creating the several useful energies man has already discovered and put to use. Compared to Freemasonry this scientific fact may be equated to the Masonic energy that fills the world today that flows from the hundreds of thousands of men and women who "orbit" around the "white fire core" of King Solomon's Temple to give the world its foundational center in virtue, honor and morality.

From the Temple symbolism, Masonry has adopted the exotically spiritual meaning conveyed by the words "High Twelve," which represents the *"beauty and glory of the day."* To our ancient ancestors, it also represented the hours on the face of the clock, which correspond to the Twelve Hierarchies, or zodiacal signs, through which our Jewish brethren contend in their Kabbalah teachings that souls enter and leave the earth. It is said that all heavenly bodies, as well as all human beings come forth through the "open door" at the twelve o'clock line – the *beauty and glory of the day.* But at what point they come forth and under whose influence is seemingly haphazardly determined by the moment of birth. Some have hypothesized that random determination to represent the unconscious element of creation – that part undertaken by the Great Architect without either our assistance or our knowledge.

Masons are builders of temples to virtue, as well as diggers of pits within which to bury sin. This transformation of the Temple symbolism has generally replaced the older temple analogies to the Kabbalah and its Tree of Life, representing yet again the alchemical-like nature of the symbolic teachings by the Craft. Drawn from multiple cultures, religions, philosophies and oral traditions, the intended meaning of King Solomon's Temple to Freemasons has depended upon what period of history is being examined.

Beginning with the Carl Jung era and continuing through to the present day, Masonry has accepted the thesis that the individual constitutes the only reality in Nature. That is not to state that unity and teamwork have become obsolete concepts, but even those essential ingredients to social welfare are now generally written about from the exclusive perspective of the individual rather than the group. What does man think? How does he think? Why does he think? And why does he need other people? This modern emphasis upon the perspective of the individual has clearly influenced Masonry's present day interpretations of the meaning of its Temple symbolism.

Today *Hiram Abif* represents that individual perspective more than any other imagery used by the Craft to communicate *knowledge.* Through his eyes, we are taught the importance of both constructing the Temple and worshipping God at the Temple altar. Light and darkness are brought to life as facets of our own person. Like the ground floor of the Temple checkered black and white, we learn to expect that we, too, are capable of good and evil. In truth neither exclusively controls our behavior and we are therefore taught the importance of choosing which force to nourish and which force to limit.

Such personalizing of the Temple symbolism may be criticized as merely reducing to a material level an important spiritual concept. But such criticism is entirely without merit, for it ignores Freemasonry's close connection to Hermeticism which inculcates the value of synthesizing opposing ideas, as well as comprehending the seeming disparities between various theses and antitheses. Here, we are reminded of that important phrase, *as it is above so shall it be below.* In other words, *Hiram Abif* teaches us the importance of personalizing spiritual concepts so that God's Kingdom on earth may eventually emerge from man's several conscious efforts.

If the Craft's Temple symbolism can also be said to represent *work,* or *labor,* in the sense that human effort must be applied to its construction, then we may also discern yet another reason why the Grand Master refused to reveal the *Word* to the ruffians. Jubela, Jubelo and Jubelum each sought something to which they were not then entitled. *Work* needed to be done by each of them before they would be permitted advancement from the Fellowcraft status to the status of Master Mason. Had *Hiram Abif* simply given them the *Word* to save his own life, the value of *work* would have been compromised for generations. Not having done so, the Grand Master insured that the *labor* necessary to accomplish the journey along the correct path toward virtue and morality is not subject to short-cuts.

Deception, deceit and trickery will not accomplish the task and should be routinely rebuffed by Masons. Such devices flow from the forces of darkness and deserve every Mason's earnest work to eliminate. After *Hiram Abif* was slain, the assassins wondered aloud what they had accomplished and finally acknowledged that they were still in a state of complete darkness. Treachery had failed to bring to light the sacred *Word.* Rather, it eventually led to the death and destruction of Jubela, Jubelo and Jubelum. Construction of the Temple and not been halted forever. Instead after a temporary pause to bury the Grand Master and replace him with a new Chief Architect, the mighty edifice was completed in its fullest splendor - a monument to virtue and morality.

It has been suggested, although by no means verified in history, that this magnificent Temple continued as the center of religious life for the Jews for more than four centuries until its destruction by Nebuchadnezzar's army in approximately 586 B.C. During periods of religious decline among the Israelites it was allowed to deteriorate and was frequently shamefully neglected. But each such period was followed by great spiritual awakenings not unlike those history has recorded to have transformed the religious landscape of our own Nation. During those periods of spiritual awakening the Temple was carefully repaired and reconsecrated with reverent and holy hands.

On several occasions the Temple treasury was plundered by foreign invaders. The golden vessels were taken away as spoils of war, or equally as often exploited by weak and corrupt kings who sought peace by paying tribute to foreign monarchs who threatened violence. These were all replenished by generous Israelites during the periods of revival to begin the cycle over again.

For Masons, the lessons from the past about the Temple teach the importance of establishing a center where man can worship the Great Architect. In the hands of *Hiram Abif*, as well as under the direction of his successor, Adonhiram, the construction was splendidly beautiful and richly ornamented so as to leave no doubt in anyone's mind that it was God's dwelling place. The Jewish tradition of establishing such a center of worship closely followed the Egyptian tradition, each dominated by a pure priesthood that would intercede with God on man's behalf, just as had Abraham on behalf of the people of Sodom. That priestly purity was deemed so important to both the Jews and the Egyptians that revolts were staged at times when the righteous perceived the erosion or complete destruction of the recognized High Priesthood. Some contended that the priesthood was a birthright, while others held the strong belief that priests should be elected from a society of men and chosen because of their demonstrated virtue and morality. As we will learn later, this difference of opinion about the purity of the priesthood led to revolt, violence and great social upheavals.

From the Gospel of Matthew we are informed that the infant Jesus was taken out of Israel and into Egypt by his mother and father ostensibly to escape the wrath of King Herod. Some writers on this subject have speculated that the real purpose was to insure Jesus' education at the hands of a "pure priesthood." Regardless of where the truth of that matter actually rests, the symbolic importance of the Temple serving as the center for worshipping God is inescapable.

For Masons, the Temple also represents the individual whom Jesus reputedly equated with serving as the flesh and blood house wherein the soul given by God actually dwelled. Speculative Masons no longer erect magnificent edifices from stone, but instead build character, virtue and morality. It is these that enable each and every Mason to serve mankind as virtual individual centers of worship. As true as it is that man does not live by bread alone, neither does he live apart from the Great Architect who has impregnated his human creatures with His own *fire-spark*. In that God has chosen to dwell within each man, woman and child, each person has a work to reverently perform in repairing that spiritual temple not made with hands. For guidance about how best to perform that work Masons may look to the Grand Master *Hiram Abif,* who has set an example for all Masons to follow.

Chapter 13
MAKING GOLD FROM BRASS

A very old manuscript suggested that Masonry originated at the hands of alchemists and Hermetic philosophers. Indeed, it is highly probable that the allegory depicted in Masonry's Third Degree contains a rather precise alchemical formula. Whether or not one agrees with that theory may entirely depend upon the definition of the word "alchemy."

Originally, alchemy was regarded as an operative science whereby gold was made from brass or other metals. Secret formulas are said to have circulated among a select few throughout Europe which had been secretly handed down from generation to generation. The precise manner for making gold from metal was reputedly recorded in those secret formulas and nowhere else, most of which were transmitted orally. Consequently it became extremely important that what was said was accurately remembered word for word.

Reasons for pursuing that science have not been clearly recorded in the surviving writings leaving modern-day authors to speculate about the motives. For purposes of this work it is wholly unnecessary to recite those speculations, for in truth the actual motivations of operative alchemists have been lost and will likely remain concealed forever in the mists of time. However it is important to understand the alchemical significance of something referred to as *the universal agent*.

The scientific method for turning metal into gold allegedly required the presence of a special chemical substance. When heated properly and accurately assimilated into other necessary ingredients, that special substance was said to have caused a miraculous transformation. Without it, metal would have remained metal. Also, unless the secret formula was followed precisely gold would never appear. Lacking any further scientific description that substance has simply been known throughout the ages as *the universal agent.*

Several writers have agreed that *Hiram Abif* represents a *universal agent,* for without him King Solomon's Temple would not have been erected. While such a claim seemingly ignores the Masonic tradition that the Temple was completed by Adonhiram, it is allegorically correct to state that the great Grand Master was an essential ingredient. Had he not commenced construction, fabricated the holy vessels and attended to the supervision of the craftsmen, the Temple would very likely have turned out quite differently.

Within most Masonic circles the very name of *Hiram Abif* is symbolic. To those Masons it means something akin to *my Father, the Universal Spirit, one in essence, three in aspect.* That meaning leads us to return to the central message of the very ancient *dying god* symbolism that was re-enacted in several of the mystery schools. In each, the martyred *dying god* proved to be the necessary ingredient, or *universal agent,* for the continuation of human life after death. Without the *dying god* man would never be transformed from his material death to an eternal spiritual life.

Although the ritual in Masonry's Third Degree does not directly recite that the Grand Master was resurrected, it may be argued that it impliedly does so by acknowledging that the spirits of all men return unto God upon material death. Rosicrucian legend further contends that *Hiram Abif* is a radical name representing fire which is mysteriously combined as *the universal agent* with the light of the Sun, air and water to form the cosmic forces necessary to sustain human life. While all four elements are essential, fire alone represents the light of God in Nature with which all human beings are impregnated.

An old family German prayer memorializes this mystery, as follows: *O holy and hallowed Trinity, Thou undivided and triple Unity! Cause me to sink into the abyss of Thy limitless eternal Fire, for only in that Fire can the mortal nature of man be changed into humble dust, while the new body of the salt union lies in the light. Oh, melt me and transmute me in this Thy holy Fire, so that on the day at Thy command the fiery waters of the Holy Spirit draw me out from the dark dust, giving me new birth and making me alive with His breath.* By aid of this prayer we may more easily discern that both the lost alchemical formula and *Hiram Abif* himself are to be regarded primarily as allegorical symbols – not as real things or people.

One of the oldest versions of the alchemical allegory is contained in the *Emerald Tablet of Hermes*. In it the Grand Master is actually referred to as the *universal agent* or ingredient essential to the divine regeneration of humanity. *Hiram* is also regarded by the *Emerald Tablet* as the only person who is truly knowledgeable about Nature's secret operations. His importance to the manner and method of regeneration is spelled out more particularly in the quasi-recipe that follows in the Tablet. That recipe describes how the world was first created, the path to follow to reach the hidden road to spirituality and also how the concept of the Trinity contains the whole wisdom of the world. In other words, the *Emerald Tablet* holds a valuable clue about the centrality of *Hiram Abif* to man's transformation into a divine being.

The *universal agent* is sometimes also referred to as the *Philosopher's Stone* – the object of several fanciful novels and tales about magical occurrences throughout the universe. Some people contend that such a stone actually exists, but has remained hidden from the masses for centuries to prevent its misuse. More likely, the stone, too, is intended to be symbolic of something we are expected to rediscover through study, prayer, meditation and contemplation. If, as Solomon is quoted in the book of Ecclesiastes as having stated: "There is nothing new under the sun;" then all that ever was or ever will be known awaits rediscovery by man. In that regard, we should remember that it is not God's will to conceal anything from man, but to insure that important matters pertaining to the spirit and soul are transmitted to men who have proven themselves *worthy and well qualified*.

Here, much is to be gleaned from the Holy Bible about man becoming *worthy*. From the Gospels we learn about the parable of the ten foolish virgins who failed to prepare themselves for the bridegroom's visitation. We also read that Jesus cautioned against tossing pearls before swine and that he who has ears should "hear" the importance of that message. Both are intended to impart wise and serious truths about the necessity of becoming *worthy*, or of being transformed from a wholly material being to a divine entity in the making. It is within this context that one discovers the true relevance of the *universal agent, Philosopher's Stone* and *Hiram Abif*, which represent the active transforming ingredient.

That oft-maligned figure in alchemy, Paracelsus, perhaps unfairly accused of practicing black arts, frequently wrote that man's philosophical transformation was as important to man's longevity as were his scientific advancements in the field of medicine. Indeed, the great alchemist was himself a physician whose uncommon mixtures of chemicals into healing potions so confounded his colleagues as to have led several of them to accuse him of being in league with Satan. Such accusations are somewhat difficult to understand when we consider that Paracelsus cautioned us to praise God perpetually, live a temperate life and beware of all sinfulness. Those hardly amount to invitations to follow in the footsteps of the devil.

In his work entitled *Man and the Created World*, Paracelsus claimed, in the manner of a true alchemist, that man was not born out of nothingness. Paracelsus found from the Holy Bible that God took mother earth and formed man. But some additional substance was used, for dust and dirt alone has never been known to yield a living, breathing human being. Among alchemists and Rosicrucians that substance, or *universal agent*, is the very fire-light, or spark with which the Great Architect has impregnated all humanity. Both disciplines speculate further that God's creative power is symbolized by the element of fire.

To the extent that Freemasonry attributes to *Hiram Abif* the alchemical status as *universal agent*, it is interesting to note that the fraternity teaches that certain of the Grand Master's character traits are important to emulate, especially if man is ever to change and become *worthy and well qualified* to learn the things that remain concealed by our Supreme Ruler of the Universe. We read in the book of Genesis that when the earth was still nothing but water, the spirit of the Lord moved upon the face of those waters and God breathed His own fire spirit into man's being. The Great Architect thereby established man as His dwelling place – a lesson also reputedly taught by Jesus.

Man is the ultimate example of the creation of something valuable out of something coarse and common – figuratively, gold from base metal. The world is as God created it, who like a potter molding clay fashioned all kinds of creatures and gave unto man His own essence. But man's nature does not permit him to immediately discern that he contains a spark of the blessed fire-light, for the grossness of matter eclipses the light within him. Thus it is that all men must transform their gross matter into a finer substance in order for their golden spirit or soul to shine forth for the world to see. In this manner, according to Paracelsus, all things may eventually be endowed with the spirit of life and realize their fullest potential.

Speculative alchemy also teaches us that the Great Architect is the original *alchemist,* who picked up the substances of the earth and blended them to produce man. Then man was filled with His spirit. But understanding the importance of that spirit requires another ingredient – the *universal agent.* Without it man may never fully develop into the spiritual being intended by the Great Architect, for the recipes of good human behavior are otherwise lost. Without the *universal agent* man has no Godly exemplar and is entirely adrift in a sea of darkness. Until man has something from God to study, absorb and emulate, he has only himself upon whom to rely. In that state of existence he may forever remain as brass, or a tinkling cymbal, instead of one day attaining a state of golden refinement in the image of the Supreme Grand Master.

To the alchemist, then, we may offer our gratitude for revealing the necessity of having a great teacher in our lives. The Dead Sea Scrolls record that those who left those holy records for our learning were at one time guided by such a person – a *Teacher of Righteousness.* Although neither the Scrolls, nor history reveals the name of that person, we nevertheless unequivocally understand that the presence of such a person of and from God is essential to our personal transformation from a state of darkness to a state of living in the light. *Hiram Abif* is given to Freemasons as such a person whose piety and charity transcend his human existence. Masons do not learn the lessons of the dead from their past Grand Master who instead teaches lessons about how to live, love, care and contribute to the welfare of all mankind.

Many in Masonry resist embracing *Hiram Abif* as a symbol of the Son of God for fear that in doing so they will either dishonor their religion, or substitute the Grand Master for the Messiah, the Christ, or some other similar religious figure. Such is not the case and no Mason need ever fear that his reverence for the slain Grand Master will ever result in moral or spiritual harm. *Hiram Abif* is nothing more and nothing less than the Freemasonry's symbolic *Teacher of Righteousness,* for without the lessons taught by his life Masons might never know the spiritual importance of the *five points of fellowship,* or the holy significance of the evergreen *acacia*. No Mason should feel guilty about embracing the Masonic allegory about the resurrection which is presented to us by the Craft as a lesson in dedicating ourselves to becoming something better than we are.

There remains something more to be learned from the science and philosophy of alchemy. It pertains to the actual transformation of material substances, i.e., changing brass or base metals into gold. Here, we return to the ancient legend of Gilgamesh and the biblical stories recounting that some men lived to seemingly unbelievably ages. To what was such longevity attributed? How did those legendary men actually live so long? Is there some ancient alchemical formula at work here, or possibly some more scientific answer?

Most modern-day medical doctors contend that man has the ability to live 100 years – possibly longer, but certainly no shorter a period. A visit to your local rest home or assisted care facility will most likely confirm for you that many men and women are currently living well into their nineties. News media occasionally record the rather unusual circumstance of a person living to the approximate age of 120 oftentimes telling us that such people lived in conditions, settings and environments with which most of us are entirely unfamiliar.

Current research into genetics promises a key to unlock the door that may lead us all to living even longer lives, yielding important information about man's predilection to disease and how best to guard against its onset. Adequate exercise and a proper balanced diet have also emerged as significant contributors to longevity. Modern science also informs us that there is yet much more to learn about this subject. While all of this is enormously interesting and quite likely extremely important to humanity, none of it adequately explains how men and women of antiquity lived for hundreds of years. Are those stories false? Are they allegorical? Or is there some hidden alchemical explanation?

Medieval tales tell us about secretive men wearing pointed hats who employed even more secretive chemical formulas used to manufacture gold from base metals. It is claimed that certain European nations banned those practices, not for religious reasons, but to avoid the collapse of national economies. We also read legends claiming that Tubalcain, Pythagoras and King Solomon were *practical alchemists* who understood the ancient chemical formulas and thereby possessed unique gold-making skills. Quite naturally a similar legend that is associated with Solomon continues to attract much attention, for classifying him as a gold-maker tends to explain how it was possible that his Temple to God contained such vast quantities of gold.

Hypothetically assuming that the legends are true in their entirety, it is fair to look further into the purposes or motives behind such gold-making activity. For some greed likely prompted their activities. For others perhaps the excitement of applying a scientific chemical formula provided sufficient motivation. But for men such as Pythagoras and Solomon those motivations do not fit well with the principles, values and character traits that history attributes to them. Freemasonry reveres both men not because they made gold from brass, but because their lives serve as important symbols of virtue, honor and morality.

While not much is truly known about Pythagoras, it is well-known that entire philosophical schools were created by him during his lifetime and by his students following his death. Not even his many detractors ever claimed that the great philosopher was greedy. Although it is written in the Holy Bible that Solomon took a wife or two that prudence dictated he should not have taken, and that he worshipped multiple gods, he has never been criticized for being greedy.

Assuming that alchemy is a real science based upon demonstrable mathematics, why would men such as Pythagoras and Solomon acquire and use the science if not to merely accumulate wealth and ornamentation? The true answer may never be proven by direct evidence. But there is a good deal of circumstantial evidence that we may either accept or reject depending upon its convincing force.

It has been a custom among many of the ancient religions to ingest certain foods and substances in the course of performing various holy rituals. That custom and practice continues today among religions throughout the world. Today most people who continue the custom believe that the practice is symbolic. But some religions impose a literal and almost superstitious understanding upon the meaning of the ritual.

Those narrower religions have claimed for centuries that men who ingest the offered substances consume a divine essence and in turn become a part of the divine. In other words, for those exotic practitioners ordinary food and drink is magically transformed into the pure essence of the Great Architect. The truth about such a transformation of substances is not universally accepted among Freemasons or any other group of people. However, the historical truth that supports the symbolism is extraordinarily difficult to deny.

We learn from the book of Genesis that the person known as Noah engaged in a ritual ingestion of "blood." Based upon an even more ancient ritualistic practice, the "blood" he allegedly ingested was neither human nor animal blood. Rather, it was believed to have been a divine essence: an essence that not only connected man to God, but that also added years to man's life. That essence, simply called "blood" owing to its life-sustaining properties, is said by some writers to have actually consisted of a substance derived from liquid gold.

Neither Noah nor any other ancient holy man taught or practiced the actual consumption of human or animal blood. Indeed, continuing from the days of Noah until the time of Moses and beyond the Hebrews regarded the consumption of blood to be contrary to strict dietary laws. Holy men were even selected to oversee the preparations of foods to insure proper compliance with those laws. However, Noah did pass on the ritual practice of ingesting the divine essence during the ceremony the Jews refer to as *The Table of the Bread of The Presence*.

The antiquity of this ritual extends to well before the time Noah is reputed to have lived and also appears to have been a part of the more ancient Egyptian Mysteries. For the pharaohs who lived long before Noah, gold was evidently exceedingly important, as was more recently revealed to us by the abundance of golden artifacts discovered in the tomb of Tutankhamen during the early Twentieth Century archeological excavations in Egypt.

In approximately 1450 B.C., Tuthmosis III established the *Great White Brotherhood* whose members were curiously preoccupied with the ingestion of a white powdery substance derived from an alchemical transformation of gold. This *Great White Brotherhood*, which has nothing to do with race, ethnicity, or creed, is frequently cited by several different writers as the forerunner of the Rosicrucians. All of the available evidence suggests that it was those ancients who first referred to the ingestible substance as *Star Fire*.

The substance is believed by some to consist of an active ingredient within the human body that causes the brain's pineal gland to secrete *soma* – a substance that certain scientists have concluded promotes longevity. Interestingly the *Star Fire* or white powder that is yielded by a formulaic combination of liquid gold with specific base metals was identified long ago by our ancient ancestors as necessary to sustaining a long life. If it is so that we are continuing to search for possible motivations for Solomon's involvement in alchemy, or gold-making, none could have been more important to him than a long life.

Originally the ceremonial ritual of ingestion was reserved for royalty, as were the elaborate funerary and mummifications of deceased kings, queens, princes and princesses. In time, the ritualistic inner circle was extended to include members of the so-called High Priesthood. Throughout King Solomon's reign the participation in the ritual was actually limited to the one High Priest. The attendant ceremony was conducted within the veiled confines of the *Sanctum Sanctorum*.

Today, any person who attends a church service that offers communion and is qualified by that church to accept *Eucharist*, or who has otherwise been invited to *The Table of the Bread of The Presence* may participate in what we now know to be the successor to this great ritual. All who willingly prepare and avail themselves may participate in the ritual of enlightened consciousness. What remains unfinished for us is insuring that all who participate also understand that the ensuing enlightenment is of the utmost importance to mankind's spiritual improvement.

In alchemy's *fire* symbolism, the color *red* represents gold. The *Star Fire* substance has been equated with female menstrual blood which is believed to be the alchemical equivalent to the *Philosopher's Stone*, or the substance necessary to transform base metal into gold: the literal *Gold of the Gods*. To the ancient alchemists, such as Paracelsus, the metals employed were not merely base substances. Rather, they were regarded as living essences, or secretions, which if red in color were considered to be of nobility. If assimilated properly according to a *secret formula* they would consistently yield gold. It was believed by such men that this was the route to true *knowingness*, for the only personal god anyone could possibly know was the god within each living being revealed by the unmistakable golden color that attached to each man's aura.

While most of this symbolism has been lost to us as a result of the demise of Gnostic Christianity, a certain amount of the ancient and original knowledge continues to be preserved by the Rosicrucians, and is also recorded in Talmudic and Rabbinical lore. However we can no longer turn to any single source for elaboration upon the medical science of *living substances* that was once practiced among the ancients. Since we do not know how that science worked, or whether or not it actually contributed to human longevity, those who currently study practical *alchemy* are extremely secretive because none of those practitioners wish to see the science entirely eliminated or ridiculed. Yet, in spite of those obstacles to learning the truth, recent discoveries about the properties of *melatonin* and *serotonin* are exceptionally relevant to that study.

Melatonin is produced naturally by the human pineal gland and is activated within the body by another chemical known as *serotonin*. Working together those substances enhance and boost the body's immune system. Most people who buy *melatonin* across the counter today do so under the belief that its regular use will promote more consistent sleep patterns. While that appears to be the experience of many who regularly ingest the substance, science has also reported that high *melatonin* production also heightens energy, stamina and physical tolerance. It represents the body's most potent and effective antioxidant, which is necessary to the warding off an assortment of cancerous diseases. If such effects upon the human body are continuously verified, *melatonin* may prove to be a link to a lost chemistry once practiced by the ancient alchemists.

Those ancient alchemical practitioners included members of the High Priesthood, sometimes referred to as the *magi*. Gold and frankincense (closely associated with pineal secretions such as *melatonin*) were the traditional substances of those practitioners together with myrrh which was ingested as a sedative. As we read about the travels of such *magi* in the New Testament Gospels, perhaps this new information may shed new light upon the holy significance of the *three wise men* that visited the newborn Jesus and left behind gifts of gold, frankincense and myrrh.

As a sedative, myrrh symbolized death rather than a sleeping aid to be given to babies. Death, or *daath,* as that term is used in the Kabbalah of the Hebrews, actually signified *higher knowledge*, or that state of regenerative existence that follows man's material life. Accessing that higher knowledge before death has been the exercise of a select few, as well as the goal of many mystical ancients who participated in alchemical gold-making.

Freemasonry's emphasis upon self-study and the formation of independent opinions about divine and eternal matters did not occur by happenstance. Neither did it develop simply as the evolution of the Craft's support for man exercising his natural spirit of freedom. Rather, there is a more scientific reason which is interestingly connected with this very same alchemical practice of making gold from base metals.

Modern medical research has concluded that the pineal gland is an organ of thought that permits all humans to acquire an inner perception which lends itself to the formation of earthly conceptions of eternal ideas. In certain circles of wisdom the pineal is also regarded as the *Eye of Wisdom* which represents intuitive knowledge. Heightened self-awareness contributes to a heightened inner vision, which in turn teaches us the possibilities of formulating our own ideas about divine and eternal concepts.

Becoming aware of spiritual matters is the true goal Masonry intends for us to achieve by inculcating within us a thirst for knowledge. It is the very same goal intended by the ancient Egyptian Mysteries as allegorically expressed in the Osiric legend. Precisely when and why that legend evolved into the Hiramic Legend is not presently known. However, it is abundantly clear that the central message imparted by both is that during the lifetime of all humans each is engaged in the process of *becoming.* More simply stated we are all undergoing a process of change – physically and spiritually. As we emerge from the wombs of our mothers, grow from infants to children to adulthood and advance to old age we are engaged in the process of dying, which is nothing more than changing from a material to a spiritual existence.

Throughout that physical process we are also experiencing a changing spiritual awareness. Just as the assassins of *Hiram Abif* went from callous murderers to penitents so, too, are we all becoming something newer and better as a consequence of our respective life experiences. It is fair to wonder whether or not mankind is *becoming,* or changing when it appears from man's recorded histories that some people actually seem to become so hideous that they attain the height of evil at the moment of their own deaths. The answer to that question is not concealed in the mists of speculation; it lies firmly in the grasp of observable physical reality. That such evil eventually dies in and of itself represents change, or man *becoming* something other than the physical embodiment of evil.

The ingestion of substances created during the alchemical process was historically reserved for those referred to as *master craftsmen* – the same appellation ascribed to *Hiram Abif.* Some writers have equated those substances to the biblical *manna* reportedly consumed by the Hebrews during their sojourn in the desert with Moses. Others have called it the *bread of life* which today occupies a prominent place as a *sacrament* in many Christian liturgies. In Grail lore, as well as in certain passages in the Holy Bible, those substances are also referred to as a stone. For example, in the book of Genesis, Melchizedek is depicted holding a cup with a peculiar stone inside. Also in the book of Revelation, an unusual white stone is depicted. Today mankind knows that stone as the *Philosopher's Stone.*

Alchemists reportedly used such a *Philosopher's Stone* to transmute base metal into gold. Spiritual men of the relevant age believed there was no difference between physical and spiritual transmutations and consequently renewed the custom of the human ingestion of gold-making substances for the purpose of advancing their own spiritual awareness – to *become* more complete spiritual beings. For that purpose a different type of gold was ingested than what we generally know it to be. It was of a much higher quality and according to legend the recipe for its making was known only to the *master craftsmen.*

Was this the real secret the assassins were trying to obtain from *Hiram Abif?* Has Masonic legend obscured this real purpose by casting the *master craftsmen* as builders of stone edifices? If so, why would such concealment have been made in the first instance? As obviously speculative as is this proposition, it deserves our serious consideration.

To further complicate matters, it appears that the geometry revered by Freemasonry may also have derived at least in part from the science of gold-making. In *Rosarium Philosporum,* an alchemical writing, the making of the *Philosopher's Stone* is actually described in terms of geometry. This process, too, was reputedly known only by the *master craftsmen,* who according to Sumerian legend had been charged with the responsibility for making the substance previously referred to as the *bread of life.*

When it was ingested the substance reportedly had an extraordinary effect. The chemical reaction in the human body is said to have stimulated the pineal and pituitary glands to such an extent that the body generated enormous levels of both melatonin and serotonin – two substances that some medical researchers have connected with human longevity. Within the Sumerian community the *master craftsmen* were responsible for perfecting the technique of producing this magical substance – this *bread of life.*

Those who have delved into this subject have of necessity been well-schooled in this Sumerian legend. Although none of the existing Masonic literary works describe it in specific detail, the fact that the majority of those works characterize the Hiramic Legend as an alchemical formula strongly suggests that those writers have at least considered the possibility that *master craftsmen* in Freemasonry are the heirs of the Sumerian *master craftsmen.* There does not appear to be anything in present-day Masonic ritual that verifies that assumption. No matter how closely one inspects that ritual, he will not find any reference to gold-making. However, Freemasonry does abound in symbolic lessons about the *bread of life,* regeneration and the act of *becoming.* Are those lessons hinting further at something else that has been lost to the Craft? The answer to that question awaits further study.

Chapter 14

SIGNALING FOR HELP

Upon arriving at *Hiram Abif's* grave, King Solomon and Hiram of Tyre were so overwhelmed with grief that they wailed and gestured toward the heavens. The words and gestures chosen that day have been inextricably woven into the fabric of Freemasonry. It is unlikely that any Master Mason will ever forget their importance. Indeed history records that Masons have flown to the aid of the person uttering those words or making those same gestures. Both serve as symbols of a Mason's highest duty to another Mason – the duty to give aid when another Mason's life is in peril.

The nature of this Masonic duty has been extensively argued and is often misunderstood. One retired United States military officer, who was not himself a Mason, remarked that during his years of active service he had been wary of having Masons in his command, because he understood that they believed they owed a higher duty to each other than to other military men alongside whom they might have to enter into combat. He had arrived at that conclusion after learning that Freemasons were taught that they were bound together by an indissoluble tie and had pledged aid to a fellow member of the Craft if needed. How that notion originated in that man's mind is a complete mystery, for it inaccurately assumes that Masons are taught to be disobedient and to serve their country dishonorably.

But that man is not alone in his mistaken belief. Even some writers about Freemasonry have posited erroneous notions about treasonous complicity among Masons who found themselves on opposite sides of the battlefield. One speculation holds that a British General intentionally lost a battle that led to England's ultimate defeat in the Revolutionary War rather than go to battle against brother Masons serving in the American Revolutionary Army. Another similar speculation contends that Freemasons captured other Masons as spies for opposing militaries and later helped those spies to escape. The fact that no verifiable act of such high treason has ever been discovered strongly suggests that none ever occurred. No fraternal organization has come under as much scrutiny as Freemasonry which continues to absorb body-blows of scorn and false accusation from its legion of detractors. Rest assured that if such misdeeds were verifiable, we would have read about them by now in some blog on the Internet, or in a scandalous literary revelation about the "truth" behind Freemasonry.

The verifiable truth is that Masons have fought in wars for centuries, sometimes killing members of their own fraternity. Many have proven heroic while others have behaved as cowards. Most have obeyed the orders of their superiors, while some have been discharged from service because of their disobedience. General Benedict Arnold even betrayed his country and was exiled to live out his life in England. However, another of Arnold's brothers, General George Washington, became the undisputed father of our country. In sum, the evidence before us reveals that while Masons are human and just as capable of erring as any other human, for the most part they have not only served their country admirably, they have oftentimes been at the front lines of the battles for freedom, justice and social awareness.

As opposed to massive acts of treason and disobedience, history instead records acts of uncommon kindness generously given by one brother Mason to another even during the stress of war. During America's Civil War unusual charitable acts were engaged in by Masons who served in militaries of both the North and the South. For example on or about June 11, 1863, among the gunboats of the North that were peppering Port Hudson, Mississippi, was the *USS Albatross*. Two of the officers aboard were Masons; the captain and his executive officer. Delirious, the captain shot and killed himself. Believing he would want a Masonic funeral, the executive officer went ashore under a flag of truce, met two Masons who were then living in the area of the shelling and asked for their assistance. Both the Master and Senior Warden of the local Masonic lodge were then serving as officers in the Confederate Army. Neither man hesitated to afford a fallen brother the honor of a Masonic burial, even though the decedent had fought for the enemy. Afterward the men returned to their duty stations and the warfare raged on. Even after the War ended the Daughters of the Confederacy kept that Mason's grave fresh with flowers.

Masonic ritual teaches Masons that there are certain signs, or modes of recognizing a Mason, that are not openly communicated to non-Masons. In fact, such ritual makes it possible for one Mason to know that another Mason is in immediate need of help. While non-Masons would merely look on in wonderment if that ritual was demonstrated, another Mason would rush to assist his friend and brother.

The results of misunderstanding how the duty of aid and assistance must conform to other equally important Masonic obligations are described later in the chapter entitled *Admonishing a Brother.* Masonry teaches the importance of aiding and supporting each other. Loving charity is at the heart of those teachings, but that obligation must be undertaken responsibly. It is not acceptable to aid and abet the commission of a crime, to assist another Mason to escape justice, to violate the laws of the land, or to betray one's country. Those who do so and offer the excuse that they are acting as true Masons are entirely mistaken in that belief.

In performing Masonic obligations, Freemasons are not asked to leave their common sense and learning behind. The same is certainly so when responding to a *signal of distress.* Flying to the relief of a fellow Mason demands at least as much prudence as one would exercise when crossing a busy street on foot. No man is required to throw himself over a high place and fall to his certain death simply because another Mason has just jumped from a building. Neither is a Mason asked to violate any law of the land in which he lives while performing any Masonic duty.

It is perhaps helpful to review the origin of the Masonic *signal of distress* to better understand its true meaning. The Hiramic Legend reveals that the signal was first used when King Solomon saw the gravesite of his beloved *Hiram Abif.* Solomon was deeply saddened by the death of his dear friend was nearly moved to tears upon seeing the body. In keeping with the tradition of the times, he thrust his arms in the air and wailed his grief to the Great Architect above beseeching His answer about what should be done.

This allegory teaches us that when we are distressed we should turn to the Supreme Architect of the Universe for assistance. While God comforts the spirit and soul man is expected to put his own muscle to work to help ease his own plight, as well as the physical suffering of others.

Human society is as much a creation of the Great Architect as is the solar system of the heavenly universe. If the bond of gravitational force was suddenly severed, the stars and planets would likely fly off in chaos. So, too, would society flounder if the social moral bonds were cut.

The *signal of distress* also serves to emphatically remind us that faith in morality and virtue, as well as faith in God, is essential to man's spiritual development. Our Great Architect has decreed that human life shall be properly spent in a social condition. Public spirit and community welfare depend upon that condition. Giving to others in order that as many people as possible may be safe and comfortable is as important to that social condition as is the offering up of our prayers. When human strength and wisdom fail, we are ever reminded that the power of prayer is at our disposal and that our petitions to the Supreme Architect of the Universe serve as the ultimate *signal of distress.*

As King Solomon stood at the head of *Hiram Abif's* grave wailing to the heavens with his arms outstretched, his actions served to remind everyone present of his unparalleled faith in God. Solomon believed that the Great Architect would answer his plea and soothe his anguish. The path would be made clear and the Great King would soon know what to do. In his heart and soul he knew that God was certain to answer this *signal of distress.* That imagery and symbolism also highlights the clear distinction between the faith of Solomon's generation and the rationalism that today seemingly pervades men's consciousness.

In Solomon's day a man's senses were as important to him as his intellect. In today's climate of rationalism, truth is determined more by the human intellect than by the human senses. Indeed, the present-day condition among men provides us with the very definition of the word "rationalism." The man of today may boast that he has freed himself from superstition, but in so doing he may have very well also eroded his spiritual values to an extraordinarily dangerous degree.

Masonry's *signal of distress* is transcendent. Although it is much more than a mere call for human assistance, a literal interpretation of Masonic ritual would suggest that it is nothing more. Masons freely obligate themselves to rush to the aid of another Mason, but the message about God's role in that aid has become so subtle and subdued in its expression that one could easily conclude that the *signal of distress* exclusively pertains to human endeavor – not God's response. While every Mason is free to adopt that interpretation, the Hiramic Legend offers much more to be considered.

Anthropological studies provide us with significant lessons about what happens to primitive societies that are exposed to modern civilization. As civilization creeps into the lives of primitive people they slowly experience a wasting away of their spiritual lives. That is not meant to suggest that civilization is evil, but to illustrate the importance of each present-day Mason assiduously evaluating the lessons of ancient Masonic symbolism for the purpose of making past spiritual lessons the lessons of today. Primitive societies experience severe declines in the aftermath of the advancement of civilization. Moral and spiritual traditions evaporate. Previously undiscovered tribes of men and women are very quickly diminished, deprived and demeaned as their former innocent, almost child-like practices are replaced by the intellectualism and rationalism that represent the peaks of prominence experienced in the modern world.

All men share the same experiences as the tribal communities which continue to be invaded by modern-day civilization. The impact is significant to the Mason who desires to reconnect with both the specific values espoused by the *signal of distress* symbolism, as well as other Masonic symbolism that originated in ancient times. But present-day Masons generally do not understand what they have lost, for the spiritual leaders of the religions they have followed from birth have unfortunately become more interested in preserving institutions than probing the spiritual truths concealed within the Masonic symbols. Consequently it is left to the Craft to demonstrate leadership in that great pursuit. Suffice to say, the exploration of those mysteries requires more than one or two authors writing books upon the subject. Members of the Craft must commit themselves to contribute to that effort, if mankind is ever to benefit from the truths concealed within the Masonic mysteries.

Faith does not exclude thought and man need not fear that science will somehow compromise his spiritual beliefs. If we carefully reflect upon all that we presently know and list the universe of things that we do not know, Freemasonry comes closer to establishing a baseline for attaining further spiritual knowledge than does any other presently known discipline. While the *signal of distress* may have meant one thing to King Solomon and something quite different to the Mason living in today's world of rationalism, it may also signify to us the necessity of regaining that which we have lost during the advancement of civilization.

In earlier ages, as instinctive concepts welled up in the minds of men, the conscious mind integrated those concepts into a coherent psychic pattern. When Solomon governed his kingdom human instinct was regarded as something given to man by the Great Architect. Today it has been relegated to the status of guesswork, because human intellect is more often deemed to be superior. As Solomon stretched forth his arms and loudly prayed to the Great Architect to reveal what should be done about *Hiram Abif*, he knew that his human intuition would accurately interpret God's response. Such beliefs are too frequently disparaged by today's rationalists who might be expected to quickly label such acts and beliefs as "nutty," "off-base," or "deranged."

Present-day Masons frequently speak in purely physical terms. That is to be expected since it is the natural outgrowth of today's formal education which prefers to teach by way of laboratory experiments to demonstrate "truths." More attention is paid to what man knows, how men act and the need for men to offer of their time in order that others may prosper. Too little attention is paid to the spiritual side – that side that asks men to get in tune with the Great Architect and to become *intuitively* aware of what He wants men to do.

But for Masons, the word "matter" remains dry and almost inhuman. It seems irrelevant to any discussion about the spiritual truths concealed by the symbolism of the *signal of distress*. The ego-thoughts of man have nearly replaced true faith in the Great Creator. Interpretations of Masonic symbols, as well as many other sacred symbols from the past, have been relegated to exercises in "rationalism," as opposed to the spiritual pursuits originally intended.

A man who openly chooses to engage in a prayerful life is often characterized as a "kook" whose ideas are unworthy of serious consideration. Religious institutions of various denominations have not helped the situation by promoting unrealistic demands that biblical allegory be accepted as actual fact. The well-educated present-day person quickly recognizes that such demands are seriously flawed. In turn real spiritual truths manage to be lumped in with the fiction and tossed out the door. The well-educated man of today learned long ago that there is no Santa Claus and has moved on to the pursuit of less spiritual endeavors. The loser in all of this is civilization which has been deprived of its best and brightest spiritual minds.

Unlike those religions, Masonry has identified and pursued a much different path, especially with regard to the *signal of distress*. Recognizing that many men feel spiritually isolated, the Craft retains the use of symbols to impart wise and serious truths. Where religions have abandoned the symbolisms associated with the Great Architect, Masonry has sought to rediscover them as a part of mankind's spiritual connection to "the above."

Consider all that has been lost and then think about how best to rediscover it. Thunder is no longer generally regarded as evidence of an angry God. No river in the world is believed to possess a spirit. Snakes are not presumed to embody wisdom and mountain caves no longer serve as abodes for demons. Each of those beliefs has been tossed upon the trash heap of antiquity where it has been left to rot. No voices speak to men from stones. Man rarely communes with nature. What has happened to the primitive spirituality? Is man doomed to an existence defined by "rationalism?" Or, has primitive spirituality simply become irrelevant?

During the past 40 years, mankind's advances have been largely attributable to the development of a sophisticated scientific understanding about matter. Technological advances far exceed social and spiritual advancement as the age of enlightenment has ever so slowly given way to the age of micromechanical devices. Everywhere in the world that one chooses to walk the busy city streets, men, women and children of all ages can be seen with cell phones glued to their ears. Corporate boardrooms have the capability of conducting business meetings across the world via video systems without people ever leaving their offices. Information about any subject that one desires to investigate is instantly available on the Internet. Miniaturized electronic devices power and operate complex military training systems, as well as weapons of war. Without question these advancements have greatly benefited society. But have they also tended to dehumanize the human spirit?

As long as man determines to remain aloof from nature, he will remain spiritually isolated and out of touch with his emotional and unconscious identity. This condition or state of man places an entirely new importance upon the meaning behind Freemasonry's *signal of distress*. Our present-day world fails to challenge us about how best to get in touch with our inner souls. Consequently, our generation is like generations in the past that failed to meet man's spiritual needs. However, no generation other than ours has had to cope with such a broad spectrum of distractions that invite men to pay more attention to material passions than to spiritual pleasures. To a very large extent, mankind has lost the ability to cultivate healthy spiritual growth.

The ruffians slew *Hiram Abif* after being frustrated by his refusal to give them what they demanded – the key, or password that would permit entry into a world into which they were not then permitted to enter. In so doing, Jubela, Jubelo and Jubelum abandoned all spiritual truths and soon found themselves isolated from the world in the mountainous caves of Palestine. As King Solomon later raised his arms in a *signal of distress,* it may be said that he was intuitively imploring the aid of the Great Architect to help humanity of all ages to recapture that which was lost.

Our challenge today is not to discover the most accurate interpretation of the *signal of distress* symbolism, but to discover the narrow path that can lead us through the maze of material wonderment and into the world of greater spiritual self-awareness. If the assassins' cave can be said to represent human isolation, then Solomon's gesture to the heavens can also be said to represent man's first step toward rediscovering that narrow path.

In the Entered Apprentice Degree, the candidate is instructed upon the importance of imploring God's aid in all of his lawful undertakings. In the Third Degree, Solomon is represented as re-emphasizing that lesson by use of the *signal of distress*. But are there other steps that we should take toward regaining that which we have lost? Freemasonry has long contended that a most important step to first be taken is toward assimilating the varied wise and serious truths imparted by its symbols. But why should we be limited to using symbolism? Why not simply tell us in understandable words all that we must know?

In all ages men who wrote about symbolism generally agreed that diversity, or numinosity of interpretation, is largely dependent upon the application of human emotion to the challenge that is presented. In that manner the symbol becomes charged with a psychic energy that opens the door to intuition. When intuition is permitted to enter into the equation, man suddenly finds himself surrounded by a state of consciousness that transcends scientific proof. That is not to say that everything man can conjure up in his mind constitutes the fruits of intuition. To the contrary, such thoughts are more accurately labeled as fantasy. Real intuition comes after the industrious development of the intellect sufficient to enable the mind to identify certain spiritual matters that can only be comprehended non-scientifically. It is impossible to achieve that state of mind without first knowing what is and is not scientifically proven in the material world. That knowledge does not come quickly or easily to any man. Neither does it flood into our brains in a flash of sudden awareness. It comes, if indeed it comes at all, to the man who assiduously studies, meditates, prays and listens to the Great Architect's voice in nature.

In the book of Proverbs, a passage attributed to King Solomon clearly illustrates the value of intuition, or as it is called by Solomon himself, *wisdom*. *If you eat honey, my son, because it is good, if virgin honey is sweet to your taste; such, you must know, is wisdom to your soul. Proverbs 24:13-14.* Words, being nothing more than symbols, are wholly inadequate to absolutely define *intuition, wisdom,* or the exact meaning of that passage of scripture. The true definition lies beyond the grasp of our human mind, because it is not part of a mechanical system that can be learned by rote. *Intuition* and *wisdom* are not mere names or philosophical concepts. They are pieces of life that become known to us by archetypes and images that serve as bridges from the known to the unknown. Both must be explained exclusively within the context of the life experienced by each individual and thus are incapable of one simple definition.

Each human soul eventually responds to the voice of the Great Architect, but no two souls respond in precisely the same manner. Intuition is revealed differently to even those whose life experiences are very similar. In churches throughout the world where men and women are treated to the same ritual and the same doctrine, it is more frequently the case that the faith of those men and women is derived from several different influences. For example, within the Roman Catholic community one finds conservatives, liberals and moderates who each hear God's voice differently. They hear the same homily, listen to the same readings from the Holy Bible and partake of the same Eucharist. But the individual response to what is taught is rarely identical.

The same is true in Islamic communities where even members of the same sect have differing beliefs about God's demands on human behavior. Jews are equally divided into arch-conservative, orthodox, moderate and liberal points of view about religious doctrine. Those divisions and differences defy any reasonable attempt to define the entire faith of the Christian, Islamic or Jewish religions. When such attempts have been made in the past, the conclusions frequently resulted in discovering the difficultly of the task that is involved. Suffice to say, people receive different intuitions about life and man's relationship to the Great Architect.

Chapter 15
A JUST SENTENCE

After discovering the assassins hiding in a cave, the pursuing Fellowcraft rushed upon them, bound them in fetters and took Jubela, Jubelo and Jubelum before King Solomon for trial and judgment. There was no trial by jury during Solomon's reign. He was the sole judge and jury and from his decision there was no appeal.

In shame, the assassins hung their heads as they stood before their irate King, each chancing a glance to catch a glimpse of his co-conspirator standing alongside. "What have you to say," Solomon bellowed, "are you guilty, or not guilty of killing the Grand Master?" The assassins meekly admitted their guilt. Slamming his gavel upon the table, Solomon leaped to his feet and shouted, "Hold up your heads you vile and impious wretches and receive your sentences." The Mosaic Law was clear – *an eye for an eye*. Nothing would serve the ends of justice other than execution.

The Fellowcraft led Jubela, Jubelo and Jubelum from the chamber and hauled them through Jerusalem to the outer gates. Without further ado, each assassin was put to death. The Hiramic Legend discloses that each was executed in accordance with their own words. Jubela had his throat cut from ear-to-ear and bled to death. Jubelo's left breast was torn open and his heart was ripped from his body. Jubleum's body was cut in two and his bowels taken away and burned to ashes.

Masonry points to this allegory as imparting something much more important about virtue and morality than the assassins' gory deaths. Justice demanded atonement for *Hiram Abif's* premeditated murder. Had Solomon declined to act, he would have betrayed his duty as king and breached his obligation as a Grand Master. The allegory does not describe Solomon as either joyful or reluctant to perform his duty. Blessed with more wisdom than any man who had lived before or after, Solomon knew the importance of justice. Without it mankind would be horribly out of balance with God.

In Scottish Rite Freemasonry, *equilibrium* has been described as the *Royal Secret* – a secret that is available for discovery by all Masons who achieve the thirty-second degree of Scottish Rite Masonry. In the Hiramic Legend, *equilibrium* is nothing less than perfect justice. That Masonry attaches different lessons to the same symbolism should come as no surprise, for many different truths are derived from the same implements and tools of architecture employed in Craft symbolism.

Symbols were the universal language of ancient theologians and were the most favored method of instruction. Like nature, symbols address human knowledge through understandings absorbed through the eye and by the mind. The most ancient expressions of religious knowledge were passed on visually through pictures and other symbols. Everywhere one looks today, men, women and children have personal computers within their reach and by a simple keystroke can access knowledge from numerous different sources. Televisions have become necessities for every American household and promise the instant communication of worldwide events. Video tapes and digital video discs offer recorded histories that one may view at his or her leisure. Aural messaging (listening) has become obsolete as most people receive their information through their eyes in much the same manner as did their ancient ancestors.

Lessons taught in the past revealed the secrets of the Sphynx to the man or woman who searched and understood the correct symbols. Ancient sages, both barbarian and Greek, often employed the identical symbols or combinations thereof to convey different lessons. Jesus mesmerized his audiences with parables that conveyed stories intended to teach lessons about virtue, morality and the grace of the Great Architect. Many believed that because so many different interpretations were possible from one symbol the man who possessed the gift of *correctly* interpreting symbols should occupy a very special place in society. When we consider that the biblical characters known to us as Joseph (Jacob's son) and Daniel (the prophet) were selected by rulers of governments precisely because it was believed they each had that special gift, we may understand the historical importance behind interpreting symbols.

The ancient Egyptian Mysteries consisted of a series of symbols the explanation of which resided in the truth each individual who witnessed them believed them to hold. Soon sacred commentaries crept in rendering individual interpretations irrelevant. Even Freemasonry has knelt at the altar of common understanding from time-to-time and selected interpretations of its own symbols that enjoyed "official approval." When it did so, the Craft behaved much in the same manner as did every other religion, philosophy and psychology that demanded acceptance among its members of a common doctrinal interpretation. However, while the fraternity does offer interpretations of its symbolism for consideration none is currently regarded as exclusive. Were it otherwise free thinking would be curtailed and a tyranny of the mind would prevail. The Craft abhors both and teaches neither.

Precisely where the *justice allegory* of the sentencing of the assassins fits into this picture is somewhat elusive. There are only so many ways to interpret that episode, but none offers a more important Masonic lesson than the *justice/equilibrium* interpretation. A legitimate discussion about the numerous possible meanings of the allegory could follow, but it is wholly imprudent to suggest that there is any lesson more important to derive from this symbolism than the lesson about *justice.*

Constituting the *equilibrium* or balance between light and darkness, *justice* is demonstrably linked to Hermetic philosophy. As it has been repeatedly stated, Masonry seeks to find a synthesis among competing concepts as opposed to compelling acceptance of one interpretation above all other interpretations.

Any person who has either participated in a lawsuit, or who has witnessed courtroom proceedings has attained some appreciation for the meaning of *justice.* Solomon understood it to mean the correct consequence that must applied to human wrongdoing. Americans understand that it can mean several different things at several different times.

In a courtroom where legal battles are fought, *justice* is the correct result or "verdict" that follows an application of the law to the facts of the specific case. In a political contest, *justice* is generally considered to be consistent with the fact that the political party one holds in high esteem won the election. In a more religious context, *justice* means that your particular religious point of view has been widely adopted as true and accurate. And, in a human relations perspective, *justice* conveys the notion that there is a right and a wrong connected with every human event. Is any of this truly *justice*, or is it merely the way some wish to define *justice?*

Universally regarded as one of the four cardinal virtues, *justice* has been criticized as something reserved for the very rich who can buy anything they desire. It has also been hailed by the poor as the saving refuge. Some well-informed people will point to some highly publicized lawsuits over the last several years to support the argument that only the rich get *justice.* Others argue with equally convincing force that *justice* is all that stands between the powerful rich and the weaker poor classes who find it humiliatingly necessary to beg in order to survive. Neither end of this spectrum accurately reflects the *justice* administered by Solomon.

Nobody paid Solomon to make his decision. The three assassins were not poor; they were Fellowcraft in the service of the King. The *justice* administered that day was administered without regard to station in life, or wealth. As legend records, it was administered because it was correct and just. As such this episode in the Hiramic Legend is intended to symbolize pure *justice,* or the decision between right and wrong that best achieves equilibrium between the two. A horrid deed had been accomplished – the Grand Master *Hiram Abif* was cruelly murdered. *Justice* demanded a correspondingly correct consequence. Nothing would bring *Hiram* back to life, but his murder demanded just condemnation of his assassins.

As pure, simple and honest *justice,* the *justice* administered by Solomon serves as an example of the kind of *equilibrium* the Hiramic Legend intends for Masons practice. Solomon's judgment borrowed from what each individual assassin thought he deserved. Each was put to death in the manner chosen he chose for himself. Here, we are taught that even a guilty man should be offered a voice at the time of his sentencing. Of course not every condemned man will act as contritely as did the assassins. Indeed many who have murdered and then sentenced have asked for no punishment at all. Yet *equilibrium* or balanced fairness does not require the guilty to select his punishment. It merely requires that the voice of the guilty man be heard and that his words be considered.

This Masonic lesson also imposes broad duties upon world governments to set fair standards, for *justice* without fairness is no *justice* at all. When men are charged with criminal conduct, incarcerated, tried for their alleged crimes and sentenced without ever having the opportunity for their voices to be heard, there is no *equilibrium*. There is only tyranny. When those who sit in judgment of others are partial, biased, or corrupt so is the *justice* that they pretend to administer. When judges see only black and white and nothing in-between, the *justice* they hand out is incomplete. When officers of courts of law owe greater allegiance to the institutional government than to the people, individual *justice* gives way to the tyranny of the majority.

In all of man's history there has never been one perfect system of *justice*. That fact is not an indictment of any man, woman, or government; it is merely a truth that should compel all men never to become complacent about seeking real *justice*. The *justice* of Solomon might not have actually occurred in the manner depicted in the Hiramic Legend– if, indeed, it ever actually occurred. After all *Hiram Abif* is a fictional creation drawn from the ancient mysteries and the events attributed to his life may never have actually taken place. Consequently, Solomon's *justice* is really just a goal: it has never been man's reality.

Americans point with pride to their system of *justice*, which incorporates the concept of "trial-by-jury." The English are equally proud of their system of *justice*, which although not utilizing trial-by-jury provides broad individual rights to fair notice and "due process." Other systems of *justice* found in other countries around the globe are harsher in some respects, more lenient in others and quite similar in yet other facets. It is safe to state that none are perfect and that quite likely none ever will be perfect. But actual perfection should never be man's goal. Rather, man's goal should be to consistently strive to apply perfect *justice*.

Masons will quickly associate the punishments Solomon ordered for the ruffians with their own Masonic vows. For by making those vows, each Mason has consented to submit himself to the same *justice* should he be judged an offender. In so doing, the Mason has freely consented to symbolically receive a specific punishment. Upon first reflection that may seem too harsh or unfair, especially since a Mason may theoretically receive a death sentence even if his offense does not rise to the same level as the slaying *Hiram Abif*. However, when examined closer there is no unfairness; there is real *equilibrium*.

In each instance we observe a simple law of nature: for every act there is a consequence. The penalties assumed by each individual Mason should he violate his Masonic vows are symbolic. The Craft never intended that they be carried out literally. However, the same was not the case for the three assassins: the sentences that originally fell from their own lips were the actual sentences imposed – or so it would appear. In that *Hiram Abif* is fictional, he could not have really been murdered and no man could have really been sentenced for his death. Thus, even those sentences of death serve as symbols of something else; something much more profound.

Throughout history despotism has proven to be one of the great personifications of evil. When we pause to carefully consider and understand the meaning of *despotism* we may be surprised to learn that it describes *any force that controls men by manipulating their necessities, follies, or passions*. History does not merely record the despotic enslavement of humanity; it also reveals the abrupt encirclement of entire civilizations by doctrines, thoughts, ideas and habits. In many instances governments that once began as responsible servants of the people have made a complete reversal and reduced its citizens to servant status. Benevolent rulers have all too frequently transformed themselves into demonizing tyrants. The rule of loving kindness has all too swiftly given way to the terrorizing of the citizenry until they accepted a particular doctrine, thought, idea, or habit to the exclusion of all others. Man's voice and vote have also frequently been silenced and freedom of choice has all too often been replaced with no choice at all.

With this history serving as our inspiration, the assassins in the Hiramic Legend may be said to represent three specific forms of despotism: the priesthood, politicians and the ignorant mob. While much has already been written about those three in my first book *Meditations on Masonic Symbolism*, it is useful to also consider that each form of despotism lies at the heart of the symbolic sentencing of Jubela, Jubelo and Jubelum, and penalties for breaking a Masonic vow. In sum, each appeal to our human sensibility, for it is by our human senses that we acquire the meaning of all things, including the meaning of *equilibrium,* or justice.

As they sat quietly in the caves of Palestine awaiting the fate *Divine Providence* held for them, Jubela, Jubelo and Jubelum likely recalled their own vows and the penalties for breaking them. Instead of weighing some hypothetical wrongdoing for which they might one day be expected to pay a price, they faced a far more certain reality. They had just conspired to kill *Hiram Abif* and their brother Jubelum had slain the Grand Master. Once hopeful of concealing their guilt, they were now consumed by thoughts of the justice they must soon face. Theirs was much more than a crime against humanity; it was a crime against Masonry.

The candidate for Masonic degrees, like the ruffians who painfully weighed their own guilt, is expected to carefully consider the important connection between his vows and the concept of justice. Every human act results in something and every wrongful act should result in some penalty. For example, man should not expect to breathe in the air, if he has spoiled the atmosphere. The simple beauty of a forest of tall trees may no longer be appreciated if the grove is chopped to the ground. Fields and meadows can no longer offer peace of mind when they are covered in concrete. Our own human sensibilities intuitively inform us about these truths and our personal experiences offer us a basis for understanding their just reality.

But mere human understanding about the concept of justice does not go far enough to explain how justice originated. When and how did it occur? Is justice a random accident or freak of nature? Is its origin included within the origins of our universe? When the Great Architect first created man from the dust, did He also teach him *equilibrium?* A careful consideration of the Hiramic Legend reveals a possible answer which may actually prove central to the lesson about King Solomon's sentencing of the assassins.

While some may disagree with the contention that Blue Lodge Masonry owes its origins to the ancient Egyptian Mysteries, none will seriously dispute the ritual similarities between the two. In the Egyptian Osirian Legend we are introduced to a fictional character named Anubis, also known as Sirius, who appeared in the shape of a dog to assist Isis in her search for the body of Osiris following his murder and mutilation at the hands of another fictional and evil character known as Typhon. To Sirius or Anubis, the ancient Egyptians attributed the discovery of the laws from which mankind first learned justice. This simple allegorical explanation was likely provided either as an allegorical concealment of the known origins, or was the result of a complete lack of knowledge about those origins. Regardless, man was never intended to believe that Anubis, or any other one person or character thought up the idea of justice and then taught it to all humanity. Rather, mankind's attention is invited once again to a more plausible scientific answer — an answer taught by lessons learned from the study of the Metaverse.

The definition of Metaverse used here is *the cycle of the evolution of all known and unknown universes, including our own.* As man meditates and contemplates upon creation and seeks to understand what came first, the chicken or the egg, he may eventually encounter this emerging science that directly relates to the origin and destiny of all life. Astronomers have observed through todays powerful telescopes that bursts of light in the atmosphere are oftentimes the signs of the creation of new stars, planets and universes. Similarly, many of those same heavenly bodies have been observed collapsing into "black holes" in space there to presumably die. This cycle repeats itself over and over and is thus reminiscent of the birth, death and rebirth of all human, animal and plant life.

The emerging science of the Metaverse embraces the premise that everything is connected, including the things from the past and present, as well as those things to come in the future. That premise holds that each life cycle informs or influences the next life cycle, i.e., passes on the lessons previously learned. For example, one scientific model suggests that our universe learned something from ancient universes as the old gave way to the new and evolutionary changes resulted. Not all older universes supported human life, any more than do all present-day universes. Something was *learned* along the creative journey that informed or influenced our universe about how to support, sustain and even assist in the creation of new life. It is equally plausible, if there be any truth in this emerging science that human habits, traditions, cultures and knowledge have developed in much the same manner. Exactly how, where and when that occurred is not presently known and may not soon be discovered.

As opposed to using the symbolism of a dog-shaped figure named Anubis, Masonry uses the venerable Solomon to serve as Freemasonry's version of the first man to give humanity lessons in perfect justice. This esteemed Grand Master and King of Israel also taught the Craft about the almighty force and importance of truth – a Divine attribute that Masonry recognizes to be the foundation of every human virtue. From Solomon we also obtain a hint about the origins of all creation, for it was by his prayerful request that the Great Architect blessed him with a wisdom that was never before known among men. Indeed, Solomon's wisdom has not since been displayed by any living human being. Thus we find ourselves compelled to inquire about wisdom herself in order to shed further light on the origin of creation.

The Holy Bible contains repeated passages about wisdom and in the *Song of Songs* describes wisdom as a woman without a name. Ancient Egypt called this woman Isis, the wife of Osiris and astronomically analogized her to the moon – Osiris representing the Sun. Isis was said to be the reflection of Osiris, just as the moon reflects the light from the Sun. Both symbols are of immediate interest to our present inquiry, for that which is reflective passes on something – light, energy, wisdom - that originally emanates from another source. As such, they are uniquely consistent with the premise associated with the emerging science of the Metaverse - that which has come before "informs" of "influences" succeeding generations.

All that we have investigated herein clearly suggests that justice did not simply randomly appear as a virtuous concept. Rather, it must have a history, an origin and an application that quite likely precedes the creation of man. Some may wish to call it the essence and character of a loving God who cannot be anything other than just and fair. If so, the *equilibrium* taught us in the Hiramic Legend is nothing less than that essence of the Great Architect which is passed on to generations of men who are created in His image and contain within themselves a spark of the Divine. We need not hear someone tell us what *justice* is, for the God within us "informs" us about its Divine nature.

Chapter 16

GRAND MASTER HIRAM AND THE MESSIAH

Various authors and commentators about Freemasonry have speculated that *Hiram Abif* is intended by the Craft to symbolize Jesus Christ. The reasons offered in support of that contention are primarily based upon the Hiramic Legend's symbolism of a *resurrection,* or raising of the dead similar to Jesus' own resurrection, as described in the several Gospels. Although the answer to the question of whether or not Jesus is at the core of that Masonic symbolism may never be learned once and for all time, there are as many dissimilarities between the Christ and *Hiram Abif* as there are similarities for our consideration. Indeed, there is a dissimilarity so striking that it simply cannot go overlooked: while most modern Christian religions teach that Jesus was Divine, Freemasonry makes no such claim about the slain Grand Master.

When King Solomon finally determined that he was ready to commence the great construction of an elaborate temple for God, he was surprised and delighted to simultaneously receive a congratulatory letter from Hiram of Tyre. In it the King of Tyre also offered his assistance to Solomon, who was keenly aware that the Phoenicians were both skilled metallurgists and master builders. The edifices that dotted their homeland in Canaan were not only skillfully erected; they stood as monuments to exquisite art and beauty. Only the temples in ancient Egypt rivaled the Phoenician workmanship that was increasingly recognized throughout the region as the most exceptional that any kingdom had to offer.

Solomon asked King Hiram to lend him a man who was well skilled in the building arts and who could also plan, organize and superintend the planned massive temple construction. Without a moment's hesitation Hiram selected *Hiram Abif,* known in the land of Canaan as the son of a widow and renowned as a most skillful artificer in metals and construction fabrics. He is reputed to have descended from Tubal-cain, said to have been the first artificer in metals and of the eighth generation from Adam; the first man into whom God allegedly breathed life. When this master builder placed the finishing touches on his constructions, it seemed to those who viewed *Hiram's* work that the edifice had actually been touched by the Divine.

Although most of the foregoing is allegorical there is very little therein that is either consistent with or reminiscent of the Gospel stories about Jesus. Whereas *Hiram Abif* was a master builder, it is written that Jesus was taught carpentry by his father Joseph. Unlike the slain Grand Master there are no temples or stately edifices that Jesus is credited with having built. Although parables attributed to Jesus' teachings touching upon the concept that man is inwardly a Temple of God, there is nothing anywhere written in the many Holy Writings that places Jesus at the construction site of any stately edifice. Moreover, the Gospels fix Jesus' time on earth at approximately the first century whereas according to the Holy Bible Solomon, King Hiram of Tyre and *Hiram Abif* lived centuries before. (The precise dating of the lifetimes of these men is subject to enormous doubt and worthy of further research).

Prior to the commencement of the construction, Solomon instituted *lodges,* or meeting places for the different classifications of workmen. They were segregated into three distinct groups: Entered Apprentices or bearers of constructions materials; Fellowcraft or those who labored on the mountaintops and in the rock quarries to extract construction materials from the earth; and Masters or overseers of the work who superintended the work. This ingenious organization of workmen into organized groupings is said to have contributed to the peace and harmony that allegedly prevailed among all of the workmen during the seven years the Temple was said to have been under construction. Each *lodge* regularly met in different apartments of the Temple before the entire edifice was completed. Situated atop this masterful organizational chart were the three Grand Masters: Solomon, King of Israel; Hiram, King of Tyre; and *Hiram Abif,* who was designated as the chief designer and inspector of every facet of this enormous undertaking.

Before he commenced his public ministry, Jesus is reputed to have assembled his own workmen consisting in part of the *Twelve*, or those men whom the Holy Bible refers to as Apostles. Following the episode famously described in the Gospel attributed to John as the *Wedding at Cana,* Jesus led his followers on a path that was intended to figuratively build the Kingdom of God on earth. This was no ordinary kingdom but one that was to result from the expansion of all human consciousness sufficient to lead all men to know that a piece of the Divine resided inside each of them.

While doing so, Jesus imparted many truths about God's characteristics and taught all who listened about the everlasting love that the Creator held for all of His creatures. But unlike the moments of fraternal intercourse *Hiram Abif* is said to have enjoyed, the Holy Bible does not describe a time when Jesus enjoyed a time of peace and fraternal harmony. His journey was punctuated by discord among his own followers, challenges from the Jewish priesthood and harassment by the myriad Roman legions that occupied Palestine. The Holy Scriptures relate that eventually the discord and disharmony led to his crucifixion at the hands of vicious Roman soldiers. While there are similarities between the deaths of *Hiram Abif* and Jesus, those similarities are insufficient to confirm that the Hiramic Legend is intended to represent the Christ. Discord and disharmony have contributed to the deaths of hundreds of thousands of men, women and children who have had nothing at all in common with either the slain Grand Master or Jesus.

Hiram Abif and Jesus actually represent different, although not entirely disassociated, schools of spirituality. In the so-called higher degree rituals of Freemasonry, we learn allegorically that the first three Grand Masters were initiated into a sacred and very secretive society of men. Solomon is said to have been initiated at or near the building of the Temple. By then both Hiram of Tyre and *Hiram Abif* had already been initiated into that same great society or order. Although present-day Masons are not precisely informed about the nature of that order, diligent study may confirm that it was the very same order into which Pythagoras and many of the Egyptian Pharaohs were also initiated. The ritual performed for Solomon is said to have been the same ritual used to transform the Pharaohs into gods.

Initiation was considered by the ancients to represent a mystical death or symbolic descent into the *lower regions* where every evil stood ready to lay claim to the candidate's soul. After conquering those evils during the ritual the initiate was said to have been *regenerated,* or *born again* to live a life of purity. Upon completing his ritualistic journey the candidate was deemed worthy of the Great Architect's unbridled protection.

That initiation was an essential part of entering into schools which taught the truths of primitive spiritual revelation including truths that disclosed the existence and attributes of the *One True God*. The immortality of the human soul, as well as the existence of rewards and punishments after death was also taught in those same mystery schools. The initiates were educated in the importance of Nature, the arts, sciences, morality, government, philosophy, philanthropy and metaphysics. Public scorn was heaped upon those who refused admission after having been invited to be initiated. Such men were most often thought to be odd, profane and unworthy of either future public employment or private confidence.

Everywhere and in all their various forms the mystery schools were funereal, i.e., dignified and solemn. Each school symbolically celebrated a mystical death and restoration to life that pertained to a heroic person. Although the details differed from country to country and school to school, the essence of the message was always the same. Their commonality is firmly rooted in astronomy and mythology both of which some believe also gave rise to the Hiramic Legend.

Although some writers have speculated that Jesus, too, was initiated into the Egyptian mysteries, scant supporting evidence may be found in the Holy Bible. The Gospel of Matthew alludes to a time when Joseph and Mary quickly immigrated to Egypt, ostensibly to avoid those who wished to kill their young son. Some authors have expanded upon that story and portrayed Egypt as the home of the true priesthood; that Jesus was the rightful heir to the throne of David, who was actually an Egyptian pharaoh; and that Jesus was thereby schooled in the spiritual arts in the *"true church."* If that was so, that schooling would have necessarily also included his initiation into the Egyptian mystery school.

In support of that contention, those writers have also singled out the passage in the Gospel of Mark suggesting that Jesus was conferring initiatory (Masonic?) degrees on a young man who ran away with an apron about his waist at the very moment Jesus' captors descended upon him in the Garden of Gethsemane. For many Freemasons this is very thin evidence let alone sufficient proof to conclude that Jesus had any connection with either the mystery schools, or Masonry. Yet without conclusive evidence one way or the other, it is wise and prudent to keep an open mind until convincing proof is actually made known to us.

Comparing allegories and then straining to stress the similarities in order to arrive at a reasonably verified assumption that *Hiram Abif* represents Jesus is unproductive even though it remains a captivating subject of speculation. Freemasonry is not a religion and does not promote any particular religion over any other. Each Mason is encouraged to choose, follow and practice the religion that best suits his own temperament and spiritual comfort. Thus, what is the point of such exercises? Is it to establish that Freemasonry is a Christian fraternity to the alienation of our Jewish, Islamic, Buddhist and Hindu brethren? If so, the exercise is not at all Masonic and should be replaced by a richer esoteric consideration about what is truly the importance of the Hiramic Legend.

There is a significant contrast between the ancient rites of initiation and the equally ancient hero myths that may assist us to better understand which one provides the thematic foundation for Masonic symbolism. Simply stated the issue is whether of not *Hiram Abif* is more a symbol of the mystery schools of initiation, or a contraction of the ancient hero myths. Ancient history and the rituals practiced in several contemporary societies have provided us with a wealth of material that can help answer that question.

Rites of initiation have been frequently employed in some cultures to symbolize the separation of children from their parents. For example the transformation from childhood to adulthood is symbolized in the Jewish rituals of *bar* and *bah mitzvah*. The three degrees of Masonry, at least in pertinent part, represent the three stages of human life which is also a transformation from one human condition to another. On the other hand, the hero myths suggest something quite different and have little, if anything to do with a transformation from childhood to adulthood. Instead the hero myths suggest an archetype of the dying god that symbolizes Divine grace. In essence, those myths provide that although all men will eventually succumb to a material death, they are assured by the grace of the Great Architect that they will never truly die. According to the myths that hero assumes mankind's guilt, suffers and dies for that guilt, and then is lifted by Divine grace into an everlasting life. That concept is precisely at the core of the Christian Church's teachings about Jesus. Nothing remotely similar is represented in Freemasonry by the Hiramic Legend.

The rites of initiation that pertain to Freemasonry promote an inward inculcation of virtue and morality and serve somewhat like a second parent for the candidate. Once the candidate is initiated into Masonry, he discovers a rich substitute for the lessons he quite likely first learned at his mother's knee. The lessons in morality originally taught him by his loving mother are re-discovered in the three Masonic degrees. Each lesson enables the candidate to draw upon an abundant source of virtuous energy to identify and accomplish the destiny and purposes of his own life's journey.

Similarly, in many primitive tribal rites of initiation the candidate is symbolically transported back to the deepest level of his original mother-child identity (or to that state of mind referred to as the "ego-Self") and is compelled to suffer a symbolic death during those rites. The similarity of those rites to the Hiramic Legend is vivid. As those rites progress, the initiate is ceremonially rescued from that state of mind by the rite of rebirth or regeneration. In similar fashion, *Hiram Abif* is eventually raised from his grave during the Masonic rites. Upon careful reflection might that also serve as a symbolic representation of the transcendence of the ego-Self? Of course, the truth of that postulate is for each individual Mason to eventually decide for himself.

Whether found in primitive tribal groups or within more complex societies, this particular ritual invariably consists of some representation of death giving way to life. It is nothing less than the passage from one stage of existence to another. In the Hiramic Legend the ritual is not confined to the rites of passage for the youthful, but also symbolizes the numerous passages that man also encounters at different stages in his earthly existence. In sum, Masonry teaches that man is constantly *becoming;* he is always transitioning from what he is to what he will next become.

At critical stages in those periods of transition the archetype of initiation is activated to provide a meaningful change in the attitude of the initiate that will ultimately result in him feeling more spiritually satisfied than he did during his previous state of being. Masonry's use of a symbolic spiral staircase is intended to remind the candidate that man is constantly changing spiritually: mankind either advances, or declines. The outcome is entirely dependent upon the choices made during the earthly journey. Either way, man finds himself confronted with an entirely new spirituality that, on the one hand brings him closer to the Great Architect, or on the other hand more vastly separates him from the Divine presence.

The archetypal patterns of initiation, known throughout history as the *mysteries,* are woven into the texture of those ecclesiastical rituals that require different manners of worshipping the Supreme Ruler of the Universe at birth, marriage and death. These are best demonstrated by the very real experiences of living people who, whether or not they are Masons, unconsciously duplicate the major patterns found in the rites of initiation.

In young people this is best demonstrated by what psychologists call the *ordeal* or *trial by strength,* and is readily apparent to us when we witness a competitive athletic or sporting event. In more mature individuals this is best evidenced by personal sacrifice, or suffering on behalf of a greater cause or for another person. In the aged it is frequently demonstrated by the quiet suffering of those gripped in the throes of a terminal illness. In each case man strives to succeed to prove his worthiness: a work of life that is at the heart of the Hiramic Legend.

There is a striking difference between rites of initiation and the hero myths that also adds another dimension to our exploration into whether or not *Hiram Abif* was intended to represent the Messiah. In mythology, the typical *hero* exhausts his efforts to achieve his ambitions. He is ultimately regarded as having been successful even if immediately following his accomplishments he is punished or slain because of his hubris.

We are informed by the synoptic Gospel writers that Jesus was criticized by the religious establishment of his day for having arrogantly equated himself to God. According to that establishment, by so doing Jesus earned his crucifixion at the hands of the Romans. In direct contrast, the candidate for Masonic rites of initiation is asked to voluntarily relinquish his willful ambitions and desires and submit to the *ordeal* or physical challenge of the rite. The candidate in the ancient rites was required to endure without any promise of success, which is precisely the lesson taught us by *Hiram Abif*. The motivation for doing so is the desire to contribute to the expansion of human consciousness about the goodness of the Great Architect for the purpose of better enabling mankind to one day live in a state of pure fraternal love. As such, the Masonic candidate is regarded as a warrior for *light* who devotes his life to battling against the forces of *darkness*.

The candidate in the ancient rites of initiation was required to be prepared to die, as was the Grand Master *Hiram Abif*, who defiantly refused to reveal the secrets of a Master Mason to Jubela, Jubelo and Jubelum knowing that by doing so he would surely die. The purpose of this symbolism is to create a hope and belief in the candidate that his material death following a life of virtue will give birth to the continuation of morality and one day achieve an environment on earth wherein men may live together in peace and harmony.

The presence of an altar during all rites of initiations, ancient and present-day, symbolizes an intention to implore God's aid to conform human behavior to His message about loving our neighbor. It is upon that altar that the candidate's mistakes of the past are symbolically sacrificed in favor of a future life grounded in virtue and morality. The rebirth that follows the symbolic raising from the grave during the rites of initiation is more about invigorating earthly and material life than it is about transitioning to the Heavenly Jerusalem where all spirits reunite with the Great Architect.

Early Christian churches regarded Orpheus, the Greco-Roman successor to the Dionysus religion, as the prototype of the Christ. Freemasonry has never equated *Hiram Abif* to Orpheus. Like his predecessor Dionysus,

Orpheus held the promise of a future divine life for all mankind. To the contrary *Hiram Abif* held the secrets of a Master Mason. Like both Dionysus and Jesus, Orpheus was considered God incarnate. *Hiram Abif* was not a *god* he was always a man – a Master Builder whose talents were in architecture.

Jesus was born of a virgin who, according to theology, remained so even though married to a living husband: *Hiram Abif* was the son of a widow. After his death and resurrection, Jesus returned unto heaven and his body was never discovered. *Hiram Abif* was found in a shallow grave by the Fellowcraft, raised from the grave and transported to the Temple grounds where he was eventually buried with great pomp and ceremony.

Most will agree that the common ground for comparing the Grand Master to the Messiah is the *raising from the grave*, mistakenly referred to by some in Freemasonry as the *resurrection*. Masonic ritual does not equate that *raising* to the *resurrection*, but some Masonic writers have planted that seed for our continuing consideration. As a consequence we are compelled to ask the question: is the Masonic symbolism of rebirth the same as resurrection? Perhaps it is, perhaps it is not, but the truth is far from certain one way or the other. We may be left to forever wonder, which is likely as accurate as Freemasonry would wish to make any of its potentially religious symbolism.

Without question there is an enormous difference between the rites of initiation and the so-called hero myths. However, each symbolizes something extraordinarily significant to mankind's spiritual advancement. Initiation symbolizes a commitment to spiritual change in earthly matters in order that a man might best prepare himself for divine existence after death and to pass on to succeeding generations a better foundation upon which to continue building God's Kingdom of fraternal love.

The hero myths represent mankind's hope for life after death. Are the two so desperately distinct that we should strive to point out their differences? Or are the two similar enough that we should permit all Masons to draw their own independent conclusions about the matter? Freemasonry's commitment to the freedom of choice provides the answer, but we will not simply avoid exploring the comparisons and contrasts under the guise of that freedom. Rather we will dig deeper to determine all that we can learn from our rich Masonic symbolism.

A thorough examination of the biblical Jesus reveals a distinction between his essence as a man and his enduring theological importance. That distinction is what primarily separates those who embrace the Christian religion from those who revere him but embrace other religious faiths. Of central importance to the matter is the question of Jesus' divinity.

Since 325 AD, the Christian Church – prompted by the Roman Catholic Church - has accepted him as the *Son,* consubstantial with the *One True God.* In that year the Roman Catholic Church *confessed* at the first ecumenical council held at Nicea that Jesus was God incarnate. At the second ecumenical council held in 381 AD at Constantinople that confession was reiterated and expanded. From that time forward all Catholics and most Protestants have worshipped Jesus as Lord and God.

Not too surprisingly, those who embraced other religions were at once amused, confused and outraged. To many of those people such a conclusion was nothing less than outright heresy and blasphemy. How could anyone have the arrogance to declare that any human being, let alone a revolutionary named Jesus from the rebellious land of Galilee, was God? There is little wonder that such harsh sentiments eventually resulted in the eruption of violence.

Ever evolving human intellect once regarded God as an entirely separate entity who, having created man was different from man and rarely became involved in man's personal affairs. In that viewpoint God was a "big picture" entity concerned more with "connecting the dots" between the beginning and end of time.

Throughout all of history men have engaged in serious reflection about God and at various times changed their opinions about Him. The watershed point of that evolving thought occurred when some religious thinkers began to consider that a spark of the Divine existed within each and every person. Once that thought began taking root, it was not difficult for man to also wonder whether or not some men had more of that spark within them than did others. That same thinking has resulted in many of our established religions concluding that they, not competing religions, constitute the one true religion. For generations intellectual and physical battles have been waged and continue to be fought today in hopes of securing religious supremacy.

Lest Masons become too complacent in their belief that *Hiram Abif* is free from such controversy, we should carefully review some rather ancient and revealing parochial allegories about our slain Grand Master. We begin that review with the ancient *mysteries* that had their foundation in rites once practiced by the Persians, Indians and Egyptians. Present-day historians continue to regard that part of the world as the cradle of western civilization where some form of Masonry was once secretly practiced among the enlightened members of society. The exact nature of that form and practice is presently unknown, but the meetings were undoubtedly well guarded to make certain that no profane eavesdroppers overheard the ceremonies.

From those meetings ideas about the Great Architect flooded the many schools of philosophy and houses of worship revealing to everyone that the Almighty was truly a multifaceted Creator. At times, the Supreme Ruler of the Universe was merciful, terse, loving, disciplining, peaceful and warlike. The Old Testament is littered with such descriptions of God's character in mind-numbing fashion. So diverse are His characteristics that the human mind cannot possibly fathom how a loving being could also inflict war, disease and famine upon His creation. But according to one Persian allegory, *Hiram* proved the key to man's hope of eventually comprehending the incomprehensible.

One of the principal objectives of the ancient *mysteries* was to communicate true and correct ideas about God to a select few. The ancient Persians portrayed *Hiram* as both the King and Master who taught those ideas to both Moses and Pythagoras. Did he do so as a *Son of God*? Does this allegory also suggest that *Hiram* was Divine, as Jesus was considered Divine? Such possibilities merely invite further unconfirmed speculation. Since there has never been an ecclesiastical declaration, such as that made by the Council at Nicea, proclaiming *Hiram* to be Divine, those speculations must remain unresolved for the time being. Suffice to say, that to Masons *Hiram* represents the beauty and glory of the day, which owing to his personal integrity, piety and reverence for sacred things, also represents a highly developed spirituality the potentiality for which resides in every man. The extent to which that spirituality may be developed during any man's lifetime is entirely dependent upon both the grace of God and the choices each man makes.

Our Jewish brethren are faithful in their theological belief that the Messiah has yet to come to earth. They have been chastised, criticized, and condescended to because of their refusal to believe that Jesus, or any other man, is God. The founder of modern-day Christianity was a Jew named Saul, referred to in the New Testament as an Apostle of Jesus whose name was later changed to Paul. Unlike the *Twelve* who followed Jesus during his lifetime, Paul is reputed to have become an Apostle upon encountering the spiritual Jesus long after the earthly Jesus had reputedly been put to death. It was Paul who wrote that Jesus' Divinity constituted a stumbling block for the Jews. And it was not only the Jews that he pointed out when accusing them of spiritual ineptitude. Paul rigidly concluded that all religions and bodies of men that rejected Jesus' Divinity were less spiritual than those who embraced him as the only Son of God.

As all Masons know, and as has been stated elsewhere in this work Freemasonry does not promote any one religion at the expense of any other religion. The Craft steadfastly refuses to be dragged into disputes about God which threaten the freedom each man should have to approach the Great Architect in his own way and to enhance his own spirituality in a manner that he alone chooses. Whether or not the Masonry that Albert Pike suggests was practiced before the days of Moses, it is certain that today's Masons do not preoccupy themselves with speculations about whether or not *Hiram Abif* symbolizes the Messiah. It is sufficient for Masons to know that the slain Grand Master symbolizes honor, virtue, integrity and fortitude even when facing death. When a man nurtures and develops such personal characteristics to the extent that they become habitual, he may be assured that he has done all he can do to develop the spirit within him. The rest is up to God.

There is another matter common to both *Hiram Abif* and Jesus that is likely extraordinarily important to Masons. It is the matter of the Temple. King Solomon engaged Hiram of Tyre and *Hiram Abif* to build a Temple to serve as the house within which the God of Abraham, Isaac and Jacob would dwell. The entire Masonic allegory about the Hiramic Legend is centered upon that Temple, as well as upon the importance of expanding the human spirituality represented by the Temple.

Similarly, Jesus was trained in the Temple (albeit the successor to King Solomon's Temple - Herod's Temple) and instructed there on both the Holy Scriptures and the ideas of God. In a particular passage of Holy Scripture, upon finding that the Temple had become a common marketplace, Jesus flew into a rage and violently cleared the halls while loudly declaring that no man should ever again so denigrate God's house. Later we are informed that he also carried that thought over to a parable about the human body, instructing his disciples that like the stone structure itself, man should treat his own body as though it was God's Temple.

This Temple symbolism is intended to convey both an appreciation for establishing physical houses of worship, as well as for the spiritual evolution of human consciousness. However, it is to that latter representation that Masonry's Hiramic Legend truly pertains. For as King Solomon raised the body of *Hiram Abif* for more decent internment, Masons also bear witness to the instruction that the act of raising the body of the slain Grand Master also signified the expansion of human awareness. Each candidate who participates in the Masonic ritual eventually becomes profoundly aware of his own personal responsibility to awaken his spirituality for the purpose of aiding and promoting the continuing erection of God's Kingdom on earth.

It is this awakening that constitutes the great spiritual work that *Hiram Abif* so eloquently personifies. Throughout history this work has taken place as a function of the simultaneous action of two contrasting forces: the forces from *above* and *below*. Those forces represent the continuous revelation to man by the Great Architect and the effort of each man to thereupon erect his own spiritual superstructure – divine will working together with human will.

Human spiritual evolution continues to be the product of the collaboration of revelation and humanism. In Indo-Tibetan terms this phenomena is carried out by Avatars, on the one hand, and Buddhas, on the other hand. The Buddha awaits revelation by the Avatar which is then added to the existing state of spiritual consciousness, or awareness.

Hiram Abif and the Temple symbolism are nothing less than Masonry's substitute for Buddhas and Avatars. The Grand Master knelt each day at the altar in the *Sanctum Sanctorum* to allow God's voice to enlighten his soul before continuing with his labors. That act of spiritual respiration is intended to serve as an object lesson to all Masons, who are encouraged by the Craft never to enter upon any great or important undertaking without first invoking the blessing of the Great Architect.

The greatest religions in history embrace this same lesson but symbolically express it differently. Esoteric Islam (Shi'ism and Sufism) awaits the *parousia* or coming of the twelfth Imam who is believed to be the entity who will bring full revelation to man at the end of time. Believing Jews await the first coming of the Messiah for a similar purpose. And, as we have already been informed, our Christian brethren anticipate the second coming of the Christ, which is said to coincide with the eventual establishment of God's Kingdom on earth. Considered together, each represents an attitude of anticipation that permeates all of the major religions.

Without being nourished and directed from above, this human anticipation here below would have long ago exhausted itself. Suffice to say it is not exhausted but it has experienced an energetic increase from generation to generation. It aspires to a reality and is not content to remain a mere illusion or fantasy. It inspires the creation of Temples, both external and internal, upon which the greatest exertions of spiritual energy are applied in anticipation that the Great Architect will never cease to unveil His revelations until the day mankind has been made fully aware. In sum, to Masons *Hiram Abif* is illustrative of the importance for each man to walk with God and circumscribe his human behavior within the limits defined by the Great Architect.

The continual yearning for human freedom is at the heart of the lessons of the Temple imagery. The specific nature of the freedom taught has absolutely nothing to do with the notion that everyone should be empowered to do anything at any time. To the contrary, *Hiram Abif* represents a disciplined freedom – one that is defined by the laws of the Great Architect which if followed will set all men free from the limitations of their grossest desires. In his assumed role as Messiah, Jesus set men free by relieving them from the worry that human death constitutes the annihilation of existence. Similarly, in his role as the "beauty and glory of the day," *Hiram* exemplifies the narrow path that men should walk toward both enjoying their personal freedom and ensuring its continuation for generations to come. Each allegory compliments the other and invites a deeper contemplation upon what God truly has in mind for all of us.

One of the more tumultuous yet highly productive periods in human history occurred during both the American and French Revolutions. Each resulted in a violent change in government and shifted power from a monarchy to the people. Historians have written volumes about how those conflicts added to human consciousness by illuminating the minds of all men about what it actually means to be "free." Nothing less the same individual freedom is at stake in both the Synoptic Gospels and the Hiramic Legend. While men may forever argue for or against the use of violence against human beings to gain that freedom, none will argue that once gained, extraordinary efforts must be used to retain freedom's benefits.

Once people gain their freedom it is essential that they secure it and not entrust its protection to any one person. The progress of personal freedom throughout the world is tangible evidence that human spiritual consciousness is expanding. Scottish Rite Masonry teaches that one of the worst personifications of evil is tyranny or despotism. In so doing it seeks to inculcate by the dramatic exemplification of lessons in virtue and morality a deep commitment to defending personal freedom in the countries where each Scottish Rite Mason lives. That teaching represents a call to work for the advancement of human consciousness; to seek also the advancement of all mankind against the scourges of poverty, enslavement, repression and hate.

Masons experience the allegory of the raising of *Hiram Abif* from the grave and, among other notions, conclude that one significant purpose is to vigorously promote love as the substance that cements mankind. The Gospel stories about Jesus' resurrection primarily emphasize it as the penultimate sign of God's love for His created children. If there is a direct parallel relationship between Jesus and the slain Grand Master it is that each represents the Great Architect's love. It is this same transformation of love from idea to habit that constitutes both the work of Masonry, as well as the work that will eventually erect God's Kingdom on earth.

Chapter 17

THE SEAFARING/WAYFARING MAN

After brutally murdering the Grand Master *Hiram Abif*, Jubela, Jubelo and Jubelum decided to make their escape out of King Solomon's kingdom to avoid being captured and brought to justice. Stressfully huddling together they bickered about what next to do and were told by their Jubelum that their best chance was to travel by a circuitous route to Joppa, a seaport town, and hire a boat to take them to the land of Ethiopia. Without hesitation each agreed and upon arriving at the docks encountered a seafaring man who appeared to be in charge of the boat they wished to hire.

Jubelum stepped forward and asked where the handsome boat was bound. "Ethiopia," the seafaring man said, adding matter-of-factly that it was sailing immediately.

"Do you take passengers?" Jubelum inquired. The seafaring man eyed the assassin carefully trying to take his measure. The man in front of him did not look like any ordinary passenger. He was dressed as a *Temple* workman – much different than most travelers he encountered. Like everyone else in the entire Kingdom, the seafaring man knew that a fabulous edifice was being erected by the mighty King to serve as a house for the One God of Abraham, Isaac, Jacob and Moses.

"I do, if you have King Solomon's pass," the seafaring man carefully answered.

Trying hard not to show his disappointment, Jubelum turned, strode back to his fellow assassins and whispered to them what he had been told. "What pass is this?" Jubela and Jubelo asked. "We have never heard of such a thing – what shall we tell him?"

Jubelum held up his hand for silence lest. "I will offer him an incentive," he suggested, turning to slowly walked back to the weathered seafaring man. "We have no pass," he said finally, "but we will pay you any sum of money you require." Shaking his head the seafaring man said, "My friend, I am sorry. You cannot go without King Solomon's pass, for it is strictly forbidden." Jubelum again returned to his fellow assassins and after a brief conversation said, "Let us turn back into the country."

The seafaring man makes his appearance in the Hiramic Legend at precisely the moment when the ruffians desperately need to make their escape. It is he and nobody else who stands between them and the hope of escape. However, because he was also a man of virtue and morality, he abided without a moment's hesitation to King Solomon's command that he must demand a particular pass from those seeking to leave the Kingdom. He did not know at the time that the order was given to prevent the escape of *Hiram Abif's* murderers.

After Jubela, Jubelo and Jubelum were compelled to turn back into the country to seek a hiding place, each of them eventually noticed the nagging noise in going on in their heads. Their consciences were loudly calling out to them. Eventually those consciences betrayed them, as each eventually let loudly fall from his lips words that later sealed their fate.

Had the seafaring man failed to hold firm to Solomon's charge to demand a password, the assassins' eventual remorse, pleas for forgiveness and resounding confessions of their souls might never have occurred. Each could have easily lived out the remainder of his natural life without ever having to confront his personal sin. There would have been no justice and no adverse consequence for killing the Grand Master. Equally important there would never have been an opportunity for the ruffians to receive forgiveness from the Great Architect.

The image of the stubborn seafaring man with arms folded across his chest, a scowl on his face and shaking his head from side to side symbolizes a force over which we humans have no control – a force capable of reminding us about our human failings. Although that force did not by itself bring about a reformation in the three assassins, it put that process in motion.

Good and evil arises from man's love or rejection of the Supreme Ruler of the Universe. That is not to simply state that each person has within himself the power exclusive of all other forces to distinguish good from evil. Rather, it is a matter once again of the choices that men make. Jubela, Jubelo and Jubelum could have chosen to obediently go about their work at the Temple, but instead they plotted to kill *Hiram Abif.* They rejected God, turned away from His love and embraced hatred.

If that same conduct could ever result in the finality of things, i.e., that man has the last word in all that is done on the face of the earth, and that God is irrelevant, it would also terrifyingly signify that the Creator has walked away and left us alone to fend for ourselves. The lesson of the seafaring man is intended to teach us that the Great Architect has not walked away. He is always present and engages Himself with all creation. This truth is sometimes referred to in theology and philosophy as *Divine Revelation.*

The give and take that goes on between the Creator and His creature is not always initiated by man's prayer. Sometimes the Great Architect seeks out man, makes His presence known and lovingly blocks the path which if followed would lead to certain destruction. The seafaring man blocked that path for the assassins when he turned them away at the dock. Is he thus meant to represent Divine intervention? Does the Great Architect make use of some of us at different times in our lives to serve as "seafaring" men for other wayward travelers whom we encounter during life's journey? If so, are we always faithful to the task?

Our ancestors who embraced the Hermetic philosophy taught us the fundamentals of Divine respiration: *as it is above, so shall it be below.* Mankind is in a constant state of give-and-take with the Creator – taking His lessons and inspirations and giving them to the world through the lives we lead. Freemasonry's emphasis upon *charity* teaches that same lesson one hundred times over. Whence came the inspiration to build hospitals for suffering children, homes for the poor and aged, or clinics for those with speech defects? Some man or body of men had the idea and then put that idea to work. But where did the idea originate? Why would any man care about any other person? Our Hermetic ancestors would answer "*because God cares,*" again underscoring the principle that *as it is above, so shall it be below.*

However, if such ideas originate from above are we also to understand that God actually intervenes in our lives? The lesson of the seafaring man clearly indicates that He does. But does He do so whether or not we have first invited Him? Again, the lesson of the seafaring man suggests to us that the answer is "yes."

The three ruffians did not ask to be turned away: they asked for passage to Ethiopia. They did not wish for the denial of their request; they eagerly sought to convince the steadfast seafaring man that they must leave the Kingdom. That which thereafter occurred in their lives was entirely contrary to the *idea* of escaping detection that they first formed in their own minds. Who was responsible for the interference? If it was not mere happenstance or coincidence, it must have been the result of Divine intervention.

During their search for the assassins, the Fellowcraft first traveled away from the Temple toward the seaport town of Joppa. Like the ruffians, the Fellowcraft also recognized that escaping by boat would be the quickest way to put a great deal of distance between the pursued and their pursuers. As they entered the town they met a wayfaring, or traveling man whom they hailed.

"Hello," said one of the Fellowcraft, "have you seen any men pass through who looked like workers from King Solomon's Temple?"

The wayfaring man reflected a moment before answering. "Yes, I believe I have," he said finally, pointing toward the docks. "There were three men dressed like *Temple* workmen talking with a seafaring man over there."

"Where did they go?" the same Fellowcraft asked.

"I know they did not get on any of the boats," the wayfaring man replied. He pointed toward the distance to the east. "They must have turned back into the country."

The Fellowcraft whispered among themselves and quickly concluded that the men described by the wayfaring man were the assassins. "This is important information," one of the Fellowcraft said, "I think we should immediately return to the Temple and report this to King Solomon." Everyone agreed and they immediately returned with the news.

Solomon listened carefully to the report of his Fellowcraft. He suspected that they had something to do with the Grand Master's disappearance. "That means the murderers are still in the Kingdom," he said finally. "If what you say is true and you are not the real murderers, you should be able to find those assassins. Search everywhere you can and find the murderers and the body of *Hiram Abif.*" Pointing a finger at them he continued, "And if you do not, I will assume that you are the real assassins and act accordingly." The Fellowcraft bowed respectfully in shuddering understanding that if they did not find either the deserters or the body of the Grand Master they would be put to death.

Like the seafaring man, the wayfaring man represents an external force that eventually leads to the capture of Jubela, Jubelo and Jubelum. Both symbolize the interaction between the Great Architect and His creatures. Using the information passed on by the wayfaring man, the Fellowcraft eventually discovered the ruffians cowering in a cave in the mountains of Palestine and dragged them before King Solomon who imposed the death sentence for their heinous crime. The convergence of two distinct Divine and external forces eventually result in *equilibrium,* or the imposition of justice for the violation of God's laws.

But the wayfaring man represents something more. He is not merely redundant or complimentary to the symbolism of the seafaring man: he is necessary to God's plan in and of himself. Without the wayfaring man, the Hiramic Legend might well have ended without the Fellowcraft ever discovering the assassins. We know from our own personal experiences that although we are often aware of the challenges at hand, we do not always discover the solution. The wayfaring man represents a solution and signifies the fulfillment of *hope.*

Knowing about the purpose of life is essential to all men if they are ever to understand how to live correctly. Unless man understands the order of which he is a part, humanity may never accomplish the greatest good of which it is capable. With the wayfaring man, we eventually attain a just result in our story. The field of today's endeavors is bounded on the one hand by the unknown of tomorrow and on the other by dead history. Only the present is relevant for us; the past is dead. What about the future? It lies at the feet of the wayfaring man.

Sometime during their lives most men become concerned about life, death, or possibly both. Plato, as well as other ancient philosophers from an assortment of philosophical schools, was primarily concerned about life and told us in his writings that it was imperishable. He also told us to look beyond ourselves – the matter and dust that physically makes us what we are – and to pay attention to the truth that within each one of us there is a piece of the Divine that will never die. He also informed us that in a physical sense life as we know it results from the temporary association of the *above* with the *below*: the incorporeal with the corporeal. Human bodies, being corporeal, occupy space and an interval of time. Incorporeal bodies, such as the gods of the philosophers, are not limited by time and exist in a timeless environment.

The caves within which the assassins concealed themselves symbolize the mundane powers of the sensible world in that the rocky openings remind us of that which leads us into darkness. The passages that lead man into and out of such caverns represent beginnings and endings to humans – similar to the representations of the winter and summer solstices. The northern passage, very much like the *North* in a Masonic Lodge, represents the premature descent of man. However, the south passage, symbolized by the *beauty and glory of the day*, is referred to by ancient philosophers as the avenue of escape for immortal souls.

One symbol remains unexplained: the olive branch, which although not specifically appearing in the Hiramic Legend is represented by the cave in which the assassins secreted themselves. The olive branches sprouted above those caves.

The olive is regarded by the ancients as the plant of Minerva, the Roman goddess of wisdom. The olive branch was routinely situated atop gates, arches, or caves to signify the wisdom that sits atop the universe. It also represents the winner of the race of life – he or she who has well run the race and won in the sight of God.

Together, the seafaring and wayfaring men represent the cycle of necessity, i.e., the period of time or condition of existence through which humanity must pass before attaining conscious immortality. Just as the news from the wayfaring man was essential to discovering the ruffians' hiding place, so, too, is it essential that mankind pass through the *valley of death* to finally discover the equilibrium or balance between *light and darkness*. Some assert that philosophy alone can bestow upon every man, woman and child the precious gift of immortality, in spite of also having benefited from the grace of the Grand Architect, for without incorporating the lessons of philosophy into every person's life, mankind never becomes worthy of such immortality. Such is also a lesson of the Hindus, who preach reincarnation, or the return of souls for the purpose of further indoctrination. Yet when all else is stripped away the bare essence of man's quest to understand death is left for all to ponder.

It has been written that as long as man believes in death, there is no life; and that what man regards as existence, i.e., the human body, is actually nothing other than the gloomy vestibule of oblivion. Of course such thinking is founded upon the conclusion that human death results in oblivion. That conclusion has been argued against by Buddhists and Christians alike, as well as many others, who variously have decided that human death is either but a dream from which one will eventually awaken, or the passage to a more rewarding existence. Both of those arguments derive from the evolution of human consciousness that enables generation after generation to benefit from the truths discovered by the human mind and spirit.

Those truths are not limited to the concept of immortality, for being immortal is simply a means to an end – the infinite opportunity to achieve perfection. If those truths were so limited the fact that man goes on living after he is dead would suggest that he would continue to experience the miseries of the material world. The teachings of Christianity and Freemasonry converge at this point to inform us that such is not the case.

The wayfaring man also symbolizes the importance of taking direction from those who possess greater knowledge, information and wisdom. Though in hot pursuit none of the Fellowcraft actually knew which way the three assassins had traveled. An educated guess took them to Joppa, but from there without actually seeing Jubela, Jubelo, or Jubelum they knew not which direction to travel next. Had not the wayfaring man told them what he had seen, they would have cast about blindly likely failing in their search and suffering the wrath of King Solomon upon their return to the Temple.

In his numerous philosophical writings, Kant frequently ponders such deep subjects as *pure reason* and the *a priori* understanding of all things. His philosophical explorations are premised upon his firm belief that for all things there is a universal truth – perhaps several distinct universal truths for several distinct challenges. While Kant never identified that source or sources as God, he did describe *pure reason* and *a priori* understanding as transcendental, i.e., things beyond the limits of human thought.

The wayfaring man represents information beyond the limits of knowledge – he knew something about the three assassins that was not known to the Fellowcraft. The importance of that symbolism is immediately evident, as it signifies Masonry's encouragement of generations of human beings to seek knowledge beyond what they already know.

The teachings of the Holy Bible encourage the same pursuit of the unknown. While it is certainly easy to accept that there are things we may never know, it is important that we not instantly succumb to that notion. The prophets of the Old Testament were able to offer up timely predictions about the future which were based upon "unknowable" facts. Jesus taught that there was nothing that could not be known. Thus it is not so much a question of whether or not we should pursue the "unknowable" but how such a pursuit should best be made.

Ask and it shall be given unto you; seek and ye shall find; knock and it shall be opened unto you. This well-known passage of scripture not only appears in the Gospel of Luke (*Luke 11:9*), it is also presented in ritual to initiates during the conferral of Masonic degrees. Precisely how a Mason should *ask, seek* and *knock* is developed more fully in Masonic ritual. Suffice to state that Masonry promotes an approach to the task that is very diverse. Prayer, meditation, contemplation, obtaining knowledge from books and people, and placing one's mind and being in a state of virtue and morality are parts of that diverse approach. But none of those attributes are capable of being instantly mastered. Such mastery requires time, dedication and work – hard work.

The wayfaring man seemed a likely source about the unknown whereabouts of the assassins, but the Fellowcraft could not be certain that he would actually know anything useful. They first had to *ask* and once they heard what he had to say, they then had to *seek* the ruffians whom they eventually discovered concealed in the mountains of Palestine. Once they made their discovery, they then *knocked,* or rushed upon the murderers, seized and bound them and took them before King Solomon. Masonic legend tells us that had they not been so fortunate in making their discovery, each one of the Fellowcraft would have been executed instead of the true killers. In other words, had it not been for the wayfaring man justice would have been thwarted.

Chapter 18

NO MAN IS AN ISLAND

The ritual dramatization about the legend of *Hiram Abif* opens with a beautiful display of harmonious activity. The Temple is under construction by men who, working without any noisy tools of iron, have been wisely segregated by Solomon into cheerful working parties. Each man had an assigned task which he performed to the best of his capability. Discord was nonexistent. If one word could suffice to describe their situation at the time it would be *solidarity*.

Although Solomon's well-oiled operation was all too soon interrupted by conspiracy and murder, it stands as a symbol to the world of what men can accomplish when they work in a spirit of harmonious unity. No undertaking can ever be successfully completed without teamwork and talented leadership. Masonry not only inculcates those characteristics, it also teaches that teamwork may best be accomplished by men dedicated to the pursuit and achievement of a common goal. Petty disputes, piques and quarrels – while definitely a part of the normal human condition – must be circumscribed and quelled if that common goal is ever to be achieved.

The lesson about *human solidarity* is not meant to be limited to Masons. It is intended to serve as a roadmap for mankind to follow in all of its travels. For Masons, as well as for all societies of men, women and children, those travels eventually bring each one face-to-face with the concept of social justice. Solidarity depends first and foremost upon man providing the living conditions necessary to promote social justice. That represents one of the basic ingredients of solidarity and is best accomplished by men who work for the common good rather than for their own self-interest.

Masonry compels us to frequently examine whether or not society is in proper equilibrium, i.e., balanced between the interests of the person and the interests of society as a whole. Solomon was intent upon building the most ornate Temple to serve as God's house and structured his organization of workmen for the purpose of best accomplishing that goal. Similarly, governments have formed at various periods in history to provide for the necessities of men and their leaders, including the structures within which each might dwell. But Solomon also put in place something more that has not always been mirrored by manmade governments: safeguards to protect each man's personal dignity.

Social justice may only be attained when men respect each other's transcendental dignity. That transcendental dignity presupposes that every human being has natural or divine rights which he is entitled to enjoy simply because he exists. Those rights are sometimes referred to as *God-given,* because they flow from each man's dignity as a creature of the Great Architect. Solomon recognized that those rights must be protected and preserved and established a working environment that required every *Temple* workman to be obedient to his superior, affectionate with his peer and condescending to his inferior in rank or office.

The defense of those rights, as well as the defense of the dignity of every person, has been entrusted by the Great Architect to all of us. Every human being owes a duty of respect to every other human being regardless of race, sex, age, religion, or creed. This was the law long before Solomon sought the assistance of Hiram of Tyre to build his Temple. It was passed down to mankind by the Great Architect when He first uttered the *Word* that gave rise to His glorious creation. As such, these rights of the individual are superior to the rights of society as a whole. Masonry teaches that governments must honor that superiority, if they wish to achieve social justice. Those governments that do not wish to so act risk being labeled as criminals against the laws of nature.

The moral legitimacy of every authority, whether ecumenical, theological, or fraternal, rests upon the enactment of safeguards to individual primacy. Nothing less was ultimately at stake when the Founding Fathers of the United States of America met in Philadelphia to negotiate among themselves the terms and conditions of this Nation's declaration of independence from England. For a time, the uprising of the citizens during the French Revolution was promoted by a similar sense of responsibility to individual and personal dignity. As history sadly records, that period later proved extraordinarily bloody and unnecessarily vengeful. Garibaldi looked around him and saw human oppression in every quarter, as he determined to lead his Italian brethren from governmental domination to a life filled with individual freedom. In each instance, as well as in hundreds of others like them, the failure or refusal to recognize individual rights undermined the moral legitimacy of government and resulted in horrific violence and death.

It is one of Masonry's roles to remind men of good will about man's natural-born spirit of freedom and to protect the rights that flow from God to every man, woman and child. Respect for the individual person arises from respect for the principle that everyone should look upon his neighbor as another self and earnestly endeavor to insure that that neighbor enjoys the means for living life with dignity.

That same mutual respect was at work in quarries during the building of the Temple, except in the single instance that resulted in the death of the Grand Master *Hiram Abif*. No legislation can ever eliminate the fears, prejudices, pride and selfishness that obstruct the establishment of truly fraternal organizations like Freemasonry. That ceases only when people embrace their neighbor as a "brother" and heap upon him the greatest acts of charity of which they are capable.

The duty to actively serve one's neighbor is not reserved for Masons alone. It is a duty incumbent upon all men especially when serving the disadvantaged. We would do well to recall the words of Jesus wherein he stated, *as you did it to one of the least of these my brethren, you did it to me. Matthew 25:40.* Mankind serves God best by insisting upon social justice for all men not just for the brightest, the wealthiest, or the most powerful. By definition *human solidarity* means a condition whereby all men from all stages of life freely respect the dignity of each other.

Men owe that same duty of respect to people who think or behave differently. There is no particular way a man must appear before he is entitled to respect. Also no man need act or behave in any particular manner to deserve another's man's respect.

Masonry teaches us that forgiveness is Divine. For their part in the initial conspiracy to kill *Hiram Abif,* each of the twelve Fellowcraft could have been punished. Instead they were all forgiven their crimes and reintegrated into the workmen who later completed the *Temple* construction under the guidance of Adonhiram. By forgiving those Fellowcraft, King Solomon exemplified the love necessary to maintain solidarity – a love that Masons are taught should be extended to our enemies as well as to our friends.

Human solidarity is incompatible with a hatred of enemies, the reviling of others, or the unwillingness to actively work to reform the misbehavior of others. That is not merely a Masonic duty – it is a human duty owed by everyone to each other. History has too frequently recorded societal conditions wherein misfits and nonconformists were tossed aside without any effort having been made to embrace them as neighbors. Men and women have been enslaved simply because they were deemed to be low creatures owing to their color, religion, sex, or politics. Human beings who committed crimes because they were unable to control their passions or desires have been labeled for the remainder of their earthly lives as "irredeemable." Entire civilizations have been perceived as threats to the existence of other civilizations and societies and thus continue to remain at what seems a perpetual distance. All too often the feeble, diseased and incapacitated human beings of this world have felt the brunt of rejection instead of brotherly love – derision in place of respect. The lesson of the Hiramic Legend demands a much different approach by men and Masons alike.

Created in the image of the One True God, all men have the same nature and origin. Mankind is called by God to participate in the same Divine beatitude and therefore enjoys equal dignity. The Supreme Ruler of the Universe has not conferred different rights upon the different individuals He has created. In fact it appears that He has intentionally created human beings to be different but has never decreed that they be treated unequally.

Every form of social or cultural discrimination based upon color, religion, sex, age, language, or social condition must not only be circumscribed, they must be eradicated. Simply stated, those human indignities are incompatible with human solidarity. Solomon did not configure his workmen on that basis. Rather, he grouped men according to their abilities to contribute to the construction of the Temple.

When he comes into this world, man is unequipped with everything he needs to survive and thrive. He is wholly dependent upon others, including the government and society within which he resides. Those who reject that importance of providing that support and bluntly adhere to the notion of "every man for himself" have yet to become charitable human beings. Those who become absorbed in their prejudices and need to find someone else less worthy have not yet learned that all of God's creatures were equally created. No society or government in the annals of human history has long survived after structuring a strata of the socially privileged that denies others the respect, dignity and Divine rights to which they are entitled.

Differences among individuals most often arise because of age, physical abilities, intellectual or moral aptitudes and the distribution of material wealth. Although not all of Solomon's workmen received equal wages, those of equal rank were treated equally. Even those of different rank were treated with equal fairness.

Most men recognize that each individual has been endowed with different talents. Today the reason for those differences is beyond our comprehension. However, the importance of promoting social intercourse among individuals of different rank is not. Differences among people actually encourage acts of great generosity, uncommon kindness and the sharing of goods and services with others. It is those acts that tend to foster the mutual enrichment of all cultures and all people.

Most if not all of the inequalities arising from human conceptions and beliefs are simply inherently wrong and are opposed to the natural order of human existence. No intelligent being seriously believes that some humans are more akin to the animal kingdom than others and thus deserve to live in conditions of abject poverty and servitude. No enlightened individual with an ounce of integrity may contend that his skin color, religion, sex, or social status makes him superior in God's eyes. Those are the notions of the unenlightened and are blatantly false premises upon which some men unfortunately continue to feed their egos and self-interests. They are also the notions frequently identified with past generations from which Freemasons such as Washington, Bolivar, Garibaldi and Danton sought to free their people. And, they are the notions of enslavement which must give way to feelings of brotherly love and affection, if human solidarity is ever to be achieved.

Unity neither implies nor requires that all men think alike. Nature and the evolution of human consciousness dictate otherwise. We read in the Gospel of Luke that some who had witnessed the slaughter of certain Galilean citizens by the Roman governor, Pilate, believed it was the just punishment by God upon those who had lived badly. We also read in the same sacred source that the same conclusion was made about those who perished at Siloam when a tower fell crushing them to death.

More recently, a self-professed man of God proclaimed that the disaster wrought by the Hurricane Katrina in New Orleans was the result of the Creator's disgust with the sin that ran rampant in that city. Jesus himself rebuked that sentiment in an earlier age and opened our eyes to the truth that the natural world of *cause* and *effect* is a world of its own. Nothing man can do will change the natural laws.

When asked by his young protégé, "What is the color green?" the wise old man stroked his chin and thought awhile before answering. "What do you say it is?" he finally asked.

Every living adult human who is not color-blind has learned to distinguish one color from another. We have been taught that distinction by some other person, as nothing in nature would assist any person to ever know the name of a color. Someone pointed to an object and said that the color we observed was green. The human mind remembered the distinction and eventually understood it without having to be reminded. But, can anyone really explain what green is? If someone viewed the world through the eyes of another might not green actually appear to be red?

Although we may never know the answer to that question, it is possible to more fully appreciate the possibility that differences exist in the way people view everything in the world. Human consciousness is experienced only by the person contemplating it. That one person evaluates the finite and ponders about the infinite perhaps eventually drawing conclusions about it just like the person who learned about colors – by listening to what someone else has said.

Carl Jung sought to expand mankind's understanding by introducing the concept of "unconsciousness" – the opposing notion to "consciousness." In so doing, he sought to put man in touch with his dreams and compelled him to ask himself whether or not his consciousness is influenced in any manner whatsoever by his unconsciousness. While a great deal of study remains to be conducted, the best man can presently conclude is that there is much we do not yet know. There may also be much that man may never know by any means other than *faith*.

The principle of human solidarity is best articulated by examples instead of words. Its true meaning may best be understood by examining the hundreds of thousands of examples of friendship and social charity practiced among Masons and their families. Men and women of financial means lovingly contributing of their wealth make possible better lives for those less fortunate. It is those acts of genuine love that may best define human solidarity, for giving symbolizes one person's determination to treat other people as *another me*. Freemasonry teaches that like the laws of *cause* and *effect*, the law of human solidarity is also a law of nature. When that law is violated, the consequences may include human violence, widespread hatred, uncommon jealousy and devastating despair.

Socio-economic problems that have beset every generation can actually be eliminated. They cannot be ended by keeping the poor at arm's distance; by separating Christians from Jews, Muslims, or any other religion; or by insisting that others think in the same manner. Indeed solidarity means the exact opposite. Rich and poor alike can associate and help each other – the one with his wealth and the other with the thankful industry that is given in return. Employers and employees have extraordinarily common ground – the one generously pays for services rendered and the other gives of his loyal work. Leaders in government enjoy a special relationship with the citizens whom they lead – the leaders enact and execute just and fair laws while the citizens respond by promoting prosperity, happiness and connectivity in all that they do. International solidarity is both the goal and requirement of the moral order and is also governed by the same natural laws of *cause* and *effect*. When nations get along with each other peace prevails – when their disputes rage out of control, war and deadly destruction follows.

The Hiramic Legend also teaches that the virtue of human solidarity is more than the sum total of how men deal with their material goods; it is more about dealing with spiritual goods. By spreading the spiritual goods of mankind, Freemasonry opens new paths to the development of temporal goods – the *effect* of which is to better promote the public welfare. The slow and steady advancement of human consciousness, or spiritual awareness, can be observed in the evolutionary roadmap of human history. It consists in large part of taking one step forward, then a step or two backwards before again advancing several steps.

Regardless of its slow pace, spiritual awareness is advancing generation by generation. In the same way that Solomon completed the building of his Temple to God following *Hiram Abif's* death, so, too, has Masonry picked up the cudgels dropped by a fallen brother to carry on in his place. Each generation has added something of value to what has gone before it bringing to mind the deeper meaning of the Old Testament symbolism about the river that flowed out of the Garden of Eden.

Chapter 19

HUMAN STRIFE

On the day following *Hiram Abif's* murder, King Solomon entered the Temple unaware that the crime and its attempted cover-up were still in progress. Glancing around the room he saw workmen wandering about in a daze. Spying Hiram of Tyre, he shouted, "What is the cause of all of this confusion?"

"The Grand Master *Hiram Abif* is missing," the King of Tyre answered. "For some reason he has not drawn any designs on his trestle board since yesterday."

Solomon was instantly overcome with a sense of disaster. "I fear some accident has befallen the Grand Master," he said finally. "Have the workmen search every single apartment in this Temple. And as a matter of precaution, also have the roll called of all of the workmen."

After careful search *Hiram Abif* was nowhere to be found. The roll call also oddly revealed that Jubela, Jubelo and Jubelum were missing. Since the commencement of work on the Temple none of the workmen had ever missed a day's labor. All work had ceased and King Solomon was now becoming increasingly alarmed.

"Send out a search party and see what you can learn," he ordered looking directly at Hiram of Tyre. Slumping onto his throne he stared blankly, his mind doing its best to absorb the possible reasons for this conflict and contention.

Masonic tradition informs us that this was the one and only occasion of confusion and disorder during the Temple construction. Not even the rains had kept the men from their work. But without the guidance of their chief supervisor, there was little the men could do but stand around and wait for order to be restored.

The lesson taught by this symbolism is not wholly unique to Freemasonry. Conflict and contention among men as well as sorting out potential solutions has been a subject discussed by nearly all major philosophers, heads of government and religious leaders. We are immediately reminded of the passages from the book of Genesis wherein we are told that about the time when God returned to inspect His human creatures in the Garden of Eden after Cain slew his brother Abel. The peace and harmony He intended had been interrupted by an act of human violence requiring His immediate attention. Scripture informs us that God angrily banished Cain from His kingdom and sentenced him to wander the world. Similarly, after *Hiram Abif's* assassins were arrested and brought before him, King Solomon had them taken away and executed.

The laws of nature dictate that *need* causes contention unless that *need* is either filled, or curtailed. Here, within the confines of King Solomon's Temple, that *need* is represented by the desire of the Fellowcraft to obtain the Master's Word from *Hiram Abif* even if doing so required murdering the Grand Master.

Contention is nothing more than the collision of opposite interests. One side has one set of desires which are opposed by the other side. Both sets of desires represent opposing *needs*. The desire of the ruffians for the *Word* symbolizes what can happen when those opposing needs collide. Of course, real life examples are available in abundance.

The French author Victor Hugo wrote about a man he named Jean Valjean in his famous novel, *Les Miserables*. According to the story, Valjean fell upon hard times and did not have enough money to feed either himself, or his child. Casting aside his personal virtue in favor of his *need*, Valjean stole to satisfy that *need*.

Sadly, such instances are not limited to literature, but have been repeated by real men experiencing similar *needs*. Stealing to satisfy that *need*, while possibly pointing out the existence of inequality and unfairness among men, is diametrically opposed to the theft victim's *need* to be safe in his possessions. Thus, a conflict and contention arise that in this example requires a further analysis and synthesis of two distinctly different points of view. Just as God and King Solomon resolved the contentions they experienced with Cain and the murderous ruffians, this particular conflict and contention also demands a similar resolution.

As we read further about Jean Valjean, we learn that Hugo has provided us with a discourse about various possible resolutions as well as the possible consequences that might follow some of those possibilities. Valjean was arrested, prosecuted, convicted and unceremoniously thrown into jail. Even after Valjean's release, his torment continued at the hands of a man named Javert whom Hugo cast as an unbending police inspector. Javert hounded Valjean after learning that he was a formerly convicted criminal who allegedly later stole from his friend, benefactor and employer – the kindly Bishop Myriel. All who have read this marvelous literary tale know its conclusion – overcome with remorse after discovering Valjean's innocence, Javert eventually committed suicide.

But a more significant philosophical feature of Hugo's work teaches us both the importance of resolving conflict and the strong human emotions that frequently stand in the way. In Hugo's story, Valjean's *need* intersected with certain characteristics found in many people: strong determination and dangerous intentions. Freemasonry's Hiramic Legend also offers us a story about conflict and contention that arises out of the confrontation of determined personalities presented to us in the form of the three assassins and *Hiram Abif*. That conflict and contention was fueled by the dangerous intentions of Jubela, Jubelo and Jubelum. The purpose for both Hugo's symbolism and that related to *Hiram Abif* is not to merely explain the causes of contention, but to teach the importance of compromise and the settling of disputes. If we read our history books long enough we will discover that rarely has history revealed a satisfying result from unresolved conflict.

On the eve of World War II during the late 1930's men of good intentions struggled to find ways to avoid all-out war. The conflict that loomed ahead threatened to engulf every single man, woman and child and to forever change the way people and their governments regarded each other. Those valiant efforts at compromise now occupy the unenviable place in human experience of representing the epitome of appeasement.

In today's parlance *appeasement* conjures up images of cowardice, self-deception and weakness. It tends to suggest acts of giving in to the unjust demands of another. In fact at one time *appeasement* meant something very different. Literally interpreted, *appeasement* simply means calming, reconciling and conceding wherever and whenever appropriate.

While *appeasement* is very likely a poor choice of words to describe the resolution of conflict, the words "calming" and "reconciling" are not. If it is true that danger plus strength promotes contention, it is equally the case that reducing the conflict, easing the resulting tensions and discovering common ground leads to conflict resolution. Persistence in making unreasonable demands, even if those demands are earnestly held as something akin to principle, never ends in good fortune. It may end with one side being beaten down, but the sense of injustice will likely simmer and later erupt in renewed conflict and contention.

Was there a way in which the murder of *Hiram Abif* could have been avoided short of the Grand Master yielding to the threats and giving the Master's Word to the ruffians? Has any Masonic lodge ever engaged in such a discussion and arrived at a universally accepted conclusion? The answer is a resounding "no." But with the benefit of some hindsight and a goodly portion of wild speculation, perhaps one can think of a way that murder could have been prevented.

It is highly unlikely that *Hiram Abif's* murder could have been unilaterally prevented. More likely than not something would have had to have transpired between the Grand Master and at least one of the three assassins to ease and eliminate the conflict and contention among them. Either some form of persuasion by one side or the other, or some form of compromise by both sides would have been essential. The Hiramic Legend, while teaching the importance of conflict resolution, does not contain even the faintest hint of either persuasion, or compromise. Brute persistence in unreasonable demands was met by an unyielding refusal to bend. Murder was the result, followed soon by the execution of the murderers. Nothing was accomplished and the *Word* was lost. Similarly, on the eve of World War II the necessary ingredients for peace were missing and hundreds of thousands of human beings eventually perished.

In our daily lives conflict resulting from differing opinions or disparate interests arises all around us. According to several ancient philosophers and most present-day thinkers who are seriously dedicated to discovering the best and most efficient methods of conflict resolution, before doing anything else mankind must first decide how important it is to always be the winner of an argument before humanity may can expect to make significant progress. If it is always important to be the winner in every dispute, the ability to resolve conflict will remain elusive.

Governments throughout the world have never learned that lesson and their failure to do so have understandably resulted in repeated wars, unnecessary bloodshed and the separation of men from each other. Too, within most societal circles it has sadly become entirely unacceptable to adopt an attitude of resolving conflict at any cost. Rather, most nations continue to act upon the premise that each and every conflict must be *won.*

The ancient sages knew that the only way to avoid contention was to seek and discover common ground. They also knew that continually voicing a difference of opinion merely inflames the passions – it resolves nothing. Most disputes arise when one or more persons exercise mean intentions and assiduously assert only their basest self-interest. Without question it is not always possible for combatants to find common ground. To the contrary, it is more frequently the case that unless a neutral third party mediates or arbitrates the dispute escalates to unforeseeable heights. Some people have to be told they are behaving badly by someone they trust and rely upon before they will ever believe it to be so. It is with this truth in mind that Masonry teaches Masons to *whisper good counsel* into the ear of an errant brother Mason.

Only a man who is held in the highest esteem can possibly serve as a mediator or arbitrator. Otherwise the process will more likely than not fail. Without such people injustice, violence, outrage and lawlessness will reign and peace will never have a chance. Masonry seeks to inculcate the importance of virtue and morality for no greater reason than to offer to the world a reservoir of men who are honest and who are regarded as such by those around them. The goal of the fraternity is to produce reliably honest men who can actively assist others to arrive at peaceable solutions to otherwise irresoluble disputes. How grave is the miscarriage of justice to discover a Mason who contributes to conflict rather than to peaceable resolutions.

The most prominent obstacle to conflict resolution is truth – that is truth as man perceives it to be. Without question truth presents the most troubling challenge to any peacemaker, for it is frequently unwise to insist that one yield that which he perceives to be true simply to settle a dispute. An even greater challenge is posed by the need to confront those who hold that all or most important affairs of men are subject to absolute truths or certitudes. The man who has no room in his consciousness for doubt can prove an extremely difficult challenge to successful negotiations. While most Masons who have immersed themselves in the teaching and symbolism of the Craft understand the significance of *relativism* to truth, there are many both within the fraternity and outside of Freemasonry who bristle at the notion that any truth could ever be regarded as *relative*.

The most important tenet imparted by the holy men in history is the principle of *brotherly love*. When *brotherly love* is absent or inhibited in any conflict or contention, one should proceed cautiously with attempts at resolution. A Mason should be capable of telling the difference between a man who really loves his fellow man and a man who merely professes to do so. His own conduct reveals the truth. The man who has the best opportunity to help others discover common ground is the man who demonstrates by his own conduct that loving others is his chosen way of life.

But what about other truths, such as the so-called truth that the Great Architect prefers one form of worship above all others? Perhaps the real truth on that subject is that men have for ages successfully manipulated other men by making them think that God prefers one religion over all others. But can such a statement ever be uttered in a hostile environment when it is obvious to everyone involved that such a sentiment will surely be rejected? The answer is unequivocally "no," but the reason that it is unequivocal is not simply because it is not the truth. The real reason is that hurting another person's feelings over any subject is entirely contrary to *brotherly love*. History has proven from numerous events in the past that even men who claim to be dedicated atheists may find common ground with God-fearing men if that common ground is based upon *brotherly love*.

The Hiramic Legend imparts an equally compelling wisdom about humanity that must always be carefully considered when conflict requires resolution. From time immemorial it is been our human experience that men do not always see things in the same light as other men. To some even a sweet smelling perfume is noxious. As humans our minds are not wired to operate in the same manner. The stark contrast offered by the examples of the humbly defiant *Hiram Abif* and the rudely violent ruffians is intended to symbolize and illustrate that difference. Consider this question: was there any possibility for the Grand Master to persuade the assassins to think as he did about virtue, honor, patience and integrity? Or for that matter could Jubela, Jubelo and Jubelum have handled matters differently in hopes of getting *Hiram Abif* to see matters their way?

Political and diplomatic leaders around the world have known about this differential entrenchment for centuries. Their schools and fields of endeavor teach them a way of handling this obstacle. That way or approach is technically called *mutual influence*. Simply defined, *mutual influence* means the imposition of opposing points of view upon others, as well as the requirement that those opposing points of view eventually act in harmony. It is important to take note of the fact that the definition does not require harmony. Rather, it requires that men act in harmony whether or not they maintain opposing points of view. The distinction is monumentally important to understanding what constitutes the most effective methods of conflict resolution.

In order for one person to exert influence over another, no matter the poisonous nature of the relationship, both people must behave sincerely and possess a disciplined determination not to act judgmentally. In this we may have actually identified how both *Hiram Abif* and the three assassins could have improved their chances for conflict resolution. The Grand Master told his attackers to stop acting rudely and violently and patiently await their time to receive the secrets of a Master Mason. Did his comment come across to his attackers as judgmental and provocative? Or would it have mattered had he uttered less judgmental words? For their part the assassins fared no better and guaranteed the Grand Master's defiance with their threats of death and dishonor. Neither side to this conflict appeared willing to accept the other and at least try to act in harmony. There is little wonder that murder was the result.

To successfully exert *mutual influence* both sides are first compelled to assume an unselfish attitude. There is a saying common in today's use that seems very appropriate – *this isn't about you or me, it is about us!* The important truth that we may discern in that modern-day phrase is contained in the word "us." *Mutual influence* is very much about *us* and has very little or nothing at all to do with *me* or *you* individually.

King Solomon did not so much motivate the Temple workmen by instilling a sense of individuality as he did by promoting teamwork and working toward a common goal. Most men who have worked successfully in politics and diplomacy on the world stage have learned this essential truth about most men: when motivated to work together for something everyone believes in men cheerfully work together without conflict. Is there an important lesson somewhere in this truth that can be used in conflict resolution?

As simple as it may seem to be to grasp the significance of acting unselfishly, it is actually very difficult to consistently do so. The tendency to drift toward selfishness is sadly far too common among men. Not even the harmony and good order established for the Temple workmen by Solomon lasted indefinitely.

Fifteen Fellowcraft eventually entered into a conspiracy to extort the secrets of a Master Mason from *Hiram Abif.* But what did Solomon do to restore Temple harmony after the heinous murder of his beloved fellow Grand Master? The lesson we learn from that effort is illuminating.

After sentencing the assassins to death, Solomon appointed Adonhiram as *Hiram Abif's* replacement. We learn from Masonic tradition that as a consequence peace and tranquility once again prevailed. The Temple construction was completed; Solomon had kept his faith with God; and King Hiram of Tyre paid the craftsmen their wages thereby insuring that every workman was treated fairly. At that time in history all seemed peaceful and very tranquil. But if we read farther about Masonic tradition we will discover that the peace and tranquility did not last long and Solomon was again called upon to exercise his uncanny wisdom to resolve conflict.

As a reward for his faithful and diligent service, Solomon gave Hiram of Tyre twenty cities in the land of Galilee. When Hiram went to inspect his new properties he discovered them to be shabby, impoverished and largely depopulated. He angrily stormed into Solomon's chamber and demanded an explanation. The muscles in his jaw tensed as he spat out his displeasure for having been so horribly deceived by the man he once considered to be both a comrade and brother.

"Did I not keep my bargain with you and provide skilled Temple workmen who were paid from my own treasury?" Hiram of Tyre asked. "Is this how the great King of Israel whose wisdom is without peer cheats his dearest friend and ally?"

The truth of the matter was that Solomon had not taken care to know very much about the gifted cities before he transferred them to his dear brother. But the anger on Hiram's face told Solomon that the King of Tyre would not be easily assuaged by such an excuse. To resolve the conflict Solomon knew it was essential that *mutual influence* be brought to bear.

Solomon knew that he had to act selflessly – yet in spite of earnest prayer exactly how to do so momentarily escaped him until the occurrence of an unforeseen event. While striding about Solomon's chamber in his intemperate tirade, Hiram discovered one of Solomon's valued servants eavesdropping on their conversation.

"Who is this?" Hiram demanded, yanking the trembling Zabud from behind the chamber curtain and throwing him at Solomon's feet. The great King's heart sank.

"It is my faithful and valued servant, Zabud, whom I raised in my service from," Solomon quietly remarked. He knew that the law of his kingdom required the imposition of death upon anyone caught eavesdropping on the King.

"Your majesty," Zabud implored falling to his knees. "Forgive me, for when I saw the King of Tyre in a rage racing into your chamber, I ran behind to protect you. The fierce look on his face told me he intended you great harm."

The King of Tyre nevertheless demanded Zabud's death and Solomon knew that if he failed to keep the law, conflict and contention would reign. He was resolved to do his duty until the King of Tyre unexpectedly calmed down, set aside his own selfish interests and influenced a much different result. Responding to Solomon's sincere apology at having giving away such dilapidated cities, Hiram's was eventually overcome with a sense of *brotherly love*.

"Worry not, my brother, about your valued servant, Zabud," Hiram said throwing an arm around Solomon's shoulder as they strolled about the chamber. "Your friendship and brotherly affection are more important to me than all of the cities in your empire. I behaved rashly and out of self pity unfairly believing the worst about your intentions. But I now clearly see that you have always cared about others more than yourself. You have cared more for me than I have cared about you. Zabud is to be spared and I will make the cities in Galilee which with the improvements I have planned will one day be a jewel."

Masonic tradition tells us that the King of Tyre was a man of superior virtue. Naturally given to the same base human inclinations as the rest of us, his displeasure with what he first regarded as an unworthy gift caused him to instantly lash out at hits friend and brother. At the outset it was all about *him* and not about *us*. Once he realized his error in virtue the conflict and contention was quickly resolved.

While such good behavior might be expected from men of superior virtue, what can we say about those men and nations who are not quite so virtuous but are nevertheless embroiled in conflict? Is it rational for us to expect that all men who behave badly will sooner or later realize their mistake and act on the basis of what is best for *us?* Is irredeemable evil among men something that only exists in fiction, or is it possibly a dreadful fact of human existence? If such evil does exist, how can the concept of *mutual influence* be made relevant when it appears?

Our material world is littered with opposites – the good and the bad; light and darkness; and in ancient Chinese philosophy, the *yin* and the *yang*. Where the bad or darkness prevails, it may not be enough to simply take the high road and hope that the good and light will prevail. Although all men are capable of behaving well, history is replete with examples of men who have demonstrated that behaving badly is their normal behavior. That propensity to act badly also applies to some nations, governments and politicians. How can *mutual influence* possibly be relevant to resolving conflicts when the people and entities involved are intent upon behaving badly?

If humility, selflessness and truthfulness are essential to the success of *mutual influence,* we must discover their comparable substitutes when attempting to resolve contentions with amoral and arrogant people. The lack of humility implies the persistence of pride, a characteristic that is both potentially good in nature and inherently bad when there are no boundaries. If we are willing to attack that pride and erode a prideful personality the tactic might actually prove to be effective. It is equally possible that such an attack could backfire and result in a stronger sense of pride. Even the Grand Master *Hiram Abif*, for whom the word "pride" was a badge of honor not disrepute, resisted when threatened by vile and impious wretches. But placing in jeopardy that which one holds dearest just might make a difference – it could lead to establishing *mutual influence* in the most difficult conflicts. But first we must understand some basic but extremely important truths about the human psyche.

"Selflessness" connotes several related concepts: caring about others more than yourself; and caring more about something else than yourself. Even the most dedicated egoist has something he cares about more than himself. For example, power may be important to the politician; advancement in rank may be just as important to the diplomat. If you stop to think about it carefully you will likely discover that there is something more important to you than *you* – what is it? To effectively create and act upon *mutual influence,* one must first discover that which is most important to the people involved in the conflict.

"Truthfulness" is not necessarily entirely about absolute *truths.* Within the context of conflict resolution it is more accurately defined as that which corresponds to reality. In conflict resolution unless the conflict concerns men of superior virtue, the matter of determining precisely what all sides to the conflict mutually agree is *real* is paramount.

In the present-day political climate in the Middle East, the need to behave rationally and not employ weapons of mass destruction is seemingly a mutually agreed upon reality. Whether people should embrace Judaism, Christianity or Islam is not reality, for it is wholesale folly to believe such a thing could soon be mutually agreed upon. But for now achieving mutual agreement upon the disciplined resistance to the annihilation of the human race is a realistic expectation. The simple truth of the matter is that unless men in power exercise restraint the human race will be exterminated. Rational men understand this truth and it is therefore rational to believe that it is possible that men in that part of the world will mutually agree not to destroy each other.

But what if those in conflict are not rational but are instead quite deranged? How is *mutual influence* relevant in that instance? Masonry and its symbolic degrees do not directly teach us how to deal with such aberrations in our world. Rather, Masonry pertains to affairs among men of high morality and excellent virtue. But Masons are not taught to ignore the deranged, the delusional, or the pathological mind. Indeed, it is possible that Jubela, Jubelo and Jubelum were deranged. Masons are told to use the power of brotherly love even when dealing with deranged minds.

Man is a naturally social creature. Psychologists tell us that is so regardless of whether or not the man is sane. He desires others, with whom he can communicate, break bread and behold. It is also a part of his nature to want the respect and attention of others – to feel as though he belongs in society and that his life is worthwhile. When these desires come under attack, it is natural to expect that he will become defensive and combative.

The very elderly who struggle each day to simply get by provide us an excellent example. When the productive years have streaked by it is difficult to accept that there is nothing more to be contributed. The need to be respected for what they have done and who they are is as relevant to the elderly as it is to the young. Therefore conflict and contention involving the elderly cannot be resolved by ignoring the need for attention. In truth it is the same for men, women and children of all ages. It was certainly true of the Grand Master *Hiram Abif* who resisted the humiliating confrontation with the three assassins whom he must have perceived as belittling the virtue and integrity upon which he had built his entire life.

To resolve any conflict it is essential that those involved remain flexible, if *mutual influence* is ever to be brought to bear. Masonic tradition informs us that *Hiram Abif* was inflexible in his unfeigned piety to God, which at first glance might suggest that he was ill equipped to resolve his conflict with the ruffians. Such is not the case, however, for the flexibility required to resolve conflicts does not also require the abandonment of morals, virtues and values. Rather the flexibility that is required consists of setting aside willfulness, self-interest and the disregard for other points of view. Everyone can adopt such an attitude without ever abandoning valuable principles.

One of the more typical occurrences commonly encountered during conflict resolution is failure. But it is important to understand that failing is a part of the process – not the end. History is replete with examples of virtuous men who admonished foolish tyrants to stop acting cruelly only to be rebuffed. The lesson from that history is not that resolution fails upon meeting initial resistance, but only when men fail to persist in bringing about a reformation.

Masons are taught a valuable lesson in this regard when placed upon the *five points of fellowship,* for the purpose of whispering good counsel into another Mason's ear is to assist that man to reform his errant behavior. Whispering once may not be enough for some men, because stubborn resistance to change is common. However, it is absolutely critical for the man who wishes to resolve conflict be equally stubborn – not inflexible, but committed to bringing about a reformation. There is a distinction between the two.

We read in the Holy Bible that there is a time and place for all things. The book of Ecclesiastes records the following wise commentary by King Solomon in Chapter Three: *{T}here is an appointed time for everything, and a time for every affair under the heavens {.}* The New Testament memorializes the revolutionary idea endorsed by Jesus that a man must constantly forgive his brother. Speaking to his disciples about how to handle a brother who consistently does harmful things and later apologizes, he said, ... *if he wrongs you seven times in one day and returns to you seven times saying, 'I am sorry,' you should forgive him. Luke 17:4.* Unfortunately it is far too frequent the case that men in conflict do not easily forgive each other.

Ancient Chinese philosophy teaches that when there is no way to win a dispute it is better to bear the situation with patience. The wisdom of that philosophy has been proven repeatedly throughout history. Generations of men have gone to war because of the lack of sufficient patience resulting in horrible violence, death and destruction. Evidently the influence of *mutual influence* had no chance, because one side or the other in the conflict decided to wait no longer for a peaceful resolution to unfold. Although it is sad but all too often the case that the use of force to compel a resolution is frequently chosen by politicians and rulers of governments, the imposition of one's will upon another by means of war generally results in new conflicts and contentions requiring yet again renewed efforts at patient resolution. Practicing the art of wisely forgiving others returns to favor when men finally tire of war.

Solomon forgave the twelve Fellowcraft their conspiracy, embraced them as loyal workmen and reintegrated them into the Temple work force. Masonic tradition teaches that peace and tranquility returned to the work place just as it had existed before *Hiram Abif's* murder. Recognizing that there always exists the possibility that people will change their ways, Solomon acted wisely in assisting the twelve. He resolved the conflict and contention and proceeded to erect what has been described as the most magnificent Temple ever known to man.

It has often been stated that if one is fond of contention, evil awaits. All men have been taught at one time or another during their lifetimes that selfishness is a human impulse that must be circumscribed or controlled. That is so because of the evil selfishness generates when men ignore other men, fail to extend respect to others and otherwise subjugate and diminish the value of the thoughts and feelings of other human beings. Selfishness also interferes with the development of *mutual influence* and replaces it with a sense of loathing, anger and suspicion – evils that in turn spawn unrelenting conflict and contention.

Through the symbolism of the *five points of fellowship* the Hiramic Legend teaches us the conditions that must be present before *mutual influence* may prevail: man must be prepared to so dedicate himself to the welfare of his fellow man that he will go on foot and out of his way to be of service; when praying to the Great Architect, he must pray for the welfare of others, as well as for his own; he must be trustworthy, faithful and loyal to the interests of others just as he is faithful to serving and protecting his own interests; when another man falls, or stumbles in his pursuit of virtue and morality, he must also find extended to him the helpful hand of another who is intent upon giving all necessary support; and, every man should labor with the commitment of enabling others to reform their bad behavior by extending endless forgiveness, limitless patience and boundless love and affection. No conflict or contention can long remain unresolved when men *mutually influence* each other by practicing the principles taught by the *five points of fellowship*.

Chapter 20

LEADERSHIP

From time immemorial man has struggled with the challenge of deciding how best to manage societies of people. Historically, monarchies have predominated, but there have been many other choices. Tribal chieftains, dictators, assemblies and popularly elected officials have from time-to-time led the multitudes. The Hiramic Legend also offers helpful lessons for us to consider by cautioning us against seizing upon choice at the exclusion of all others. Different times and different societies may demand different governments. If the saying that *the devil is in the details* has any present-day relevance to this issue, it is because it clarifies for us that the manner in which people are led is frequently more important than the title of the government.

All that man is or can ever hope to become depends upon his relationship with the Great Architect. No person or body of persons is greater than God. Oddly enough, however, it seems that man is actually incapable of worshipping a concept of God that is greater than what his ego conceives. Thus *man* or *self* would actually appear to be at the core of man's consciousness. Man's spiritual awareness is framed by his own image – seemingly the reverse of the scriptural teaching that God created man in His image. Even the various societies that constitute the *multitude* are first and foremost centered upon the concept of *man* – or what every man hopes to become.

From Masonic tradition we learn that Solomon called upon King Hiram of Tyre after looking about his kingdom and discovering that the skills he required to construct the Temple were not possessed by anyone in his kingdom. We know that it was the Hebrews and not the Phoenicians who wished to build a Temple. Yet Solomon's most skillful laborers were found among the Phoenicians King Hiram brought from the land of Canaan. Being foreigners those laborers did not serve at the pleasure of either Solomon or his people - they served at the pleasure of the King of Tyre. But it was their labors that enhanced the beauty of the Hebrews' spiritual worship.

What are we to understand from this allegory about leading the *multitude*? First, if we carefully consider the environment that existed during the building of the Temple we learn that Solomon took charge of his generals, or supervisors – he did not take charge of the workmen. Although he was the reigning monarch throughout all of Israel, he chose not to directly lead the *multitude*, but delegated that task to the Phoenicians he supervised. Second, the Temple was not erected for the *multitude*; it was erected to serve as a house where the Great Architect would dwell. There was nothing being built for the people unless one considers the opportunity to worship a confined God from afar as a benefit. Finally, it required the murder of a general – *Hiram Abif* – to trigger action that, at least in part, may be viewed as relevant to the *multitude*.

Hiram Abif was a noble spirit who led his workmen by prayer and personal example. In so doing he embodied virtue and morality to the highest degree; so much so that his example serves today as the exemplar to all Masons. Although never a king, *Hiram Abif* undeniably was the moral leader of all of the Temple workmen. His suffering at the hands of the ruffians symbolizes the resolve all men must possess if they hope to free those whom they lead from tyrants.

The chapter entitled *The Ruffians* identifies the types of tyranny represented by each of the three assassins. Jubela symbolizes the priest, or holy man who binds his followers in chains of doctrine. Jubela represents the politician who smoothly seduces and manipulates his supporters. And Jubelum calls to mind the brutal and horrifying mob-mind that sweeps the righteous and unrighteous along upon a river of vengeance and blood. Neither monarchs nor generals can defeat such enemies without the aid and assistance of the *multitude*.

The warfare that is necessary is not one of bullets, bombs and destruction. Rather it is warfare conducted by peaceable means intended to control and alleviate disaster. *Hiram Abif* represents "beauty," not ugliness. He stands for peace not war and as such symbolizes the best hopes for all societies. Violent warfare leads to the destruction of all that man has built, as well as the lives of men created by the Great Architect. Such violence is the very antithesis of the Hermetic motto, *as it is above so shall it be below*. But peace preserves all that God and man have touched and promotes spiritual growth among individuals and societies alike.

Undeniably the *multitude* is in need of leadership, for without it chaos and anarchy will eventually run amuck leaving in their wake aimlessness, despair and disorder. Throughout history mankind has been fortunate to have never lacked men who desired to fill that need. Unfortunately many of those men have proven to be more self-serving than selfless and consequently have contributed to disorder, repression and miserable thoughts among the *multitude*. On less frequent occasions mankind has greatly benefitted from the leadership of men committed to promoting the welfare of the people. At those times societies have experienced periods of enormous prosperity in terms of economic wealth and emotional well-being. It is this latter type of leadership that *Hiram Abif* symbolizes – a leadership that is founded upon a strong upright embrace of moral courage.

An interesting contrast during recent times more clearly illustrates the significance of the distinction. Though each man battled against the United States and its allies during World War I, the leadership traits of Baron Manfred von Richthofen and Hermann Goering stand in stark contrast and actually assist us to understand the traits Masonry seeks to inculcate. The Red Baron, as Richthofen was known, was regarded as a man of simple and honorable purpose by the men who served in his command. His devotion to his men was paramount and caused him to reject an opportunity to leave the battlefield for a life of comfort and heroic public relations. Goering, on the other hand, was once diagnosed after being committed to a psychiatric ward for the morphine addiction he acquired after having been shot in the groin as a man wholly lacking in moral courage. His bravado was intended to cover up his own cowardice and he was loathed by most whom he led.

The similar example of moral courage displayed by *Hiram Abif* has been instilled in the hearts of every Master Mason. His example is held high and pointed to as our true aspiration and encompasses piety to God, fidelity and an unflinching loyalty to the obligations willingly accepted. If mankind wishes to embrace a definitive criterion for leadership, whether it is in the realm of politics, the military or in business, there is no better exemplar than *Hiram*. The man who possesses true moral character will never disappoint those whom he leads.

In Chinese philosophy we learn that the ancients taught that even military leaders who would excel must be possessed of such a noble spirit that will convince the civil monarchs of his capabilities. Such is seemingly a fantasy to our minds, for far too frequently such leaders are selected because of their obsequiousness – their awkward submission to the flawed leadership of those who have the power to appoint.

In striking contrast we learn that *Hiram Abif* was selected by Solomon because he possessed both the talent required and the noble spirit necessary to lead. Men follow such a man with dedication, commitment and unfailing loyalty. Government leaders throughout the present-day world might learn a valuable lesson from the Hiramic Legend – but unfortunately most governments persist in the avoidance of men of noble spirit.

Over the years many have either suggested or forcefully promoted the notion that the people, or the *multitude,* have no need of a centralized leader – one man, or one body who tells them how to act. According to those voices, the people themselves can best decide how to act, react and behave. Here, it is wise for Masons to recall the caution advised by Albert Pike, who characterized the uncontrolled mob as the rough equivalent of a misdirected tyrant. One need travel no farther back in history than the French Revolution to discover the horrors that can result at the hands of the unruly mob.

Intrigue, conspiracy and the guillotine ruled the day. Men and women met behind closed doors and argued about the fate of the monarchy. Political leaders met separately to review, discuss and argue about the constant demands by the people for new and different freedoms. Few men of moral courage attended either of those secret sessions and their absence proved devastating to the hopes for peace, civility and human charity.

One such man did step forward, only to eventually be manhandled by the mob and sent to a gruesome guillotining. His name was Georges Danton, a Mason and distinguished president of the Committee of Public Safety. Danton was born of modest ancestry but was fortunate enough to have been sufficiently educated to have been admitted to the Paris bar of lawyers. When the Revolution was finally launched, Danton made his first appearance as president of the Cordeliers Club – a center of popular sovereignty, or rule by the *multitude*. The Cordeliers were the first to accuse the monarchy of hostility to individual freedom and led the radical faction.

Danton voted to send King Louis XVI to his death and played a conspicuous role in the creation of the infamous Revolutionary Tribunal which, although having initially disarmed the vengeful populace, became the Revolution's instrument of terror. In time all executive power for the nation was seized by the Committee of Public Safety where Danton displayed a more Masonic type of moral leadership. He instilled a sense of respect for the *multitude* and its hopes for vast freedoms that were then unknown anywhere in the world except in the newly formed United States of America.

Alas, Danton was more like Thomas Jefferson than in his devotion to the revolutionary aspirations of the *multitude*. Suffice to say, Danton finally went too far in his dedication to the masses deciding for both him and those whom he led that the people knew best and could better distinguish right from wrong than could any government of men. Danton was not only proven wrong, he unwittingly wrote his own death sentence.

Eventually, Danton was arrested, condemned and beheaded beneath the dreaded guillotine – the very same instrument he earlier endorsed to rid the world of the dictatorial King Louis XVI. Although he is remembered today as one of Masonry's guardians of individual freedom, history holds him in questionable regard for having forfeited the moral leadership he once exerted.

Masonic tradition teaches that there are several components of the Masonic definition of *moral leadership*. Most importantly that definition begins with an exploration of the beautiful variety of different ideas, attitudes, faiths, hopes and aspirations that identify the different cultures of the *multitude*. While those ideas differ from country to country and, region to region some are held in common. The most excellent example is religion which defines the moral boundaries within which most every idea, attitude, faith, hope and aspiration is formed.

Masonic tradition also teaches that *Hiram Abif* was a man of enormous virtue whose *moral leadership* is exemplified by the lessons taught in the Hiramic Legend. However we are never informed about his religious affiliation other than that he was a Phoenician who presumably practiced the religion of his people. Yet the Temple workmen were not at all likely to have embraced that same religion. The slain Grand Master's *moral leadership* would have been lost forever never to have served as a lesson to succeeding generations had he insisted that the Hebrew workmen worship Moloch, or any other Canaanite god. More likely than not he would have encountered resentment, hostility and possibly outright rebellion.

The numerous religious beliefs of the *multitude* regularly contend with each other for attention. When those disparate beliefs come up in conversation they far too frequently become the source of contentious dispute. Throughout history it seems that most, if not all wars have been fought in the name of God. But in the sole instance of the reign of Solomon the worship of multiple religions resulted in peace during his reign. The difference seems to be that Solomon enjoyed a unique wisdom we now call *moral leadership*. That wisdom is lost among most other historical monarchs owing primarily to an odd but repetitive intolerance of differing religious points of view. In fact it is intolerance that seems to be the real cause of most of the wars that have been waged throughout man's entire history.

But is that fact suggestive of the additional fact that man should avoid religion? Before answering that question it is fair to also ask how any leadership can be labeled *moral* if it is not guided by some religious belief. The answer actually lies in the knowledge that the Great Architect speaks to men in many different tongues – a truth first revealed to us in the Old Testament's story about the Tower of Babel.

From that story, as well as numerous others that follow in scripture, we learn that all men have within them a spark of the Divine that will never die. Each and every person possesses a substance of the Great Architect that contains its own spiritual *DNA* or knowledge that grows as it learns new lessons through spiritual senses. Should those lessons never be learned, the spirit and soul would shrivel.

The *moral leadership* demanded by the *multitude* understands that most men are heavily burdened with enormous egos. Interestingly, Masonry teaches that man is the center of the universe; a lesson that arises out of the further understanding that all men possess a spark of the Divine. But Masonry also teaches that self-pride tends toward the dark side and ignites feelings of hatred and anger. When man permits those emotions to rum rampant among the *multitude* chaos is not far away. How we manage human pride is as important to *moral leadership* as is the management of contending religious beliefs. If we consider the matter carefully, we see that both are closely related; a fact that suggests that management of human pride is extremely important to creating an environment of religious tolerance.

An interesting challenge is presented to us when the *multitude* demands that its leaders adhere to one specific religious belief. Many political governments have historically been ruled by theocracies, or governing boards controlled by a priesthood. Those governments demanded religious purity which seemingly led to the marginalization of non-conforming beliefs. In such societies, the people have been compelled to dress in a certain manner, communicate with each other in a definite way and worship God in an identical manner. Those who have violated such strict requirements have frequently been criminally prosecuted and severely punished.

This challenge also pertains to whether or not *moral leadership* can possibly thrive in such a closed political environment. Lest one simply conclude that we are speaking about any specific nation or country, it is fair to note that such conditions may also exist in any region, any neighborhood, or any house of worship. When considered in that context, the answer to the challenge is not easily articulated.

The Masonic allegory about building the Temple of Solomon teaches us not only how best to govern a country or nation, but also how best to govern our relationships with foreign countries and nations. It is very possible for the *moral leadership* of the *multitude* of one country or nation to lose its moral quality when that leadership encounters a foreign people. Adhering to Judaic, Christian, or Islamic fundamentals within a country whose *multitude* embrace one of those religions would appear relatively simple to accomplish. However, insisting that countries or nations foreign to those religions also embrace one of them will likely result in violence. Such violence will in turn result in a complete failure of *moral leadership*. When violence reigns peace has no chance to succeed.

History records that men of many different religious faiths have demonstrated *moral leadership*. Such leadership has never proven to the exclusive province of Christians, Jews, Moslems, Hindus, or Buddhists. In fact respect for differing points of view is a trait held in common by all such leaders, who have also learned the value communicating with potential adversaries rather than fighting with them.

Through a parable the New Testament teaches that if a man is sued by his neighbor, it is best that he settle the dispute before going to court. The meaning is clear: men must find ways to resolve disputes that do not result in violent conflict. When that lesson is applied to our examination into the relationship between *moral leadership* and the *multitude* the parable opens our eyes to the importance of always seeking peace and harmony.

The Hiramic Legend also imparts a caution to us about leaving the matter of governing the *multitude* to inferior or incompetent people. Such people do not possess either the intellect or the wisdom necessary for the task. *Hiram Abif's* several refusals to give into the demands of Jubela, Jubelo and Jubelum may be interpreted as a refusal to hand over the means of leading the Temple workmen to three Fellowcraft who had not yet demonstrated their merit. His steadfast refusal to do so resulted in his own death and serves as an example to us about the extent to which men should go when resisting the entrustment of government to incompetents, sycophants, or egomaniacs.

Whenever possible the *multitude* must also participate in the exercise of *moral leadership* by selecting those who should govern. Too frequently, however, the *multitude* proves ineffective in making such choices. Those who are eventually selected to govern continue to exhibit a hodge-podge of good, bad and indifferent leaders. In some instances that failure results in tyranny, terror, repression and slavery. Whenever man is subjected to such results of failed leadership the potential lingers for violent revolt by the *multitude*. History is littered with examples of such violent revolutions which have rarely proven either successful or beneficial to mankind. More often than not such violence merely results in the horrid and unnecessary sacrifice of the lives of men, women and children.

In his memorable literary work entitled *House Divided: The Story of Freemasonry and the Civil War,* the renowned Masonic author Allen E. Roberts included texts from speeches delivered on the eve of war by various Grand Masters in various Masonic jurisdictions. Not one man among them advocated violence or the massive overthrow of the federal government, including those Grand Masters from southern states. Exercising *moral leadership* each of those leaders recommended caution, unending dialogue and compromise. Such lecturing proved unpopular in some states where men expressed tenacious political and social beliefs that were diametrically opposed to the beliefs held by others. To each Grand Master's credit, being popular was not as important as was the exercise of *moral leadership.* Leaders who are centered in virtue and morality are content to tell the *multitude* what he needs to hear, which is not always what it would like to hear.

What lesson may we learn from those Grand Masters about the pursuit of liberty and freedom? And once we discover the answer, how does that lesson square with the lessons taught us by Washington, Franklin and other Freemasons who led this Nation in revolt against England? Is violence acceptable or not? Is it so that men should never go to war for any reason? Or do some reasons justify the intentional sacrifice of hundreds of thousands of men, women and children? Does the Hiramic Legend teach us anything about this subject?

If it is so that *moral leadership* is lost any time those who govern the *multitude* lead them to war, it should be equally true that war must be avoided at all cost – not just some but all wars. However that does not appear to be the lesson taught by any Masonic source. Rather, we are informed that all reasonable efforts at peaceably resolving conflicts should be employed. But what are we to do if peaceable efforts fail? Should we willingly surrender values, lives and moral authority?

In Roberts' work, the Grand Masters he wrote about exhausting all avenues that could possibly lead to peace. Not one of them urged the abandonment of battlefields until the outcome later proved obvious. They had spoken their words of caution and fulfilled their responsibilities of *moral leadership* and once the outcome of the conflict became evident they spoke again about the need to stop the senseless slaughter of the losing combatants.

Neither Washington, Franklin, nor any other well known Freemason of the American Revolutionary advocated war as a first step in responding to England's repressive measures. Rather each of them advocated restraint, patience, communication, dialogue and making every effort to peaceably resolve differences. They exercised *moral leadership* and continued to do so after all peaceable measures failed when after the war had been won they participated in the establishment of a government that empowered the *multitude*.

Harry S. Truman continues to be criticized for ordering the use of atomic weapons to destroy masses of Japanese near the end of World War II. Those critics claim that once he issued those orders he lost his moral authority to lead. Did he? Regardless of how one views the conspiracy theorists' versions of American complicity in the commencement of war, it is significant that Truman was not a part of the presidential administration when that war commenced. His order to drop "the bomb" was delivered during a period of war, not during a time of peace. While it resulted in massive casualties it likely also hastened the end of a horrifying conflict that had engulfed the world community. Does a leader who resolves violent conflict by violent means lose his moral authority? Nothing in either the Hiramic Legend or any other Masonic lesson supports such a conclusion – although the loss of life, any life, is enormously regrettable.

One of the more profound lessons imparted by the Hiramic Legend is the notion that human existence is not limited to one lifetime. Indeed, it might be that man lives several lifetimes and that each new lifetime is intended to permit us to improve upon the last. If that is so, it is more likely than not true that there are some principles and values that transcend human life. One of those appears to be human freedom which the Great Architect refuses to infringe upon.

A man once asked his religious leader why God permitted bad things to happen. The religious leader responded by reminding the man about a relevant parable found in the Gospel of Matthew. There, we read the story about weeds sprouting up amidst wheat – an allegorical lesson about human development. Neither God nor any of His missionaries yanked the weeds from the ground but instead permitted them to grow alongside the wheat.

A present-day parable more clearly illustrates the point that the religious leader was trying to make. Imagine if you were to sit down at your own dinner table and there were places set for your entire family – your wife, son and daughter. As you all were seated you suddenly noticed that Johnny, your son, was missing. The telephone rang and the person on the other end of the line told you he was from the Weed Patrol. You were then also told that Johnny would not be coming home because it was discovered he would do something in the future that would seriously harm another person. How would you feel about that?

One might imagine several possible answers by the man, such as *thank heavens – now we do not have to waste more time, money and energy on that louse.* Although possible, that is not likely to be your real response. Most likely you would feel a sense of enormous loss – your son would never be coming home – the Weed Patrol got him.

Such things do not happen merely because God refuses to intervene. Human free will is actually at work. People can change their behavior and oftentimes do so after learning from their mistakes and failures. Even if a person fails to improve other people may be prompted by the example to change and become productive workers God's vineyard. Thus it is that attitudes, ideas, behaviors and actions by all men have an impact upon the future. Mankind will either inherit a world filled with *light* or one that is cast in varying shades of *darkness*. The choices each person makes during their lifetime will set the stage for what is to come. Consequently each person's sense of right and wrong, virtue and sin will dictate how that person behaves now and in the future. There are certain constant principles, values, virtues and moralities that are important to the positive evolutionary change of all mankind.

Returning to President Truman's moment of decision, the moral authority at that moment cannot be decided by simply concluding it is wrong to kill. While that is a true statement and has forever been memorialized in the Ten Commandments, the question remains whether or not killing on all occasions results in a loss of *moral authority*. The Hiramic Legend teaches that it does not, for if it were otherwise King Solomon would have sacrificed his *moral authority* when he sentenced Jubela, Jubelo and Jubelum to die for having slain *Hiram Abif.* Instead, his sentence is regarded as just by the Craft because it restored equilibrium between *light* and *darkness.*

The *multitude* is best served by leaders who exercise the moral courage to do that which is right when the occasion to act arises. Precisely what it is that is *right* is not easily reduced to a formulaic list. It depends upon all of the circumstances, as well as the judgment of history, for it is the future that will either benefit or suffer the ill effects. Masonry teaches that the best way man can assure that he is being governed by *moral leadership* is to insist upon men of merit to serve in that role – not men of incompetence, or men who seek only to serve their own interests, biases, religious ideas, or personal ambition.

Chapter 21

FULFILLMENT

Everything we are told about the building of the Temple symbolizes *work*. In Masonry, God is referred to as the Great Architect of the Universe; the workmen are busy *building* the Temple; the principle emblems of Masonry are *working tools;* the first *worker* in brass is venerated in the Third Degree of Masonry; when Masons meet they are said to be at *labor;* and the primary duty of a Master of a Masonic Lodge is to set the Craft to *work*. In sum, a Mason is fulfilled by his labors and his ancestors remind him about *forgotten labors*.

Each of the workmen at King Solomon's Temple labored during the daytime and rested at night. While the restful sleep was essential it was the work that fulfilled them, satisfying their hunger to be productive human beings. An ancient proverb teaches that courtesy and righteousness are duties everyone should fulfill. They are duties taught by the example of *Hiram Abif,* who kneeled at the altar every day at *High Twelve* to worship the One True God and pray for the wisdom necessary to exercise courtesy, righteousness and leadership.

Both Hiram of Tyre and his devoted artificer *Hiram Abif* introduced Solomon's Hebrew followers to the courtesies and righteousness they had learned from the Phoenician Cosmogony. Like all others before them, it was regarded by the men of Tyre as the *Word of God*. Written in astral characters it displayed God manifested in multiple planetary Divinities who communicated the profound mysteries of Divine Intelligence through demigods. Their doctrines resembled those of the ancient Sabeans whom many assert were led by the famous Queen of Sheba, who once encountered Solomon during her reign.

The Phoenicians adopted from the Hindu Vedas the story about Chrishna, the Redeemer who was cradled and educated by Shepherds. That story told about a tyrant who lived at the time of Chrisna's birth and ordered all male newborns to be slain. Having survived Chrishna later performed wondrous miracles, raised the dead, washed the feet of his followers and always exhibited a humble spirit. It was also told that he was born of a virgin – a story not at all unlike the Christian version about Jesus. How odd and ironic it was that Solomon should encounter such people with such stories about man's relationship to God and to have learned their courtesy and righteousness during the building of the Temple.

But it was the Phoenicians – those people led by King Hiram of Tyre and symbolized so vividly by *Hiram Abif* – who taught the wise King of Israel the lesson of *fulfillment*. Even before the great Temple was ever conceived, the Phoenicians assisted their Israelite neighbors in the pursuit of their holy enterprises. Their willingness to do so was primarily owing to the great tie that bound them together indefinitely – the principal leaders of both nations were initiates in the same mysteries. Moses was most assuredly so or he would not have been permitted to marry, as he did, a daughter of the Priest of On. It is written that Joshua followed Moses into the mysteries and later led the Israelites to victory in numerous battles and wars. Both King Hiram and *Hiram Abif* are also described as initiates, as King Solomon had to have been before being permitted to marry the Egyptian princess who became his wife.

Together, the Israelites and the Phoenicians founded the Colleges of Artificers which some Masonic writers believe was the originator of a Masonic ritual no longer in use. Like the Etrurian and Roman Colleges, the Colleges of Artificers served as the great laboratory for testing the value of labor to mankind's spiritual character and physical development. It is from that respect of labor that Masonry has chosen to center its principal ritual upon an act of construction – the building of a great edifice where the One True God would forever reside upon earth.

The fundamental thesis offered for human *fulfillment* is premised upon the notion that there is a perennial nobleness and sacredness in work. Masonry's symbolic employment of Solomon's Temple teaches that while there are several different classifications of labor all men *fulfill* themselves by working. Even when engaged in the coarsest sort of labor, man's soul begins to understand harmony the moment he starts to work. A sense of usefulness, worth and purpose give him vitality and urge him to strive to accomplish greater deeds. Every living human being has some noble thing to accomplish during his or her lifetime. Leisure, luxury and a lifetime that feeds upon the work of others results in a vast emptiness and profound disappointment in the soul. If man will not work when he is able to work, what is his value to either himself or those that surround him?

From the three classifications of Temple workmen we also learn that labor inspires more labor and tends to assist in the promotion of an individual worker from one station in life, or degree, to a higher station. Entered Apprentices or bearers of burden who by their work have proven themselves worthy are promoted to the classification of Fellowcraft. As hewers on the mountain and in the rock quarries those Fellowcraft may by their own excellence eventually become overseers or supervisors. Each classification of work has its own worth and nobility which leads to newer and higher levels of accomplishment in the process of human *fulfillment*.

Mankind's greatest potential for harmony is closely connected to work. It is said that every great and important undertaking requires wisdom to conceive of an idea, strength to bring that idea into fruition and a beautiful soul or spirit that is dedicated to serving both. Neither is greater than the others and none exists without the others. While various writers have written that some work is more meritorious than other work because it promotes virtue rather than human genius, mankind is never *fulfilled* until it receives the benefits from both. Virtue induces brotherly love, peaceful co-existence and wholesome communication among the people. But genius gives us great works of art, fantastic technologies and scientific discoveries that improve the way in which all men may live. It is so exceedingly unfair to ask which is the better that Masonry simply teaches that both are necessary for man to feel truly *fulfilled*.

The Hiramic Legend teaches that *fulfillment* is dependent upon a specific course of conduct that differs from individual to individual. Not all of the Temple workmen served as overseers. The majority worked at lesser duties but none would have proven successful without the success of the others. This concept of team work exists throughout Masonic symbolism and is intended to inspire each Mason to both identify that which he can best accomplish with others and how best to succeed.

One first selects the task to be performed and then commits himself to its completion. Masonry offers its members many varied projects within which one may apply his talents. Those projects frequently include the education of other Masons in Masonic and secular studies, charitable works that benefit both the fraternity and the community at large, and participating in symbolic ritual ceremonies. The success of each project depends entirely upon the success of the team.

It has been said that duty is with us always and such is certainly true for all men who commit to be active in the performance of Masonic projects. Such should be no less true for all men in all walks of life who work with others to improve mankind's existence. While Masonry's fundamental lesson about *duty* rests upon the notion that all work is worthwhile, the equally important lesson is that unless one man performs the duty he has freely accepted, the team around him will fail.

Had the Entered Apprentices decided to go fishing instead of carrying the stone from the rock quarries there would not have been any materials with which to build the Temple. Similarly if the Fellowcraft had simply determined to nap instead of hewing the rock from its quarry beds, there would not have been any stone for the Entered Apprentices to carry. And if both classes of workmen ran away there would have been no need for the overseers who would suddenly discover that there was no construction to supervise.

This lesson teaches us that all men are connected in their work and must labor in harmony if any great work is ever to be accomplished. But simply knowing we must seek harmony is not always enough to inspire men to conscientiously perform their duties. Indeed not even lessons about the rewarding personal spiritual benefits of labor are sufficient to compel all men to work. Some will choose to remain idle regardless of the extent of encouragement to become involved in something other than self indulgence. Such is the nature of the freedom of choice with which all men have been imbued by the Great Architect.

Not even the Wisdom of Solomon could wholly eliminate stragglers, neer-do-wells and faithless team mates. Three of his workmen chose to scheme and murder instead of perform their duties. Twelve others plotted with the murderers and for a time also abandoned their own labors. We are told that all work stopped until the intrigue was fully resolved and did not commence again until Solomon selected Adonhiram to lead in the place of *Hiram Abif.*

This natural ebb and flow – labor and interruption – is precisely how our earthly community has lurched through history building God's kingdom on earth brick-by-brick. At times man has strenuously applied his best and most sincere efforts at advancing the causes of peace and harmony. Each time he has, something or someone interrupts his work with of war, chaos, or turmoil.

Several of the world's major religions including those of the Hindu and Chinese have connected this phenomenon to each human soul by teaching that all souls repeat the cycle of life and death on earth. The doctrine taught is referred to as *reincarnation* and relates that each incarnation commences where the previous one ended, filled with the lessons of the former. The new incarnated life then advances, declines or remains unchanged depending upon the choices each person makes during his or her incarnation.

Obviously if that doctrine is true some men are *fulfilled* sooner than others while some never achieve *fulfillment* regardless of the frequency of incarnations. Not even those who embrace *reincarnation* can be counted upon to become good team mates. Like all humans some will choose self indulgence and some will accept the challenge to act as a good social partner.

From this truth about human nature another truth emerges: while duty surely is with us always, not everyone feels duty-bound. Nor is that truth likely to ever change. The Hiramic Legend imparts this same message in hopes that Masons will learn not to be overly anxious about being disappointed by others. Instead man must learn to factor into each life experience the potentiality that many of the ups and downs he will encounter will be the result of others failing in the performance of their work. To assume otherwise ignores human nature and will only lead to frustration. When frustration sets in, one's own performance can fail.

However the lesson taught us about *fulfillment* by the Temple workmen is not limited to knowing about the shortcomings of others but includes a cautionary warning about our own tendency to indulge in self applause. Nothing can be more irritating than to work alongside another person who labors solely to attain personal attention. Worse still is losing ourselves to those same temptations and then feeling the sting of a just rebuke from another Mason whispering good counsel in our ear.

It has oft been written that Masons are practical philosophers. When we compare Freemasonry to the first philosophers we learn that they, too, devoted their energies to instructing men about duty and the principles of virtue. Much more may also be learned from those original thinkers, for soon after the precepts they taught became commonplace, human nature prompted some to distinguish themselves from their fellow philosophers. This resulted in the emergence of absurd systems of thinking and the development of doctrines that many continue to find dangerous.

Once certain talents were revealed some philosophers secured the applause of many. Several of the other thinkers who heard no applause for themselves were overcome with jealousy and determined that they, too, would grasp honors and recognition. The challenge for public recognition that followed was more complex to resolve than even the challenge of replacing a non-productive worker.

It eventually became necessary for the reading public, as well as the dedicated philosophers to address the inherent weakness in character that became so pervasive. It is natural that men want to be recognized; to receive the applause of the world for their endeavors; and not to leave the outcome to chance. Rousseau identified some of those men, including Diogenes, Protagoras and Hobbes – men he marginalized as purveyors of dangerous doctrines that he contended were actually intended to become so poisonous that knowing the author would be easy. It seems a startling notion that some men will actually choose to live in the *darkness* merely to attain fame. But the truth that some men do so is so apparent that it is difficult to ignore.

The Hiramic Legend tells us what awaits the pretender – men like Jubela, Jubelo and Jubelum who discard merit in favor of instant success at any cost. Eventually all such men fail although for some it requires more time to achieve their downfall.

The three assassins never acquired that which they sought from *Hiram Abif;* an allegory that clearly suggests to those who hold the power to confer honors and recognition for the *fulfillment* of work should do all within their power to avoid the temptation to lavish such honors upon the unworthy, the pretenders, or those who refuse to work for the recognition. When Albert Pike described Freemasonry as a laboratory for *work,* he also furnished Masons with a reason why they must labor. Unless men dedicate the talents they possess to creative endeavors, their failure will impede mankind's development. If all Masons sincerely dedicated themselves to consistent productivity it is likely that the fraternity would never experience concerns about membership, raising money for its charities, or supporting the growth of social communities. However like non-Masons, initiates into the mysteries do not always give of themselves. That fact should not be regarded as a source of regret, but as an inspiration to do better. It remains a fact of human nature that must slowly be overcome. When the "stones" of the Temple are finally laid laid, the edifice will stand strong against the elements.

Man's thirst for success can produce either *fulfilling* results, or personal destruction. Masonry has never taught its members that desiring to be successful is inherently wrong. To the contrary, the Hiramic Legend is intended to inspire men to be as successful as possible in all of their endeavors. The Grand Master *Hiram Abif* was not a failure in his work – he was one of the most celebrated artists of his time. Had he not been skilled in metal work and the construction of beautiful structures he would never have chosen by either Hiram of Tyre or King Solomon to lead the Temple workmen. But his thirst for success was tempered by an enormous capacity to impose the greatest virtue and morality upon his environment. One need merely review the Masonic legend about his daily life to understand how he was able to do so.

Each day at *high twelve* he entered the *sanctum sanctorum,* or Holy of Holies to kneel in prayer to God at the altar. This most accomplished man understood the importance of humbling himself before his great Creator and consequently included petitions for the welfare of others in his silent prayers.

"Give me guidance to create the plans for the workmen to follow," he prayed, "and please sustain each of them in their work and lives."

This daily display of *Hiram Abif's* reliance upon the Great Architect became his touchstone for building his own spiritual temple. While the Masonic legend does not describe whether or not the Grand Master was an avid reader of scripture, it seems certain that the Holy Writings were inscribed in this allegorical figure's heart. Love of God; love of mankind; and love of work – it was these three that distinguished *Hiram Abif* from all other men. By embracing those same three virtues, each and every Mason, man, woman and child can hope to also enjoy a similar distinction and *fulfillment*.

While it is essential to point out man's natural character weaknesses, our constant reflection on those will tend to weaken our resolve to try and do better. If too much reflection is had about weaknesses, some may begin to believe that there is nothing one can do to change nature.

"Why should I even try?" one might ask of himself. The correct answer is that life is about work; work is about trying; and trying leads to success. That is precisely the attitude with which *Hiram Abif* approached his duties as the leader of the Temple workmen. Each day before he entered the *sanctum sanctorum* he inspected the progress of the work to see if anything was necessary to improve upon either the strength of the structure or the beauty of its adornments. Each day he tried to understand what next needed to be done then performed the task necessary to complete the work. Until his death that routine never changed leaving for us the best example about how to persevere toward *fulfilling* our destiny.

Chapter 22

GRADUAL PROGRESSION

G ive me the secrets of a Master Mason," Jubela angrily demanded as he accosted *Hiram Abif* near the south gate of the unfinished Temple. The Grand Master refused setting in motion the violent events that followed. Those events illustrate a significant component of Masonic teachings. Taught by degrees only, Masonry inculcates into each candidate's heart and soul the importance of developing into maturity without skipping the many intervening steps. Jubela, on the other hand, was intent upon advancing as quickly as possible even if doing so meant that someone as distinguished as *Hiram Abif* died in the process.

So many people share the same impatience and are intent upon become an overnight success. Sadly those people miss out on the joys of *developing gradually*. Masonry educates its initiates in three distinct stages: the *Entered Apprentice Degree*, the *Fellowcraft Degree*, and the sublime degree of *Master Mason*. Each degree or classification contains numerous lessons about life, history, philosophy, science and theology that become foundations for lessons offered in succeeding degrees. Most men who have enjoyed living the Masonic experience for many years agree that learning and re-learning each of those lessons can be a lifetime venture. But one must not be in a rush throughout this journey, for the joys to be experienced may best be realized when one allows himself to slow down and allow the *light* to gradually replace the *darkness*.

The Hiramic Legend's emphasis on this important truth is as important to non-Masons as it is to Masons, for the desire to rush to success is shared by all men. The absurdity of that desire is obvious to anyone who recalls that the greatest artists known to man first had to learn to draw; the finest artisans were required to study as apprentices under the steady guidance of proven masters; and every person who ever served mankind as a professional had to go to school, pass examinations to test his competence and demonstrate to proven practitioners that they had sufficiently mastered the knowledge necessary to perform the work.

Developing gradually is nothing other than advancing step-by-step. *Hiram Abif* refused to convey the secrets of a *Master Mason* to Jubela, Jubelo, or Jubelum, because neither of those Fellowcraft had completed the steps necessary to advance to that degree. His refusal teaches us never to yield to the temptation to help another skip life's essential steps. Rather we are reminded about the importance of building success upon a solid foundation of knowledge.

If we pause to speculate about how the three assassins might have acted if they had been successful obtaining the secrets to which they were not entitled, we actually begin to witness the disaster that awaits all who try to bypass life's gradual progression. Had the ruffians received those secrets without first learning the lessons taught by the *Entered Apprentice* and *Fellowcraft* degrees, the foundation provided by those lessons would never have been laid. Jubela, Jubelo and Jubelum would have proven to be no better, because neither of them would have known what to do with the *Word* had it been obtained. They would never have known the truths that a Fellowcraft can learn from the study of the liberal arts and sciences, or been enabled to apply those truths to the benefit of others. The best they would have accomplished would have been the wearing of a title – *Master Mason*. Merely wearing that title would have resulted in nothing more significant than the momentary soothing of selfish pride.

History is filled with stories about men who sought undeserved status and praise and wound up leading their followers to ruin and disgrace. Napoleon Bonaparte rose the rank of general in the French Army while still in his late 20's. His lack of experience and horrible temperament caused the slaughter of many of his soldiers. Historical hindsight reveals that he was unfit to wear the title of general and is prominently remembered for his pride and arrogance rather than for any contribution he may have made to mankind.

The ancient Roman Emperor, Nero, thirsted after power, acquired it and led tyrannically and extravagantly. Adolph Hitler turned his hatred of the Jews into a theme for governmental rule. John Quincy Adams, although enormously intelligent, could never control his impatience and pettiness resulting in his failed United States presidency. Hideki Tojo became the most influential military leader of Japan before and during World War II and led his nation to collapse and ruin.

While other examples abound, these well-known historical figures serve as prime examples of the consequences for failing to learn important lessons in virtue and morality before attempting to tackle the difficult task of leading governments and armies. None of them exemplified the beauties that flow when leaders patiently participate in *gradual development*. Each of our poor examples insisted that things had to progress as they dictated and at the pace they demanded. We need look no farther than to those men to understand the horrid consequences of impatience, arrogance, ineptitude and intemperance.

It has been said that no one is wise who is not as fully acquainted with the extent of ignorance as with the extent of wisdom. That is so because in mortal concerns wisdom is an inconsequential area of rationality existing in an infinite expanse of ignorance. More simply stated, life offers us much to learn and we have an obligation to educate ourselves step-by-step so that we may, each one of us, contribute to the present and future welfare of humanity. That was one of the principal reasons why *Hiram Abif* courageously stood his ground and fatally resisted the demands of the three assassins.

Assimilating all of the liberal arts and sciences presented to us in the *Fellowcraft degree* is an impossible task if it is also expected that only a brief period of study is required. This part of our lives is not merely symbolic – it is a truth of nature. Yet that truth has too often been overlooked in several Masonic jurisdictions which have recently yielded to rapid advancement through the Masonic degrees. Suffice to say that the challenge to *develop gradually* is not limited to the secular or non-Masonic world. It is among the several challenges that presently hold much of Freemasonry in their grasp.

All the great manifestations of nature are the result of slow and frequently imperceptible degrees of growth. Contrariwise, the works of destruction and disaster have seemingly occurred in an instant. The great earthquake that shook San Francisco released awesome energies of destruction that sent panicky men and women running in all directions. Tornados that touch down without warning frequently leave a trail of mangled buildings in the flash of an eye. Hurricanes that sweep across the oceans careen into coastal lands unexpectedly wiping out entire cities.

The story has been told about the wandering barbarian of the ancient past who knelt to the ground in England and idly scraped away the earth so that the acorn in his hand would have a home where it could grow. Human events outpaced the slow growth of that seed which continued its upward climb long after the barbarian had died. The years marched onward and the once tender shoot fed by dews and the light of day sprung forth into full maturity. All the while history witnessed such events as the Norman invasion, the parceling of the land by William the Conqueror among his barons, the greatness of Richard Lion-Heart and the wresting of the Magna Carta from the dark King John beneath the strong shady limbs of the tree that grew from the spot. That tiny acorn *developed gradually* to serve its great purposes of witnessing and participating in great events that occurred during centuries of time.

Knowing the slow process by which the Great Architect achieves great results, we also know that He does not often expect to complete the building of an edifice in one human life span. God has chosen to create and has selected a slow and steady progression to that end as opposed to working to attain instantaneous results. So it is, too, for mankind whose greatest accomplishments have required generations to complete. The seemingly endless cycle of birth, life and death has remained a consistent truth of nature throughout those generations. That which one man planted generations ago men generations later have harvested. From this truth we learn another: like the Great Architect, man must build slowly if he is to accomplish great things.

The Hiramic Legend reinforces this truth by its focus upon the building of King Solomon's Temple. It required two chief architects and two lifetimes. After *Hiram Abif* was slain his successor Adonhiram continued the work until the great edifice stood as testimony to man's diligent creativity. We are not told by the allegory how many other workmen at the Temple died before it was completed. However the Jewish historian Josephus informs us that the construction continued for seven difficult years – a span of time within which young men grow to physical maturity, mature men yield to old age and the aged eventually die. Like the barbarian's acorn that grew from generation to generation, the great Temple exhausted youthful energy and delivered aging men to their grave before it was completed to serve its purpose.

Our Masonic *mysteries* had an origin which we are taught then *developed gradually* into the truths it teaches today. It began in ancient China, evolved further in India, migrated to Chaldea then on into Egypt through the Hyksos lineage and later within the Sinai Peninsula under the guidance of the man known to the world as Moses and to some as Ahkenaten. The rituals practiced today are the result of that evolution. In that our origins are in part rooted in ancient China, Freemasonry has also been greatly influenced by the old philosophy known as *I Ching*.

The Chinese masters from that time and place taught that all development should proceed step-by-step in an orderly fashion. Oftentimes matters, ideas and projects require the consumption of a lot of time to cultivate the proper environment for further advancement. The relevant allegory offered by the *I Ching* is that of a young maiden smitten with the idea of marriage.

As the story unfolds it is made clear to us that while she is certain to be married, she must wait for the appropriate time. True love, mutual understanding and harmony must be laid, just as the craftsman lays the first stone of a building in the northeast corner. The allegory transforms into a story about an ancient king who bides his time to permit events beyond his control to unfold before he proceeds to consolidate his power.

This allegory serves as a lesson in the patience necessary to competently create something, for without such patience destruction could be instantaneous. An impetuous person might miss the opportunity to achieve his destiny if he behaves rashly. Just as Masons are taught that fortitude is a desired virtue that is equidistant between rashness and cowardice, many people have simply ignored this truth.

Frequently man needs other men to accomplish a goal – a truth of nature that requires us to spend time with others to develop the trust necessary for working together. Recent events in American politics reveal the potential for failure when developing trust among people is ignored. The chance to improve upon a better health care system went awry in the 1990's because people did not understand the importance of assembling supportive allies. Most of the world has heaped scorn upon this country because the President unilaterally chose to inflict war before forming a supportive coalition. A Great Depression descended upon this country and the world when another American President refused to form a world-wide consensus about how to manage trade taxes and thereby foolishly damaged the world economy. In each instance the outcome might have been different had men understood the importance of *developing gradually.*

Several virtues converge when a favorable environment for slow and steady progress is finally put in place. First and foremost the choices made along the way are guided by the virtue of *humility*. Second, the virtue of *perseverance* is essential when traveling the bumpy road toward success. Third, without *confidence* in one's personal powers to decide and persuade others to join the pursuit progress may never be made. And last, but certainly not least, *faith* in God's loving power is as essential to success as is any other virtue.

Man was not intended to live an isolated life. He is by nature a social being and history records that his greatest accomplishments have been the result of grand coalitions of like-minded people who worked together in pursuit of a common goal. What madness and chaos would have resulted at the building of King Solomon's Temple had some or all of the workmen decided to follow different plans drawn upon a different trestle board? Consider also the disaster that would have befallen those men had some or all of them not taken the time necessary to learn the necessary skills. A workman who had never before seen a hammer would not have known what to do. But by proper preparation, confident and persuasive leadership, the workmen endeavored from the same set of plans and constructed what Masonic tradition informs us was the greatest edifice of its time.

One reason that Masonry's esoteric work has remained secret is to insure that when those secrets are revealed, the person receiving them has progressed to the extent necessary to understand and implement the hidden truths. The necessary progression is nothing less than mastering the proper temperament, or wisdom that resists extreme influences. It is that wisdom that Plato once referred to as the science of all sciences from which flows the ability to distinguish the known from the unknown and how best to learn that which was heretofore thought unknowable. Masonry teaches that such wisdom is not merely the knowledge of things but the understanding about the *condition of knowledge* which may only be acquired when one *develops gradually*.

The Ten Commandments contains an extraordinary commentary about the nature of such wisdom. By inference we are taught to respect and honor our elders – not simply because respect and honor are good traits, but because those behaviors inculcate a respect for those who have lived long lives – those who *developed gradually*. If it is so that Masonic esoteric knowledge pertains to the inherent nature or condition of knowledge and is limited to those fully acquainted with the profound issues discussed throughout all philosophy and theology, it must also be so that our wise elders are important to gradual development.

Chapter 23

MASONIC ORIGINS

The Masonic legend of *Hiram Abif*, while entirely allegorical, conceals within its ritualistic expression the secrets about the true origins of the Craft. One will never become fully knowledgeable about those origins without first becoming engulfed in the rich symbolism used in the conferral of Masonry's third degree. While the history of the building crafts and their guilds during the medieval period is enticing to those seeking a beginning point for this fraternity, it is inaccurate and incomplete to conclude that such is the case. Much to the contrary, the origins of Freemasonry are closely linked to Abraham, the biblical Patriarch. Although the original teachings of Abraham's era have been corrupted through time, Freemasonry serves as a guardian of the theology embraced by Abraham's sacred family.

It is not coincidental that Masonry embraces both the cosmological and mathematical tenets commonly practiced during Abraham's lifetime. Indeed, the ritual of the Hiramic Legend contains many of those elements. Some are also evident in the ritual of both the first and second Masonic degrees. Whereas present-day mainstream thinking rejects astrology and numerology as useless and heretical, both sciences are deeply embedded into the fabric of existing Masonic ritual.

No Entered Apprentice can easily forget the symbolism of the *covering of the lodge,* or its relevance to the study of the skies. Similarly no Fellowcraft will likely ignore the lessons he learned about the numbers 3, 5 and 7. And without doubt few if any Master Masons will hesitate to ponder the significance of the number 12, or the moonlit night beneath which the three assassins met to discuss a corpse that lay in the *rubbish of the Temple*. The origin of these lessons lies with none other than the Chaldean Shepherds from who Abraham drew his understandings about the *One True God*.

Those lessons were passed down to those Shepherds by way of a man called Enoch, whom the Holy Bible records as the son of Jared an ancestor of the celebrated Noah. Additional information about the theological connection between Enoch and Abraham is given to us by Pythagoras. Masonic tradition informs us that Enoch and Pythagoras stand as bookends to Abraham and serve to explain both the Patriarch's relationship to Masonry, as well as the reason why he accepted the truth about the *One True God*.

The fundamental theological and philosophical premise running as a common thread through all three is that human beings are not merely immortal – they have always existed. Just as the *alpha* and *omega*, man has no beginning and no ending. The souls of all men have existed in the embrace of the Great Architect from time immemorial. As those souls entered and exited earth they did so through the cosmos, or galaxy and the points of entrance and exit are more clearly defined for us by the Zodiac. This conclusion explains why the ancients, as well as many modern Masons who possess the ancient knowledge, spent so much time carefully perusing the skies. It also offers an explanation about the upheavals in Egypt that eventually resulted in two separate exoduses, both of which are recorded in the Holy Bible, as well as other Holy Writings.

This entire theology/philosophy originated with Enoch, who constructed a temple and presided over ritualistic ceremonies that were forerunners of modern-day Freemasonry. As we will learn much of the ancient knowledge has been corrupted throughout the ages leaving most Masons entirely without any understanding about their roots. Several Masonic writers have touched upon this topic in various literary works, but none has brought together the many threads that combine to form the fabric of Freemasonry.

To learn more about Enoch, we must first confront his legend and reality. Numerous ancient Jewish, Christian and Islamic sources relate a story about the goodness of Enoch. It has been written that he was of such virtue and morality that God spirited him away rather than permitting him to experience the throes of death. It has been said that he lived until the age of 365 and was so highly regarded by the Great Architect as to have been honored by being re-named *Metatron*. Various Muslim scholars have suggested that during his lifetime Enoch worked as a tailor. Other Jewish authors describe him as a son of Cain – the disgraced biblical personage who is said to have slain his own brother, Abel.

Whether or not Enoch was a real person, a fantasy, or merely a composite of several real people there is no doubt that he represents the man who first developed the theology/philosophy that is embraced by present-day Freemasons. Biblical genealogy places Enoch in the family of Jesus. Freemasonry encourages its members to make frequent visits to the scriptures, as they are regarded as the *rule and guide* of their lives. Thus, without regard to Enoch's reality, his symbolism is extraordinarily important to understanding the reason why Abraham unhesitatingly embraced the *One True God*.

The earliest Masonic references to Enoch are set forth in two ancient manuscripts: the *Indigo Jones* manuscript and the *Woods* manuscript which were written at the beginning of the reign of the English monarch, James I. The *Indigo Jones* manuscript, which may be obtained from Masonic book dealers who also handle antiquities, was written in approximately 1607 and is highly recommended reading, for in addition to mentioning Enoch and other well-known Masonic concepts, it discusses the importance of the *twelve signs* of the Zodiac. The *Woods* manuscript, written at an earlier time, discusses the importance of the liberal arts and sciences, the knowledge of which has been variously threatened by floods and other natural disasters. From these two manuscripts evolved a ritualistic degree in the Ancient and Accepted Scottish Rite known as the Royal Arch of Enoch.

That ritual depicts Enoch as the preserver of knowledge at the time of the Great Flood. He deposited writings into a column that set forth all that was known about the sciences. That column was later discovered during the building of King Solomon's Temple and serves as the basis for the allegory about the *secrets of Freemasonry*. The discovery was made on Mount Moriah - a fact that tends to explain the significance of that location to Masonry. The discovery and translation of the writing known to us as the *Book of Enoch* by Scotsman James Bruce also lends greater insight into the theology/philosophy that captured Abraham's attention.

The *Book of Enoch* contained magical and astrological formulae that had been assembled from a variety of different authors. It offered information about the harmony of nature and why harmony was important to understanding the nature of the *One True God*. The regular motion of the stars and the change of seasons lent further evidence of God's creative rhythm which has been absorbed into Masonic ritual.

In the *Fellowcraft Degree,* or Second Degree of Freemasonry, we are taught that nature is managed by the mathematically beautiful laws of geometry. By the use of geometry man may actually trace nature into its deepest recesses and discover precisely how the planets move in their respective orbits. The orderliness of it all first determined mankind to adopt discipline in everything that he did – from forming social networks with other human beings to the development of a theology that tended to reveal God in His fullest splendor.

But more than mere scientific curiosity captured the imagination of the first Masons. The comings and goings of the spirits and souls through specific portals in the heavens led the earliest observers of the sky to develop a science that would enable them to better understand this aspect of the Great Architect's creative power. Chapters 72 through 82 of the *Book of Enoch* are entirely devoted to the movements of various heavenly bodies which are said to have been drawn from Enoch's dreaming visions. That *Book* and those visions were revered as sacred texts by the early Christians and, although substantially modified by him, appear in various forms throughout the writings of Saul – also known to some as Josephus Flavius, or the Apostle Paul.

Most significant to the cosmology adopted by Masonry, the *Book of Enoch* details a meeting between Enoch and the Angel Raphael during which Enoch was instructed in the secrets of nature. The Angel Michael paid them a visit during the same time and led Enoch by the hand into a separate compartment where he communicated to him the secrets of righteousness. In the process, Enoch learned about the importance of the "mystic rose," which later is revealed to us as a symbol of the Christ. But contrary to some theological beliefs that symbol was never intended to refer to a specific person: rather the secrets taught to Enoch revealed to him that "Christ" referred to that spark of the Divine that resided within each and every human being. The attribution of the "Christ" designation to Jesus occurred much later in history – long after Enoch, Abraham and Pythagoras had passed from this earth – and resulted from the writings of Saul-Paul.

Enoch was the first person in history known to have spoken about angels. Lest we dismiss as fantastic any further discussion about angels, we should recall that both the Old and New Testaments of the Holy Bible openly discuss them. So, too, do each of the Holy Writings for many of the religions man has accepted from the beginning of time.

The word "angel" means "messenger" one of whom, *Aseph,* is recorded in the Holy Writings as having provided the music heard at the consecration ceremonies for King Solomon's Temple. The *Book of Enoch* reveals that the "angels he knew were a classification of beings he called "Watchers," who are nothing less than the "Giants" referred to in the Holy Bible's book of Genesis. These beings were regarded as intermediaries between God and man and were recognized as relevant influences by the ancient Egyptians of Abraham's era.

The *Book of Enoch* also records that Enoch received comprehensive instruction about astronomy from the Angel Raphael. He was taught that the sun moves around the sky during the year and illuminates certain portals or windows to that realm that exists beyond the heavens. It is recorded that six such portals were revealed in the east and equal number in the west. This phenomenon thoroughly engaged Enoch who demonstrated his growing obsession by writing down everything he was told by the Angels Raphael and Michael. It is these writings upon which the Chaldean Shepherds constructed their theology/philosophy that was eventually embraced by Abraham. In painstaking detail Enoch carefully recorded day and night skies; the movement of the stars and planets; and the hemispheric changes as winter gave way to spring, spring to summer and summer to fall. Those records also reflected the amount of daylight in each day of each and every season.

It was from those records that man began to more carefully study the importance of the winter and summer solstices – astronomical concepts that are of great importance to the Hiramic Legend. *Hiram Abif's* raising from the grave in part represents the activity of the sun as it arises from winter to travel to its greatest height in the heavens at the summer solstice. To Enoch that course of astronomical travel represented the continuity of life: all that lives dies and eventually rises again. As the sun passed through several different Zodiacal complexes of stars, its journey also symbolized how the varying powers and forces attributed to each Zodiac influenced the sun's behavior. It was from this phenomenon that the Chaldeans and ancient Egyptians decided which power of the Great Architect was most prominently deserving of mankind's greatest attention. Indeed, the High Priests of Upper and Lower Egypt constructed entire theologies upon the conclusions they drew from that phenomenon.

The great pending debate among those holy men during Abraham's lifetime was whether the Zodiac Taurus (the bull) or Aries (the ram/sheep) constituted the predominant theological influence. Feuds raged among both the priests and the people and eventually resulted in the expulsion of one set of believers from Egypt. Without question during Abraham's time, religion was the greatest challenge to the stability of the lives of all people. If that sounds familiar to other times and places, including present-day societies, we may at once recognize that differences of opinion about religion are not a new challenge.

The ancient Egyptian writer Manetho informs us that the Egyptian priesthood led their people to worship a bull-deity commencing in the Second Dynasty. It was during this religious period that the legend of Osiris, Isis and Horus was introduced to *initiated* society. Referred to as *Apis,* the bull-deity was symbolized by Osiris who also represented the *resurrected man;* the virtual embodiment of human immortality. As noted in an earlier chapter, some Masons observing the *Third Degree of Masonry* connect the Osiric Legend directly to the Hiramic Legend.

The so-called cult of the *Apis Bull* has its roots in the early beginnings of Egyptian civilization. Some contend that this animal was selected because it symbolized strength, virility and the type of fighting spirit that ordinary people hoped their own pharaoh would possess. A drawing of a bull was often seen with a sun-disk situated between its horns in such a configuration that conjured up notions of an *ankh,* or resurrection-cross. *Apis* was originally considered to be the herald or forerunner of the chief god *Ptah* in much the same manner as present-day Christians see John the Baptist as the forerunner of Jesus Christ.

Apis was also unmistakably connected to *Taurus,* the great bull symbol that is contained in that heavenly Zodiac. It is situated in the sky between *Aries* to the west and *Gemini* to the east. It also represented a specific astrological period that paralleled a host of social, cultural and political developments on earth. By the time Abraham appeared on the world scene Egypt had been worshipping the *Apis Bull* or *Taurean* influence for nearly 1,000 years. The religion taught to the masses was premised upon the influences of this Zodiacal sign resulting in dogmas, doctrines and the construction of enormously elaborate temples. The great *Sphinx* was erected during this era and allegedly contains within its stone construction the secrets and essence of that period – secrets that are associated with mathematics.

It is written that the *Age of Taurus* lasted from approximately 4286 BC to approximately 1850 BC. Abraham is said to have lived between approximately 1812 BC and approximately 1637 BC. If those dates are approximately accurate, Abraham came into this world three centuries after the *Age of Taurus* ended. However Manetho records that during Abraham's lifetime the Egyptian society was actually on the verge of recognizing the transition from one astrological age to another – that of the Zodiac *Aries*. Perhaps the chronology associated with Abraham's life is inaccurate. But if it is accurate over 300 hundred years had passed since the *Age of Taurus* gave way in the heavens to the *Age of Aries*. Nevertheless the dogma and doctrine that had been constructed by the priesthood during that age had not evolved or changed in the slightest. Indeed the people had become quite comfortable with their religion and were not easily persuaded to change.

A dispute erupted marked by isolated incidents of physical violence. According to the priests who recognized the transition from *Taurus* to *Aries* the change in the heavens dictated that the old religion must evolve into a new form of worship. After all, those priests stated, the precession in astrology demanded that man respect the new Divine influences foretold by the precession. It was all part of God's grand plan for creation.

The Thebans of Lower Egypt backed the common people in Upper Egypt resulting in a political coup for Thebes. The people were split down the middle: southerners against the northerners with the northerners labeled as heretics. The southerners who lived in Upper Egypt cemented the dispute by crowning and anointing their own pharaoh – a Hyksos, or *Shepherd King,* and an adherent of *Aries.*

The dynasty of Abraham began at the same time and in the same region – an occurrence historically embraced by both Josephus and Freemasonry. It marked the beginning of the theology that would continue down through the succeeding ages that would study the importance of mankind's embrace of the *One True God* – the Great Architect whose evolving influences upon man on earth were symbolized by the precessional evolutions in the Zodiac. Was Abraham the newly crowned and anointed Phaoroh? Some writers have speculated that he was.

Thus history and Masonic tradition inform us that the widely accepted allegory about "lowly" shepherds influencing the religious development of man is actually symbolic of the more important figures, such as Abraham, who not only grasped the importance behind the theology of *Aries,* but acted in a manner that helped it to flourish. Masonic tradition also contends that there was a rivalry between Abraham and the pharaoh in Thebes – Terah, Abraham's father. The two did not see eye-to-eye about the transition from *Taurus* to *Aries* and allowed their differences to drag the Egyptian people into prolonged warfare.

While Biblical genealogy is questionable, at best, the book of Genesis clearly states that the man known as Jacob was one of Abraham's grandsons. Some authors have concluded that Jacob was also a pharaoh of Upper Egypt just like his grandfather. *Aries* was still losing to *Taurus* in overall influence throughout Egypt. But during his time Jacob held the line, worshipped in the temples of the *One True God* and witnessed the installation of his brother Esau as the pharaoh of Lower Egypt.

The book of Genesis conveys the story about those two brothers, each a son of Abraham's son Isaac, whose jealousy toward one another was compounded when Jacob tricked his father into anointing him instead of the older Esau as the rightful successor. Esau departed the land in anger swearing vengeance. The warfare that ensued between them and their armies eventually compelled Jacob to lead his weaker forces entirely out of Egypt and commence a treacherous journey that eventually led them to the land known as Canaan.

Along the way, Jacob continued the use of houses of worship constructed to employ the east-to-west configuration originally constructed by Enoch. That design was intended to symbolize the manner of the sun's travels through the Zodiac – the precessional evolutions of the skies. In so doing Jacob perpetuated practices later inherited by Freemasonry and paid due recognition to the relevance of that cosmology to the comings-and goings of human souls. It also became important to Jacob and the ancients to learn how best to nourish those souls while on earth to assist the Great Architect to complete His plan.

History records Jacob's escape as the first *exodus* out of Egypt. The disruption was prompted by nothing less than religious strife. Esau's followers embraced the priesthood of *Taurus* while Jacob's people were persuaded that the heavens of *Aries* foretold such a change in the future that demanded that they, too, change their manner of worship. But Jacob did not depart from the land quietly – a fact that leads us to another story recorded in the book of Genesis.

We are informed by the scriptures that because Pharoh had resisted the demands of a man called Moses to permit the enslaved Hebrews to leave Egypt, God sent a destroying angel to slay the first born of the Egyptians. To protect the Hebrews from this calamity Moses directed that lamb's blood be swiped across the threshold of every Hebrew's house. As the story unfolds, the destroying angel passed by those houses and entered into the homes of the Egyptians killing each and every first born offspring.

The story holds two points of interest for us. First, in answer to the question why use lamb's blood, we need only reconsider the religious tensions that existed between the followers of *Taurus* and the followers of *Aries* – the ram versus the lamb. The traditional interpretation of the story is intended to connect with New Testament scripture about the *Lamb of God* – the present-day Christians' symbolism for Jesus the Christ. Ancient history also records something very different, which brings us to the second point of interest.

As was stated previously, Jacob did not leave Egypt quietly; instead he inflicted much death and destruction to the land on his way out slaughtering many men, women and children. He ordered his army to behave so viciously that Esau would think twice before sending legions to follow and attempt to kill the retreating people. Jacob's actions may be viewed more as protecting his own people from the ravages of their enemy – the followers of *Taurus*. This interpretation also sheds a different light upon whom or what was the *destroying angel*.

The stories of the Old Testament and the writings of Josephus reveal that Jacob's armies subsequently wreaked havoc throughout the land of Palestine as the people pursued their journey. Jacob led the second most powerful army in the world at that time and used it to protect and further the interests of his people - the followers of *Aries*. History records that Jacob did his job well, for the cosmology of his followers has been woven into the fabric of Freemasonry, as revealed in the Hiramic Legend.

A sword pointing to a naked heart is presented as an emblem to the candidate for the Master Mason degree to teach several valuable lessons. Perhaps the most significant is the lesson about the Great Architect's influence upon the sun, moon and stars and His promise to reward those who both understand the meaning of that influence and yield to it. That lesson imparts the understanding that God is always creating – the world and all that is in it is undergoing constant change. Men are changing from self-serving louts to helpful brethren. Institutions rarely continue to support tyrants, but turn instead to men who work for the benefit of all mankind. Religions have turned away from beliefs that the universe is earth-centered and have slowly begun to adopt the understanding that the heavens are central to all existence. It was nothing less than this very change in attitude and behavior that was at the heart of the religious conflict between the ancient followers of *Taurus* and the ancient followers of *Aries*.

As a further illustration of Masonry's embrace of the influences of *Aries*, the importance of cosmology to the Craft is revelaed in the Twenty-Fifth degree of Scottish Rite Freemasonry – a degree that cannot be conferred upon a man until he was received the degree of *Hiram Abif* – the sublime degree of Master Mason. The galaxies known as *Cancer* and *Capricorn* were regarded by the followers of *Aries* as the gates through which souls passed from heaven to earth. The great Masonic patron Pythagoras contributed to that cosmology with this insight: the dominions of the planet Pluto assert their influence over those souls as they descend from heaven. Indeed all of the celestial bodies are believed by many to constitute Divine elements from which mankind has learned about the immortality of the soul and that all souls pre-existed their time on earth.

After Jacob had led his followers safely out of Egypt that country was left without any legitimate heir to the royal line of Shepherd Kings. However, not all of the followers of *Aries* had departed. Many decided to remain in the land of their fathers. It was impossible for them to leave behind lifetime friends, familiar surroundings and the one language they best understood. But they were not forgotten by Jacob, who later masterminded the infiltration of his own son Joseph back into the land of Esau.

The story in the Old Testament notwithstanding, Joseph's return to Egypt runs parallel to Jesus own "return" as it is described in the veiled allegory of the New Testament. Both men were heirs to the royal line and both returned to the land of their fathers for similar reasons. Joseph's smartly disguised return was intended to result in his eventual occupation of the throne that rightfully belonged to the Shepherd Kings – not the pretenders who had descended from Esau. The details surrounding this fascinating historical episode may be read elsewhere. Its greater importance to Masonry concerns the reason why Jesus travelled to Egypt. That youthful journey, also concealed in allegory within the Gospel of Matthew, was actually for the purpose of exposing him to what was then regarded as the true priesthood – not to escape Herod, who was not even alive at the time. Jesus' family correctly concluded that the priests in their land were mere pretenders. Precisely how the corrupted empire established by Esau remained the land of *true* priests is a matter of great importance to Masons and may be best learned reading about the life of Moses.

Among other things the Grand Master *Hiram Abif* symbolizes that true priesthood. Even the manner of his worship, described in part in present-day Masonic ceremonies, serves to remind us about the manner in which those *true* priests worshipped. The distinction made here between *true* and *false* priesthoods is drawn from the period in ancient Egypt during which the followers of *Taurus* refused to give way to the Divine elements in the heavens that altered the Zodical influences upon the sun. When the sun began to rise each day in the Zodiac of *Aries* thereby giving rise to a belief that history was then entering into the age of the *Lamb of God,* the followers of *Taurus* refused to be persuaded, rejected the so-called plans of the Great Architect and exchanged them for their own ideas. The priesthood that supported those ideas was referred to in the days of Jesus' youth as the *false* priesthood. It was only the *true* priesthood, symbolized by *Hiram Abif,* from whom a royal descendant such as Jesus could receive competent and reliably holy instruction.

The center of cosmological understanding in ancient Egypt was situated in the City of Heliopolis. There, the famous *sun temples* were first constructed during the third dynasty. Heliopolis also served as the center for training the priesthood and the pharaohs. Many of the Heliopolian priests chose not to leave the country during Jacob's first *exodus*. To them, it was more important that they continue their labors tracing the motions of the heavens so that mankind might better comprehend the plan of the Great Architect of the Universe.

Masonic tradition informs us that none of those priests yielded to the demands of the *Taurean* priesthood to relinquish their manner and method of worship. To have done so would have amounted to yielding the very secrets of the universe to ignorance and darkness. Some were slain for their refusal to conform, but even in the face of death we are told that none submitted. If that sounds vaguely familiar to Masons who know the story of *Hiram Abif* and the ruffians, it is no mere coincidence.

The ancient traditions of the *true* priests remained intact for ages having been passed from one generation to the next. The Heliopolian tradition of observing the skies continued filling everyone who chose to learn with the knowledge that God is a creative force, not a captive who slavishly serve's mankind's preferences.

It is for man to understand God, not the other way around. As God evolves and increasingly reveals Himself and His plan, we are expected to respond by embracing His change; not to reject it in favor of the conservative theological comforts we currently embrace. It is precisely this truth to which Jesus is said to have alluded when he equated his generation with people who had become too intoxicated and unable to clearly think and act.

King Solomon's Temple was constructed in a manner that is said to have copied the design of the Tabernacle made famous in the story about the exodus led by Moses. Its construction is described in elaborate detail in the first book of Kings of the Holy Bible. Upon closer inspection those details set forth a plan for construction that is nearly identical to the ancient *sun temples*. When we add to that fact the legend that *Hiram*

Abif went into the Temple each day at *high twelve,* we discover yet another parallel to Freemasonry that is neither accidental nor coincidental.

Twelve has long been regarded as the perfect number whose greatest symbolic relationship is to the concept of *rule.* For example, consider the saying, "For as the sun rules the day, and the moon and stars govern the night, so do their passage through the twelve signs of the Zodiac complete the great circle of the heavens." When this phrase is substituted for the corrupted phrase presently used in Masonry its greater significance to the Craft is clear. *Twelve* is also part of the phrase that identifies the sun at its highest point in the daily sky – *high twelve* – the very time *Hiram Abif* went into the *Sanctum Sanctorum* to pray to the *ever living God.* When a candidate for Masonic degrees is added to the room, there are *twelve* participants in the ritual.

Like the ancient *sun temples,* Masons regard King Solomon's Temple as the place where the secrets of God's design are communicated to holy men and then translated by them onto a *trestleboard* for use by the workmen. The truth here intended is that God speaks to man through His own creation. Those who have ears will understand; those who do not may forever remain deaf. Thus it was in this manner of entering the temple and "speaking" to God that both *Hiram Abif* and the Heliopolian priests conveyed the plans of the Great Architect to their followers.

To avoid detection and harassment by the *Taurean* priests, the priests of *Aries* substituted the word "shepherd" for the word *Aries.* Throughout succeeding ages and continuing on into today's world the use of the word "shepherd" wherever it appears in the Holy Writings was originally intended to refer to a follower of *Aries.* This ruse continued throughout the days of Joseph and assisted the Arians to establish strongholds in Jerusalem and Egypt, where, as we are told by Josephus, that ancient land was once led by one man and his eleven brethren – Joseph and his brothers.

Manetho, the famous Egyptian historian and priest, wrote about a subsequent period in Egypt – a time years after Joseph had reinstated the so-called true royal blood line. Specifically, Manetho depicted a second *exodus* from the land by "lepers" and "cripples." Smaller in number than the *exodus* by Jacob and his followers, this emigration included certain *true* priests whose worship in the manner of *Aries* had been discovered. These were the "lepers" or people who refused to embrace the doctrine of *Taurus*. Manetho's description of those people reveals an overt intolerance in the land toward anyone who believed differently than the *Taurean* priests. Once the "lepers" were discovered they were forced to leave the country. But as was the case during the first *exodus*, not all *true* priests departed – many who had not been "found out" remained to secretly continue the same tracings of the heavens.

The people of the second *exodus* were led away by two men known in the Holy Bible as Moses and his brother Aaron. In reality one of those brothers had become pharaoh. His true name was Akhenaton, known in history as the sun-disk pharaoh, who rose to power by marrying into the royal blood line. He embraced the teachings of the Heliopolian priests and embarked upon a campaign to rid Egypt of *Taurean* worship leaving nobody to wonder that the "Shepherd Kings" had recaptured power throughout the land. Whether Akhenaton was actually Moses or his brother Aaron has been the subject of some dispute. However there is no dispute that the pharaoh ran headlong into a roaring conflict with the *Taurean* priests who became intent upon removing this heretical tyrant as quickly as possible.

The religion Akhenaton wanted to establish, including the worship of *Aten* whom Akhenaton referred to as the *One True God,* has erroneously been described by some writers as the first monotheistic religion. In truth, Aton was merely the name selected by Akhenaton to describe the same *One True God* worshipped by his ancestors Abraham, Jacob, Joseph and the other Shepherd Kings. The theology was the same, but for the first time in history a pronounceable name was lent to *He who shall remain nameless.* Clearly made of stern stuff, Akhenaton could easily have opted to not make such a public proclamation about religion and by stealth eventually eliminate the *false* or *Taurean* priesthood. Instead he courageously faced his enemies, who subsequently proved equally tough and determined in the protection of their religion.

Forced to move his monarchy to the part of middle Egypt that became known as Amarna, the continuous religious rhetoric from his camp eventually prompted the Theban *false* priests to press the military for Akhenaton's ouster from all of Egypt. But before he was finally forced to leave the country, Akhenaton erected a temporary temple dedicated to the worship of *Aten.* The temple was later carried away by the people during what we now known as the second *exodus.*

That temporary temple is referred to by present-day observers as the *Tabernacle of Moses* after which Masonic tradition informs us King Solomon's Temple and present-day Masonic lodges were patterned in their construction. Although Akhenaton tried mightily to do so, he found that changing the religious beliefs of an entire nation was impossible and finally led his people on the well-known journey attributed to Moses and described for us in the Old Testament. As was so after the first *exodus* several of the Arian priests refused to leave the country and remained in Heliopolis. Secretly they determined to continue the survey of nature and the heavens so that mankind would benefit from understanding all that the Great Architect chose to reveal.

The religion embraced by the emigrants of the second *exodus* was based upon the theological and philosophical teachings of the Arian priesthood and the Shepherd Kings. Masonic tradition informs us that the rituals or liturgies that were adopted were based the rituals and liturgies used by Enoch, Abraham, Isaac and Jacob. Those rituals employed various symbols that were intended to reveal unalterable truths about God and the universe.

Perhaps the most significant of lesson learned by those who witnessed the rituals convinced man to *awaken* to the presence of God, or the spark of Divinity that resided within him. That *awakening* continues to be expressed in present-day Masonry through the Hiramic Legend. It was also a significant part of the rituals used by the Arian priests remaining in Heliopolis, as well as the priests who traveled with the emigrants of the second *exodus*.

The precise nature of those teachings is not generally known to those who have not been initiated into Freemasonry. Indeed they may not be revealed to anyone who has not been initiated. What can be revealed is that the secret science and mysterious emblems of initiation have always been connected with the heavens, the spheres and the constellations. To fully understand the truths taught by that secret science that *connection* must be carefully and diligently studied.

In the hands of the ancient priests of the Shepherd Kings, those symbols revealed truths about God and the universe. In the centuries following the second *exodus* the interpretations have become garbled and now amount to little more than *lost words*. Such was not the case, however, when Jesus traveled from Jerusalem to Heliopolis for instruction by the Arian priests.

Masonry and the Arian method of worshipping the Great Architect took a major detour during the Babylonia captivity of the Hebrews. By the time of the war preceding that captivity the religion most prominently associated with the Arian ritual was referred to as Judaism. From the days of the second *exodus* the priesthood successfully adapted the ritual to the ever evolving religion that finally absorbed it. During the captivity the original religion had all but vanished and was known only to a dwindling few elders by the time King Cyrus of Persia allowed the captives to return home.

During captivity the manner and method of the priesthood also changed. It changed so dramatically that it bore little or no resemblance to the aging Arian priesthood that had escaped captivity and remained in Jerusalem. When the captives returned to the land of the fathers a violent competition broke out between the priesthood of captivity and the Arian priesthood remaining in Jerusalem. By strength of the sheer superior number of followers, the priests of captivity wrested control of the religion from the Arian priests and began the process of indoctrinating the people in a new brand of Judaism.

It was during the Babylonia captivity that the *Word* was *lost*. Thereafter theological and religious struggles persisted resulting in terrorism, hostility, violence and bloodshed. Sects erupted all over the land laying claim to the *truth* and casting accusing fingers at the so-called pretenders that controlled the religious practices. The resulting tumult and unrest was so vehement that the conquering Roman Emperors struggled with the challenge of how best to control the situation. The raging disputes throughout the land frequently resulted in death and property damage. When that death and damage began to affect the Roman soldiers the decision was made to appoint minor-monarchs or sub-kings to rule over the people as Roman surrogates.

One of the more famous of those surrogates was Herod the Great who followed his father, Antipater, to his throne. Since Antipater was not of the Shepherd King royal bloodline, he appointed Hyrcanus as High Priest – a man known to have descended from a lineage of Egyptian Arian priests. Political intrigue and behind-the-scenes machinations by Hyrcanus eventually led to the marriage between his grand daughter Mariamme and Herod the Great. Thereafter a colorable claim could be made that the *true* priesthood was connected to the Herodian bloodline. Unfortunately Herod the Great proved corrupt and later had his own sons and Mariamme murdered severing the holy ties that might otherwise have prevailed. It is within the scope of these historical events that we find the allegory about John the Baptist.

Precisely who that person was has been the subject of debate among historians – a debate which will not herein be engaged or resolved. Suffice to say that Masonic tradition reports that John – or whatever his name really was - was a descendant of the Arian priesthood; his death presaged the death of Mariamme; and he had a connection to Jesus. However, he did not live during the era of Herod the tetrarch (Agrippa II), as has been suggested in various passages of scripture in the New Testament. He was actually among the troublesome priests with whom Herod the Great had to deal. He was also Mariamme's brother – both having directly descended from the priesthood of the Shepherd Kings.

It was into this political turmoil that Jesus was born. Masonic traditions vary about his origins, but one holds that he was descended from the royal bloodline of the Shepherd Kings and lived in the region known as Gamala. Consequently the familiar biblical stories about shepherds and magi visiting him at his birth are more easily understood. This was no ordinary child; the shepherds were not merely tending flocks of animals; the magi were not simply highly interested in celestial movements; and the symbol of the bright star is meant to convey something much more important than as a mere signal that something important had occurred in a land called Bethlehem. He who has ears must listen!

Herod's murderous assault upon the royal bloodline was well known throughout the land. His evil intentions of wiping out the ancestry in its entirety were central to the concerns in the home of the young Jesus. His parents knew that the Arian priesthood was still active in Heliopolis and spirited the youngster out of the land for his personal protection, spiritual instruction and initiation into the mysteries. Because of his ancestry, he was feted there as the new *Son of God* in the same manner as Akhenaton (Moses), Joseph, Jacob and Abraham before him. This event is alluded to in the Gospel of John which describes Jesus as the true *light* that illuminates every man who comes into the world. His importance to Masonry is equally without parallel.

Educated in Heliopolis he learned the ways of the oldest religions, the movements of the stars and the complexities of the cosmos. Jesus also became proficient in what is known as sand writing – a skill alluded to in veiled allegory set forth in the New Testament. He also became so skillful in building that he proved deserving of the title *cornerstone* – a title reserved for very skilled architects, who were also known as *carpenters*. The title of *architect* was also given to Akhenaton – a word that derives from the Egyptian word *tekh* alluding to the mixing together of bread and wine. The highest of all deities was referred to by the Helipolian priests as the *Architect of the Universe* – a name that is well known among Masons.

The Arian ritual practices were also given to Jesus during his initiation into the mysteries – practices that had been lost as a result of the Babylonian captivity. From those mysteries he learned about the symbolic importance of *raising* a man to the sublime degree of Master Mason. The New Testament seemingly records Jesus' personal participation in that ritual in a veiled allegory about a man named Lazarus. The Gospel of Luke also contains a brief allusion to Jesus' participation in a similar ceremony at the time of his arrest. When he finally returned to Judea he carried with him the secrets of the universe and walked the land as a man of royalty – a fact he kept as quiet as possible; going so far as to deny his station in life when examined extensively by the Pharisaic priesthood before his death.

Masonic tradition also informs us that while at Heliopolis, Jesus learned that the cosmos is constantly in motion. Another age would soon arrive and replace both the *Taurean* and *Arian* influences. That new age is known to us as the Age of *Pisces*. Astrological history records that while this age arrived in approximately 498 A.D., cosmological movements toward that age commenced as early as approximately 222 B.C. Jesus had received advance warning from the Heliopolian priests about the advent of this new age that promised to be as revolutionary as all others. Symbolized by the sign of a fish, that coming age was resisted as fiercely as was the coming of the Age of *Aries* revealing once again the challenges man must encounter when change is inevitable.

Like Akhenaton before him, Jesus returned to his homeland with an enormous responsibility. Not only would he one day have to assert his royal claim to the crown, he also was compelled to prepare the people for a change in the manner and method of worshipping the Great Architect of the Universe. The symbolic *raising* of *Hiram Abif* from the grave serves to remind the discerning Mason that God is in charge; it is His cosmos, not ours, that moves across the heavens; it is His voice to which we must listen; and it is to His command we must obey. Having begun his young life as a *Lamb of God*, or child of *Aries*, Jesus henceforth determined to become a *fisherman* and in so doing enlisted others to also become *fishers of men*.

The word *Nazerene* refers to the Essene sect as well as to a contraction of the Aramaic word *Nasrani*. To us it means *little fishes* that are standing or walking on water. This lesson in cosmology adopted by Masonry also alludes to the heavenly truth that the Age of *Pisces* will one day yield to the Age of *Aquarius*. While some interpret the allegory of Jesus walking on water as evidence of his unusual powers, it is actually intended to reveal that while Jesus walked the earth in the Age of *Pisces*, he stood on the foundations (water) of the Age of *Aquarius*.

Some contend that Jesus was married at an elaborate ceremony in a town called Cana. Indeed the Nag Hammadi collection of literary works appears to confirm that event which is described in both the Gospel of Mary Magdalene and the Gospel of Philip. To the extent that wedding ceremony is important to either Freemasonry or the world at large, if true it serves to illustrate that Jesus behaved as did his forefathers who were of the royal bloodline of the Shepherd Kings. Like his forefathers, Jesus embraced marriage and the production of offspring. Additionally, he held women in such high esteem as to follow the ancient Egyptian tradition of including some in his own priestly inner circle. To the extent celibacy has become a part of certain religions it has nothing to do with Jesus. Neither does it have any place in Masonry.

According to several Masonic writers Jesus' death at the hands of the controlling Romans had little if anything to do with either a concern about public uprisings, or the challenge he allegedly presented to the institutional religion of the time. His death was more about making certain that claimants to legitimate kingship, such as Jesus, were thoroughly eliminated.

For years Rome had become accustomed to installing men of its own selection to control the people of Jerusalem. Those years had not gone by without friction any more than had the years since Rome conquered Egypt. The ancient land of the pharaohs was subdued in approximately 30 BC while Jerusalem was not brought to its knees until approximately

6 AD. While the Heliopolian priests secretly continued their divine labors in Egypt thereby perpetuating the ancient practices of the original Shepherd Kings and Arian priesthood, the Romans did not encounter any open resistance to its right to govern the people and the land. The situation in Jerusalem eventually proved much different.

Among certain religious sects, especially the sect known as the Essenes, legends persisted about a *messiah,* or as the Egyptians called him, *Mes-sah*. The literal translation of the Egyptian word is *son of divine king*. All the kings of Egypt were regarded in some respect as the *Mes-sah*, but the one spoken of in the Essenes' legends was more akin to a spiritual king – one who combined the royal bloodline with the *true* priesthood. It was this person about whom rumors spread throughout Jerusalem gaining the keen attention of the governing Romans when the name of Jesus was mentioned in the conversations. Previous pretenders had arisen throughout the land, but this particular man was different and everyone who had been in his presence had become imminently aware of that difference.

Few of the secret texts survive to the present day describing the details of Jesus' murder. The Holy Bible offers a fascinating story, but the truth about the episode is even more gripping. In its aftermath Masonic ritualistic practices were driven farther underground than ever before and did not publically surface again until the year 1717 when the religious environment throughout the British Isles made safe its reappearance.

The true facts surrounding Jesus' death may be, as follows: together with his brothers and the *fisher men* he had assembled, Jesus embarked upon a plan to regain the throne that belonged to the Shepherd Kings. The plan assumed the possibility of failure once Jesus stepped forth and told the populace who he was and why he was there. Such a failure included the distinct possibility that Jesus would be killed. If that occurred he would *rise again* in the form of his brothers and *fisher men*, conquer the minds, spirits and souls of the people and regain the throne through another royal bloodline descendant.

For various unforeseeable reasons that plan failed in its entirety. Jesus was murdered by the Romans; one of the brothers committed suicide; the *fisher men* scattered; and those who remained loyal to the cause were so weakened that they were eventually overcome by men intent upon using the occasion to consolidate Roman power.

Chapter 24

ADVANCING ANCIENT FREEMASONRY

It is a mistake to conclude that the practice of ritual Freemasonry was limited to the Chaldean Shepherd Kings, Abraham, the *Hyksos* pharaohs, Akhenaton and Jesus. While those events were unfolding in the Holy Land, the Masonic ritual, symbolism and philosophy was breathing life into other corners of the world. The migration was the result of the number of initiates throughout the land who took with them the best of their respective Enochian Temple educations as they traveled the world. Perhaps no figure looms larger on that stage than Pythagoras another prominent patron of Freemasonry who transported of the mysteries of China to India and later taught the lessons derived from those mysteries at various philosophical schools throughout much of ancient Greece.

Pythagoras was born on the Greek Isle of Samos where the tyrannical government eventually prompted him to travel to China and India, as well as into the heart of the ancient Egyptian priesthood. In each of those environments he closely associated himself with the recognized holy men and carefully studied everything each imparted about God and the universe. Pythagoras was no ordinary man and his deep sense of piety and reverence for holy matters was immediately noticed by other mystery schools. Soon he received many invitations to be initiated into the deeper *mysteries* which he quickly accepted.

While in China he was schooled in the philosophical lessons that eventually comprised the *I Ching*. That philosophy instructed men about nature, the laws of the universe and the various forms that *equilibrium* assumed. It was later transformed by Confucius into the practical lessons about life that continue to enjoy a unique place of prominence in Chinese civilization.

Pythagoras next traveled into Egypt and absorbed the lessons taught there by the High Priests. Again he was invited into the *mysteries* which he found to be very similar to the Chinese *mysteries,* but with certain exceptional distinctions. The Egyptians proved more inclined to adopt the notion that the Divine spirit was separate from the creation, including mankind. On the other hand the Chinese seemed to see the hand of the Great Architect everywhere they looked.

It would be an enormous error to conclude that Pythagoras later became nothing more than the sum total of his education and initiations. In reality he was much more and went on to display talents for mathematics, astrology, astronomy and cosmology. Perhaps his greatest passion was for music which he translated into mathematical equations. Those equations later became the foundation for proving the manner in which the planets and stars moved. It was those very same equations separately arrived at by others that provided the basis for the cosmological studies of the Chaldean Shepherds from whom Abraham drew his understandings about the *One True God.*

In addition to the philosophy Pythagoras passed on, he also embraced a theology that Abraham discovered and wholeheartedly embraced. That theology was premised upon a certain numerology that was founded upon the belief that the essence of being is number. The one and only creative force was identified by the number "one." It is from this Pythagorean numerology, as well as from Pythagoras' own instructions about the significance of the cosmos that the Chaldean Shepherds adopted the theological concept of the *One True God.*

Further study by each reader into the Mithraic mysteries and the histories of France, England and Scotland will shed more light upon Masonry's progression. However unless one becomes immersed in the Masonic ritual and understands its history and substance he will never know either the Craft's true origins, or its *secrets.* As Holy Scripture states: *ask and it shall be given you; seek and ye shall find; knock and it shall be opened unto you.* One needs only to ask to be made a Mason and once he is he may begin to learn the remainder of what cannot be written.

Part 2
Masonic Philosophy

INTRODUCTION

During his journey along life's path illuminated by the shining light of Masonic Symbolism, a Mason is informed by his elders that he is symbolically traveling from west to east in search of that which has been lost. Exactly what it is that has been lost has long been the subject of diligent research by Masonic scholars, who seek to identify Masonry's origin, the true genesis of its philosophy and the truth or falsity about certain legends that have recently gained popularity.

The spiritual truths Masonry teaches have been written about, examined and digested by philosophers, mages, clerics and men of science who have been schooled in the traditions of both western and eastern culture. By telling the candidate for Masonic degrees that he is traveling from west to east, Freemasonry incorporates the spiritual doctrines and dogmas derived from those traditions. Each one contains both truth and error requiring a careful study of how one tradition relates to another and how synthesizing the several disparate spiritual concepts can eventually result in separating truth from error. The manner in which that study may best be pursued includes personal meditation upon the various wise and serious spiritual truths imparted by Masonic Symbolism.

Masons should be particularly careful not to adopt anything as a spiritual truth unless confirmed by personal meditation, prayer and study. Understanding what is true and that which is false rarely occurs.

While the reasons are many, each is grounded in the blind acceptance of doctrine.

People frequently embrace specific religions and philosophies simply because they have also been embraced by their parents, spouses, friends and family. Such blind adherence to doctrine has littered the historical landscape with war and brutal violence. When it comes to matters pertaining to God and the human soul, people are not as naturally tolerant and loving of one another as one might expect. Tolerance is a learned behavior and begins with gaining an understanding about what the word really means.

Part 2 of this book continues a Masonic exploration of the many virtues and moral behaviors that when put into practice define a person as a Mason. Those morals and virtues are drawn from the many traditions of western and eastern cultures that have so richly contributed to the Craft's symbolism. From Egypt, India, Persia, the Orient, Greece, Rome, as well as all other points east and west, man's encounters with God have been memorialized in rituals, liturgies, works of art and sacred writings. Masonry has drawn from the masters of all ages and sought to instill an understanding in its members that each man, woman and child is embedded with a part of God – a divine spark - that we are supposed to eventually understand, love and strengthen.

Societies have historically thrived during times of heightened fraternalism. Within our own nation clubs and organizations have emerged over the course of our history to become bulwarks of charity and social responsibility. Membership in those fraternal groups has, at times exceeded all reasonable expectations; while at other times it has sunk to depths that have left even the most optimistic in a state of confusion and bewilderment about fraternalism's relevance. But during periods of significant social advancement, membership in Masonry was also significantly higher than at other times. Although the precise reasons why this is so are currently the subject of ongoing research around the world, the inescapable fact is that society's advancement is strangely linked to Freemasonry.

Chapter 25

A Man Plucked Off His Shoe

*"Now this was the manner in former times in Israel
concerning redeeming and concerning changing
for to confirm all things; a man plucked off
his and gave it to his neighbor..."*

Ruth 4:7

During the ceremonies of the Entered Apprentice Degree, the candidate is instructed about the above-referenced passage of scripture, which is meant to indicate both the confirming of a contract, as well as the commitment to fully perform the terms and conditions of that contract. In Freemasonry, this symbolism is intended to convey the sanctity of the contract made between the candidate and the Masonic institution when he assumes his vows. For the Israelite of Ruth's era there was nothing more essential than shoes, or sandals without which men and women were compelled to walk across hot sands, dirt and rock. Consequently, giving a shoe to another person not only conveyed the importance of the commitment, but a sense that the person to whom the shoe was given was as important as the person giving it.

This symbolism is repeated throughout Masonry by way of different lessons, because it is the purpose of the Craft to ensure that each Mason appreciates the importance of his vows and promises. Entire charitable institutions rely upon the keeping of such commitments. Hospitals operated by Shriners would vanish if Masons suddenly decided it was unimportant to care for the helpless. Homes for the aged would no longer receive funding if groups of Masons turned their backs on the needs of others. Members of individual Masonic lodges would never experience random acts of kindness by their brethren if Masons concluded that self interest was more important than assisting others. It is the agreement, or covenant made by each Mason that guarantees that the world will experience the fruits of Masonic labor. Yet, as with other Masonic symbolism, there are also other esoteric lessons to be learned from the scripture found in the book of Ruth.

"Plucking off one's shoe and giving it to another" also symbolizes *redeeming* and *changing* and is equally important to Masons. For those who regularly attend religious services and observe as the collection plate is passed, it is intriguing to note how often people toss in some change, a dollar or two, or perhaps nothing at all. To some simply having attended the service is sufficient enough, for it represents the sacrifice of time, if nothing more. Similarly, the Mason who works for a living has quite likely observed fellow employees voice support for the needy during holiday times, but how often does he observe real acts of charity – the giving of time, food, shelter and compassion? It is within this realm that *redeeming* and *changing* apply.

Theologians frequently remind their audiences about man's original fall from God's grace, commonly referred to within those circles as "original sin." The villain here is *temptation,* about which much has previously been written. Temptation represents the transition from obedience to disobedience. The man who has given in to the temptations that have invaded his life is truly in need of *redeeming* and *changing* to recapture his original obedient nature. The Holy Writings offer us the allegory of Adam and Eve in the Garden of Eden to convey to us the importance attached to all men making an effort to subdue the passions and to keep them within due bounds toward all mankind.

In the book of Genesis, Eve listened to the voice of the serpent, saw that the tree of knowledge was good for food and took and ate what she desired in complete contravention to God's command. There is no greater symbolism of disobedience recorded anywhere in our Holy Writings, or elsewhere in any other traditional story. The voice of the serpent represents the living being whose intelligence is most advanced and whose consciousness is turned toward the horizontal, or material plane rather than the vertical, or spiritual plane. The intelligence of both Adam and Eve before the *Fall* was entirely vertical. Their eyes had not been opened to their own "nakedness" and they were conscious of everything vertical, or of God. After the *Fall,* their understanding about their condition changed radically. Suddenly aware of their nakedness, fig leaves were adjusted to cover the most private of human body parts and their entire consciousness was consumed with things related to the material plane.

Here, the serpent symbolizes the principle of power apart from God. The remainder of the histories and stories set forth in the Holy Writings relate to man's journey back to the living God. Temples are erected in His name; prophets admonish generations to obey His laws; wars are waged in His cause; men suffer in obedience to His word; and, man searches for a *messiah* to deliver salvation. Along the way, man also discovers that the true principle of obedience is devotion without reserve to the sole voice from above. It is precisely at this juncture that Freemasonry generally steps aside to allow Masons and their families to seek their own route to salvation, for be it ever known to all men at all times and in every place that Freemasonry is not a religion.

Those who follow the Jewish faith find the way to *redeeming* and *changing* through the law of Moses, including the Ten Commandments. Buddhists travel the road of inner serenity, as do the Hindus, each seeking the peace within themselves that illuminates the soul. Christians resolve to accept the divinity of Jesus Christ. Moslems attempt to align themselves to the teachings of Mohammed and his descendants to ensure a proper place in the world of obedience to God. But what of the Mason who has not selected a formal religion to follow? If he does not adhere to a particular dogma, is his journey from the *Fall* back to obedience destined to fail? Freemasonry tells such a man that he will not fail, if he devotes himself without reserve to the sole voice from above – the voice of the Supreme Architect of the Universe.

All human existence is about choices – the choice to live in the *light,* as well as the choice to live in *darkness.* Mankind is offered a plethora of religious doctrine from which to choose and is surrounded by the philosophies developed by the greatest minds that ever lived. History, literature and science also weigh in lay before each and every person a literal banquet of choices. He who has chosen well has selected the path that leads him directly back to obedience. Man is both *redeemed,* or reclaimed by the Creator, and *changed* when he resolves to ask God to reveal His will; seeks to understand how to apply that will to his own life; and, knocks at the door of the Great Architect with faith that the door will be opened. One never opens the door by force. One waits for it to be opened by God's will.

It is relatively easy to discern the obedient person. He avoids anger and replaces it with kind words to his fellow man. He acknowledges his own faults, apologizes for his slights to others and resolves to do better next time. He freely gives of his precious time to serve, comfort and compassionate others. He visits the widows, orphans and elderly. He avoids disputes and builds harmony. He understands different points of view and keeps self-pride well under control. And, he regularly kneels in humble praise and supplication to the Almighty Father of the Universe – the one living God. Simply stated, he is a Freemason.

Chapter 26

A Man, Freeborn...

> "...Cast out this bondwoman and her son; for the son of this bondwoman shall not be heir with my son..."
>
> Gen. 21:10

It is said that neither a slave, nor one born in slavery can be admitted into the rites and privileges of Freemasonry. That is so in the first instance, because no one legally bound to another can voluntarily assume the covenants of the Craft. In the case of the second instance, it must be assumed that any person born in a servile state, even though he may afterwards become free, inherits a degradation of mind and enthrallment of spirit which disqualify him from performing the duties of a Mason with "freedom, fervency and zeal." Thus, every candidate for Masonic degrees is first introduced to the lodge as a freeborn man.

As true as the foregoing may be, it does not go far enough in interpreting what Freemasonry intends being freeborn to symbolize. It is equally important to also understand how this relates to Masonry's attitude toward despotism and mankind's ceaseless pursuit of freedom. Within the teachings of the Craft we learn that life is a law of Nature and that he who imposes his own selfish desires upon another man's natural born spirit of freedom is a criminal against the laws of Nature.

To succumb to the infiltrations of the immense "me" of the despot is tantamount to sacrificing freedom on the altar of materialism. If a man does not resist those infiltrations, he is doomed to be absorbed by them making the world less free than it was before.

Against what threats to freedom does a Mason stand? And, how does a Mason manifest his resistance to such threats? War and rebellion are far from the thoughts of a true Freemason. Peace, harmony and good will toward all mankind are his motto. He is obliged by his vows to pay due obedience to the laws under which he lives.

When the United States of America was on the brink of civil war in the late 1850's, Grand Masters from many states spoke about the need for all man to take a deep breath and find a way to avoid bloodshed. Not one openly promoted the commencement of hostilities – whether his constituents resided in the North, or in the South. Yet, once war began, Masons on both side of the great divide fought and died in battle after battle.

Masons are united in eternal hostility to tyranny and despotic power. Those evils are not solely found among history's legendary tyrants, such as Hitler, Stalin and the beasts of today who slaughter their own kinsmen for the purpose of consolidating and perpetuating political power. Rather, they are found everywhere men act to reduce the life of the many for the profit of one. Tyranny and despotism has been found to reside in churches, as well as in castles. Wherever life is extinguished, compressed, stifled, corrupted, or diminished to suit the will of one over many tyranny and despotism reign. It is these that weaken the soul of humanity and shackle the will of every free person. It is these that Freemasonry abhors and resists. That resistance is personified by the inculcation of universal benevolence, tolerance and love of all mankind.

Where darkness reigns in the heart of men that is where the light of Masonry must shine brightest. We are reminded of the parable in our Holy Writings which teaches us that a shining lamp must not be placed where it cannot be seen. The unwarranted taking of human life is not mitigated by taking lives either in revenge, or in a misguided effort that it is so necessary to defeat our enemies. Masonry does not teach "an eye for an eye," but love in place of hatred; peace instead of war; and tolerance as opposed to domination. It is that lamp which must be kept in the open for all to see.

Yet, in a peaceful manner Masons have for centuries vowed to resist arbitrary power and rule. That is not a call to war any more that Mahatma Gandhi called his people to war against the colonialists in India. Rather, it is a vow to use the means available to peaceably effect change; to personally remain the absolute master of one's voice, vote and opinion; and never to allow another to dictate in matters of conscience.

Perhaps the greatest threat against man's freedom comes not from monarchs, dictators, or evil minded rulers, but from the generally well-intended people who permit themselves the unseemly luxury of besmirching another person's good name. In legal circles, such conduct is called libel or slander. Around the water cooler of many workplaces it is simply called gossip. On prime time television, it is often referred to as good journalism.

An idle tongue wags caring not that the story about the man in the corner is only half true. Suddenly another human being is imprisoned by the disapproval of many and may not easily free himself even if he successfully proves the story false. Too many will say, "Where there is smoke, there is fire," and the damage will therefore be irremediable. However, a Mason assumes vows obligating him to protect a brother Mason's good name – a vow that is much more meaningful in this age of instant communication than ever before. A breach of fidelity here could leave a mark on another brother that may never be erased. It matters not that the breach actually involves a truthful statement about another brother's failings or flaws. That is not the test in Masonry, for those in the Craft know that there is more than enough misery to be spread amongst all of God's people. A breach of the vow occurs wherever there might be a chance that another brother, his family or friends will be held in low regard on account of something said by another brother. The reason is simple: such a breach involves the potential compromise of another brother's freedom.

Thus, to be *free born* means something more than being born free, or never having worn the chains of slavery. All men are by Nature intended to be free and it is this truth to which the phrase *free born* pertains. Men have made slaves of other men, but God has never done so. Men have created prisons to house offenders – not so with God. If it is true that man is placed here on earth to learn that which God desires of him, then man must also learn how to keep all men free. We do not speak here of opening the doors for dangerous criminals to roam and victimize society. But, we do admonish society to set aside its frustration and work ceaselessly to understand why man offends others unlawfully and how best to peaceably effect a change in behavior. Such will not occur instantaneously, or even in a generation. The stain of poverty, violence and fear is difficult, indeed, to remove and may require several lifetimes of several generations. But, regardless of the difficulty, this must be a fundamental objective of every Mason — to labor against all that threatens to enslave mankind.

Chapter 27
A Passage Of Scripture

*"And I tell you, ask and you will receive,
seek and you will find, knock and the
door will be opened unto you."*

Luke 11:9

During the ritual of the Entered Apprentice Degree, the candidate's attention is directed to the above-referenced passage of scripture, which he is told is applicable to his personal situation at the time of his initiation. A man must ask to be made a Mason; he will never receive a specific invitation to become a member. Before entering a Masonic lodge, the candidate is required to knock at the entrance. Once appropriate identifying words are exchanged, the candidate is allowed to enter and commence his pursuit of the beauties of Freemasonry.

Although Masonry does not teach what a Mason ought to believe concerning God, man and nature, it does teach him how to ask, seek and knock in order to arrive at that which one seeks to know about God, man and nature. It is after one has received, found and gained access to what was to him previously unknown that he *knows*. The aptitude for "knowing how to know" is a trait essential for every Mason, without which the pursuit of truth may lead down an endless chain of blind alleys.

That aptitude is characterized by certain spiritual exercises which should be consistently practiced if one is to ever succeed in knowing about God, man and nature. Common spiritual exercises form the link which unites Freemasons. It is not common knowledge common which unites them, but the similarity in each Mason's experiences during his pursuit of God, man and nature. If three people from different countries were to meet each other, having made the book of Genesis, the Gospel of St. John, and the vision of Ezekiel the subject of spiritual exercises for many years, they would do so in brotherhood, although the one would know the history of humanity, the other would have the science of healing and the third would make a profound Kabbalist.

That which one knows is the result of personal experience and orientation, while depth, or consciousness is what one brother Mason holds in common with another brother Mason. The aim of spiritual exercise is depth; to plunge into the most profound aspects of the Holy Writings, to breathe their air, to participate as an eye-witness and to admire the beauty of the layers of thought. The Essenes participated in spiritual exercises that explored both the exoteric and the esoteric interpretations of ancient scripture. In so doing, they plumbed the depths of the Zohar making such use of it that the words came alive; symbolism became reality; and, that which had been previously hidden from mankind's view was made visible to all who observed the conduct of the practitioners.

The questions posed are what should we ask? How should we seek? Where shall we knock? The most important response is to identify our ideal; our purpose. It has been posited that all reality is merely that which has been subjectively created by our minds. Yet, there is something terribly disorienting about the idea that all our experience is subjective. If all we experience is simply a reflection of ourselves, then what do we have to hold on to? If expectations are merely self-fulfilling prophesies, if reality is our own creation, then are we not caught in a vicious circle of our own selves? Before we begin answering the question what should we ask, we must decide what we want.

The Holy Writings instruct us that if we wish peace to prevail, we must act peaceably. If we desire love in the world, we must love our neighbor. If we demand that the needs of the people must be met, we must be generous in our own dealings with our fellow man. The lessons we are this taught reveal that how we think about God, man and nature dictates whether or not mankind will be benefited, or despised. Do you wish to ask for yourself, or for your brother? Do you desire to feed your passions, or to serve mankind? One request is answered by God; the other is left unanswered. Can you discern why that happens?

Several writers of the ever popular self-improvement books tell us that we only need visualize that which we truly want and it will come to us. Highly competitive professional athletes hire psychiatrists and psychologists to help them properly focus upon their goals. Jesus is reputed to have taught that it is useless to look without for the kingdom of heaven, for it is found within each person. The Holy Writings relate stories about people who could move mountains because of the faith they exercised. Everywhere one looks today, the concept of "mind-over-matter" thrives.

The spiritual exercises Masons are taught are fundamentally structured to achieve one objective: the brotherhood of man. Homes for the poor and desperate are a reality because over the years, men committed to the welfare of others visualized such a charity, raised money to support it and hired capable men to build the facilities. Educational endowments that are now so common place in the fraternity began as an idea; a thought that some one person, or several people had together. Speech therapy centers, eye foundations and hospitals for crippled children that now abound throughout the world all began with an idea that led to action which resulted in the providing of valuable services to other less fortunate people. The foundation for such thought was the overwhelming sense of brotherly love and affection by one human being for another.

When we *ask,* do we ask properly? If that which gently courses through the mind is the thought of how best to serve our fellow man, the spiritual exercise has been successful and we can correctly expect to receive. When we *seek,* of what are we in search? A mind that concentrates on God and His *agape love* desires nothing greater than to know it's Creator and thus to imitate Him. When we *knock,* to what place are we seeking admission? Entry into a world of practical sense enables us to prudently put into action that which the mind has conceived, which clarifies more completely the Masonic phrase, "…wisdom to contrive."

A Freemason's engagement in Masonic spiritual exercises is also aided by his sense of synthesis; the sense of orientation and acquisition of knowledge of essential facts in every domain. While the metaphysical sense operates within a realm referred to as the "concept of God," the Freemason's sense is oriented toward the "living God" – the spiritual, concrete fact of God. Our Creator is not an abstract concept; it is not a notion, but rather a true sense of *being*. We do not ask of a concept; we ask of a living God. We do not seek a notion; we pursue a living Creator. And, we do not knock at the door of an abstract thought; we seek entry to a place where real wisdom may be attained.

It is a horrible tragedy for a soul to seek always and everywhere that which is concrete. Man was intended not to devote himself to absolutes, because he is not God. Rather, man is intended to absorb all there is to absorb and then to ask God to assist us all in pursuing the many paths of truth that He has prepared for us.

Chapter 28

ADMONISHING A BROTHER

*"Yet count him not as an enemy, but
admonish him as a brother."*

2 Thess. 3:15

One of the most distinctive duties or ethical obligations of a Mason is to whisper good counsel in another brother's ear. A Freemason is particularly charged to tell an erring brother about the consequences of that which he is doing, as well as to seek a reformation in his brother's conduct. As such, this lesson teaches us how we are to handle situations when one brother Mason has done something wrong, or has evidenced an intention to do so.

Admonitions from one brother Mason to another are never to be given with self-sufficient pride, or in derogatory and imperious tones. The language of brotherly love does not include derisive phrases, or accusatory lectures. Rather, brotherly love demands that we express genuine concern for the welfare of the brother with whom we are speaking. The occasions that require admonishment are not also occasions for demonstrating how worthy you are and how unworthy is your brother.

Neither does brotherly love entail the mere putting together of words intended to impart one brother's displeasure with another brother. That is not enough to dispatch the Masonic and ethical obligation to whisper good counsel and endeavor to bring about a reformation. The Masonic obligation requires the brother delivering the admonishment to be persuasive with an attitude of mercy unrestrained.

Yet, when taken by some to its logical conclusion, this obligation may seem to require overlooking one brother's offenses, or even becoming complicit in the commission of another brother's crimes. Such is not the case and never has been a part of Masonic ethics. It has never been the duty of a Mason to break the law, or violate his trust with all Masons around the globe withersoever they are dispersed. To the contrary, every Mason is taught to be law-abiding, to conform to the rules of the Craft and to live by the laws of the land in which he resides.

In some instances a Masonic admonition must, or should be followed by some public exposure of the offense so that justice may occur. The matter of who should make that disclosure has been a subject of great debate. Here, several Masonic virtues converge and must be wisely assimilated to arrive at a Masonic course of action. They include maintaining the secrets of a brother; abiding by the laws of the fraternity; abiding by the laws of the nation; and adhering to the precepts of justice. The possibility for confusion is enormous and the consequences for failing to understand exactly what is required of you as a Mason could prove catastrophic.

It is initially important to understand that while one of the three principal tenets of Freemasonry is brotherly love, the fraternity is not a rehabilitation center for those who commit crimes. Recall that the other two of the three principal tenets include not only brotherly love, but also relief and *truth*. The four cardinal virtues include temperance, fortitude, prudence and *justice*. Truth and justice have nothing in common with deceit and concealment.

If one brother Mason becomes aware that another brother Mason has committed a crime, what is his obligation? It is not to ignore that brother, but neither is it to condone, support, or conceal that fact from the Masonic lodge of which he is a member. Masons do not assist a brother to escape *justice*, or to avoid telling the *truth*. The first obligation, then, is to whisper good counsel into the offending brother's ear that he should make a clear confession of his deeds to his Masonic brethren. The second is to convince him that the Masonic course he has chosen to guide his life demands that he be prepared to accept just punishment and to work toward a reformation of bad behavior.

In their enthusiasm to abide by the duty to help a fallen brother, some Masons have interpreted that obligation as endorsing the concealment of offenses from all others, including the lodge to which they belong. While the purpose of doing so may be to help the fallen brother to avoid embarrassment and humiliation, such avoidance does not constitute *truth* and *justice*. Indeed, there are no circumstances whereby one brother Mason is to countenance the outright breach of Masonic obligations. That is not whispering good counsel and it certainly is not helping a fallen brother to recapture the virtues he chose when he selected Freemasonry as the path for his life's journey.

Yet, it must also be considered that Freemasonry does not either ask Masons to inform upon other Masons, or to become spies for the Craft. Both are an abuse of the tenets of Freemasonry and can lead to confusion, discord and anger among the brethren. Consequently, it is essential to exercise prudence and wisdom to insure the continuance of brotherly love and affection. When information about one brother's misbehavior first comes to your attention, if you know that brother well, you must confront him in a friendly manner, listen to what he says to you by way of explanation and then, if the misconduct so requires, ask him to join you in telling one or more of the trusted elected officers of your Masonic lodge about what has transpired. If he refuses, it remains your duty to pass along the information to the lodge leadership.

The duty to admonish a fallen brother has several important purposes. In addition to seeking a reformation in the personal conduct of the offending brother, the performance of that duty also seeks to protect the integrity of Freemasonry. The mosaic pavement teaches us that human life is checkered with good and evil. That is so for Masons, as well as for the rest of humanity. We cannot expect men to be better than they are – they will fail, succeed, behave well, and act poorly – that is human nature. Masonry's primary reason for existing is to provide the working tools necessary for enhancing man's chances for succeeding and behaving well.

The success Masonry seeks to enhance is spiritual not material success. Since spiritual success demands that a person look within himself to know who and what he is, the act of admonishing a fallen brother is one of the most loving acts any brother can perform. The paths to spiritual enlightenment are richly illumined by right knowledge, right aspiration, right speech, right behavior, right livelihood, right effort right mindfulness and right absorption. When we err in any one of those endeavors, we have the right to count on a true and trustworthy fellow Mason to come to our aid. When we do not see, understand, or even believe the error of our ways, we can count on another brother Mason to whisper good counsel in our ear that we may right ourselves and continue along our paths, straight and true.

The message of the duty to admonish a fallen brother is simply this: you are important; you count, not only as a human being, but also as a spirit and soul that in time will be reunited with God. One man, even though he has received all of the degrees of Freemasonry, is no match for the evil that permeates the material world. But, he is secure in the knowledge that he is not alone. Should he fail, or falter in his journey, His God and another brother Mason will be there to whisper good counsel; to reinforce the tenets of brotherly love, relief and truth; and to remind us that without justice, man is no higher than the animals God created him to govern.

Chapter 29

CIRCUMSPECTION

"See then that ye walk circumspectly, not
as fools, but as wise,..."

Eph. 5:15

Every ethical and religious organization requires the spirit and practice of *watchfulness,* but with a Mason it becomes a positive duty, and the neglect becomes a heinous crime. No member of the Craft who has passed through the Entered Apprentice Degree can ever forget the warning not to let carelessly fall from his lips any of the hidden mysteries of Freemasonry. Considered from a very human perspective, the admonition to be *watchful,* or *circumspect* includes the admonition to guard against negative thinking.

Freemasonry encourages every Mason to exercise his natural-born spirit of free will to love his fellow man. As Masons, vows are exchanged in this regard and each brother understands that he is bound to every other brother by ties that are never to be dissolved. But, the duty to give of one's love is not limited to the giving of the same only to other Masons. Once initiated into the Craft, a Mason has a life-long duty to love his neighbor as he does himself.

It has been stated that a person's self-worth cannot be verified by others. One must first learn to love himself, or herself before one can effectively love one's neighbor. Our world is filled with people who sadly are infected with a horrible social disease — low self esteem. Perhaps you are like many of those people and have grown up believing that the idea of loving yourself is wrong.

From an early age, many of our churches teach young children that they are sinners and have fallen short of the grace of God. Others are vilified by so-called loving parents who call them "bad," and thus grow into adulthood believing that to be so. Many try to succeed and fail, but refuse to try again never knowing that failure is as natural for the growth of the spirit as is success. With obstacles such as these, there is little wonder why too many never achieve present-moment happiness in their lives.

Giving love to others is directly related to how much love you have for yourself. Since your own happiness cannot ever be wholly dependent upon anyone other than yourself, it is important that you become secure in yourself. Masonry teaches men how to achieve that level of security. Men who once feared standing before a gathering of people to deliver a talk discover how much easier it is to do so in the company of the brethren assembled. Those who too frequently discovered that their talents were not valued by others quickly learn how much those talents are needed by the Craft. In Freemasonry, there is enough work to go around, as well as enough encouragement to continue to apply yourself to become better at what you do and more loving of others. The central lesson learned that is essential to enabling a man to adequately love his neighbor is that a Mason is permitted to choose to be himself and never worry about satisfying others about his worth.

The origin of those loathsome feelings associated with low self-esteem is not difficult to identify. They are the natural consequence of negative thinking. Wondering if you are well liked; worrying that others will not approve what you wear or how you comb your hair; and dithering with anxiety, because you do not believe you have become what others expect you to become are all examples of negative thinking. Before you can love yourself, and then your neighbor as you do yourself, you must *circumscribe* those negative thoughts. If one pays attention to the lessons offered by Freemasonry, one will learn how to do so.

Masonic ritual inculcates the knowledge that at no time and under no circumstance is self-hate healthier than self-love. As Masons we are taught that God embraces all of the children of His creation and disinherits none. Even when you behave in a manner that you despise, apply positive thinking to your condition and learn from your mistake. Resolve not to repeat the same error and try your best. But, never tie your mistakes to your own self-worth. The Mason who is less than letter-perfect in his ritual is no less valuable to the Craft than the Mason who infrequently errs.

Freemasonry also teaches its members the importance of recognizing that you have choices in life. The Craft ritual instructs about *light* and *darkness, truth* and *falsehood,* and *honor* and *shame*. It is never the case that a man lives his life in the *light,* guided by *truth* and *honor* unless he chooses that path. When we understand that free will includes the concept of having a buffet of choices in life, we also understand that we do not need to drift along with the current that threatens to throw us over the cliff. As Masons, we are taught not to ever let that happen.

By exercising the power of positive thinking and remaining resolute and *circumspect* in that endeavor, we can alter self-destructive behavior. An insight obtained during a Masonic lesson must be practiced repeatedly until it becomes habit. Only when we make a positive application of the lesson learned will we effectively change our own behavior. In so doing, we also discover that we have taken command of our present moments – that time and space we are allotted within which to be either happy, or unhappy.

Choice and present moment living are fundamental to our loving ourselves in the most efficacious manner. Although Masons must never forget their duties and responsibilities to the widows, orphans and needy, they must also not forget that those duties and responsibilities will be dispatched more Masonically, if the Mason performing them is loving and caring in all aspects of his life. The responsibility for what you are and what you will become is yours. The great work of Freemasonry begins with the greater work on yourself, which can only be accomplished when negative thinking is replaced by positive thinking.

Once you have embarked upon your Masonic path of *circumspection* test yourself periodically by asking some or all of the following questions. Do I really believe that my mind is my own? Am I capable of controlling my own feelings? Am I motivated from within rather than from outside influences? Do I need the approval of others to become a true and good Mason? Do I accept myself for what I am? Am I a doer, or a critic? Can I love myself at all times? Am I free from guilt? Do I freely welcome the mysterious and unknown? Are there other equally valuable lessons in Freemasonry that I should learn? When you can truthfully answer "yes" to each question, you may be assured that you are on the correct path toward *circumspection*.

Chapter 30
CLEFTS OF THE ROCKS

> "And they shall go into the holes of the rocks, and
> into the caves of the earth, for the fear of the
> Lord, and for the glory of his majesty, when
> He ariseth to shake terribly the earth."
>
> Is. 2:19

All of Palestine is made up of mountains that abound in caves, caverns and deep clefts, which anciently were used as places of refuge or as dens for robbers. Every Master Mason will also recognize the *clefts of the rocks* as the location where three ruffians are said to have concealed themselves after completing a murder that symbolically shook the foundation of Masonry. In the accompanying allegory, we learn that those in search of the assassins, upon hearing their anguished voices, charged into the craggy crevices to capture them and bring them to justice before King Solomon. Those clefts have a more profound meaning to Masonry than merely having served as the hiding place for the three miscreants.

The symbolism of the ruffians is intended to bring each one of us face-to-face with three well-recognized threats to individual welfare and social progress: kingcraft, priestcraft and the ignorant mob-mind. The evil threatened by each is discussed more thoroughly in *Meditations on Masonic Symbolism*. Here, it is the manner in which those ruffians concealed themselves that offers additional philosophical insight into other pitfalls and dangers not as easily discernable.

From time immemorial, Masons have attempted to interpret the true meanings associated with each of the tools and implements of architecture it has employed to represent and communicate wise and serious truths. Pythagoras provided us with his extraordinary insight into the esoteric meanings, while Pike endeavored to memorialize those meanings in a few volumes of literary genius. Yet, as we probe deeper into the efforts of our Masonic ancestors to offer clarity, we learn that symbols were continually added to the body of work making accurate interpretations ever more difficult to achieve.

In time, well-meaning men attempted to reduce the meaning of Masonic symbolism to comprehensible levels and in the process accomplished the trivialization of much that may have become forever lost. For example, presenting a symbol to the eye of another without also offering some framework within which to understand its meaning makes it susceptible to imprecise interpretation. While that state of affairs is not unique to certain schools of philosophy (the dialogues of Plato are one very good example), there was an original purpose for each of our Masonic symbols that has become concealed in contradiction and incongruity.

The true relationship of the *clefts of the rocks* to the evils represented by the ruffians may forever be hidden from our view. However, there is no mistaking the fact that at a minimum the symbolism serves to caution Masons against adopting any particular dogma or doctrine without first making a critical inquiry. Pythagoras taught that religion should always be pursued in tandem with philosophy, because God resided in the minds and souls of men as much as he resided in the churches where priests crafted theological doctrines. Simply stated, the Pythagorean School spoke against accepting any religion, dogma or doctrine without first having subjected it to critical thinking.

That is not to say that Pythagoras specifically endorsed the pursuit of any particular doctrine over any other. He did not; but he did endorse mankind's pursuit of God – in Nature, in mathematics and in philosophy. When we reflect upon the *clefts of the rocks* as the hiding place for the three evils represented by the ruffians, we are reminded to search those hiding places within our own minds where bias, prejudice and hate lay in wait to snatch us from the embrace of virtue. Bringing God into the equation by loving prayer casts a bright light upon those darkened crevices and enables us to more clearly see which ruffian we must pursue, capture and forever banish from our thinking.

The Masonic experience consists of a never-ending personal quest for further enlightenment. Obstacles are frequently encountered, but none are greater than those that take secret refuge in our minds. When we pass beyond the habit of learning and drift toward the hardened belief that we have finally acquired all of the answers to our questions about the meaning of life, barriers to our further enlightenment are erected. Masonry teaches us to knock down those barriers, to assume a more humble spirit and recognize that mankind has yet to learn the true pronunciation of the ineffable name of Deity. Our Christian brethren may correctly ponder why it is that Jesus did not lay out specific plans about which school of thought, which method of worship and which religion best served God's plan for humanity. It is insufficient in that regard to strain at scripture for a subtle interpretation about whose church is embraced by God. If there was such a church, it would have been explained very clearly. That such a clear explanation has never been discovered likely conveys the truth that no one thought, school of thought, doctrine, dogma, or religion is preferred over any other.

Originally, the symbols of Masonry served as tools for *masters* who employed a Socratic method of teaching. Those *masters* built spirits, souls and minds rather than stately edifices. They were referred to as geniuses of the speculative schools – practical philosophers who taught men how to critically examine propositions for the purpose of discovering that often times there is no correct answer, only more questions. Masonry seeks to challenge men to return to that manner of thinking, because the symbols used by the Craft should be studied without any expectation of eventually discovering a single answer.

As an example of that manner of thinking, Plato wrote in his discourses about *piety*. His selected style of writing featured two men talking with each other, challenging the conclusions arrived at by each. When it came to *piety,* the two speakers discovered that while each thought he knew the answer, neither could provide a concrete definition. Its true definition simply remained in the mind of the beholder, similar to the manner in which the definition of beauty remains in the eye of the beholder.

What ruffians are hiding in the *clefts of the rocks* in your minds? Do you believe you know more about life than your neighbor? Do you believe that your philosophy, religion, or political preference is more correct than that of your neighbor? If so, what do you intend to do about the false pride clinging to its hiding place within you? How will you dispatch the arrogance that causes you to think that you are better than anyone else? Our Masonic allegories taught us how King Solomon handled such ruffians. What lesson in that regard did you learn from him? How will you use that information?

Chapter 31

CLOUDED CANOPY

> "Then shall the King say unto them on his right hand,
> Come, ye blessed of my Father, inherit the kingdom
> prepared for you from the foundation of the world."
>
> Matt. 25:34

In the first degree of Freemasonry, the Entered Apprentice is instructed on the "covering" of a Masonic lodge and provided with an interpretation of its symbolism. That interpretation is not meant to be definitive. Rather, it is hoped that it will inspire each individual Mason to investigate further and possibly discover other interpretations that he may prove to be equally vital.

Masonic tradition holds that every Masonic lodge is symbolically "covered" by the *clouded canopy, or star-decked heavens*. To illustrate that point, many lodges have colorful artwork painted onto the ceilings depicting the sky, moon, stars and other astronomical delights. During a lesson drawn from ritual, the Entered Apprentice is told that all good Masons hope at last to arrive at those heavens. In his pursuit of that goal, the Mason is assisted by the theological ladder which the Patriarch Jacob, in his vision, saw reaching from earth to heaven. The three principle rounds of that ladder are denominated *faith, hope and charity,* which are intended to become the principle characteristics of every good Mason.

As with most Masonic symbols, the *clouded canopy* communicates another more spiritual meaning to the discerning eye. The principal function of a canopy, when considered as a material object, is to protect those beneath it. In day-to-day experience, it essentially serves as either a ceiling, or a roof. However, when considered from a spiritual perspective the *clouded canopy* offers a springboard for meditating upon the difference between man's material state and that which is above. Such meditations invariably include weighing the difference between humility and the human ego.

Although Masons are taught the virtues of assuming a humble demeanor from the beginning of their Masonic careers, successfully achieving such a demeanor is often quite daunting. Being in a state of humility implies consciousness of the difference and distance between human and divine consciousness. Comprehending the fact of such a difference can lead one to more acutely understanding the awesome power that resides with our Great Architect. We are at once in awe and in fear of such raw unlimited power, which also inspires us to praise our God, thank Him for His blessings and pray for the strength and wisdom necessary to love Him more completely.

It is said that there is a *canopy* that separates the human from the Divine, which at the same time unites them. That *canopy* serves to remind man that he is not God, but has a relationship with God. The former is essential to curbing that state of mind known as "megalomania," while the latter strongly implies that a Mason united with God serves as the best opportunity for the light of love to shine in the material world.

This *canopy* is also represented in Masonic teachings by the *Tabernacle of Moses*. Composed of the "skin of humility," that *Tabernacle* not served as a house of worship to the Hebrews of the Exodus, it also served to protect against the danger of killing love through ontological identification, i.e., through identification of self with the Divine. It is the attempted obliteration of the difference between self and God that has resulted in the most horrible abuses practiced in man's history.

Tyrants and dictators throughout the ages have proven the truth about this observation, often with the most horrid consequences visited upon their subjects. Adolf Hitler sought not only to purify mankind by eliminating all but the Aryan breed, he acquired all the knowledge possible to enable to him call upon the powers of God and make them his own. Josef Stalin annihilated the Russian Orthodox Church, demanding that his subjects worship only him. The early Roman Emperor, Flavius Theodosius, believing himself the very messenger of God, issued edicts that resulted in the eradication of "pagan" worship and the rich Gnostic library situated in Alexandria. Theodosius single-handedly also brought about the destruction of the Serapeum, the ancient Egyptian temple of worship. In each instance, the destructive force of megalomania was unleashed in the world proving yet again that ancient adage that in the wrong hands, power corrupts absolutely.

He who faithfully practices the principles and virtues taught in Freemasonry is consistently aware of his the necessity to correct his own failings. The *point within the circle* reminds him to keep his passions, prejudices and personal interests within due bounds. The *compasses* reminds him to circumscribe his desires. The *lambskin apron* reminds him of that purity of character that is essential to his gaining admission into that celestial lodge above – that lodge beyond the *clouded canopy* where the Supreme Architect of the Universe forever presides. The Freemason approaches each related task with humility of mind, completely aware that but for the grace of the Great Architect, he would fall from his flight as surely as a wounded sparrow.

The profound message delivered by the symbolism of the *clouded canopy* is that in due time man is destined to travel on a plane that is not limited by time. During our earthly existence, we learn the importance of comprehending ourselves as a piece in the puzzle of history. We contribute of our talents, establish our ideals and know not whether or when the goal will actually be achieved. Time limits what we can accomplish; timelessness, or that plane beyond the *clouded canopy,* promises the opportunity for limitless accomplishment. The limitations of time also inculcates the virtue of patience and prompts each one of us to learn as much about history, science, philosophy and theology so that we may understand where our individual lives fit within God's plan for the universe.

The dual symbolism of Saint John the Baptist and Saint John the Evangelist prompt each Mason to learn of what message each man is a symbol. Saint John the Baptist represents the beginning of the messianic period, while Saint John the Evangelist symbolizes the New Jerusalem. The Baptist introduces Masons to the *God within,* whom we encounter with a due and deliberate reverence. As Jesus instructed his followers, the kingdom of God is not to be discovered beyond the horizon; it resides within the heart of man. That knowledge sets free the individuality of each human being and motivates every knowing person to search within for the presence of the Divine. The Evangelist builds upon that profound theme by introducing us to the *Heavenly Jerusalem* – that house not built with hands, eternal in the heavens. As such, it is not so much a place as it is a state of being which we begin to create while on earth venturing through this vale of tears.

"Man that is born of a woman is of few days and full of trouble. He cometh forth like a flower and is cut down; he fleeth also as a shadow and continueth not." This profound lesson drawn from the book of Job reminds us to be ever conscious of the meaning of the *clouded canopy.* Whether or not we are ready, we will pass from this earthly existence. That which awaits the Mason who has labored to love his Creator and cherish his brother is no mystery at all – love and service to a higher degree. But, that which awaits he who does nothing to love and serve his brother is a continuing journey to learn the simpler lessons God has provided. For some, the path traveled leads a greater twisted distance to a much shorter destination. For others, the path is narrow and straight and leads the traveler to his destination on time – to the realm beyond the *clouded canopy.*

Chapter 32

DEATH

"Man that is born of a woman is of
few days and full of trouble."

Job 14:1

Some who study Freemasonry from afar say that Masons have an extraordinary fascination with death. They also say that the Craft is too often morbidly clothed in dark garments during some of its ritualistic degrees. To the outsider, the fact that the subject of death is represented in Masonic symbolism is sufficient proof that the fraternity leans too heavily toward the occult and all too frequently neglects the living, flesh and bone reality of human life. However, to Masons who are experienced in the teachings of the Craft, death is merely a symbol of a completed initiation. It also stands as the great *secret* of all time – a secret that can not be disclosed even if one desired to, for no known living person has returned from the grave to tell his story.

The Masonic idea of death, like that of the Jew and Christian, is not accompanied by gloom. The dark garments worn during several Masonic degrees are not intended to signify that death is the equivalent of darkness. Rather, the garments themselves signify the sadness a compassionate person feels at losing a loved one to the passage of death. The difference is obvious to the discerning eye. On the one hand, Masonry regards death as the beginning of new life, while on the other hand, death also inspires the deepest sense of love for those who have passed away and will not be seen again in this earthly existence. The fact that new life should inspire great sadness is actually the product of one of the most natural human emotions.

From the beginning to the end the rituals of Freemasonry teach and symbolize the concept of man's immortality. If a Mason pays very close attention to the lessons in those rituals, he will also learn that Freemasonry absolutely and unequivocally repudiates the notion that death is nothing more than annihilation. This subject is central to the Third Degree, which in part teaches that there is a part inside of each human that lives forever.

Much has been written about various philosophies surrounding death, all of which is clearly useful to anyone interested in understanding the relationship of material existence to spiritual life. Rudolf Steiner has written in his classic entitled *Theosophy* about how all life is connected: material to soul, and soul to spirit. Simply stated, life consists of three segments – physical, soul and spirit – which although existing on different planes, or behind separate veils, share corresponding "environments." There is no beginning and ending, at least not in the sense that is commonly understood. Man did not suddenly appear and then just as suddenly vanish forever to be forgotten. Quite to the contrary, the esoteric or hidden meaning behind the Gospel of John inspires us to contemplate the truth that all that God created is never dashed to pieces and thrown upon the trash heap.

The Masonic symbolism of death demands a most serious study by the Mason who desires to understand its true nature. Certainty of immortality issues from the participation experienced in that which is intrinsically indestructible, imperishable and immortal. It is fair to ask, whence such certainty came. How can one possibly know such things to be true? In most instances where interpretation of Masonic symbolism is explored, the matter of experience becomes profoundly significant. Man cannot truly know something to be *true* unless and until he experiences that something for himself. While that is an accurate statement, it is not complete any more than it is complete to state that if immortality cannot be scientifically proven, it is nothing more than mere fantasy.

Each of us who received a religious education during our early years was taught that there are some matters that must be taken on *faith*. While faith is central to Masonry and constitutes one of the three principle rounds of Jacob's ladder, a Mason need not rely alone on faith to understand the truth about death being the gateway to new life. Our own intuition confirms the fact.

A survey of theosophy reveals that there is a similarity between physical sensations, i.e., touching, feeling, seeing, smelling and tasting, and intuition. We are so familiar with the physical sensations that rush over us each day that we hardly notice that which we are sensing. Intuition, on the other hand, requires practice for it relates to the consciousness of our souls and pertains to the spirit. You will know that you have experienced intuition, if when thinking back in time, you can recall a circumstance when you had an unexplained feeling that something was about to happen – and it did happen.

Those who practice to heighten their sensitivity to intuition build their sensory capacity to equal that of their physical sensations. In fact, one relates to the other in the following manner: through the physical senses, man absorbs the stimulation from the outside world which causes certain feelings to well up within him, followed by an almost instinctive comprehension that somehow everything he has beheld is all related. Intuition is not the ability to foretell the future; it is the ability to understand the spiritual present.

Another example of the type of intuition that confirms the truth about death constituting a gateway to life begins with understanding the "I" that separates our physical existence from our spiritual existence. While Masonry teaches the importance of team work to accomplish greater charitable works, it also teaches the importance of understanding who you are. At some point in your life you suddenly became aware that you are you, and that there is a very big world that surrounds you. The Masonic rituals you experienced during each of your degrees were experienced by you, not someone else. You have a specific and very special identity that nobody else can ever experience. Within that special identity you have a strong instinct to survive – to never, never, never die. Like all human beings, you were born with that instinct and grew to understand its presence within you. It is an instinct for continuing life, not an instinct for annihilation.

That instinct constitutes the very foundation for your intuition, for it was given to you at your birth, has grown with you throughout your life and has never left your side. You know you will always live, not because you wish it to be so, but because your instinct and intuition tell you so.

Masonic symbolism inculcates an understanding that all human life has an immortal part – the spirit or soul of man. The Craft chose to make immortality its central tenet not to cheat and deceive you about that which is true, but to reveal to you why it is true and thus why it is important to construct the days of your physical existence with that truth in mind. The Great Creator has not provided us with rules to follow for daily living for a temporary purpose. Those rules and guidelines are a roadmap to eternity. When you consider that the laws of the universe are as consistent as are the theorems of geometry, you cannot help but also comprehend the eternal and everlasting application of those laws. Why? For whose benefit? If we end in annihilation, what sort of vanity and trickery is this? If our lives end forever, what good are eternal laws, rules and regulations?

Freemasonry provides us with yet another symbol by which we are enabled to answer these, as well as all other similar questions. The pommels or balls situated atop the two pillars, Boaz and Jachin, are valuable instruments for both improving the mind and giving it the most distinct idea of any problem. They also enable us to solve the same. Have you figured out how? What does this lesson actually mean to you? If you never gave it another thought after first hearing it in a Masonic lodge, it is time you went a little farther in your studies.

The pommels and balls represent globes. Besides serving as maps of the outward parts of the world and the heavenly stars, they illustrate the truth about planetary relationships. Those truths reveal to constancy of both the laws of the universe and the theorems of geometry. In other words, Masonry teaches that the science of the universe is living proof of the immortality of man, for man was created in God's image as the center of the universe – the big "I" of all creation. It is upon this truth that Masonry builds its foundation of charity for all mankind; of hope in the future of our immortal spirits and souls; and of faith that everything that God has created was never meant for destruction. Everything was meant to live, die and live again – just as we are taught by the pommels and balls situated atop Boaz and Jachin.

Chapter 33

DESPOTISM

*"Put them in mind to be subject to principalities
and powers, to obey magistrates, to be ready
to do every good work."*

Titus 3:1

Freemasonry holds that one of the worst personifications of the principle of evil is despotism. That contention is held so strongly that our Scottish Rite Masons eventually vow eternal hostility to tyranny, which is nothing more than the imposition of the selfish desires of one man upon man's natural-born spirit of freedom. Masonry defines the despot as a criminal against the laws of nature who reduces the lives of many to his own will, replacing himself for the state and the voice of the people.

Although such vile immorality imposed upon humanity by certain governmental leaders is worthy of hostility, the Craft does not intend that Masons should rise in armed conflict every time a despot emerges. Neither does the fraternity wish to limit a Mason's understanding about who, or what is, or may become a despot. Heads of state, religious leaders, proponents of a particular school of philosophical thought, or even the bully down the street may fit the Masonic definition of a despot. The Masonic principles of positive thinking and positive emotion are more often Masonry's recommended weapons as opposed to guns and bullets.

Though the individual despot may vary from head of state to the bully down the street, it is not difficult to discern the character traits common to all despots. The tyrannical ruler of nations has left his indelible mark upon the pages of history: the people he or she governed suffered repression of freedoms, humiliation, outrage and often became the victims of murderous rages. The religious despot has also littered the historical landscape with such obscenities as warfare waged against innocent human beings in the name of God. Philosophical tyrants frequently have resorted to the demeaning tactic of unfairly marginalizing thought that differs in any material respect with the thought promoted by a particular philosophy. Equally agonizing, the bully down the street threatens to physically beat anyone who does not pay him or her the respect he or she demands.

Revolutions have been fought to stop some of these examples of despotic power. Yet, in the long term it is neither war nor revolution that will prevent the future emergence of other despots. If freedom is to permanently replace repression, the principles of Freemasonry must be put into practice by people and nations.In other words, as with most other matters upon which Masonry weighs in, it is more important that each individual is armed with the tools necessary to resist arbitrary power and rule than it is to arm the masses with weapons of human destruction. Freemasonry is about building the Temple; it is not about tearing it down.

From time immemorial, Masonry has offered lessons that are intended to improve how men think, feel and act. It is these to which we turn for a more enlightened understanding about how best to deal with the despots we encounter in our lives. For example, the First Degree of Masonry offers instructions about the four cardinal virtues: temperance, fortitude, prudence and justice. During the ritual in the Second Degree, candidates are introduced to the power of Pythagorean geometry – the true beauty of morality. And, in the Third Degree, Masonry reaches out to impress upon our minds the fact that true immortality cannot be based upon anything other than honor and virtue. While these three degrees principally reach out to each individual Mason and seek to affect his thoughts and feelings, the principles derived from those lessons are equally valuable to the worldwide community.

Because everyone cannot become a Mason, the world may only experience the benefit of those Masonic principles when they are put into action by Masons. Every faithful Mason who does so changes not only the environment where he lives, he also contributes to changing the environment of the entire world. To prove our point, consider the possibilities of the dramatic impact the lessons from the three Masonic degrees may have upon society.

To be temperate, one must constantly keep guard over his passions. This does not mean that Masons are expected to become monks. Rather, when living life to its fullest extent, a Mason is expected not to do anything that brings shame on himself, or the fraternity. No hard and fast rules are set forth – the Mason knows what that means: everything in moderation. In other words, *temperance* teaches one not to be extreme in his or her points of view about matters relating to politics and religion. Do you think the world today could benefit from a broader practice of this virtue? If so, faithfully incorporate it into your daily life and miracles will happen – despots will be vanquished.

When exercising fortitude, one must necessarily act courageously and not unreasonably permit fear to alter the course of his or her conduct. If any one emotion has caused more pain and suffering throughout history, it is without question the emotion of fear - fear of humiliation, fear of being laughed at, fear of losing, fear of being wrong, fear of rejection, and so on and so forth. Fear can cause a person to actually adopt extremism in place of temperance or tolerance. Fear can also cause one to support an immoral purpose, to embrace the hatred of others, or to even regard God with disdain and suspicion rather than with unfailing love. In short, fear can become the despot's greatest weapon against those who seek his removal.

Prudence teaches us to regulate our lives and actions agreeable to that which is reasonable. Undeniably that which is reasonable will vary from circumstance to circumstance, as well as from time to time. Yet, if one presented with a choice of action will simply pause to reflect upon the consequences of each choice, the more reasonable of the two will become obvious. Despots prefer that their subject behave impetuously and give little thought to the consequences of poor choices. Masonry asks us to weigh carefully the choices life presents and to do the best we can to consistently select the more reasonable option. Do you believe that there is too little evidence that prudence is alive and well in our world today? If so, be a force for change – resolve not to act impetuously in any matter that is significant to the welfare of others.

Justice is that standard that requires us to render unto every man his just due without consideration to such things as race, color, religion, or creed. Masonry does not merely demand that we are fair with our friends – we are also expected to be fair with our enemies, as well. But, justice also requires that men act with mercy, which is not commonly found among depots. Indeed, one would be hard pressed to find very many examples from the past when despots have behaved justly toward anyone other than themselves. True justice first requires the setting aside of self interest. Masonry teaches that it is impossible for man to act in the in the best interest of others when he first insists upon protecting his own interest.

While focusing upon geometry during the Second Degree, Masonry does not intend to merely the mathematics taught in schools. Rather, the geometry taught in Masonry instructs upon the beauties that flow from Pythagorean philosophy. One extraordinarily important maxim from that philosophy is that life is a law of nature and, as a consequence, it is in man's nature to always be free. Pythagoras believed that it was essential for mankind to comprehend the laws of all nature, including the laws pertaining to the heavens and the stars. From a study of nature, Pythagoras believed that man would eventually come to understand that for every act there is a consequence; for each cause a predictable effect will follow. The wise Mason understands that lesson and by virtue of his own experience has learned what conditions must exist in the world around him before he may enjoy true peace and freedom – before all men can live in a world without despots.

Those conditions are best exemplified by the lessons about immortality drawn from the Third Degree. Masonry embraces the truth that life as created by God never ends. It changes, as every human being should know, but it never terminates. Since the despot's greatest weapon is fear, once all men also embrace the truth about immortality fear's grip on the soul of all societies is seriously weakened. If you will change, but never die, of what is there to fear? Perhaps one will answer that even if I shall live forever, there is still the chance that I can lose prestige, standing, respect, a job, money or valued possessions, if I do not act as the despot demands. Yet, that proposition assumes a life without God – a life without the warm touch of His grace. Masonry does not teach such an assumption. To the contrary, Masonry boldly acknowledges that the history of man is a history about human beings ever evolving spiritually to enable all mankind to be regarded by the Great Architect as his best, closest and dearest friends.

It is that to which Masonry aspires. It is that condition in the world that the despot most fears. It is to that end that you have been called into existence, my brethren. Embrace the knowledge and live it in the world – despots will vanish before your very eyes.

Chapter 34

DIVESTED OF ALL MINERALS AND METALS

"And there thou shalt build an altar unto the Lord thy God, ..."

Deut. 27:5

Candidates for degrees in Freemasonry are required to enter a Masonic lodge without any metallic substances on their person. They are also instructed that King Solomon's Temple was erected without the aid of any iron or metallic tools. Eventually they learn about the Masonic importance of the biblical character Tubalcain, who is described in the book of Genesis as the first artificer in metals. Explanations about each of these subjects are provided during the ceremonies, but those explanations are merely preliminary to the deeper meanings, which are veiled in the mysteries of the Craft that each candidate must explore for himself.

Freemasonry's relationship to the science and philosophy of *alchemy* has been written about extensively by this and other Masonic authors. Indeed, if one lifts the veil of Masonic mysteries high enough, he will see beneath it an alchemical formula that is essential to the Third Degree allegories. The alchemical significance of divesting a person of all metallic substances, as symbolized in Masonry, is that it prepares the candidate to be transformed into a new man. As lustration, or baptism symbolizes the completion of man's commitment to spiritual renewal, so too does the divesting of metallic substances symbolize man's readiness to learn and become reborn.

Divestiture further acknowledges the need to rid oneself of the resulting impurities that an adherence to the material side of life inflicts upon man's soul. Freemasonry seeks to provide a candidate the tools necessary to make his material life consistent with his spiritual life. God never intended for man to select one as opposed to the other – to choose either to live in the world or in the spirit. Rather, the Great Architect intended that all men would live a spiritual life in the body and environment in which he was placed by Nature.

If the science of *alchemy* may be said to refer to the transformation of substances and elements, then the philosophy of *alchemy* may be said to similarly pertain to the transformation of men from non-spiritual to spiritual beings. As such, the importance of *alchemy* to Freemasons is not so much the substantive alchemical philosophy as it is what that substantive philosophy actually symbolizes. It is not enough to merely understand that it symbolizes change. It is far more important to understand that it symbolizes the need to learn how to change and how to make the necessary changes.

Freemasonry selects tools of architecture, or tools of iron from which to teach wise and serious truths. The plumb, level and square are implements used for construction and together with the other several tools of iron selected by the Craft teach a candidate the *what and how* of transforming himself from a non-spiritual to a spiritual being. For example the plumb admonishes us to walk uprightly before God, which means that we must learn and follow His laws, which laws include the laws of Nature. The level teaches us that we are traveling a path that eventually will lead us to a world beyond this material existence – a place from whose bourne no traveler returns. We are thereby taught that something is expected of us; something other than living a life filled with luxury and indolence. The square symbolizes justice, equality and truth and thereby teaches the importance of acting fairly toward all men at all times.

Your universe is created by the thoughts and feelings you experience in your daily life. This is the great lesson of *alchemy* and one of the centerpieces of the ancient mysteries that Freemasonry embraces. If you think and feel virtuously, you attract virtuous things into your life. If you permit negative thoughts and feelings to permeate your being, you will attract negative things. Freemasonry teaches us to contemplate the plumb, level and square, as well as the other tools of architecture, which we use to build good thoughts and to construct excellent feelings. When those lessons are learned, the Mason becomes all that he wishes to become — and even more.

The lodge room is Freemasonry's laboratory — the place where experiments in brotherhood ultimately become transformed into creations of social love. In the lodge room, one brother Mason listens to the cares and concerns of another brother Mason and then works to help relieve those conditions. The thoughts and feelings generated by that one encounter carry over into matters outside of the lodge. Homes for the aged appear, eye foundations emerge, clinics pop up around the globe to aid the speechless and hospitals abound everywhere to care for injured children.

But, there is a personal responsibility associated with becoming all that you want to become. First and foremost, a Mason must learn patience — nothing happens over night. Second, a Mason must employ perseverance on a daily basis. It does little good to think and behave virtuously for a day and then to behave badly for days thereafter. Commitment to excellence of thought and emotion is a lifetime commitment. Third, a Mason must place his brother ahead of himself, for to think and feel selfishly will result in attracting only those people who think and feel similarly. If you wish to attract abundance, you must give of yourself abundantly. Finally, a Mason needs to be acquainted with the true meaning of the word *love*. It begins with a love of God, being thankful for Him, His creations and His gift of life. It yields to a love of self and then culminates in the love of other human beings as deeply as one loves himself.

Thus, transforming our material lives into equally spiritual lives is the great work of Freemasonry. It begins with the divesting of all *minerals and metals* — that baggage in our lives that we accumulated before we were introduced to Masonic thought and Masonic emotion. As Shakespeare has stated, "Think well, act well, and live well." If you do, you will have discovered the true essence of Freemasonry.

Chapter 35

EQUILIBRIUM

"...for ye are the temple of the living God;..."

2 Cor. 6:16

In Royal Arch Masonry, as well as in the 32nd degree of Scottish Rite Masonry, candidates are instructed upon the importance of achieving spiritual balance. Referring to it as the *Royal Secret,* Albert Pike defined that spiritual balance as *equilibrium.* Royal Arch Masons know it by the phrase *living in the light* and symbolize it with the keystone. Many experienced Masons, whose dedication to the workings of the Craft are beyond reproach, mistakenly interpret *equilibrium* in a very secular context, i.e., living only a part of one's life for God, which is not at all the meaning intended by the fraternity.

It is hard to envision what living part-time for God means. Does it mean that one day we attend church services and the next day cheat our brother? Or, can it possibly mean that we should spend part of our lives forgetting about God? Neither of those satisfies the achieving of spiritual equilibrium. At best it seems to authorize a certain spiritual laziness, which Masonry has never endorsed and never encouraged in its members.

Equilibrium refers to balancing the human soul with the spirit and is symbolized in a Masonic lodge very early in a candidate's Masonic career by the two pillars, Boaz and Jachin. Some writers have used the words "soul" and "spirit" interchangeably, but doing so neglects the important spiritual distinction between the two. The "soul" is the heart of man which can die with the body, if not properly attended to during one's life. On the other hand, the "spirit" is the part of the Divine that lives within us and which will never, never, never die.

As Pike has written, "Freemasonry is the subjugation of the Human that is in man by the Divine; the conquest of the appetites and passions by the moral sense and reason; a continual effort, struggle, and warfare of the spiritual against the material and sensual." *Morals and Dogma.* That is not a call to living part-time for God, but a challenge to fight the battles of light and darkness every second of every day in every environment in which a Freemason finds himself.

The fundamentals of the Kabbalistic scheme are based upon the assertion that the human spirit, once descended through the heavens to earth, is in a state of material imprisonment and is under the constant influence of evil passions. Kabbalistic thought has exerted a tremendous influence over both Christian and Jewish thought from at least the mediaeval period to the present. Its theories are inextricably interwoven with the tenets of alchemy, Hermeticism, Rosicrucianism and Freemasonry. In material part, those theories teach man how he may achieve balance in his life, or acquire spiritual *equilibrium.*

As it was originally intended, contemplative Kabbalah evolved for the purpose of revealing to man through his higher intellectual faculties and ability to engage in abstract reasoning the spiritual essence within himself. Such was known to Sir Francis Bacon, as well as to many of the Freemasons who founded the Royal Society in England, who encouraged and promoted man's pursuit of knowledge. Candidates are instructed in the Fellowcraft Degree (a Masonic degree that some believe was created by Bacon) about the importance of studying the liberal arts and sciences. In the greatest tradition of Kabbalistic thought, those studies should be undertaken by each individual Mason for the purpose of learning about that which is inside of him so that he may eventually distill light from darkness and live each day for the benefit of others.

It is correct to inquire whether or not the concept of *equilibrium* leaves any room for rest and recreation. Here, Masons may reflect upon the lessons imparted by the Twenty-four Inch Gauge. The human body requires sleep; the mind cannot always be engaged in study; and within the period of every twenty-four hours of a day, the batteries that propel us through life need to be re-charged. This, too, is a part of *equilibrium* and as such should also have a place in every Mason's life as an important feature of the *Royal Secret.*

In the *Sepher Yetzirah,* also known as the Book of Creation, the author takes the reader back to the days of Abraham and instructs about how the Supreme Architect of the Universe intended man to achieve spiritual balance in his life. From it we learn that out of the spirit of the Living God emanated air; from the air, water; from the water, fire; from the fire, the height and depth, the East and the West, the North and the South. Everything that flowed from that one Divine spirit is in perfect balance and harmony without which the universe would not exist.

The Mason who learns these lessons well and who places them into practice in his daily life will not necessarily end his struggle. To the contrary, his struggles may very well become greater, because he is more aware of their existence. However, when human strength and wisdom fail during those struggles, Divine assistance is vouchsafed us through the medium of prayer. Man is incapable of succeeding in his struggles without the assistance of the Supreme Architect. That assistance is not part-time and is not needed only on occasion – it is essential to survival and constitutes the very essence of *equilibrium.*

Here we return to the Masonic symbolism of the point within the circle for the purpose of more clearly understanding the extent of our struggles in life. In Christian theology, the point, line and circle depict the three separate spheres of heaven, earth and hell. Heaven is the spiritual plane where God dwells; earth is where the material nature of God thrives; and hell is where God is the least powerful. As opposed to representing three separate places where the spirit of man may eventually travel, heaven, earth and hell represent three possible states of man's condition while living on earth.

In the physical or earthly state, matter dominates resulting in the need to exert enormous spiritual energy to manifest light over darkness. It is said that within the material plane of existence, spirituality constitutes one-fifth of an individual's life-force – a fact which if true that hardly represents the state of *equilibrium* Masonry asks us to achieve. Instead, that fact clearly implies that we must exert ourselves more intently to compensate and overcome our natural-born spiritual deficiencies. In this regard, the point within the circle also represents the spirit of man trapped within the material plane which always seeks freedom from its imprisonment.

The Craft teaches us that life is labor and that labor is desirable for man's state of spiritual well-being. This is not a part-time effort, but a full-time job. *Equilibrium* is not attainable with a half-hearted effort. It is attainable only by dedicated hard work. The question for each of us is how hard are we willing to work?

Chapter 36

FEAR NOT

"In God have I put my trust: I will not be afraid what man can do unto me."

Ps. 56:11

The first word uttered by a candidate for Masonic degrees upon entering a Masonic Lodge declares his faith in God. Without that declaration the form and beauties of a lodge would be forever concealed from him. So, too, would be the hidden beauties of Freemasonry. That declaration also professes the candidate's undying trust in God – a trust that is symbolically tested during the ritual used in each of the three degrees of Masonry.

In the First Degree, the candidate is released to the custody of a person whom he cannot see and in a sightless condition is caused to be led in paths he has never before traveled. His conductor is merely identified to him as a true and trusty friend upon whose fidelity he can, with the utmost confidence, rely. The candidate is taught a most important lesson about Freemasonry – it is safe to trust a brother Mason; as safe as trusting in God.

During the Second Degree, the candidate is taught the importance of the symbolic Middle Chamber of King Solomon's Temple, which he may only enter by demonstrating his worthiness and knowledge. Here, Masons learn that knowledge is the gift of God and that the benefits we receive from knowledge are to be shared with every man, woman and child with whom they come into contact. That is so, because Divine Wisdom is at the root of all we can ever hope to learn and know, the comforts from which are not be denied any of God's creatures.

Yet, it is during the Third Degree that the candidate learns how to rely upon God – how to fear not what man can do unto him. During the ritual, the candidate learns that he will no longer have someone to pray for him. He must do so by himself. The true and trusty brother who had previously served as his guide is replaced with the invisible presence of the Deity. Here, Masons are prepared for *traveling abroad,* or in the social and professional circles in his life outside of a Masonic Lodge.

When we reflect upon the progression of the Masonic lessons about trusting in God, we are reminded about the parallel lessons taught during the natural state of human existence. A child is born into the world unable to care for itself. Throughout its early years, it receives the loving care of its nurturing parents and thereby learns how to trust in someone to make it feel safe, secure and very much loved. There comes a time when the child must leave that safe environment and journey alone into the world. It is then that the child truly learns in whom to place its trust.

Throughout the history of mankind, nothing has rendered men more powerless than fear. Those who either assumed authority over others, or embarked on a path toward doing so quickly learned that the imposition of fear upon men made them easy to subjugate and manipulate. Monarchs, legislatures, churches and employers have at various times used fear to gain power, hold power and gain compliance with their different demands. In so doing, they acted as enemies of freedom, for men who act or fail to act out of fear are never truly free.

What is it that causes you to fear? Is it ill health or the steps you must take to keep good health? Could you withstand the humiliation and pressures of losing your job? Does your religion make unreasonable demands upon your behavior and emotions so that you fear falling from God's grace? Or, do you fear that others do not like you? Such disordered thinking can also give way to anger and resentment – two products of fear – and result in the loss of friends and the loss of peace of mind.

Albert Pike wrote about how essential it is for man to embrace virtue and honor in their lives. He wrote that good men were made better by so doing and that others around them also greatly benefited from the resulting acts of kindness, charity and goodwill. He also wrote about how quickly virtue and honor vanish when fear is allowed to creep into man's consciousness. A kind word is often quickly and irrationally replaced with an unwarranted harsh criticism. The helping hand is suddenly withdrawn replaced with a vacant uncaring air. Those who ordinarily rushed to instill harmony where bickering once reigned now look over their shoulders to see who is spying on them and who will report them to those who can harm them.

With such consequences clearly in focus, it becomes easier to fully comprehend the importance of *fearing not what man can do unto you*. As Masons, we learn to pray as though everything depends upon God and to act as though everything depends upon us. Thus, Freemasons have acknowledged from time immemorial that prayer and action are two very well known secrets to aid in achieving good mental and physical health. It is essential to know that both must act together. Prayer without action by he who prays is as useless as faith is without acts.

Fear is a natural reaction to that with which we are unfamiliar. When pain is potentially involved, it is most natural to, at least, feel a great deal of trepidation. Imagine for a moment the plight of the Grand Master Jacques De Molay as he awaited certain torture, most clearly already having been told precisely which instrument would hurtfully probe which delicate parts of his body. Without doubt, he felt fear. Yet, as we are informed by ancient history, he eventually overcame that fear, declared that he would not profess the misdeeds attributed to him and his Knights Templar and was subsequently burned alive at the stake.

What is it that enables men to overcome fear? The heroic efforts of the soldiers at Iwo Jima, or those who stormed the cliffs at the Normandy invasion stand out to generations as examples of unflinching bravery. To the military man the answer is clear – he fights because of his comrades in arms. But, why do we resist fear? Most of us are not in combat and thus not at war. The answer is that we have so conditioned our faith and our minds that we know that we, like all men, will die. Our passing from this material life was ordained before we were born. It matters not so much how we die, but how we live.

Freedom is a gift of God. We can accept it, or reject the entire premise. Fear forces us to make a choice. Many select slavery and yield. Others believe that freedom is a matter of choice and therefore choose to act free, even though they may be in a horrendous state of fear. Man is but of little time here on earth. Yet, his spirit lives forever. We ought not to care so much about our welfare here on earth as to sacrifice the great gift of freedom God has given us.

Men of courage are men of freedom. Men in fear are men in bondage. The Holy Writings is replete with allegories about deliverance from bondage – not submission to slavery. We have been created to become men of God, not men subjugated to the will of those who would use fear to strip us of our natural born spirit of freedom,

When ill health strikes, fear not. You will live. You may even live awhile longer here on this plane. If you do not, it matters not, for you have always been and always will be a life force.

When your fortune fails and you are worrying about how to live one month to the next, fear not. No one has guaranteed you a life without turmoil. However, you have been guaranteed that God will give you strength. Pray and act as though you will succeed. Should you feel threatened, whether by an employer, a priest or holy man, or a bully, fear not. No man has been empowered by God to impose his own selfish desires upon any other man. The only manner in which that succeeds is when the man allows it to succeed.

My brethren, Masonry offers us a plan for how best to succeed in life. That plan is centered upon the four cardinal virtues of temperance, fortitude, prudence and justice. None of those virtues may be successfully practiced by a fearful man. Thus, Masonry admonishes us to be steadfast – not fearful. Had Hiram Abif feared death, he would have quickly revealed the secrets of a Master Mason when first assailed by the ruffian at the south gate.

How quickly do you surrender?

Chapter 37
ANGLE OF A SQUARE

"Learn to do well; seek judgment, relieve the oppressed, judge the fatherless, plead for the widow."

Is. 1:17

In Freemasonry, the square is often referred to as a symbol of morality. To an Entered Apprentice Mason, it is one of the *three great lights;* to the Fellowcraft, it constitutes one of his *working tools;* and to the Master it is a symbol of his office. In each of those presentations, the square is intended to inculcate morality, truthfulness and virtue. There is also one additional presentation which teaches us that we are in a constant state of change, or growth. Nothing on earth is in its final state. Rather, everything is always *becoming* something new and different.

As a part of his ritualistic lessons as a Master Mason, the candidate is instructed about the importance of *forming the angle of a square,* i.e., carrying to its end the formation of the virtuous man, which is an improvement upon the man of original Creation. While the lessons about morality, truthfulness and virtue are imparted to the candidate as goals to be attained, the companion lesson about always *forming the angle of a square* teaches that action is necessary if those goals are ever to be attained. Consider the lesson from the Fellowcraft Degree: "from a point to a line; from a line to a superfice; and, from a superfice to a solid."

Action is to an idea as breathing is to living. If one does not breathe, he will surely die. If an idea is not put into motion, it will never achieve fruition. Morality, truthfulness and virtue are learned skills – they are not the product of either having good genes, or a fanciful imagination. The humorist, Mark Twain, once said that just because one can blow air through a trumpet, that does not mean he should play the trumpet for the entertainment of others. To do so requires more than the talent of blowing – it requires learning, discipline and *skill*. Thus, when we are in the process of *forming the angle of a square,* we are inevitably disciplining ourselves at the same time we are learning and acquiring the skills necessary to attain the desired result.

It is fair to ask where one should go to best learn the skills that will enable him to act as morally, truthfully and virtuously as possible. Is it within the confines of a church, Masonic lodge, school, or family home? The answer is not an easy one to give. Frequently churches, lodges, schools and family homes impart a mixture of both what is needed and what should be avoided.

Very often churches offer a definition for morality, but behave hypocritically thereby confusing the sensitivities of those who rely solely upon a specific religion or church for their lessons in life. Masonic lodges offer a relatively free environment within which one may grow, but frequently cloud that environment with a foggy array of big egos demanding that attention be paid to *me,* not to you. Schools usually can be counted on to provide safe surroundings within which students may improve intellectually, but recently many school grounds have proven to be breeding grounds for malcontents, violence and even murder. Sadly even the family home – that secure, warm, loving place where everyone should love one another without reservation – too frequently falls short producing physically and mentally abused children, who become maladjusted adults. The unmistakable conclusion to be drawn is that there is no one perfect site where one can go to acquire the necessary skills to *form the angle of the square.* Each environment has its benefits and its distractions.

Since ancient times, philosophy has strived to separate the good from the evil. Parents often choose to send their children to private, rather than public schools, because they believe, correctly or incorrectly, that there those children will receive the best education. Families select "safe" neighborhoods within which to live believing, correctly or incorrectly, that they are thereby best providing for everyone's safety. Nations seek to isolate other nations both politically and economically, because they believe, correctly or incorrectly, that those in need of isolation practice evil.

In the Holy Bible, a parable is recited which is intended to demonstrate to the discerning reader that a seed must rot away before it may bear fruit. But, what exactly does that passage of scripture mean by the word *rot?* In philosophical terms, to rot away is the precedent to being born and to being able to transform the forces of nature in such a manner that morality, truthfulness and virtue become like living organisms. It matters little which environment one selects within which to make that transformation, as long as that environment is well-suited to the disposition of the individual involved. To some it is the church, to others it is within the lodge, at school, or among the cherished members of one's family. Yet others find that all such environments contribute something to the personal process of transformation.

Masons are not told where to go to learn the skills necessary to *form the angle of the square.* They are clearly not told that all that is necessary may be discovered within a Masonic lodge. Quite to the contrary, they are instructed that while Masonry has a history, literature and philosophy, much is to be learned elsewhere. When one reads the works of Plato, he can acquire the skills necessary to discuss, listen, absorb, discriminate and act. If another chooses to read the literary works of Albertus Magnus, who was the mentor to St. Thomas Aquinas, he acquires the skill necessary to comprehend the relationship of God and Jesus to Nature and precisely why that relationship is important to apply in every spiritual undertaking. The studies of astronomy, arithmetic, logic, grammar and rhetoric potentially enrich the mind with valuable information necessary to acquire the skills of communication by suggesting that everything and everyone is *connected.*

While *forming the angle of the square,* we must acquire the skill of listening, if we are ever to attain morality, truthfulness and virtue. Masonry teaches the importance of that fact by instilling in the candidate the importance of being *silent.* To test your own listening ability, try answering this question for yourself: do you hear what someone else is saying, or do you simply wait until that person is finished so that you can talk? When talking with your wife or child have you ever been guilty of saying, "just get to the point?" If you answer "yes," you have yet to acquire the skill of listening, the importance of which Masonry teaches by imparting the necessity for silence.

In the studies of a Fellowcraft Mason, the candidate is guided by reason, love and faith – a trinity essential to *forming the angle of the square*. Throughout history, correctly or incorrectly, mankind has been guided more by what he believes than by what he knows – by faith more than by reason. If you examine what has transpired in your own life, you may agree. Few take the time necessary to determine whether or not that which he believes has been scientifically proven to be accurate. Most believe the sun will always rise in the east, not because they understand astronomy and the related science, but because it has always been so throughout their lives. While that example happens to be scientifically proven, other things you believe may not.

If we are to acquire all of the skills necessary to improve upon our talent to exercise morality, truthfulness and virtue, it is important that we understand how to use reason and love. Reason requires that we exercise our intellect; that we consider the pros and cons of each action we intend to undertake. Love asks us to exercise compassion and to view every other individual as another self. Neither one of those traits, or habits is normally discovered to exist in a person as a matter of Nature. Rather, they are acquired skills. It is human nature to act impulsively – not to think about the consequences of what we intend. Similarly, it is human nature to think of ourselves first, and then to consider the needs of our brethren. To properly *form the angle of the square*, it is absolutely essential that we practice, practice and practice yet again so that reason and love become as habitual to our behavior, as faith is to our spiritual nature.

Chapter 38

FRATERNITY

*"Neither shall thy name any more be called Abram,
but thy name shall be Abraham; for a father
of nations have I made thee."*

Gen. 17:5

From the moment he is initiated as an Entered Apprentice, a Mason is instructed upon the importance of remaining free. The initiate quickly learns that freedom is a quality of life that the Craft takes very seriously. Each Mason is informed at some early point in his Masonic career that he must endeavor for the remainder of his life to be the sole sovereign over his earthly destiny. He also learns that from a political perspective, while Freemasonry abstains from generally expressing preferences, the Craft emphatically endorses liberty, freedom of speech, freedom of religion, freedom of association and a free public education for all citizens.

Albert Pike wrote that where two or several of these sovereignties associate, the State begins, requiring each to relinquish a portion of his personal sovereignty. *(Morals and Dogma)*. However, even in the act of relinquishment, the individual gains, for he participates in the establishment of a union whose ties shall never be dissolved. That union is called *fraternity,* a word that conveys both a definition of unity, as well as an understanding about how to accomplish human unification.

The Masonic meaning of *fraternity* is quite likely much different than the meaning you acquired while attending school. In colleges across the nation, campuses abound with fraternities that offer male students social acceptance, camaraderie, fellowship and a central place or house to sleep, study and party. Women are not left out, for most of those campuses offer the same environment to female students through an assortment of sororities. Many who join Freemasonry have at one time also been members of such fraternities, as well as other social fraternal organizations, such as the Moose or Elks lodges. While certainly not denouncing or demeaning any of those fraternities that perform many valuable services to the societies in which their members live, the meaning of *fraternity* to the Craft is profoundly philosophical.

Lamenting about how communities of seemingly good people could quickly morph into vicious, death-dealing armies, Manly P. Hall wrote about a new fraternal order he hoped would eventually sweep the world. In his book entitled *Lectures on Ancient Philosophy,* Hall called his new order the *gospel of identity.* The premise for his new gospel was that all life forms are the manifestations of one God. Using that premise, Hall expanded his thinking to include the notion that all people were evolving to one identity, one government and one new world order. Such thinking foretold of a new age and, indeed, the Ancient and Accepted Scottish Rite entitled its publication *The New Age.* It foretold the fulfillment of a Masonic hope – *a brotherhood of man under the fatherhood of God.*

Hall's *gospel of identity,* while subject to denunciation as fanciful thinking, at best, or, at worst dangerous in its promotion of forsaking individual freedoms, is relevant to each one of us when considered in light of lessons set forth in the Holy Bible. As a teaching drawn from the First Great Light of Masonry, its significance in shaping individual conduct must be carefully considered. In the *book of Genesis,* God calls forth Abram from among the masses and upon finding him worthy changes his name and promises that, *"In you all the nations of the earth shall be blessed."* (Gen. 17:5). That covenant was not with many people on behalf of many nations, but with one holy and worthy man on behalf of all men.

The meaning of *fraternity* to Freemasons at least includes the notion that as members of the nations referred to in scripture, we are also heirs of the benefits God has promised - *...all nations of the earth shall be blessed.* But, what does Freemasonry teach us about how we are to be blessed? What, if anything are we to do? Cain slew his brother Abel and, as we are informed, was condemned to wander the world. The sons of Jacob through their brother Joseph into a well and left him to die. They suffered the ravages of famine and death as a consequence. To the contrary, the men described in the Holy Writings who treated their brethren well were, in turn, treated well by God and Nature. To us as Masons, the lesson is evident: treat your brother as you would have him treat you – then you will be blessed.

But the concept of one Abraham being the father of all nations also teaches us valuable lesson about how man is expected to live, especially when compared with the lessons taught us by Nature. We believe as men that equality is the foundation to human liberty. But, true equality in all things leads to chaos and disorder where jealousies and personal interests push aside justice, compassion and love. The *equality* taught us in Masonry holds that all men of all aptitudes shall have equal opportunities in life. Freemasonry teaches tolerance of other opinions – it does not teach that harmony and freedom are achieved when the presence of all opposing opinions forces mankind into a moral gridlock. If, as it has been said, Hermeticism is the true philosophical ancestor of Freemasonry, then we must harken to the lessons of that credo – varying ideas and opinions must be synthesized into a cohesive structure whereby all men are free to equally pursue each and every opportunity providence has made available to us.

If you would be wise, as King Solomon was wise, you must learn the thoughts and desires of your brethren, as well as the thoughts of the members of your family, neighborhoods, houses of worship and work places. As humans, we are first brought together to differ, then to listen to the difference and then to make a difference by coming to an agreement. It is sad that the word *compromise* has fallen into such disfavor in our world of today. To compromise a position means to some the very abdication of all that is correct in favor of all that is false. The arrogance of such an assumption is self-evident – no one has a right to make the assumption that his point of view is correct and yours is incorrect. We do, however, have the right, and indeed the obligation as human beings to advocate for the position we believe is most correct. But once the advocacy ceases, as a *fraternity* of God's children we then have the obligation to come to a peaceful agreement – to achieve compromise – to abide by the teachings of our Hermetic philosophy – to synthesize and harmonize.

Freemasonry does not free us as men from the responsibility of embracing the difficult task of discovering the right path that will lead us from chaos to confusion. Suffice to say, there is no silver bullet, or magic potion that will ease the way. The adjustment of mutual rights and mutual wrongs is as difficult for us as it is for nations around the globe who do not see eye-to-eye on much of anything. Freemasonry teaches us that the difference lies in how we feel about the human beings with whom we have differing opinions – and that is a feeling about others that must be learned, for we are quite naturally a very selfish lot and enjoy pandering to our own interests. How natural is it for an entire body of men to work industriously all of their lives and then to give of that wealth so that crippled children may be healed at no cost to them? Is it not more natural to spend what you have earned on yourself and also to chastise the poor for being poor? Freemasonry teaches us that *fraternity* is not about self-interest. Rather, it is all about someone other than you – a lesson that may take a lifetime to learn, if, indeed, it ever is truly learned.

If truth were to be told, humans have an extremely difficult time placing faith in other humans. When a medical doctor recommends a specific course of medical action, we generally want a second opinion. Before hiring a person to handle our money, we seek assurances that he or she is ethical, honest and, above all else, bonded! Masonry does not ask us to leave our common sense at home – asking for a second opinion and seeking assurances of honesty are prudent courses of conduct. That we are compelled to make them prudent courses of conduct precisely proves the truth about the difficulties we have we faith in others. Freemasonry offers you the tools to improve that faith through both understanding and working on behalf of *fraternity*.

Not all of the workings of *fraternity* are benign and harmonious. Threats to freedom do exist and are very real even in today's society. Wherever light exists in the world, darkness hides in the corner waiting for its opportunity to absorb the light. Demagoguery and despotism, two evils that Masonry has combated against for ages, still demands the Craft's attention. Where they exist, the pen of Masonry is expected to bring them to light; to accuse them; to prosecute them; and, to eliminate them as best as possible.

By nature, man is cruel. But, *fraternity* replaces cruelty with justice, compassion and love. By nature, man enjoys seeing others suffer. *Fraternity* builds hospitals, homes for the aged and clinics for children in need of learning how to speak. History reveals that man kills man for pleasure and political gain. *Fraternity* embraces all men – not just who think like us, or look like us – all men. *Fraternity* builds Masons by providing the network within which the *gospel of identity* may be preached and put into action. Masons build *fraternity* by forging a *brotherhood of man under the fatherhood of God* – by following in the footsteps of Abraham so that all nations will truly be blessed.

Chapter 39

FRIENDSHIP

"A man that hath friends must shew himself friendly; and there is no friend that sticketh closer than a brother."

Prov. 18:24

During a moment in the ritual of the Entered Apprentice degree, the initiate into the mysteries of Freemasonry is told about the symbolism of two hands clasped, and of two human figures holding each other by the right hand. That description focuses primarily upon the significance of the right hand as the *seat* of fidelity. However, the joining of human beings and the clasping together of their hands evokes a vivid image of two friends. Masonry teaches us many virtues and inculcates high-minded values that each of us may ponder, meditate upon and deeply reflect upon the many splendid truths. But being an experiential body, one of the most important truths it teaches is that active friendship among men is as important as are the three principle tenets of Freemasonry – brotherly love, relief and truth.

What greater gift can one man give to another other than his commitment to being a friend? That commitment carries with it the unspoken further commitment to unconditionally love the other person.

Masons do not befriend each other because they think alike, pray in the same manner, accept the same theology, or even vote the same way at the polls. Rather, Masons befriend one another because they are inhabitants of the same planet and were created by the same God. The country of origin, sect, or opinion has absolutely no role in determining friendship.

Pythagoras taught that friendship was the truest and most nearly perfect of all relationships. He declared that in Nature there was a friendship of all for all; of gods for men; of doctrines one for another; of the soul for the body; of the rational part for the irrational part; of philosophy for its theory; of men for one another; of countrymen for one another; that friendship also existed between strangers, between a man and his wife, his children and his servants. To Pythagoras, all bonds without friendship were mere shackles for which there was no virtue in maintaining. Relationships to Pythagoras were essentially mental rather than physical whereby a stranger of sympathetic intellect was a more valued companion than a blood relative.

The bonds and ties of the material life we know break far too easily. Man is born, lives his life and then passes away – all too swiftly. But, through eternity one bond remains forever secure- the bond of fellowship. The bond created by the clasped hands never dies, for that bond is of the spirit and eternal soul.

To have a friend is good, but to be a friend is better. If the candidate learns correctly, the lessons of Masonry teach him how to be a better friend. A friend does not complain when you make a late night telephone call – instead he asks, "What took you so long to call?" A friend does not have to be asked for a ride to a destination – the offer is made the instant the need becomes known. A friend is never too busy to make time – his time is your time. There is no subject that is unsafe to talk about with a friend – with your friend you are never in danger. In other words, friendliness is next to Godliness, for he who serves man also serves the Great Architect.

Yet, since all in this world passes away, what is it about friendship that Masonry teaches shall endure for all ages? What is the lasting meaning of becoming a friend to another human being? Is it to create memories? No, because those shall also fade and pass away. Rather, it is to teach the soul how to become God's friend, for that is the primary purpose for which mankind was created.

The tradition that has unfolded from the study of The Emerald Tablet of Hermes Trismegistus has delivered to Freemasonry the *Hiram Legend,* which is central to the Third Degree. In that legend, *Hiram* symbolizes the Universal Agent, or power that is eternally building and unfolding in the bodies of all mankind. The use or abuse of that energy is the cornerstone of all Masonic teachings, as well as the key to all things found in Nature. *Hiram* represents that energy that some have called *ether,* which constitutes that hypothetical substance or element that carries the impulses from God through the universal nervous system of infinite space.

The early *Hiramic Legend* reveals that it is that substance which also constitutes the mysterious manner in which Moses, the prophets, Jesus and other holy men communicated directly with the Supreme Architect of the Universe. Solving that mystery will also solve the so-called *Great Problem* – that puzzle presented to candidates for degrees in the Scottish Rite of Freemasonry. This ether instills energy in the three essential processes of human life – thought, emotion and action. Should we eventually understand how it works and how we may participate in its working, we would also be able to communicate directly with the Divine. It is this that the *Hiram Legend* refers to as *the lost word.*

In the pre-Christian dialogue of *Asclepius,* Hermes states, "...in the after times none will pursue philosophy in singleness of heart." (*Asclepius* i; trsl. Walter Scott, *Hermetica,* vol. i, Oxford, 1924, pp.309, 311). That statement is nothing less than a call to action – the third in the trio of essentials for all human life. It invites us to be curious (thoughtful), useful (emphatic in our emotion) and to befriend the Great Creator by giving Him the glory or credit for all that we achieve (action). The call to action compels us to seek knowledge not for the mere sake of obtaining information, but to better love God and become His friend. Curiosity, even if useful, is not enough for the deeply committed Mason, for it is nothing more than vain, foolhardy and baneful if it fails to serve the Supreme Architect.

There can be no greater knowledge to be attained than that of the ether, or *lost word.* Masons are encouraged to pray, not for the mere purpose of instilling rote piety, but to learn how to listen for God's voice. Good friends do not engage in one-way conversations. That is a speech, not a conversation. Instead, friends speak then listen and so on until the entire conversation is completed. So it should be during prayer with God. The Holy Bible teaches us that it is God who first calls to man – not the other way around. God calls out and man responds, either by thinking, feeling and acting, or by ignoring that which he has heard. All men are the image of the Great Creator and either think, feel and fail to act, which is vanity, or act to implement the impulse sent through infinite space by the Divine. When all religions say that man is constantly in search of God, each means that man is constantly in a quest to learn how to communicate with God – how to engage in a conversation with a dear friend.

When we are once again exposed to the symbolism in the Masonic Lodge of two humans holding each other by the right hand, we should meditate further upon the eternal nature of friendship. Although we shall all pass away from this material world, we shall never pass from the presence of the Great Architect. Though we may wonder what form or shape we shall have after our death, we need never wonder that regardless of form and shape, we will either be God's good friend because we learned our lessons well on earth, or find that we are in need of still further education. He who requires more learning after death is on an interrupted journey.

Chapter 40
GRIP OF THE LION'S PAW

> "Judah is a lion's whelp: from the prey, my son, thou art
> gone up: he stooped down, he crouched as a lion,
> and as an old lion; who shall rouse him up?"
>
> Gen. 49:9

In the tribal benediction pronounced upon Judah and the tribe of which he was the founder, the term *lion's whelp* symbolized strength. Therefore, the emblem on the banner of the Tribe of Judah was a lion. The same symbolism is found in Masonic ritual and has enjoyed several philosophical and theological interpretations.

To our Christian brethren, the phrase "Lion of the Tribe of Judah" refers to the Messiah, who is said to have brought light and immortality into the world. To our Jewish brethren, Judah was the fourth son of the patriarch Jacob and represents the *fourth point* discussed in ancient Freemasonry. Both Kings David and Solomon are also said to have descended from the Tribe of Judah. However, there is a more ancient usage of the *lion's paw* that may have application to the Masonic mysteries.

Candidates who successfully passed the Mithraic initiations were called *Lions* and were marked upon their foreheads with the Egyptian cross, or *ankh*. Throughout the entire Mithraic ritual references were made of Mithra as the Sun God, who came to earth to offer himself as a sacrifice for man and by his death giving men life eternal. After initiation, the candidate was hailed as one who had risen from the grave and was permitted to learn the secret Persian mysteries that originated with Zarathustra.

Although popularized by the Romans and the belief that at least one Roman Emperor was initiated into the order, the *Rites of Mithra* was of Persian origin and later migrated into Southern Europe. "Mithra" is the Zend-Avesta title for the sun and he/she dwelled within that orb. Mithra was both male and female and, as a deity, represented the "feminine principle." That phrase has been more recently popularized in the work of fiction by Dan Brown entitled *The Da Vinci Code*. However, as opposed to representing the Holy Grail, as did Mary Magdalene in Brown's work, the female side of Mithra represented Nature while the male side represented the sun that bathed Nature so that flora and fauna would grow. With this understanding it is easier to also understand the connection between Freemasonry and the *Rites of Mithra*.

From Masonic symbolism, Masons are taught that *sacred* Pythagorean geometry connects man to nature by teaching him about its most concealed recesses; how things in nature are connected; and that numberless worlds surround mankind which the Great Architect of the Universe has connected through the laws of nature. It is correctly stated that a survey of nature first caused man to study symmetry and order which led to the discovery of every useful art. Freemasonry also teaches that the *Supreme Intelligence* pervades all nature and which is further described in the book of Revelation as the *Sea of Glass*.

The *Rites of Mithra* also gave Freemasonry the symbolism of the lesser lights, i.e., the sun, moon and Mercury (later replaced with *Master of the lodge*). That symbolism is intended to explain the natural order of hierarchical authority – as the sun rules the day and the moon governs the night, so should the Worshipful Master, with equal regularity, rule and govern the lodge. Yet, even with such pervasive evidence of the Mithraic influences on Freemasonry, what is the significance of the *grip of the lion's paw?*

Those initiated into the Mithraic mysteries passed through three important degrees. In the first degree, the candidate was taught about his own spiritual nature which must be manifested through disciplined conduct. In the second degree, the candidate was instructed that he represented the mediator between good and evil, light and darkness and was sent into a dark pit to wage battle against the beasts of lust. Finally, in the third degree, he was provided a cape with designs of the zodiac, including the sign of Leo, which represented a lion. The candidate is said to have risen from the grave by the power generated from the sun's influence on Leo – or the strong *grip of the lion's paw*. In that other Mithraic symbolisms are found in Masonic symbolism, the possibility that this symbolism also originated from those rites cannot be ignored. Yet, even so, what is the symbolic importance to Masons?

Mithra derived from the teachings of Zarathrustra which taught that good and evil existed in the world side-by-side. Masons are taught by one of its "ornaments" that human existence is checkered with good and evil. Real life experiences prove that to be so – the battle between good and evil was vividly on display during the Second World War, as well as during the course of other well known conflicts. The *Rites of Mithra* also teach that eventually good will prevail over evil, as symbolized by the energy of the sun rising each day in the east. It is said that that great orb is enabled to rise because of the strength of the Leo residing in its orbit – the *grip of the lion's paw!*

As Freemasons pass through the three degrees necessary to finally achieve the status of Master Mason, they become starkly aware that the Craft demands of them a participation in exercises intended to make them morally straight – good soldiers for the cause of good in the conflict between good and evil, light and darkness. Symbolically rising from the tomb of transgression, the candidate is at last acknowledged as being sufficiently prepared to exemplify goodness to the rest of the world. Whether or not he makes as good use of those tools as have Master Masons in ages past is strictly up to the individual candidate. He may choose goodness or evil, light or darkness; and in so doing either creates the temple wherein the Supreme Architect of the Universe will reside, or the tomb into which evil will eventually be cast.

The Mason who best learns this lesson shows to the world that he was raised by the *grip of the lion's paw*.

Chapter 41

INTOLERANCE

"Are ye not then partial to yourselves, and become judges of evil thoughts?"

Jas. 2:4

Early in his Masonic career, a Freemason is instructed upon the exercise of brotherly love and told that he is to regard the whole human species as one family. That family includes the high and the low, the rich and the poor who, as created by one Almighty Parent and inhabitants of the same planet, are to aid, support and protect one another. Throughout the remainder of his Masonic career, the Mason will receive countless additional instructions about the relationship of brotherly love to the concept of tolerance, especially the concept of religious tolerance.

Most people, including most Freemasons, generally regard themselves as tolerant of other people's religious beliefs. If asked that question during a town meeting, or in any other public setting it is not likely that many would hesitate to raise their hands in proof of their tolerant nature, if for no other reason than to avoid appearing to their friends and neighbors as being socially unacceptable. Indeed, as opposed to merely feigning sincerity, it is likely that most people actually believe they deserve to be labeled as tolerant, especially if they happen to be citizens of the United States.

Our Nation's Constitutional protection of the freedom of religion is taught to American school children at an early age. Churches of several different denominations dot the landscape, as do the synagogues and mosques. While our society can hope that such fundamental devotions to the concept of religious tolerance are accurately representative of how we act as citizens, the truth actually depends upon how one defines *religious tolerance*.

Wikipedia, an Internet dictionary, suggests that the word *tolerance* is a recent political term used as an antithesis to the word *discrimination*. That same source goes on to describe *tolerance* as a word most people would rather avoid using; a word that is evidently universally disliked, because it starkly challenges us to understand that it means much more than merely accepting differing opinions.

As an example of that distaste, one person with an excellent reputation for good character who had recently discovered the joys of a particular religion, replied with a resounding "no" when asked whether or not the new religion brought a deeper sense of tolerance. "To be truly tolerant, as I understand the meaning of that word," that person said, "would require me to be dishonest to both my religion and the beliefs I hold to be true should I accept other religious points of view."

Here, we have struck upon another definition of *tolerance,* one that has sadly enjoyed widespread acceptance throughout the world: a definition that clearly implies that being religiously tolerant means not having any firm beliefs in matters of morality and God. The basic misunderstanding behind that definition is based upon the misconception that one gives up anything other than ego and self-pride when other similarly held religious beliefs are *tolerated.* Such is not the case, at least not from the perspective of Freemasonry.

When you tolerate other religious beliefs you are not required to adopt those beliefs as your own. Neither is it required that you find any particular truth in those other beliefs. Although the failure to do so may expose you as a very unwise and narrow person, unwilling to discover the tremendous value in diversity, that alone does not necessarily render you intolerant. To be tolerant you simply need to be willing to extend religious freedom to people of all religious traditions even though you may disagree, in whole or in part, with the teachings of those other religions.

The ritual selected by Freemasonry to impart wise and serious truths has no single source. It is not Christian, Jewish, Islamic or Hindu. It does, however, find its source in each of those religions, as well as several others. Moreover, its beauty is richly augmented by wonderful philosophical schools from the past. Ancient Egypt contributed such symbolism as east-to-west, the divine nature of the Temple, the immortality of mankind and the resurrection. Our Hebrew brothers added the symbolism of the one God, which was later reinforced by Mohammed and other Islamic writers. The Hindus led us to adopt the symbolism of the beauty of the world around us, so rich and thoroughly satisfying as to be deserving of return visits after death in the manner of the reincarnation of souls. Pythagoras and Plato tendered to the Craft the concept of mankind's unity with God and nature. Among its many valuable spiritual contributions, Christianity taught the Craft to educate its members about the inner soul, the mind of man and the freedom of everyone to choose good over evil, light instead of darkness. As a consequence, Freemasonry's ritual is the result of the synthesizing of different beliefs and different points of view. Consequently, it is no surprise that the fraternity both promotes religious tolerance and literally breathes it into the hearts and souls of its members.

In the Fellowcraft Degree, the candidate is instructed upon the value of earnestly seeking knowledge from the various liberal arts and sciences – grammar, rhetoric, logic, arithmetic, geometry, music and astronomy. That instruction carries with it the implication that one should avoid doctrinal adherences to conclusions that are subject to change when that which was previously unknown shed new light on the matter. The tyranny of doctrine casts an ominous shadow over religious tolerance, because unchangeable doctrine has no room for new light.

When asked if new archeological discoveries might bring a change to existing church doctrine, one prelate recently answered "no." It is not difficult to understand the reason for that answer. Change in the fundamental facts inherent in any given doctrine could undermine a church's credibility. Accordingly, the best defense against such change was, and continues to be intolerance. The result of such a posture was illustrated most graphically during that period of history known simply as "The Inquisition" – a period when prelates and kings roamed the civilized world searching for heretics to burn and torture. The Inquisition led to mass killings of Jews, gypsies and supposed witches, as well as others who were deemed not to have sincerely embraced the specific doctrine then in power.

Sadly, events like the Inquisition have permeated man's history. In Rome, those who adhered to the tenets of the fledgling Christian religion were hunted, tortured and killed by those now referred to as the "pagans." Later, after the Emperor Constantine anointed Christianity as the approved state religion, the tables were turned. Pagans were hunted by Christians and the period of torture and death was relived. Catholics and Protestants continue to kill one another in certain parts of the world, even though each religion claims to be Christ-centered. Certain Islamic sects hate each other and send death squads to eliminate the "enemy."

Freemasonry teaches that each religious doctrine contains truth and error, and will forever do so as long as doctrine remains unchangeable. Thus, Freemasonry bears a close affinity to Hermetic philosophy, the origination of which is attributed to Hermes Trimegistus. That philosophy is of an esoteric nature consisting of mysteries that are expressed in symbols. Certain disciplines drawn from that philosophy have attempted to become complete doctrines: Kabbalah, astrology and alchemy are but a few. When such intellectualization of Hermetic philosophy attempts to establish unequivocal concepts it commits an abuse that is neither adopted by the philosophy itself, nor Freemasonry.

In Freemasonry, there are no theories; there is only experience, including the experience of interpreting symbols. Mystical experience is the root; the experience of acquiring knowledge may be considered the sap; and putting into practice the lessons learned from the interpretation of symbols constitutes the wood. An important lesson in this regard may be derived from the rich symbolism found in the book of Revelations, also known as the Apocalypse of Saint John.

The key to understanding the Apocalypse is to practice it by making use of it as a series of spiritual exercises that awaken deeper levels of consciousness. The seven letters to the churches, the seven seals of the sealed book, the seven trumpets and the seven vials signify a course of spiritual study. To understand those studies, one must place himself in a state of consciousness suitable to receiving revelations: concentration, inner silence, consciousness connecting with sub-consciousness, followed by summarizing that which has been learned. Such effort at synthesizing, so well established in the Masonic interpretation of symbols, is incompatible with intolerance. Rather, it is highlighted by a sense of change; an awareness that no one man, one philosophy, or one religion embodies the entire truth. All that is, or ever was, is not and never will be known in its entirety.

To Freemasons everywhere in the world, the development of a tolerant state of consciousness is central to the promotion of brotherly love. One cannot love his brother, if he hates his brother's religious doctrine. One cannot aid and support his brother, if he concludes that his brother's pitiful condition is God's will visited upon he who practices false religious doctrine. And, one cannot rejoice in the welfare and successes of his brother when he arrogantly believes that he walks in truth while his brother follows the path of darkness.

Tolerance, then, is more than simply putting up with someone else's differing religious belief: it requires embracing and loving the difference.

Chapter 42

JACOB'S LADDER

*"And he dreamed, and behold a ladder set up
on the earth, and the top of it reached to heaven:
and behold the angels of God ascending and descending on it."*

Gen. 28:12

In the Entered Apprentice Degree, the candidate sees and hears Freemasonry's lesson symbolized by the star-decked heavens, or clouded canopy which covers the material earth. This symbolism is of such significance that many European and domestic lodges continue to reinforce its lessons by painting the ceilings with stars, planets and other heavenly luminaries. Concealed within that symbolism is the additional veil to certain wise and serious truths known as "Jacob's Ladder."

We read in the book of Genesis that a man named Jacob fell asleep one night out in the open during his travels from Beersheba to the land of Haran. In his dreams he saw a great ladder with one end set on earth and the top reaching far into the heavens above. Jacob seemed to see the "angels of God" ascending and descending the ladder. As he looks higher up, he also seemed to see God Himself standing above it and heard Him promise that Jacob and his descendants would inherit the land where Jacob slept. Upon awakening, Jacob declared the ground sacred, arranged the stones he used for a pillow into a pillar and named the spot Bethel, which means house of God. (Genesis 28:10-19).

Like so many other stories in the Old Testament, for those who do not insist upon a literal interpretation, the legend of Jacob's Ladder conveys a deep concern and belief that is actually centered in a very old culture. A careful reading of the book of Genesis reveals to the discerning eye that the entire book, when read as a whole, appears to be disjointed, difficult to read as one continuum and seemingly missing some very essential background information. Recent academic research has concluded a reason for this fact that tends to more fully explain why Egypt was so important to our Masonic ancestors.

Jacob's vision was but a fragment of a richer living tradition; an ancient teaching about the link between the earthly and divine worlds. This tradition is further emphasized in Masonic ritual by the explanation given concerning the pillars named Boaz and Jachin, discussed in an earlier chapter. In this tradition we are told that the link between the two worlds has been broken. Angels with flaming swords block the entrance to the Garden of Eden and, as we read further in the story about Jacob's Ladder, Jacob is admonished against climbing that ladder to heaven. For many who read this story, it is a significant event in describing the Fall of man to sin and his need for divine redemption. Yet, the ancient tradition behind that story is much more enlightening.

The ancient Egyptians absorbed much of the earlier cultural and religious practices of Mesopotamia, from which the legends of Gilgamesh arose. Within that legend is a startling tale about men who walked the earth seemingly having come from nowhere known to mankind. They were on earth to learn what the earthly existence had to teach and once those lessons were learned, they left earth to travel to heaven to enrich that divine environment with earthly influences. (The book of Genesis actually contains a piece of this legend in the story about the "Watchers," or "Giants.") This legend later became a benchmark for Hermes Trismegestis whose philosophy known as Hermeticism emphasis the divine slogan "as it is above, so shall it be below."

According to the ancient tradition, the story about Jacob's Ladder is both instructional and insightful. Owing to the location of the sacred ground where Jacob slept, it is believed that it together with other similar sacred locations serve as the perfect conduits between the earthly and divine worlds. In other words, the ancients believed, as many believe today, that there are more sacred places to worship God than others. In part, this legend tends to shed more light on the earthly significance of Jerusalem to our Jewish brethren, as well as our Christian and Moslem brethren.

For Masons there is yet another lesson to be learned from Jacob's vision. While certain dogmas and doctrines assert the lone entitlement to bridging the gap between heaven and earth, God and man, those dogmas and doctrines are but paths one may select to complete our divine journey. There are other equally valid paths, which fact reminds us that embracing diversity is essential to establishing true freedom. More importantly, Masons are encouraged to think for themselves, pray to God on their own and develop a relationship with the Divine that is not wholly dependent about the intermediary of a specific dogma or doctrine. God created man in His image. He did not create dogma and doctrine in His image – those were created by man.

In that latter regard, the ancient writer Philo affirmed that the Therapeutae practiced what Freemasonry now preaches about the acquisition of divine knowledge. Stories from the Old Testament and elsewhere should be read for their symbolic messages, not for their literal recitation about factual history. The Therapeutae read the Holy Scriptures and sought wisdom from their ancestral philosophy by taking it as an allegory, since they also thought that the words of the text were symbols of something whose hidden nature is revealed by studying the underlying meaning.

Freemasonry teaches by the use of symbols and in so doing encourages its members to understand that God's most enduring lessons are yet to be recovered from the mists of the past. Prophets and seers have told us that mankind has merely scratched the surface of all that is to be learned. Where man once walked on foot to get from one place to the other, he may now fly. While ancient civilizations could not communicate one with another, today's nations are in instant communication. Mankind is drawing ever closer together, hundreds of thousands of people are living in urban environments and men on one end of the globe are nourishing the needs of men at the other end. Man's relationship with God, direct and unfettered by outside dogma or doctrine, is essential for men to absorb the concept of brotherly love – not as a mere concept, but as a way of life.

Such are some of the lessons learned from the Masonic symbolism of Jacob's Ladder. Can you find others?

Chapter 43

LUSTRATION

> "And Aaron and his sons thou shalt
> bring unto the tabernacle of the
> congregation, and shalt wash
> them with water."
>
> Ex. 29:4

Although this ancient rite is not practiced in the first three degrees of Freemasonry, but in the high degrees only, the symbolism of *lustration*, or washing, imparts some of the more significant spiritual lessons embraced by the Craft. From time immemorial, washing was employed as an act of devotion – even before Jesus was baptized by John in the River Jordan. Before entering sacred chambers, initiates for many of the ancient sacred rites were washed at their entrance to symbolize their purity of mind, soul and body. The act of *lustration* was also intended to demonstrate to the world that the candidate's heart was pure before God.

Over the years the original meaning of such washing has undergone changes – some beneficial, some not. In Judaism, washing has been extended to the bodies of the dead, as an additional symbol of purification for the journey to that land from whose bourn no traveler returns. In Christian churches, converts submit to baptism in the style intended to replicate the baptism of Jesus by John. Some Christian churches administer a sprinkling over the head, while others require total emersion of the body. Some religions go so far as to require *lustration* before a person may consider their soul ready for eternal salvation.

Freemasonry teaches that the truth of the relationship of this rite to an individual's salvation is between the individual and the religion he chooses to follow. Man has never had the right to compel another man to adopt any particular religious perspective. The choice of religious perspective is to be decided only by the individual and God.

More often, people select their religious beliefs based upon their ancestry, the place where they were raised and influence of their peers. Those born in a Protestant land are more likely to become Protestants. Those raised in the Church of St. Peter are more likely to embrace Catholicism. Allah is worshipped throughout much of the Middle East, and thus most who are born and raised their choose Islam. If you are born and raised in a Jewish community, you are quite likely to condemn Jesus as an imposter. Few believe in any particular religion because they have examined its tenets thoroughly and discover evidence of primacy. As Albert Pike has observed, "Not one man in ten thousand knows anything about the *proofs* of his faith. (*Morals and Dogma*).

Masonry perpetuates the symbolism of *lustration* for a very important spiritual reason that has absolutely nothing to do with the promotion of religion. In order that man may even count himself worthy to emulate the morality associated with God, he must possess a pure heart. Before man may expect the gift of eternal life, he must rid himself of the impurities he has permitted to embrace his soul. It matters not what one believes is the true path to salvation. All paths must be traveled by a pure heart.

But purity does not mean that one must become perfect, for perfection is left to God – not to man. The Mosaic Pavement teaches us that life is checkered with good and evil – all life, not just yours. The indented tessel teaches us that we are surrounded by manifold blessings and comforts, which we may each enjoy by a faithful reliance upon Divine Providence. Consequently, as Masons we are taught that there are two ingredients to the recipe for a pure heart: our own actions in conformity with the teachings of God, and God's grace which is given to us as the most precious present any of us will ever receive.

The *tarot,* consisting of a deck of cards with symbolic images imprinted on each card, illustrates a particular Arcanum, or esoteric lesson, that is symbolized by an angelic-winged woman holding two vases – one in each hand – with water flowing between the vases. Of all Masonic symbols, this *tarot* image best illustrates the manner in which man should approach God.

Frequently, when we are engaged in prayer, God is either like a school principal, or a hired servant. On the one hand, when we pray to God we realize that we are unworthy and believe that at any moment He will punish us more severely than He already has punished us. On the other hand, in His role as hired servant, God simply meets our demands, hears our requests and grants our wishes. Neither one is what God desires of us.

In the Old Testament, we are told that God favored offerings of sincerity, not holocausts, or the burning of living things. We also learn in the book of Genesis that Abraham talked with God about God's intention to destroy Sodom – the original Sin City. In that passage, Abraham demonstrates that he and God have compassion – Abraham for 50, 40, 20, even 10 worthy men – God, for all of His creation. God yields to Abraham and rewards his deep compassion. The city was eventually destroyed, but those for whom Abraham worried were saved.

Both the woman holding the two vases and the Old Testament stories reveals that God wants a relationship with us. He wants us to understand that He respects us as co-participants in His Creation. Not only has He created us in His image, He has given us a free will that He will not disturb.

In the Entered Apprentice Degree, we are exposed to a very important passage of scripture – "ask and it shall be given unto to you; seek and ye shall find; knock and it shall be opened unto you." Yet, in that Degree, we are not informed about how we should ask, seek and knock. Those lessons are revealed during the ensuing two degrees, which teach us the importance of purifying our hearts and minds before God – the lesson of the *lustration.*

Purification occurs within a Mason when he realizes that God wants to be approached as a father, or partner in Creation. Abraham's "bargaining" with God was successful, not because he promised something in return, but because he demonstrated to God that they each shared a common desire – compassion. An interest to be recognized by your fellow man, or to receive acclaim from an organization, while not entirely without merit, is nevertheless useless to God. He already respects you for who you are. There is no greater acclaim that you will ever receive. Rather, when you "ask, seek and knock," do so with a heart and mind that seeks the same goals God seeks.

How many times in your life have you changed God's mind? Abraham did, and you probably have too. Think back. Was there ever a time that you prayed about something for which you had a deep and abiding passion? Perhaps a loved one destined to die, whose death was seemingly miraculously postponed? If so, think about the circumstances surrounding that time and try to understand the lesson God was trying to teach you. If you ask, seek, or knock with a pure heart and mind, you will receive. If you ask your earthly father for a specific thing, would you expect him to hand you something different? Perhaps, if you were not in his good graces, but if you were and he could give you what you desired, he would do so – just as you would do so for your own son or daughter.

My brethren, Masonry seeks to teach you to approach God as a father – not as a principal of a school, or a hired servant. The symbolism of the *lustration* is intended to represent a sacrament, or outward manifestation of an inward truth. When your heart and mind is in tune with God, He will answer all that you ask, give you all that you seek, and open every door necessary to guide you along the proper path.

Chapter 44

MELCHIZEDEK

> "And Melchizedek king of Salem brought
> forth bread and wine: and he was
> priest of the most high God."
>
> Gen. 14:18

In Masonry, the mysterious figure from the Old Testament known simply as *Melchizedek* is connected with the order or degree of High Priesthood. He is said to have welcomed Abraham with bread and wine after the Father of the Hebrews had completed his most recent military sojourn in the land of Canaan. Masonic tradition informs us that he escorted Abraham into the hallowed halls of an Enochian Temple – a mysterious forerunner of Masonic lodges – and there initiated him into certain ancient mysteries. His holiness was so highly esteemed that, in the New Testament, Jesus is compared to him as a High Priest of the Order of *Melchizedek*. Even the official title of this Most High Priest – the King of Salem - is shrouded in mystery.

The journey toward discovering the importance of this figure to Freemasonry begins with identifying the realm of his reign. As we have learned from exploring other Masonic symbols, the word *Salem* is regarded by several historians as the Holy Land now known throughout the world as Jerusalem. The word itself means "peace," and thus the title King of Salem may also be translated to mean the King of Peace. We recall from our various readings in the New Testament that Jesus was referred to as the Prince of Peace. This connection between *Melchizedek* and the figure referred to as *Christ* is essential for Masons to comprehend, if the true significance of the King of Salem is ever to be grasped.

The next step in our journey toward discovering the truth about this mystical character concerns both why Abraham would have bothered to pay *Melchizedek* a visit in the first instance, as well as why the King of Salem is regarded by today's theologians as the ultimate High Priest. Interestingly, the answer to both of those questions is considerably significant to Freemasonry. Those answers are gleaned in part from the Dead Sea Scrolls, which contained fragments entitled the *Prince Melchizedek Document.*

At the time of his encounter with the King of Salem, Abraham was reputedly a powerful military leader of the Egyptian army and a man of extraordinarily high standing in Egyptian politics. His legions had just successfully concluded a lengthy, hotly contested battle with four troublesome kings. The men were weary and worn out and yearned to return home. Yet Abraham stopped to sit down in the presence of the King of Peace – the Most High Priest – strongly suggesting that *Melchizedek's* reputation was well-known to Abraham. It also strongly suggests that Abraham expected to gain a great benefit from the meeting. The benefit most likely related to spiritual matters, not material concerns.

Although Abraham was an esteemed military commander and man of high political ranking, he was not a part of the inner circle within the governing Egyptian hierarchy. He was a Hebrew from Ur, not Egyptian and this fact alone could easily have precluded him from ever being initiated into the ancient Egyptian mysteries. The ancient Egyptian government had always sponsored a specific religion and only "pure-bloods" were permitted to be initiated.

Melchizedek was not Egyptian. Many writers of antiquity asserted that he was literally of God's essence – not at all unlike the later attributions made about Jesus. His very name appeared to some to be a combination of *Michael* and *Zadok* – the archangel, on the one hand, and the spiritual High Priest, on the other hand. As such, *Melchizedek* was not limited to initiating men into the ancient mysteries based upon race, color, creed, or religion. Like Freemasonry today, his criteria for initiation were primarily based upon the internal worth of a man, not his worldly wealth or honors. Moreover, *Melchizedek's* God was not Amen-Ra the Egyptian sun-god. It was none other than the Mountain Lord who is reported to have later revealed His name to Moses – *I Am that I Am!*

The mysteries into which *Melchizedek* could initiate a man, such as Abraham, were not confined to one theological doctrine. They were singularly viewed as truths emanating from the One God in whom all creation may place its trust. Subsequently, ancient writings record that Hermes Trismegistus instituted the Emerald Tablet, which memorialized a purely non-doctrinal synthesis of philosophy, Kabbalism and Egyptian theology. In the years after the death of Abraham, tradition informs us that the Egyptian priesthood, then recently enlightened by the teachings of Hermes, adopted the rituals employed by *Melchizedek* during Abraham's initiation. From that time forward, although slight differences in ritual preference existed, the mysteries were the same whether conferred in Egypt, Greece, or elsewhere. Free from doctrinal restrictions, they have been regarded as nothing less than lessons in truth given to all creation by the One True God in whom every Mason places his trust.

Although many argue whether or not *Melchizedek* was a real entity, a combination of entities, an incarnation of Christ, or merely a symbol, one of the more significant aspects of his story surrounds the symbolism associated with the bread with which he received Abraham. The use of bread continues to this day in Christian religious services representing both the Christ and the Word of God. In the days of Abraham it simply represented *righteousness* without qualifying what manner of worshipping God was more righteous than any other. Freemasonry has adopted a very similar perspective.

Like *Melchizedek,* Masons believe that only God is righteous. Man-made religions, each demanding to be acknowledged as the one true religion, attempt to re-interpret that truth claiming that since it emanated from God, it alone is righteous. Freemasonry recoils at such teachings having witnessed from the dawn of creation the ravages inflicted upon humanity in an effort to conform non-believers into a state of *righteousness.* Why must man be fettered by doctrinal bindings to be considered righteous? Is not true righteousness found in the freedom of every man to his own voice, vote and opinion? When Freemasons participated in establishing a government for the newly liberated United States of America it was, first and foremost, based upon the freedoms of speech and religion. Yet, in this day of so-called enlightenment we still hear the plaintive cry that such freedoms are not *righteousness* – rather they are licenses to commit immorality.

Conformity to one approved manner of thinking, praying and speaking is too often promoted as the one true path to God. If that is so, *Melchizedek* would fail the test, for his God loved all people of all walks of life and all beliefs. If that is so, the spiritual gifts from Abraham also fail the test, for those gifts were promised by God to inure to the benefit of all of Abraham's descendants – to the children of Ishmael, as well as the children of Isaac. Much to the contrary, Freemasons know that the true lesson of the King of Salem – whether man or myth – is that each and every man, woman and child is precious in God's sight and that we, as God's servants, must never shame our declaration of faith in Him before our Masonic altars by condemning anyone because of his or her religious and philosophical beliefs.

Chapter 45

MOUNT MORIAH

> "Then Solomon began to build the house of the
> Lord at Jerusalem in mount Moriah,..."
>
> 2Chr. 3:1

During the ritual performed in the Third Degree of Masonry, the candidate is told about a place referred to as *Mount Moriah*, but is not informed why it is of interest to Masons. Masonic tradition informs us that it was the place where Abraham was about to offer up his son, Isaac, but lifted him from the sacrificial altar upon hearing the voice of God. Also, it was there that King David is said to have met and appeased the destroying angel. Masonic tradition further informs us that during the era of David's son, Solomon, Hiram Abif was laid to rest at *Mount Moriah* by his assassins, who planted an acacia at the head of the grave so that it could be readily recognized later. Each of those stories seems to tie the spot to something very important to Masonry and mankind, but the answer as to what that might be is not made clear at any time during the Masonic ritual.

To learn the answer we begin first by returning to Abraham. The Holy Bible asserts that God entered into a covenant with Abraham and that through the lineage of his son, Isaac, promised that He would establish His kingdom forever. It was there that Isaac's sons Esau and Jacob eventually came together forming the Tribe of Judah, to which Masonry attributes the origination of the enormously significant symbolism known as the *lion's paw*. Later, the Holy Writings inform us that Moses led the Hebrews to *Mount Moriah* where the royal house of Judah was to be enthroned. Along the way they encountered any number of Canaanites, Amalekites, Edomites and others who sought without success to impede their journey.

Those stories from sacred scripture symbolically convey important spiritual lessons. Central to those lessons is the notion that life is a journey back to God. Along the way we can expect to encounter our own Canaanites and the like, who jump out at us as obstacles to reaching our goal. Only by exercising unceasing faith in God may we expect to clear the path of those obstacles – a faith that finds us in constant prayer and action.

After Moses settled his community of followers near *Mount Moriah*, we are informed again by the Holy Bible that he there erected a Tabernacle within which the Ark of the Covenant was placed. That Tabernacle was the first house erected by the Hebrews for the Lord God – a tent where it is said the Ineffable One was pleased to rest. Generations later, the Hebrews were ejected from the land, but returned under the banner of David, their first king, whose men carried before them the Ark of the Covenant, which is reported to have contained nothing less than the power of God. The High Priest, referred to by the generic priestly name of Zadok, re-instituted the Ark in its holy environment and the Davidic kingdom was established. *Mount Moriah* was thereafter referred to by the Hebrews as the Rock of David. Today it is called the Dome of the Rock.

Undeniably, *Mount Moriah* has been regarded for centuries by Hebrews, Christians and Muslims as one of the holiest places in the entire world. It is to this sense of holiness that Masonry alludes by selecting the spot as a place of importance during one of its most important ritualistic degrees. It may never be known whether or not a man named Hiram Abif was ever buried there, or that such a man ever actually existed. Masonry does not expect us to confirm or deny the truth of that allegory. Rather, Masons are expected to reflect upon the spiritual significance of establishing a kingdom of men under the fatherhood of God in an environment with which God is well pleased.

Reflecting for the moment upon the change of hands through which this revered location has gone offers us further insight into the wisdom of Masonry's refusal to endorse any one religion over any other religion. For centuries too many bloody wars have been fought for control of *Mount Moriah;* religious wars that have laid waste to beautiful monuments and cut-downs hundreds of thousands of men, women and children before their lives could be fully lived. Those wars and ravages are not merely a part of mankind's past – they are being fought today in one form or another. Throughout it all, whom does God prefer? Which faction does He favor? What religion will finally emerge as the one true religion for all mankind to follow?

Embracing the differences in all men, Masonry inculcates a deep appreciation for diversity and points its members in the direction of harmonizing those differences. Raging deadly warfare will eventually subside and a winner will emerge to claim the title of truest of all religions. Throughout history, such has always been so, but new wars have always followed with new and different winners claiming the title. The lesson for all humanity is that wars and hatred result only in death and destruction, not harmony.

But, what has all of this to do with how Masons should best live their daily lives? It is one thing to know and understand the "big picture" and quite another to learn where you personally fit into that big picture. Wars, tumults and divisive disputes always involve the assertion of competing self-interest. They are the result of the immense "me" of men's egos, which demand that others pay attention to them, listen to them and abide by what they say. Masonry asks you to exercise self-discipline and to curb your natural-born ego so that you are better enabled to appreciate and understand your brother's opposing point of view. It is only by trying to become understanding of others that we eventually truly do become understanding. And, it is the process of learning that lesson that is at the core of fraternalism, or the greater love of one's brother.

Mount Moriah represents for us the center of Masonic activity where acts of kindness and loving concern for others are exchanged. It can be your own lodge, or it can be anywhere that brethren gather to bestow God's greatest gift on His creation — the love of one man for another. For us, too, it represents an important admonishment never to embrace anything of material value more dearly than we embrace another human being. There are no riches on earth more valuable than human life, which has been breathed into every person by God Himself. For that reason, no Mason should ever support or countenance any act toward any other person that is anything other than kind and loving.

Chapter 46

OPERATIVE AND SPECULATIVE MASONRY

"The labor of the righteous tendeth to life:
the fruit of the wicked to sin."

Prov. 10:16

Certain writers about Freemasonry emphatically declare that Masons were originally builders, or men who were skilled at fashioning stone for the builder's use. For them, the phrase *operative masonry* refers to men from a certain period in history who, presumably knowing nothing about the spiritual significance of our Masonic symbols, worked with squares, compasses, mallets and levels to erect buildings. In contrast, *speculative masons* are described by those same writers as present-day Masons – men who have suddenly discovered the spiritual significance of the tools our blue-collar ancestors evidently knew nothing about. Some support for that contention is believed to derive from Masonic ritual itself, which purportedly offers the candidate a distinction to consider between operative and speculative Masonry. We are informed that our ancient brethren wrought at the building of King Solomon's Temple and other stately edifices, but that we today are only speculative Masons.

The history of the English guilds also provides an additional basis for concluding that operative Masons were originally skilled builders who saw no spiritual significance in the tools with which they worked. For them, the *secrets of masonry* exclusively pertained to the various skills associated with stonemasonry. However, without regard to whether Freemasonry sprung from those guilds, or is actually the heir to the *ancient mysteries* found in the initiatory rites, if today's Mason is simply told that his Masonic ancestors were simply originally builders, he is deprived of the more significant lessons in esoteric symbolism offered by comparing and contrasting operative Masonry and speculative Masonry on a spiritual level.

On one level, all Masons, past and present, are both operative and speculative. The speculative side of man learns the philosophical, theological and spiritual lessons that Freemasonry teaches, while the operative side of man puts those lessons into action. In that Freemasonry has adopted the Hermetic habit of synthesizing contrary or competing concepts, it is essential that the Mason understand how he is to bring the lessons he has learned into the world where he lives.

Albert Pike wrote that the message found in the Emerald Table attributed to the Great Egyptian Hierophant, Hermes Trismegistus – equilibrium is achieved after the assimilation of different concepts – is the great lesson Masonry imparts to humanity. For example, Pike observed that *wisdom,* as described in the Kabbalistic Books, Proverbs and Ecclesiastes is nothing less than the Creative Agent of God. As the Creative Agent, *wisdom* is active, not passive – it is in the present, not of the past. Creation is an ongoing phenomenon in which all mankind participates to a greater, or lesser degree depending upon each man's state of enlightenment. Thus, Freemasonry is as *operative* today as it was when our ancient brethren wrought at the building of stately edifices.

Pike, as well as other Masonic writers, encouraged Masons to develop both their operative sense, as well as their speculative curiosity. For Masonry to impart anything of lasting value to humanity, Masons must think then act. One cannot exist without the other, if man hopes to contribute anything to his brethren. In so doing, those writers have variously invited us to each synthesize three antitheses or antimonies: (1) *idealism – realism;* (2) *realism – nominalism;* and (3) *faith – empirical science.*

The idealist considers everything as so many forms of thought, while the realist affirms that objects of knowledge have an existence that is independent of thought. For example, the realist answers "yes" to the question of whether or not a fallen tree in an isolated forest makes a sound – the idealist is not so certain. When all is said and the quarreling about which is correct has subsided, the Masons is left with the unshakeable knowledge that both have a common source in the Great Architect. Actions built upon both considerations are, therefore, regarded as valid by God. However, the failure to act on either notion gives nothing to the world.

Realism relates to the school of occidental thought which attributes objective reality to general notions that are usually designated as "abstract." Mediaeval philosophy designated it as "universalia" – all things pertain to the universal. Nominalism, on the other hand, admits that only "particulars" are real. The problem was explicitly analyzed by Plato, who first observed on behalf of realists: "I see a horse, but I don't see horseness." According to Plato, "horseness" merely exists as an idea and is not real other than as a form of thought. Horses aside, the philosophical struggle becomes important when we ask ourselves, "What came first, genesis, or creation?" The differing concepts also draw grave significance from the discussion about which is more important, the individual, or society. To Freemasons, the problem is again resolved by reference back to the Supreme Architect of the Universe – Masons confess His superiority in all matters and trust that thought coupled with action will make real to all mankind God's enormous love.

It is written in the Gospels that if one has faith as a grain of mustard seed, he may move mountains. Empirical science takes a grain of hydrogen and releases its energy thereby reducing a mountain to dust. The first is speculative, the second is operative. Mankind has not yet learned to use the immense powers of the mind to generally move mountains. However, science has unleashed the power of the atom for man to build or destroy. Yet, that science did not act alone as if by magic. Learned men applied their knowledge to the task and discovered a secret of Nature that is potentially good and evil. Nothing of the atom, of hydrogen, or even of the spherical shape of the world would be known to this age had not men of a previous age thought and acted. Thinking without doing would have produced nothing. And so it is also when one acts without first thinking. The speculative side of man serves the operative side, and vice versa.

Freemasonry teaches that nothing is impossible. If a man dreams a condition for his future, he will attain it when God and that man's soul work together. But, to sit idly by and wish for something to happen without acting together with God leads nowhere. The surest way to make true the prayer for world peace is for each man to avoid war and embrace peace. The best way to insure an answer to a prayer for alleviating hunger is to give of what you have so that the hungry may eat. While praying that poverty may vanish is laudable, the most efficient way to eliminate its ravishing is to donate to causes that support the poor.

In the book of James, man is informed that faith without works is dead. But, it is not the faith itself that is dead. If one fails to put his faith to work, the beneficial effects of that faith will never be known to anyone. It will amount to nothing more than wishful thinking. Masons do not embrace such fantasies. If they did, the world would have no hospitals operated and funded by Shriners. The aged, widowed and orphaned would have no place to call home. And, the speech impaired would have no clinics to go to and cure their ailment.

When the thoughtful, speculative Mason places his thinking into operative action the world becomes a better place. When he fails, darkness prevails to the detriment of all humanity. Consider your actions and resolve never to hide your lamp beneath a bushel. You are a Mason and should act like one.

Chapter 47

PERSEVERANCE

"For so is the will of God, that with well doing ye
may put to silence the ignorance of foolish men."

1 Pet. 2:15

During a particular degree ritual ceremony, Masonry employs a series of symbols revealed together that concludes with a vivid image of *time* standing at the back of a woman patiently unfolding the ringlets of her hair. Masons are concurrently instructed that "time, patience and perseverance will accomplish all things." That symbolism is intended to impart both an exoteric, as well as an esoteric message.

No man can seriously question the practical value of patience. Acquiring a patient demeanor oftentimes saves one from the embarrassment that results when anger threatens to cause him to blurt out in public regrettable words of derision. Patience in the workplace also enables one to complete a task efficiently and effectively. Tender and quiet emotions foster friendships, whereas impatient nagging and prodding tends to destroy relationships. If the rational thinking man is given a choice, he will likely prudently select patience over impatience, because the rational thinking man knows that harmony in all things is essential to peace of mind.

Similarly, most men are familiar with that phrase of encouragement first heard in our youth: "If at first you do not succeed, try, try again." Nothing in life is often accomplished easily. That which is easy is not often as meaningful to us as are those things that required the exertion of great effort. Abraham Lincoln, this Nation's sixteenth President, failed at business, failed at politics, suffered a nervous breakdown and eventually was elected President – not once, but twice. Like George Bailey, the leading character in the Frank Capra movie, *It's a Wonderful Life,* Lincoln's life was important to those around him. Had he given in to any of his failures or setbacks and vanished from the public eye, the landscape of American life and politics would most assuredly be substantially different today.

The ancients recognized that all life is in various stages of *becoming*. It is said that grains of sand are in the process of *becoming* human in consciousness; humans are in the process of *becoming* planets; planets were in the process of *becoming* solar systems; and planets were in the process of *becoming* solar systems. Life has no choice in the matter – the laws of Nature dictate that with the passing of time, such changes are inevitable. In this context, perseverance assumes a slightly different meaning. Whereas Lincoln freely chose to run for public office after being defeated, the grains of sand that the ancients believed were in the process of *becoming* simply awaited the passage of time. In each circumstance, *becoming* requires time and patience – it does not occur instantaneously.

Freemasonry recognizes that the concept of perseverance is directly related to the concept of destiny. Both practical and philosophical alchemy concern the changing of substances over a period of time to attain a different more desirable substance. Employing the correct chemical formula, brass is eventually converted to gold. Likewise, employing the correct state of mind man converts dark and evil thoughts to kind and good works. Both results represent the *destiny,* or expected effect caused by the application of the best formula. However, neither result will follow unless the one applying the formula persists in his effort until the desired effect is accomplished. Ancient Freemasonry concluded that that truth had equal application to spiritual matters.

The theological and philosophical studies of the ancients consist of layer upon layer of the deepest meaning that man is capable of understanding. Yet nowhere in any writings presently available to mankind does one definitive work exist on either of those subjects. In order to arrive at the deepest meaning one must read vastly, listen carefully and meditate with determination.

After Pythagoras died, Plato was initiated into the "Greater Mysteries" and was sent out into the world at age 49 to continue the work once performed by Pythagoras himself. Following Plato's death, disciples who called themselves neo-Platonists continued to explore new philosophical avenues, thus proving to succeeding generations that regardless of the genius of one or two men, arriving at that which constitutes the *deepest meaning* remains a work in progress that each individual Mason is obligated to pursue. If it is not pursued, the meaning will be forever lost.

Author Manly P. Hall, both a Freemason and highly respected philosopher during his time, wrote about the *Bembine Table of Isis,* an Egyptian hieroglyph believed by some to conceal the key to sacred alphabets. Many learned men have studied the *Table,* but to date none has deciphered the code completely. The master secret contained therein awaits discovery – perhaps by some newly initiated Mason who applies a great sense of *perseverance* to the task. Perhaps that new initiate will only add to what has already been discovered offering to those who follow in his footsteps after his death yet another piece to God's puzzle. However, if no one makes an effort, nothing more will ever be known –rather, all will be lost.

How many men have lived their lives to completion without ever realizing their destiny? How many others have lived out their lives contrary to their destiny? And, how many more simply did not care what they did with the life God gave them? Following both World War I and World War II, several writers bemoaned the loss of so much human life which not only deprived families of loved ones, but also deprived society of the beneficial accomplishments the young dead could have made. As tragic as that harvest of death was, it is more tragic to find those who have had a chance to fulfill their promise by living through adulthood, but failed to contribute anything positive to mankind.

In his writings about reincarnation, Edgar Cayce, the famous occultist, seer and healer from the early 20th century, described the meaning of past failures and accomplishments during previous lives to certain of his "patients." In each instance, Cayce chronicled both acts of valor as well as acts constituting breaches of faith. He did so to enable his "patients" to learn how best to live their present lives. Some heeded his revelations, others did not. Those who did lived happy and productive lives. Those who learned nothing from the past died without ever having improved upon the lives Cayce believed they had previously lived.

One does not need to either accept or reject the notion of reincarnation to understand the important lesson from Cayce's studies. A man who seeks to learn and then use that which he has learned to serve his brother has done all he can possibly be expected to do to fulfill his own destiny. On the other hand, a man who persists in sloth, self-interest, or pride will merely have wasted his time – he will not have left anything upon which others can build.

Masonic tradition informs us that in the time of King Solomon, three Masters were once sent to explore the ruins of a temple said to have been built by Enoch. They discovered and then fearlessly explored a deep shaft sunk into the earth. Descending through nine arches, they finally reached a chamber hewn in solid rock where treasure had been hidden before the Great Flood. A description of that treasure may be acquired after an initiate has risen to the Masonic rank of *Perfect Elu* and will not be further revealed here. The importance here is for the reader to understand that the ancient Masters could never have reached the hidden vault if they had failed to master all of the requisite lessons in Freemasonry and applied those lessons to their personal lives.

The reward of the practice of virtue and upright living is nothing less than spiritual fulfillment. What remains for you as the inheritor of the ancient system we call Freemasonry is to persevere in learning how to apply that which you have discovered.

Chapter 48

POT OF INCENSE

"Let my prayer be set before thee as incense; and the lifting up of my hands as the evening sacrifice."

Ps. 141:2

The burning of incense was a part of worship common to all ancient nations, including the Hebrews, the Egyptians and the Hindus. Among the Hebrews it was also a symbol of prayer, of holy devotions and of the purity of affections in divine worship. Masonry retains this ancient symbol in the form of the *pot of incense,* which is intended to teach us that our hearts should continually glow with gratitude to the Great Architect. The gratitude expected of us is further symbolized by the act of making a sacrifice.

Our ancestors regularly sacrificed to the Divine Wisdom intending the ritual to be act of loving appeasement. In the Old Testament, sacrifices were made in many different ways. Cain and Abel each offered their respective sacrifices to God and we are informed that Abel's was the more pleasing. Abraham was about to slay his own son, Isaac, on an altar, again to please God. The High Priests of Israel variously offered holocausts of grain and animals to both atone for the errors of their people and to please the Deity. In each instance, man attempted to give something of value, beauty and importance to God as a demonstration of his loving gratitude to the Great Creator.

Masonry regards the practice of burning incense as a particularly significant form of sacrifice – but why is that so? In early human history, the burning of incense became important to many religions around the world, not just to the Jews and the Hebrews. The best known incense materials in those days were frankincense and myrrh. Interestingly, in the New Testament story about the birth of Jesus, the *magi* brought the infant child gifts of those substances. It is this story that leads us to discover a reason that Freemasonry employs the *pot of incense* as one of its more important symbols – not because Christians regard Jesus as Divine, but to impart another ancient, wise and significant truth.

When frankincense burned it produced a white smoke which was presented as the purest offering to God. It was also associated with the legendary phoenix, the bird that rose from the ashes of death to renewed life. Those ashes were said to have been produced by the burning of frankincense. As such, it is a symbol of regeneration, which Masonry teaches is proceeds from the dying material body. Myrrh was used to embalm the body, or prepare it for regeneration, and as such was highly regarded by the ancients as a necessary ingredient for the proper anointing of mortal bodies before they passed on to the great reward with God. Freemasonry adopts as its most central truth the fact that life never begins and never ends – it always was, is and ever shall be.

Some Masonic writers have concluded that the ancients had a better understanding than do we in this present-day age about how to increase mankind's longevity. For example, the substance referred to as *manna*, consumed, as we are informed in the Holy Writings, by the Israelites during their sojourn with Moses, may have been more nourishing than we once believed. For years, the priests and royalty of regimes in Mesopotamia and Egypt consumed an alchemically refined substance referred to as *mfkzt*. It was regarded as a valuable mineral product that possessed qualities that made the human body stronger and enabled it to exist longer. Modern day researchers are now asserting that this mineral product is the so-called *bread-of-life* that has become the centerpiece of many religious ceremonial rituals. To make *mfkzt* one must refine metal to a pure white gold, in which state it actually is said to have a negative weight.

Perhaps it is because gold yields *mfkzt* that it was presented to Jesus by the *magi* together with frankincense and myrrh. The importance of these facts to Masons is unquestionably related to regeneration, or as some would call it – the resurrection.

The *pot of incense,* then, represents much more than a mere ritualistic sacrifice to God giving thanks for what He has provided. It is intended to remind us to be very grateful that the law of Nature – God's law – renders it impossible that we should ever die. Once a Freemason acknowledges the truthfulness of that law, he cannot help but ponder and meditate upon what that truth means to him. Does it provide us with a license to live vile and immoral lifestyles? Does it free us to act toward our fellowmen in any manner we choose, whether for good or for evil? Or, does it impose upon us grave responsibilities to become obedient to the laws of Nature – to God's law – and constantly strive to live in such a manner that the lives of others are made better?

The sacrifice Masons should consider making is the freedom to choose to live badly. If you will live forever; if you have always lived and truly will never die, then logically you can choose to live badly. Men throughout history have done so. Yet, according to the lessons of antiquity adopted by Masons, the light of God shines even on them. But, have you considered the great likelihood that in the living of your own life you are also creating *heaven?* In other words, have you ever reflected upon the possibility that what you create here on earth is reflected above? The Hermetic saying *as it is above, so shall it be below,* does not work one way – it is a roadmap to a two-way street. *As it is below, so shall it be above* is equally true in Hermetic philosophy, which forms a significant part of Masonic philosophy.

Each and every human life has an enduring impact upon future generations. The precise manner of that impact flows from the decisions made by each individual during the course of his or her lifetime. One can decide to violate the laws, hurt people and provide a source for hatred and discontent. One may also choose to be lazy and let others do the work, thereby becoming a charge on the resources of others. Or, one can choose to learn, become good at something that serves the welfare of others and find untold joy in watching how his or her conduct has a positive impact upon others.

The symbols and lessons of Masonry teach us that the results of lives lived either poorly or well also affect future spiritual life - the life that continues to exist long after the material body has decayed and died. Some have decided that it is best to simply wait for God to establish His kingdom on earth, believing that nothing they may do could possibly have an effect upon when mankind will actually enjoy the benefits of living in God's kingdom. But, my brethren, such thinking suggests that mankind has nothing to do with God, His creation, or the future He has planned for us. According to that school of thought, God is merely amused by us and will soon tire of our silly behavior, wave His hand and instantly make things better without our help. Perhaps He will – but perhaps something more is required of us who have been created in His image – we who have within us a Holy Spirit, or piece of God Himself.

Masonry has never taught that man can sit by idly and watch as evil deeds prevail. Rather, Masonry has always taught that a Mason has an important work ahead of him – a work that must be calculated to promote brotherly love, relief and truth. In Freemasonry, the word *sacrifice* is intended to describe selfless good deeds performed by one person for the benefit of another person. The fraternity does not dwell upon offerings of food, animals, or humans as a propitiation or worship. Nowhere in the Commandments has the law directed us to make such sacrifices, or otherwise to bargain with God as though obtaining His love and approval could only be had by resorting to commercial trickery. To the contrary, we have been directed to love one another; to love God; and to provide for the welfare of each other.

As our ancient brethren sacrificed to the Divine Wisdom during their ceremonial worship, so do we as Freemasons sacrifice from the *pot of incense* - literally and figuratively. During certain Masonic ceremonies, candidates dip their fingers into a bowl, press a few particles of incense between their fingers and then drop them onto a hot-plate. The sweet aroma released during the burning is intended to remind us of the pleasantness we release into the world of today and tomorrow when we circumscribe our desires, keep our passions within due bounds, extend aid to the needy and relief to the poor. Have you considered what work you may do today that will make it possible for God's kingdom to rein tomorrow?

Chapter 49
RUBBISH OF THE TEMPLE

> "...let us lay aside every weight, and the
> sin which doth so easily beset us,..."
>
> Heb. 12:1

Although no reference to the rubbish of the temple is found in the Holy Writings, the legend has been preserved in Freemasonry as a part of the morality lesson flowing from the stories about the building of King Solomon's Temple. Masonic tradition relates that hindrances to the workmen appeared repeatedly, primarily arising out of material and worldly things. Those hindrances have been presented during Masonic ritual to illustrate certain distractions that retard mankind's moral and spiritual growth.

Here, theology converges with philosophy in further illustration of the synthesis of ideas commonly found in the ritual, or liturgy of the Craft. To the theologian, the rubbish of the temple represents sin, or that state of being that separates man from the Supreme Architect. Entire writings have been devoted by various denominations to "original sin," "the differentiation of the types of sin," consequences of sin and even redemption from sin. Though differing in many other areas, most theologies agree that man was originally tempted by worldly things, drew away from God, experienced death as a resulting fact of life and is sorely in need of redemption from his folly to restore himself to the divine relationship his Creator intended. Freemasonry draws upon various philosophies to send the similar message that all men are imperfect and, as a consequence, should rely upon the grace of the Supreme Architect.

The "blue degrees" of Freemasonry, as well as certain degrees and orders of both the Scottish Rite of Freemasonry and the Knights Templar explore the consequences of sin, as well as the rewards derived from mankind's redemption. For example, a body is buried in the rubbish of the temple and is eventually raised from the grave. Also, a great temple is laid to ruin by enemies of God's people only to be rebuilt again because the divine spirit moves monarchs to empathize with the sufferings of those whose entire lives are dependent upon temple worship. The lessons from each teach similar truths: time, patience and perseverance will accomplish all things.

However, if a Freemason merely accepts such lessons as the sum total of that which is to be learned, he misses another layer of equally prominent symbolism. Gnostics believed that "sin," or that condition of man represented by the rubbish of the temple, was missing the mark of truth. Speaking negatively falls into that category. To correct such error, it is important to the gnostic to rephrase speech to state an affirmative. As an example, a person might argue that he or she is against war. Constituting negative speech, such a statement would also constitute sin to the gnostic. Instead one would offer the same sentiment in affirmative language, such as, "I favor peace."

Both the Holy Writings and certain evolutionists concur that when it is said that God is slow, it is meant that the Supreme Architect has fashioned into creation the principle of stability – a pause between the dynamic of perpetual cause and effect. When we "miss the mark," or set in motion negative *karma*, the consequences are not always immediate. Often there is time for us to change our minds, to listen to our hearts and reflect upon what we have done – much the same as did the Twelve Fellowcraft. Anger may be converted to mercy leading to healing and a higher quality of life.

The ultimate aim is redemption and hence unification. Some theologians, as well as many philosophers have written that there either is no hell, or that damnation is not eternal regardless of the evil committed. The light of heaven and the fires of hell are but two emanations of the same Holy Spirit which aim to educate and therefore liberate the soul. In other words, not even the rubbish of the temple can restrain a positive spirit. However, he who persists in negativity buries himself deeper within the bowels of that rubbish.

Masonic ritual symbolizes the burial in three separate locations of the deceased body of a legendary person regarded as illustrious by the Craft. The removal of the body from one location and internment elsewhere symbolically suggests the migration of the soul – removal from the rubbish of the temple and placement at another location and so on. As such, the symbolism also suggests that there are certain lessons to be learned after death that have an impact upon the future of the soul. Those lessons seemingly apply to both the living and the dead, for in Masonic ritual it is the people who are living that move the dead, or assist in the migration. Among other obligations this duty imposes upon Freemasons the obligation to pray for departed brethren. Such acts of perpetual kindness assist in shedding the rubbish of the temple for both the living and the departed.

The rubbish represents the undesirable habits and traits that we acquire throughout life. It is the result of the bad choices selected by each one of us as we work our way through each day. Instead of smiling, we choose to frown. Rather than thinking a kind thought about another person, we reflect with glee upon his or her misfortune. As opposed to placing the interest of others first, we are consumed by our own selfish desires. There is not one single person who has not at sometime made a decision that is undesirable. However, there are many who change their course of conduct and in so doing redeem themselves from concluding their earthly existence beneath a heap of rubbish.

Similar to other symbols and symbolism used in Freemasonry, the rubbish of the temple also serves to remind us that it is imperative that we remain in control of our minds. Our thoughts lead to ideas which translate into physical action. One thinks he will stand up and walk, determines to do so, lifts his body from the chair and strides across the room. It is the mind that is the impetus for every action.

Jesus is reputed to have taught his disciples that that which resides within each of us is holy and therefore must be given the same care one also gives when attending to holy matters. Buddha informed his followers that the divine was within and only comes to light after great mental effort. Plato influenced his readers to exercise the mind, because it was the seat of man's existence. For these great teachers, as well as for Freemasons, it is essential to improve the mind; to feed it with good thoughts; and, to exercise it diligently in the service of our fellow man. In so doing, we also rid ourselves of the rubbish that tends to settle in and around the Temple, or mind of man.

Chapter 50

SHIBBOLETH

"...Say now Shibboleth:..."

Judges 12:6

The word *shibboleth* signifies a stream of water, or a full ear of corn both of which are derived from the idea of a plentiful harvest resulting from an abundance of water. As it appears in the Old Testament of the Holy Bible, *shibboleth* was employed as a pass word to distinguish friend from foe. In the book of Judges we learn that the Gileadites under Jephtha, who had just won a hard-fought victory over the revolutionary Ephramites, adopted this word to test soldiers fleeing across the River Jordan. The Ephramites, being of a different tribe than the Gileadites, fatefully mispronounced the word and were killed on the spot. This story is embraced by Freemasonry, as is the word *shibboleth*, to impart an important spiritual truth.

As a pass word, *shibboleth* was intended to reveal members of an opposing party – people who had not properly attained the right to be included in a specific group or organization. Masonry makes a very similar use of the same word, but as a fraternity does not intend to permanently exclude anyone simply because he does not know how to use it properly. Any man who professes a belief in the Supreme Being may be accepted into the Craft. The door to Freemasonry is always open to he who knocks. Thus, rather than teaching a lesson of exclusion, *shibboleth* is intended to teach Masons that there are matters we know and matters we do not know. As to the latter, Masons are expected to become better informed.

Freemasonry is frequently called both a science and a philosophy. While that is certainly an accurate statement, it is important to understand exactly how Freemasonry defines the word *science*. In lessons about other Masonic symbols we learned that there is a very clear distinction between geometry as a mathematical science and what has come to be known as Pythagorean geometry. One is purely empirical, while the other incorporates spiritual truths to assist in understanding that which empirical science cannot explain. It is this to which Masonry alludes by the use of the word *science*. In Freemasonry, empirical knowledge is augmented by pertinent spiritual concepts.

When we consider the word *shibboleth*, we learn that Masonry does not necessarily stop its exploration of knowledge where empirical science ends. If the scientific laboratory fails to yield the answer, the research does not end. To the contrary, the conclusion of the empirical quest is quite frequently merely the beginning of a further Masonic quest.

As an example, it is well to consider what the French physiologist E. H. Du Bois-Reymond has provided to us. In 1882, Du-Bois Reymond wrote that there were seven enigmas that one would never comprehend through empirical science: the essence of matter and energy; the origin of motion; the origin of sense-perception; the question of free will; the origin of life; the purposeful organization of Nature; and, the origin of thought and language. Although Reymond may be correct in his assumption regarding empirical science, those seven enigmas are often explored and considered in both Masonic ritual and Masonic literature. Those explorations do not, however, constitute the development of a theology, which unlike empirical science states to the world that it can answer each of the seven enigmas with the dogmas and doctrines found in religion. The Masonic quest seeks something other than the answers provided by those two polar opposites. It is to that middle ground that the word *shibboleth* applies.

Masons are instructed by the rich ritual and literature its forebears and authors have provided about how best to avoid the confusing paradox presented by the contrast between empirical science and theology. The first discipline poses the danger of knowing nothing, while the second discipline poses the danger of thinking that one knows everything. It is precisely at this juncture that Masonry steps into the discussion and introduces a profoundly active Hermetic thought. This thought and action is referred to by many writers as the practical philosophy of Freemasonry.

Within the context of the practical philosophy of Masonry, the word *shibboleth* reminds us that the best lessons in life flow from real life experiences, not merely from conclusions derived from reflection and meditation. Real flesh-and-blood warriors attempted to pass over the River Jordan with real weapons that were intended to be used to inflict a very real death on their foes. It was for those dangerous realities that the Gileadites selected *shibboleth* as their pass word to distinguish friend from foe.

Practical Masonic philosophy imparts to the individual Mason the importance of assessing the lessons of real human experiences. For example, a real authentic faith in God can be enjoyed when men turn to Him in prayer during times of fear, need, or gratitude. The overwhelming sense of peace that follows is the human experience of being faithful to God. Also, when men join the exercise of free will with the exercises of imagining and intellectualizing, they learn that they can make things happen, or they can fail in their efforts. Both success and failure can teach us valuable lessons about life, but not unless each is actually experienced. Reading about the success and failure of others goes only so far and cannot possibly replace the thrill of victory, or the agony of defeat we experience when we apply ourselves to the accomplishment of a task.

While there is an enormous philosophy and science to be learned from Masonic symbolism, it is labor, or the effort of each individual brother that both delivers the benefits of the Craft to mankind and impresses its truths upon the hearts of the brethren. Thus, there is a clear distinction between Masonic labor and Masonic reflection which transcends empirical science. Masonic labor is the physical exertion that is influenced by the combination s of free will, thought and faith in God. Masonic reflection interjects an individual's personal interpretation into the message communicated by a symbol or theory. That interpretation often results in either good works, or bad acts.

It is not difficult to understand why one of the *ruffians* in a Masonic ritual exclaims, "*This is no time for reflection: what shall we do with the body?*" The work at hand was nothing less than the immediate disposal of a corpse – and not just any corpse, but the corpse of a murdered man of great stature. Reflections upon motive or reason were useless to accomplishing the task. Nothing would suffice other than grabbing a spade, digging a hole and burying the body.

The lesson subsequently learned by those *ruffians* was that hateful acts have dreadful consequences. No amount of reflection on their part could have altered the decision of their judge to have them taken without the gates of the city and there executed. The only time reflection could have saved them was if it had come before the horrible act of murder and caused the men to act differently.

Empirical science is incapable of testing good and bad, light and darkness, because they are moral concepts best tested by the laws of Nature and God. Masonic science, however, embraces those laws, applies them to the lessons one may discover in the study of Masonic symbolism, and opens yet another door that may lead to new and different truths. Thus, when a Mason utters the word *shibboleth*, it signifies to other Masons that he, too, is following the same path – the path of practical Masonic philosophy.

Chapter 51

STONE OF FOUNDATION

"Where wast thou when I laid the foundations of the earth?"

Job 38:4

The *Stone of Foundation* constitutes one of the most important and complex symbols of Freemasonry. Referred to in a number of Masonic writings about the legends and traditions of Freemasonry, it also holds an important place in Jewish Talmudic writings. While this symbol is more often discussed in connection with the higher degrees of Masonry, it is intimately connected with the legend about the construction of King Solomon's Temple and consequently is important to understanding the first three degrees of Masonry. The *Stone of Foundation* should not be confused with other stones symbolically used by the Craft, such as the *Cornerstone*, the *keystone*, and the *capstone*.

According to the legend of the building of Solomon's Temple, the *Stone of Foundation* was placed within the foundations of the Temple and later, after the building of the Second Temple, or Temple of Herod, was re-located in the Holy of Holies, or Sanctum Santorum. It was reportedly shaped in the form of a perfect cube and was inscribed with the

Ineffable Name of God. Talmudic writers say that it was laid by Jehovah as the foundation of the world.

Masonry recognizes that there are several legends as to the origin of the *Stone of Foundation* and has patterned some of its higher degrees after the legend associated with Enoch. Masonic tradition teaches that he made a triangular plate of gold upon which he engraved the Ineffable Name and placed it within the deep caverns of an underground temple that was situated on Mount Moriah. From there, the *Stone* eventually found its way into Solomon's Temple and then into the Second Temple. Because it contained the Ineffable Name, the *Stone* is closely associated with another Masonic symbol – *the lost word*.

On a more philosophical and esoteric level, the *Stone of Foundation* also represents the spirit of Freemasonry, which some writers claim walked with God before the universe was spread out, or the heavens were unscrolled. It is from this interpretation that the *Stone* leaves its most indelible footprint, for it is here, as well as elsewhere, that the notion originated that Freemasonry has secrets worth guarding. The secrets attaining to the *Stone* go well beyond the "modes of recognition" that the Craft openly admits are held secret. They relate to the philosophical side of Masonry which throughout the known history of Freemasonry has experienced a rather chilly reception from both members of the fraternity and non-members. Only recently have university professors and learned Masons begun to more carefully explore those secrets in a widespread effort to identify the Craft's true origins.

The elements of Masonic history have proven to be very elusive. There are chronological periods that appear as though they should exist which have not yet been located. A dark interval of time lies between modern day Freemasonry and the days the ancient and original mysteries were first practiced. So dark and vacant is that separation that many Masons are content to deny that the Craft has any relationship whatsoever to anything other than the guilds. Yet, the *Stone of Foundation* remains ever present inviting us to explore its mysteries further in an attempt to more fully comprehend Masonry's true position.

The secrets of the *Stone* appear to be closely related to the Ineffable Name, or *lost word*. As such, they apparently relate to man's relationship with God; God's creative power; and, God's non-discriminating love for all that He has created. Albert Pike wrote of his own opinion on this matter and stated that because most Masonic symbols have lost their original meanings, the true philosophy of God has been irretrievably lost. Perhaps that was so for Pike, who spent his lifetime studying Masonic symbolism, and perhaps it will prove to be so for all of us living today. But, to conclude that the true meanings of the Craft's symbols are "irretrievably lost" is tantamount to declaring defeat in our pursuit of Masonry's true position. Thankfully, those who persist in the quest today have ignored Pike's doomsday pronouncement.

The *Stone of Foundation* means something more than that it was placed inside of a Temple. To begin your own personal quest for the meaning, first ask why would anyone wish to conceal this object? If it contained the Ineffable Name, why keep hidden that which is unknown? If it is truly unknown, then why be concerned about who might possess it? Unless, of course, one believed that deciphering the "code" would result in either acquiring or losing great power. But, what sort of power would that be? Power to rule over men; to rule the world; to have anything and everything your heart desires? The answer most clearly lies with the Ineffable Name itself.

A thorough study of the Kabbalah will lead the student through the complex maze of the *Yud He Vav- He* – the Hebrew letters said to constitute the Ineffable Name. While its true pronunciation is unknown, from time immemorial theologians and philosophers have studied the deeper meanings of each word and how each word relates to each other word in the whole Ineffable Name. Very generally, *Yud* represents the first cause of creation; *He* the cooperating partner in creation; while *Vav-He* is the result of the union of the first two. A lifetime may be spent exploring the great complexities that lie beneath this simple explanation, but suffice to say the general interpretation offered here clearly suggests that the Ineffable Name is the root of many religious and philosophical doctrines and dogmas.

When applied to the ancient Egyptian Mysteries, the relationship of the *Yud He Vav-He* to Osiris, Isis and Horus is uncanny. Similarly, the Christian notion of Joseph, Mary and Jesus seems to be significantly connected, as does Trinitarianism in all of its permutations. What appears to have been taught about God since the beginning is that He has an intimate loving relationship with all of His children. The *Yud He Vav-He* reveals that our Great Architect is quite clearly more the God of love than He is a god of revenge and warfare – the only God of all creation.

The placement of the *Stone of Foundation* into a secret location is reminiscent of the ancient pagan practices. Gods were venerated in secret places with appropriately secret rituals. Thus, one may see a commonality between Solomon's act of concealing the *Stone* and the secret worship by the pagans, who are here defined as those religious persons who practiced a religion that is dissimilar to modern day Christianity. To those people, God was supported in all of His efforts by lesser gods, who were often identified as *master builders* constructing the creation under the supervision of a *chief master builder*.

Freemasonry has at least three sources for its legends, two of which may be regarded as pagan, while the third is very much Christian in nature. The first is the Dionysiac artificers, the second the Roman collegia, and the third the Rosicrucians. The Dionysians were the master builders in the ancient world and likened man to a rough ashlar which was to be trued by tools not made with hands. The Roman collegia were the inheritors of the Dionysian bent toward building who fashioned enormous cities the ruins of which still stand as reminders of that era. The Rosicrucians delivered to Europe the mysteries of Egypt and Persia and at Damascus preserved the secret philosophy of the Rose of Sharon – a symbol of the Christ.

If you examine the roots of Masonic thought, you will find that one thought rises above all others – *truth beareth away the victory!* Truth is eternal and imparted to every candidate for Masonic degrees as a Divine attribute – the very foundation of every virtue. Undeniably, it is *truth* that is at the core of the meanings we are intended to glean from the *Stone of Foundation*. But, Masonry teaches us that no one religion or any one person revealed to mankind all that is true. Those revelations have come to us through a diverse assortment of religions, theologies and philosophies.

Moses did not originate a new religion for Israel. Rather, he adapted the Egyptian Mysteries to the needs of his people. Buddha did not reject the esotericism of the Hindu Brahmins. Rather, he adapted that esotericism to needs of the masses in India. Neither Pythagoras, nor Plato originated philosophical geometry – they merely drew from others, applied what they had learned and sought to improve upon that knowledge. Out of all of that knowledge truth is created and will continue to be created as long as man learns, applies, adapts and improves upon what others have done.

Each Mason has at hand those lofty principles of universal order upon whose truth the faiths of mankind have forever been established. The *Stone of Foundation* represents the secret doctrine that only God knows, but that man may discover if he will but listen, learn and apply that which he has learned. It is this that is at the core of all Masonic education, as much as it is so that man need go no farther to identify the beginnings of Freemasonry than to find the beginning of man's search for *truth*.

Have you begun that search for yourself?

Chapter 52

STRENGTH

"So Hiram gave Solomon cedar trees
and fir trees according to all his desire."

1 Kings 5:10

The banner that hangs from the pillar of the Senior Warden's station in the west of every Masonic lodge room contains the word "strength." Symbolically, the banner of "strength" stands between the banner of "wisdom" on the Worshipful Master's pillar in the east, and the banner of "beauty" on the Junior Warden's pillar in the south. As such, "strength" represents one of the three principle supports of a lodge of Freemasons. Indeed, it is the duty of every Senior Warden in every Masonic lodge to strengthen and support the authority of the Worshipful Master.

The Senior Warden also symbolizes Hiram, King of Tyre, who according to Masonic legend aided Solomon, King of Israel, to build the holy house of the Temple. Together, the two kings are also said to represent power and wisdom acting in harmonious combination.

Of the orders of architecture esteemed by Masons, the Doric column symbolizes "strength," because of all the orders it is the most massive. Hiram stands as the figure of strength, because his supply of material and workmen strengthened and supported Solomon in the building of the Temple. Other layers of esoteric meaning lay beneath the surface of this symbolism and await discovery by the Mason who is willing to search for more *light*.

Drawing from its rich association with the ancient Egyptian mysteries, as well as our brother Pythagoras and his followers, Freemasonry encourages man to explore God's revelations in natural religion - the religion of humanity that stems from what the philosophers and theologians refer to as *non-fallen Nature*.

By a disciplined study of the symbol of strength we may also discover two essential principles: *opposition,* which flows from friction and produces energy; and, *concordance,* which delivers fusion and also produces energy. These two opposing forces, or strength, are well-known in the scientific community, although oddly fusion has proven to be more scientifically theoretical than real.

The history of man reveals that enormous energies of a psychic nature are released into the world through warfare, which are directly associated with behavioral conflicts of interests and rude pretensions. Energies of an intellectual nature pass from a virtual state to a state of reality whenever controversy arises. All "truth" that is discovered from such *oppositional* force springs forth from a clash of opinions, which is not actually "truth," but simply a result of combative intellectual energy. Unvarnished "truth" is revealed through a *fusion* of opinions, that is through a harmonious blending of ideas, not through clashes of opinion.

During warfare men, women and children die because of violent human conflict. Once the will to continue warfare expires, peace or a period of no war prevails. Several historians who have witnessed and read about violent warfare have concluded that for peace to reign, it is absolutely necessary that men, women and children must die. Yet, those historians have either failed to note, or intentionally ignored the fact that people die from warfare only because mankind has not yet learned how best to employ the energies of *fusion,* or harmony.

Masonry teaches that quarrelling will never lead to truth. It may eventually subside and result in a state of non-quarrelling, but the negative energies released are wholly non-conducive synthesis or harmony. As long as one does not make peace his or her primary objective, everything accomplished by the subsiding of quarreling is both tenuous and fragile. Freemasonry's message that mankind must embrace diversity represents the Craft's greatest strength, for the lesson learned is that polemic conflicts are non-productive and when discovered to exist, should be immediately eliminated from a Masonic lodge.

It is from the *fusion,* or harmonious blending of opinions that truth flows. Past Masonic writers taught that *conversation* is the opposite of *controversy* and is the essence of *fusion* and synthesis. All real conversation calls upon God, the Supreme Architect and transcendent center of all existence to mediate and is therefore based upon the underlying principle found in the Gospels: "Where two or three are gathered in my name, there also am I in their midst."

Freemasonry also encourages the personal study of the Kabbalah to better understand the creative role that conversation and *strength* can play. The *Zohar* (considered by many to be the definitive work on Kabbalah) was written centuries ago to explore the deeper meaning of the *Torah* and man's relationship to the Supreme Architect of the Universe. Some authors attribute the original source of Kabbalah to the ancient Egyptians and assert that it is this that constitutes what is known as the "Egyptian Mysteries." The guiding organizational symbolism of that material is referred to as *the tree of life,* the complex study of which includes, but is not limited to the consideration of philosophy, theosophy, theurgy (oftentimes also referred to as "divine magic") and numerology.

With respect to Freemasonry's use of *strength* as a part of its symbolism, the Kabbalah's numerology offers additional insight into its intended meaning. In Kabbalah the number five is labeled *Gevurah* – "might" – which several ancients have identified as the symbol of creative power. Here, the relationship to Freemasonry's allegory about Hiram, King of Tyre, lending his support and materials to Solomon for the purpose of constructing the Temple is most remarkable. *Gevurah* is regarded as a formative force, just as was Hiram of Tyre's power. Had he not aided Solomon by rendering his power to be used in harmonious combination with Solomon's wisdom, it is not likely the Temple would have been built.

Thus, an important interpretation that Masons can glean from *strength* is something far different from notions of mere raw physical power. Rather, *strength* consists of an advanced spiritual power that understands the importance of *fusion,* or the assimilation of diverse ideas into a positive creative force both within a Masonic lodge and abroad in the larger general societal population.

As such, the Mason who is elected to serve as Senior Warden is expected to conduct himself in such a manner that arguments are quelled at his instruction, harmony reigns where controversy once held sway, and ideas are put into action so that by aid of the *wisdom,* or authority of the Worshipful Master they become reality.

Look to the west, my brethren. Strength, harmony and powerful support for peaceful projects begin there with the Senior Warden and are sent up to the east through the deacons only. Without *strength* wisdom is ineffective. Both must co-exist before a Masonic lodge can become a creative force to the benefit of its members and the community it serves.

Chapter 53
SUN, MOON AND MASTER

*"And he shall be as the light of the morning when the sun riseth,
even a morning without clouds; as the tender grass springing
out of the earth by clear shining after rain."*

2 Sam. 23:4

Three small lights, known to Freemasons as the *three lesser lights,* decorate every Masonic lodge. They are likened to the Sun, Moon and Master of the Lodge for no less than two purposes: to illustrate the perseverance a Master should exert when leading his lodge, and to provide the only light by which a candidate for degrees may see the Holy Bible, square and compasses. The former purpose constitutes an *exoteric* symbolism while the letter represents an *esoteric* interpretation. Both impart important lessons to every Mason, but the *esoteric* meaning draws us closer to understanding Freemasonry's relationship with those, like the ancient Egyptians, who made the Sun and Moon central to their mysteries.

Some religious writers have mistakenly accused all of the ancients who used the Sun and Moon as a central feature of their worship of Deity to be idolaters. Other religious writers have gone so far as to label those ancients as heretics. In truth the Egyptians, and quite likely the Assyrians and Babylonians, too, viewed the Sun and Moon as heavenly symbols of the Great Creator, whose real name was said to be unpronounceable. Among those people the Sun was usually symbolized by the figure and nature of the zodiacal constellation through which it passed at the vernal equinox. Thus, for nearly the past 2,000 years the Sun has been symbolized by Pisces, the Two Fish. For the 2,160 years prior to that Aries, the Ram symbolized the Sun. Prior to that period, Taurus, the Bull was the ruling sign.

In *Morals and Dogma,* Albert Pike provided us with a detailed description of the celestial environment during the time Zoroaster was initiated into *the mysteries.* Pike wrote that at the precise moment Zoroaster was inducted, the Sun appeared emerging from the back of Taurus. During this period, the religion practiced by most ancient Egyptians was centered upon the symbolism of the Bull known as *Apis,* considered to be the Sun God. If the allegories in the Old Testament continue to sustain validation by modern day theologies, then it may also be noted that the Hebrews, too, amassed writings littered with traces of the very same astrological influence. The same is true of the Christian religion.

Centuries before Constantine anointed Christianity as the state-approved religion, the so-called pagans revered the constellation of Aries referring to it as the *Lamb of God which taketh away the sins of the world.* Aries was also called *Savior,* or *Lord* – names used to symbolize God, as did Aries itself. Later, during the Christian era when the Sun was in Pisces, a new symbolism became prominent – that of the fish. Jesus himself was frequently called the *Fisher of Men.* Indeed, St. Augustine taught that the Greek letters making up the word *Fish* was literally interpreted to read 'Jesus Christ, Son of God, Savior, and Cross.' In part, this is the reason certain Christian sects of today observe Friday as the sacred day of the Virgin (also seen in the Zodiac as *Venus*) when they shall only eat fish and not meat. The sign of the fish was one of the earliest symbols of Christianity; and when drawn in the sand, it informed one Christian that another of the same faith was nearby.

Thus, it has been seemingly so for thousands of years that the Sun in its path has influenced whatever form of worship man offers to the Supreme Architect of the Universe. But what is the role of the Moon? Exactly how does that heavenly body fit into the scheme of worship?

And, why is it used in conjunction with the Sun in Masonic symbolism? Pike suggests that the relationship symbolizes nothing less than magic – the exact and absolute science of nature and its laws, which makes clear the Masonic imperative to study the seven liberal arts and sciences (grammar, rhetoric, arithmetic, astronomy, logic, music and geometry), as well as the Holy Writings. Yet, there is also an equally fundamental philosophical connection to be considered.

There are two distinct systems of astrological philosophy. The first is referred to as Ptolemaic and regards the earth as being at the center of the solar system. For the Ptolemaics, the Sun, Moon and planets revolve around the earth. That system has been proven incorrect, yet for many years it was believed accurate and provided the basis for viewing even spiritual matters from a strictly materialistic perspective. The other system is called the heliocentric, which continues today to be considered the accurate consideration of the movement of the heavenly bodies. The Sun is at the center and the Moon and all of the planets revolve around it. From the heliocentric philosophy notions about the higher intellectual and spiritual faculties of man have arisen. Man is no longer considered the center of the universe. Rather, God assumes His correct position as the center of all existence.

The ancients saw both the Sun and Moon as symbols of God. The Sun was divinely illuminated by its own light generated from within which radiated outward to give life to all living things. The Moon reflected the Sun's light when the Sun could not be seen and had unique generative powers. While they were viewed and regarded separately, sometimes with male and female components, they were together considered Nature's most recognized symbols of Deity.

In addition, the Moon has acquired certain other attributes, including that of *wisdom,* which was most often embodied in the fictional person of Isis, whom the ancient Egyptians regarded as the sister and wife of Osiris, as well as the mother of Horus and the sister of Typhon. Each of those fictional characters played out parts in an allegory intended to conceal deeper mysteries that continue to be unknown to all but a few. In that allegory, lessons about immortality, or the continuing nature of all life were communicated to the few whom the High Priests deemed worthy of such knowledge. Some scholars about that era have today concluded that the allegory itself may have actually been a representation of real people ruling and governing a much earlier world.

Represented in the ancient Egyptian allegory by the Moon, Isis was venerated as the *Virgin of the World,* a theological concept perpetuated to this day by the Catholic Church's veneration of the *Virgin Mary.* In Freemasonry, the *Virgin of the World* is sometimes shown standing between two great pillars – Boaz and Jachin – symbolizing the fact that Nature attains productivity by means of polarity, that is, the harmonizing of opposite forces. As wisdom personified, Isis stands between the pillars of opposites, demonstrating that understanding is always found at the point of equilibrium and that truth is often crucified between the two thieves of apparent contradiction.

As the Moon is robed in the reflected light of the Sun, so Isis, like the virgin described in the book of Revelations, is clothed in the glory of the illuminated Sun. Much more can be read by the aspirant to knowledge about the Moon's relationship to water, the eternal symbol of regeneration, its influence upon other celestial bodies and how it inspired such Naturalistic religions as Druidism. In Freemasonry, the Moon, as represented by Isis also plays a significant role in the mystery surrounding the famous *Lost Word.* In one Egyptian occult myth, Isis is said to have conjured the invincible God of Eternity, *Ra,* to tell her his secret and sacred name – which he did. By means of that name, or word, Isis was able to demand obedience from other invisible, but superior deities.

While modern man may entirely disregard the allegories and symbolism from the past and judge them to be misguided, Freemasonry has continued to impress their importance upon the minds of men. The Holy Bible, square and compasses are taught to be regarded for sacred and virtuous purposes – but first under the light cast by the *three lesser lights.* We are thereby cautioned to consider that which we today regard as *truth* as the evolved expression of that which yesterday was also taught as *truth.*

Plutarch wrote that: "He alone is a true servant or follower who after he has heard and become acquainted with the ways of God searched into the hidden truths which lie concealed under them and thereby examines the whole by the dictates of reason and philosophy."

Consider then the fact that Freemasonry does not instruct that the Sun, Moon or Master of the Lodge is more important than the other – or even that together they are more important that the *Three Great Lights*. It is not a matter of discovering that symbol which is more important than any other. Rather, the Masonic quest involves an examination of all of its symbols and a meditation upon how each relates to the other, teaching all mankind to similarly view all humanity. The Holy Writings emphasize that point by noting that while all men exercise different talents, each is derived from the same source.

Chapter 54

TEMPERANCE

*"See then that ye walk circumspectly,
not as fools, but as wise."*

Eph. 5:15

Temperance is one of the four cardinal virtues taught to candidates during the ritual performance of the Entered Apprentice Degree. It is wisely impressed upon the conscience and memory of the initiate in one of the most solemn portions of that degree. Specific emphasis is made upon the effect of dissipation in paralyzing and deforming the mental faculties to the point that the "secrets" of Freemasonry might be divulged in an unguarded moment. While *temperance* also may pertain to abstaining from hard drink, Freemasonry does not require total abstinence, but rather promotes moderation in all things.

Oftentimes referred to as the due restraint upon the affections and passions which renders the body tame and governable, *temperance* also frees the mind from the allurements of vice. Throughout its many spiritual lessons, Freemasonry explores the truth that during his lifetime man is beset with a host of opposing influences: light versus darkness; good versus evil; and, holiness versus sinfulness. Perhaps the most important lesson arising out of those explorations is that mankind will always be confronted by those obstacles, which Masonry assists in overcoming. Saint Anthony the Great confirmed that teaching when he said, "without temptation there is no spiritual progress."

Temptation belongs as an integral part to the exercise of human free will, which is both inviolable and inalienable. It is fundamental to most choices men make during their lifetimes that at least one available option falls into the categories of darkness, evil, or sinfulness. In his work entitled *Sermon on the Annunciation of the Blessed Virgin Mary,* Saint Bernard of Clairvaux (the original benefactor of the original Knights Templar) wrote that because he is an image of the Great Creator, man is free and remains so throughout eternity.

That freedom can become either a blessing, or a curse depending upon how it is exercised. When correct choices are made, man lives a very blessed life. When incorrect choices are made, man suffers. In our world of today, societies and individuals make good and bad choices each and every day. When a nation's government acts to feed the hungry or to relieve the suffering of the poor and ill of health, it ensures itself of being blessed. On the other hand, when such a government chooses to inflict war, death and destruction upon another body of human beings, it sends a very foul odor up to God. When one man or one woman reaches out to another human being with tenderness, love and mercy, that person's life is blessed. However, when one tosses insults at another person, or otherwise mistreats that other person, his or her own life becomes more miserable than he or she could have ever imagined.

The lesson about *temperance* taught in Masonry is a lesson in the consequences of mankind's exercise of free will. The Major League baseball player who freely chooses to ingest unlawful performance-enhancing substances can expect to be suspended from playing the game he loves best. The corporate executive who chooses to cheat on his taxes or to steal from his company's stockholders can expect a lengthy prison sentence. Similarly, the man who gives of his own bounty to others can expect to see hungry people become well-fed, sick people healed and poor people provided with the necessities of life. In short, the consequences of good choices are good results.

But, lest one come to believe that the lesson about *temperance* is solely a lesson about how man may benefit his life by his own conduct, it should not be forgotten that Freemasonry also teaches the truth about the wonderful consequences of personal labor performed in conjunction with perfect faith in God. Faith, too, is a product of man's exercise of his innate free will. One either has faith in the Great Architect, or he does not have such a faith – the choice is up to the individual. Men who eventually become Masons openly profess their faith in God and are thus expected to behave as men of faith – not like animals, brutes or misfits.

Freemasonry inculcates the practice of invoking God's blessing before embarking upon any great or important undertaking. Prayer, such as this, is also a matter of choice – one either prays, or one does not pray. Masons pray, not only when gathered together, but also when alone at work, at home, or abroad in the society in which each lives. Thus, Masons are also expected to behave as men of prayer – men who act in conjunction with their faith in God. The truly *temperate* soul practices prayer and faith so regularly that those behaviors become ingrained and the basis upon which the exercise of free choice is made.

Temperance, then, is nothing less than the constant application of virtue and morality to each and every act done by a human. Is it an impossible standard? Nothing that pertains to God is ever impossible. However, if the virtue is never practiced, it will never become a part of the fabric that becomes man's decision-making center. Masons know that simply because something is difficult to accomplish does not mean that an effort to accomplish should never be made. If that was a Masonic byword, there would be no hospitals for indigent children, homes for indigent aged people, or clinics for children who cannot properly be understood when they speak. *Temperance,* then, is also about making an effort to make a difference.

As a creature made in the image of God, man is suppose to become healthy, wealthy and wise. To become *temperate* does not mean that one also becomes sullen, withdrawn, or impoverished. Those are not the conditions associated with the consequences of better behavior. Rather, they are the consequences of ignorance. Although it certainly is the case that virtuous and moral humans can have as much suffering in their lives, as do the unvirtuous, it is also the case that the suffering is less noticeable. The man of virtue is forever cheery, uplifting to others and an inspiration to those around him, regardless of his own personal sufferings. While he may be unhealthy in body, he is healthy of spirit and of more value to Creation than the healthy man who exercises unhealthy habits.

Temperance is a matter of the degree of the spiritual attributes exhibited by an individual. Would you refer to a man as *temperate*, if he habitually appeared drunk in public, but regularly showed up at a church on Sunday? Probably not, even though showing up for church services demonstrates a certain spiritual awareness. On the other hand, would you describe a man as *temperate*, if he contributed time and money to the poor, regularly prayed to God and always attempted to make correct choices in life? Probably so, because even though that same man likely has his faults, as do all humans, the degree of his exhibited spirituality is very high.

But, does Masonry teach us to merely appear to be *temperate*, or does it seek to instill within us a desire to be as *temperate* within ourselves as we are to the world? The answer is clear – the *temperance* taught in Masonry is as much about the real you, as it is about the person that others regularly see. Believe it or not, people recognize the difference and you can be assured that, sooner or later, the person sitting next to you will figure out who you really are. Thus, the *temperance* demonstrated by you must either be genuine, or it becomes nothing at all.

The essence of one's identity as a human being consists of three parts: body, soul and spirit. We each possess a physical body that forms the boundary line of our material existence. Each of us also possesses a soul which assimilates all that the body senses: sight, sound, taste, hearing and feeling. The spirit is not only nourished by righteous behavior and grows accordingly; it is also the center of our *temperate* nature. Even-handedness, pleasantness and graciousness each derive from *temperance* and each flows from the spirit within man. As a Mason grows in the understanding of the teachings of the Craft, his spirit expands and he becomes more just, more likeable and much more courteous to his fellow man.

It is those qualities that not only define a quality person and good Mason; they also constitute the very attributes of the spirit life that not only lives in the present, but also in all eternity. Faith may be lost to sight and hope may end in fruition, but charity, or *temperance*, extends beyond the grave through the boundless realm of eternity. The lessons we learn in Masonry not only prepare us for the world of today, but enable us to enter the spiritual world of tomorrow. My brothers, I pray that you will learn them well.

Chapter 55

THE ACACIA

"I will plant in the wilderness the cedar, the shittah tree, and the myrtle, and the olive tree; I will set in the desert the fir tree, and the pine, and the box tree together:"

Is. 41:19

The symbolism of the *acacia,* or evergreen is well-known throughout Freemasonry. It was planted to mark the spot of the burial of a celebrated artist important to Masonic teachings. A sprig of evergreen is used by the Funeral Master during every Masonic funeral ceremony. The *shittim-wood* that was reputedly used by the children of Israel in the construction of Moses' Tabernacle, as well as is the building of the Ark of the Covenant is a species of the *acacia.* Being a thorny tamarisk, it also grew around the dead body of Osiris in the Egyptian legend and constituted the *crown of thorns* crushed to the brow of the Christ during his Passion. In all of those events, the *acacia* represented immortality, because of its tenacity of life. Without question, the tamarisk was extraordinarily difficult to kill.

The ancients identified the *acacia* with the more sensitive plant known as the mimosa. A Coptic legend informs us that the mimosa was the first of all trees and shrubs to actually worship the Christ.

Indeed, some of the early fathers of Christianity used the tree to symbolize the Christ. As such, the ancients meant to convey the notion that trees, plants and shrubs were living, breathing life forms that were animated with the Divine Light.

Trees are often mentioned in both the Old and New Testaments, as well as in the writings of the so-called pagans. As examples, we find messages about creation hidden with such symbols as the Tree of Life, which represents the spiritual point of balance or equilibrium, and the Tree of Knowledge, which represents polarity in the form of good and evil. Moses heard the voice of God emanating from a burning bush. Buddha received his illumination while under the bodhi tree and the consecrated rod of Hermes was nothing more than a type of tree.

Philosophers and priests were frequently referred to as trees. The very name of the Druids allegedly means "the men of oak trees." Initiates into certain Syrian mysteries were called "cedars." In fact, the famous "cedars of Lebanon" described in the First Degree of Masonry were initiated sages which constituted the true supports of King Solomon's Temple. If one listens closely to the lessons in the First Degree, he will hear that the three pillars in the lodge symbolically represent the Worshipful Master, Senior and Junior Wardens – originally regarded as three exceptionally wise and talented men who spiritually led the Entered Apprentices, Fellowcrafts and Masters, or overseers of the work.

As opposed to symbolizing specific people, Freemasonry uses the *acacia* to represent certain principles of spirituality that all people should aspire to attain. First, it is the emblem of the vernal equinox, or annual resurrection of the sun from the death of winter. Second, it signifies purity and innocence – traits also embodied in the legendary character Hiram Abif. Third, it typifies human immortality and the regeneration of life. The evergreen represents that immortal part of man that survives the destruction of the physical body and which will never, never, never die. Finally, it is the revered emblem of the ancient Egyptian Mysteries, to which Masonry owes much of its foundation.

The legend of Hiram Abif is liberally drawn from the Egyptian Mystery ritual of the murder and resurrection of Osiris. As such, the sprig of *acacia* also represents to Hiram's resurrection to all Masons. In the Egyptian legend, the chest containing the body of Osiris, who was viciously murdered by Typhon, was washed ashore and lodged in the roots of a tamarisk, or *acacia*. The tamarisk grew into a mighty tree enclosing within itself the body of the murdered god. Some writers have theorized that this legend is the basis upon which the story was based about the sprig of *acacia* left at Hiram's grave. Others also have asserted that the present-day Christmas tree is a continuation of the mystery of the evergreen.

Among Freemasons the essential lesson taught by the *acacia* pertains to the permanence of the human soul. The theme of permanence is bundled up into the various theologies and philosophies arising out of the notion of the resurrection. Today, certain religions teach that when a human dies eventually both his soul and material body continue in a heavenly environment. Other religions hold that only the soul continues to live. Most accept the contention that souls always were and ever will be living organisms. Regardless of the interpretation one selects regarding an afterlife, Freemasonry attaches an equally important significance to this life.

For centuries, men have asked the same question: what is the purpose of human life? Hundreds of thousands have joined Freemasonry over the years in hopes of learning an answer, but have learned that the Craft returns them to their churches, synagogues, mosques and other places of worship to seek more knowledge. As a candidate passes through the degrees of Masonry, he is informed that true knowledge is never to be found in one place. A man must search everywhere there is knowledge to understand his relationship with the Great Architect.

During that search, it is like that the inquiring mind will, sooner or later, stumble across the teachings of Origen, who lived, wrote and instructed between 185 A.D. and 254 A.D. At one period in Christian history, Origen was regarded as the most accurate of all interpreters about the human soul. Although later discarded by the Church as a heretic, he originally taught that souls repeat themselves in material incarnation – a teaching that now is termed reincarnation. Origen believed that each human being contained a spark of the Creator that had no beginning and no end. In his literary work entitled *De Principils,* Origen wrote: "Every soul…comes into this world strengthened by the victories or weakened by the defeats of the previous life. Its place in this world as a vessel appointed to honor or dishonor, is determined by its previous merits or demerits. Its work in this world determines its place in the world which is to follow."

Without either accepting or rejecting reincarnation, Freemasonry makes a similar demand of its members about how each should live the life given them. Masons are called to live spiritually strong lives; not lives weakened by self-centeredness. When Pike wrote that every man had a work to do, he challenged every Mason to not only make the best of the circumstances in which he found himself, but to do so by serving others. Pray for others, feed the hungry, give to the poor, lavish love upon your neighbor and provide for the spiritual growth of your family – it is these that Masonry inculcates into the hearts and souls of the honored members of the Craft.

The *acacia* reminds us that while our lives are not limited by time, our material existence is time-controlled. No man knows how much time he has, but he should know that time is running out. If a good work is to be done during this lifetime, it must be done today, for tomorrow is in God's hands. While we breathe, stand, walk and talk we may do something that improves the lot of our brethren. When time shall be no more, that work will be done by those left behind and we ourselves shall give no more. Though life shall always continue beyond man's earthly existence, man's ability to love, give and share with others will stop when his body returns to the earth and his soul goes to God.

Chapter 56

THE ALL-SEEING EYE

"Behold, the eye of the Lord is upon them that
fear Him, upon them that hope in His mercy;..."

Ps. 33:18

Masons are taught to carry on their Masonic activities and to live their lives under a sense of the omnipresent and omniscience of God. The symbol of the *all-seeing eye* serves as a reminder of the faith Freemasonry has devoted to this fundamental premise. It also serves to teach us that although our thoughts are hidden from others, they are well known to the Supreme Architect of the Universe.

Both past and recent literary works on Freemasonry have explored the significance of the *all-seeing eye* as it symbolically appears in the cultures of several societies. Here, in the United States of America the currency used in commerce bears the symbol of a pyramid at the top of which is affixed an *all-seeing eye*. Some have speculated that not only is such a symbol representative of this Nation's Masonic roots, it also signifies that a secret society of men constitute the real governing power here and around the world. While only the first part of that speculation has any truth behind it, it is intriguing to observe that institutions, such as Freemasonry, are often presumed to have originated each of the symbols they employ.

The *swastika* serves as a prime example of a symbol that acquires meaning simply by virtue of having been used by a very high profile organization. Throughout the modern Western world, that symbol is associated with German Nazism, which ravaged humanity with as much evil as history has ever described. That association has all but eclipsed the symbol's historical status as a sacred sign in the Dharmic religions. Thus, what was once a sign of love has become a symbol of hate – the values of the organization using the symbol have come to define the symbol itself for future generations.

The same may be said of Freemasonry's use of the *all-seeing eye.* When enclosed within a triangle, the symbol is commonly interpreted as representing the eye of God keeping watch over mankind. Its usage may be traced back to the ancient Egyptians who referred to the symbol as the Eye of Horus – son of Osiris and Isis in the Osirian mysteries. From that time forward, religions around the world have incorporated the sign, including Christian Catholics, Latter Day Saints, Judaism and Oriental worships such as Cao Dai found in Vietnam. But, it is Freemasonry that has become most closely identified with this symbol since Thomas Smith Webb first referred to it in an article he wrote in 1797 for *The Freemasons Monitor.*

Traditionally, Freemasonry has not used a pyramid in connection with the *all-seeing eye,* which casts doubt on the Masonic connection to the symbol as it appears on American currency, the protestations to the contrary by former Vice President Henry Wallace notwithstanding. Wallace claimed that in 1935 President Franklin D. Roosevelt was inspired by the Masonic *all-seeing eye* when he had it incorporated into the dollar bill. Roosevelt himself never made such a claim and did not ever endorse Wallace's assertion.

While believing in such a connection offers great opportunities for writers of Masonic fiction, it is more likely the case that our forefathers used the symbol as the Eye of God who watches over the affairs of mankind. To presume otherwise without more solid evidence of the same is akin to also presuming that Catholics use the symbol because of its Masonic connection, or that Latter Day Saints do the same for like reasons. But setting the record straight regarding this symbol should not in manner diminish its true Masonic significance.

The *all-seeing eye* is embraced by Freemasonry because it is a non-denominational symbol of Deity. Masonry regards no man on account of the religion he selects and does not promote the notion that God is the captive of any one form of religion, the approver of one over another, or the hater of one as opposed to another. When Masons pray or reflect upon God within a Masonic lodge they do not apply a Jewish, Christian, Islamic, or any other theological doctrine to Him. Neither do Masons confine God to the concept of Nature. Rather, He is worshipped as the Great Creator and lover of all humanity and Nature. In that regard, Masons apply themselves to become God's partner in extending His love and in continuing with His creation.

The *all-seeing eye* also symbolizes the heart, or soul of man, which Freemasonry symbolizes in other settings as the center of synthesizing knowledge and the human will. God waits there to meet man and assist him in conducting himself in a manner that best serves His plan. When man greets God there in humble contemplation, he is moved to incorporate the three principle tenets of Masonry into his daily life – brotherly love, relief and truth. However, if man passes up the chance to meet God in his heart, the unfettered imposition of that man's will to put his knowledge into action has a very good chance of not adding anything of value to love, relief and truth.

In Freemasonry the "heart" that is intended is not that of emotion, or the faculty of becoming passionate. Those we are taught to circumscribe and to keep within due bounds toward all mankind. Rather, the "heart" Freemasonry intends is that which Indian esotericism refers to as the middle center of the seven centers of man's psychic and vital constitution. It is nothing less than the "twelve-petalled lotus," or heart center that represents love. Thus, it represents not what man can become, but what he *is* – a creature of God who exists for the purpose of loving God and all His creation.

In Freemasonry, that love is manifested throughout the world in the numerous charities supported by every man, woman and child who embraces Masonic tradition and values. Under the gaze of the *all-seeing eye,* Masons everywhere work to provide societies around the globe with medical care, education, housing, physical and emotional care, as well as leadership in the family, government and workplace. In so doing,

Freemasonry consistently makes a positive contribution to the definition of the *all-seeing eye,* unlike the Nazis who denigrated the sacred symbol of the swastika.

If the symbol of God has become for the world the symbol of Freemasonry, that stands as a tribute to the morals and virtues which are held dearly by every Mason. Do nothing, my brother, which would ever tend to tarnish mankind's opinion of our venerable institution. Make loving kindness your daily practice; make loyal service to mankind your objective; and make the worship of God central to your life.

Chapter 57

THE ANCHOR AND ARK

"Which hope we have as an anchor of the
soul, both sure and steadfast, and that
entereth into that within the veil."

Heb. 6:19

In the third degree of Masonry where the ceremonies relate largely to life and death, man's journey over the sea of life is symbolized by *Noah's Ark,* and his hope of immortality and a safe landing in the haven of eternal security is symbolized by the anchor. Considered together, the *anchor and ark* are emblems of hope grounded in a well-spent life. As such, those symbols are a part of the many different symbols Masonry employs to teach the importance of structuring human life upon principles of morality and virtue.

Masonry interprets the *anchor* to mean the force of morality – not merely the idea of morality. As a force, it is the magnetic attraction of the heart toward truth and virtue in a manner similar to the directional pointing of the needle on a compass. Just as a true compass will lead a wayward mariner from rough seas to a hospitable harbor, so too may morality guide us throughout life from darkness to light. We are assured of being well-grounded in our daily activities when we patiently assess the choices each day offers us and wisely select the choice that is the more moral.

The Masonic *ark*, or vessel that carries us along throughout our lifetimes, is constructed of honor and duty, not wood. By never losing sight of those essential virtues, we may avoid a disastrous shipwreck. A Mason who does lose sight risks sinking and forever disappearing without ever being honored for his goodness of heart and deed. Should the Supreme Architect then demand an accounting from such a Mason for what he has done with his life, regret and shame are likely to sweep over him like a drowning sea.

It is said with ample authority that all of the forces of Nature are, or may some come under man's control. Similarly, the book of Ecclesiastes from the Old Testament teaches us that there is nothing new under the sun. Considered together, the two thoughts suggest that mankind is in the process of rediscovering what was once known – rediscovering that which was lost. The lessons of the *anchor and ark* are intended to spiritually equip us to make those discoveries – to please God so that He will not withhold from us the opportunity to learn wisely and then apply that which we have learned so that yet more wise truths may be rediscovered.

The manner in which the Dead Sea Scrolls have been revealed to the average person is an example of what is meant here. Those priceless documents from ages past were first discovered in the 1940's. Excerpts were not made publicly available for years after that and many of the documents making up this treasure trove of knowledge have never been made publicly available. The answer to the question "Why?" aids us in learning how one becomes "worthy" to know such things.

Merely desiring to know something is not always enough. Knowing how to learn a lesson does not always mean that lesson will be learned. The truth behind these statements is not intended in any manner to be mystical, or metaphysical. Simply stated, sometimes there are real live forces working against you in your endeavors – forces that intend to keep you from accomplishing your goal. In the case of the Dead Sea Scrolls, various researchers, theologians and politicians have determined that, for whatever reason known only to them, the general population is not capable of handling the knowledge those unrevealed scrolls possess. That determination has been made most likely because systems, institutions and doctrines of religion are at stake. Unless those who have control over the missing knowledge change their minds, years from now that knowledge will still be a mystery to all but those in control.

It is correct to ask what all of this has to do with the Masonic *anchor and ark*. The answer to that question is based upon the extent of a Mason's obligation to others. Morality, honor and duty are fundamentals which if put into practice will eventually change men. Not merely some men, but all men. For, if Masons practice their Craft effectively they also teach others, by example and deed, how man was intended by the Creator to live his life.

Masonry teaches that truth is a Divine attribute and the foundation of every virtue. The power of kings, monarchs and governments around the world is not comparable to the almighty force and the importance of truth. Our reality here on earth, as well as in heaven above rests in the unerring truth that is never subject to the variations and vicissitudes of time and fortune. Burning all of the publications deposited in the library at Alexandria did not make those publications untrue. Determining that one religious doctrine is paramount to any other does not change the truth that all doctrines are worthy of consideration and reflection. Deciding that the world requires one form of government over any other form will never alter the truth that all forms of government have, at one time or another in the history of mankind, proven efficient, fair and just.

It is these truths that Masons must not only adopt, but must live for the world to see, learn and change. When Masonic values eventually change the world, men will no longer hide important knowledge to protect personal interests. But, it is only when such change is actually effected that men will truly become "worthy" of knowing all that is hidden. That is the natural state of being the Creator has provided us. As a part of Natural law, it cannot and will not deviate.

Either change is made, or truth will remain stifled. The outcome is in your hands. As your *ark* travels through this vale of tears will it leave behind lessons in morality, honor and duty for others to learn? Will the *anchor* of hope for all Masons, as well as all mankind, be dropped from your vessel? My brother, you have an important work yet to accomplish. Consult the Holy Writings, learn the lessons of Masonic symbolism, live those lessons for your circle of friends and family to see and commit yourself to being for change – for change that removes barriers to knowledge – for change that eliminates fear as a motive for concealing the rediscovery of all that we once knew.

Chapter 58

THE BEEHIVE

"Wherefore we labor, that, whether present
or absent, we may be accepted of him."

2 Cor. 5:9

Of all the hieroglyphical emblems explained to a Master Mason none is more significant than *the beehive*. Symbolizing industry and labor, *the beehive* is said to teach us that work is required of all men and creatures on earth, as well as of the creatures in heaven. It serves as a reminder that true happiness and prosperity are found only when man labors diligently for the common good. So important is that labor that Masonry regards the man who refuses to work for his neighbor as a drone – a useless member of society who is unworthy of being protected as a Mason.

Throughout history, the bee has been regarded as a symbol of wisdom. As the bee extracts pollen from the flowers, so does man extract wisdom from the events in his daily life. The insect is also considered sacred to the goddess Venus and is one of the many life forms for whose origin cannot presently be traced. In that bees are ruled by queens, they are also viewed as representative of the so-called feminine principle. Yet, Masonry holds more closely to the symbolism that relates to industry and labor – for very obvious reasons.

The Great Architect has not created a world filled with rich men and women. Rather, the earth largely consists of humans who are so poor that each must toil ceaselessly for a meager subsistence. It is precisely for this reason that Masonry holds work in such high esteem. It honors the worker who produces, as opposed to the person who simply consumes that which the labor of others produces.

The *law of attraction,* so well known to Masonry from time immemorial, theorizes that man's life consists of that which he makes for himself. The theory rests heavily upon positive thinking, but positive thinking without work to accomplish the task is as dead as the Apostle James found faith without works. Thought lays out the plan that work will accomplish. One does not serve mankind without the other.

As odd as it may seem, in truth almost all of the noblest achievements in the world have been made by people of poor means. Poets, scholars, artisans and artists whose roots extend deeply into the poverty stricken highways of the world have produced works of genius. There is nothing glorious in the world that did not first require labor, either of the body or the mind. Without it there would be no pyramids in Egypt to set the mind to wondering; no temples or houses of worship to clear the soul before devoting to God; no canals, highways or air terminals to transport commerce; and no memory of the past or hope for the future.

Freemasonry also teaches that we should encourage our offspring to labor, if we truly desire to provide for the greatest chance for their future happiness. Man was not created for luxuries, neither was his mind suited for indolence. He who pampers his body and mind with luxuries and indulgences sends the wrong message to his children. *The beehive* represents work, not the accumulation of wealth. Is your legacy to be an example of self absorption, or one of serving mankind? Do you wish to set your children on the path to indulgence, luxury and vice, or is it more important to you that they become good citizens serving others? Masonry teaches that the service to all mankind is the noblest destiny of man. It also teaches that wealth is to be used to heal the sick and strengthen the poor of spirit. It is these lessons that *the beehive* seeks to impart.

It is man's nature to desire distinction – to feel important and needed. Whether at work, at home, or in a Masonic lodge, man wants to show that he not only belongs, but that he also has something important to contribute. Masons are not taught to run from those natural feelings, but to apply them in their lives in a positive manner. The perversion of these desires results in striving to accumulate titles, money, honors and public acclaim. The positive application of those desires results in housing for the aged, hospitals for ill children and free clinics for those who need assistance in speaking so that they may be clearly understood. It is the latter application, not the former perversion that promotes real progress for all humanity.

Edgar Cayce, the famous seer of the 1920's, '30's and '40's, underscored this truth during his readings of "patients'" past lives. Whether or not one accepts or rejects the notion that a human being, such as Cayce, could ever possess such abilities, or that souls incarnate, die and are reincarnated is entirely irrelevant. Rather, even if nothing more than symbolic of what was in his mind, the readings relating to work and industry are instructive to Masons.

Cayce interviewed several persons whom he reported had, in previous lives, held significant positions of power and leadership in places of government. He also reported that in other previous lives, those same entities had lived in poverty, or were relegated to a lesser station in life. Without exception the poor and lowly, because of their work and industry, made greater lasting contributions to society than did those who enjoyed positions of power. The reason for such a result was not because the people themselves were defective, but rested squarely upon the fact that God expects us to serve others, not ourselves.

The beehive also teaches us that every man has a work to do in himself. That work is nobler than the fashioning of wood or marble – it concerns the shaping of the human soul. Freemasonry refers to that work as *the work of virtue,* without which man lives his entire life without ever fulfilling his true destiny. No Mason should ever deem his life doomed to mediocrity, meanness, vanity, or unprofitable toil. In the great providence of the Supreme Architect of the Universe there is enough good work for every man. He needs but to think it and then to do it.

Masonry has always sought to ennoble common life. The rich and the poor, the high and the low, who as created by one almighty parent and inhabitants of the same planet are to aid, support and protect each other. What is done in private is oftentimes more important to the progress of humanity than that which is performed in public. The anonymous gift to hospitals where doctors straighten the twisted limbs of our children; the quiet soft prayer spoken on behalf of another in need; and the humble giving of one's time to heal another's distresses are at least as valuable to the advancement of the human soul as are the more public decisions made by legislators, business executives and community leaders.

Placed in its proper perspective, *the beehive* symbolically emphasizes one word that is well known among Masons. That word is *duty*. The bee that gathers the pollen does so because that is its duty. The bee that builds the hive does so because it must. And the queen presides over all of the activity because that is the proper order of things necessary to fulfill the duty of the hive. Each has a work to do that if unperformed renders the work of the entire hive incomplete.

Chapter 59

THE COMMON GAVEL

> "For we know that, if our earthly house of this tabernacle
> were dissolved, we have a building of God, an house
> not made with hands, eternal in the heavens."
>
> 2 Cor. 5:1

A Freemason can ask no more than to have the opportunity to prove that which he is; to become the dream that is his inspiration. One has no right to ask God for wisdom, or to demand happiness. Like all men, Freemasons are given a gift by nature through which they learn all things and become their dreams – the privilege of labor.

The common gavel is explained in Masonry as being an instrument used by operative masons to break off the rough and superfluous parts of stones. As such, it is an instrument used for building edifices. In its esoteric sense, it also represents an instrument used in Freemasonry to build dreams.

Life is the span of time appointed to all human beings within which to accomplish something. Every fleeting moment is an opportunity to make progress toward that achievement. Every fit of laziness, apathy, indifference and slothfulness is an opportunity lost.

Man is climbing an endless flight of stairs with his eyes fixed on the goal situated at the top. Most cannot see the goal, but have nonetheless learned an important lesson – as one builds his own character he is given strength to climb the stairs. Therefore, the work of a Freemason is to build character – the character of all men encountered in the span of a life.

Building things, especially spiritual things, is the worthiest work man can find. Out of the mists, the Supreme Architect of the Universe stretched forth his finger, selected man as the being among all of His creation who would become the instrument of His hand. Man was appointed to be the builder of His temple, instructed to raise pillars, construct tile floors and ornament the divine dwelling with metals and jewels more splendid than anything known to mankind.

Through His instruments Solomon, King of Israel and Hiram, King of Tyre, the Great Architect tapped Hiram Abiff on the shoulder and set him to work as His master builder. God pointed to the clouds, the streams of heavenly light and instructed Hiram to make the building from those substances and not to use an axe, hammer, or other tool of iron in its construction. What was set in motion on earth was also built in heaven – that spiritual house not made with hands. "As it is above, so shall it be below."

The ancients taught that when man desires something here below, forces of realizing that goal are also set in motion above. The Essenian Teacher of Righteousness instructed his followers that such forces are God's reward for mankind's behavior. He who seeks such a reward from material goods as already attained that to which he is entitled. He who refrains from practice good deeds merely to receive the praise of his fellows will gain God's favor. Freemasons use the common gavel to build quietly and without regard to whether or not mankind will praise his efforts.

One can easily imagine Hiram Abiff constructing the idea for the Temple in his own mind. Perhaps the task seemed daunting at first, but straightening his shoulders he grasped the trestle board in his hands and drew the plans for building God's dwelling. With divine hope, footings were laid. From the formless clay, molds were cast, sacred ornaments were designed and slowly the structure began to take shape. Yet, completion of the building was not to be for Hiram.

Turning upon him, the three left their Grand Master dying in the midst of his labors. Using the same tools that had been used by the workmen to create; the three destroyed the Master Workman leaving the Temple unfinished. What sort of reward from above was this? Perverted thought, uncurbed emotions and destructive action had converged to deprive Hiram of the life given by our Creator. Thought, desire, action — these three — left the Temple in ruins.

We learn from the Holy Writings that David, King of Israel desired to build the Temple, but because his own desires had resulted in many wars and much bloodshed, that distinguished privilege was denied him. The task fell to his son, Solomon whose wisdom and determination before God resulted in the completion of the task. Now, both David and the Master Builder Hiram were dead — again, what sort of reward from above was this?

Our common gavel is also a symbol of *justice,* that standard or boundary of right which enables us to render unto every man his just due without distinction. Within the realm of justice one learns that for every action there is a consequence, or *reward.* Undisciplined thought, unleashed emotions and careless action not only thrust the Temple into ruin, they threaten to throw lives held under their spell into complete chaos. Poverty is the just reward for imprudent spending. A life without friends is the just reward for angry backbiting. And, poor health is the guaranteed lot for he who disregards the deleterious effect of his bad habits.

The Gospels set forth in the New Testament of the Holy Bible illustrate the steps man must take in order to experience goodness and blessedness. We are told the story of Jesus, who while spending 40 days in the wilderness was sorely tempted to give in to his material desires. Each temptation was resisted resulting in his being coroneted by God with a royal crown. According to the story, his reward for controlling his passions was to be seated at God's right hand.

But, what about those who commit acts of evil? Is there no hope; no redemption? What does the common gavel teach us in that regard? When the three assassins awoke to the horror they had just committed they cried out to God, who had compassion upon the children of His creation. Figuratively, they were handed a tiny lamp, marked Hiram's grave so that it could be found, grieved loudly and professed their remorse. They freely admitted their crime and submitted to execution. Even in time of trouble, the Supreme Architect administered to them and saved them with an everlasting salvation – for He permits all to call him *father*.

When we reflect upon the lessons about virtue and justice taught us by the common gavel, we should also remind ourselves that Freemasonry is not just a social order that enjoys a history stretching back a few centuries. The ancient mysteries perpetuated in Masonic ritual, of which the common gavel is but one symbol, confer powers on those who participate that mold their destiny. As a science of the soul, whose authority over man's unwieldy natural spirit is symbolized in the common gavel, it becomes a universal expression of divine wisdom.

As you think, contemplate and learn try to examine what parts of your own behavior need the common gavel. What rough and superfluous parts need to be knocked away to expose the beauty beneath? Freemasonry is the privilege to work – to work at improving so that by improving one may better serve humanity.

Chapter 60

THE EAST

> "The Lord by wisdom hath founded the earth; by understanding hath he established the heavens."
>
> Prov. 3:19

In ancient Craft Masonry, wisdom is symbolized by the East, the place of light, being represented by the pillar that stands in the east as a support of the lodge, and also by the Worshipful Master. Wisdom is also symbolized in the fraternity by King Solomon, who is famed as the wisest man that ever lived. The wisdom Solomon possessed was something much more than simply excellent knowledge. God had so blessed this Son of David that the power of his wisdom was almost divine; a creative energy that actively worked miracles in the lives of King Solomon's subjects. Although certainly not expected to replicate such Divine miracles, each Master of a Masonic lodge should never forget that he represents the goal all Masons strive to achieve – Divine Wisdom. As such, the Master is an example to the brethren he leads and will inevitably leave either a lasting good impression upon the minds of every member of his lodge, or a bad example none wish to follow.

True wisdom is not a system or a creed and thus cannot be entirely learned by the adherence to any single approach to acquiring knowledge.

In Freemasonry, wisdom is more correctly defined as an infinite search, or rather approximation that is inspired by each man's individual intellectual and moral progress. In Masonry, also, knowledge is convertible into power, as axioms are converted into rules. But, contrary to popular belief, knowledge is not power. Wisdom is power and is served by knowledge, the best use of which is to make a man mature into a state of wisdom.

To limit oneself to merely knowing the rituals of Masonry is of little value, for by itself the ritualistic liturgy is simply many words and many sentences strung together. Even to comprehend the several meanings of Masonic symbols is of little value unless the meanings we glean from those symbols add to our wisdom. Man may spend a lifetime studying a specific science, history, or philosophy committing to memory each and every salient detail. Yet in the end, if that study adds little to his own wisdom, he has accomplished very little. Freemasonry has identified wisdom as being that state of mind and attitude whereby a man may correctly assess and determine truth from falsehood. In that regard, Masonry seeks to teach a man about his rights, interests and duties – lessons in truth that genuinely add to personal wisdom.

When we read about the history of King Solomon, we are not terribly interested in learning how much he knew of astronomy – though he knew a great deal about that subject – or how well read he was in the political science of his era – though he was also extremely knowledgeable in that field, as well. Rather, the stories of interest to us as Masons are those that are central to his character and describe how well he understood people; how easily he mastered justice; and, how dedicated he was as a sovereign to leading his nation. The knowledge Solomon acquired during his lifetime yielded the greatest genius in wisdom history has ever witnessed. During his lifetime, peace and tranquility pervaded the world owing in no small measure to that wisdom.

If the example of the Craft's legendary founder is followed, the true Mason should become a man who helps Freemasonry to implement great purposes. No man is too unenlightened, or under-educated to add to the glory of Masonic charity. A smile, polite nod of the head, or small donation of money contributes as greatly to Masonic charity as do the enormous good deeds of Grand Masters and their entourage. Yet, it requires wisdom to understand that fact to be a truth, as well as to determine what one can do, when it can be done and precisely how to do that which each man possesses the ability to contribute.

There are several benchmarks of wisdom for which each Mason can look for in his life. If you have achieved even one of those goals, you are headed in the correct direction toward attaining wisdom. For example, the wiser a man becomes, the less likely he will be inclined to submit to restraints on his conscience and intellect. Freemasonry imposes not the duty of rote submission, but demands that each member comprehend the importance of freedom – not merely as an abstract hope for man's material state of being, but as a true spiritual, mental and intellectual state of being. No true Mason will ever permit any one person or body of persons to dictate to him in matters for which he alone is accountable and responsible. Rather, he will rely upon the convictions of his own conscience and the judgments of his own intellect and thereby emerge as a true soldier of liberty.

Liberty and freedom are twin curses to the ignorant. Therefore, the Mason who desires true freedom must also acquire great knowledge of many subjects – music, science, mathematics, history, philosophy and theology are but a few such subjects. In the Fellowcraft Degree, the candidate is told about the various liberal arts and sciences and encouraged to make them a life-long study. Does he? If he does not, does he understand the consequences? If he does not, why have you, my excellent wise brother, not so informed him? Do you not wish him true liberty and lasting freedom?

As a practical matter, understanding certain essential aspects of today's political science, like the political science during the era of King Solomon, is of enormous importance to attaining wisdom. Political science, as opposed to political party preference, is truly a law of nature. People interact on the basis of behavioral propensities and boundaries erected for the purpose of defining that which is and that which is not acceptable in cordial society. The science applied to understanding how those propensities and boundaries relate to each other is referred to as "political science." In his day, Solomon understood what his people desired and the limitations of what he could deliver to his people. That understanding was the root of the wisdom history attributes to his reign.

As Masons, we are confronted with the necessity to understand similar needs both within a Masonic lodge and within the society where we live our daily lives.

The political science that should be of interest to Masons has for its object the determination of what human institutions are necessary to secure and perpetuate the protection of personal, religious and political freedoms. Freemasons have united in eternal hostility to tyranny and demands for every person a free voice and opinion in all public affairs. That he may do so, the individual Mason obligates himself to keep himself free, to promote free government in the country where he lives and to be complete master over his own voice, vote and opinion. Thus, shall he forever be the true soldier of liberty.

In Masonic lodges, the East symbolizes the wisdom essential to preserving the Divine Truth that is embodied on earth in freedom. Without ever consciously thinking about whether or not it is of God, men everywhere prefer freedom to slavery. Freedom is a law of nature and he who sets out to deprive another of his natural-born state of freedom is a criminal against the laws of nature. The man or Mason who understands this truth possesses true wisdom. The man who fails to understand that truth, regardless of the extent of knowledge he has acquired, is wholly unwise.

Look to the East, my brethren. Learn freedom through obedience and secrecy. Acquire habits of virtue and morality. Abide by the laws of the fraternity you serve and the land in which you live. Thus, will you ever be a source of true wisdom to your fellowman.

Chapter 61

THE FALL

> "It is like the precious ointment upon the head,
> that ran down upon the beard, even Aaron's beard;
> that went down to the skirts of his garments; As the dew
> of Hermon, and as the dew that descended upon the mountains
> of Zion:"
>
> Ps. 133:2-3

The dew referred to in the passage from the book of Psalms represents to Freemasons the influences of Divine grace given to us by God. It reminds us that we have all fallen short of what is expected from us; that we have fallen from paradise, much as did Adam and Eve in the Biblical story about creation. It also reminds us that while we are all God's creatures, we have within ourselves the power to do acts of great good, or greater evil.

If the paradise in the Biblical account is understood as an actual place on the terrestrial, or material plane, and if man's "Fall" is similarly understood as having taken place on this plane, the capability to do evil arises from something within ourselves; something quite possibly passed down to us from generations of ancestors. Thus understood, the tendency toward evil within man relates to the flesh, not the spirit, which is at war with the body.

However, it is the body which, rightly, has more reason to be ashamed of the soul inhabiting it, than the latter of the body. For, the body is a miracle of wisdom, harmony and stability, which does not merit the scorn, but rather the admiration of the soul. Can the soul boast of moral principles as stable as the body's skeleton? Is the soul as indefatigable and as faithful as the heart which beats within the body every day without taking a break? And, if this does not suffice to change scorn into respect, then one may recall, if he is Christian, that Jesus once inhabited and honored this flesh, as did Gautama Buddha.

Freemasonry does not promote a man's struggle against the body, but rather against the seed of evil sown within the soul. The virtues taught Masons are calculated to teach us that good and evil exist side-by-side; not only in the world within which we live, but within our very hearts. Like the alchemist, Masons are taught how to refine the good within themselves so that each may become a positive, rather than negative influence upon those with whom he interacts. We do these practices in virtue for the sake of our soul's reunion with our God.

This principle of positive asceticism is not unique to Freemasonry; it is universal. Everyone practices it. A scientist who shuts himself in his room with a view to pursuing his studies does so because he is taken up with the truth that he is seeking and not because he wants to deprive his body of sun, air, or the outside world. Positive asceticism is, therefore, truly an exchange of good for better – a message certainly not lost upon Freemasons.

The dew of Hermon and the dew that fell upon the mountain of Zion so familiar to those who study the lessons of the first degree of Freemasonry, emblematically reveals that God has given to us the Divine grace of knowledge by which we may truly exchange the good for the better. If the Fall of Man symbolically represents original sin, as many believe, that original sin has something to do with knowledge; either the lack of it enitirely, or the misuse of it in the manner of disobedience. The potential for greater evil within us is realized when we choose to exercise our free will separate and apart from the will of God. This is what child psychologists have called "presumptuous audacity" when describing a misbehaving and disobedient child.

The Book of Genesis informs us that mankind was originally placed in a garden "in order to till it and keep it." Gen. 2:15. For Masons, a garden is symbolically associated with a state of cooperation and equilibrium between the spirit and nature. It is, therefore, incumbent upon all Freemasons to cultivate and maintain the world – to will and to be silent as by the grace of our great Creator we watch how our hands, guided by His grace, mold cooperation and equilibrium. A state we call "brotherhood."

Chapter 62

THE GREEN MAN

> "Unto what is the kingdom of God like? And whereunto shall I resemble it? It is like a grain of mustard seed,...and it grew..."
>
> Luke 13:18-19

The construction of Rosslyn Chapel, located north of Edinburgh in Scotland, was commenced in approximately 1446 by William Sinclair, who was reputed to have been a Knight Templar that was likely engaged in warfare in the Holy Land. While neither of those facts has been confirmed, the chapel he constructed is filled with images of stone that when viewed as a whole leaves the distinct impression that the site is religious. However, it is definitely not a Christian site and does not easily fit into any current well-known religious motif. It is, in a word, unique revealing evidence that the architect was very much involved with initiatory mysteries.

One of the stone images carved into the interior of the chapel symbolizes a *Green Man,* which in certain religious studies has been associated with so-called pagan religions. After carefully studying those images, it appears more likely that the *Green Man* is consistent with a more Masonic interpretation of the Deity than of any other religion or philosophy.

The depiction is clearly that of a man's head with leafy vines growing from inside extending outward through the mouth and traveling upward forming a dense bushy vegetation.

While the figure certainly could symbolize the never-ending cycle of seasons and regeneration commonly found in other clearly defined pagan symbols, its origin is Greek and Roman. To them, the *Green Man* represented the full flowering of education and thus was inspirational to those contemplating the pursuit of knowledge. The *Green Man* later found his way into Christian symbolism where he represented the immortality of the spirit and the resurrection of Jesus. Regardless of whether the *Green Man* represents Jesus linking Heaven to Earth, or the more simplistic pursuit of knowledge, it is undeniably the case that he also represents the growth of man's spirit.

Freemasonry's affinity to the pursuit of knowledge has never been solely because it benefits he who learns, but because it eventually benefits those with whom he who learns comes into contact. Masonic writers who have explored both the science and philosophy of alchemy have also provided us with insight into how the *Green Man* represents the benefit of one man's knowledge to another man's welfare. Freemasonry has consistently adopted the belief that the Supreme Architect of the Universe manifests Himself through human growth – the urge moving from within a human being to a manifestation of action.

There is no greater miracle than that produced by the tiny mustard seed, which when planted in the Earth produces a bush many thousand times its own size. The Holy Bible contains a parable that uses the tiny mustard seed to illustrate an important spiritual truth about the strength of faith. In Freemasonry, the Craft teaches that the Supreme Architect manifests Himself through an infinity of forms which is implanted into the dark material earth. One of those forms is art, which Masons are taught to both understand and create.

Art is a seed of man's spirituality, for from a simple sentence in a masterful work of literature, or from one line drawn in a painting flow messages and ideas that those who either read, or observe may interpret for their respective personal improvement. It is the basis for mankind's regeneration, or transmutation from a state of unknowing to a state of knowing – much like the ancient alchemists transformed tin into gold.

Thus, the *Green Man* symbolizes the wisdom which man acquires from the knowledge he has gained as a direct result of his growth in spiritual matters commencing with the mustard seed, or smallest particle of spiritual knowledge imparted to him.

It is fair to inquire at this point about what art a Mason should explore. Should it be an examination of the Da Vinci painting *The Last Supper,* which excited so much interest in the recent titillating books and movies about the legend surrounding the ancient Knights Templar? Is it the full and complete absorption of all literary works written by Albert Pike? Or, are you expected to absorb other types of art and discern the messages about God from those? While the answer that all art is important to man's growth is inexact, it is the truthful answer.

Academics around the globe are presently engaged in a concerted effort to identify the historical beginnings of Freemasonry. They do so by pursuing several avenues that promise empirical certainty once fully analyzed. However, since Freemasonry includes a diverse quantity of disciplines, it is not at all likely that the true origins will ever be discovered without a thorough evaluation of the symbolism Masonry has selected throughout the ages to impart wise and serious truths. One famous Masonic writer has gone farther and asserted that the origins of Freemasonry will never be traced, because that origin is veiled in superphysical mystery. Whether or not we will ever know the complete truth about Freemasonry's origin, one may begin the effort by pulling that veil aside and studying the diverse symbols of the Craft, as well as the various works of art created from the depths of man's soul and spirit.

There are essentially two methods whereby man may grow: by observing Nature, or by creating and appreciating art. The true artist patterns his or her work after the laws of Nature, either adopting all that Nature has revealed, or assimilating so much of that which exists in Nature as is necessary to complete the artist's intended design. It is from such designs that mankind learns the place of humanity in the *Magnus Opus* of all artwork – the grand design of the Supreme Architect of the Universe.

The art of deciphering Masonic symbols may be employed to unlock unsuspected wisdom that was quite likely originally possessed by those who lent those symbols to the fraternity. Ancient books with erroneous paginations, as well as a host of secret alphabets used throughout the ages should be included in the deciphering effort. For, subtle methods were often used to conceal divine truths from the uninitiated. By way of specific example, consider the literary works of Shakespeare, which some believe were actually the works of Sir Francis Bacon: that renowned Rosicrucian and Freemason, who is said to have been the legitimate son of Elizabeth I; dedicated to the charitable workings of the Craft; and in desperate need of "political cover" to avoid detection as the author of such politically inflammatory writings as those found in several of the Shakespearian plays. What is the truth? Can it be ascertained by studying the artwork itself? Is it worth knowing? Answers to those questions may only come to those who take the time to explore the works and decide for themselves.

The symbolism of the *Green Man* also teaches us that growth is experiential, that is, it may only be experienced to fully understand. Such is also so with regard to the "secrets" of Freemasonry. Those "secrets," like understanding what growth means, cannot be revealed even if someone actually chose to sit down and explain them to the entire world. Like death, Freemasonry can only be "experienced," and thus the "secrets" remain hidden from all who choose never to enjoy the experience. That is so with our *Green Man,* for it is from his mouth that vegetation grows and around his head that the resulting busy growth twines. He grows, he experiences and he becomes wise.

Chapter 63

THE HEAVENLY JERUSALEM

> "Thy kingdom come. Thy will be
> done in earth as it is in heaven."
>
> Matt. 6:10

When the human soul, having had the experience of union with the Great Architect, turns toward its neighbor and toward Nature, not in order to merely think or contemplate, but in order to act it becomes like the soul of a *magi* – those ancient wise men whom the Holy Writings tell us visited the infant Jesus. Tradition refers to this occurrence as *sacred magic*. Freemasonry refers to it as *brotherly love*. In either case, this occurrence constitutes the convergence in man of that which he has learned by his own hard work and that which God has revealed to him as a matter of grace.

In the Third Degree of Masonry, the Craft is taught that an immortal soul resides within each one of us. The certainty of that fact is revealed to the brethren in the allegorical Hiramic legend, which also conveys the notion that the number *three*, or the concept of *trinity*, represents the various stages of Divine revelation. Masonic tradition, like the traditions found in other ancient mysteries, calls this "the descent of the heavenly Jerusalem."

In contrast to the symbolism of the *Tower of Babel,* which in part conveys materialism, or man's pursuit of his earthly desires, the symbolism of the *heavenly Jerusalem* represents the final stage of the transformation of the whole of humanity to a balanced spiritual existence. Hermeticism, Christianity and Judaism each embraces the philosophy of conversion of the human soul by understanding that *light* and *darkness* exist side-by-side requiring mankind to separate the wheat from the chaff – to enhance that which is good and suppress that which is evil within each person. This is not a task to be undertaken by churches on behalf of its members, or governments on behalf of its citizens. Rather, Freemasonry teaches that this is an individual task that can only be completed by each individual person.

The "descent of the heavenly Jerusalem" comprises the most intimate experiences of human souls, as well as the evolution of our planet. It represents the radiation of grace from above upon earthly creation, as well as creations response to that radiation. Mankind may use its freedom of will and choice to accept, or to reject that which is offered from above. The longer it is rejected, the longer the descent will take place. When it is completed, the entire human civilization will be transformed into a celestial city.

The quest for this Jerusalem is not a search for a place. It is a journey toward a new state of being where the laws adhered to are those of heaven. We see those laws at work every day when we pause to enjoy Nature. But, those pauses are too infrequent and are enjoyed by few people. The life of the modern world does not permit such indulgences. Rather, constant communication is the order of the day, as men and women walk the streets hurriedly chatting away on cell phones glued to their ears and completely ignoring the humanity and Nature around them. Freemasons wonder whether with people believing they have so little time for anything other than feeding earthly desires a new heaven and new earth will ever be created, in spite of the prediction of its imminent arrival in our Holy Writings.

When the descent of the heavenly Jerusalem is completed, nothing will remain concealed. Everyone will be like Jesus' disciples, to whom he said that all things were revealed, but to others they were concealed in parables and allegory. There is nothing that will remain secret, or unknown, for everything that takes place in subjective intimacy will one day become objective reality. It is a law of Nature that every subjective thing will at some time become objective – that human aspirations, thoughts and feelings will become fulfilled. As the prophet said, "For they sow the wind, and they shall reap the whirlwind." (Hos. 9:7).

It is a fair question to ask what you can do to hasten the descent. But, before receiving the answer it may be best to first explore the things about you that thwart that descent. How recently have you demanded a change in your brother without considering the changes required of you? Have you in recent memory either tossed an angry word at a brother, or spoken badly about him behind his back? What is it that you do in Masonry, other than pay your dues? With so many things about you that need changing, would it not be best to become more patient? Is it possible for you to become more patient with your brother, yourself and with God?

During his earthly ministry, Jesus encountered the Samaritans, who were at that time regarded as heretics. His own followers chided him for wasting his time in their presence, for no matter how hard anyone tried, the Samaritans would not change their religious point of view. Rather than walking away from those people, as many in his camp advised, he spoke with them, taught them, reached out to understand them and gave them his love. Jesus was not in a rush with the Samaritans, or any other people who also needed his guidance and good counsel. He demonstrated patience, teaching us the value of that extremely important virtue.

When you return to assessing yourself, do you recall your last occasion of intolerance? Was there someone, or some group of people about whom you openly expressed disgust, annoyance, or frustration? If so, was that because their behavior did not conform to your expectations? The driver on the freeway who cut you off never said he was sorry, did he? The people in the vehicle alongside of you did not seem to care that their boom-box annoyed you, did they? Is that why you lost your patience?

Freemasonry teaches that men should labor not so much to accomplish something in their lifetime, but to provide either a foundation upon which others may build, or to add to a foundation originally begun by others centuries before you were born. The Craft more favorably embraces the tortoise than it does the hare, for patient attendance to morality and virtue in everything one attempts is demanded of anyone who wishes to hasten the descent of the heavenly Jerusalem.

The first and most important lesson to be learned is the meaning of patience, for without it you contribute nothing to the Great Architect's plan. Patience is the ability to endure waiting, delay, or provocation without becoming annoyed or upset. Indeed, the increase of patience in a man is a holy work, enhanced by God's grace and the Holy Spirit He has breathed into your existence. As the Apostle Paul stated in his writings: "Love is patient."

The degrees of Masonry teach the candidate valuable lessons over a period of time – not at once. A man changes because of his exposure to Masonry over time – not on the very evening of his initiation. From time immemorial, men have worked to lay the foundation of *light* that one day will entirely replace the darkness in the world and fulfill the "descent of the heavenly Jerusalem." The precise day or hour is unknown to anyone. It is only known to our Divine Creator. You cannot assist the process unless you, too, are willing to patiently face anger, hate, tyranny and blasphemy. Your impatience, though certainly understandable as a human emotion, will set back the clock, not move time forward.

As Freemasons, let us try to be a little more like the Great Architect, who patiently showers upon the deserving and undeserving alike his compassion and mercy. He embraces all with the affluence of His love and rejects no one. If we are so loved, should we not so love one another? The fulfillment of the spiritual change Freemasonry endeavors to accomplish depends upon you and no one else. If you do not do your job and acquire greater patience in everything you undertake, you are directly responsible for thwarting the great goal of the Craft – a true brotherhood of man under the fatherhood of God.

Each Masonic lodge is an island within a disjointed community. There, on that island, the lessons God intended all mankind to learn and employ may be experienced – not merely learned, but truly experienced. Yet, leaving the providing of that experience to others deprives humanity of all you have to offer. Can you set aside your discomforts, annoyances and grievances long enough to join your brethren in making a difference? You may be surprised at what you learn about yourself, mankind and the Supreme Grand Master of the Universe.

Chapter 64

THE HIDDEN MYSTERIES

"Knowledge of the mysteries of the kingdom of God
has been granted to you; but to the rest they are
made known through parables..."

Luke 8:10

In each of the three degrees of Blue Lodge Masonry the candidate acknowledges his obligation not to reveal the manner and method used by Masons to impart knowledge of the *hidden mysteries* of Freemasonry to anyone who is not entitled to receive them. Throughout history that "Masonic obligation" has been the source of scathing accusations hurled at the fraternity that it is a dangerous secret society, or in the alternative, that it has heretical secrets known only to its members. Those accusations have resulted in attempts by non-Masons to marginalize the Craft and attribute devil-worship to its followers. So-called holy men and kings have even been prompted to hunt down, burn, torture and kill Freemasons. Yet, if the world had known then what is known today – that Freemasonry conceals nothing that is not wholly available to every man, woman and child - perhaps such ruthlessness would not have occurred.

Writers who have woven Masonic themes into literary works of fiction and non-fiction, while perhaps legitimately speculating upon matters of public interest such as whether or not Jesus married Mary of Magdalene, or that the original Knights Templar discovered the Holy Grail, have contributed to the public fascination with the prospect that Freemasonry continues to conceal something that is extraordinarily valuable to all mankind. Indeed, something great and glorious is concealed, or *hidden* by Freemasons, but it has absolutely nothing to do with Jesus, Mary of Magdalene, or the Holy Grail. And even though that "something" is and always will remain *hidden,* it is equally available to non-Masons. Anyone who takes the time to journey down the proper path will discover what is *hidden* without the need for any Mason to violate his obligation.

During the journey toward discovering the *hidden mysteries* valued by Freemasons, one inevitably encounters that mystical sect known as the Essenes. Since the discovery of the Dead Sea Scrolls in 1947, even though much of that information has not yet been made publicly available, a great deal of material about this sect is now in the public domain. For example, we now understand that the Essenes were of the eclectic sect of philosophers and held Plato in the highest esteem. They believed that true philosophy, the greatest gift of God to man, was scattered throughout all sects and that it was man's duty to gather it together and present it as the unified word of the Almighty.

The writings of the Essenes were laced with mysticism, parables, enigmas and sophisticated allegories. They studied both the esoteric and exoteric meanings of the Holy Writings, which they found in the Old Testament just as the Gnostics found in the New Testament. Christian writers, as well as allegedly Jesus himself, recognized that all scripture had an *inner* meaning, as well as an *outer* truth.

The passage of scripture taken from the Gospel of Luke at the head of this article makes it abundantly clear that the public teachings attributed to Jesus were different from the private teachings he imparted to his inner circle of Apostles. Even within that inner circle, it is reputed that some received a *light* not otherwise given to other Apostles. That *light* represents what the world now refers to as the *hidden mysteries,* because it is not freely meted out to those in the *outer* circle; those who are left to decipher the kingdom of God for themselves from the several allegories, stories and parables set forth in the Holy Writings.

In some intellectual circles, as well as in certain Masonic literature, it is insinuated that Jesus was killed because he improperly divulged the *hidden mysteries* which he had vowed to conceal and never reveal. Under that belief, he was not killed merely because he challenged Roman rule, or the religious dogma taught by the Pharisees. Consequently, the question is frequently asked: did Jesus practice Freemasonry? The answer depends upon one's own assessment of the available hard evidence.

Jesus did participate in the baptism of Saint John the Baptist, who is regarded by Masons as a patron of the fraternity. While he often criticized the Pharisees and Sadducees, Jesus never once mentioned the Essenes, whose doctrines bear a striking resemblance to Jesus' teachings, as well as to the teachings of Freemasonry. It is also asserted that at the time of his arrest Jesus was then in the process of conferring a Masonic degree upon a candidate. "Now a young man followed him and fled wearing nothing but a linen cloth about his body." Mark 14:50-51.

That particular passage does not appear in any of the other three accepted gospels and no further explanation has been added anywhere in the Holy Writings to help us understand precisely what was going on between Jesus and the anonymous young man at this critical point in Jesus' life. Perhaps Freemasons discern a similarity to an aspect of Masonic ritual, perhaps not. To understand the nature of the *hidden mysteries,* it is not essential that the question be answered one way, or the other.

The forms and ceremonies used by the Essenes were symbolical, just as they are today in Freemasonry. According to Philo, they had four degrees; were Jews by birth; and held a greater affection for each other than was true of members of any other sect. Before there was a Christian religion, they fulfilled the Christian law, "Love one another." They despised riches and made certain that no single member had more material goods than any other member, all of which were held in common. Their piety toward the one living God was without compare, which they ritualized in mysterious ceremonies and initiations about which very little is known. However, like Freemasonry, it was within the symbolism of those ceremonies that the *hidden mysteries* could be revealed.

This extraordinarily well disciplined and highly organized sect did not simply appear on the scene at about the time Saint John the Baptist preached than did Freemasonry erupt in 1717 with a fully mechanized ritual. Passages from the Dead Sea Scrolls reveal that members of the sect wrote about the Pharaoh Akhenaton and monotheism and quite likely practiced forms and ceremonies related to the one living God at a time much earlier than even the patriarch Jacob. Other passages make clear the fact that the *hidden mysteries* could only be accessed through specific use of certain arts, parts and points similar to what has been described of the ceremonial practices of the mystical High Priest and King of Salem, Melchizadek. Owing to the relationship of Saint John the Baptist as a patron of Freemasonry, it is fair to conclude that the Craft bears at least a strong an affinity to the Essenes.

When the relationship of the Essenes to Freemasonry is so understood, it is also easier to understand why the manner, sequence and method of Masonic ritual is only explained to those who are initiated into the fraternity. In other words, while the *hidden mysteries* are not held private, the manner Masons employ to know and study them is something that can only be learned by a member of the Craft. But what are those *hidden mysteries?* Why should any man, woman, or child care to know and understand them? The best way to answer both of those questions is to begin with an explanation of what it takes for any person to fully comprehend the Mysteries.

It is not enough for a person to simply become God-intoxicated. As long as the mind remains disorderly, ignorant and ill-disciplined, any effort to comprehend the *hidden mysteries* will be in vain. Because of the necessity for a higher level of consciousness to enable a more sophisticated synthesis of all God has made available for man to study, Freemasonry has adopted the system of Pythagoras, whom Masonic writers have described as having himself been a Mason. Under that system grammar, rhetoric and logic are taught to cultivate and improve the mind. Mathematics, geometry, music and astronomy are also inculcated and a system of symbols is derived therefrom. This outline for the cultivation of intellectual insight should be strictly followed.

However, the cultivation of intellectual insight is not enough. There remains a step to be taken during which the cautionary scripture tale about the Tower of Babel should be kept in mind. Man builds his intellectual powers at the hands of human workmen until he reaches the top story of that tower. Here, communion with the Supreme Architect of the Universe takes over, for no man can peer behind the veil concealing the *hidden mysteries* unless permitted to do so by God. Thus the steps for any person to take include educating the mind about all that God has created and then clearing the mind for direct instructions from the Deity through meditative prayer, as opposed to petitioning prayer.

Ask, and it shall be given you; seek, and you find; knock, and the door to all understanding of the *hidden mysteries* will be opened for you. You simply need to know how to ask, where to seek and the manner in which you are expected to knock.

Chapter 65

THE HUMAN SOUL

*"If a man die, shall he live again? all the
days of my appointed time will I wait,
till my change come."*

Job 14:14

The symbols of Freemasonry open our hearts and minds to the many virtues available to each of us to aid in our individual pursuit of life and love. But, what if anything does those symbols seek to tell us about the human soul? Is mankind simply an accidental occurrence, a freak of nature and the unexpected consequence of some *Big Bang* that resulted in outer space eons ago? Indeed not – at least not to Freemasons who teach a doctrine of man's immortality. No man who has been raised to the sublime degree of Master Mason can ever forget the lessons about the truth of the human soul.

Man is seemingly surrounded by injustice and all too often discovers that those in whom he has placed his greatest trust have abandoned him for the sake of commercial greed. To many, the shocking impact of such a discovery is horribly disappointing, for the injustice and unfairness is frequently visited upon us by those who have achieved the highest levels of material accomplishment and openly profess to also be men of God.

Such experiences call into question the extent to which the human soul has advanced since the days when he first emerged from the caves and exchanged animal skins for a business suit.

Is it idle to hope for any great progress of humanity toward perfection? Are the advances in civilization nothing more than increases in selfishness and self-centeredness? Does man's freedom merely give him a license to slight or backstab his closest friends and business partners? Amidst the consequences of such human vanity and self-conceit, the Ancient Craft of Freemasonry correctly inquires – *whence came we, and whither are we going?*

When Freemasons look forward to the *acacia,* that evergreen which budded and bloomed at the head of the grave of that celebrated artist whom the Craft reveres, they are reminded of the immortal part; the spirit or soul of man that will live when time shall be no more. That human soul is regarded as the inspiration of the great Divinity whom all Masons adore. How man became an "inspiration" of God, or what that phrase even means is a mystery greater than life itself. To the extent such a mystery truly exists, it is because there is human consciousness in existence ready and able to pose that question.

What if in the midst of all the elements and their various formations there appeared a magical sculpture that revealed the secret, or mystery of the universe? Likely, some would rush to identify it as the *Great Masonic Secret,* but they would be incorrect. What if the features of that sculpture expressed the Great Architect's thoughts and feelings? More likely than not, men everywhere of every religion, creed and doctrine would cherish that sculpture as though it was God, or at least an inspiration of God. There is such a sculpture – the human being.

Freemasonry teaches that the human being is a mirror reflection of creation. Within every person's very being lies all of the secrets of the universe, sometimes buried deeply within the unconscious mind. Of those secrets there is none greater than that God exists – a truth every Mason professes openly during his initiation into our ancient and honorable fraternity. When we closely examine the several interpretations of the many symbols used in Freemasonry, we also learn that the single most important undertaking for every human being is to become

God's companion. With complete awareness of our unity with the Great Architect, the purpose of our coming into being is to share in the responsibility of continuing the process of creation, to add to the glory of life by the manner in which we reflect the creative energy of God which flows within each one of us.

Each human being represents God's attempt to become aware, in a finite material body, of the nature of infinite creative forces. That is one of the messages Freemasonry means to convey when it teaches that the human soul is the inspiration of God. Each experience by each human being is very important to God, and within the heart of our own being we sense the Great Architect's reaction to our own individual responses to every experience in life. God awaits our recognition of His presence, which comes from within – from the human soul that silently and constantly honors the loving presence of the Divine.

The *level* teaches us that deep down we are more alike than different. We share the same survival instincts, the need to be loved, the same task of leaving the home of our parents, and of facing death. The human story is universal, yet no two stories are exactly alike. We are individuals and our task in life is to develop and express our own individuality. This oneness, or unity requires that we love God and one another – but in our own way. This universal requirement for living independently has important implications on the human soul.

Freemasonry's lessons about diversity and its rich contribution to our freedoms and liberties is more clearly understood when one acknowledges that God expresses Himself in multiple individualities. The Great Architect is millions upon millions of souls – and then some. The lessons from the Master Mason degree also teach us that each soul is an expression of God – unique and individual. The life of an individual human being is a symbolic manifestation of its soul; both a piece of God and a miniature replica of the Great Creator. It is a fair question to ask how can so many pieces, or human beings, each asserting his or her own individuality also express the whole of God?

For a person to be himself, or herself, requires self-acceptance and a lack of self-consciousness. Giving no thought to being a separate "self," life becomes one's "self." Such an ideal, when put into practice, exemplifies the Masonic teaching that Freemasons should live their individual lives like no one else can, while embracing all of life in a spirit of love. Experiencing and loving life as yourself results in you reaching out with your own unique perceptions and talents to live each moment. The "you" referred to here is not the separate person you have constructed in your own mind – it is the bigger "you," the divine "you" that is your material link to the soul God has given you.

The human soul grew that separate "you" in order to better experience itself in full material awareness. Our conscious minds are intended to be driven by our soul, a truth that also corresponds directly with certain passages from the Holy Bible which tell us not to worry about what we shall eat or wear, because we are as dear to the Creator as are the birds in the sky. When Freemasonry asks you to give without expectation of receiving anything in return, it is because Freemasonry also teaches us that the human soul will make certain we receive all that we need.

Chapter 66

THE LEVEL

> "That which is altogether just shalt thou follow,
> that thou mayest live, and inherit the land
> which the Lord thy God giveth thee."
>
> Deut. 16:20

In Freemasonry, the level is the symbol of equality, not only among members of the Craft, but of all humanity. The fraternity teaches that mankind is the offspring of God, created in His image of one blood. As such, each person is born with certain inalienable rights to life, liberty and the pursuit of happiness. Those who wrote this country's Declaration of Independence and Constitution were not implementing man-made justice when incorporating such sentiments into our laws — they were enacting fundamental principles given us by the Most High.

Freemasonry's love of equality does not mean that it also endorses the destruction of distinctions based upon merit, or that rank is somehow inconsistent with the Craft's belief. Without question, all men are created equal by nature. Each is subject to the same infirmities associated with human existence. All are embraced b y God as His children and are ultimately destined to be judged equally and impartially according to His immutable laws. But some men, by training, discipline and the proper use of their God given talents rise above the ordinary and are entitled to enjoy a different status. Every man, woman and child has the opportunity to so advance, which makes this equality of opportunity not only consistent with divine and human laws, it is the very cement and support of civil society.

The level also serves as the emblem in the jewel worn by the Senior Warden of a Masonic lodge and reminds those in attendance at a Masonic meeting that all have gathered *on the level.* That phrase has also acquired significance in the day-to-day parlance in civil society. When one speaks about another as being *on the level,* he generally means that he believes the person about whom he is speaking to be truthful, honest and forthright.

Although Freemasonry did not invent those virtues, it inculcates them from the time a candidate for Masonic degrees first knocks at the door of a lodge until he is translated from this imperfect life to that celestial lodge above where the Supreme Architect of the Universe forever presides. Albert Pike, as well as other Masonic writers, has gone so far as to say that Freemasonry is the first apostle of equality. During this Nation's formative years, Thomas Paine wrote an essay complimenting the Craft for its unflinching commitment to a government without tyranny, or religious restriction. Yet, there is something more about the significance of the level – something that holds a more personal about the meaning of the level for each and every Mason.

Masonic lodges have a sweet smell about them. Brotherhood is in the air and the principle of equality finds a perfectly welcome spot at the altar of obligation and prayer. Those sanctuaries are no different than any other meeting place, as far as furnishings go. But, the people are different. In a Masonic lodge one man regards another person whom he has just met for the first time as a long-lost friend. The Masons who gather there were not born to be different from other men. Each has his own cross to bear; each has enough sin in his past to condemn him. Yet, there is something special about the purpose-driven lives noticeable in the people who comprise the congregation. Harmony is worked at; kindnesses are freely given; smiles are easily flashed; and, men care not whether you reside in high society, or mingle daily with the middle class that makes up your neighborhood.

Within those lodges men meet upon the *level*; the rich and the poor; the high and the low; who, as created by one Almighty parent and inhabitants of the same world are to aid, support and protect one another. Men of diverse creeds, different interests and disparate occupations share a mutual respect and true regard for each other. Freemasonry lifts those men to a higher level than they would have ever believed themselves capable of reaching. Once there, each Freemason more clearly sees and understands the true meaning of the word "equality."

No two people are, or should be treated differently in a Masonic lodge. Impartiality and fairness are, or should be accepted as routine by all members. For that reason alone discrimination is unknown among the members of the Craft, sincerity and plain dealing distinguish them; and, with heart and tongue they join in promoting each other's welfare and rejoicing in each other's prosperity. No one is precluded from participating in the lodge's activities and equal access is given to the *hidden mysteries*.

Yet, the virtues symbolized by the *level* are not intended to be limited to the Masonic lodge room. The concept of equality, or of treating others with equal respect, is to be put into action by every Mason outside of the lodge room. At work, when others jump on the bandwagon to crucify a fellow worker, the Mason among them may be expected to demand common courtesy, compassion and empathy. In social circles when the conversation turns to criticizing a friend who is not present, the Mason among them may be expected to encourage restraint. When anger, disharmony, or disrespect of any nature rears its ugly head, it will not be a surprise to those who know that by word and example the Mason in the crowd promotes peace, harmony and goodwill.

Thus, as with all other virtues taught in Freemasonry, the lessons in equality taught by the *level*, instilled and nurtured within a Masonic lodge, achieve the greatest good for all mankind when lived in the world by the Mason himself. It comes as no surprise to followers of the Craft that Freemasons expect of themselves that each will be the change they expect to see in the world. In so becoming, each Mason brings light into the world and yields himself to become God's vessel for extending extraordinary grace to all creation.

Chapter 67

THE PERAMBULATION

*"And it came to pass at the seventh time, when
the priests blew with trumpets, Joshua said
unto the people, Shout; for the Lord
hath given you the city."*

Jos. 6:16

As an indication that they are *duly and truly prepared* to be initiated, passed and raised in the first three Masonic degrees, candidates for Freemasonry are caused to circumambulate the lodge. Also referred to as a *perambulation,* the candidate's travels during the degree is one of the more important ritual tasks to be performed. Hymns and prayers are recited, drawn from passages in the Holy Writings. Depending upon whether he is being initiated as an Entered Apprentice, passed to the degree of Fellowcraft, or raised to the sublime degree of Master Mason, as candidate's *perambulation* becomes increasingly extensive. It is fair to ask both why this tradition is followed and what it symbolizes.

The scripture cited above is from the book of Joshua and refers to the circumambulation by the priests prior to the collapsing of the walls of Jericho. Since it is not likely that mere trumpet blasts caused stone to crumble, either the trumpet symbolizes a much more powerful force, or the entire episode is intended to convey a wiser and more serious truth.

In his recent book, *Lost Secrets of the Sacred Ark,* Laurence Gardner hypothesizes that the trumpet represented a powerful fusion force emanating from the Ark of the Covenant. While that may be true, there is presently no way of either confirming or denying that possibility. However, in that the Old Testament, as well as the entirety of the Holy Bible is littered with allegorical tales, it is equally likely that Freemasonry, which has been in existence longer than Mr. Gardner has been writing, adopted the allegorical meaning as the foundation for the present day *perambulation* by candidates in Masonic lodges.

During ancient rites of the worship of Deity, designated holy men moved solemnly around sacred objects in a circular manner. Such movement was an integral part of the ritual used by the Hindus and Buddhists. In Islam, circumambulation is used during holy services at Mecca. In each, the movement was intended to represent the spiritual transition of man from daily life to spiritual perfection. That transition was to be accomplished in stages as each man moved more closely in his life and education to the spiritual energy of the Deity.

This ancient custom is retained in Masonry, but its meaning has been generally forgotten. In some present-day Masonic organizations a tension exists between those brethren who wish to pursue the esoteric lessons taught by the Craft and those brethren who prefer a strict adherence to Masonic ritual, which has evolved over at least the past two centuries. Some in the esoteric camp say that the rigid adherence to ritual neglects the more important tenets of sacred ancient philosophy. Certain adherents to the "ritual-only" camp believe that Masonry is practiced in its purest form by working to attain "word-perfect" ritualistic performance. In classic Hermetic tradition, both are equally correct and incorrect.

It is perilous to work in Masonry under the belief that an adherence to Masonic ritual is not Masonry and, therefore, should be relegated to the junk-heap of past relics. It is no less perilous to ignore the fact that Masonic ritual enjoys a sacred connection with the religions and philosophies of the past. More often than not, if one looks carefully into the Masonic past, he will discover that there exists a holy union between the approved ritual and the esoteric knowledge it is intended to convey. Indeed, a Mason may actually discover new joys in attending ritual performances once he learns more about the rich sacred past.

The candidate's travels, or *perambulation* of the lodge room, are intended to symbolize the state of spiritual attainment associated with the aid of each of the first three degrees of Masonry. As an Entered Apprentice, the newly initiated Mason learns to humbly submit himself to the fact that knows little, if anything, about what the Craft teaches. In his state of ignorance, the initiated candidate is introduced to the tools of learning that, when studied under the guidance of the more experienced brethren, will eventually enlighten his spirit.

A Fellowcraft is presumed to have mastered the rudiments of Masonic symbolism and at least be knowledgeable about the fact that Masonry uses symbols to impart wise and serious truths. His spirit is in need of solid food and, thus, the candidate is led to the study of the liberal arts and sciences, which he is expected to read and understand through the prism of spirituality instilled by Masonry. While continuing to require spiritual food, the Master Mason is expected to take the lessons he has learned and usefully offer them to the community in which he resides by living the spiritual life he has been taught. The *perambulation* not only symbolizes the candidate's spiritual state, but also the three stages of preparation necessary before the world may expect to benefit from that spirituality.

In ancient religious practices, the *perambulation* was believed to a necessary precedent to calling forth the presence of Deity. This once pervasive practice survives today in several of the occult cultures and has fallen into general disfavor. Masonry does not employ the *perambulation* in hopes that it will magically cause God to appear, for the Craft understands and teaches that the Great Architect is always present. The purpose today is to provide the candidate and brethren with a ritual practice that focuses the mind upon that presence and instills a prayerful attitude throughout the entire ritualistic performance.

Freemasons around the globe are keenly interested in discovering the roots and origins of the Craft. University professors throughout Europe, as well as elsewhere are researching historical archives inspecting new information and re-examining already existing material in hopes of one day being able to declare with certainty *whence came Freemasonry.* More likely than not, those roots and origins will not easily be discovered without first understanding that Masonry is about man's relationship to God.

From time immemorial, man has questioned himself about God's existence. The fraternity of Freemasons consists of men who have decided that He does exist and who openly profess their faith in His existence. A man cannot become a Mason without a belief in the Supreme Being. Even though he already possesses faith in God before joining the Craft, a candidate may not have a very developed idea of what that means to himself, his family, his friends and his country. While Freemasonry does not teach such a man about the existence of God, it does teach him how God relates to His creations and how we who are created in His image may benefit those with whom we come into contact each and every day.

What is stated here may be tested by you in the setting of your own lodge. The next time you are seated in a lodge room and observe the ritualistic *perambulation,* silence yourself and allow God to speak to your heart throughout the entire performance. There will be plenty of time to talk to the member sitting next to you after the performance is concluded. Consider the stages of your own spiritual development and try to identify your spiritual strengths and weaknesses. Later, work very hard to improve upon your strengths and to eliminate your weaknesses. If you try this exercise in lodge on a regular basis, more likely than not you will discover that you are practicing real Masonry and in the doing also discover the basis for the origins of the Craft to which you belong.

Chapter 68

THE PLUMB

"Let thine eyes look right on, and let
thine eyelids look straight before thee."

Prov. 4:25

Freemasons are instructed that they are to "act by the plumb" at all times throughout their Masonic careers. The plumb is an instrument made use of by operative masons, or masons who actually erected temples, cathedrals and other mighty edifices, to arrive at truly perpendicular lines. It has also been adopted in Speculative Masonry as one of the principle "working tools," or implements of architecture intended to convey wise and serious philosophical truths. As such, it is a symbol of rectitude of conduct and inculcates integrity and upright moral behavior.

The Freemason who chooses to adhere to the precepts of the Craft is guided by the unerring principles of truth. The plumb is symbolic of the necessity for each man to carefully select moral and spiritual values as his ideals from which he will not deviate even in the face of adversity. It is the matter of the *ideal* that is most important to Freemasons, because it serves as the blueprint around which each man will, or should design his respective attitudes.

Plato considered the dynamics of selecting a principle, or *ideal*, that is built upon by the powers of the human mind. In so doing, he explored the impact of willpower on the pursuit of a worthwhile *ideal*. Suffice to say that Plato concluded, as have other writers, that the fulfillment of any *ideal* is directly proportionate to what one *wills* to accomplish.

It is easy to say pick and ideal, design your attitudes to keep them positive and take a walk when you are feeling blue. It is easy to say, but hardly easy to do. If we are depressed, tired, sick, or frightened maintaining a positive outlook can become enormously difficult. Anyone who says you can always do that which you will to do simply has not been in tough situations.

To believe that you can do anything you choose, or will to do also sounds grandiose. From our own life experiences, it does not seem right that by sheer strength of will one can expect to always have things his or her way. In fact, it sounds selfish, manipulative a just a bit deluded. So what does Freemasonry expect from us in this regard? It is one thing to accept the scriptural proposition that faith can move mountains, but it would also seem that greed could destroy the mountain. Moreover, we are taught that self-centered willfulness produces darkness rather than light.

The plumb reminds us not to veer too far from right to left, or from left to right during our journey throughout life. We are to seek to achieve balance in all matters, which also requires us to heal or remove negative attitudes. However, simply trying to rely upon raw willpower can be counterproductive. Tapping into a higher form of will can prove to be a better strategy and produce a Freemason's *ideal*. Relating to a higher will, first expressed in the form of an *ideal*, also helps guide behavior according to spiritual values and leads to the use of higher powers of the mind. The higher form of will represents the true will, or dynamic, propelling force within every soul – the God within. It has the same freedom of choice as its Creator and if deferred to will guide, develop, change and motivate human behavior.

The *will* is also the agent of obedience that teaches us to become subject to certain outside influences that are beyond the individual self. Where selfishness derives from self-centeredness, selflessness springs from spiritual influences contained in ideals. Before a Freemason can accomplish the ideal of selflessness he must understand what the Craft requires of him when it demands *obedience.*

Obedience rivets the will-to-greatness of the heart silencing personal desires. It is what is meant by the phrase "circumscribing our desires." True obedience is the very opposite of tyranny and slavery, since its root is the love which flows from faith. That which is above serves that which is below and that which is below obeys that which is above. Thus, obedience is the practical conclusion to that which one recognizes as the existence of something higher than oneself. Whosoever recognizes the Supreme Architect of the Universe, obeys.

Such obedience is visibly practiced in certain religious orders. For example, the chela follows his or her guru in India and Tibet. This is also true of the absolute obedience that the hassidim have toward their tzadekim in the Jewish Hassidic communities. It is exemplified with a Masonic lodge wherein the assembled brethren are taught obedience to the master – not obedience to tyranny, but obedience to the service of others.

The plumb is also the emblem appearing on the jewel worn by the Junior Warden during all approved Masonic events. It is, therefore, the Junior Warden in every Masonic lodge who symbolizes obedience to faith, integrity and honor. He also symbolizes the proper Masonic *ideal,* which is to radiate outward beyond the lodge room to the rest of the world as the "beauty and glory of the day."

Chapter 69

THE PURITY OF THE LILY

*"And upon the top of the pillars was lily work:
so was the work of the pillars finished."*

1 Kings 7:22

The plant so frequently mentioned in the Old Testament as the "lily," often used as an emblem of peace and purity, was actually the lotus lily of Egypt and India. It also occupies a special place in Freemasonry as one of the ornaments adorning the two pillars in King Solomon's Temple known as Boaz and Jachin. As such, the lily has maintained the same symbolic meaning as it enjoyed in ancient Egypt and India.

As was so in ancient times, Fellowcraft Masons are also taught that, owing to the retired situation of its growth and it's purity, the lily adorning the pillars represents "peace." Quite frequently, the lily appears in esoteric writings in combination with the "rose," such as in the *Song of Songs* that appears in the Old Testament. There, in a series of love songs between a king and his bride, the bride relates that she is the rose of Sharon and the lily of the valleys. (*Song of Songs 2:1*). Throughout the ages writers have disagreed about the identity of the king and bride. Some have stated a belief that the king is Solomon and the bride one of his several wives. Others have variously interpreted the king to mean Jesus, while his "bride" was either the Roman Catholic Church, or Mary Magdalene. However, it is unnecessary to adopt any particular interpretation as the best in order to fully appreciate the symbolic meaning of the "lily."

By ancient definition, the word *Sharon* symbolically describes another spiritual dimension known as the Orbit of Light. In that dimension, mankind is exposed to a peculiar realm of advanced enlightenment primarily associated with what is known as *Star Fire gold,* a substance referred to in alchemical literature as a lunar extract of Anunnaki goddesses. A lesson from this symbolism, essential to Freemasons, is that true peace is intimately linked to what is known as the House of David.

The pillars Boaz and Jachin appearing in the porch of King Solomon's Temple were not structurally necessary to the building itself. They were intended to be purely ornamental and as such to convey a deeper spiritual significance. Boaz, representing strength, was actually the husband of Ruth, who became Boaz's widow and bore a generation of persons that included King David. Jachin was the name of the first High Priest to serve in King Solomon's Temple. Used together, Boaz and Jachin are intended to symbolize legitimate kingship and priesthood.

We learn from the great Jewish historian Josephus that purity of the priesthood was extremely important to that segment of Hebrew society referred to as the *Zealots*. From days of old, the legitimate priests descended from the symbolic characters we know as Melchizadek, Zadok and Aaron. Kings descended from Ruth and her ancestors and heirs. The perceived lack of priestly purity during the first century eventually led the Zealots to wage furious warfare against their Roman invaders ending in the mass suicide by Zealot defenders at the fortress known as *Masada*.

We also learn from Josephus and other ancient historians that during the period of Jewish captivity, which occurred well after both David and Solomon had gone to their rest, the Hebrews ceased to be ruled by the House of David. Followers of Jesus hoped that he would re-establish both the kingly and priestly legitimacy. Many became disillusioned by his crucifixion and continued to be watchful for the coming of the expected messiah.

Seemingly lost amongst the factual investigations by ancient, as well as modern historians, is the truth that Boaz and Jachin actually reflect a spiritual consequence, not a material reality. Some may dispute that contention and point to arguments that Jesus, a descendant of David and the priestly line, had brothers, sisters and at least one child, who allegedly had others whom today, while remaining unknown to all except a few, constitute the true bloodline. While such may or may not be true, the resolution of that issue is also unnecessary to fathoming the significance of the lily to Freemasons.

Purity and peace are two consequences of active love, which is the true essence of God. The House of David, while possibly of material relevance to this, or some subsequent generation, symbolizes that which should occupy a Freemason's primary attention – establishing a lasting relationship with the Deity. Such a relationship is meant to go beyond an intellectual engagement with the Divine Mind and result in the material acquisition of the essence of the Divine – love.

Mankind's history has been littered more with violence, destruction and hatred than it has been filled with times of pure peace. When Freemasons speak about the Kingdom of God they speak about a material environment wherein men, women and children may live in happiness, respect and peace. Love of others as another *self* is the required condition of purity so essential to peace, so necessary for happiness and so much at the core of every Masonic oath sworn to by every Freemason.

Some religions teach that the world will end and God will descend from the heavens to rule. Such lessons implant in the mind visions of a God fed up with mankind, angry with the repeated failures at achieving peace and prepared to impose His dominion on all creatures. Those He finds unworthy will, some believe, be cast aside as so much chaff among the wheat to burn in eternal damnation. Prophets and preachers from time immemorial have scared the human race with such stories about a whimsical God. But, that is not the behavior of love; that is not a just reaction; rather, that is the behavior of a tyrant, not a divinely loving God.

Freemasonry teaches that God is kind, gentle, beneficent, embracing, soothing, compassionate, sympathetic and forgiving. He invites us to Himself – He never forces Himself upon His creatures. When we respond, we discover a new life filled with concern for others, for Nature and for the future – we discover God, our one and only King and High Priest symbolically presented to us in the lesson of the lily.

Chapter 70
THE ROLE MODEL

"You shall love the Lord your God with all your
heart, with all your soul, with all your mind,
and with all your strength."

Mark 12:30

If asked to name a hero or two most admired during our youth, the answer would likely be very predictable. Mickey Mantle was a great baseball player; Muhammed Ali reigned as heavyweight boxing champion and was self-proclaimed as the greatest; and today Tiger Woods can hit a golf ball farther and straighter than any other person on earth. The criteria for many who select a hero would probably include accomplishing one or more of the adventurous similar feats similar as those three professional athletes. For others, great musical skill, dominant business acumen, or political popularity might be the necessary ingredient. In Freemasonry, we look for other qualities in men who would become role models – qualities that are more spiritual, but no less spectacular.

It is doubtful that a Masonic Hall of Fame would include only men whom we would consider to be saints, for all men are susceptible to various faults and errors. However, those who have struggled with their faults and have best succeeded in demonstrating to the rest of humanity how to circumscribe their desires and keep their passions within due bounds toward all mankind would be more likely to be voted into our Hall of Fame. It is those men who would likely become role models to every true Freemason. The traits that separate them from other men and women include their unfeigned piety and their undying love of God – a piety and love that shines through the darkness of their human shortcomings.

The first word you ever uttered upon entering a Masonic Lodge declared your faith in God. Without that profession of faith, neither the form, nor beauties of Masonry would have been disclosed to you. Indeed, the truths revealed by the Craft would have always remained hidden from your sight forever.

Later, as a Mason you vowed to live in the light and become obedient to the laws of the Supreme Ruler of the Universe. The words that passed from your lips came directly from your heart and you meant to keep each and every vow that you made. Yet, as the days, months and years passed by you may have noticed that you became less diligent in keeping those promises and vows. Careers had to be pursued; children needed to be raised; and you found little time for attending to Masonic activities. As it was true for you, it is also true that most Masons come up short in keeping their vows. The true Masonic hero, or role model, is the Mason who has achieved the greatest equilibrium in his life in spite of his shortcomings, failings and errors.

Like many other worthwhile organizations, the numerous Masonic bodies hand out various honors and awards to its deserving members. Some are elected to office by the vote of their brethren; others are recognized for their steady contributions to their lodges; and some are singled out for their unselfish contributions to the community in which they live. However, no awards or honors are, or ever should be passed out to acknowledge that any one Mason exceeds any other in his piety and love of God.

Awarding a divine life is solely within the province of the Great Architect – not of man. Only God may judge how well a man nurtures his spirit and soul thereby bringing light into the world around him. As a consequence, one need never expect to awaken one day and discover that a Masonic Hall of Fame has been established identifying by name those

Masons who have been the most pious and God-loving. Rather, it shall always be so that each Mason will be singularly and quietly responsible for his own actions and for eventually becoming the best Masonic role model that he can become.

Have you ever considered what it is about you that most people admire? If you know the answer to that question, are you satisfied with it? Does that answer, in whole or in part, have anything at all to do with the extent of your piety and love of God? If so, you are to be congratulated. If not, you may need to make some changes in the way you lead your life.

Do you understand what it means to have piety and love for God? If so, you have already become a role model. If not, is it not time that you finally learn what it all means? Far from teaching that a pious and God-loving man must lead a withdrawn, contemplative life, Masonry teaches us that divine life is to be lived robustly.

It has been said that saints never aspire to mere meditation, but rather aspire to *life*. God gave man life; He has provided us with roadmaps about how to live that life; and, He is said by our Christian brethren to have given His only begotten Son so that we would always have life. If you have been thinking that becoming pious and God-loving meant that you would have to become odd and withdrawn from the family and friends you most love, Masonry teaches that you have been very mistaken.

The robust life of *piety* is outlined for us by the three principle tenets of Masonry: brotherly love, relief and truth. If lived well, that life can become the best role model, not only for present and future Masons, but for all mankind. By regarding the whole human species as one family, a Mason is compelled to curb his biases and prejudices against other races, creeds and religions. While such men are extremely difficult to find, from the earliest times of recorded history Masons have been taught how best to take control of and subdue their natural desires for their own peace of mind, and for the benefit of all mankind. Imagine the difference those men would make in today's world, if they would merely put into daily practice the Masonic lessons they had learned.

A pious nature reveals itself to the world by relieving the distresses of others. To soothe the unhappy, to sympathize with their misfortunes, to compassionate their miseries and to restore peace to their troubled minds is the great aim of Masonry. It is as though the hand of the Supreme

Architect himself has reached down to caress the needy when men act to relieve another man's distresses.

Truth is a divine attribute and the foundation of every virtue, but is often times one of the most misunderstood words in the human language. Some leaders in government believe that *truth* is what the people need to know, as opposed to what has actually happened. Well intended people of all walks of life frequently sanction the so-called *white lie,* because it tends to promote a better good, if some things remain concealed. But, neither of those definitions satisfactorily defines *truth* – which can never be subjected to any variations or vicissitudes of time, or fortune. Neither are those definitions entirely inaccurate, for truth springs from the spirit and soul of man, not merely from the words that fall from his mouth.

Whether or not a Mason is regarded as God-loving in the eyes of his brethren is most often dependent upon how dedicated he is perceived to be to that which is *true.* The *truth* referred to here has little, if anything, to do with that which is correct versus that which is wrong, but is related more importantly to a spiritual state. Doctrines are not at all concerned here – rather, the *truth* possessed by the Masonic role model is founded upon the prudent investigation of diverse ideas. Masonic *truth* acknowledges that mankind still does not know how to pronounce the ineffable name of Deity, which symbolizes the further *truth* that no single religion, creed, or doctrine can ever capture or define God's infinite nature.

Practicing brotherly love, relief and truth requires much more than merely thinking good thoughts. It requires doing good deeds, living life to the fullest and never losing confidence in the Masonic lessons you have learned. In short, it requires aspiring to become a Masonic role model to others.

Chapter 71

THE TEMPLE

*"...for ye are the temple
of the living God..."*

2 Cor. 6:16

As every member of the Craft knows, the Temple of King Solomon is central to the allegories and lessons taught in Freemasonry. In its most basic sense, the Temple symbolizes man's desire to praise God, as well as God's willingness to dwell in an edifice, or body that is erected by faithful followers. Passages in the Holy Bible describe the Temple in both literal and spiritual terms.

On the one hand, the Temple is described as a real edifice where people gathered. On the other hand, the Temple also represents the human heart that is to be made ready for the dwelling of the Holy Spirit. It is a relatively easy matter to understand these lessons, but is there another more fundamental reason Freemasonry has selected this specific Temple and not some other temple or structure as the centerpiece upon which to build rich symbolism?

Throughout history mankind has struggled with the chore of selecting between two very clear options: the pursuit of material power versus obedience to God. Royal castles generally symbolize the pursuit of material power, while temples and cathedrals often symbolize the yielding to God's will. Notably, Freemasons are not depicted anywhere in history or literature as builders of castles, but as builders of temples and cathedrals. Without question the characteristics most desired by Freemasons are obedience to God and service to our fellow man. However, the question remains – what is the most accurate Masonic meaning associated with King Solomon's Temple?

Before the Temple became the center of activity for the early Hebrews, temples dotted the landscape of ancient Egypt and served as settings for spiritual pursuits. At that time, Egyptian society did not maintain defined divisions between religious, governmental, commercial, or social interactions, because both the spiritual canons and more mundane day-to-day laws were believed to have been delivered and endowed by the "gods," who served the one Almighty Creator. The typical Egyptian temple was manned by a diverse company of attendants, clergy, students, healers and laypersons who performed the daily tasks of maintaining the temple and organizing daily activities for the people. Interestingly, certain tasks assigned to selected individuals are similarly performed in present day Masonic lodges.

Like present-day *tilers* who stand guard outside a Masonic lodge room, sentries referred to as *Sau* were posted outside Egyptian temples. Their duties included serving as doorkeepers of the main sanctuary ensuring that only dedicated clergy and pharaohs entered the consecrated *inner temple*. That sanctity was also maintained by the early Hebrews who strictly limited entry into the *sanctum santorem,* or Holy of Holies to those few men designated by the king as High Priests.

The Egyptian *Sau* also performed the temple closing rites so that the cosmic order evoked by the ceremony could be maintained and thereafter taken into the world of the living to vitalize the environment. That vitalization occurred when worshippers returned to their daily lives and exhibited to their family, neighbors and friends the virtues taught during the ceremonial liturgy. Like the Hebrews who followed, the ancient Egyptian temple worshipper was expected to be a vehicle for God's love – a concept that currently finds acceptance in the doctrines of several religions.

Other Egyptian temple officers also bore striking similarities to their present day counter parts found in Masonic Lodges. For example, the presiding officer of an ancient Egyptian temple was referred to as the *temple master*, who like the pharaohs were considered to have descended from divine beings and governed the temple with the consent of the gods. The counterpart to the chaplain in a Masonic lodge was the *sentyt*, or oracle, whose duty it was to call upon divine forces to bless both the ceremonies and the worshippers in attendance. It was within this environment that Moses was believed to have been educated. Available writings relate that he was later enlightened by his own vision of the one God which was worshipped by his followers in the Tabernacle that was situated due east and west upon Mount Sinai.

Certain authors, as well as the renowned master of psychiatry, Sigmund Freud, have speculated that Moses was actually a pharaoh named Akhenaton. Akhenaton is depicted as a descendant of the biblical Joseph, the powerful *vizier* of Egypt and son of Jacob – a person who also figured prominently at an Essene community located at Qumran. He challenged the current religious climate by erecting temples to the Aton and demanding that only Aton be worshipped. As opposed to being merely a whimsical choice among the many "gods," Akhenaton's choice of Aton was predicated upon a change in the cosmos. For hundreds of years, Egyptian religion had been based upon the worship of the Appis-bull, or *Taurus,* because the bull ascended in the sky with the sun. At or near the time that Akhenaton ascended the throne, *Aries* had astronomically replaced *Taurus.* High priests commenced preparing the people for a change in the centerpiece for religious worship – the bull was to be replaced by the ram.

According to the legend presented by some authors, because the people were in serious revolt over the change in religion, Moses (Akhenaton) was compelled to abdicate his throne, leave Egypt with his followers and establish a kingdom near Mount Sinai where Masonic tradition informs us he erected a Tabernacle. Although it is not presently possible to verify that speculation, that legend may shed some light upon the answer to the question – why is King Solomon's Temple, which replaced Moses' Tabernacle, and not some other temple or cathedral, so essential to Masons? Among other reasons, it may have been the first temple erected to the One Living God, in whom all Masons profess a profound belief

In a further effort to provide a more viable answer to the question, Masonic literature has frequently described the similarities between the Tabernacle and Solomon's Temple in matters of construction, architectural arrangement and furnishings. At initial glance, such matters may appear too trivial to have any relevance to the matter. However, such a hasty conclusion could prove misleading and cause us to overlook a deeper significance of the ancient Egyptian temple to Freemasonry.

Like the Tabernacle and Solomon's Temple, the ancient Egyptian temples regarded esoteric construction, holy vessels and sacred architecture as absolutely necessary for establishing the proper spiritual environment for religious worship. That notion was not merely the result of wild superstition, or of a fanciful belief in the arts of magic. Rather, the idea of making a temple a place of the highest purity has been held by mankind as a special rite for centuries.

Unique rites of consecration involving the use of corn, wine and oil, or similar substances were employed by both the Mesopotamian priests and the priests who were responsible for erecting and maintaining Enochian temples. Today, many Christians regard the human body as temples that must be purified to permit the Holy Spirit to dwell therein and grow strong. Some go so far as to state that Solomon's Temple is intended to remind Freemasons of their individual responsibility to conduct themselves with honor, dignity and virtue. Regardless of how one presently views Solomon's Temple, like the ancient Egyptian temples it serves more significantly as a symbol of the brotherhood of man under the fatherhood of God.

Similar to ancient Egyptian temples, Solomon's Temple served as the center of both religious and commercial life. Only the designated high priests were allowed once each year to visit the Ark of the Covenant in the Holy of Holies where the *Shekinah,* or divine presence sat upon the mercy seat. Lay people gathered in the outer temple to praise God while tradesmen worked the booths that lined the exterior selling everything from livestock to mercantile goods. If society had anything worthwhile to offer during the eras of the ancient Egyptian temples or Solomon's Temple, it was offered to the people at the temple.

Without question, the temple is intended to remind all Masons that the One Living God is at the center of life. Yet, even with this understanding about why a temple is used in Masonic symbolism, it does not explain why King Solomon's Temple specifically receives special recognition. Freemasonry has not selected Moses' Tabernacle, or some ancient Egyptian temple – it has selected King Solomon's Temple to the exclusion of all others to serve as a centerpiece of Masonic symbolism. Why?

No one has discovered the ruins of Solomon's Temple, rendering the truth of its existence archeologically unproven, much the same as is true of Noah's Ark. Some have contended that the only reason such proof has not been forthcoming is because the Temple of the Mount is situated on top and excavations have not been allowed. That is true recently, but the original Knights Templar are believed to have extensively excavated the site during the first crusade and nothing about Solomon's Temple has been reported from those digs.

Of course, it is possible that no one has looked in the correct place. One recent writer has speculated that Solomon's Temple was actually Egyptian and has been archeologically discovered in the region anciently referred to as Lower Egypt. That writer also speculated that Solomon was also an Egyptian Pharaoh, a son of David, who according to the same author was also a Pharaoh who lived under an Egyptian name. Such speculations may or may not eventually be proven scientifically, but whether or not true, it is irrelevant to resolving the puzzle about why Freemasonry has chosen Solomon's Temple as a Masonic symbol.

Was it the structure itself that was so important? Is there something unique about King Solomon, the era, the religious climate, or the politics of the time that cause Freemasons to seize upon this temple?

The great Jewish historian Josephus informs us that peace and tranquility pervaded the world during Solomon's reign. If so, Solomon's power must have also pervaded the world – he must have been the most powerful monarch of his age.

He also transcended the restrictions of religious doctrine. Solomon worshiped many gods, admired the Canaanite kings divine appointment to power and also found the concept One Living God fascinating and convincing. In those matters Solomon was a very unique individual. He synthesized different systems of religious belief and even ignored political decorum within his own realm to offer a special place of importance to the Canaanite king Hiram of Tyre. Solomon also possessed unsurpassed wisdom – a gift from God that followed Solomon's specific prayer to be able to know right from wrong so that he might better be the enabled to serve his subjects. Yet, there is something more about Solomon that is equally intriguing.

We read in the Old Testament at *1 Kings 3:1* that Solomon married the daughter of the Egyptian Pharaoh and took her to the City of David. Although the Holy Writings shed no light upon whether or not that marriage resulted in Solomon also being initiated into the Egyptian Mysteries, history has not often recorded the marriage of Egyptian princesses to anyone other than an Egyptian of high importance. The Mysteries were, indeed, reserved for such men and purposely hidden from the commoner. Unfortunately, while the speculation is inviting, it leads us nowhere, because the relevant passages of scripture tell us nothing further about the details attendant to Solomon's marriage. However, we are informed about something even more intriguing - the ceremonial practices of the high priests appointed by Solomon mirrored those of the Egyptian priests in ancient Lower Egypt.

Like the temples erected to the one god Aton by Akhenaton, Solomon's Temple did not contain an idol, or representative image of God. Rather, it contained only the Ark of the Covenant and the overshadowing Shekinah. As such, Solomon's Temple symbolizes the hearing ear of God which is regarded so reverently by Masons – what Freemason can ever forget the instruction, "no man should ever enter upon any great or important undertaking without first invoking the blessing of God."

In arriving at an understanding about why Freemasonry has specifically selected Solomon's Temple over all other temples it is not important to be certain that it ever existed, that it was Hebrew or Egyptian, or that it was situated at the site where we now behold the Temple Mount. It is not the fact of its existence that matters – it is the truths that it expresses which are important to Masons. Of primary significance to us, the Supreme Architect of the Universe is not depicted in Solomon's Temple, or other Masonic symbolism as man, woman, or any other figure or idol. His face is unknown. His name remains unpronounceable. He is the great "I Am" who may only be experienced, not seen. In Him is the great secret that no living man can speak, because no living man knows it. He is the sphinx, enigmatic, unsolvable by the human mind that was, is and forever shall be. To know Him is to accept the unknowing and enjoy the contentedness of His everlasting love for all of His creation. The name we attribute to Him is but a substitute to be replaced by the true word or name when He decides to reveal it to us.

Chapter 72

THE TOWER OF BABEL

*"And they said, Go to, let us build us a
city and the tower, which the
children of men builded."*

Gen. 11:4

In Freemasonry, men are taught the importance of circumscribing their desires, as well as the necessity for keeping their passions within due bounds toward others. That lesson is not only valuable to the manner in which humans live alongside of each other, but also to the manner in which they humble themselves before the Great Architect of the Universe. Unleashed human passions and desires have proven to be the source of most of mankind's sufferings, especially when fueled by pride and conceit.

The biblical story about the Tower of Babel is intended to illustrate the consequences that can be expected when men build their lives upon a material foundation, as opposed to building them upon a foundation supported by the love of God. The connection of that story to Masonry is inescapable, for Freemasonry teaches about the benefit of a brotherhood of man living under the fatherhood of God. In that regard, from the time a Mason is initiated into the Craft he is taught the importance of never becoming wise in his own conceit.

The builders of the Tower of Babel sought to erect a city and tower to the heavens as a tribute to man's material success and divorced themselves from any concern about God. Some modern-day writers have equated that endeavor to the efforts of present-day scientists to make and extend human life without God – an accusation that may or may not be meritorious. Nevertheless, the significance of the symbolism to us as Masons is that pride in unsound theories is worse than living in ignorance.

To Freemasons, the word *pride* has both a positive and a negative connotation. On the one hand, it is well to take pride in the numerous charities Freemasonry supports throughout the world which benefits all of society. Yet, on the other hand, pride in self and boastful arrogance is both unseemly and destructive. It is to the negative connotation that Freemasonry directs the candidate's attention for the purpose of inculcating essential virtues.

Like the builders of the Tower of Babel, the prideful man seeks to mold for himself a crown of glory. You have likely heard such a man, quite possibly even in the midst of a Masonic meeting. He is the one who is always correct in what he says and does – you are always wrong. He knows the ritual better than you and is willing to shout out that fact during a sacred ritualistic performance. He also knows how you should be living your life, because he is wise and you are not. That man also demands to be recognized for his greatness among his inferiors – the man who complains because he did not receive an award, an acclaim, or a special acknowledgement. He can also be counted on to tell you that you do not know as much about man's relationship to God as he knows and therefore should listen with care to what it is he has to say. Does that description sound familiar? Do you know such a man? Is he you?

The Tower of Babel compels us to return to the basics – all men have sprung from the dust and to dust they all must return. All men err, even the proud man. Everyone suffers and pride cannot heal the pain. Is there any man born who has not, or will not die? When a man reasons on a ponderous subject matter, is he not inevitably forced to question his own conclusions? However, the builder of the Tower is ignorant of these truths and blindly adheres to the proposition that matters always are as they appear to the individual. There is no external truth to the Tower builder. The only truth he understands is the truth he himself has constructed.

Put another way, Masonry teaches that God is light and in Him there is no darkness. He is supremely just and the thing, or creation most like Him is the man who has become as just as it is humanly possible to become. But, what does that actually mean? Who defines the word "just?" Is it a question of examining the concept of my injustice toward you, or yours toward me? Or is it a matter of examining justice and injustice themselves? The former is defined by my personal experience, while the latter is defined by a more universal, philosophical and divine perception. Within the context of our present symbolism, the former is an example of building the Tower of Babel, while the latter requires an analysis of cause and effect according to the laws of Nature.

There are two patterns considered in the story about the Tower. One is divine and supremely happy; the other has nothing to do with God and constitutes the pattern of the most profound unhappiness. There is a price to pay for living a life according to the way you believe things ought to be, rather than according to the way God meant them to be. If you would avoid paying that price, you must learn what it is that God wants. It is in this realm that Masonry aids its members by revealing God's desires through, among other things, Masonic symbolism.

Pride in oneself is not man's heritage. A country existing under the principle of *one nation under God* does not bequeath to its citizens a legacy that promotes self-interest. The building erected upon self-interest, like the Tower of Babel, will eventually crash to the ground fatally injuring all who dared to climb aboard. If humanity's true government is to be in the hands of the wisest and best – at some time in mankind's future – it will not be founded upon anything other than *one humanity under God,* or more specifically upon *a brotherhood of humanity under the fatherhood of God.*

Why do governments, institutions, or fraternities of men at various times fail? Each establishment is related, at least in part, to the fundamentals that adhere to each other establishment. So, what do they share in common when they fail? A failure of freedom? A failure of purpose? A lack of vision? Which one could it be? In truth, it is a combination of each when God is left out of the equation. For, when God is locked out, justice does not exist, compassion cannot be found and love has left the building. Governments, institutions and fraternities decay when unsupported by justice, compassion and love – in other words, when man abandons God.

As the compasses and square teach Masons to circumscribe their desires and to keep their passions toward all mankind within due bounds, they also teach us to communicate consistently with the Great Architect. Some churches refer to this as *praying constantly*. But, Masonic communication with the Great Architect involves more than prayer. It involves living a life that is directed by the Supreme Ruler of the Universe – it involves living a life of love for others, as opposed to love of self. Lest one forgets that which is taught elsewhere in other Masonic symbolism – the love of others begin with a just, compassionate love of self. Not a prideful loving, but an appreciation that you are created in the image of God and have an assignment during your lifetime to reflect that image in everything you do every time you do it.

Chapter 73

THE VALE

"He discovereth deep things out of darkness, and bringeth out to light the shadow of death."

Job 12:22

Among the ancients the term *vale* was a symbol of deep things, or secrets. Concealed within the etymological meaning of the word is "that which lies remote from sight, such as counsels and designs which are deep or close." Masonic tradition informs us that our ancient brethren assembled on the highest hills and in the lowest vales. It is said that by so doing, they could observe the approach of those who were not entitled to hear, or view the dramatization of the ancient mysteries.

When a Masonic lodge is said to stand in the *lowest vale*, it is intended to convey that the secrecy which it applies to its work is actually the concealment in symbolism of the most ancient truths about man's relationship to God. A careful study of esoteric Freemasonry reveals that the *lowest vale* implies that the beautiful cosmic allegories exemplified during Masonic ritual actually perpetuate the teachings of the some of the oldest *Mystery Schools*, including Zend-Avesta and Pythagoras. It has never been intended that much of the exoteric work conducted in a Masonic lodge should be kept secret from non-Masons.

The *deep things* symbolized by the *vale* are ageless and lay at the very heart of the reason Freemasonry has existed from time immemorial. Masons explore Nature to quietly learn how better to serve mankind. As the school for the study of such *deep things,* Freemasonry is free of the limitations of creed and sect. It seeks to include rather than exclude and considers the ceiling of its lodge to be the boundless realm of the stars and heavens. Its walls consist of he ends of the earth and its floor is made up with the mosaic pavement checker boarded with crossing currents of human emotion.

Similar to the officers in a Masonic lodge, who progress from the lowest rank to that of Worshipful Master, all of the ancient *Mystery Schools* had spiritual hierarchies, or planes through which Nature expressed herself to the world. Each truth is believed to be clutched tightly to Nature's bosom and held closely within the *vale* where every Masonic lodge performs its true work of applying the principles learned from the symbolisms used during each ritual exemplification.

The only secrets Freemasonry holds unto itself and its brethren are those found in the *vale.* Some who are unschooled in the *deep things* taught by the Craft expect to find treasure, religious relics and even royal lineage directly related to the Christ comprising that which the fraternity holds dearest. Such, however, is not the case. Rather if one was permitted to peek behind Freemasonry's veil, he or she would discover God, Nature, the universe and man's relationship to all.

It should come as no surprise to anyone that something precious is concealed from men. When the Hebrews prepared the Ark of the Covenant, two Cherubim were carved into the woodwork representing guardians of the divine presence visiting within. The book of Genesis describes how God guarded the Garden of Eden following the expulsion of Adam and Eve. The true pronunciation of the name of deity was known only to the High priests, who communicated it in a whisper once a year to selected candidates for greater spiritual enlightenment. These are examples of protecting the pathway to God, much as the Knights Templar are reputed to have protected the pathway for pilgrims making their way to the Holy City. Yet, that which is guarded in Freemasonry, i.e., its symbolic ritual, is available to all who would search in the right place.

Birth is not the beginning of life anymore than death constitutes life's end. The duty to work has been given to all mankind, not to merely keep everyone busy, but to teach man how to serve his fellows. Work is mankind's vehicle for helping the Supreme Architect of the Universe to create. The work conducted by Masons in the *vale* is instructive to all those present that have ears with which to listen. There are no magical sequences of words, or chants to deliver that Freemasonry believes calls down the presence of God. God is present wherever a Temple has been erected for that purpose and purified from the degradations of material existence. No priest stands over a cup passing his hand over its contents to bring down the consubstantial power of the Almighty. Instead, the work in the *vale* incorporates the best mankind has developed from the beginning of time to develop a harmonization between the conscious mind and the subconscious thoughts.

The initiates of antiquity were, indeed, far-sighted. They realized that nations come and go, golden ages of enlightenment are followed by dark ages of repression and religions evolve from the doctrines of the past. The dogmas deemed to be absolute truths today are not the same truths held dear by the ancients. We live in a world of change whether we like it, or not – a change entirely attributable to the creative powers of the Great Architect. With the needs of posterity fixed firmly in their minds, the ancients endeavored to make certain that *knowledge* and *wisdom* were preserved for application in whatever kingdom, empire, or dogma that might hold sway over the people in the future. From that endeavor, the Masonic symbolism available today was made possible. Therefore, he would unveil the *ancient mysteries* must search in the place where they were originally concealed – within the ritual of Freemasonry.

During the era of Plato, Aristotle and Philo philosophy and religion were not considered separately. Thus, it was necessary for the curious to familiarize themselves with both the depths of philosophic thought and the origins of theology. The *mysteries,* or *deep things*, taught in the *vale* of Freemasonry are so profound and so potent as to be capable of revelation only to those who approach the study with no personal ambition, or hidden agenda. They embody the last remnants the most sacred teachings known to mankind which were once believed lost.

The entire history of Christian and pagan Gnosticism is concealed within the symbols of Freemasonry. Undoubtedly, the Gnostics were prolific writers, but because they incurred the wrath of the early Christian

Church very little of that literature has survived. When that institution ascended to power, it destroyed all available records. Within the past 60 years, man has recovered some of those writings upon the discoveries of the library at Nag Hammadi and the Dead Sea Scrolls. Yet, much of the wisdom and knowledge remains lost only to be discovered through the proper interpretations of Masonic symbolism. Those discoveries continue every week of every year when Masonic lodges meet in the *vale* and share spiritual experiences during the revelations by God through symbolic ritual.

Chapter 74
THE VOLUME OF THE SACRED LAW

"And Peter said to him: Aeneas,...; rise and
make your bed. And he immediately rose."

Acts 9:32-34

From the time of his initiation into the fraternity, a Freemason is repeatedly reminded of his responsibility to regard the Holy Book as his guide throughout life. He is not, however, instructed to adopt everything contained in the Holy Book as doctrinally literal, for to do so results in disputes, division and dissension about the "correct" interpretation. Instead, the Freemason should constantly remind himself that the Holy Book is intended as a guide about how to love.

One of the greatest acts of love set forth in the many stories of the Holy Bible relates to what the Apostle Peter did at a place named Lydda. There, Peter found a man named Aeneas who was paralyzed and had been bedridden for eight years. Peter's spiritual act of healing was an act of pure charity. He neither asked, nor received anything in return for the use of his sacred powers. The sole aim of his effort was to restore to movement another person who had been unable to move.

There is also a significant relationship of the square and compasses to the Holy Book that directly impacts how a Freemason should understand

and act upon the concept of *love*. Joined together, the square and compasses symbolizes the Hermetic notion: *as it is above, so shall it be below.* Applied to the concept of *love,* a Freemason is instructed to regard love as the genuine confluence of human will and divine will. In other words, the love a Freemason is to express should be the product of both his own personal determination to so act, as well as the operation divine guidance, which is found contained within the volume of the sacred law.

The Greek word *agape* has been used in different ways by contemporary and ancient sources to describe divine, unconditional, self-sacrificing, active, volitional and thoughtful love. Plato used the word to denote love of spouse and family. Early Christians used the word to describe the special love for God, as well as for the love God has for His creation. *Agape,* therefore, defines the love a Freemason is taught by the use of the square and compasses situated atop the Holy Book.

The Supreme Architect's works of creation, as well as the changes of life each of us experiences is spread before mankind as the gifts of His infinite love. The love of God is working toward the completion of a plan that is beyond all thought and imagination simply because it is too glorious for us to comprehend. God's love provides for all ages and conditions; for infancy, maturity and old age; for want, weakness, joy, sorrow and even sin. It is available to all who ask His blessing, but cannot be completely fulfilled without man's help.

If all men were born paralyzed and could only lay and watch as time unfolded, there would be no arms, or legs to come to anyone's aid. If all mankind could not utter one word, there would be no good counsel whispered into another's ear. If all could never hear, no one would ever know and understand the loving words spoken by a brother. If Peter had not been present in Lydda, his presence and his voice, so essential to God's healing of Aeneas, would never have been felt. Such truths reveal another quality of the *love* required of a Freemason: incarnation.

The "incarnation" used here does not refer to the live birth of a sentient God-man, such as is so in the Christian religion in the story about Jesus. Rather, it means the convergence of two wills, distinct and free – divine will and human will. While God's sacred power was sufficient to heal Aeneas without Peter, Peter was present for some reason important to Aeneas's healing. The divine will needed his will in order to give birth to the power that lifted Aeneas from his sick bed. Similarly, Peter could have done nothing to heal Aeneas if his will had not been united with that of God. This form of "incarnation" refers to the person who transforms himself from a self-centered individual to a person dedicated to the service of others.

Once a Freemason understands that when his service is joined with God's love the fullness of *agape* love is possible, he more clearly understands what it is he is expected to learn from a studious reading of the volume of the sacred law. It is entirely unnecessary to adopt as literal truth the various stories set forth in the Holy Book to properly learn how to join human will with divine will. Too, it is vanity to attempt to decipher from scripture which religion, or which church God prefers. It is sufficient to learn that service to others exercised after prayer to God is the foundation of all true love.

To achieve a complete appreciation about how one joins his or her will with the will of God, one must meditate upon the scriptures. As opposed to reading the Holy Book as a history of mankind's material pursuits, it should be regarded as a series of instructions designed to enlighten man's introspective knowledge about God. The ancient Egyptian adepts taught their initiates how to commune with the "sons of God" who existed in what was called the Far World, or "other side of the river." Entire portions of such ancient books as the Book of the Dead and the Book of Enoch were devoted to instructions on how to commune with God in His presence. One need not believe or disbelieve the possibility of doing so. It is sufficient to learn that making an effort to meet with God in prayer requires considerable study of the symbolism contained in the Holy Book.

Chapter 75

THE WEEPING VIRGIN

"The Lord by wisdom hath founded the earth;..."

Prov. 3:19

Masonry uses the symbol of *a virgin weeping* to mark the final resting place of Hiram Abif. As such, she represents the unfinished state of the Temple following the death of Hiram, who was the architect of the work. The death of that celebrated artist and the resulting consequence to the Temple were sources of great sadness for King Solomon, as well as an inspiration to him to somehow forge ahead and complete the unfinished work. Yet, while you could accept *compassion* and *perseverance* as the lessons of that symbolism, you might miss a more profound esoteric meaning if you decided to look no farther.

This use of a feminine figure in this instance to symbolize a wise and serious Masonic truth is unique to all of the symbolism employed elsewhere by the Craft. Nowhere in either past or present usage has a woman been selected by Masonry to convey a spiritual lesson. For that reason, as well as others, the symbolic significance to the fraternity of *a virgin weeping* is enormous.

Manly P. Hall, the renowned philosopher and dedicated Freemason, wrote in his epic *The Secret Teachings of All Ages* that the Craft's weeping virgin was intended to represent Virgo, one of several constellations of stars that make up the zodiac. Suggesting that the Hiramic legend actually evolved from the Osiric legend used in the ancient Egyptian mysteries, Hall noted that the female figure Isis, the wife of Osiris, was represented in the zodiac by Virgo. In astrology, Virgo represents purity and service. Virgo operated in the heavens under influence of both the sun and Mercury, two heavenly bodies that the ancient Egyptians also employed to represent Osiris and Horus (the son of Osiris and Isis), respectively. While Hall's description certainly tends to support his speculation about the origin of the Hiramic legend, it does not go far enough to inform us how to make a practical application of this truly significant symbolism.

The manner in which Masonry's employs a woman weeping at the loss of Hiram Abif is similar to the more metaphysical use of that same symbolism to represent the importance of disciplining the human body to become obedient to the dictates of the immortal soul. That said, the question still remains - why does Masonry specifically portray this female as a virgin, and what is the practical application in my life? While there are several possibilities, one possible reason for the portrayal lies in the fact that the Divine state of virginity – that state of being toward which all humanity should strive - consists of the harmonizing of three principles: the spirit, the body and the soul.

The Holy Bible offers further insight into the significance of a female virgin when, in *Proverbs* the Virgin speaks through Solomon and teaches the world that she is a partner with God in the creation of the earth. Prov. 8:22-30. Those passages of scripture also teach us that the Virgin also cooperates with the Divine in the theological miracles of the redemption of the human soul. Various female figures from Isis to Sophia and Mary have represented the incarnate principle of virginity, or so-called non-fallen human nature, which is nothing less than the creative *force* of God. The female figure has also been described by some philosophers and theologians as the central symbol of such desirable human qualities as individuality, purity of creative thought, and wisdom. Some present-day religions have even adopted the female figure as a concrete living individual who, although generally unseen by humans in the material world, actually loves, suffers and rejoices for all of God's children in perpetuity.

Masonry recommends that each Mason draw his own religious interpretation of this symbolism, if he chooses to do so, based upon the religious doctrine that most appeals to him. The choice made is entirely irrelevant to the importance of the weeping virgin to the Craft. For us in Masonry, she represents the loving intensity and purity of heart with which Masons should approach the task of fulfilling spiritual aspirations. She also represents Mother Nature, who watches over earth's creation, which she cooperated in with God.

Such qualities as love and purity are not new to us. They are most often found in mothers, who carefully and lovingly guide the children they bore into existence into adulthood. Having been the principle actor in the miracle of human birth, what mother would not be found weeping if her adult son or daughter met an untimely death? What son or daughter would hesitate to move heaven and earth to please their mother? There is no closer bond between humans than the loving bond that exists between a mother and her child. Masons may view their weeping virgin in the same light.

The unfinished state of the temple for which the virgin weeps represents the failure to completely erect a place of holiness. Hiram Abif was not allowed to complete his task, because he was murdered. But, what excuse does the complacent listless idler have to offer? Hiram had no choice; the listless idler has a choice – he can make himself aware of his uselessness and after a genuine expression of remorse for his failings take the necessary steps toward completing the building of his own spiritual temple.

Where do you fit into this picture? Do you fall into the category of men who sneer at the lowly beggar, shamelessly exude false pride, cheat your brother, assume vulgar speech as your habit, or stand idly by while religious institutions – the veritable houses of God – abuse children and unapologetically incite deadly wars? If you do, the virgin weeps for you, for you are in serious spiritual peril. She extends her hand to you, which if grasped in yours will assist you in rising from your pitiful lowly state to a new life of love and purity.

Like earthly mothers, who can be extremely protective of their children, the weeping virgin also hopes that you will take the steps necessary to protect your soul. As she watches over the tomb of Hiram, she watches over the tomb of transgression in which you may be buried, ever hopeful that by giving yourself to a life of love and pure action, you will rise from that tomb and shine as the stars forever and ever. If you desire to make a practical application of the lessons derived from this symbolism, strive to understand how God wants you to treat others, then put that understanding to work.

Chapter 76

TOOLS OF IRON

> "And the house, when it was in building, was
> built of stone made ready before it was brought
> thither: so that there was neither hammer nor ax nor
> any tool of iron heard in the house, while it was building."
>
> 1 Kings 6:7

From a lecture delivered during Masonic ritual, we learn that during the building of King Solomon's Temple there was not heard the sound of ax, hammer, or any tool of iron. That was so, because the whole building was completed with the aid of wooden mauls that had been specifically prepared tap into place stone and wood-work that had been carefully hewn and carved. When the entire structure was completed, it appeared to be more the work of the Supreme Architect of the Universe than that of men. This allegory has immediate relevance to a Mason's construction of his own spiritual building, of which King Solomon's Temple is the archetype.

The manner in which the Temple was put together is symbolic of the peace and harmony that should prevail among Freemasons when laboring together. It also symbolizes that all men, whether or not they are members of the Craft, should so conduct their individual lives that anger and discord are but a bad memory of a very distant past. In other words, Freemasons are encouraged to demonstrate within a Masonic lodge, as well as when abroad in the world, how to live in peace with oneself, as well as with others.

In order that man may live in complete peace and harmony, he will eventually learn what Freemasonry already inculcates: the spiritual self has absolutely nothing to do with any specific religious affiliation. This is one of the reasons that Masons avoid speaking about religion when assembled together. Becoming sufficiently spiritual, such that the notion of peace dominates your thinking and mood, requires one to transcend reality – to rely upon something other than the five physical senses. One cannot hear, touch, smell, see, or even taste harmony, or that state of equilibrium we call *peace*. Rather, inner peace results from the mind, which we know from the teachings in the Fellowcraft degree to constitute one of those numberless worlds around us that often defy logic.

But, what does the manner in which King Solomon's Temple is said to have been built teach us about how to achieve inner and outer peace? For the builders themselves, that decision was easy, because it was made for them by the three Grand Masters. Those overseers simply instructed that no tool of iron be used. In our personal lives, those three Grand Masters are replaced by the triune God – recognized as such in Freemasonry by reference to the unpronounceable name which consists of three syllables. Everywhere in our own Holy Writings we read that God determined that man should live in peace. But, by the perverse exercise of free will, man decided to live otherwise. He carelessly decided instead to demand vengeance when he was wronged; to desire an eye-for-an-eye as his justice; and to deprive the living of their precious life if they disagreed with the manner in which he thought. Freemasonry asks us to revisit the allegory about the three Grand Masters and leave there more determined to act as God intended us to act.

Freemasons should understand from the teachings of the Craft that man is a spiritual being having a human experience; not merely a human being having a spiritual experience. The difference is significant, for the former teaches that our minds is where we process all of our experiences, while the latter suggests that we are the center of the universe around which all other men revolve. A touch, kiss, or caress means little unless the mind interprets each of those as acts of sensual and loving kindness.

Your mind is all that you have for relating to the world around you – *as you think, so shall you be.*

The builders who worked at the direction of the three Grand Masters during the construction King Solomon's Temple could have decided, either as a group, or individually, to disobey the Grand Masters' instructions. Had they done so, the story passed along to us would be about loud clanging noises in the Temple while it was building. However, the builders in our story were obedient to the guidance from elsewhere and harmony prevailed. Thus, our story is as much about obedience, as it is about peace and harmony. The latter did not occur at the building of the Temple without the former.

Civilization has learned throughout the ages that chaos is a threat to both mankind's safety and its' emotional well-being. Order and symmetry in all things is essential for peace and calm to prevail. Masonry teaches that man first learned these lessons by observing nature, the heavens and the immutable laws of God. Each season gives way to the next without a quarrel. Trees brown and leaves fall to the ground only to be replaced by new green foliage that appears at exactly the correct time of year. The planets move in their respective orbits around the sun, for to do otherwise would likely result in a massive stellar collision that would doom the universe. Wherever man looks at nature, he sees balance, order, peace and harmony. But, when he looks at his fellow man he becomes fearful, for his fellowman has the same power as he does to decide to scowl rather than smile; to spew out anger rather than speak kindly; or to physically strike for the purpose of inflicting injury rather than wrapping an arm around the shoulders in a loving embrace.

The builders at the Temple did not fear one another. To the contrary, they were joined together in brotherhood. The common bond among them was fraternalism, which requires that instead of focusing upon what one man dislikes about another man, he determines to love that man regardless. Only the most committed Pollyanna would conclude that there were no differences of opinion among the builders at the Temple. Those men came from different cultures, and from different tribes within different cultures. Some believed in multiple gods, while others held a belief in the one God. Yet, Masonic tradition informs us that they did not focus on those differences, but on how best to work together to actually complete the building of the Temple. Whether or not such men actually lived and actually worked in such harmony is not important. However, the lesson derived from that allegory is imperative.

In that tools of iron symbolize noise and chaos, it is easier for us to understand what Freemasonry is attempting to teach us. Mankind's most desired state of being is that of peace and harmony. As opposed to waiting for a miraculous event to occur, for men to suddenly become tolerant beings, for doctrines to merge, or for hatred to vanish, each person has the power this moment to determine the future happiness of his or her existence. Decide now that there is never a good reason to be vengeful, to be mean to another person, to spew out hateful words, to criticize in a hurtful manner, to inflict physical violence upon another, or in any manner whatsoever do anything that is not kind and loving. Once those *tools of iron* are removed from your personal behavior, you will be surprised to see them disappear from the lives of those with whom you interact daily.

The structure of King Solomon's Temple is intended to remind us that our goal in this life is to adapt our lives to our spiritual nature. The steps we take each day to build our own spiritual temple should remind us that our bodies, minds and souls are one. Along the way, it is important to stop and experience that unity within ourselves, for Freemasonry imparts to each of us the necessity to not merely know how to act and behave, but to conduct our daily lives accordingly. If there is not to be heard the sound of ax, hammer, or any tool of iron during the building of our own spiritual temple, then we must discipline ourselves to live peaceably and quietly.

Describing how Masters of a lodge should govern, Albert Pike provided the following list in his work *Morals and Dogma:* (1) urge upon your brethren the practice of morality; (2) urge your brethren to love one another, to be faithful to their country and to obey the laws of the land; (3) respect all forms of worship, tolerate all political and religious opinions and venerate God; (4) fraternize with all men and assist the unfortunate; (5) think well, speak well and act well; (6) make the wise and the good your model; and (7) do that which thou ought to do and let the result be what it shall be. None of those tasks can ever be accomplished within a realm of chaos. The Master who has failed to look within himself to discover his unity with all that God has created will never muster the calm, quiet peacefulness necessary to build his spiritual temple without aid of those noisy tools of iron.

Correctly believing that a Mason requires a guiding and helping hand to learn about his spiritual nature and then to put that spiritual nature to work in the service of humanity, Freemasonry has adopted Masonic education programs throughout all of the United States. Perhaps more personal, one brother Mason will inevitably discover in his Masonic travels another brother Mason who is wise in the ways of the spirit and who is willing to impart that wisdom when asked. Our lodges are not merely places where bills are paid and Masonic degrees are conferred. They are also hallowed chamber within which brethren joined together by the strongest ties of fraternalism share that which is inside of them – the spirit, or soul of man, which bears the nearest affinity to that all pervading spirit of Nature and which will never, never, never die. You will be surprised what you receive when you ask, amazed at what is set before you when you knock and startled by what you will find when you seek. In this manner, my brethren, you may learn how to set aside those tools of iron and build in peace.

Chapter 77
TRUTH IS A DIVINE ATTRIBUTE

"And ye shall know the truth, and
the truth shall set you free."

John 8:32

The primary object of Freemasonry is the search for *truth,* which is generally symbolized in Masonic ritual by *light* and the *Word.* From his initiation onward, the Mason pursues his search for the *Word,* which is, in its fullest realization, the knowledge of God. The ancient Hebrews who embraced the Kabbalah taught that if man understood the meaning of the name of God, *YWHW,* he would understand the entirety of divine knowledge. Saint Paul, the founder of traditional Christianity, similarly taught that Jesus Christ is the *truth* manifest in the written word. Beginning with the Entered Apprentice Degree and continuing throughout all Masonic ritual, a Mason is taught that truth is a divine attribute and the foundation of every virtue.

Truth constitutes the very cornerstone of all that is good and righteous and may be regarded as the most profound concept embraced by Freemasonry. According to Masonic ritual, it is fundamental to both the four cardinal virtues of temperance, fortitude, prudence and justice, and the theological virtues of faith, hope and charity. There is no attribute higher than *truth* taught in Freemasonry, and quite possibly no other attribute that is less understood.

Within the story written in the Gospels about Jesus' confrontation with Pilate, the governor of Judea is reported to have asked rhetorically, "What is truth?" Indeed, throughout history it seems that mankind repeatedly asks itself that question before arriving at convenient answers. For example, young students in American classrooms have for years been taught the story about George Washington chopping down the cherry tree. The young George is reputed to have rushed to his mother's side to tell her what he had done after felling what must have been a tree that was given great status by the Washington family. In addition to giving us the impression that George was a truthful person from an early age, that tale is also a lesson in morality: telling the truth, even when the truth might get you in trouble, is an important ideal and principle.

Certain writers on the subject of self improvement have suggested that the truth about certain subjects, if revealed to others, may be so harmful to a person that it should be concealed. Those particular writers have explored the effect of such awkward disclosures on the growth of the human psyche and have concluded that some truths are too inimical to warrant revealing them. Without question, each person has something he or she has done during their lifetime that if revealed to the world around them could diminish their standing within the community in which they live. Yet, whether or not that "something" is ever revealed, it is still *truth,* because it actually happened. Concealing the fact will never change that truth. It will merely serve to keep some others from knowing.

While the foregoing does relate to a form of truthfulness, disclosure versus concealment, the *truth* that Freemasons are told is a divine attribute is not necessarily conjoined with the notions about whether or not a person should, or should not relate the true facts about a particular event. Rather, Freemasonry explores an answer that may be given to the question attributed to Pilate: "What is truth?" The correct answer flows from a closer examination of the relationship of the quest for *truth* with the benefits derived from prayer and benediction.

For the Craft, benediction is more than a simple good wish made for others. It is the putting into action of divine power transcending the individual thought and will of one who is blessed, as well as the one who is offering the blessing. Freemasonry describes this as essentially a sacerdotal act. The Kabbalah compares the role of prayer and benediction to a double movement, ascending and descending similar to the circulation of blood in the human body. Man's prayers rise toward God and after being divinely oxidized are transformed into benedictions which descend below from above. In other words, a benediction is God's spiritual answer to our prayer.

That lesson is reinforced in other symbolism used in a Masonic lodge room. The pillars of Boaz and Jachin situated at the entrance to King Solomon's Temple correspond to the two functions of prayer and benediction. One represents Severity and the other mercy, because it is severity which stimulates prayer and mercy which blesses. The blue blood of Boaz ascends and the oxidized blood of Jachin descends. The two columns thus have a practical significance for Masons – they also represent spiritual respiration.

"Truth and intelligence are the eternal attributes of God, not of the individual soul," wrote Albert Pike in *Morals and Dogma*, as he pondered the mysteries of the Royal Secret. Drawing upon earlier writings by ancient Indian sects, Pike expressed the belief that God and the individual soul are distinct. Therefore, the practice of prayer from below followed by benediction from above was, for Pike, an ancient truth that was the very cement and support of every virtue. From this context we at last draw our Masonic understanding about what truth really is – God's response to our prayer.

One cannot truly become temperate unless he or she first prays to the great Creator for the ability to comprehend right from wrong. Indeed, the ability to make that distinction was precisely the *wisdom* for which Solomon prayed. God's response constitutes His blessing. Also, one cannot truly act with fortitude, weigh challenging situations prudently, or deal justly with others unless prayer is followed by His blessing – His benediction. Thus, the truth Masons are taught to seek results from man's personal interaction with God. Man asks; God answers. Truth is not revealed to those who do not ask, seek, or knock. Man cannot safely rely upon the fact that God will act regardless of our interaction with Him. He may; He may not. Mankind was imbued with a free will that like other laws of nature is rarely interrupted by divine intervention. Otherwise there would be no free will — there would simply be God's will.

The respiration of the soul — the give-and-take of prayer — is that state that St. Paul referred to as "freedom in God." It is a new way of breathing. During benediction, one freely breathes in the divine breath and lives a life of virtue; a life of brotherly love, relief and truth. *Truth*, then, is memorialized by our freely acting to bring to life the lessons of the Beatitudes; affection for our kindred, tenderness for our friends, gentleness and forbearance toward our inferiors, pity for those who suffer and forgiveness of our enemies. It is these that are the divine attributes that are the foundation of every virtue.

Chapter 78

"What Do You Most Desire?"

> "...but the Lord shall be unto thee
> an everlasting light,..."
>
> Is. 60:19

In each degree of Freemasonry, the candidate is asked what it is that he most desires. The answer is always the same: "light." Symbolically, the word "light" means knowledge, but in Freemasonry it specifically means knowledge about man's relationship with God, nature and humanity. Since Freemasonry does not claim to possess all knowledge, it has no secret scrolls to pass along, or hidden codexes to share with new candidates. Instead, Freemasonry gives the candidate the necessary tools whereby he himself can explore the glories of God, nature and humanity for himself.

To assist the candidate in his quest for light, Freemasonry offers yet another symbol from which a spiritual exercise emerges: "darkness." If one listens carefully to what is said about being brought into the light, one also hears that he is necessarily brought out of darkness. In order that the candidate may better understand what this truly means, consider this thesis: it is essential to *create* light from darkness. That thesis supposes that the light that any person holds is polarized at two poles between which there is only darkness.

Within the domain of human consciousness there actually exist two kinds of darkness. One is more commonly referred to as "ignorance," while the other is the darkness of higher knowledge. The problems of ignorance are left to the schools to resolve. It is the latter darkness of higher knowledge with which Freemasonry is concerned.

Seldom in history has man suddenly attained higher knowledge of God to such a degree that he is intellectually fine tuned with the Divine. There were several traveling the road to Damascus they day Paul *suddenly* attained divine enlightenment. Yet, none other than Paul were so instantly drawn to the Lord's bosom. Like most of the rest of us, they, too, likely traveled a slower path toward enlightenment. Freemasonry regards such a slow path as normal and thus provides the very useful tool referred to as the neutralization of binaries to assist the candidate and Mason along the way.

The complexities of that tool may be simplified by clarifying it as a meditative *synthesis* of opposing ideas. That process was illustrated by the use of opposite poles and colors by the German scientist Wilhelm Ostwald in his work entitled *Die Farbenfibel* published in 1916. In his example, Ostwald visualized the north pole as red in color, becoming seven different colors as he reached the equator, then completely black by the time he ended at the south pole. The north pole was called the *white point* while the south pole was referred to as the *black point*.

By analogy, we are able to conceive of the *white point* as representing wisdom and the *black point* ignorance. Wisdom is nothing more than the synthesis of all sciences of human knowledge. Platonism is oriented toward this *white point*, while at the other end of the spectrum the *black point* can be represented by nihilism. The zone wherein the process of synthesis occurs is darkness of higher knowledge, or the realm of spiritual unknowing. Once the process of synthesizing is completed, the darkness is replaced by light, or the realm of spiritual knowing.

It is within that realm that one discovers what Freemasonry refers to as *prudence*. Prudence is the constant awareness of being between two darknesses – the darkness of the *white point*, on the one hand, and the darkness of the *black point* on the other hand. Prudence also teaches us that moving from spiritual unknowing to spiritual knowing is a slow process, necessarily so to avoid the candidate and Mason from being blinded by too much light at one time. By way of yet another analogy, it is much like learning mathematics in school. Before one can master algebra, one must learn to add and subtract. The initiate is not someone who knows everything. He is a person who bears the truth within a deeper level of his own consciousness that is revealed to him step-by-step.

Prudence never elaborates a system of belief, which is precisely the reason Freemasonry never instructs that one religion is preferable to any other religion. To the contrary, prudence is occupied only with synthesizing particular problems at deeper levels of consciousness. That is why the enlightened Master Mason if often able to offer a dozen different answers to dozens of different questions giving them spontaneously and without much regard or care for mutual agreement. That is so, because the quest for the whole truth begins with the proposition that nobody knows the whole truth. Therefore, there is no knowledge that is off limits to a Mason's personal scrutiny.

The darkness where synthesis occurs is the region of deeper consciousness, which philosophers have for ages referred to as the "gift of Perfect Night." From the inner darkness comes the revelations of spiritual truth, which constitute the "gifts of Perfect Night" in all their splendor. It has been also said that the search for those gifts, or the act of synthesizing opposites, is equivalent to the search for peace among nations, among people and among ideas.

Part 3
Lessons In
The Masonic Lodge

Introduction

Like Masons around the world, California Freemasons promote health care, homes for the aged, education and public education. However, within each California Masonic lodge the most important emphasis is placed upon promoting man's understanding of God and his relationship to the Deity.

Grounded in a synthesis of ancient philosophies and religions, Masonry embraces its own literature and history. The allegories it portrays in its rich rituals reveal truths derived from that synthesis and teach that new truths are yet to be discovered.

Freemasonry is known throughout the world as an "ancient system" and fraternity that transmits knowledge by symbols rather than through the written word. That was so for the ancients, because written material was extremely limited until relatively recent times. As in times past, knowledge is currently passed on through Masonic ritual, or demonstrations and dramatizations using Masonic symbols. That ritual is performed within closely guarded lodges that may only be attended by initiated Freemasons. The ritual is secret, but the lessons taught are for everyone.

The primary purpose of a Masonic lodge is to provide a venue for creating Masons – teaching them about philosophy, comparative religion, liberal arts, science, grammar, rhetoric, astronomy, geometry and music.

For Masons, the greatest and most sacred of these is the study of geometry. Why? Perhaps within the following pages several reasons will be disclosed. If not, the complete knowledge merely awaits you're initiation into the most ancient and profound fraternity that has ever existed.

For now reflect upon the fact that geometry treats of the powers and properties of magnitudes, in general, and is symbolized by the letter "G" suspended directly above the chair where the lodge Master sits. Of all the liberal arts and sciences, geometry is enriched with a consistency and unswerving truth about spatial relationships not found elsewhere in other disciplines. That fact is intended to inspire Masons and everyone who reflects upon it about the unswerving truth of the Deity. It is neither a Christian, Jewish, or Islamic Deity – rather it is the One True God in whom it is worth placing your trust – a God that disinherits none of his children but embraces them all.

A Freemason is a man of the age of 18, or older, who professes a belief in one Supreme Being, and who has been voluntarily initiated into the Craft by a solemn symbolic ceremony performed by members in good standing of a Masonic lodge. The candidate initially proceeds in his Masonic journey as an Entered Apprentice exploring and absorbing the basic Masonic fundamentals.

Next, the candidate advances to the second degree as a Fellowcraft and commits himself to acquiring a broader understanding of the liberal arts and sciences. Finally, upon advancing to the third and sublime degree of Master Mason, the candidate is exposed to the valuable lessons about the distinction between mortality and immortality. He is also encouraged to investigate the reality about his own soul.

During his Masonic journey, the candidate for professes several vows of fidelity and honor, the specifics of which relate exclusively to Freemasonry and are therefore are kept "secret" from non-Masons – it is, in fact, one of the few "Masonic secrets" not revealed to the world at-large. The candidate commits himself to serving the Deity and his laws; promoting the welfare of all Masons, their widows and orphans; and working to make the world where he lives a better place.

Chapter 79
WHAT IS A MASON?

"Thou shalt have no other gods before me."

Ex. 20:3

Numerous articles have been written in various Masonic periodicals describing, discussing and examining a host of characteristics and personal attributes common among Freemasons. At the head of the list is usually the fact that Freemasonry is a "fraternity" that assists its members to improve themselves as trustworthy citizens; to responsibly participate in the communities in which they live; and devotedly serve educational foundations, charitable enterprises and free health services sponsored, managed and operated by Masons. However, few focus squarely upon that which truly sets Freemasonry apart from other worthwhile community service organizations.

Indeed, Freemasonry cares for the poor; sponsors educational scholarships; supports and maintains hospitals, clinics and residential facilities for senior citizens and the disadvantaged; and even offers free eye transplants, surgeries and general care to members and their families. Yet, the same is true of several other organizations that share in a like-minded manner Freemasonry's dedication to giving. Those endeavors are not only worthwhile, they are essential to the quality of life we most desire to perpetuate in our great Nation. Nevertheless, they do not uniquely distinguish Masons from others. That "uniqueness" may be found in the manner each Mason approaches and shapes his personal relationship with the Deity.

Masonry does not teach men to believe in one God, to behave according to a specific moral code, or to engage in acts of loving kindness we call "charity." A candidate for the degrees of Freemasonry is expected to bring those beliefs with him when he joins the fraternity, where he will find them encouraged and reinforced. Any candidate who expects Freemasonry to teach him the true path to God will soon realize his error. Masonry leaves those matters to the Rabbis, the Priests, the Ministers and the Imams.

History has taught the world that arguments about religious differences among men can wrench apart the harmonious fabric of society and plunge whole nations into violence, death and despair. Consequently, Freemasonry itself is not a religion and refuses to promote any one religion to the exclusion of others. Rather, Masons believe firmly in each man's freedom to choose the religion most suited to him – a freedom that is regarded so reverently that it is among those cited in the First Amendment to the United States Constitution. It is this belief that truly distinguishes Freemasonry and the members who are called "Masons."

A study of the American Revolutionary War and of the times preceding it reveals that even our original thirteen colonies had a difficult time with the concept of freedom of religion. In fact, each colony had its own state-sponsored religion with the right to tax citizens for the support of each respective religious denomination. That state of affairs mirrored the reality around the globe: nations everywhere sported state-sponsored religions and often criminalized deviations from the practice of that religion. Since there was then no model anywhere on the face of the Earth from which our Founding Fathers could learn the importance of "freedom of religion," one must look to the institution of Masonry itself and discover exactly how that concept became a cornerstone of our Nation's First Amendment.

During the era of 1776, only Freemasons espoused the idea that men should be free to pursue whatever religion they chose. A study of the people central to forging our country's Declaration of Independence, Bill of Rights and Constitution discloses that many held membership in Freemasonry in common regardless of their varied and respective views about church and religion. That fact is the very reason that from the outset of its existence, our Nation's laws have provided the widest latitude among society for the worship of God.

History also teaches us that Masons have regularly labored in the protection of that freedom, while many religions have labored to perpetuate their institutions to the exclusion of others. Freemasonry does not sponsor any particular religion, while many religions persist in attempting to convince "non-believers" of their error. Yet, Masons are not irreligious. Freemasonry encourages each individual Mason to attend, serve and support the church and religion of his choice. Ironically, Freemasonry has far too often been condemned and falsely persecuted by some for promoting such free choice. Indeed, throughout history certain segments of society have violently attacked Masons as being heretical simply because Freemasonry as an institution does not and never will endorse any specific religious dogma to the exclusion of all others.

As a fraternity, we should fondly think about our Masonic predecessors who taught each of us that no man's particular "error," i.e., view of God and theology, should be preferred over the "error" of another.

The next time you are asked," What is a Mason?" instead of offering the stock reply, "a member of a fraternal society dedicated to self-improvement and charitable works," remember that your Craft's greatest contribution to the formation of this country was the expression of the belief in one Supreme Being, who desires that each man inherit His blessings, and who asks that each person respond to His call freely, deliberately, and uniquely.

Chapter 80

TRAVELING IN FOREIGN COUNTRIES

"For we know that if our earthly house of this tabernacle were dissolved, we have a building of God, an house not made with hands, eternal in the Heavens."

2Cor.5:1

Masonry is a succession of allegories, the mere vehicles for great lessons in morality. It speaks in symbols and sheds light upon "secrets" no living person can fully discern – future life after death. Ancient Craft Masonry provides the necessary "working tools" for use in our daily lives; "working tools" that can prepare us to eventually welcome death, not as a grim tyrant, but as a kind messenger sent to translate us from this imperfect world to that all perfect celestial Lodge above where the Supreme Architect of the Universe forever presides.

The ritual performed during the sublime degree of Master Mason explains to the candidate that the lessons taught him are intended to enable him to "obtain wages while traveling in foreign countries." Masonic writers have frequently interpreted this symbolism to mean that while living on this Earth, we are to conduct our lives as men of character, integrity and piety. Yet, while that interpretation is certainly substantial, it is incomplete.

Consider this passage from sacred scripture: "Man that is born of woman is of few days and full of trouble. He cometh forth like a flower and is cut down. He fleeth, also, as a shadow and continueth not." In other words, our earthly existence has a beginning and an ending. It consists of a wonderful journey through this world, this material plane, this identifiable land from the day of our birth to the time of our demise. As Master Masons, we are further instructed upon the truth that our death does not result in annihilation. Indeed, we are "translated" into a new and different existence – a "foreign country" – where the soul of man will continue a journey that we can neither presently know, nor fully understand.

It is while traveling in that realm that Masons anticipate receiving "wages:" that celestial land "from whose bourn no traveler returns." Thus the term "foreign country" has a profound spiritual meaning to weighed and considered as seriously as we weigh and consider the lessons of morality applied to our earthly existence. From the square and compasses, we are reminded of the truth: "as it is above, so shall it be below." The lessons learned lead Masons to conclude that the morality we learn to live here below will, if lived well, entitle us to "wages," or reward when we travel above.

In Blue Lodge Masonry, the lessons derived from the various symbols teach us what the Ancients instructed the elite: when physical life ends, man is resurrected to a new and different existence. Masons are inspired to make this life a credit to the future by extending charity, or love to all mankind, regardless of race, religion, creed or doctrine. As spiritual beings, we should also anticipate the fullness of new life as the just reward, or "wages," of our faithfulness. That fullness is expected by Masons to the brightest light emanating from the presence of God when we are once again figuratively asked, "being in a condition of darkness, what do you most desire?"

Although Freemasonry is not a religion and has never been promoted as a substitute for religion, it does offer a road map for the religious man to follow. From sacred scripture we learn that, "(P)ure religion and undefiled before God is this: to visit the orphans and widows in their time of affliction and to keep ourselves spotless before the world." (Jas.1:27). This passage represents the very foundation of Masonic charity. When we practice such Masonic charity we may be assured that once the Supreme Architect finally brings us from darkness to that eternal light, we will be deemed faithful and worthy of the "wages" He will provide us while "traveling in that foreign country."

Chapter 81
BEAUTY: THE DESIGN OF GOD

"For the Lord taketh pleasure in His people:
He will beautify the meek with salvation."

Ps. 149:4

Operative Freemasonry's chief objective in architecture was to accomplish beauty and symmetry, as was accomplished in the building of King Solomon's Temple. Speculative Masonry emphasizes the beauty of character and the virtues of true manhood. Symbolically, "beauty" is one of three principle supports of a Masonic Lodge. It is represented by the Corinthian column, the most beautiful of the ancient orders of architecture, as well as by the Junior Warden, who symbolizes the meridian sun – the most beautiful object in the heavens. Fellowcraft Masons are instructed during the second degree of Freemasonry that five original orders of architecture were studied by Freemasons. The Corinthian, created by the Greeks, was considered the more beautiful of all of the orders. Hiram Abif, who Masonic tradition informs us was the the Grand Master in charge of the building of King Solomon's Temple, is for that reason also represented by the column of beauty.

Lessons in Freemasonry teach us that as a symbol, "beauty" is intended to inspire us to study and attain a deeper understanding about the dignity of human nature, as well as about the vast powers and capacities of the human soul. Our attention is invited to the literary works of all great writers, including Plato and Aristotle, not merely those whom we refer to as "Masonic authors," such as Albert Pike and A. E. Waite. Although man is encompassed within a dome of incomprehensible wonders, he is given an array of freedoms and choices. He is certainly more than a mere object upon which God's light is to fall. Rather, as human beings we respond to that which stimulates us to action – the good as well as the evil. On the one hand, the response can be a loathing of mankind in general, or merely of certain specific people because of true or imagined infractions. Whole nations and religious bodies have ventured into violent and deadly conquests simply because those upon whom horror was inflicted thought, behaved and believed differently. On the other hand, the more beautiful response, the response Freemasonry encourages, recognizes that although man is faulty by nature, we are all conducted by the same divine radiance emanating from the Great Architect of the Universe. God's light shines upon everyone including the good and evil.

All of the ancient religions recognized a tension between light and darkness; good and evil; order and disorder. The Deity, universe and human intellect may best be understood as a complete and harmonious organism. Mankind is called to assume its role within that organism that while we are unique individuals we are all proceeding through life with our own share of pain, sorrow, illness and suffering. To Masons, it matters not that we suffer, it matters how we handle our suffering.

Like the beauty of a developing human soul, beauty in architecture is distinctive. Who can legitimately challenge the majesty of the spires atop the churches situated throughout Europe where the Operative Masons labored so extensively? And, who can question the distinctiveness of a human soul that seeks to attain wisdom and knowledge for the purposes of serving his fellows, his country and his God?

Within the confines of each man's suffering, the soul truly yearns to shout, "Thank you, Father of All Creation, for finding me worthy to be tested." And once tested, to be found worthy in spite of our personal sorrows and needs to teach and share wisdom with others; in short, to serve mankind to God's glory. Indeed, my brother, that is the "beauty and glory of the day" – and the noblest work of man.

Chapter 82

THE RUFFIANS

> "And ye shall know the truth, and
> the truth shall make you free."
>
> John 8:32

At the heart of the mysteries of Freemasonry lies a legend from which one learns how three unworthy craftsmen working at the Temple of Solomon entered into a plot to extort from a famous Freemason a secret they had no right to know. No man can sit in witness of that pertinent ritual without sensing that there is, indeed, a secret which each Master Mason has not yet won the right to know from the Great Architect of the Universe. That secret relates to how, when and in what manner good will be victorious over evil.

To those who trace Masonic symbolism to ancient Sun worship, the three Ruffians, or unworthy craftsmen, are the three winter months in the year that plot to murder the beauty and glory of summer. To those who find the origins of Freemasonry to lie in the Ancient Egyptian Mysteries, the legend is a drama about Typhon, the spirit of evil, who slays Osiris, the spirit of good, and who to Typhon's dismay is ultimately and triumphantly resurrected to life. Others will find a connection between the legend to the life and death of Jesus, who was put to death outside the city gate by three of the most ruthless "Ruffians" known to man – the Priest, the Politician, and the Mob. Some may identify the Ruffians, or assassins as the three renegade knights, who falsely accused the Knights Templar and thereby aided King Philip of France and Pope Clement to abolish Templarism and slay its Grand Master.

Albert Pike, that giant of Masonic philosophy, identified the three Ruffians as the greatest enemies of individual welfare and social progress ever to exist: kingcraft, priestcraft and the ignorant mob-mind. The first enemy strikes a blow at the throat, the seat of freedom of speech. The second enemy stabs at the heart, the home of freedom of conscience. And, the third enemy fells its victim dead with a blow to the brain, which is the throne of freedom of thought.

Of the three Ruffians, perhaps the most terrible, ruthless and brutal is the ignorant mob-mind. It is so easily inflamed, so hard to restrain and so willing to wreak havoc where peace once prevailed. No tyrant or wicked priest can reduce a nation to slavery until it is first lost in the darkness of ignorance – the fruit of the mob-mind. Pike concluded that when the Ruffians murdered the Great Mason, they symbolically robbed not only their fellow craftsmen, but also themselves of the most precious secret of personal and social life – the knowledge to not only understand right from wrong, but to do good rather than evil. Pike believed that to be so because he knew that what men are together is determined by what each is alone.

One cannot get to the heart of real truth until it is admitted that there is within man himself a certain moral perversity; a spirit of mischief, which does wrong deliberately and in direct contravention to that which is known to be right. Here, truly is the real Ruffian most to be feared – the one who can be overcome only by self-discipline, the practice of that which is virtuous, and prayer for Divine assistance. It is that Ruffian of the dark, lurking in our own minds and hearts, who leads us to hurt rather than help a brother, who lays us up in idle inactivity when duty calls, and who must be taken without the gates of the city and executed from our very minds. We dare not appease him, turn a blind eye to his mischief, or tolerate his presence in our innermost being. Otherwise we, too, shall be felled dead at his feet.

Chapter 83

THE MYSTIC TIE

"Behold, how good and how pleasant it is
for brethren to dwell together in unity!"

Ps. 133:1

Many symbols, as well as the several tenets of Freemasonry that they represent, are termed "mystical," because they are known and understood best by those men who have received the rites of the Order. In a similar sense, the term "mystic tie" refers to the sacred and inviolable bond that unites Masonic brethren. This tie stems from the vows of eternal brotherhood made by each Mason, irrespective of differences in religion, race, or nationality. Men of the most discordant opinions in worldly matters are united into one fellowship, meet at one altar, combine their energies to work charity and are thus called "Brethren of the Mystic Tie."

Freemasons are reminded of that mystic tie during the conferral of the Entered Apprentice Degree, as the candidate for initiation is conducted once around the lodge room to demonstrate to the Worshipful Master and brethren that he is duly and truly prepared for inclusion into membership. As the initiate takes his vows and the cable tow is removed, the brethren are also reminded that the physical ties among people are less significant than the spiritual bonds of loyalty and fraternal affection. Those spiritual ties are emblematic of the tenderness with which the Supreme Architect of the Universe embraces all of His children with the affluence of His love. Care and concern for a brother in Freemasonry, then, inclines the spirit of man to a sense of caring for God.

The mystic tie in Freemasonry, unlike the symbolic silver chord referred to in the Old Testament of the Holy Bible, which is severed upon man's death, once forged is never broken – it is truly eternal. As a reminder of that truth, Freemasons celebrate a ritualistic memorial for a departed brother uniting themselves with that brother's passing to the Celestial Lodge above.

Freemasons are also reminded of their strong ties of brotherhood when they read and absorb Masonic writings, learn about the good deeds performed by past great Masons and marvel at the numerous institutional charities established by Freemasons long before the living were born. Indeed, the very practice of Masonic ritual reminds every Freemason that mankind is destined to participate in the greatest mystery of all – the gift of eternal life. When it is understood that all men are so destined, it becomes easier to also understand that it is incumbent upon us to accept men as God has made them, the world as He has made it, and make the best we can of all.

Chapter 84

AN EMBLEM OF INNOCENCE

"Your lamb shall be without blemish..."

Ex. 12:5

Masonic tradition informs us that in all ages the lamb has been deemed an emblem of innocence. Hence, it is required that a Mason's Apron should be made from lambskin to symbolize the innocence a Freemason is to retain and exercise throughout his lifetime. In the higher degrees of Freemasonry, as well as in the chivalric degrees, the lamb serves as a symbol of the biblical Paschal Lamb of the Jewish Passover, which is also a symbolical archetype of Jesus, who is regarded as the Christ by our Christian brethren – the spiritual "Lamb of God."

Freemasons are required to strive after perfect innocence in all life's relations, especially in Masonic relationships. The pure white lambskin apron worn by Masons during all Masonic approved assemblies is intended to constantly remind us of that very requirement and duty. That apron constitutes the first gift bestowed upon a candidate for degrees in Freemasonry. It also represents a Mason's responsibilities.

In ancient Israel, the apron, or "girdle," formed a part of the vestment of the priesthood – known in Gnostic circles as the Vestments of Zadok. Like a Freemason's apron, those aprons were also white and made from lambskin.

White denoted purity and the lambskin denoted innocence. While Masonic ritual teaches a connection with operative class Masons, who variously wore aprons to protect their clothing from being soiled, the lambskin's significance as a priestly garment cannot be overlooked. It is from that priestly connection that a Mason's responsibilities toward mankind flow.

Like the Ten Commandments given by God to Moses, Freemasonry also has another Decalogue, which constitutes both a Masonic law to initiates, as well as a Masonic definition of the phrase "purity and innocence:" (1) God is eternal, of supreme intelligence and inexhaustible love, and is therefore to be revered and honored by the practice of the four cardinal virtues, temperance, fortitude, prudence and justice; (2) a Freemason's soul, like the souls of all mankind, is immortal – he is not to do any act that would degrade it; (3) Freemasons are to war against vice unceasingly, submit to the light of wisdom and knowledge, and do unto others that which we would have them do unto us; (4) Freemasons are to pay respect and do homage to the aged, instruct the young, and protect and defend infancy; (5) a Mason should cherish his wife and children, love his country and obey it's laws; (6) as a Freemason, the man you call a friend shall become a second self; (7) Freemasons are to avoid and flee from insincere relationships; (8) Masons are not permitted to allow any passion to become his master; (9) a Mason should hear much, speak little, and act well; and, (10) Freemasons are to study to know men, to learn about themselves, to be just, and to avoid idleness. The most important lesson learned from this Decalogue is to love one another, for its is also written in the sacred writings, as well as in the hearts of every Mason that he who claims to live in the light, yet hates his brother, is still in darkness. The Freemason will understand when such a man is also described as continuing to wear his "hoodwink."

Brethren, do not believe that you can affect nothing; do not despair; and, above all else, do not become inert. Many great deeds are accomplished from the small struggles in life. Misfortune, isolation, abandonment, and poverty are life's battles whose heroes are those who work each day to lessen their sad effects upon man and society. The lambskin, then, reminds each Freemason to become a priest, a soldier, a brother and a friend – pray with an innocent heart, war against vice with a pure conscience, and embrace a brother and friend with inexhaustible love.

Chapter 85

JUSTICE IN A GREAT MEASURE

"To do justice and judgment is more acceptable to the Lord than sacrifice."

Prov. 21:3

The lessons of the Entered Apprentice degree teach us to act uprightly in our dealings with all mankind, and to never fail to act justly toward ourselves, our brethren, or the world. Justice, then, is the cornerstone upon which we are instructed to erect our Masonic superstructure. For, justice in a great measure constitutes the cement of civil society. Without it, universal confusion would reign, lawless force could replace equity, and social intercourse might no longer occur.

Through His wisdom, God has given to each of us the opportunity to follow His plan for just relationships. A Freemason need look no farther than the Ten Commandments how we may participate in His plan. If tempted to steal what belongs to another, we are to resist. If we give in to the temptation, we are to repay what was taken, make amends with our neighbor and sin no more. Man is tempted by many similar passions arising from lust, greed and vanity. Freemasons are taught that it is not only forbidden to grant control of oneself to one's passions, it is unjust.

To the law of God, Freemasonry adds an imperative contract obligation upon every Mason. Upon entering the Order, or fraternity, the initiate binds himself by a solemn vow to every other Mason in the world. The initiate becomes a brother to others he does not and may never know. He becomes responsible to families he may never see. He promises to aid widows and orphans who are not yet widows, or orphans. In essence, he becomes obligated to people other than himself to whom he owes duties of kindness, sympathy and compassion.

In return for his vows, the initiate becomes entitled to call upon every other Mason in the world for assistance when in need, protection when in danger, sympathy when in sorrow, attention when ill, and a burial when dead. These constitute reciprocal responsibilities of the fraternity to the initiate and are emblematic of the just dues to be given, as a standard or boundary of right, to every man by every Mason.

While performing his just duties, a Freemason is uniquely guided by principles of impartiality to act toward other men, women and children without regard to their race, religion, creed, or political beliefs. It is not for error in such beliefs or walks of life for which we chastise our brother (they are his beliefs and as such are his to hold), but for his intolerance of others and when he lacks charity toward all mankind.

Freemasons do not accuse fellow brethren for exercising a different philosophy. Rather, a lack of kindness to others is accused, as is a lack of sympathy, or a lack of integrity. Freemasons do not love their brethren because they think alike. Rather, brethren are loved simply because they are brethren. And, Freemasons do not return an unkind act with yet another – they restore troubled souls with compassion

Within the world itself, Freemasons are also expected to treat all human beings as brothers; especially those who are hateful, spiteful and wish everyone ill. Societies establish laws to guide the people who live within them. God establishes laws for all to follow, regardless of the society within which one lives. So, too, does Freemasonry extend it's "laws," or rather it's harmonious tenets, that every Mason may know that he is as much "at labor" outside of his lodge as he is when he is inside.

As Freemasons, we are also taught to regard the laws of the land in which we respectively live as deserving of our complete and unhesitating devotion. Thus, it is not for the Freemason to pick and choose which laws to follow, but to follow all of them and make equal application of them all. Masons are expected to act for the preservation of freedoms whether in the form of public education, or the selection of houses of worship, and to judge each other by the extent of charity freely given. When given in a great measure, the good it serves is limitless. The old are comforted, the ill healed, orphans have fathers, widows are not alone, and God's justice is meted out to every man, woman and child.

Chapter 86

WISDOM: THE FIRST GREAT PILLAR OF MASONRY

> "If any of you lack wisdom, let him ask God,
> that giveth to man liberally, and upbraideth not;
> and it shall be given him."
>
> Jas. 1:5

In Ancient Craft Masonry, wisdom is symbolized by the "East," the place of light, which is also represented in a lodge by a pillar that stands in the east as the great support of a lodge – the Worshipful Master. Wisdom is also represented in Masonic tradition by King Solomon, who prayed to God that above all things in His power to give, he most desired the wisdom God could provide. Therefore, wisdom is recognized in Freemasonry as divine power – the creative energy of Deity. In short, wisdom seeks, by observation, experience and reflection to know things in their essence.

The lessons in Freemasonry teach us that it is necessary for a man to learn wisdom so that he may contrive, in other words to create. Above all else, Masonry invites each of us to consider the dignity of human nature and to ponder the vast powers and capacities of the human soul. The opposites in the world challenge each of us, not to fathom why they exists as much as to support the one and defeat the other. Good health is promoted by Masonic hospitals while illness is chased away. Joy is brought into the life of an isolated widow who is honored at a luncheon, eliminating, even if only for an hour or two, the ravages of sorrow. Brethren rejoice in the success of each other and lend a listening ear when one brother is overwhelmed by failure and disappointment. Life is promoted while death is put in its place as nothing more than a translating event.

One seems never to know the true meaning what it is he or she has until it is lost. Too frequently, people fail to appreciate the wealth of meaning found in the fond sayings of a parent, a child, or a friend, until that parent, child, or friend is no longer alive. Yet, to the truly wise person, nothing that is sincerely loved is ever lost. Instead of counting absence as loss, the truly wise meditates upon the memories, using the mind to resuscitate the dead and to animate visions of the past.

True wisdom recognizes the fleeting nature of our earthly existence. Humans are mortal, but there is a spiritual part that never dies. Our lives are lived here on earth as we choose while eternity yawns before us. Amidst the unseen presence of our ever loving God, each man's mind gives him the character by which he may judge how well he has lived and how worthy he is of eternal life. If he is truthful to himself, the wise man knows he is unworthy, but that God's love has endured transforming him from a person in the dark to a luminous individual who lives in the light.

The wise man despises selfishness, apathy, indifference and inaction. It is these that make men and Freemasonry ineffectual, as if like the pyramids they were doting with age and had forgotten the memory of the best traits most admired in those who have before us.

To better embrace wisdom, a Freemason can seek to revive within himself those faded impressions of generosity and self sacrifice. No man can suffer and be patient, struggle and conquer, improve and be happy without first having hope and a complete reliance upon the beneficence of God. His beneficence teaches us that extending joy to others is the just return of the grace given to us. The wise man learns how to act toward others by clearly observing and imitating how the Great Creator acts toward him and all creation.

Chapter 87
CHASTITY

> "Neither shalt thou desire thy neighbor's wife,
> neither shalt thou covet thy neighbor's house, his
> field,...or anything that is thy neighbor's."
>
> Deut. 5:21

From time immemorial, one of the chief characteristics of Freemasonry has been its uncompromising demand for adherence by its members with the seventh and tenth Commandments as a matter of promoting personal purity. In a peculiar devotion, Freemasonry stands for the protection of the *chastity* of womanhood, as every Mason knows by virtue of the sacred vows he has assumed. The deeper meaning of those vows relates to the obligation it imposes upon each individual Mason to himself remain chaste.

This sacred vow requires putting into daily practice a life completely devoid of covetousness and indifference. Succinctly stated, living a chaste life means living in conformity with the spiritual law. When a person does so, he or she is regarded as being *chaste*. It is entirely irrelevant whether that man or woman is married or celibate.

Contrary to popular belief, the practice of chastity that is imposed upon Masons is not solely related to matters of sex. Rather, it bears equally on all other domains wherein there is a choice between light and darkness, good and evil. For example, fanaticism is a sin against chastity, because a fanatic is carried along in his or her path by a dark and violent current. The French Revolution, initiated on ground of justice, became an orgy of perverse collective intoxication, as did the revolution in Russia. Nationalism, whether rearing its head in Nazi Germany, or elsewhere around the globe, is similarly a form of collective intoxication drowning the conscience of the heart. Therefore, it is wholly incompatible with the state of chastity.

When a candidate for degrees in Freemasonry is brought from darkness to see the light by which Masons work, he is immediately introduced to the characteristic of chastity. The square and compasses remind us to circumscribe our desires and keep our passions within due bounds toward all mankind. That obligation also requires that a Mason avoid ever participating in the collective intoxication of fanaticism, to obey the laws of the country in which he resides and to conduct his affairs with all mankind in a just manner.

One can easily miss the significant point of chastity, if one fails to see that it is a part of the characteristic of charitableness. Along the Masonic journey, each Mason is taught to regard his fellow brother as another self. When a Mason or any other person does so, he or she is exercising chastity, in that he or she is acting in conformity with the spiritual law of doing unto others that which you would have them do unto you. Chastity, then, may be regarded as that state of being in which man is content with what God has given him, and being content, he is made whole.

Chapter 88

HARMONY: THE MUSIC OF MASONRY

> "I will sing of the mercies of the Lord forever:
> with my mouth will I make known thy
> faithfulness to all generations."
>
> Ps. 89

Freemasonry's archetypal definition of harmony — beauty, symmetry and order in matter and spirit — is best demonstrated by the rich and consistent application of beauty, symmetry and order in the world of music. Of all things to which we are daily exposed, bad music, unappealing music, or noisy music can rankle our nerves quicker than can an unkind remark by another person. Some people avoid attempting to play a musical instrument, or to sing a song, because they do not want to create an ugly sound. But, in the hands of a skilled musician, an instrument can be nearly brought to life filling the concert hall with the most melodious beauty, the most perfect symmetry and the most structured order that is referred to as harmony.

There exists a true relationship between Freemasonry and music. One published author has devoted an entire tome to that study, which he aptly entitled, "The Harmony of Spheres." The concept of planets and stars harmoniously filling the cosmos is like the harmonious mingling of tones which produce to the most vivid imagination an overwhelming sense of well being. Philosophers, astronomers and mathematicians have been duly inspired over the years by melodious musical harmonies, which in turn have provided mankind with a rich poetry and literature upon which men have meditated from times of antiquity to the present day.

Astronomy and harmonics, which is concerned with the movement of sounds, each employ arithmetic and geometry to measure the quality and quantity of principle movements. It is within both of those disciplines that one may discover Freemasonry's unique relationship to music, revealed in the writings of such Masonic patrons as Ptolemy and Pythagoras. Ptolemy proved heliocentricity by mathematics, while Pythagoras may have been the founder of music when he applied harmonics to geometric progressions to prove that all sound was based upon mathematics.

Everything that is governed by natural law partakes of some rational order with regard to its movement. Expanding upon his notions of a sun centered universe, Ptolemy applied mutually consistent disciplines of spatial symmetry to musical harmony and concluded in a posthumously published work that the movement of sound, like the movement of stars, is governed by certain harmonic relationships. Pythagoras applied his exceeding knowledge of mathematics to a study of conjunct tetra chords and octave ratios, reasoning that there is a special relationship between Freemasonry's sacred numbers 3, 5 and 7, and tonal consonance. That is, the numbers 3, 5 and 7 are essential to harmonious music. When those numbers are not present, the sound produced is ugly, chaotic and unstructured. Both Ptolemy and Pythagoras respectively inferred from their studies that harmonious music has a beneficial impact upon the human soul.

Masonic orders routinely employ music during their ceremonies. The connection to Freemasonry's rich mythical past is made plain: men with Masonic educations have applied the lessons of Freemasonry to discover that the harmonious intersection of melodious sound with splendid doctrine creates a harmonic power that feeds the soul with thoughts of loving kindness. Consequently, in order that a Mason might completely enjoy and understand the lessons offered in degree ritual, it is strongly recommended that each ceremony be accompanied by the playing of harmonious melodies.

Chapter 89

TRIUNE SYMBOLISM

"Therefore speak I to them in parables: because they seeing see not; and hearing not neither do they understand."

Matt. 13:13

Many of Freemasonry's most sublime truths are conveyed to us in veiled allegories and are made visible to us by the accompanying ancient symbols. The greatest of these, the "Lost Word," is concealed within various groups of three symbols, each group building upon the other to teach us the Masonic meaning of the word "trinity." Each group may be considered as a vehicle of information necessary to aid in the comprehensive struggle to learn about God, nature, the government of the universe and about the existence of sorrow and evil. After careful study and reflection, one may more specifically understand the "principle of First Cause" of all things – that which is often referred to as the "absolute," or "Word."

See, hear, and understand what Freemasonry says about trinity. Three pillars figuratively support a lodge: wisdom, strength and beauty. The Egyptians and Hebrews based their respective civil policies upon the wisdom of selected priests, the power and strength of civil chiefs, and the resulting harmonious prosperity of the State. The duration, or term of Masonic apprenticeship was three years, because the Ancient Mysteries required three years' preparation by a candidate before he could be initiated. The alarm at the door of a lodge is given by three raps. There are three moveable and three immoveable jewels; three principle officers in a lodge, three great and three lesser lights; three journeys by the candidate around the lodge; three questions put to the candidate prior to his admission into a lodge; three letters in the tetragrammaton of the Hebrews, or ineffable Word; and three syllables in the substitute for the "Lost Master's Word," which could be communicated only when King Solomon, Hiram, King of Tyre and Hiram Abif were all present.

In a more material fashion, the number three also represents unity and each group of veiled allegories demonstrates how the number three actually "forms one:" one lodge; one body of brethren; one "Word;" and, one God. Freemasonry teaches three theological virtues: faith, hope and charity – neither of which exists apart from the other two in the conduct of a Mason while fulfilling his duty to God, his country, and his neighbor.

Blue Lodge Freemasonry offers three degrees to worthy candidates, neither one of which can make a complete Mason without the other two. Those three degrees of Masonry are also a reflection of yet another truth: there are only three discrete "degrees" existing in the universe that are within man's perception and comprehension – the physical realm, intelligence and morality.

Freemasonry speaks in symbols and teaches the eternal principles of morality. The truths of its philosophy teach us what God and nature are, and what we are, and lift us into a sphere of intellectual independence and religious freedom. Toleration of diversity is one of Freemasonry's greatest "secrets." Without it, men of differing beliefs could never act in one brotherhood under the Fatherhood of one God, as Freemasonry has done always. Triune symbolism teaches us the certainty that God disinherits none of His children, but permits all to call Him Father.

Chapter 90

KNOWLEDGE – A MASONIC DUTY

*"Bow down thine ear and hear the words of the wise,
and apply thine heart unto my knowledge."*

Prov. 22:17

Freemasonry teaches that each man possesses a Divine and human nature, represented by the triangle. Human nature is depicted on one line of the triangle, the Divine on another and earthly matter on the third. Knowledge, or the relationship of each side of the triangle to each other side, is symbolized by light. Ignorance is symbolized by darkness. When a candidate for the various degrees of Freemasonry declares his desire to enter into the mysteries of Freemasonry "in search of the light," then later declares his desire to "search for more light," he literally means that he is there to acquire knowledge.

To learn, to attain knowledge, to be wise is a necessity for every truly noble soul. To teach, to communicate that knowledge to others is equally the impulse of a noble nature and the worthiest work of man. The monuments of genius and learning are more durable and lasting than the monuments to power. These maxims, as well as others found in Freemasonry encourage Masons not only to learn what has been set forth by our Masonic writers, but to also seek the light elsewhere.

Learning is a Mason's duty, because by acquiring knowledge man prepares himself to serve his neighbor, his brother, his family, his country and his God. To attain that which is unknown to others and to keep it locked tightly within our hearts is akin to place a lamp under a bed where it cannot shine. The noblest destiny of every Freemason is to take that lamp from beneath the bed and let it shine for others to see. What one man knows will likely prove helpful to another either to solve a personal problem or fathom a great philosophical expression.

Our Nations' Founding Fathers, several of whom also happened to be Freemasons, were mostly regarded as "Renaissance men," that is men who were learned in the arts and sciences. Diversity of knowledge was their character and the imprint of that diversity may be seen today in the symbolism associated with the original architecture in our Nations' capitol. Every culture, religious thought and ancient truth is commingled, memorialized and seamlessly blended. Search the obelisk that is the Washington Monument. Study the columns supporting the Capitol Building. Witness the grandeur on display at the several Smithsonian Museums. Each piece to the puzzle stands separately, but is seen as a whole and harmonious system.

Freemasons are not required, or even asked to become the smartest, brightest and best. Rather, Masons are simply taught the virtue and joy of learning. Each person progresses at a different pace, displays different interest, expresses different talents and contributes a piece to the puzzle that is eventually answered – "serve your brother with all your might, with all your heart and with all your soul."

Chapter 91
A Point

"For God,...commanded the light to shine out of the darkness."

2 Cor. 4:6

In Masonic teachings, a "point" is used to symbolically illustrate several truths. The point within a circle is intended to convey (1) the eternity of God, and (2) the circumscribed boundaries of one's behavior. When applied to the more esoteric concepts arising out of the study of geometry, the "point" alludes to a man's potential. Fellowcraft Masons are instructed that a point is the beginning of all geometrical matter. Rather than simply accepting that obvious fact, Freemasonry asks us to look deeper into the meaning of that symbolism.

Throughout the studies in Freemasonry, references to "above" and "below" repeat themselves. The manner in which the square and compasses is arranged within a lodge is a prime example: the square is pointed downward, or to the "below," while the compasses is directed upward, or at the "above." Hermeticism has long taught that the above" and "below" signify the conjoining of Divine will with human purpose. In Freemasonry, the most important goal to which a Mason aspires is to be entirely in sync with the Great Architect; to align human will with Divine will and thereby serve all mankind with the greatest loving kindness imaginable. In alchemy, that conjoining of wills constitutes the correct mystical blending of the infinite with the finite mind – the illumination of darkness with supernal light which has no beginning and no end.

While God endures forever and is not confined by the dimension of time, such is not so for man, who being a part of the material world has a material beginning and a material end. The "point" symbolically demonstrated in Freemasonry is also meant to imply that there is a starting point for man's understanding of and relationship with God. For some, it is at the knee of a devout parent; mother, or father. For others, it begins after years of ritualistic attendance at religious houses of worship. And yet for others still, the commencement of a relationship with God begins during the evolution of understanding that results from a prolonged exposure to Freemasonry. Regardless of the path, the result is usually the same: man begins an earthly journey in the light.

It is that light which enables man to see the truths lying in wait behind the various arrangements of symbols in Freemasonry. The greatest of these is the truth that there is life after physical death. Consider the "raising" in the Third Degree; contemplate upon its meaning and understand the truth it conveys. Freemasons are also informed from lessons in that degree that an acacia should remind us that we are each invested, by virtue of our creation, with a spirit or affinity that will never die.

Consider the potential, or starting point, illustrated by the Third Degree of Freemasonry. A Mason is free to abandon his personal point of view, to renounce his personal will at any time during his life and to feely follow the wisdom taught by the Supreme Architect of the Universe. A Mason truly has no greater obligation during his material lifetime.

Chapter 92

WHENCE CAME YOU?

"And behold, I propose to build an house unto the name of the Lord my God."

1 Kings 5:5

Masonic catechism replies to the question "Whence came you?" in the following manner: "From a Lodge of the Holy Saints John at Jerusalem." From the Jewish historian Josephus, we are informed that when he captured Judea, King David renamed the city "Jerusalem." As we also know, King Solomon's Temple, like the Tabernacle erected at Moses' command, was situated due east and west – a geography that lends revealing information about why the city was named "Jerusalem." Far from a mere historical lesson, the reason touches upon the essence of a specific belief system that delivered us Hiram, King of Tyre and Hiram Abif who together with Solomon are considered Freemasonry's first three Most Excellent Grand Masters.

The first known form of name for the renamed city was "Urushalim" – "uru," meaning "founded by," and the suffix "salem," or "Shalim," which is the name of the ancient Canaanite god of Venus in its evening setting. Interestingly, both Hiram of Tyre and Hiram Abif were Phoenicians and

Canaanites. Thus, the very name "Jerusalem" effectively means the place dedicated to Venus in her evening setting.

However, Solomon's Temple faced the opposite direction toward Venus rising in its role as "Morning Star." That is so apparently because of the importance of the Sun's symbolical association with the Divine. It is also true, because the "Shekinah," or presence of the Divine, was visible only in the east as a pre-dawn astronomical phenomenon. Astronomically, "Shekinah" represents the concurrence of Venus and Mercury, which is exceedingly rare and does not occur with mathematical precision.

Using state-of-the-art computer software, technicians have recently "dialed back" the time clock to learn what was present in the skies during certain notable events. Surprisingly, the "Shekinah" phenomenon was present on the dates attributed in history to the exodus of the Jews from Egypt; at the building of King Solomon's Temple; and, during the time attribute as the birth of Jesus.

The Ancients placed great religious significance upon Venus, variously describing the luminous planet as the manifestation of the female component of the Deity (an attribute arguably continued by the Catholic Church in its Story of Mary, the "Mother of God"), the symbol of fertilization, and the Light of Divine Glory. Ancient Canaanite worshippers, as well as Egyptian mystics and early Druidic societies astronomically "timed" the appearance of Venus' light in the eastern pre-dawn skies and calculated roughly 40 year intervals between the appearances. Coincidentally, the number "40" occurs exactly 40 times in the Holy Bible.

The Temple of Solomon was constructed with a dormer, that is a small window situated in a position whereby sunlight could be let inside the Sanctum Santorum. That light was also referred to as the "Shekinah" and shone upon the Ark of the Covenant, which remained inside the Holy of Holies until the Temple's complete destruction by invaders. Solomon adopted Hiram of Tyre's reverence for the Divine Light, secured it for Israel, and caused it to dwell in the Ark at Jerusalem. The lineage of that belief system traces itself directly to both Saint John the Baptist and Saint John the Evangelist – two eminent patrons of Freemasonry.

Chapter 93

THE PRINCIPLE OF BROTHERHOOD

"A man that hath friends must shew himself friendly: and there
is no friend that sticketh closer than a brother."

Prov. 18:24

The principle of brotherhood and the obligation of a distinct affection for fellow members are characteristics common to many fraternal organizations. Too often brotherly love is, in reality, treated as a mere abstraction, an indefinable something that is not truly practiced. In many instances, if it is practiced at all, the individuals involved are motivated by selfish interest, such as manipulating others to give aid, or to be made to feel guilty for refusing.

A candidate for degrees in Freemasonry, however, will likely discover that the tenets of brotherly love, relief and truth taught him are regarded by the Craft "Masonic ornaments," that is the sheer foundation of an institution built upon the great principle of love. The mode and manner of the practice of these principles is detailed in words which are illustrated in symbols so that there may be no cause for error in understanding, or failing to practice. No Mason is likely to forget the "Five Points of Fellowship" or the interesting incidents that accompany their explanation; and, as long as he is controlled by his knowledge and retains this memory, he is not likely to fail in his duties of brotherly love.

Benevolence is sometimes defined by other Masonic writers as the expression of goodwill to others which results in great deeds of kindness. It is prompted by the emotion of love inculcated in the divine command: "Thou shalt love thy neighbor as thyself." A benevolent disposition suffers uneasiness at the suffering of others, abhors cruelty under every guise and pretext and seeks to relieve those conditions. It becomes universal when it yearns for and strives to secure the welfare of all men – friends and enemies alike.

Freemasons are taught to look upon all mankind as having been formed by the one Great Architect of the Universe in a spirit of love and sympathy. They are also taught to discharge the duties of benevolence in the widest and most generous scope. Masonry is an internal principle intended to regulate outward conduct. Masons are encouraged to become essential – to work for the benefit of others, to labor for our neighbor's

best interest, to never become satisfied that we have given enough, but to pray for the strength to ceaselessly be a brother.

Chapter 94

IN UNITY

"Behold, how good and how pleasant
it is for brethren to dwell together
in unity."

Ps. 133:1

Freemasonry recognizes certain inalienable rights of men of every race, creed and religion to have different opinions about all of the vital issues of life, including, but certainly not limited to, the freedom of thought and liberty of conscience. Genuine unity in mind and heart, as well as in the noble purposes of Freemasonry, is urged upon Masons at all times. True brotherly love and fraternalism are cultivated and a community of interest among the brethren of the mystic tie is maintained at all times.

That tie emerges from the vows of eternal brotherhood professed at the altar by each Mason. It binds Masons to brotherhood regardless of race, religion, or social affiliations. Freemasonry's devotion to these, as well as other tenets of virtue, has remained steadfast throughout times of greatest stress, including the American Revolution and American Civil War. The voice of the Masonic leadership in each era resonated with urgings to work for peace, to stay law abiding, to be tolerant and to be free. Those Masons expressed a concern to their followers that remains relevant today: our greatest enemy does not approach from without, but from within.

In his entitled "The Fire from Within," Carlos Castenada writes: "Self importance is man's greatest enemy. What weakens him is feeling offended by the deeds and mis-deeds of his fellow man. Self importance requires that one spend most of one's life being offended by something, or by someone." Freemasonry promotes the virtue of considering every other brother as another self. When that state of existence is achieved, not only in the mind, but also in deeds, it is impossible for self-centeredness to survive. With the self as the focal point, one sustains the illusion that he or she is, in fact, his or her own body —an entity completely separate from all others. It is that sense of separateness that leads men to compete rather than cooperate with others.

It is essential that Freemasons maintain a strong self-concept and feel appreciated. One does not have to abandon himself altogether to also appreciate another brother as another self. Consider the fact that having achieved the state of looking upon others as another self when one does not treat himself very well – when one behaves badly, acts dishonestly, or engages in other destructive conduct. Unless the other person is offered honesty and virtuous treatment, he or she can do quite nicely without the attention.

A problem also arises when one misidentifies who he or she truly is by simply identifying himself or herself as a body shape, a body size, by the type of goods possessed, by the number of personal achievements gained, or by a personal dogma. Mankind's gravest conflicts and wars have resulted primarily from an insistence that one point of view was more accurate than any other.

Since Freemasons voice approval of such virtues as charity and justice, it is imperative that each Mason conduct himself consistent with love and fairness toward all whom they meet. When self importance spins its vicious web and disharmony results, if a Mason is present it becomes his indispensable duty to work to promote cooperation and compromise. When someone else states different it is important that the Mason hearing consider before responding that it is not necessary that he always be right regarding every subject abut which he, too, has an opinion. When a Freemason stops to contemplate how he has spent his life, if he has acted upon the lessons taught him, he would discover that he had served God with a purpose. And when all is said and done; when the soul returns unto God who gave it, the best reward of all would be to hear those gently words, "well done, my son – you have served my unity."

Chapter 95
THE FATHERHOOD OF GOD

> "So God created man in His own image, in the image of God created He him; male and female created He them."
>
> Gen. 1:27

Freemasonry teaches that man is the offspring of God by creation; that God made mankind to be of one blood; and, that God's fatherly love for man finds its greatest expression in His redemptive plan for "fallen humanity." Religions will disagree one with the other about the precise nature of that plan, but none dispute that a plan of redemption does, indeed, exist. Freemasonry stays away from such disputes and permits each member to lean upon the religious faith of his choice for further understanding about the plan of redemption. However, the lessons of Freemasonry temptingly lure us to ponder the deeper esoteric reason why God would care.

When all is said, we are truly a pitiful race. We kill each other; starve each other; permit poverty to weaken us decade after decade; and, we barely tolerate a neighbor who fails to see religious matters the same way we see them. Yet, in spite of our shortcomings, we are constantly informed that each one of us is God's special child.

Borrowing generously from ancient Hermetic thought, certain Masonic writers have postulated that God cannot help but love us, both the good and the bad, because we are one with Him. Some insist that the Divine and human intellect are identical; that what some refer to as the Holy Spirit actually lives in our minds, which some consider to be the seat of man's soul. This notion is not peculiar to Freemasonry and Hermeticism. In fact, the same sentiment can be seen in the writings of many so-called self-improvement authors, as well as in the writings of Albert Pike himself. Consequently, in that the notion is repeated throughout time and by men and societies of differing backgrounds and dogmas, it has begun to acquire a certain status of truthfulness among all men.

As Pike observed, "...all Light is one, so all Intellect and Reason being one; each Human Intellect a minute ray of the Infinite Intellect." [Pike: Lectures on Masonic Symbolism.] Can such thinking be merely the result of human vanity and conceit, or is there a further basis in truth for literally knowing that we are, each one of us, a part of God?

Justin Martyr, a Roman Catholic, wrote during the middle of the second century that the doctrine of the unity of God is above all other doctrines. Indeed, until Irenaeus wrote in the latter second century about the theology of dualism (God existing separately and apart from man), most of those who are referred to as the Ancient Fathers promoted the belief that God, the all-being cause and creator of everything, existed in the soul of man and acted as man's conscience. Literally, that meant that God and man were one, or at least of the same essence. The ramifications of such thinking are enormous and lend further credence to the lesson attributed to Jesus – that all men are capable of achieving the highest spiritual state of "sonship" with the Father.

Today, we often hear Masonic speakers refer to Freemasonry as, "A brotherhood of man under the Fatherhood of God." It matters not if you accept a Unitarian point of view, the concept of dualism, or even notions of pantheism (God existing in everything, everywhere). It only matters that you recognize the great truth that God is, and you are because He is. As such, you are no more important and no less important to God than is your neighbor.

The important duties you owe to God, your neighbor and yourself may be found in the "Volume of the Sacred Law" (Holy Bible). When read often, it reveals how essential it is for each of us to be forgiving, nurturing, tolerant and loving. When any of those virtues are lacking in us as individuals, others with whom we have contact are deprived of intercourse with God. Indeed, when those virtues are lacking in us, we contribute darkness rather than light to mankind's collective soul and fall short of fulfilling our Masonic vows.

Chapter 96

HUMILITY OF THE MIND

"Before destruction the heart is haughty.
And before honor is humility."

Prov. 18:12

The Holy Writings teach us that all is vanity and in so doing enlighten us to the fact that worldly pleasures are fleeting and end in emptiness. A thoughtful man who considers his life's toil cannot help but reflect upon what he has wrought, what works he has accomplished, and what treasures he has accumulated. One preacher and sage observed that when he looked at all of the work of his own hands and considered the extent of his own labor, he actually saw that all was vanity and vexation of spirit – that nothing that he had wrought on his own profited him anything of lasting value.

The various rituals employed in Freemasonry teach us that all brethren should maintain freedom from pride and arrogance. It is most destructive to view oneself as wisest, most faithful, most industrious and more important as a result of a more talented nature. The good seed of harmony spread by others is thereby choked by the weeds of our own self importance. Freemasonry's ritual also teaches how much can be gained by relying upon others to also exert their unique and equally important talents; how society is so much more benefited by the working together of multiple hands and minds. The initiate for Masonic degrees does not conduct himself around the lodge room – he is assisted by others. He observes not only one pillar in the lodge – he sees no less than three. The administration of a lodge is not committed to the care of one man – a line of officers work together for the greatest good of the whole.

The first step toward acquiring any truth is to adopt a humble mind, a sense of personal ignorance, and a thirst for knowledge to use for the benefit of ourselves and others. We live in an age of ever increasing fanaticism, intolerance and rage seemingly driven by an unrelenting and crazed certainty on the part of the fanatics that they alone act in the name of God. It is the height of vanity for anyone to presume that his or her perception of God constitutes the sole and complete truth; that others who disagree are so subhuman as to deserve a swift and vengeful demise.

The well known Masonic writer, Albert Pike, once observed that, (T)he Mason does not dogmatize, but entertaining and uttering his own convictions, he leaves everyone else free to do the same; and only hopes that the time will come, even if after the lapse of ages, when all men shall form one great family of brethren, and one law alone – the law of love – shall govern God's whole universe." [Pike: Magnum Opus.] The correct path is pointed to in the first of God's Ten Commandments delivered by Moses to the Hebrews: "...thou shalt have no other gods before me." That directive may only be accurately understood by a humble heart and mind, a spirit so subdued to God's will as to faithfully know that He created everything, not simply some things, and that He loves everyone, not just some, regardless of the religion they adopt, or chose not to adopt. When we sincerely believe that He wishes all, not merely some, to live in complete peace and harmony, we have, indeed, taken the required first step toward attaining "truth."

The prayer spoken by a humble mind does not presume that the Great Architect is like Santa Claus – someone to be called upon only when we wish Him to do something for us. Rather, the prayer spoken by the humble mind seeks to know God, to be like God and to serve His will by knowing His knowledge – the knowledge of brotherly love and affection.

Chapter 97

THE FAITHFUL SERVANT

*"When thou vowest a vow unto God, defer not to pay it;
for He hath no pleasure in fools; pay that which
thou hast vowed."*

Eccl. 5:4

All Freemasons are required to be steadfast in keeping the vows of the Order. That is so, among other reasons, because Masons are expected to be sincere in the practice of all the virtues taught by the ritual, symbols and lectures. Masons are further expected to maintain unflinching loyalty to the fraternity in the manner of a faithful servant.

A faithful servant is one who keeps his vows, is diligent in his stewardship, behaves dutifully to his Master and remains loyal in the face of trial and tribulation. In the explanation of the ritual used in the Entered Apprentice Degree, faith is said to be the first rung of the theological ladder employed in Masonic education. Trust in God is required and is accordingly emphasized in each of the three degrees of Freemasonry. That trust constitutes the basis of true character and service, and thus demands a belief in something beyond ourselves, beyond science and beyond our capacity to know anything at all for certain.

Masonic ritual continually verifies the virtues of faith and trust and teaches Masons everywhere to conform their personal conduct accordingly. Candidates for Masonic degrees are blindfolded, not for the purpose of frightening them, but to teach them a valuable lesson about trusting in one who is there to guide. In the Entered Apprentice Degree, the candidate is reminded to fear not what man can do unto him, but to exercise faith that the brother guiding him will not permit him to suffer harm.

The lessons about faith and trust are not intended to remain limited to placing such in the hands of a brother. They are also intended to teach the candidate, as well as the Freemason already arrived at his Master Mason status, to permit God to lead him throughout life. One of the first questions asked of a candidate is in whom he places his trust. The response is one of the most important vows made in a Mason's career: the vow the trust in God.

The manner in which Freemasons respond to their duty to their country, their neighbor, their families and themselves evidences the true extent of their faith. How a Freemason responds to calamity, misfortune, ill fortune and the reality of his own death demonstrates the extent of steadfastness he possesses. The true measure is what others may see in the response – not what is intended, but what is actually done by the man himself. One may have the best intentions about how to behave and fall short when the time to perform arrives. To so fail is part of human nature. Theology refers to such conduct as "sin," because it is conduct that separates man from God. Yet, to fail means to have tried. And, having once tried, to try again and again and yet again without ever losing faith that the trust in God will eventually erode much of what makes us fail.

It is within our human nature to be fearful, doubting and questioning about our own faith. Man searches frequently for proof of the truth about that which he is asked to believe. That, too, is human nature. Yet, when Jesus was asked by the masses for a "sign," he responded by stating that the generation would receive nothing more than the sign of Jonah. What was meant by that saying was that man will repeatedly find that God helps him, that God is always present when He is called upon and that He will ever be a faithful servant to His Creation. We are merely asked to believe that to be true – to exercise faith and trust, which require each of us to rise above our human nature and satisfy our souls that God is truth and that nothing we have ever attained in a secular education has ever disproved His love for us.

Chapter 98

ADVERSITY

"Rejoice with them that do rejoice: weep with them that weep."

Rom. 12:15

Times of ill fortune or destitution, whether of the purse or the soul, touch the lives of every Freemason, his family and friends. It is, indeed, the mystery of this earthly existence that all mankind is destined to suffer, not because the Great Architect has willed us pain, but that we should learn important lessons about life. Poverty, ill health, times of war, moments of self doubt, persecution, fear and death itself extends ugly tentacles and threaten to grip us is a vice of depression. We have, each one of us, experienced the very best, as well as the very worst that life has to offer. Along the way we have learned that the best hope we have in coping with the very worst is the love and comfort of our families, our friends and our Masonic brethren.

Masonic tradition teaches us that such adversity must be accepted cheerfully as a test of our character and met head on with prayer and courage. We are also taught to go to the aid of a brother who is in the grasp of despair and to seek out other brethren when we ourselves are in need of comfort. Yet, to do so we must first know our brother.

A brother neglected is never truly known. A brother who is not forgiven his faults and errors does not truly exist. A brother upon whom we have turned our backs is not permitted entry into our lives. If giving and receiving comfort in times of adversity is a Masonic characteristic, Masons must often meet with their brothers, frequently speak with their brethren and easily forgive a brother a real or imagined trespass.

Anger, disharmony, or pain suffered as a result of past injustices too often influences a man to forsake another, for one brother Mason to ignore another worthy brother. When we allow such evils to separate us, who will be there to rejoice when we rejoice, or to weep when we weep?

Doubt not that such evils exist, even within the halls of a Masonic lodge. Cain first struck his brother killing him on the spot. That one uncontrolled departure from brotherly love resulted in the separation of two brothers forever. Instead of prospering and living a life full of loving emotion, Cain was compelled to wander the earth with a burning conscience. Yet, that story from the Holy Bible is but one example. History will not soon forget the holocausts, the infanticides, or the incessant march of men filled with hate from one generational war to the next.

Healing begins at home with each man's God, his family and his worthy brother Mason. If you harbor ill will against anyone for any past slight, wrong, injury, or injustice, try to be the first to pick up the telephone and call that brother. Time is running out and you may never again have the chance.

The time will come when we shall all meet again in that Great Celestial Lodge above where no man is less than any other, except the one who failed to forgive his brother. Forgiveness is a divine virtue, for every day God forgives us much, or He would not permit us to live. Prepare for the adversity to come by forgiving the brother in front of you. You will need his comfort, as he will need yours.

Chapter 99

HISTORY VS. MYTH

> "The sun shall be no more than the light by day;
> neither for brightness shall the moon give light unto thee
> but the Lord shall be unto thee an everlasting light, and thy
> God thy glory."
>
> Is. 60:19

It has been said that one of the fallacies of conventional scholarship is to insist on a rigorous and artificial distinction between history and myth. According to that distinction, "history" is regarded as documented fact, or data that will withstand assorted tests and scientific scrutiny and prove that something actually happened. On the other hand, "myth" is routinely dismissed as irrelevant, or incidental to history. Too often, "myth" is consigned to the realm of fantasy, poetry and fiction. When compared to the acceptance of history as fact, "myth" is relegated to the low rank of being a spurious embellishment, or falsification of fact. Yet, many of the most educated of the "Ancients" drew no distinction whatsoever between the two, more often than not simply referring to both as accurate recollections of past events.

Events described in the Old Testament of the Holy Bible, such as the parting of the Red Sea, or God meeting Moses face-to-face to give him the Law, are held by many people today to be mythical stories. But, there are also many who believe those same events actually occurred. In truth, there is much that is referred to as history that simply cannot be proven to have occurred. For example, the "facts" allegedly recorded by the great Jewish historian, Josephus, are littered with inaccuracies owing primarily to the inclination of Josephus to reflect a specific bias, or perspective about the politics and culture of his age. Most historians of that same era, as well as throughout later generations sought to convey how they respectively saw the events unfolding around them without regard to the truth of the recorded facts. Those "histories" are clearly biased and inevitably falsify or distort what actually transpired. For example, speculation surrounding the events leading to the assassination of President John F. Kennedy, or even the actual whereabouts of rock star, Elvis Presley, is variously couched as either historical or mythical depending upon who is telling the story.

Inquirers after Masonic truths have for ages vainly attempted to separate and distinguish history from myth as the two schools apply to the beginnings of Ancient Craft Freemasonry. Some of Masonry's most learned men continue to debunk one author, or another, because a particular work is not actually "history," but merely unproven "myth." Yet, in so doing, Masonry's greatest minds unwittingly tend to deprive the rest of us from a specific form of "light" and threaten to leave unread valuable information that may actually assist us to understand what Freemasonry truly means to the world, as well as to its individual members. If the Ancient Craft is nothing more than the sum total, or result of a sudden eruption upon the world scene in 1717, how do we account for the numerous rich symbolic stories, legends and "histories" about the glorious Temple of King Solomon? Why does Freemasonry devote entire degrees to Moses? Why do the twelve tribes of Israel play such a significant role in the organization and conduct of Masonic Lodge meetings? And, why do we continue to demonstrate a resurrection of the soul as a part of our Masonic ritual?

Historians have never interviewed the deceased to actually record how each is faring after life on Earth, yet all Masons fiercely believe in an afterlife. History has neglected to record where God came from, what He is doing, or why He cares anything at all for mankind. Yet, Masons express a zealous belief in His existence. In other words, there is much that Freemasonry claims to "know" to be true for which there is no recorded history. Indeed, much of what is "known" is informed by the soul of man – matters of faith that some would refer to as fantastic, imaginary, wishful thinking, or "mythical."

Much that is written about Freemasonry qualifies as myth, but it should neither be rejected outright, nor adopted as having actually occurred without a critical review. All that is written is intended to inspire, to influence the heart and soul, and to spark a thirst for more Divine Light. Just as the workmen at the Temple of Solomon initially threw away the stone that would prove most valuable to the construction of the edifice, we risk so doing if we reject one form of information in favor of another. It is more likely the case that the spirit that resides within each of us knows the difference and can be trusted to teach us the truth.

Chapter 100

Two Things Worth Living For

*"The labor of the righteous tendeth to life;
the fruit of the wicked to sin."*

Prov. 10:16

Writers about Freemasonry have told us that there are but two things worth living for: to *do* what is worthy of being written, and to *write* what is worthy of being read. The greater of these is the *doing*. No matter how magnificent and noble an act an author can describe, or the artist paint, it is far nobler for one to go and do that which one describes, or be the model which the other draws. In other words, when we pause to look within ourselves to assess how well we are doing in living life, the standard by which every Freemason measures his past, present and future worth is his work and the example he sets for others to follow.

Freemasonry teaches that contributing to the best interests of our fellow man is the noblest work of mankind. In the great Providence of God, in the great ordinances of our being there is opened to every man a sphere for the noblest action. More often than not that sphere is not of extraordinary heights. Rather, it is borne of the exemplification of extraordinary virtues displayed during an ordinary life. It arises most often during times of silence and seclusion, in wearing sickness without complaint, displaying sorely tried honesty that asks no praise and privately yielding advantage to another.

It is natural that all men should desire distinction. But those who seem happiest are those who seek to develop beauty. Such is the true harmony of the universe. Here below, each Mason has a work to do in himself greater than any work of genius; a work upon a nobler material than marble, or stone – a work to be created and completed upon his soul and intellect.

A great author or artist only portrays what man should do, both virtuous and commended to our mutual admiration and imitation. Yet, the practical realization of the great ideals of art include the exercise of love, piety, truth and all that is right. They are displayed in the daily routine of ordinary lives and survive as testaments to the true character of a Freemason.

Duty is always with us and forbids idleness. To work with the hands or brain according to each person's skill and capacity is more honorable that either title, or privilege. When one considers the world in its primitive creation, it is easier to understand that God was wise to give us a dark mass with which to work; an empty canvass upon which to draw the character of man's existence. Mankind is, therefore, taught and encouraged to create as God creates, to love as He loves and to add beauty to His beautiful bounty.

When time has finally run its course and we conclude this wondrous journey on earth, among our survivors who will honor the memory of the riches we have accumulated? Who will recall that we lived a life of luxury? Who will want to recount the deeds of treachery that drove us to the top? Such things are but vanity and will wash away in our dust. But that which we do for others will live forever.

Chapter 101

THE MYSTERY OF CREATION

"The heavens declare the glory of God: and the firmament sheweth His handiwork."

Ps. 19:1

Freemasonry recognizes one great "Creative Architect" in the origin of the world and the vast expanse of solar and planetary systems. For each individual Mason, the Earth and the heavens are living symbols of God's own handiwork and declare his glory. The mysteries of creation revealed in the various symbols of Freemasonry are the foundation for each Mason's personal relationship with our Divine Creator.

From time immemorial, our Ancient Craft has accepted the account of creation recited in the Old Testament of the Holy Bible as the revealed truth of God. Rather than constituting a literal truth, the story told is a symbolic recitation Masons may ponder while meditating more deeply upon the infinite nature of the Supreme Architect of the Universe.

At several points during the history of the world, men of various intents and purposes have hijacked the purity of such religions as Judaism, Christianity and Islam to impose a man-made interpretation of God's creation. To Hermetic Christians, this exercise of power by man is an exercise of the power taught by the serpent to Eve in the Garden of Eden, a theme that was repeated later in the Old Testament in the story about the Tower of Babel. Each of those religions has spawned numerous sects each in turn attempting to explain God's infinite wisdom and power using only man's very limited finite knowledge.

To the contrary, Freemasonry adheres to the notion that such shortcuts in thinking inhibits and confines the true essence of our indefinable Creator and God. Even certain scientific thought, most notably Einstein's "theory of relativity," concludes that creation is not entirely subject to human explanation. Similarly, philosophers such as Plato have also concluded that human intellect alone is incapable of fully understanding the infinite windings of creation. Religious doctrines seek to fill the void left by the inadequacies of science and philosophy, as does Freemasonry, by inculcating a belief that the truth about the infinite can only be fully discovered and appreciated through faith.

As the purer religions of Judaism, Christianity and Islam once did, Freemasonry turns to certain symbols that reveal specific truths about the heavens and Earth. It is not by accident that Masonry interprets a special relationship among the twelve (12) sons of Jacob and the twelve (12) signs of the Zodiac where the planets are domiciled at various times throughout each year. For example, the Zodiacal lion called "Leo" (whose constellation resides with the Sun – Masonry's singular symbol of sovereign authority) relates to the Tribe of Judah. During Masonic ritual, Masons are taught the significance of the "strong grip of the lion's paw."

Similarly, Freemasonry has discovered that astronomy offers further proof of the resurrection and renewal of life in the seasonal activities occurring in the heavens. In late December of each year, the Sun recedes to its lowest point in the heavens, there to remain for three days before beginning its gradual ascent to its highest point in late June. This phenomena was interpreted by many of the Ancients as a Divine revelation that death (symbolized by the winter season) yields to renewed life (symbolized by the spring and summer seasons).

In much the same vein, Freemasonry teaches, through its use of selected symbols about creation, that the true "Temple," or inner spirit of man, is in a process of constant construction. Masons are instructed that the Supreme Architect of the Universe, having once dwelled at the Temple of King Solomon, now dwells in the Temple's true successor – the heart and soul of each man, woman and child. Because none of us are perfect beings, Masons believe that mankind is in a constant condition of refinement through the lessons of honor and virtue. In other words, mankind is in a perpetual state of creation that will never die.

Chapter 102

THE AWAKENING

"O dry bones, hear the word of the Lord."

Ez. 37:4

From beginning to end, the rituals of Freemasonry symbolize and teach the doctrine of man's immortality and repute every iota of the doctrine of annihilation at death. This doctrine is at the core of the lessons taught in the Third Degree. A Mason's understanding about death is accompanied with no gloom, because he comprehends the truth that death is physical sleep for an unknown period of time, from which will spring an awakening of the body and a resurrection of the soul. Yet, as is so with all Masonic symbols, this, too, has other meanings for Masons to ponder.

In the Book of Genesis found in the Holy Bible, God and the serpent each have their say about life and death. One the one hand, God said, "Do not eat the fruit of the Tree of Knowledge, or you will die." On the other hand, the serpent told Eve, "That is ridiculous, you won't die." Here, it is important to understand whether or not the serpent simply lied to Eve, or committed fundamental error due to his misunderstanding. Stated differently, did the serpent actually state a truth found within the range of truths proper to his domain? Thus articulated, we are asked to consider whether or not there are two immortalities at issue in the Book of Genesis, as well as two different deaths – one from God's perspective and another from the serpent's point of view.

Our scant empirical experience with death reveals that it is the disappearance from the physical plane of other living beings. But, there are other disappearances within the physical plane which we call "forgetfulness," or "lack of knowledge." A core lesson taught by Freemasonry relates to the importance of knowledge to the welfare of every Mason. Therefore, even the symbolism of the resurrection should also be considered in that context, as well as in the more traditional context of immortality. In the whole of our experience, "forgetting," "sleeping," and "death" are three different manifestations of the same thing – disappearance.

One forgets, one goes to sleep, and one dies.

One remembers, one awakens, and one is born.

In addition to intellectual forgetfulness, there is also forgetfulness within the domain of the soul. An absence of faith, hope and charity shrivels the soul and darkens the spirit, moving man from the light to the darkness. Thus, it is the thoughts of the divine (symbolized by faith, hope and charity) which actually raise the consciousness of the human soul and propel it to work. Without charity, the soul is dead even though the organism within which it resides continues to breathe. It is reduced to animal and mineral qualities and bears little affinity or resemblance to that Supreme Intelligence which pervades all nature and which will never, never, never die.

Freemasonry asks each Mason to evaluate death by asking this question, "What do I myself really know about death?" That evaluation requires the use of one's memory, which is either mechanical, or moral. Moral memory is more effective, because it does not link the present to the past on a physical plane, as does mechanical memory. Rather, it links ordinary consciousness to spiritual consciousness – what is below to what is above – which is the source of our certainty about God, as well as our own immortality. Masons are taught to use their memories not merely for the purpose of regurgitating in their proper order the various words used in ritual, but to also teach the valuable lesson of expanding memory to different planes to attain a greater spiritual awareness about his own relationship to God and the universe.

Chapter 103

THE SABBATH

> "And God blessed the seventh day and sanctified it; because
> that in it He had rested from all His work which God created and made."
>
> Gen. 2:3

Throughout Masonic ritual, especially the ritual of the Fellowcraft degree, the Divine appointment of one day of rest is firmly acknowledged. For the Hebrews, the Sabbath, or day of rest, was also a day of devotion to God during which no menial work was to interfere with meditations upon His greatness. In its esoteric context, the Sabbath represents something more; something essential to a world filled with grace.

Three historical personalities have vividly portrayed the idea of what is known as the "cosmic wheel," also known to Masons as the point within a circle. They are Gautama Buddha, King Solomon and Friedrich Nietzsche. Buddha saw the "cosmic wheel" as an open circle, or as Masons will recognize, a spiral staircase from which birth, death and suffering can pass into the soul's center of rest. Solomon saw the "cosmic wheel" as inexorable fate rendering vain all human hope and endeavor – the emptiness of the world which can only be filled by God. Nietzsche saw and understood the "cosmic wheel" as a fully contained universe with no outlet — a world of eternal repetition into which no new light could shine. Nothing can be added to, or taken from Nietzsche's world. It is infinite and determinable; literally a world without God. However, in the world of both Buddha and Solomon, we notice something much different.

Although Solomon preached sadness and despair as man's lot in material existence, something inside of him defined a deliverance from woe long before Christians hailed Jesus as the Messiah. So, too, did Buddha, as well as the Hebrews themselves when they instituted the Sabbath at Moses' instruction. By the exercise of the Divine wisdom granted him by God, Solomon believed that the material world was spatial and consisted also of an as yet uncreated part. That belief was based upon Solomon's wise perception that God's infinity had a place in the already created finite world as a continuous realm of creation. That uncreated part is symbolized by one day of rest, or the Sabbath, which in Solomon's interpretation was the opening in the "cosmic wheel" — the path by which miracles occur and new life is created.

The worlds of Buddha and Solomon can be transformed. Nietzsche's cannot. A closed circle implies that there is nothing new under the sun; a cosmic hell. An open circle implies that there is an entrance and an exit to this world and that there is no eternal prison. Solomon believed that God was not unknowable, but rather knowable through the exercise of inexhaustible infinite knowledge. That is precisely why he encouraged his constituents to study, research, build and unceasingly work. The concept that we may, each one of us, come to know God's infinity is the very essence of the eternal neverending Sabbath, symbolized for us as the seventh day of creation. The Sabbath is laden with possibilities of new beginnings, new causes, new journeys and new endings. From it energies can be added to the so-called constant quantity of the phenomenal world, just as energies of this world can disappear in it.

Like Solomon's constituents, Masons are also taught the value of an unceasing search for knowledge, not solely to acquire learning, but to use it to the greater glory of our Creator, as much as to the welfare of our fellow creatures. As Masons, we understand what our Most Excellent Grand Master knew: the open circle in the "cosmic wheel" means that we will always have something new to learn.

Chapter 104
FEAR AND INJUSTICE*

"Love ye therefore the stranger: for ye
were strangers in Egypt."

Deut. 10:19

*[This article originally appeared soon after the 9/11 attacks in New York]

In this hour our Nation cries out for the soothing touch of Masonic values necessary to fill a terrible void resulting from a horrific fear that engulfed all who watched newscasts repeating with numbing regularity the awful sight of jumbo jets piloted by men with wicked intent tearing into New York's highest landmarks and sending them crashing to the ground as though they had never before stood in their place. In the aftermath, the people were left in stunned confusion fearing that others in their midst also intended immediate harm and acts of evil. As the reporters around the globe scanned the emerging pictures of those who piloted the planes, repeated their names and read their biographies, entire communities began to fear anyone among them who looked like the evildoers, or shared similar sounding names. Soon, reports about unwarranted harassment of such people flowed across the various news wires, as Americans everywhere tried to cope with thoughts of shadowy enemies stalking this great nation. It is a new age event, but sadly it is also an old age phenomena.

This attack was not the first on America. Our history is checkered with similar episodes with hateful events resulting in reservations for Native Americans, internment camps for American Japanese, horrifying lynching's of African Americans and the destruction of lives and careers during the era of "McCarthyism." Neither is this the first time Freemasons have been reminded of their duty when faced with such widespread community fears. Grand Masters from numerous states orated at the outset of our Civil War about mankind's need to pause and reflect. Brother Franklin Delano Roosevelt called upon a nation beset with unsettling uncertainty during the Great Depression to endure and thrive, boldly declaring during one of his famous fireside chats, "we have nothing to fear but fear itself."

Freemasonry echoes the same sentiment which derives from the essence of its ritual, educational literature and personal experiences in fraternalism. Our fraternity has witnesses the scourge of persecution prompted by fear. Masons should know that fear begets intolerance and that in turn intolerance begets tyranny. Throughout history, Masons have stood witness to injustice, torture and death inflicted upon mere whim, or because people thought differently, dressed differently, spoke differently, or worshipped differently. Freemasonry feels the pain of the generations of human beings who struggled mightily against oppression. Some tasted only a gruesome death as their earthly reward. These are the true enemies of mankind. Like the shadowy terrorists lurking in darkened caves and tunnels, they, too, lurk in the darkest recesses of a fearful heart.

It is said that no man is entirely without fear all of his life. Sooner or later all men become afraid of something. Masons have been provided working tools with which to combat any fear that may threaten to overwhelm. They are taught to practice charity toward everyone, not just those with whom they best get along. They are also instructed to circumscribe unruly desires and keep passions within due bounds, not only toward those whom they like, but also toward those whom they may not even know. Masons are expected to render justice universally, to extend mercy freely and to compassionate every man's misery. They do not promote fear and suspicion, but act to bring all such fears into the light that in knowing the source man is prepared to chase away such demons. In the military terms of our age, these are a few of the "smart bombs" that can be launched in man's battle against ignorance, intolerance and fear.

In the same manner in which our monumental buildings have become targets of terrorism, so too have our moral values. If we acquiesce in the unjust treatment of our neighbors simply because we fear their names, their religion, or their place of origin, we have been defeated by hatred, anger and fear. The Holy Writings make clear to us that it is far easier for man to love his friend than to embrace his enemy. Freemasons are not given an option – love thy neighbor means exactly that regardless of who or what is your neighbor.

Throughout history bigotry and hatred habitually filled the void left when a whole society permitted itself to wallow in fear. Recall the tales from that period of time known as The Inquisition. Recall how in the 20th Century an entire people were led to believe that annihilation of the Jews was necessary, proper and moral. Recall how educators, politicians and business leaders were demonized because they once inquired about communism. Such is the result of cowardice, weakness and fear. Masons must do better. The fraternity must rise above the mob mentality, reacquaint itself with its values and lead the march toward justice for all, not just those whom we do not fear.

The Masonic mission in this hour is clear: in words and deeds Freemasons must stand united in the renunciation of unfair harassment of any man, woman, or child solely on account of one's name, place of origin, color, or religion. When the voice of bigotry is heard in the streets, the Masonic voice of unity must rise higher. When hatred bubbles to the surface in social intercourse, Freemasons must openly plant seeds of kindness. When one person suffers unjustly in the presence of a Mason, the entire Craft has failed.

By doing your duty when the going gets rough, a Freemason not only lives his values, he demonstrates that his moral fiber is tough, sturdy, resilient and unbending. Stay strong, my brothers, for this, too, shall pass and our fraternity will be scrutinized by others intent upon showing to the world that Freemasonry is hypocritical – that it stands for values it does not practice. Your oaths and vows demand that you never allow that to happen.

Chapter 105

THE FIRST GREAT LIGHT

"...I have found the book of the law
in the house of the Lord..."

2 Kings 22:8

The symbols studied in Freemasonry reveal the many truths surrounding the concept of the Trinity and, among other ways, conceal them within the number "3." The number "3" may at some times represent the Triune God, at others the three states of harmony, and yet on other occasions the three primary "trunks" of the Tree of Life. Equally central to Masonic thought are what is termed the "Three Great Lights of Masonry;" the Holy Bible, square and compasses. The first and greatest of those lights is the Holy Bible, or as is often said, "The Holy Writings."

Freemasonry does not promote any one formal religion or belief system over any other and therefore tolerates the use of Holy Writings other than the Holy Bible. The Torah and Koran are excellent examples. If at any time the Craft of Freemasonry concludes that one book is more fully inspired than any other, Masonic Law provides that is sufficient reason for selecting the one found to excel. In most American, English and European lodges, the Holy Bible is selected. In California, regardless of which Holy Writings are selected, the Holy Bible must also appear alongside upon the altar.

Many, if not most symbols used in Masonry are taken directly from the scriptures contained in the First Great Light, or Holy Bible. The virtues and morals promoted by Freemasonry are also interpreted from its teachings. As such, the Holy Bible is regarded as the symbolic revelation of the very Word of God, which if ever lost will leave mankind in utter darkness.

In Masonic ritual, the brethren are also taught that if the Word of God is ever lost, it is an absolute Masonic duty to recover it through arduous research, intimate inquiry, meditation and prayer. Indeed, a significant part of Masonic ritual emphasizes the fact that even though the Word of God is available in the form of the Holy Bible, if man determines never to read its pages, the Word is as good as lost, for it is never learned. Therefore, the Masonic duty referred to is one of consistent reading of the scriptures and prayerful reflections upon their meaning.

The loss of the Word of God may also be viewed in an historical context, which further veils the concept of divinely radiated truth. Certain Masonic ritual reveals that during the so-called Babylonian Captivity, the Torah and scriptures were lost to the Hebrews, but was later discovered when they returned to Jerusalem and commenced construction of the Second Temple. Paulinian Christianity teaches that the Word, present to the world in the person of Jesus, was again lost when Jesus was crucified only to be yet again rediscovered through the inspiration of the Holy Spirit. Other Masonic ritual further incorporates this same notion of loss in the portrayal of that celebrated artist who was murdered.

In each instance, the inescapable lesson for every man is to pursue the truth with fervency and zeal. Among Masons, the adequacy of that pursuit is measured by the extent to which the individual progresses from initiation through full development in the mysteries of Freemasonry. The Holy Bible, or First Great Light, is the definitive symbol of Divine Truth. The system of belief each man selects as his "religion" will dictate for him how he will interpret that truth. Freemasonry asks its members to understand that all such systems of belief have some merit and therefore should be studied to enable the individual Mason to synthesize and in so doing to assist the spiritual evolution of all mankind.

Chapter 106
SECRECY AND SILENCE

*"Even a fool, when he holdeth his peace,
is counted wise: and he that shutteth
his lips is esteemed a man of
understanding."*

Prov. 17:28

Contrary to popular belief, Freemasonry is not a secret society though it has been railed against as such during various periods of volatility in world history. Neither does it seek to conceal its existence from the rest of the world. The names of the membership may be known to all who are interested. Every state within the Nation has a Grand Lodge of Freemasonry and a website on the Internet. One need simply make a keystroke and there you have before your own eyes a full display of all who proudly wear the honor of being a Freemason. Too, many Freemasons wear easily identifiable jewelry as a further display of their membership in that honorable institution. The element of secrecy applies solely to the ritual used in the degrees of Freemasonry, the manner in which one brother Mason may know another, and to the interpretations of the various symbols and legends made use of during Masonic education. The tenets and truths that Masonry teaches are as open to the world as though Masonic meetings were town hall events rather than carefully "tiled" (carefully secured) events.

Yet, even though it is not a secret society, Freemasonry does regard secrecy and silence as necessary safeguards against those who wish to bring down the fraternity. To speak of such is not at all paranoid when one pauses to recall that a king and a pope conspired to burn Masonic ancestors at the stake and wipe them from the face of the earth. Precisely why that occurred is not the topic of this article, but it is illustrative of the reason secrecy and silence enjoys a place of respectability in the Order. Perhaps equally important is the fact that Freemasonry instructs in the same manner as one would pursue a comprehensive study of mathematics. Before one can comprehend algebra, he or she must learn to add and subtract. For a period, algebra is "concealed" until the proper building blocks are in place to insure that the best chance to learn the truth about algebra is present.

The improper use of certain Masonic "secrets" by the uninitiated could seriously detract from the fraternity's message about charitable brotherhood, undermine the credibility of the many truths embodied in fraternal doctrine and unjustly injure the reputations of hundreds of thousands of virtuous brethren. Therefore, while an uninitiated person may justifiably inquire about the origins of Masonry and its virtues (some writers have alluded to the actual discovery of early Masonic scrolls containing great truths about God that lie hidden beneath the floors of King Solomon's Temple, pointing to those discoveries as the genesis for adopting secrecy and silence), the wisdom for demanding secrecy and silence for certain matters is indisputably correct.

By requiring the exercise of secrecy and silence about the mysteries of the Order, Freemasonry follows principles that were in place in all of the ancient mysteries and systems of worship of the Deity. The Egyptian and Judaic priestly orders are excellent examples. In Ancient Egypt, no "profane" was ever permitted into the ceremonies that instructed men about the resurrection of the dead. In the Judaic culture, only the High Priest was permitted into the Sanctum Santorum, or Holy of Holies situated within King Solomon's Temple. He was the only person within that society who could speak the ineffable name of God once a year into the ear of an initiate while loud music prevented it being heard by anyone else.

If you study well, you will learn that there is nothing sinful, immoral, or contrary to the laws of God about such requirements. To the contrary, secrecy and silence wisely anticipate that holy knowledge derived from ritual and symbolism may best be understood by a candidate for Masonic degrees who is guided along his Masonic journey by serious minded "elders," who point him in the direction of the correct path. Masonic requirements of secrecy and silence also serve to safeguard that ritual and symbolism as pure "vessels" of truth to be sipped from during the presentation of the degrees as fine wine. If one is worthy of becoming a candidate for Freemasonry, he need only knock and the door will be opened unto him. He need merely ask and he shall receive all of the mysteries he proves worthy to receive. Those who choose not to knock and not to ask have no need to view the contents of Freemasonry. They would not be understood by a faithless heart.

If you seek further justification for Freemasonry's rules of secrecy and silence, consider also this fact: multitudes of thousands of men of the highest intelligence, of the most enlightened ranks and of the most profound piety have, without compunction of conscience, obeyed these rules for hundreds of years. As a result of that faithfulness, it remains possible for a true and enlightened heart of faith, hope and charity to beat within the soul of every Freemason.

Chapter 107

SO MOTE IT BE

> "But without faith it is impossible to please Him: for he that cometh to God must believe that He is, and that He rewards them that diligently seek Him."
>
> Heb. 11:6

Masonic prayer frequently concludes with the ancient phrase spoken by all Masons in attendance, "So mote it be," which is another way of saying: "The will of God be done." Or, it is also a way of acknowledging that whatever be the answer of God to a Mason's prayer, so be it – the answer will always be wise and correct.

This ancient phrase has at least two meanings. First, it represents the assent of every Mason uttering it to the will of the Supreme Architect of the Universe. He is counted wise and brave who, baffled by the trials of life when disaster follows fast, can nevertheless accept his lot as a part of the will of God and say, though it may be difficult to do so, "so mote it be." Secondly, the phrase also represents the assent of God to a Mason's aspiration. We can endure many hardships, perhaps anything, as long as we feel that God knows, cares and feels for us. These two meanings constitute elements of a Freemason's true faith, emblematically represented in Masonic ritual by the first rung of that theological ladder, which Jacob in his vision saw reaching from earth to heaven.

Perhaps the best indications of a Mason's faith in the Supreme Being are his acts of prayer, as well as the manner in which he prays. The simple act of prayer demonstrates a hopeful reliance and repose in the unknown and further shows a belief in and pursuit of immortality. It also denotes Freemasonry's universality and connection with the laws set forth in the Holy Writings, as well as our belief in God, which every man must openly express before he can be made a Mason. To be effective, this simple act of prayer should be coupled with the proper prayerful attitude, or manner, which does not include begging God to merely do what it is we want Him to do. The proper attitude is one of humble contemplation which leads us to do God's will and not our own.

The role of prayer in the work of Freemasonry is not perfunctory. It is not a mere matter of form and rote. It is vital and profound. As an initiate enters a lodge room, prayer is offered for him to God in whom the initiate is instructed to place his trust. In a later Masonic degree, during a candidate's figurative condition of crisis, the candidate must pray for himself, either orally or mentally as he prefers. These specific acts of prayer are not simply ceremonial – they each constitute the basic faith and spirit of Freemasonry.

A Mason should never be ashamed to pray. When all is said, prayer is a part of the sanity of life. It refreshes the soul and clears the mind. Oftentimes there is more wisdom in a whispered prayer than in all the libraries of the world. God knows our needs before we speak them to Him. Yet, we ask of Him anyway, if for no other reason than to become better acquainted with our best Friend.

Grant us, Almighty Father of the Universe,
Ardently to desire, wisely to study, rightly to
Understand, and perfectly to fulfill that which
Pleases you.

So Mote It Be!

Chapter 108

LABORARE EST ORARE

"The labor of the righteous tendeth to life: the fruit of the wicked is sin."

Prov. 10:16

Operative Masons labored at the building of stately material edifices. We who now call ourselves Speculative Masons are taught the importance or working to erect a superstructure of virtue and morality. Each one of us is aided in that task by the principles conveyed to us in our various lessons in Freemasonry.

From first to last, Freemasonry is *work*. The institution venerates the Supreme Being, oftentimes referred to as the Great Architect of the Universe; commemorates the *building* of King Solomon's Temple; employs emblems fashioned after *working tools* used by masons and artisans; and preserves the name of the first *workers in brass* as one of its fraternal passwords. When brethren meet together, they are said to be *at labor*. The Master of a Lodge is figuratively seen as the overseer who *sets the Craft to work* and gives them the necessary instruction whereby they may proceed in their *labors*. Thus it is that Freemasons everywhere are consistently instructed that there is a perennial nobleness and sacredness in *work*.

There exists in both philosophy and theology a distinction between static concepts and fluid *work*. The static, or closed universe that exists without change, ignores the great truth that God is a creative force. He is the beginning, the present and the future. The ineffable word is said to be His true name and regardless of whether one adopts the Greek, the Latin, the Islamic, or the Hebrew pronunciation, God is change. Change comes from *work*, which improves upon the static, placing it into constant motion.

In addition to this truth, Freemasons are also reminded of yet another truth: *faith without works is dead.* From time immemorial, Freemasons have been invited to look within themselves, to study religion and philosophy, and to meditate upon the great goodness of our Great Architect of the Universe. But for Masons, that alone is insufficient to support their status in our world as *practical philosophers.* There is no virtue without activity and exertion, whether physical or mental. To learn for the mere sake of learning is useless, because the gift – that which was learned – is not passed along to others by the action we know and refer to as *labor.*

The *work* referred to herein is both literal and philosophical. It was well that God gave the earth to man as one dark mass whereon to labor. It was also well of Him to provide rude and unsightly materials in the ore-bed and the forest for him to fashion into splendor and beauty. It is better for the Mason to work while he lives than to simply enjoy life as it passes by; to live richer and to die poorer. Our Christian brethren will well remember the Sermon on the Mount and the lesson that one who gives everything of himself is truly blessed. It is best of all to banish from the mind that empty dream of indolence and indulgence.

A Freemason routinely addresses himself to the business of life and considers it the school of our earthly education. He has also settled the question for himself that as a man of freedom and independence, gained by the sweat and toil of his ancestors, he is far from exempt from *labor.* Masons build; they are in motion; they promote change; they create; they imitate their God in every manner possible.

Chapter 109

THE SQUARE AND COMPASS

*"And it was in the heart of David my father
to build an house for the name of the
Lord God of Israel."*

1 Kings 8:17

Knowledgeable Masons quickly recognize the Square and Compass, two of the Great Lights of any Masonic Lodge. In combination, they constitute the oldest, simplest and most universal symbol in Freemasonry. They are so recognizable as literally symbolizing Masonry that years ago, when a business firm attempted to adopt the Square and Compass as a trademark, the U.S. Patent Office refused permission on the ground that, "...there can be no doubt that this device, so commonly worn and employed by Masons, has an established mystic significance which is universally recognized." Indeed, nearly everywhere in Masonic ritual, as in the public mind, the Square and Compass are seen together as never being far apart. Since the Compass is an instrument composed of two arms, some Masonic jurisdictions refer to it as a "Compasses."

It is elementary to even the youngest Entered Apprentice that the Square is an emblem of morality, and that the Compass teaches men to circumscribe their desires and keep their passions in due bounds toward all mankind. While Masonic interpretations are well known, tracing the origin of Masonic use of these symbols is much more problematic. To simply attribute Masonic use of those instruments to tradition is not at all satisfying to the inquiring mind. As is so with most symbols in Freemasonry, nothing definitive is written about the Square and Compass in Masonic history. Therefore, one is required to use logic and intuition in conjunction with what Masonic history that does exist to discover the probable truth.

While some may disparage conclusions necessarily based upon a belief that the Knights Templar were "founders" of Freemasonry, it is undeniable that in today's Craft, Freemasonry honors Knights Templar and, likewise, Knights Templar venerate Ancient Craft Masonry. Thus, some well recorded early Templar history is useful when considering the origin of the Square and Compass.

One of the oldest symbols known to the ancient Knights is the Seal of Solomon, also more popularly known as the Star of David. The Seal held special significance to the old warrior monks, accounts of whom are articulately set forth elsewhere in writings by prominent Masonic authors. Since Bibles were generally unavailable during the Middle Ages, it is deemed quite likely that the ancient Templars took their oaths while placing their right hands upon the Seal.

Even before the French and Papal persecution compelled the fleeing Templars to institute secret "modes of recognition" as a life saving measure, the old Knights veiled the deeper meaning of relevant symbols, such as the Seal, in allegory. (Interestingly, Freemasonry, too, has adopted allegory as its tool of secrecy, providing yet another piece of evidence that the Templars and Freemasons have some common source of origin.) In its most recognizable form, the Seal appears as two interwoven equilateral triangles. Being equilateral, each side of each triangle is of the same precise length as each other side. The secret meaning of the Seal would correctly have been veiled to appear one way to the outside world, while representing something quite different to the initiated. For example, consider many of Da Vinci's artworks, the most famous of which is "The Last Supper." To the initiated, the character pointing heavenward with his index finger has a very significant esoteric meaning. The uninitiated simply sees it as a finger pointing upward.

To lend a Masonic view of the symbol, thereby completely changing the Seal's appearance, nothing more is required than omitting the horizontal bars from the interwoven triangles. If you draw the remaining figure for yourself, it should not escape your notice how similar the symbol is to Freemasonry's Square and Compass. Although not definitive as to its origin, by any means, this similarity may not simply amount to random coincidence when it is recalled that each institution venerates the other.

In order for the occurrence to be a coincidence, it would also have to be a coincidence within a coincidence. For, if you have drawn your figure correctly, you will note the position of the "legs" of the "compass" derived from the Seal, with one "leg" above the "square" and one beneath it. That precisely copies the position of the Square and Compass as it is used in the Fellowcraft Degree, which was once regarded as the degree of full membership in the brotherhood of Freemasons.

Assuming that the Square and Compass was derived from the Seal, it is also logical to wonder why the Seal would have been so significant to ancient Templars. The use of the Seal, or Star of David, as a Jewish symbol is of fairly recent vintage. Early rabbinic literature has found no historical support for the claim that it represents the shape of King David's shield, as once was thought to be true. Nevertheless, the interwoven equilateral triangles have appeared in very ancient literature and artworks, some pre-dating the arrival of the Templars.

Wholly apart from Judaism, the symbol was quite common during the Middle Ages as a sign of good fortune. Furthermore, various scholars have identified a deep theological meaning hidden within the symbol: the top triangle strives upward toward the Supreme Architect of the Universe, while the lower triangle strives downward toward the real world. That symbolism is common in Hermeticism – "as it is above, so shall it be below." When accepted in this context, Freemasons will surely recall the fraternity's special call for universality which permeates all Masonic ritual.

If the Holy Bible is the rule and guide of our faith, as all Freemasons are taught, the Square used as an emblem of morality in conjunction with the Compass representing regulation of conduct consistently displays implications of universality. Is it not so that the three Great Lights of Masonry suggest, promote and inculcate faith, hope and charity? Nothing can be more universal.

Chapter 110

THE 47TH PROBLEM OF EUCLID

> "Bow down thine ear, and hear the words of
> the wise, and apply thine heart unto
> my knowledge."
>
> Prov. 22:17

Master Masons are instructed that there are a series of hieroglyphic emblems about which they are expected to inform themselves. Simply defined, a hieroglyphic emblem is a pictorial representation that is intended to convey a specific knowledge. One of those emblems is the 47th Problem of Euclid, authored by Pythagoras, an ancient friend and brother who in his travels throughout Asia, Africa and Europe was initiated into several orders of Priesthood. He was also raised to the sublime degree of Master Mason.

Pythagoras was also schooled in Hermeticism, the tradition of synthesis that explains the divine concept of "as above, so shall it be below." Hermeticism teaches that man should seek to apply the infinite wisdom of God to the finite environment in which he resides on earth. As a student of that tradition, Pythagoras' scientific explorations were as much the result of his search for divine truth, as they were a quest for mathematical reality. To him, mathematics was the core of divine order in the universe. Therefore, the principles of the celebrated 47th Problem of Euclid constitutes a key to Masonic geometry, not only with respect to external forms, but also with regard to the moral and intellectual powers and capacities of man.

The matter of the 47th Problem is this: if any triangle has one right angle, the squares of the two shorter sides, when added together, will contain precisely the same area as the square of the longer third side, also known as the "hypotenuse." The Problem establishes the clear relationship that exists among length, breadth and thickness. The triangle unites the squares which when applied to Freemasonry symbolizes the unification of the three lodges of the Entered Apprentice, the Fellowcraft and the Master Mason into one complete whole. Thus, it is a perfect picture, or hieroglyph representing the perfection of the three degrees of Masonry when considered together.

Various historians have suggested that the application of the 47th Problem of Euclid resulted in the precise form of the Tabernacle of Moses, as well as the form of the Holy of Holies standing within the Temple of King Solomon. Closer inspection by several Masonic writers reveals that it also provides the true form of both the Master Mason's apron and the jewel worn by the Worshipful Master. As a consequence, when a Mason sitting in a Masonic lodge views those symbols, he is reminded that taken together, they represent that order and beauty which reigns forever before the throne of God.

Also for consideration by the contemplative Freemason, the understanding of this celebrated Problem is central to an appreciation of the relationship of one degree of Freemasonry to all other degrees. They are each building blocks without which the other two would be without form. When it is noted that the world was first without form and void, the 47th Problem of Euclid may also be seen as a figurative formula for the "DNA" that scientists have recently come to recognize as central to life itself.

Before a Mason can achieve the "perfect square" of a Master Mason, he must have first proceeded along the oblong paths of the preceding degrees. In other words, he must evolve according to the knowledge that he acquires. The "perfect square," emblematic of truth and morality, may only be acquired after absorbing the progressive lessons in virtue offered in the symbols and lectures of the Entered Apprentice and Fellowcraft degrees. Once those lessons are entirely understood, the Master Mason is sufficiently equipped of spirit and mind to see the truth of Freemasonry's venerable mysteries. Thus, even a Master Mason should once in awhile return to study the lessons taught in the preceding degrees to make certain he has learned all that he should.

Freemasonry also looks to the 47th Problem of Euclid as a basis for concluding that all philosophical and religious thought is worth consideration and respect. The Problem teaches that any one particular perspective about God is not incorrect, or correct. Rather, it represents where the person holding that belief is in relationship to mankind's evolving understanding about man's relationship to the Deity. As humans, we cannot know whether that place is advanced or retarded – we may only regard it as the place one is in his or her understanding about his or her relationship to the divine. Therefore, all places are to be respected, because they are all divine, at least in some part.

Chapter III

THE LETTER "G"

> "O Lord our Lord, how
> excellent is thy name
> in all the earth."
>
> Ps. 8:9

One of the most familiar, as well as most significant symbols in Freemasonry is the letter "G," which is always visible in the east suspended above the Master's chair. Masonic tradition explains that this symbol has at least two very profound meanings. First, it is the initial of the name of the Supreme Architect of the Universe – the great God of all Masons. Second, it also represents geometry, the science by which the labors of all artificers are calculated and formed. For Masons, geometry contains the determination, definition and proof of the order, beauty and wisdom of God's creation.

The great Pythagoras concluded that the mathematics of geometry, so precise and unerring in the theorems to which it gives rise, was also intended to inspire mankind with a spiritual knowledge. That knowledge, that all of God's creation from beginning to end has a clear, carefully calculated plan that adheres to a specific set of reliable rules, is something Pythagoras was certain that man was able to decipher, if he studied and meditated properly. His belief is consistent with the several passages of scripture found in the Holy Bible which teach us that there is nothing that God will not reveal to His children. The sole requirement is that the children ask for such knowledge with a pure heart.

Thus, in its dual symbolism, the letter "G" represents to Masons the creative genius of God, His unity with creation, the unity of heaven with earth, the unity of the divine with the human and the unity of the finite with the infinite. The latter was the subject of Albert Einstein's "relativity theory" about which he first wrote in 1905. In further contemplation of those truths, Freemasons everywhere engage in common acts of charity and refuse to accede to the undervaluing of this life as being somehow insignificant; worthy only as a stepping-stone to a future heavenly existence. To the contrary, Freemasonry teaches that devotion to God and that which is above includes devotion to all earthly life, especially to the causes of virtue and social justice.

The letter "G" also serves as a reminder to each Freemason that life is real, earnest and full of duties yet to be performed. In sum, Masonry propounds that life is the beginning of immortality and is meant to be commanded and controlled, not neglected, despised, or ignored. The measure of a man's devotion to God, virtue and duty is taken by evaluating his various actions toward others. That measure does not count idleness, the pursuit of self interest, or the useless wringing of self-pitying hands. Such attributes are found only in the pagan, or heathen heart — the breast in which God dwells only in name, if he dwells there at all.

Chapter 112

BOAZ AND JACHIN

> "And he set up pillars in the porch of the Temple: and he set up the right pillar. And he called the name thereof Jachin: and he set up the left pillar, and he called the name thereof Boaz."
>
> 1 Kings 7:22

The above quoted passage of Holy Scripture alludes to the erection of two huge shafts, or pillars of bronze, within King Solomon's Temple by Hiram, a man of Tyre and the son of a widow from the tribe of Napthali. Those pillars stood in relief as works of art, not as supports for any part of the structure itself. Boaz stood on the left and Jachin loomed on the right of the entrance to the Temple, just as they do today within every Masonic Lodge. As works of art, Boaz and Jachin were originally intended to serve as symbols of the unification of strength and virtue. They also represent a unification of Hebrew and Canaanite religious practices symbolized by the very persons of both Solomon, King of Israel and Hiram, King of Tyre.

Boaz signified "strength," while Jachin, a derivation of two Hebrew words, "Jah," the poetical term for Jehovah, and "Iachin," meaning "establish." Taken together, they mean "God will establish." Used in prayer set forth in the various Masonic writings, they become emblematic of the

Supreme Architect's eternal loving power: "O, Great Architect. You are mighty, and your power is established from everlasting to everlasting." As one gazes upon the representations of Boaz and Jachin within a Masonic Lodge, one should also try to see the invisible arch connecting them to be none other than the hands of God.

The ancient Order of Melchizedek established a holy priesthood to serve as God's hands on earth. That priesthood continued through to the Hebrews, eventually to a person symbolically named "Zadok," who is intended to represent the continuity of the priesthood established by God. Viewed separately, Boaz and Jachin individually signify the "kingly" and the "priestly" characteristics of the Deity and inspire us with a due reverence for His works. Christianity holds that Jesus joined those two characteristics unto himself, thus becoming for his followers both King and High Priest of the Order of Melchizedek.

The ancients utilized similar pillars to represent the unification of diverse people into one spirit. In the days of Abraham, the Egyptians erected one pillar in Upper Egypt and another in Lower Egypt to symbolize the uniting of the vastly disparate people of high standing, on the one hand, with the people of low standing on the other hand in the pursuit of one government and one religious truth. The people from both regions were polytheistic, as were most people of that era. They selected different "gods" and attributed greater or less significance to each as they chose. None fully believed that the others string of gods was either properly aligned, or equally powerful with their own. Yet, in spite of those vast differences of opinion, history clearly implies that the Egyptians realized that compromise, toleration and attempts to achieve harmony were greatly important to the welfare of the government and to the happiness of the individual.

Freemasonry acknowledges the tremendous contributions by the Ancient Egyptian culture to both civilization and religion. It emphasizes many of the concepts held dear by those Egyptians as fundamental to a just society. A population that seeks to accommodate different beliefs and permit the open expression of different opinions will more likely than not live peaceably. To the contrary, a population that rigidly excludes any but the selected beliefs and opinions will likely descend into civil war. Such has been the history of our world from time immemorial.

As Freemasons acting in today's societies, let us remember the true significance of Boaz and Jachin: God has said, "In strength will I establish this mine house and kingdom forever." That strength derives from the solidarity of the people, which in turn derives from the loving, kind, tolerant respect one displays to another. It derives from the Masonic principle of "synthesis," or the ability to live side-by-side in peace and harmony with those who neither think like us, nor look like us.

Chapter 113
FROM DARKNESS TO LIGHT

"Then, God said, 'Let there be light, and there was light."

Gen. 1:3

Prior to the commencement of each ritualistic degree in Freemasonry, the candidate is placed into a symbolic condition of darkness. There, he discovers that he must rely upon other senses than sight to comprehend what is transpiring. More particularly, the candidate is encouraged to learn how to first conceive God's truths in his heart before beholding the beauties of His creation with the eyes.

In that Freemasonry has also equated the condition of darkness to being in a state of evil, or living in ignorance, it is important for the candidate to also learn the relationship between right reflection and correct action. That is, when one absorbs a specific subject matter, it becomes a part of that person sufficient to influence physical acts. By learning to so read and absorb the lessons taught by God's revelations about what is good and what is bad, the Mason enables himself to develop an instinctive ability to act according to what is right, that is in the light.

The Entered Apprentice Mason is instructed to consider the volume of the Holy Writings as the "Great Light" in his life; to regard it as the unerring source of truth; and to govern his actions by the Divine precepts therein contained. Anyone who has taken the time to read passages therein knows that they must be read slowly to be understood. That is so, because the concepts expressed about our living God are so sophisticated that they are best understood by the "heart," that is, the soul of man. In fact, once the heart has been conditioned to understand those passages, the eyes can actually take in the words at a more rapid rate. They are but the lens through which the soul of man sees, hears, and absorbs God's most elegant truths.

In the First Degree of Freemasonry, the candidate also learns that the "covering" of a lodge, the clouded canopy or star-decked heavens, is intended to remind him to have faith in God, hope of immortality, and charity toward all mankind. Therefore, the "light" to which Freemasonry alludes radiates most brilliantly when emanating from faith, hope and charity, which further illuminates the truth about the resurrection from physical death. If death is darkness, then life is represented by light. Eternal life is represented by eternal light – that radiance from above that so pervades everything as to forever eliminate the darkness. Thus, eternal light is the appropriate symbol for the immortality of the soul.

The Holy Writings, or "Great Light" in Freemasonry, also teaches that just as a body without a soul is dead, so also is faith without works. In its simplest context, that truth means that it is not enough for a man to believe that God loves all His children. To know that God loves all and to hate your own brother implies that such a one walks in the dark, not in the light. It is not enough to simply know that charity is essential to the welfare of our fellowman; one must actively seek out opportunities to practice charity. Therefore, charity is the handmaiden of faith, because it constitutes the "works" without which faith is dead.

Masonic tradition informs us that every Masonic Lodge extends from east to west and from north to south to denote the universality of Masonry, and to teach us that a Mason's charity should be equally extensive. The arrangement and situation of a lodge itself is also a Masonic symbol; a source of great radiant light – one that acts as a constant reminder of that purity of life and conduct so essentially necessary to gaining admission into the eternal presence of our God.

Chapter 114

CORN, WINE AND OIL

*"[He causeth]...wine that maketh glad the
heart of man, and oil to make his face shine,
and bread (corn) which strengtheneth man's heart."*

Ps. 104:15

Masonic tradition informs us that the wages of a Fellowcraft Mason are corn, wine and oil; the corn of nourishment, the wine of refreshment and the oil of joy. If we do not inquire further into the true meaning of this combination of symbols, it is likely that we will overlook the deeper Masonic message it conveys.

Antiquity teaches us that corn was a symbol of the resurrection, which is at the heart of lessons taught us in the ritual of the Third Degree. Oil was anciently regarded as a symbol of prosperity and happiness. In the Jewish tradition everything appropriated to the purpose of religion in both the Tabernacle of Moses and Solomon's Temple was consecrated with oil to foster public rejoicing and festivity. Corn, or bread, was oftentimes used as a symbol of life, for it was by bread that man sustained his physical existence for the purpose of developing his spirit and soul.

Corn, wine and oil are also the elements used during the consecration of new Masonic Lodges to dedicate the new Lodge to the service of the

Great Architect of the Universe. Writings by several esoteric Freemasons reveal that angelic powers are released within a new Lodge at the moment of consecration which can guide even the most unwilling Freemason along the path of righteousness and service to mankind.

The less mystical Freemason can appreciate a different interpretation of this combination of symbols on a more material level. As an emblem of food, corn reminds us that we are nourished by bread and the hidden Manna of Righteousness; wine, the emblem of refreshment, reminds us that we are to be refreshed daily with the Word of God; and oil, the emblem of Divine anointing, informs us that we are to rejoice with joy in the riches flowing from God's grace.

In that charity is regarded in Freemasonry as the "greatest of the three principle rounds of Jacob's ladder," which extends beyond the grave throughout all eternity, Freemasons will do well to also understand the lesson to be derived from this combination of symbols about how we are to treat others. The carrying of corn, wine and oil in a procession to consecrate a new Masonic Lodge may remind us that in the pilgrimage of life, we are to give bread (corn) to the hungry, cheer (wine) to the sorrowful, and consolation (oil) to the sick and afflicted.

As is true with most matters Masonic, the wages of a Fellowcraft Mason are not intended to be hidden away. They are to be displayed in the light and given away free of charge to all we encounter who are in need. In so doing, Freemasons participate in the continuing creation and offerings of love practiced by our Great Creator.

Chapter 115

THE LOST WORD

"In the beginning was the Word, and the Word was with God, and the Word was God."

John 1:1

According to the mystical history of Freemasonry, there once existed in the ancient craft a Word of surpassing value. It has been described as the unpronounceable name of God. Known only to a select few, its true meaning was concealed to such a great extent that the meaning was eventually lost. Those who once possessed the word were rumored to have the ability to exert enormous power.

Moses was directed to speak it as a name to Pharaoh and it appeared hundreds of times in the Hebrew books of different periods. Masonic tradition informs us that when, as a result of falling into disuse, the word was lost, the original Most Excellent Grand Masters of Freemasonry, Solomon, King of Israel, Hiram, King of Tyre and Hiram Abif, the widow's son, adopted a substitute for temporary use.

As with most symbols used in Freemasonry, this, too, is subject to several differing interpretations. The lost Word is believed by many to constitute Divine Truth. Hermetic Christianity teaches that the whole of God may be known to those who know and understand the ineffable name of God. Therefore, the pursuit of knowledge is essential to the person who would know the Word and know God.

One form of such knowledge may be derived from learning what God is, what we are and how everything relates to the whole. Though mostly ignorant about his own essence, man has ventured throughout time to speculate about God's nature, to dogmatically define the Supreme Being in creeds, and even to hate those who will not accept a particular point of view about Divine Truth. Yet, true knowledge of God's Divine Essence is impossible. Nevertheless the numerous man-made conceptions about God are significant revelations of man's intellectual development.

Limited to our own finite conceptions, as well as the finite conceptions expressed by other men, Freemasons are to study other ideas, exchange differing points of view, and attempt to understand what is truly meant by the words unity, brotherhood and charity. This pursuit is not purely theological, but extends to all of the liberal arts and sciences – how each relates to the other and how the sum relates to our perception of one great and powerful cause of being.

Unity itself has proven to be a concept difficult to put into action. Though the same sun shines on the earth to yield a plethora of fruits, plants and animals, none of which are alike, yet each owing its existence to the same source, man finds it difficult seeing his neighbor as another self. As Freemasons, we are reminded by the symbolic mosaic pavement that we are surrounded by opposites; by the position of the square to the compasses that there is both light and darkness; and, by the trestle board that there is a correct path we should follow – the path of brotherhood. If Freemasons observe the lessons taught them, they will know to apply knowledge in a manner that acknowledges the inalienable rights of all people, of all faiths and of all creeds. The founding fathers of this great nation held such beliefs worthy of a revolution against tyrants who would compel men to their way of thinking and their way of life – an example of integrity well worth emulating.

God permits all to call Him Father, and He disinherits none of His children. If you believe, as some believe, the He exists apart from man, then you are compelled to act according to His laws and love your neighbor, as He loves all of us. If you believe, as yet others believe, that God exists with us and within us, then you are compelled to act according to the laws written in your hearts. Both beliefs dispose man to act upon the truth that as inhabitants of the same planet, we are to aid, support and protect one another.

Freemasons do not regard their neighbors as simply Hebrew, Christian, Moslem, Buddhist, Republican, Democrat, communist, or fascist. Those are creeds, religions and political labels that merely define points of view, some with which we agree and some with which we disagree. But, the man possessed of any such creed, religion, or political persuasion is still permitted to call God "Father," and is not disinherited by Him.

To whom, then, should go the benefits of our knowledge? They should be showered upon every man, woman and child, especially the poor, the widows and the orphans. Pray for justice to all of these, my brother, and you will have done God's work – you will have taken an important step closer to knowing the lost Word.

Chapter 116

THE INDENTED TESSEL

*"Now faith is the substance of things hoped for,
the evidence of things not seen."*

Heb. 11:1

During the First Degree of Masonry, the candidate's attention is directed to the "ornaments of the lodge," consisting of the mosaic pavement, the indented tessel and the blazing star. The mosaic pavement is intended to be emblematic of human life checkered with good and evil. It teaches that all humanity is imperfect in the eyes of God – at once capable of great acts of charity, and also of terrifying acts of brutality and murder. Yet, while journeying through this vale of tears, incapable of escaping the terrors wrought by mankind, Masons are reminded by the symbolism of the indented tessel that man may be set free from those terrors by a faithful reliance upon Divine Providence, hieroglyphically represented by the blazing star.

Examples of the rewards of relying upon God are sprinkled throughout the Holy Bible. When warned by God about a vast flood, Noah acted and by doing so demonstrated that he was a proper object for selection by God as an heir of righteousness. When Abraham was called to pack up and leave his familiar surroundings for a country he had never before seen, he did so. God rewarded his faithfulness by entering into a covenant with Abraham to treat Abraham's descendants as heirs. Moses led an entire Hebrew population from Egyptian slavery by faithfully relying upon God. Righteous to the end of his days, Jesus taught that the Kingdom of God was found within every man who professed faith in God.

Freemasonry embodies the same truth in the symbolic lesson intended by the indented tessel. The candidate is taught that the beautiful tessellated norder or skirting surrounding the mosaic pavement is emblematic of the manifold blessings and comforts one may hope to enjoy by a faithful reliance upon Divine Providence. In other words, good conduct is rewarded by God when performed with the pure intention of serving God's purpose. This symbolism suggests to the discerning Mason that even suffering can be a "manifold blessing" – perhaps not for the suffering person, but certainly for those who have the privilege of acting to relieve that suffering.

Since the beginning of man's history, wars have been fought and lives lost for the purpose of ensuring that other lives were saved. Throughout the ages, men and women have intentionally sustained diseases incurable during their lifetimes to help comfort and assist those suffering already from the same incurable disease. The blessing that was derived was to a later generation, which discovered the cure because of the sacrifices made. An entire generation suffered through the Great Depression with little or nothing in the way of material comfort. Those who survived taught a new generation important lessons about thrift and the social responsibility for caring for those who cannot care for themselves.

The greatest secret of Freemasonry is grounded in the hope and belief in something we cannot ever "know" to an empirical certainty – life after death. Is life after death a "manifold blessing?" Is it something you, as a Freemason, "know" to be true? Is faith the basis for that "knowledge?" If so, you have also discovered the commonality between "knowledge" and "faith."

Masonic writers have scoured the ages examining the Egyptian Mysteries, the Mithraic Mysteries, Hebraic teachings, Greek philosophy, dogmas from the Orient, and Christian writings to understand the full extent of the steadfastness with which people who partook in each discipline dedicated themselves to faith in God. None had ever seen God's face, felt His breath, or heard His voice. Yet, each believed He was the source of all that is good and dedicated themselves to practicing faithfulness and recording that faithfulness in the rituals that have been passed down form time immemorial.

Similarly, it is also by our faithfulness and dedication to Freemasonry's work on behalf of God that those who follow this era will acquire a better understanding of God's loving kindness. Indeed, brethren, each generation of men is an "indented tessel;" a manifold blessing and comfort to those who follow. Man's opportunity to contribute to the welfare of generations that will follow is God's truest and finest gift to each of His creatures.

Chapter 117

FREEDOM, FERVENCY AND ZEAL

"For he...was clad with zeal as a cloak."

Is. 59:17

As taught in the First Degree of Masonry, operative Masons were once required to serve their master with freedom, fervency and zeal. It was only in that manner that they could be certain to serve the master's interest instead of their own. In speculative Masonry, that same phrase is used to convey the notion that those three virtues are to be exercised whenever we serve the Great Architect. They are best demonstrated when our actions are consistent with advancing morality and by promoting the happiness of our fellow creatures.

Although Freemasonry states to the world that it is not a religion and does not promote any one established religion above any other, the Webster's New World Dictionary, Second Concise Edition, offers insight into why some insist that Freemasonry is a religion. The word "religion" is defined as "any object that is seriously or zealously pursued." Freemasonry has long had its accusers who state that the fraternity seeks to establish a "New World Order" under the banner of a new religion that will require its members to abandon Judaism, Christianity, Hinduism, Islam, or any other specific system of belief in and worship of God. To prove their point, some of those accusers cite various passages in the writings of esteemed Masonic philosophers, such as Albert Pike. In response, Freemasonry often argues that it is tolerant of all systems of belief and worship of one God and demonstrates that sincerity by extending charity to all regardless of race, creed, or religion.

Yet, as Freemasons it is important that we embrace rather than ignore, or try to conceal the fraternity's dedication to "zealously tolerate, to love with "zeal," and to work for God as a "zealot." Pike has written that every Masonic Lodge is a Temple of Religion; its officers – ministers of religion; its teachings – instructions in religion. Pike so taught not because Freemasonry replaces Judaism, Christianity, Hinduism, Islam, or any other religion, but because Masonry promotes the duty of every Mason to adopt Masonic teachings and live them to the world through the religion of choice with enthusiasm, which is a synonym for "zeal."

Freemasonry teaches that there is, indeed, a "religion" of toil. It does not replace Abraham, Moses, Jesus, Mohammed, or any other great religious person. Rather it signifies that Masonry incorporates the virtues practiced since time immemorial which pervaded the thoughts and actions of each of those great leaders, as well as others. Masons are also taught that their pursuits and occupations, when performed faithfully, actually promote God's great design. Nothing less was taught by any of those great leaders. Masons are repeatedly reminded to advocate fairly and honestly with a feeling of sincere belief that it is God's justice that will prevail, not our own personal interests. Freemasonry further instructs that books, whether they are about Masonic history, philosophy, literature, or any of the arts and sciences convey a sense of "religion," if what is absorbed instills pure, noble, virtuous and patriotic sentiments. When he listens to what he is taught, a Mason learns that society itself, with all its diversification in belief systems, is a "religion" where, as here in our country, there exists a sacred belief in our fellow man, and where, again as here, we repose perfect confidence in the integrity of another person.

It is within the halls of the Temples, or Lodges, that Freemasons inculcate faith, hope and charity. With "zeal," Masons are taught disinterestedness, affection, toleration, patriotism, devotedness and an undying love of the Supreme Architect. Masons greet one another with joy; they are lenient to each other's faults; they carefully regard and respect each other's feelings; and, they are always ready to aid each other's wants and needs. That is the true "zeal," or as Webster has defined that word, "religion" which was revealed to the Ancient Patriarchs and which Freemasonry taught centuries ago. It will continue to be taught by Freemasons until time shall be no more.

If unworthy passions and selfish, bitter, or vengeful thoughts enter here, they are intruders within our Masonic Temple and most unwelcome. They are strangers and trespassers, not invited guests. If one is Jewish, these teachings resonate because they are also presented in the synagogues. The same is so if one is Christian, Hindu, or Moslem. Freemasonry seeks not to replace any one of those systems of belief. Rather, it seeks to bridge the gaps among them, to give to every human being the opportunity to learn with "zeal," regardless of the place of worship, or the system of worship employed. To Freemasons, there is only one God and we all live in His embrace.

Chapter 118

TUBAL-CAIN

"The eighth man from Adam; the first artificer in metals."

Gen. 4:22

The Old Testament of the Holy Bible reveals that Tubal-cain was a son of Lamech, a descendant of Adam's son, Cain. He was described as an artificer in brass and iron. Masonic tradition embraces Tubal-cain as the founder of smith-craft, who likely worked in the implementation of metals into devices used for both war and peace. It is further speculated that he launched the Bronze Age, an historic era of enormous significance to mankind's ascent.

Many of the characters identified in the Book of Genesis who allegedly walked the earth before the time of Moses may not have actually existed. Many historians, both religious and secular, have come to the conclusion that most, if not all, represented either symbolic characters, or were composite characters, that is several people made into one being. That is particularly so with regard to Adam, Eve, Cain and Abel. In both the Kabbalah and Gnostic writings, each of those individuals is primarily regarded as a specific emblem of heavenly and earthly traits.

Cain and Abel are regarded jointly as examples of light and darkness, good and evil, while Adam and Eve represent both the earthly prototypes of man and woman, as well as the dual nature of God, in other words his active and passive being. If Cain is figurative only, so also may be his so-called descendant Tubal-cain, for history cannot definitely conclude that Cain and Lamech ever actually existed. As a consequence, Tubal-cain himself may be yet another in a long line of Masonic symbols calculated to inculcate some type of spiritual awareness.

Within the various writings about Freemasonry there is a definite metallic streak associated with some of the Masonic ritual. As the Entered Apprentice will recall, he was divested of all minerals and metals before entering a lodge of Free and Accepted Masons. No tool of iron was used to assemble King Solomon's Temple. Chalk, charcoal and clay – extracts from the metallurgical process – are used to emphasize freedom, fervency and zeal. More specifically, clay is our Mother Earth which provides us with both the metals and the refractories to contain them at high temperatures. From charcoal we derive heat energy to smelt and refine those metals. From chalk we obtain the flux to alloy with the gangue then separate it from the ore.

Metallurgy as a science is closely associated with the philosophy of alchemy, which is to be distinguished from the so-called alchemical science. Scientific alchemy, or the changing of metal into gold, is largely disfavored as a pure science and more often viewed as a base form of magic. Philosophical alchemy, on the other hand, is very closely studied by Freemasons for its spiritual content. The "philosopher's stone" is the entire body of philosophic knowledge from which man's crude intellect grasps important truths about himself, his relationship to other human beings and his relationship to the Supreme Architect of the Universe.

Today's disciples of the symbolic Tubal-cain include tool engineers who provide the expertise necessary to design and devise the machines, methods and tools used to cast, forge and shape all metals. Therein lies a close association with Freemasonry, because all of the "working tools" are also essential to the fabrication of metals. For example, a tool engineer does not work without a rule, square, or compasses. Like Tubal-cain's art of metallurgy, this art also unfolds the secrets of nature and science teaching us what God and nature are, and what we are. God has provided us the materials in the firmament, the stars, planets and zodiacs, which we should be inspired to use to develop the knowledge necessary to accomplish our own Divine work.

Freemasonry instructs that most implements may be used by man for great good or greater evil. Here, we return to the symbolic significance of the original brothers Cain and Abel, who begin the story of man with a lesson that our existence which is given us as a gift of our Great Creator is forever fraught with good and evil. The sharpened edge of an implement may cut stone to assist in erecting a house of worship. The same sharpened edge may also plunge deep into flesh and bone fatally wounding another human being. A mallet can serve to either join together parts of a building, or crush another man's skull. In each instance, the good or the evil results from the attitude of the person using the implement.

In the hands of a Freemason, the "working tools" are forged and malleated in his hands to eventually promote peace, goodwill, harmony, health and happiness. The mind of a Mason is disciplined by the lessons he is taught to employ the "good" attitude when using the tools and to turn away from the temptations to give in to the "bad" attitude. In other words, Freemasonry is about using ordinary substances to make gold; using his mind to serve his fellow man; using his soul to serve his God.

Chapter 119

FREEDOM AND RESPONSIBILITY

"But God be thanked, that ye were the servants of
sin, but ye have obeyed from the heart that
form of doctrine which was delivered you."

Rom. 6:17

During the presentation of the First Degree of Freemasonry, the candidate is instructed upon the importance of freedom and the responsibility he has, as a Mason, to use it wisely. Freedom is the power, rooted in reason and will, to act or not act, to do this or that, and so to perform deliberate actions on one's own responsibility. By the exercise of free will, one shapes one's own life. Freemasonry teaches that human freedom is a force for growth and maturity in truth and goodness; it attains its perfection when directed toward God.

Yet, as Freemasonry also instructs, the world is made up of opposites, a truth that equally applies to the concept of freedom. As long as freedom has not bound itself definitively to its ultimate good – God – there remains the possibility of choosing between good and evil, and thus of either growing in perfection, or failing in wrong doing. The more one does what is good, the freer one becomes. Consider the example of our Grand Master Hiram Abif, whose habit of doing good cemented in him a necessity to always protect his integrity. His example also teaches that there is no true freedom except in the service of that which is just and good. Consequently, choosing to disobey and do evil is an abuse of freedom that inevitably leads to slavery of the human soul.

Freedom makes man responsible for his acts to the extent they are voluntary. Progress in virtue, knowledge of the good, and self discipline enhance the mastery of the will over its acts. Imputability and responsibility for an action can be diminished, or even nullified by ignorance, inadvertence, duress, fear, habit, or other social factors. However, every act willed is imputable to its author and even the best among us fall short. Consider that the prophet Nathan questioned King David after he committed adultery with the wife of Uriah and had him murdered: "What is this you have done?" All men are accountable and responsible for both the good they do, as well as for the evil into which they descend.

Freedom is exercised in relationships between human beings. Freemasonry recognizes that every person, created in the image of the Supreme Architect, has the natural right to be recognized as a free and responsible being. In many jurisdictions, Masons are referred to as "Free and Accepted" in further recognition of the dignity to which mankind is destined. Everyone owes to each other a duty of respect. Freemasons also recognize that the right to the exercise of freedom, especially in moral and religious matters, is an inalienable requirement of the dignity of the person. To become valid, this right must be recognized and protected by civil authority within the limits of the common good and public order.

Chapter 120

THE FELLOWCRAFT

"Now therefore ye are no more strangers and foreigners,
but fellow citizens with the saints, and of the
household of God."

Eph. 2:19

Masonic tradition informs us that in operative Masonry there were two classes of workers, Masters and Fellows. Fellows denoted those men who were generally less skillful than those called *masters*. In its etymological meaning, the word *fellow* signifies one bound to another by a mutual trust; a follower; a companion; or, an associate. In speculative Freemasonry, the man who ascends to the Second Degree is referred to as a *Fellowcraft*. Like the Entered Apprentice, the Fellowcraft is preparing to ascend to yet another and higher degree.

While the First Degree of Masonry emphasizes the necessity of purifying the heart, the Second Degree, or Fellowcraft Degree, promotes the cultivation of man's reasoning faculties, as well as the necessity to improve one's intellectual powers. In that regard, the Fellowcraft is taught that Freemasonry is a struggling march toward what is known as "the light." The Fellowcraft soon learns that the march is not for individuals alone, but is also naturally pursued by nations, or whole groups of people working together toward a common goal. To give a nation the franchise of intellect, or light, is the only certain way to perpetuate freedom. It therefore falls to each Fellowcraft to learn, to obtain knowledge, to become wise and to serve the interests of fraternal charity rather than self interest.

It is written elsewhere that the true Mason is an ardent seeker after knowledge and knows that both books and the antique symbols of Masonry are vessels which come down to us full-freighted with the intellectual riches of the past; and that in the lading of these argosies is much that sheds light on the meaning of Masonry and proves its claim to be acknowledged as the benefactor of mankind – born in the very cradle of the race. Fellowcrafts are encouraged to study the meanings flowing from those antique symbols and to learn much more. The streams of learning that flow full and broad must be followed to their heads in the springs of the remote past. The history of man's ascent, the origin and evolution of his religions and the wisdom imparted by his ever developing philosophy announces a truth also essential to a free society: "God is above all and the Father of all; in the presence of His infinity, human distinctions are infinitely insignificant." In short, Fellowcrafts are expected to eventually understand, in the heart as well as in the mind that men best prosper when they live as a brotherhood of man under the Fatherhood of God.

The origin of the ceremonies used during the conferral of the Second Degree of Freemasonry is not precisely known. Some attribute them to Sir Francis Bacon, others to Sir Isaac Newton, both of whom were members of the Royal Society in England, which promoted the sophisticated pursuit of science and the liberal arts. If true, there is little wonder that during that ceremony a candidate's attention is directed to architecture, geometry, astronomy and other arts and sciences. In each discipline, one learns about symmetry, order, consistency and the impact of the heavens upon the earth. The latter, viewed from a Hermetic perspective, also invites the candidate to understand the phrase, "as it is above, so shall it be below."

Chapter 121

WITHIN THE LENGTH OF MY CABLETOW

*"I draw them with the cords of a
man, with bands of love..."*

Hos. 11:4

Freemasons are, by nature, generally possessed of boundless good intentions. But, each of us is limited by our own capacities and the time we have available to us. Our commitments to church, family, work, and the community in which we live restricts what each of us may give to our Ancient Craft. Consequently, because all our other endeavors are equally important, Masons should be vigilant against overextending themselves; promising more than each can deliver; and delivering less than our best. Such, in and of itself, has the potential to marginalize the Mason who so errs bringing down upon him discredit to his well-earned good reputation and scorn to the covenant of fraternity.

The cable tow is used symbolically in Freemasonry to express that fraternal covenant, which is also emblematic of the great covenant God made with Abraham to honor his descendants. God expected no less from man, who is expected to fear God and obey His commandments. Similarly, Freemasonry requires obedience from its members in giving of oneself to duty, work, devotion and honor. Yet, much like many of Abraham's rude and disobedient descendants, who promised a greater devotion to God than they were prepared to actually give, Masons who commit to act then disappear when the time to act arrives places himself in jeopardy of being regarded as unreliable.

The phrase "a cable's length" serves as a reminder to every Freemason that there are times when it is much wiser to answer "no" when asked to engage in an activity. When time or other commitments do not prudently allow for the inclusion of more tasks, a Mason's "yes" is evidence of an exercise of poor judgment. Or, it is a signal of insecurity in the love and affection of a Mason's Masonic brethren. Neither is a virtue contained within any Masonic lesson.

Strictly a phrase found only in Freemasonry, "a cable's length" has been given the literal meaning of three miles in length, or the maximum distance required of an Entered Apprentice in attending his Lodge. In a more general sense, the phrase is emblematic of the scope of man's reasonable ability to perform any task. Therefore, we are expected to learn from it that we should carefully weigh that which we propose to undertake before doing so.

Just as Jesus taught the disciples to look inward unto themselves, we, too, can learn much about our own limitations by taking the time necessary to internally reflect upon the scope of our personally abilities. When an hour is available, one cannot very well promise two. If one is of meager economic means, it is not reasonable to expect a life devoted to philanthropy. Unskilled hands can hardly be expected to build a Temple without help from more skilled laborers. The failure of one Mason to discover his own limitations deprives the whole society of the brotherly labors that he is able to undertake.

No mason ever has, or ever will be expected to act beyond the length of his cable tow. The covenant that binds us to the fraternity does not require us to forego church, family, the community, or our employment. It simply asks us to commit to what we can do based upon the scope of our reasonable abilities. When we so act, harmony is the result, not personal recrimination. Integrity, too, is served, because Masons are being honest about what they can give of themselves. Brotherhood is increased, because vows are not broken.

When a Mason's Lodge asks him to make a commitment, it also asks him to weigh well what it is he is willing to promise and to recall that once the promise is made, a Mason's word is sacred.

Chapter 122
A Test Of Faith

"But without faith it is impossible to please him:
for he that cometh to God must believe that He is,
and that He is a rewarder of them that diligently seek Him."

Heb. 11:6

In the horrible aftermath of the 9/11/01 Attack on America we were tempted to ask, "Where was God during one of our darkest hours?" Did the Supreme Architect fall asleep when we needed Him? Did he sit idly by while lives were lost and America's way of living changed forever? Is God truly intent upon permitting evil to attack virtue and watch as we suffer?

Those questions, as well as many other similar concerns were asked by Americans across the land, as we watched the World Trade Center buckle and slowly crumble to the ground in a cloud of hideous dust. Yet, across this land, Masons also recognized that hour of sorrow as a time of opportunity; a moment in history when the virtues of our ancient craft could be practiced for the greater good of all humanity. Those who knew their God well anticipated and believed that He would reveal His power and move to defeat tyranny, terrorism and hatred, just as he had done many times before throughout history.

Freemasonry teaches that faith is the first rung of that theological ladder which Jacob, in his vision, saw reaching from Earth to heaven. It is the cement that holds the ladder together as we climb higher toward the celestial "lodge" above. Faith and trust in our God is an essential requirement for membership in our Order. Both are emphasized in every ritual degree and each stands tall as pillars of true character. As Masons, we are also taught that the Supreme Architect does not sit passively as good people are attacked, maimed and killed by angry, hateful men. Working within those who have faith, He calls the willing soul to labor and motivates that soul to chase away the darkness with intense light.

It is said that out of every act of evil, a good act follows as surely as day follows the night. Those good acts do not simply occur miraculously; they spring from a faithful breast, emblematically represented in Freemasonry by the steadfast keeping of vows and a sincere practice of the virtues revealed in Masonic symbols and ritual. The hour of opportunity at hand when evil arrives asks all men, but particularly Masons to rise above vengeance and practice justice; to apply compassion, not hatred; and to search our hearts for answers about how we can best do unto our neighbor what it is that we should that he would do unto us.

One may fairly ask, "How do we know whether or not we are faithful to God?" The profound reply is when we have freely submitted our own will to His power. Acts of high provocation require equally high acts of virtue, if man is to rise above the endless tit-for-tat inherent in the mentality of hate. When terrorists strike and spew violence across the scene, it is insufficient to simply reply with overwhelming repelling force. Of course men should defend themselves when evil approaches, but man should also see such situations as opportunities to practice eliminating the darkness with the light; of seeking to apply good in place of bad; and, of replacing evil with acts of genuine kindness. The lesson we are continuously learning is that we are all brothers and children of God; those who practice good deeds, as well as those who practice evil. We hate the evil in our brother, but we do not hate our brother, for we have all been created in God's image – not just some of us.

True faith is neither blind, nor founded upon false teachings. It cannot be perverted into misapplying wrong for right, but shine forth intently as the strongest light exposing tyranny and hate as the very antithesis of freedom and love. While history has certainly taught us that every man is capable of permitting the seeds of hatred to grow to consuming heights, Freemasonry teaches men to circumscribe their desires and to keep their passions within due bounds toward all mankind – not just toward those whom we like.

Today, perhaps as never before, Freemasonry is very much needed in our world, not simply for its unique ritual and manner of educating the soul, but for its practical principles of faith, hope and charity. Masons everywhere plant seeds of goodness on a daily basis and seek to be supportive of others as another "self." The virtue of regarding our brother as a true equal, when practiced on a widespread scale, is that all absorbing light that can forever chase away the darkness. And it can only be practiced when we sincerely believe that we are all inhabitants of the same planet who are here to aid, support and protect one another under the Divine grace of our Supreme Architect of the Universe.

Chapter 123

WHY ARE MASONS CALLED FREEMASONS?

*"A man that hath friends must shew
himself friendly: and there is no friend
that sticketh closer than a brother."*

Prov. 18:24

Masonic tradition explains that neither a slave, nor one born in slavery can be admitted into the rites and privileges of the ancient and honorable fraternity of Freemasonry. While this maxim might, at first glance, appear harsh and elitist, it derived from sound logic: one legally bound to another cannot voluntarily assume the oaths and solemn covenants demanded by the "Order." Yet, logical maxims may not precisely account for why the word *Free*mason is used. In fact, some believe that it may have derived more from notions of brotherhood than from conditions of bondage.

The obligation of a distinct affection for fellow members is a characteristic common to many organized societies of men, especially of Masons. Unlike the hitchhiker, who sticks out his thumb and only promises to ride along if you provide the vehicle and the gas, Masons are committed to sharing in the highs and lows experienced during a journey with a "brother." That commitment was never more apparent than during the Middle Ages when our Masonic ancestors were pursued like criminals by kings and prelates, who intended capture, torture, murder and the annihilation of our "Order."

That horror was not inflicted upon vagrants, liars and cheats, but was practiced upon members of an organization that once constituted a Holy Order of the Roman Catholic Church. These were not men deserving of even the mildest punishment, let alone horrendous torture, but Holy Warriors, who suffered the stress and confusion of the sudden betrayal by the their very benefactors. To escape such treachery, our ancestral brethren may have determined to rely only upon the faithfulness of true and trusty friends. Oaths and signs were likely implemented to distinguish friend from foe. Multiple places of lodging would have had to have been arranged to provide rest, shelter and food for friends and brothers on the run. In that circumstance, there would not have been time to quarrel about religious differences, or preferences: lives were in the balance. Survival had to have been paramount. In such a plight, only God could possibly know the outcome.

We know that our French speaking ancestors, who necessarily fled from France following King Philip's treacherous raids upon the Templar priories, landed among other places in England and Scotland bringing with them their rich language, which was often Anglicized by true and trusty English friends. One such French word, "frere," means "brother" when translated into English. It is recorded that both the hunted and their friends in England were referred to by the French Masons as "Frere Masons," or "brother Masons." Although it can never be known for certain, it is very possible that the French phrase was subsequently Anglicized to "Freemason."

What is known for certain is that while experiencing the horrors of treachery, brotherly love, relief and truth not merely survived – it thrived. The present day scourges of loneliness, illness, poverty, prejudice and injustice hunt down our brethren almost as fervently as did the treacherous kings and prelates hunted our ancestral brothers centuries ago. Masons and their families who suffer such calamities in their daily lives can rely upon the faithfulness of "Frere Masons" for needed comfort and support. Masonic hospitals, homes and financial endowments sustain those brethren and their families who are in need and ask nothing in return.

Our Shrine Hospitals have no accounting departments. The health care is free. Our Masonic Homes do not require payment from the destitute Masons. Shelter is willingly provided through the kind contributions of the brethren. Repayment of financial aid is not expected. It is what faithful brethren do when they are needed.

Today, Masons across our nation are fortunate, indeed, to live in a diverse world where disparate customs, ideas and traditions have spawned a growing sense of community, which in turn teaches the truth of the unity of humanity. Regardless of race, creed, sex, age, or religion we are all God's children. Masonry draws the diverse near and causes true friendship to exist among those who might otherwise have remained at a perpetual distance. We are, indeed, *Freremasons*.

Chapter 124

THE HOLY SAINTS JOHN

"And thou, child, shalt be called
prophet of the Highest: for thou shalt
go before the face of the Lord to prepare His ways."

Luke 1:76

Every Mason, from the youngest Entered Apprentice to the more enlightened Master Mason, knows that Masonic Lodges are erected to God and dedicated to the Holy Saints John. For years, writers of Freemasonry have struggled to precisely explain why it is that St. John the Baptist and St. John the Evangelist were selected as the patrons of Masonry rather than any one of hundreds of other saints. For example, St. Thomas has always been regarded as the patron saint of architecture, the five orders of which (Tuscan, Doric, Ionic, Corinthian and Composite) are studied extensively by Masons.

Each year, Masonry celebrates an annual feast for each Holy Saint John: June 24 is dedicated to St. John the Baptist, while December 27 is reserved for St. John the Evangelist. Both dates correspond with the summer solstice, on the one hand, and the winter solstice on the other hand. In the summer, the Sun is at its highest apex on June 24th and at its lowest on December 27th from which point it begins again its ascent.

This astronomy was held in very sacred regard by many of the Ancients, who saw the celestial heavens as symbolic of Divine Influence. God's light shone brightest at the summer solstice and weakest on the winter solstice.

As related to us in Holy Scripture, John the Baptist was the son of a High Priest who ministered inside the temple in Jerusalem referred to as Herod's Temple, built by the Jews to replace the destroyed Temple of Solomon. Only the most sacred from the lineage of Zadok were permitted entry into the sanctum santorum. The masses conducted their worship outside. John consumed neither wine nor strong drink, wore only hair-cloth and leather, preached repentance by a watery baptism, and taught charity, liberality, justice and fair dealing. Born a Pharisaic Jew, he nevertheless denounced both the Pharisees and Saduccees as vipers, loathing their respective but distinct emphasis on ritualistic religiosity. Though his followers traveled a path of exclusion after his death, refusing to admit anyone within their circle who did not eat the foods they ate, or adhere to the rules they adopted, John traveled a much different path. Believing that all men were of God's kingdom and that virtue was more important than ritual, John zealously led those who would follow his example to search for God's kingdom within man's soul and live life praising God and serving all men as brothers.

By deed and example, John the Baptist opened the door that led to greater enlightenment and, according to Gnostic Christian thought, presided over the baptism of Jesus at the very moment his own divine nature was revealed by God. Throughout his lifetime, John had predicted that occasion, never knowing whether it would be he, or someone else, such as Jesus, who would be "anointed." John's greatest character trait was a devout willingness to serve and sow even though he might not reap all that he had sown during his lifetime. He encouraged even his own followers to seek the source, the truly divine and conform their lives to the truth emanating from its Light.

Where John the Baptist led mankind to the door that would open hearts and souls to greater understanding, John the Evangelist opened the door that allowed us to enter and walk around the room. His apocalyptic work Revelations, set forth as the last book of the New Testament in the Holy Bible, subtly disclosed to the discerning reader that just as the Kingdom of Heaven is within us, the apocalyptic events described were intended for us to look beyond the events themselves and behold a deeper understanding about creation itself. Both the Hebrew Kabbalah and Gnostic Christianity teach that owing to his free will, man can choose to be Divine, or to embrace sin. The choices he makes impact the continuum of creation, the ongoing cause and effect of life, and can either lead to the joyful union of spirit and nature, or to utter destruction.

The teachings of John the Evangelist demonstrate great energy and poetic fire. His essential lesson to us is that virtue is its own reward, a concept embraced by Freemasons around the world. He spoke of God and man's relation to Him, not of doctrine. He seized upon the imagery in the Book of Ezekiel of a God symbolized in part by fire, or zeal for all that is holy, not upon which ritual man should select to become holy. And, he believed that man could scale the heights and ascend to his Divine destiny, rather than succumb to the enslaving bonds of a meaningless outward and rigid religiosity.

While writers will likely continue to debate why the Holy Saints John were selected as the patrons of Freemasonry, and further enlighten us in the process, Masons everywhere will continue to practice the virtues and pursue the truths taught us by these devout men of God. Look within yourself when you think of John the Baptist and discover your Divinity. When your eyes behold nature, ask the spirit within you to draw you closer to the sounds, the smells and the beauty God has created and resolve to aid Him in His continuing creation.

Chapter 125

THE MASTER'S HAT

"The rich and the poor meet together:
the Lord is the maker of them all."

Prov. 22:2

Masonic writers have offered scant insight into the tradition behind the top hat worn by every Worshipful Master of a Masonic Blue Lodge. Indeed, little information is available from which to identify the date, precise or approximate, the custom was adopted. Ancient history reveals that among the Romans, "the hat" was considered a sign of freedom.

In times past, all Masons wore hats while in lodge as a symbol of both freedom and brotherly equality. In the English and American lodges of today, "the hat" is exclusively an attribute of the Worshipful Master's costume. For a better understanding about the meaning of this custom and symbol, it is helpful to examine each object of the symbolism of "the hat" more closely.

The freedom that so clearly distinguishes Freemasonry from all other fraternal organizations is "freedom of faith," which is predominant in Masonic literature. The right of each man to worship the Supreme Architect of the Universe in the manner his heart best loves exemplifies the spirit of the Craft. Until recent times, religious freedom was unknown throughout the world except by those who defied the law of the land in which they lived and endured persecution.

Prior to the American Revolution it was against the law in most of the colonies not to go to church. Not just any church, but to the church selected by the government for each respective colony. Quakers, Baptists, Congregationalists, Presbyterians, Catholics and Jews were held to be criminals in those colonies where that specific religion was not government approved. Fortunately for posterity, our Nation's Founding Fathers adopted and implemented principles of Freemasonry to abolish state sponsored religion. The separation of church and state was, for the first time in world history, instituted as the basis upon which religious tolerance and freedom of faith was founded.

Brotherly equality, so often symbolized in Masonic lodges by the implement known as the "level," teaches us that mankind is the offspring of God; that all men are created by God of one blood with certain inalienable rights to life, liberty and the pursuit of happiness. This truly Masonic metaphysical concept, adopted by the Founding Fathers in the country's Constitution, recognizes that although each one of us possesses different gifts, we are all subject to the same infirmities, the same divine love, the same death and the same final judgment. As such, Freemasons are bound to act equitably with all human distinctions and preserve those inalienable rights for all generations.

The title "Worshipful Master," or "Master of the Lodge," far from denoting lordship, implies that the person so presiding is both a teacher of Masonic symbolism and a director of Masonic conduct. As such, he is required to lead in the interpretation and implementation of lessons in Freemasonry, the most prominent of which, again symbolized by "the hat," are freedom of faith and brotherly equality. When Masons observe the hat tipped in lodge by the Worshipful Master during ritual, they are reminded that it is the Supreme Architect of the Universe to whom they are thankful; in His name that they are influenced to respect and tolerate the rights of all humanity; and, by whose power they are to extend equality and justice in both thought and deed to every man, woman and child.

Chapter 126

THE ENTERED APPRENTICE APRON

"Your lamb shall be without blemish...!"

Ex. 12:5

Worn by the initiate in Freemasonry with the flap turned up, the apron of the Entered Apprentice represents the *Cubical Stone* surmounted by the *Pyramid*. Its triangular flap is one face of the *Pyramid* and the whole is a square surmounted by a triangle. If this apron is given to the initiate without further explanation about the true symbolism, it will remain forever very confusing.

The pure white color of the apron represents what is known as "essential light," or as the Ancients declared, the Deity Himself. The lambskin material from which the apron is fashioned symbolizes the *Paschal Lamb*, which according to Mosaic law was the most acceptable offering any man could make to God. It is held equally sacred by Christian Masons, because the white lambskin apron also symbolizes *the Lamb of God that taketh away the sins of the world*. No Freemason is considered fully "clothed," as that term is used to describe a Mason sitting in a tiled lodge, if he wears an apron of any color other than white made of any material other than lambskin. The various ornamental aprons simply do not represent "essential light."

The Masonic legend explained during the Entered Apprentice Degree adds a veil that conceals yet a deeper meaning about the upturned flap itself. During the ritual, the initiate is informed that the upturned flap was originally intended to protect certain Temple workmen from having their clothing soiled. The actual esoteric meaning is, as follows: (1) the Entered Apprentice in King Solomon's Temple worked in the Northeast Corner upon what was known as *the rough ashlar,* a rude and imperfect stone cut from rock quarries; (2) the Fellowcraft toiled in the Southeast Corner of the Temple (where Masonic cornerstones were anciently laid, and indeed still should be laid to be absolutely accurate with the past construction methods employed by our Masonic ancestors) upon the *simple cube,* or *perfect ashlar* (a smoothed *rough ashlar*) that has six faces that are perfect squares; (3) to the Master Mason alone belongs the *pointed cubical,* or square, because shaped as a *Pyramid* it represents spirituality, intellect and Divine intuition; and (4) the upturned flap is also symbolic of the mute and unexplained promise, similar to that of the *square and compasses* situated upon the altar, that if the Entered Apprentice works well and his master is content with his progress, he will in due time attain to an even higher and more perfect *light.*

When a new Masonic initiate is welcomed into a lodge, each Master Mason has an obligation to share in nurturing his progress in Freemasonry. If he is left to his own devices, it is impossible for him to learn that which is only possessed by a Freemason who has devoted time to thorough study about the Craft. If the initiate does not learn, he either leaves the fraternity, or becomes useless to the advancement of its spiritual purpose. Should he leave, where would he possibly travel to obtain the same *light* Freemasonry shines? In truth, there is nowhere for him to go. He loses Freemasonry and Freemasonry loses him. Therefore, the important duty to convey Masonic knowledge must never go ignored.

"Essential light" is creative, abundant, kind, loving and very giving. It needs no man to accomplish its purpose, because it is of God, about God and radiates from God. However, it will use, as God will use, the willing body, the working mind and the devoted spirit to spread abundant love. For ages, Freemasonry has constituted such a willing body of men and shall likely do so until the end of time, as long as Freemasons remain interested and dedicated to learning and imparting the wisdom and truth it has acquired from time immemorial.

Chapter 127
THE WINDING STAIRCASE

> "Therefore thou shalt keep the Commandments
> of the Lord thy God to walk in His ways
> and to fear Him."
>
> Deut. 8:6

Commencing at the porch of King Solomon's Temple there was an impressive series of winding steps leading up to the middle chamber of that stupendous edifice. According to the teachings of Freemasonry, there were fifteen such steps, which are significantly explained to the candidate for degrees during the Fellowcraft Degree. The extraordinary symbolism associated with those steps constitutes the basis for acknowledging the close relationship of Freemasonry to Hermetic philosophy and related religious thinking.

To every Freemason, King Solomon's Temple symbolizes a world purified by Shekinah, or the Divine presence in its feminine form, i.e. wisdom. During the Entered Apprentice Degree, the initiate passes from darkness and begins a journey through the mysteries of the Temple, which is nothing greater than witnessing the truths of the world in God's presence. The mere fact that the steps are winding further symbolizes a world consisting of a spiral, as opposed to a closed circle, representing the avenue God uses to communicate with His creation.

In the Fellowcraft Degree, the candidate makes further progress in his search for light, which is the wisdom of God, by first passing through two pillars of strength and establishment. Strength is related to King David with whom God made a special covenant to use David's ancestral line from which to deliver the Messiah, thereby "establishing" the House of David as divine. The candidate then begins the laborious climb upward, step-by-step toward the goal, which is nothing less than possessing the *Word*, or Divine truth.

Continuous self improvement is acknowledged as a solemn duty of every Fellowcraft Mason; perfection is the end sought, which can only be found at the top of the fifteen steps. Those fifteen steps are separated into a series of three, five and seven steps indicating an individual Mason's adaptation to the upward course according to each individual's "strength." At the various pauses in the progression upward special instructions are given the Fellowcraft, which are intended to aid him in his ascent and which can only be attained through a rigid course of self discipline, the cultivation of noble virtues and the fervent practice of righteousness. Intellectual growth, a knowledge of the sciences which contribute to the progress of mankind and the actual attainment of true wisdom are urged by the various symbolic explanations provided the candidate during his ascension.

The seven liberal arts and sciences represent the completion of human learning. The ultimate quest for Divine knowledge beckons the candidate to climb even farther; to recognize the existence of an intellect that transcends the limited intellect of man. The true understanding is achieved when the candidate learns that the transcendent intellect is not separate from himself, but becomes a part of his being when pursued with *faith*. The sublime lesson here is that perfect knowledge of the *true Word* cannot be entirely achieved in this lifetime. Only a "substitute" will be attained. Life beyond illuminated *truth* is given by God as our reward so that we may continue to learn, work and love.

Chapter 128

TWO PERPENDICULAR PARALLEL LINES

*"See then that ye walk circumspectly,
not as fools, but as wise."*

Eph. 5:15

During the lecture in the Entered Apprentice degree, the candidate's attention is eventually directed to a point within a circle, which is supported by two perpendicular parallel lines. The point is intended to represent an individual brother and the circle the boundary line of his conduct. The two perpendicular parallel lines represent Saint John the Baptist and Saint John the Evangelist, whom the candidate is informed were imminent patrons of Freemasonry. At a deeper level, this combination of Masonic symbols invites meditation upon the importance of living a circumspect life and precisely how such a life is in complete harmony with God and the universe.

In order that one may better understand the original source of this special imagery, it is essential to study the various ancient mysteries observed by the Chinese and Japanese. Those mysteries were founded on the same principles as the mysteries that originated in India and, indeed, were expressed by very similar rites. Among the many symbols used in those rites was a ring supported by two serpents, emblematic of a world protected by the power and wisdom of the great Creator. In time, those two serpents gave way to the current Masonic symbolism of two perpendicular parallel lines, which support the circle. Those lines are termed "perpendicular," because each forms a right angle with the circle signifying the unification of different lessons in philosophy and religion.

By the circle, we are reminded that as man walks circumspectly through life, cautious in his choice of words and deeds, he walks as God intended and in full accord with His laws. The parallel lines also remind us of the several characteristics of the Holy Saints John: a steady reproval of vice on the one hand, and a faithful effort at discharging our duties to God, including the cultivation of brotherly love among all men. The perpendicular configuration of those lines further reminds us that morality, duty and charity are tools speculative Masons use to erect their spiritual building, that house not made with hands, eternal in the heavens.

Freemasonry consistently teaches about the relationship of light to darkness, goodness to evil. God is light and in Him there is no darkness at all. Yet, whence came the darkness and why does it run parallel in our lives to light? Who permitted evil to travel a path perpendicular to good? What part does man's free will actually play in these things?

Freemasonry beckons us to struggle against the animal instincts of immorality, selfishness and contempt of others. Instead, Masons are prompted to follow the example of the Holy Saints John and in so doing to live as the Creator so intended man to live. Human beings are suppose to love life as God loves it – He would not have created that which he hated. We are expected to find joy in the performance of duty to others, just as God rejoices in pouring out His blessings upon mankind. For these, and the many other blessings, Freemasons should constantly bow their hands and softly utter a prayer of thanksgiving and high praise for all that afflicts us, as well as for all that benefits us.

Affliction and beneficence are yet another example of parallels running throughout mankind's earthly existence. Man is not always benefited by what he encounters, neither is he always afflicted. During an entire lifetime, the good most often balances out the bad. It is our endurance of the one and joyful basking in the other that builds our character, instills within us that sense of duty to others and overwhelms us with a true sense of brotherly love and affection for our neighbors.

Chapter 129

THE CABLE-TOW

"I drew them with cords of a man,
with bands of love..."

Hos. 11:4

Several Masonic writers, including Albert Pike, see no meaning in the cable-tow beyond the fact that it is used either to lead an initiate into the lodge room, or pull him outside in the event he proves unworthy. However, applying such a non-symbolic interpretation is highly unusual in Freemasonry. The entirety of a Masonic lodge is a symbol, as is every object and act, which fit together revealing truths to such eyes and ears that are prepared to see and hear.

The obligations assumed and vows taken by candidates are literally ties that bind each Mason to the fraternity. When those obligations are broken, or the vows ignored, the offending member is excused possibly never again to return. In and of itself, that fact lends meaning to the cable-tow.

From ancient history and the Holy Bible we learn that the cable-tow is the outward visible symbol of the commitment made to exercise brotherly love, relieve the distressed and always favor the truth. Its length, as well as its strength is measured by the ability each Freemason has to fulfill his obligations. As such, the cable-tow represents both a man's capacity and his character. Just as the umbilical cord is replaced by a tie of love and obligation between mother and child when severed, a candidate is bound to Freemasonry by a tie stronger than his cable-tow as soon as he completes confirming his oaths at the altar. Force is replaced by brotherly love as soon as the cable-tow is removed constituting a Masonic "secret" of safety and security. Freemasons in good standing need never again want for a roof over their head, or food on the table. It will always be provided.

But, let us not too quickly forget that a cable-tow has two ends. One binds a Freemason to the fraternity; the other binds the fraternity to the Freemason. Each obligation is of equal importance; that of the whole to the one, and of the one to the whole. The fraternity is under vows to its members to guide, instruct and train them for the effective service to the Craft, as well as all of humanity. Control, obedience, direction and guidance – these are also meanings attached to the cable-tow.

By control, Freemasonry does not mean to imply that force is involved. To the contrary, Freemasonry "rules" men as beauty rules an artist, or as love rules a lover. Freemasonry "controls" and shapes us through its human touch and moral nobility. By the same power, Freemasonry wins obedience and lends direction and guidance to our lives. At the altar, Freemasons assume vows to follow and obey Freemasonry's highest principles and ideals. Those vows are not empty promises – they are commitments undertaken upon sacred honor.

For each Mason, the cable-tow extends as far as the individual's moral principles and material conditions will allow. Of that distance, each Mason must be the sole and exclusive judge of how much he can give in the way of service to others. When the cable-tow of an individual Mason is joined with those of other Masons, a bond of brotherhood so immense is formed that no mortal can accurately measure.

Brotherhood is, indeed, one of the holiest assets of humanity. There exists an invisible cord binding together every man, woman and child. It winds its way through every human life and draws together the most disparate beliefs making friends of those who might otherwise have remained at a perpetual distance.

Chapter 130

THE CORNERSTONE

> "The stone which the builders refused is become the head stone of the corner."
>
> Ps. 118:22-23

In construction, the cornerstone is placed in the corner of two walls in a building. In operative Masonry it is considered the most important stone in the entire edifice. In Masonic buildings, it is required that this stone be situated in the northeast corner of the structure.

In ancient times, the laying of cornerstones of important edifices was completed during very impressive and elaborate ceremonies. Amidst solemn prayers and acts of consecration, dignitaries acted in concert to lay the ponderous stone in its resting place. The speculative Masonic symbolism associated with the cornerstone is no less impressive.

In form, the cornerstone must be perfectly square on its surfaces and its solid contents must form a cube. In Freemasonry, the square is a symbol of morality, while the cube symbolizes truth. The situation of the cornerstone in the northeast also conforms to an even deeper spiritual significance.

To Masons, the north has always been presumed a place of darkness. The east has consistently represented light. Therefore, the progression from north to east symbolizes a Freemason's progress from darkness to light, as he becomes more educated in the workings of the Craft.

The permanence and durable quality of the cornerstone, which is intended to last longer than the edifice itself, reminds us that while the earthly tabernacle we refer to as the human body shall one day pass away, the soul, or cornerstone of immortality, shall never, never, never die. In the Christian religion, that is also symbolized in the person of Jesus. In other religions, it is symbolized simply by the spiritual concept of Deity. In truth, both attach the same meaning and provoke the same understanding about the truth of the soul's eternal existence.

The proper setting of the cornerstone by the implements of operative Masonry – the square, the level and the plumb – further reminds us that our virtues are daily tested by temptation, trial, suffering and adversity. Freemasonry teaches that men must be so tried in order that they may one day be declared true and trusty by the Master Builder. It is then that a Mason achieves the status of being a living stone for that house not made with hands, eternal in the heavens.

After it is set into place, the cornerstone to a Masonic Building is then symbolically set apart from the structure that is to follow by pouring upon its surface corn, wine and oil. As Freemasons are instructed during the Fellowcraft Degree, those three "wages of a Fellowcraft" are emblematic of the nourishment, refreshment and joy, which are to become the rewards of a faithful performance of duty.

The proper reflection upon the lessons taught by the cornerstone reveals that taken together as a whole, they embody all that is taught in Freemasonry. From a firm foundation erected upon a prayerful life, sacrifice and the exercise of brotherly love, Masons who use the tools of the Craft lead better lives and do better work than those unskilled in Freemasonry's workings. The Mason who so acts during his earthly existence is assured of hearing words of Divine approval: "well done my true and faithful servant!" To no loftier goal need any man aspire.

Chapter 131
NETWORK, LILY-WORK AND POMEGRANATES

*"A good tree cannot bring forth evil fruit, neither
can a corrupt tree bring forth good fruit."*

Matt. 7:18

In the second degree of Freemasonry, the candidate is instructed about the symbolic importance of "network, lily-work and pomegranates." The "network," from the intricate connection of its several parts denotes unity. The "lily-work," from its purity and retired situation of its growth, denotes peace. And, the "pomegranates" from the exuberance of their seeds, denote plenty. These symbols are explained in Masonic instruction as a unit and consequently should be understood as a whole.

Masons are taught that each person has an invisible self, a spirit or soul that constitutes the true essence of man. When the body falls away and the dust returns to the earth, the spirit or soul continues. This was the central instruction given to the special elect in the Ancient Egyptian mysteries and is a truth about the God-like nature of all men that far too few know about, or accept. For that reason, as well as others, the Ancient Egyptians guarded this truth as a secret, or as a pearl that is not to be thrown before swine. A man had to prove himself worthy of receiving such instruction before he was permitted to participate in the ritual.

Like the Ancient Egyptian schooled in the mysteries, Freemasons have a responsibility, while walking through this vale of tears, to nurture the spirit, to look within and try to comprehend the enormous power and innate goodness that dwells deep within each person's consciousness. The combined symbols are emblematic of unity, peace and plenty focuses our attention upon the fruits of such nurturing in such a way that we are each enabled to assess our own spiritual growth.

By unity, Freemasonry refers to fraternal love; to the notion that all men are created equal; and to the need to preserve institutions which foster the brotherhood of man. Additionally, the "network" teaches us that when we look at that which is within, we know that the same innate goodness; the same spirit; and the same God dwells within each one of us. Thus, we come to see our brother as another self, not as another person. From this knowledge springs forth in full bloom the beauty of the Golden Rule – a rule that is so very easy for a Mason to follow: "do unto your neighbor that which you would that he should do unto you."

By use of the word "peace," one most often thinks about the physical condition of the world. When our nations and countries are not at war slaughtering innocent beings we are said to be at "peace." Yet, the "lily-work" actually symbolizes something other than world peace. It teaches us that within our inner being where our "secret center" hosts the Great Architect of the Universe, a powerful peace is available to us. Man's intellect instructs his outward behavior and is regarded as the seat of the soul. Intellect allows man to be fearful, to act cowardly, to behave bravely and even to select love above hatred. When one chooses wisely, the peace within not only calms one's mood, it also alters behavior toward others. In that state of mind, one man can truthfully declare to his friend and brother, "my peace I give you."

By considering the concept of plenty, Masons learn to consistently live "on purpose," that is with an attitude of giving service abundantly. The Davidic bloodline from which King Solomon emerged required that family members serve their fellow man. It was considered unworthy to govern for the purpose of controlling others, or to merely perpetuate power over others. Freemasons, too, have the choice to serve, or to live a life of being served by others. The former is Masonic, the latter is something else. Freemasonry does not judge the choice made. However, its symbols teach us that there are natural consequences which follow each choice made. The Holy Bible instructs that from he who has little, much more will be taken away; but to he who has much, to him shall much more be given.

From these three symbols, we also learn that there is no unity without peace and plenty. There is no brotherhood of man without one man giving to another as prompted by the Divine light within him.

Chapter 132
THE ASHERAH, OR "RODS"

> "And the Lord said unto Moses, 'Put forth thine hand
> and take it (serpent) by the tail.' And he put forth
> his hand and ...it became a rod in his hand."
>
> Ex. 4:4

One Masonic writer stated that the rod of Moses, fearful to the Egyptians as the attack of a serpent, was a scepter of righteousness to the Children of Israel. As the scripture passage above taken from The Book of Exodus implies, the rod was a symbol of Divine authority – a visible demonstration of God's power. In some religions that meaning of the rod morphed. For example, in Christianity the rod denoted a type of Christ's death to which Freemasonry ultimately points; for as by a serpent death came into the world, so by the death of the Son of Man was the serpent and Satan fully vanquished. Another provocative interpretation can be gleaned from a deeper inspection of ancient Masonic history.

A Masonic Temple is intended to be a representation of King Solomon's Temple, which displayed astronomical characteristics similar to those found within an Enochian Temple. Situated due east and west, the eastern end of today's Masonic Temple is where the Worshipful

Master sits representing the sunrise at the equinox. At the opposite end, the Senior Warden sits in the west where he represents the sun setting at equinox. The Junior Warden is stationed in the south of the Masonic Temple and represents the moon, beauty, wisdom – the feminine principle.

Several English Masonic Temples display a blazing star with the letter "G" affixed to the center of the ceiling. The blazing star represents the sun, around which is a five-pointed star which has scant interpretation among Masonic writers. However, that imagery was exceptionally important to the biblical character Enoch, as well as the so-called "Grooved-Ware People," who were an ancient society of humans who also knew about the importance of the 40-year Venus cycle. Indeed, until the atomic clock was invented, there was no more accurate means of determining time than studying the position of Venus against the backdrop of the stars.

The rods carried by the Stewards and Deacons in a Masonic lodge were originally called "wands." They represented the measuring rods which the Canaanites and early Jews called "Asherah." Asherah was the name of the goddess who was regarded as the mother of the dawn and the dusk, symbolized astronomically by Venus. The purpose of those Asherah was originally to determine the angles of the sunrise and sunset as indicated by the shadows cast from the vertically held staffs. The Deacons were originally essential for orienting the location of the Temple by finding two days a year where the shadow of the rising sun perfectly aligned with the shadow of the setting sun, i.e., the equinoxes.

In the Entered Apprentice degree, the candidate is placed in the northeast corner of the lodge room. A Deacon holds the candidate with one hand, an Ashrah, or rod with the other. In that place, according to Enochian legend, the Deacon and candidate were standing on the summer solstice sunrise line marked by the shadow of the pillar named "Jachin." In the second degree in many Masonic lodges, the candidate is placed in the southeast corner on the winter solstice sunrise line denoted by the shadow from the pillar called "Boaz." In the third degree, some lodges place the candidate on the center line representing the perfect east-west line of the equinoxes.

During the era of the original Knights Templar, as well as during the early years of European Freemasonry, the Asherah were put to practical use. In the building of the hundreds of cathedrals, Asherahs were used to measure the angle of the sun's first shadow when laying the foundation stone, or "cornerstone." That resulted in the cathedrals facing the rising sun on one of two specific days of the year – the summer solstice, or the winter solstice.

Thus, the rods carried in the Masonic lodges of today represent symbols of man's effort to measure the universe. Although each rod bears an image of the sun or moon, their significance in today's Masonic ritual is forgotten. But, to the Freemason who studies such things, those rods serve as reminders of the great emphasis Freemasonry places upon the study of science, geometry and astronomy.

Chapter 133
SEVEN: THE SACRED NUMBER

"And he had in his right hand seven stars..."

Rev. 1:16

In every religious system of antiquity, particularly in the Ancient Egyptian mysteries, the number seven held a place of veneration. The Hebrew term for seven suggests sufficiency, or fullness, thereby signifying perfection. The great candlestick at King Solomon's Temple consisted of seven holders which were symbolically derived from the ancient studies of the planets, and represented the seven presiding archangels. Christians also regard seven as sacred and believe that the seven stars mentioned in the scripture passage above taken from The Book of Revelation represent the seven true messengers of Christ. The number seven is no less revered and venerated by Masonic symbolism.

Ancient intellect attributed numbers to the creative genius of God. Mathematics was seen as the revelation of principles associated exclusively with the divine mind. Saint Augustine and Martin Luther both taught that the number seven must be considered sacred, because of its repetition in scripture. As an example, the Holy Bible states that Jacob served Rachel's father for seven years; there were seven years of plenty and seven years of famine when Joseph governed Egypt; Samson was bound with seven bands; and, on the seventh day when seven priests blew seven trumpets while circling the walls of Jericho seven times, the walls collapsed and the town fell to Joshua.

Our first Most Excellent Grand Master, Solomon, King of Israel, lectured upon the seven pillars of wisdom and taught that the number seven represented Infinite Wisdom in relationship to Infinite Power. Drawing upon those teachings, Freemasonry has adopted the philosophy that while the occurrence of such wisdom and power logically suggests that one who has the power to do good work also possesses the power to work even greater evil. Only in the hands of God are the two held in equilibrium resulting in infinite harmony throughout the universe.

Yet, humans are incapable of living harmoniously by doing both good and evil. One destroys the other. Darkness gives way to light. A lighted lamp brought into a darkened room chases away the darkness. The two cannot reside side-by-side. Freemasons are asked to understand what it means to live in the light, to understand human limitations and to promptly replace perceived cruelties with abundant acts of kindness.

Man is imperfect. The perfect number seven is but a goal that is quite possibly unattainable during this earthly existence. Within mankind's limitations, falsehoods can never become truth. Intolerance cannot beget compassion. Murder does not return men to life. Such powers reside exclusively with God. Therefore, the number seven teaches us that because perfection eludes us, Freemasons should strive to work acts of charity, to circumscribe their desires and to keep their passions within due bounds toward all mankind.

Chapter 134

THE NORTH IS TERMED A PLACE OF DARKNESS

*"But, the Lord liveth, which brought ip
and which led the seed of the house
of Israel out of the north country,…"*

Jer. 23:8

Candidates are instructed in the Entered Apprentice Degree that the three lights of Freemasonry are situated in the east, west and south of the lodge room. According to Masonic legend, there is none in the north, because King Solomon's Temple was situated in such a manner that neither the Sun, nor moon, at meridian height, could bring light into the Temple from the north. Therefore, the candidate is informed that among Masons, the north is always termed a place of darkness.

As with other Masonic symbols, this, too, invites meditation upon the questions about light and darkness, good and evil. Here, our contemplation is focused upon a new consideration about these opposites. The candidate is not told that King Solomon's Temple was situated in a particular location to serve as a geography lesson. Rather, he is so informed, because the Holy Writings symbolize the north as the direction from which evil flows.

so doing we have also assured ourselves of a very specific future: a life full of spite, revenge and conflict. On the other hand, man can select kindness, compassion, faith, hope and charity as his characteristics. The difference in the future is like the difference between night and day, light and darkness.

Radiance, or the vertical connection to supernal divinity is symbolized in Freemasonry, as well as in most ancient religions, by the Sun, Moon and Mercury (note the similarity between this array and that told the candidate about the Sun, Moon and Master of the Lodge) traveling a path from east to west. Neither of those bodies travels north to south, although during the vernal equinox, the east to west path necessarily touches distinctly upon the southern hemisphere. The spirit of divinity that is thought by many to dwell within every man is said to be strengthened by exposure to the "radiance." Forces associated with the north are said to flow from the material world only and thereby incite worldly desires for such non-spiritual things as fame, wealth and power.

May it always be so that the north is termed a place of darkness among Masons. Freemasonry seeks to instill faith, hope and charity. Masons live compassionate lives. The members of a lodge constitute a brotherhood of man under the fatherhood of God. Freemasonry seeks not to give a man a futile future, one devoid of love, peace and harmony. Wholly to the contrary, the Order seeks to instill this great commandment: love God with all of your heart and soul, and lover your neighbor as you lover yourself.

Chapter 135

THE TROWEL

> "Behold, how good and how pleasant it is for
> brethren to dwell together in unity."
>
> Ps. 133:1

The trowel is the symbol of that which has the power to bind men together. What is this unifying power? We frequently meet with men who seem to lack unity in their makeup; a spirit of disorganization or anarchy is at work in them so that they seem to live at cross-purposes with themselves. What they know they should do they do not, and many things which they do they do against their own will. They may have personal force, but it is scattered and their lives never come into focus.

Of these men we say that they lack character. Character comes from the word that originally meant a graving tool; after long use the name of the tool came to be applied to the engraving itself, and thus the term has come to stand for a man whose actions give one an impression of definiteness and clear-cuttedness, like an engraving. The trowel is intended to remind us of that true character, the essential ingredient necessary for one man to properly bond with another.

Francis Bacon so thoroughly exemplified the spirit of fraternalism, that is of men bonding together to perform works of great charity, that his memory is largely associated with the Fellowcraft Degree. Bacon was at various times in his life Lord Chancellor of England, a philosopher, an author, a statesman, scientist, orator and humorist. He was one of the prophets of the scientific revolution and instigated the formation of the Royal Society. Bro. Bacon edited the first King James version of the Holy Bible and is thought by many to actually have authored several works attributed to Shakespeare.

Bacon secretly founded the first Lodge of Free & Accepted Masons in England. He wrote the second degree ritual, which by his creation emphasized the liberal arts and sciences. In addition, he founded the first Rosicrucian Brotherhood and secretly laid the groundwork for the eventual establishment of the United States of America. Using Masonic symbolism, Bacon wrote the *New Atlantis*, which many contend contains the keys to all Masonic ritual.

Bacon's example, so essential to the true symbolism of the Trowel, was that of a Master Mason building for the future. In building for the future, one must instill in others the vital essence of one's own purpose. Bacon's dreams were realizable because the early Freemasons embraced his vision and purpose. His dreams were the cement that bound the brotherhood to the process of regeneration, that is, to everlasting renewal.

That philosophy is embodied in the three degrees of Freemasonry. From grade to grade, the candidate is led from an old to an entirely new quality of life. The candidate begins his Masonic life as the natural man and ends it by becoming a regenerated "perfected" man. He symbolically rises from the dead a Master, a just man made perfect, with larger consciousness and faculties, an efficient instrument for use by the Great Architect in His plan of rebuilding the Temple of fallen humanity, and capable of advancing other men to a participation in the same great work.

Thus, the Trowel also teaches us that the real purpose of modern Freemasonry is, not the social and charitable purposes to which so much appropriate attention is paid, but the expediting of the spiritual evolution of those who aspire to perfect their own nature and transform it into a more god-like quality. The challenge of Freemasonry is to be reborn "incorruptible" which must be preceded by the death of the lower nature. Consequently, the intention of Masonry is not the building of a temple, but the greater science of soul building using the cement of brotherly love and affection.

Chapter 136

THE WIDOW'S SON

"He was a widow's son of the
tribe of Naphtali,..."

1 Kings 7:14

It is typically held within Masonic circles that Hiram Abif, the original architect of King Solomon's Temple, was actually the son of a widow of the tribe of Naphtali, who probably married a man of Tyre after the death of Hiram's father. In that Hiram enjoys such a position of imminence in Freemasonry, it is also believed that the natural reverence Masons bestowed upon the memory of his widowed mother was the basis for Freemasonry's later devotion to the support of the widows of all Masons. The earliest recorded Masonic rituals dating back to the late 1600's include passages demanding that all good Masons make a special effort to care for such special women. Yet, as is true of most symbols in Freemasonry, that of the "widow's son" is also very relevant to man's relationship to the Deity.

In Grail lore, certain ancient writers, such as Sir Thomas Malory, explored the connection of Jesus' family to the hereditary line of King David and beyond. The stories that were associated with the rich King Arthur legends were expressed as such to protect "believers" from being accused as heretics and possibly suffering horrible deaths as a result. It is believed that tarot cards originated for the same reason and thus are also a part of the concealed expression of belief that Jesus and his family may be traced to David and Abraham.

Freemasonry's Hiram Abif is also identified in Grail lore as the Son of a Widow, personified in the character known as Percival, one of the Grail champions Malory identified together with Lancelot and Sir Galahad. Percival is also sometimes identified as a grand-nephew of Joseph of Arimathea, whom some believe is none other than Jesus' own brother James. Thus, for Grail adherents, the stories establish nothing less than a bloodline traceable to directly to Divinity.

The original Widow of the Grail bloodline was Ruth the Moabite (heroine of the Old Testament book of Ruth), who married Boaz and was the great-grandmother of King David. Her descendants were called "Sons of the Widow." In this context, Hiram Abif is revealed as a descendant of Ruth, whose ancient forerunners included Tubal-cain, the first artificer in metals. Can this be the purpose for deliberately incorporating the phrase "widow's son" into essential Masonic ritual?

The true Mason is an ardent seeker after knowledge. He knows that Freemasonry has not selected its symbols for idle purposes, but to teach valuable and important lessons about God, brotherhood and charity. The chance selection of the "widow's son" as symbolism is as likely as was the chance selection of the square and compasses. Masons are told very little about Hiram Abif and it is rather odd that such a central person should nowhere appear in the Holy Bible. Some will point to various passages and report they have there found Hiram, but nowhere is there a man named Hiram Abif who is also referred to as the "widow's son."

If we accept the Grail lore interpretation, we also acknowledge that the Grand Master Hiram Abif is as important a character as is King Solomon, whom we also know from Old Testament scripture to be a son of King David. If we reject that interpretation, we are back to square one: what does Freemasonry mean when it alludes to its most central character as a Son of a Widow? Perhaps the phrase is derived from another religious source.

Manicheanism was founded by the Persian sage Mani in approximately 240 AD. His followers believed that the world was divided into kingdoms of light and darkness, good and evil. Those followers, like the descendants of Ruth, were called "sons of the widow," which was an allusion to the Ancient Egyptian Mysteries. In the Osirian mysteries, Isis was widowed when Typhon killed her husband. Typhon was a symbol for darkness and evil, while Isis and her husband were regarded as the female and male principles of light and virtue – the condition God originally intended for His human creatures.

In the New Testament of the Holy Bible, yet another reference to a "widow's son" appears in Luke 7:11-17. There, Jesus has revived the dead son of the Widow of Nain. This woman thereafter proclaimed publicly that in Jesus, God has visited His people.

In his book entitled *The Burning Bush*, Edward Beaugh Smith observed that the phrase "widow's son" appears frequently throughout the Holy Bible, recounts the Manicheanism story and leans strongly upon the Osirian legend as the source of that phrase. Smith's premise relates to what he calls an Evolutionary Epic – a time during which the consciousness will have established in the successors of the "Sons of the Widow" that evil must be overcome by charitableness. Here, Masons at last find the primary lesson intended by this specific symbolism – charity is Masonry's fundamental goal, as fundamental as knowing that our Grand Master Hiram Abif is the "widow's son."

Afterword

Masonry reminds the world that it is not a religion. It is, however, a system that inculcates zeal in the pursuit of knowledge. More than a mere system, it is a fraternity that encourages sincere feeling of brotherly affection. The world's progress is judged by how far along mankind has evolved in its empathy and compassion. Without both, the world stagnates.

In the 21st Century, men are joining Masonry in a way seldom seen in history. Young men are becoming members even though their fathers did not. They are the future of Freemasonry and the world. Our future inhabitants of this Planet will enjoy the good and the bad of their generation. Those who embrace Freemasonry will make it a better place than before. Those who do not will hold them back. It is actually as simple as that, for our society is poised to either ignore the people next door, or to wake up and care about our neighbors' welfare.

The freedom that Abraham, Jacob and Moses sought for their people remains in doubt. Will mankind embrace the means to attain true freedom, or remain in the clutches of ignorance? Will despotism prevail, or will the people win out? The question is in doubt as of the writing of this book.

Reader, if you wish to change the world – to make it a better place than when you came into it – you must take stock of yourself. Communities evolve one person at a time and you have the choice of being a positive or negative force for that change. You can insist upon having everything your way – your religion, your politics, your point of view – or you can realize that there are other people with equally valid perspectives. When you do, you will have adopted the Masonic point of view. You will have also positioned yourself to become a part of a movement God has had in mind since the Creation – a movement to evolve from a people that are suspicious, resentful and filled with hatred to a people filled with love for their neighbor.

The choice is yours.

www.ingramcontent.com/pod-product-compliance
Lightning Source LLC
Chambersburg PA
CBHW070357230426
43665CB00012B/1147